THE WEST

Key Eras in the Transformation of the West

Map 1 Roman Empire at Its Greatest Extent, ca. 117 C.E.

Western civilization has undergone many transformations throughout its history. When the Roman Empire was at its greatest extent, the basic intellectual, religious, political, and geographic outlines of what we call the West today were drawn.

The Roman Empire at Its Greatest Extent
- Roman Empire
- Parthian Empire

Map 2 Carolingian Empire

During the Carolingian Empire, Europe experienced greater political cohesion, as the Carolingian armies successfully reunified most of the western European territories of the ancient Roman Empire, distinguishing it from the Byzantine Empire in the east.

The Division of the Carolingian Empire under Charlemagne's Grandsons

Carolingian Empire
- The empire of Charlemagne, 814
- Tribute-paying tribes
- Byzantine empire

Map 3   Europe After the Congress of Vienna, 1815

The major European powers re-drew the map of Europe with the Congress of Vienna in 1815 after the defeat of Napoleon. This map shows the dismantlement of the massive empire France had acquired under his leadership.

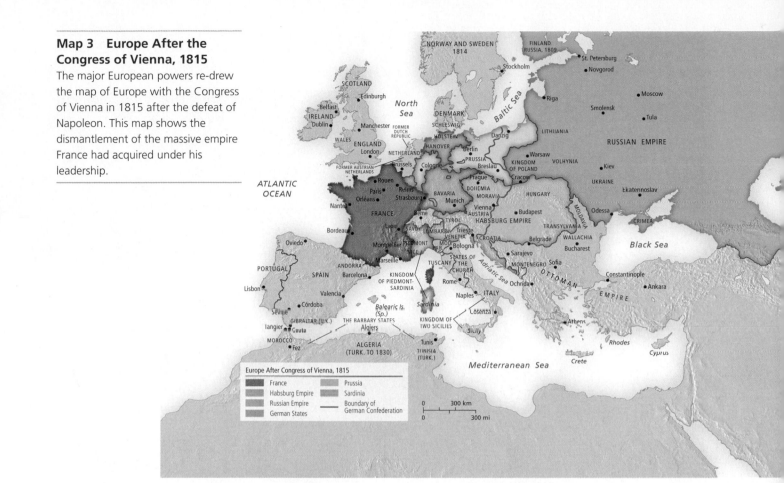

Europe After Congress of Vienna, 1815
- France
- Habsburg Empire
- Russian Empire
- German States
- Prussia
- Sardinia
- Boundary of German Confederation

0   300 km
0   300 mi

Map 4   Europe After World War I

The map of Europe changed dramatically after World War I with the collapse of the old authoritarian empires and the creation of independent nation-states in eastern Europe. What neither Map 3 nor Map 4 can show, however, is the expansion of "the West" beyond European borders to embrace cultures on other continents, including Australia, Africa, and North America.

Europe and the Middle East After World War I
- To Great Britain
- To France
- To Italy
- To Rumania
- To Denmark
- To Yugoslavia (Serbia and Montenegro)
- To Belgium
- To Greece
- Became independent
- 1914 boundaries
- New boundaries

0   300 km
0   300 mi

THE WEST

Encounters & Transformations

Second Edition

VOLUME B: 1300 to 1815

Brian Levack
University of Texas at Austin

Edward Muir
Northwestern University

Meredith Veldman
Louisiana State University

Michael Maas
Rice University

PEARSON
Longman

New York   San Francisco   Boston
London   Toronto   Sydney   Tokyo   Singapore   Madrid
Mexico City   Munich   Paris   Cape Town   Hong Kong   Montreal

Senior Acquisitions Editor: Janet Lanphier
Senior Development Editor: David B. Kear
Executive Marketing Manager: Sue Westmoreland
Supplements Editor: Kristi Olson
Media Editor: Melissa Edwards
Production Manager: Donna DeBenedictis
Project Coordination, Text Design, and Electronic Page Makeup:
    Elm Street Publishing Services, Inc.
Cover Designer/Manager: John Callahan
Cover and Frontispiece Art: Kublai Khan giving his golden seal to the Polos at his new capi-
    tal Cambaluc. From the Livre des Merveilles, c. 1413. Ms. 2810, f. 3v. Location:
    Bibliothèque Nationale, Paris, France. Photo Credit: Art Resource, NY.
Cartography: Maps.com
Photo Researcher: Photosearch, Inc.
Manufacturing Buyer: Roy L. Pickering, Jr.
Printer and Binder: Quebecor World Dubuque
Cover Printer: Coral Graphic Services, Inc.

Library of Congress Cataloging-in-Publication Data

The West : encounters & transformations / Brian Levack . . . [et al.].
    2nd ed.
      p. cm.
    Includes bibliographical references and index.
    ISBN 0-321-36404-X
    1. Civilization, Western—History—Textbooks.   I. Levack, Brian P.

    CB245.W456 2007
    909'.09821—dc22

                                        2005032587

Please visit us at http://www.ablongman.com/levack2e

ISBN 0-321-36404-X (single-volume edition)
ISBN 0-321-36405-8 (volume I)
ISBN 0-321-38413-X (volume II)
ISBN 0-321-38414-8 (volume A)
ISBN 0-321-38415-6 (volume B)
ISBN 0-321-36403-1 (volume C)

3 4 5 6 7 8 9 10—QWD—09 08 07

Brief Contents

Detailed Contents

What Is the West?   2

10 The Medieval West in Crisis   306

11 The Italian Renaissance and Beyond: The Politics of Culture   342

19 The Age of the French Revolution, 1789–1815   606

Documents

Maps

Features

Chronologies

Preface

We wrote this textbook to answer questions about the identity of the civilization in which we live. Journalists, politicians, and scholars often refer to our civilization, its political ideologies, its economic systems, and its cultures as "Western" without fully considering what that label means and why it might be appropriate. The classification of our civilization as Western has become particularly problematic in the age of globalization. The creation of international markets, the rapid dissemination of ideas on a global scale, and the transmission of popular culture from one country to another often make it difficult to distinguish what is Western from what is not. *The West: Encounters & Transformations* offers students a history of Western civilization in which these issues of Western identity are given prominence. Our goal is neither to idealize nor to indict that civilization but to describe its main characteristics in different historical periods.

The West: Encounters & Transformations gives careful consideration to two basic questions. The first is, how did the definition of the West change over time? In what ways did its boundaries shift and how did the distinguishing characteristics of its cultures change? The second question is, by what means did the West—and the idea of the West—develop? We argue that the West is the product of a series of cultural encounters that occurred both outside and within its geographical boundaries. We explore these encounters and the transformations they produced by detailing the political, social, religious, and cultural history of the regions that have been, at one time or another, a part of the West.

Defining the West

What is the West? How did it come into being? How has it developed throughout history? Many textbooks take for granted which regions or peoples of the globe constitute the West. They treat the history of the West as a somewhat expanded version of European history. While not disputing the centrality of Europe to any definition of the West, we contend that the West is not only a geographical realm with ever-shifting boundaries but also a cultural realm, an area of cultural influence extending beyond the geographical and political boundaries of Europe. We so strongly believe in this notion that we have written the essay "What Is the West?" to encourage students to think about their understanding of Western civilization and to guide their understanding of each chapter. Many of the features of what we call Western civilization originated in regions that are not geographically part of Europe (such as northern Africa and the Middle East), while ever since the fifteenth century various social, ethnic, and political groups from non-European regions (such as North and South America, eastern Russia, Australia, New Zealand, and South Africa) have identified themselves, in one way or another, with the West. Throughout the text, we devote considerable attention to the boundaries of the West and show how borderlines between cultures have been created, especially in eastern and southeastern Europe.

Considered as a geographical and cultural realm, "the West" is a term of recent origin, and the civilization to which it refers did not become clearly defined until the eleventh century, especially during the Crusades, when western European Christians developed a distinct cultural identity. Before that time we can only talk about the powerful forces that created the West, especially the dynamic interaction of the civilizations of western Europe, the Byzantine Empire, and the Muslim world.

Over the centuries Western civilization has acquired many salient characteristics. These include two of the world's great legal systems (civil law and common law), three of the world's monotheistic religions (Judaism, Christianity, and Islam), certain political and social philosophies, forms of political organization (such as the modern bureaucratic state and democracy), methods of scientific inquiry, systems of economic organization (such as industrial capitalism), and distinctive styles of art, architecture, and music. At times one or more of these characteristics has served as a primary source of Western identity: Christianity in the Middle Ages, science and rationalism during the Enlightenment, industrialization in the nineteenth and twentieth centuries, and a defense of individual liberty and democracy in the late twentieth century. These sources of Western identity, however, have always been challenged and contested, both when they were coming into prominence and when they appeared to be most triumphant. Western culture has never been monolithic, and even today references to the West imply a wide range of meanings.

Cultural Encounters

The definition of the West is closely related to the central theme of our book, which is the process of cultural encounters. Throughout *The West: Encounters & Transformations,* we examine the West as a product of a series of cultural encounters both outside the West and within it. We show that the West originated and developed through a continuous process of inclusion and exclusion resulting from a series of encounters among and within different groups. These encounters can be described in a general sense as external, internal, or ideological.

External Encounters

External encounters took place between peoples of different civilizations. Before the emergence of the West as a clearly defined entity, external encounters occurred between such diverse peoples as Greeks and Phoenicians, Macedonians and Egyptians, and Romans and Celts. After the eleventh century, external encounters between Western and non-Western peoples occurred mainly during periods of European exploration, expansion, and imperialism. In the sixteenth and seventeenth centuries, for example, a series of external encounters took place between Europeans on the one hand and Africans, Asians, and the indigenous people of the Americas on the other. Two chapters of *The West: Encounters & Transformations* (Chapters 12 and 17) and a large section of a third (Chapter 23) explore these external encounters in depth and discuss how they affected Western and non-Western civilizations alike.

Internal Encounters

Our discussion of encounters also includes similar interactions between different social groups *within* Western countries. These internal encounters often took place between dominant and subordinate groups, such as between lords and peasants, rulers and subjects, men and women, factory owners and workers, masters and slaves. Encounters between those who were educated and those who were illiterate, which recur frequently throughout Western history, also fall into this category. Encounters just as often took place between different religious and political groups, such as between Christians and Jews, Catholics and Protestants, and royal absolutists and republicans.

Ideological Encounters

Ideological encounters involve interaction between comprehensive systems of thought, most notably religious doctrines, political philosophies, and scientific theories about the nature of the world. These ideological conflicts usually arose out of internal encounters, when various groups within Western societies subscribed to different theories of government or rival religious faiths. The encounters between Christianity and polytheism in the early Middle Ages, between liberalism and conservatism in the nineteenth century, and between fascism and communism in the twentieth century were ideological encounters. Some ideological encounters had an external dimension, such as when the forces of Islam and Christianity came into conflict during the Crusades and when the Cold War developed between Soviet communism and Western democracy in the second half of the twentieth century.

* * *

The West: Encounters & Transformations illuminates the variety of these encounters and clarifies their effects. By their very nature encounters are interactive, but they have taken different forms: they have been violent or peaceful, coercive or cooperative. Some have resulted in the imposition of Western ideas on areas outside the geographical boundaries of the West or the perpetuation of the dominant culture within Western societies. More often than not, however, encounters have resulted in a more reciprocal process of exchange in which both Western and non-Western cultures or the values of both dominant and subordinate groups have undergone significant transformation. Our book not only identifies these encounters but also discusses their significance by returning periodically to the issue of Western identity.

Coverage

The West: Encounters & Transformations offers both balanced coverage of political, social, and culture history and a broader coverage of the West and the world.

Balanced Coverage

Our goal throughout the text has been to provide balanced coverage of political, social, and cultural history and to include significant coverage of religious and military history as well. Political history defines the basic structure of the book, and some chapters, such as those on the Hellenistic world, the age of confessional divisions, absolutism and state building, the French Revolution, and the coming of mass politics, include sustained political narratives. Because we understand the West to be a cultural as well as a geographical realm, we give a prominent position to cultural history. Thus we include rich sections on Hellenistic philosophy and literature, the cultural environment of the Italian Renaissance, the creation of a new political culture at the time of the French Revolution, and the atmosphere of cultural despair and desire that prevailed in Europe after World War I. We also devote special attention to religious history, including the history of Islam as well as that of Christianity and Judaism. Unlike many other textbooks, our coverage of religion continues into the modern period.

The West: Encounters & Transformations also provides extensive coverage of the history of women and gender. Wherever possible the history of women is integrated into the broader social, cultural, and political history of the period. But there are also separate sections on women in our chapters on classical Greece, the Renaissance, the Reformation, the Enlightenment, the Industrial Revolution, World War I, World War II, and the postwar era.

The West and the World

Our book provides broad geographical coverage. Because the West is the product of a series of encounters, the external areas with which the West interacted are of major importance. Three chapters deal specifically with the West and the world.

- Chapter 12, "The West and the World: The Significance of Global Encounters, 1450–1650"
- Chapter 17, "The West and the World: Empire, Trade, and War, 1650–1815"
- Chapter 23, "The West and the World: Cultural Crisis and the New Imperialism, 1870–1914"

These chapters present substantial material on sub-Saharan Africa, Latin America, the Middle East, India, and East Asia. Our text is also distinctive in its coverage of eastern Europe and the Muslim world, areas that have often been considered outside the boundaries of the West. These regions were arenas within which significant cultural encounters took place. Finally we include material on the United States and Australia, both of which have become part of the West. We recognize that most American college and university students have the opportunity to study American history as a separate subject, but treatment of the United States as a Western nation provides a different perspective from that usually given in courses on American history. For example, this book treats America's revolution as one of four Atlantic revolutions, its national unification in the nineteenth century as part of a broader western European development, its pattern of industrialization as related to that of Britain, and its central role in the Cold War as part of an ideological encounter that was global in scope.

Organization

The chronological and thematic organization of our book conforms in its broad outline to the way in which Western civilization courses are generally taught. We have limited the number of chapters to twenty-eight, in an effort to make the book more compatible with the traditional American semester calendar and to solve the frequent complaint that there is not enough time to cover all the material in the course. However, our organization differs from other books in some significant ways:

- Chapter 2, which covers the period from ca. 1600 to 550 B.C.E., is the first in a Western civilization textbook to examine the International Bronze Age and its aftermath as a period important in its own right because it saw the creation of expansionist, multi-ethnic empires linked by trade and diplomacy.
- In Chapter 4 the Roman Republic, in keeping with contemporary scholarship, has been incorporated into a discussion of the Hellenistic world, dethroned slightly to emphasize how it was one of many competing Mediterranean civilizations.
- Chapter 12 covers the first period of European expansion, from 1450 to 1650. It examines the new European encounters with the civilizations of sub-Saharan Africa, the Americas, and East Asia. By paying careful attention to the characteristics of these civilizations before the arrival of the Europeans, we show how this encounter affected indigenous peoples as well as Europeans.
- Chapter 16 is devoted entirely to the Scientific Revolution of the seventeenth century in order to emphasize the central importance of this development in the creation of Western identity.
- Chapter 17, which covers the second period of European expansion, from 1650 to 1815, studies the growth of European empires, the beginning of global warfare, and encounters between Europeans and the peoples of Asia and Africa. It treats the Atlantic revolutions of the late eighteenth and early nineteenth centuries, including

the American Revolution, as episodes in the history of European empires rather than as revolts inspired mainly by national sentiment.

■ Chapter 26 not only offers a comprehensive examination of World War II, but also explores the moral fissure in the history of the West created, in very different ways, by the Holocaust and the aerial bombings of civilian centers that culminated in the use of the atomic bomb in August 1945.

■ Chapter 28, "The West in the Contemporary Era: New Encounters and Transformations," includes an extended discussion of the emergence of European Islamic communities and the resulting transformations in both European and Islamic identities.

What's New in this Edition?

In preparing the second edition of *The West: Encounters & Transformations* we have focused on two goals: to make the textbook more teachable and to strengthen our emphasis on the encounters that have transformed the West.

Organization

We have reduced the number of chapters from twenty-nine to twenty-eight, in order to make the book even more compatible with the typical fifteen-week semester. In a number of chapters, moreover, we have made significant rearrangements of material:

■ In Chapter 3, we have discussed the Persian Empire before beginning our study of Hebrew and Greek civilizations to emphasize the argument that the latter two civilizations emerged in a political world dominated by Persia.

■ Chapters 6 through 9, which deal with the period from about 300 to 1300 C.E., have been rearranged along more thematic, less chronological lines. We have adopted this strategy to emphasize the importance of the interactions among different religious communities during a period that was crucial to the development of Christianity and Islam.

■ Chapter 17, "The West and the World: Empire, Trade, and War, 1650–1815," which appeared as Chapter 19 in the first edition, has been placed earlier in the book because it is concerned mainly with eighteenth-century developments. It now precedes the discussion of eighteenth-century society and culture.

■ In Chapter 22, "The Coming of Mass Politics: Industrialization, Emancipation, and Instability, 1870–1914," we have replaced the "nation-by-nation" narrative with a thematic approach that more effectively conveys the processes by which European elites sought both to capitalize on and control the new forces of popular nationalism.

■ Our treatment of both the Holocaust and the decision to use atomic bombs against Japan, which appeared as a separate chapter in the first edition, is now embedded in Chapter 26, "World War II." This volume still includes a far more extensive and in-depth exploration of these developments than any other Western civilization textbook.

■ New sections on "Postwar Nationalism, Westernization, and the Islamic Challenge" in Chapter 25, and "Islam, Terrorism, and European Identity" in Chapter 28 are the most striking examples of our decision to give more coverage to Islam throughout the book.

New Feature: "Encounters & Transformations"

We have introduced a new feature, "Encounters & Transformations," in about half the chapters. These essays reinforce the main theme of the book by giving specific examples of the ways in which cultural encounters changed the perception and identity of the West.

Features and Pedagogical Aids

In writing this textbook we have endeavored to keep both the student reader and the classroom instructor in mind at all times. The text includes the following features and pedagogical aids, all of which are intended to support the themes of the book.

What Is the West?

MANY OF THE PEOPLE WHO INFLUENCE PUBLIC OPINION—POLITI-cians, teachers, clergy, journalists, and television commenta-tors—refer to "Western values," "the West," and "Western civilization." They often use these terms as if they do not re-quire explanation. But what *do* these terms mean? The West has always been an arena within which different cultures, religions, values, and philosophies have interacted, and any definition of the West will inevitably arouse controversy.

The most basic definition of the West is of a place. Western civilization is now typically thought to comprise the regions of Europe, the Americas, Australia, and New Zealand. However, this is a contemporary definition of the West. The inclusion of these places in the West is the result of a long history of European expansion through colonization. In addition to being a place, Western civilization also encompasses a cultural history—a tradition stretching back thousands of years to the ancient world. Over this long period the civilization we now identify as Western gradually took shape. The

"What Is the West?"

The West: Encounters & Transformations begins with an essay to en-gage students in the task of defining the West and to introduce them to the notion of cultural encounters. "What Is the West?" guides stu-dents through the text by providing a framework for understanding how the West was shaped. Structured around the six questions of What? When? Where? Who? How? and Why?, this framework en-courages students to think about their understanding of Western civilization. The essay serves as a blueprint for using this textbook.

NEW! "Encounters & Transformations"

These features, which appear in about half the chapters, illustrate the main theme of the book by identifying specific encounters and showing how they led to significant transformations in the culture of the West. These features show, for example, how encounters among nomadic tribes of Arabia led to the rapid spread of Islam; how the Mayas' interpretation of Christian symbols transformed European Christianity into a hybrid religion; how the importation of chocolate from the New World to Europe changed Western consumption patterns and the rhythms of the Atlantic econ-omy; and how Picasso's encounter with African art led to the transformation of modernism. Each of these essays concludes with a question for discus-sion.

Encounters & Transformations

Ships of the Desert: Camels from Morocco to Central Asia

A remarkable thing happened when the Arab followers of the dynamic new religion of Islam encountered the humble beast of burden the camel. The camel helped make Arab armies lethal in battle, which meant that the mes-sage of Islam spread rapidly through conquest. In addition the caravan trade that transported goods on the backs of camels brought the Arabs into contact with a vast stretch of the world from Spain to China. In the ex-changes that took place along the caravan routes, Islamic religious ideas were widely disseminated, and Arab merchants gained access to a lucrative trade that enriched Muslim cities. The success of the caravan trade changed the very appearance of large parts of the West by making obsolete the old Roman roads and the shipping lanes that had unified the ancient Mediterranean, Europe, and North Africa in the ancient world. Narrow camel tracks replaced roads; oases and cities along the caravan routes supplanted ports in economic significance.

Before Muhammad began to re-cite, the camel had already trans-formed the life of Arabia. Camels were highly efficient beasts of bur-den, especially in arid regions, be-cause of their bodies' capacity to conserve water. Able to drink as much as twenty-eight gallons at a time, camels can last four to nine days without water and travel great distances in this period. The fat in their humps allows camels to survive for even longer without food. As pack animals, camels are more efficient than carts pulled by animals because they can traverse roadless rough terrain and cross

rivers without bridges. They re-quire fewer people to manage them on a journey than do wheeled vehicles.

Arab fighters were especially menacing because they developed the "North Arabian saddle" that let them ride the one-humped Arabian camel with comfort in battle. The new saddle required only one rider who could grasp the camel's reins with one hand while slashing downward at enemy troops with a sword in his other hand. Warriors on camels could attack infantry with speed and crushing force. By 300 C.E., camel-breeding Arab tribesmen, empowered by their new military technology, inaugu-rated the "Caravan Age." The Arabs seized control of the lucrative spice trade routes and became an eco-nomic, military, and political force by exploiting and guarding the wealth of the caravans.

After Muhammad established his community in Mecca, Islam literally "took off" on camelback. Tribes-men on camels proved an unstop-pable force as they spread Islam first throughout Arabia and the Middle East, and then with light-ning speed across North Africa into Spain and Central Asia. Camels played a significant role in the expanding Islamic economy be-cause they made long-distance trade extremely profitable. The transformations the camel brought were most evident in the former

Roman provinces wh mous Roman roads h primary conduit of la Thousands of miles o nected the provinces Empire and let troop from one front to an ever, camels changed Because these "ships do not need paved routes did not have t Roman road systems, chants bypassed then New trade routes acr and other harsh terra to camels quickly de Morocco to Central A astonishing consequ 700 paved roads start pear. Because camels walk on narrow path streets and wide mar carts and wagons tha Greek and Roman cit use. Bazaars with nar lanes appropriate to sprung up to replace and wheeled vehicle peared in these lands just roads and the stu that changed. There consequences as wel caravan traffic reache China, bringing Chin Chinese ideas to the

Question for D
How might the history have differed had not replaced the system of

The Camel Caravan
This modern photograph shows a string of camels cross-

Focus Questions

The introduction to each chapter includes a state-ment of the main question that the entire chapter addresses. It also includes a set of questions that the individual sections of the chapter seek to answer. Each of these questions is then repeated at the begin-ning of the relevant section of the chapter. The reason for this strategy is to remind the student that the purpose of studying history is not only to learn what happened in the past but also to explain and in-terpret the course of events. This pedagogical strat-egy reinforces the approach that the essay, "What is the West?," introduces at the beginning of the book.

"Justice in History"

Found in every chapter, this feature presents a his-torically significant trial or episode in which different notions of justice (or injustice) were debated and resolved. The "Justice in History" features illustrate cultural encounters within communities as they try to determine the fate of individuals from all walks of life. Many famous trials dealt with conflicts over basic religious, philosophical, or political values, such as those of Socrates, Jesus, Joan of Arc, Charles I, Galileo, and Adolf Eichmann. Other "Justice in History" features show how judicial institutions, such as the ordeal, the Inquisition, and revolutionary tribunals, handled adversarial situations in different societies. These essays, therefore, illustrate the way in which the basic values of the West have evolved through attempts to resolve disputes, contention, and conflict.

Each "Justice in History" feature includes two pedagogical aids. "Questions of Justice" helps students explore the historical significance of the episode just examined. These questions can also be used in classroom discussion or as student essay topics. "Taking It Further" provides the student with a few references that can be consulted in connection with a research project.

"The Human Body in History"

Found in about half of the chapters, these features show that the human body, which many people tend to understand solely as a product of biology, also has a history. These essays reveal that the ways in which various religious and political groups have represented the body in art and literature, clothed it, treated it medically, and abused it tell a great deal about the history of Western culture. These features include essays on the classical nude male body, the signs of disease during the Black Death, bathing the body in the East and the West, and the contraceptive pill. Concluding each essay is a single question for discussion that directs students back to the broader issues with which the chapter deals.

Primary Source Documents

In each chapter we have presented a number of excerpts from primary source documents—from "Tales of the Flood" to "Darwin's 'Descent of Man'"—in order to reinforce or expand upon the points made in the text and to introduce students to the basic materials of historical research.

Maps and Illustrations

Artwork is a key component of our book. We recognize that many students often lack a strong familiarity with geography, and so we have taken great care to develop maps that help sharpen their geographic skills. Complementing the book's standard map program, we include maps focusing on areas outside the borders of Western civilization. These maps include a small thumbnail globe that highlights the geographic area under discussion in the context of the larger world. Fine art and photos also tell the story of Western civilization, and we have included more than 350 images to help students visualize the past: the way people lived, the events that shaped their lives, and how they viewed the world around them.

Chronologies and Suggested Readings

Each chapter includes chronological charts and suggested readings. Chronologies outline significant events, such as "The End of World War II," and serve as convenient references for students. Each chapter concludes with an annotated list of suggested readings. These are not scholarly bibliographies aimed at the professor, but suggestions for students who wish to explore a topic in greater depth or to write a research paper. A comprehensive list of suggested readings is available on our book-specific website, www.ablongman.com/levack2e.

Glossary

We have sought to create a work that is accessible to students with little prior knowledge of the basic facts of Western history or geography. Throughout the book we have explained difficult concepts at length. For example, we present in-depth explanations of the concepts of Zoroastrianism, Neoplatonism, Renaissance humanism, the various Protestant denominations of the sixteenth century, capitalism, seventeenth-century absolutism, nineteenth-century liberalism and nationalism, fascism, and modernism. Key concepts such as these are identified in the chapters with a degree symbol (°) and defined as well in the end-of-text Glossary.

MyHistoryLab Icons

Throughout the text, you will see icons that will lead students to additional resources found on MyHistoryLab.com. These resources fall into four categories:

The **document** icon directs students to primary source documents that support the material they are reading in the textbook. In addition, most documents offer headnotes and analysis questions that focus students' reading.

The **image** icon leads students to photos, cartoons, and artwork that relate to the topic they are reading. Most images include a descriptive, contextualized headnote and analysis questions.

The **map** icon refers to maps, many of which are interactive and contain headnotes and questions designed to help students visualize the material they are learning. Printable map activities from Longman's outstanding geography workbooks allow students to interact with maps.

The **video** icon leads students to video clips that focus on the regions, people, or events discussed in the text.

A Note About Dates and Transliterations

In keeping with current academic practice, *The West: Encounters & Transformations* uses B.C.E. (before the common era) and C.E. (common era) to designate dates. We also follow the most current and widely accepted English transliterations of Arabic. *Qur'an,* for example, is used for *Koran; Muslim* is used for *Moslem.* Chinese words appearing in the text for the first time are written in pinyin, followed by the older Wade-Giles system in parentheses.

Supplements

For Qualified College Instructors

Instructor's Resource Manual

0-321-42735-1

In this manual written by Sharon Arnoult, Midwestern State University, each chapter contains a chapter outline, significant themes, learning objectives, lesson enrichment ideas, discussion suggestions, and questions for discussing the primary source documents in the text.

Test Bank

0-321-42731-9

Written by Susan Carrafiello, Wright State University, this supplement contains more than 1,200 multiple-choice and essay questions. All questions are referenced by topic and text page number.

TestGen-EQ Computerized Testing System

0-321-42573-1

This flexible, easy-to-master computerized test bank on a dual-platform CD includes all of the items in the printed test bank and allows instructors to select specific questions, edit existing questions, and add their own items to create exams. Tests can be printed in several different fonts and formats and can include figures, such as graphs and tables.

Companion Website (www.ablongman.com/lcvack2e)

Instructors can take advantage of the Companion Website that supports this text. The instructor section includes teaching links, downloadable maps, tables, and graphs from the text for use in PowerPoint, PowerPoint lecture outlines, and a link to the Instructor Resource Center.

Instructor Resource Center (IRC) (www.ablongman.com/irc)

Through the Instructor Resource Center, instructors can log into premium online products, browse and download book-specific instructor resources, and receive immediate access and instructions to installing course management content. Instructors who already have access to CourseCompass or Supplements Central can log in to the IRC immediately using their existing login and password. First-time users can register at the Instructor Resource Center welcome page at www.ablongman.com/irc.

MyHistoryLab (www.myhistorylab.com)

MyHistoryLab provides students with an online package complete with the entire electronic textbook and numerous study aids. With several hundred primary sources, many of which are assignable and link to a gradebook, pre- and post-tests that link to a gradebook and result in individualized study plans, videos and images, as well as map workbook activities with gradable quizzes, the site offers students a unique, interactive experience that brings history to life. The comprehensive site also includes a History Bookshelf with fifty of the most commonly assigned books in history classes and a History Toolkit with tutorials and helpful links. Other features include gradable assignments and chapter review materials; a Test Bank; and Research Navigator.

Delivered in CourseCompass, Blackboard, or WebCT, as well as in a non-course-management version, MyHistoryLab is easy to use and flexible. MyHistoryLab is organized according to the table of contents of this textbook. With the course management version, instructors can create a further customized product by adding their own syllabus, content, and assignments, or they can use the materials as presented.

PowerPoint Presentations
These presentations contain PowerPoint slides for each chapter and may include key points and terms for a lecture on the chapter, as well as full-color images of important maps, graphs, and charts. The presentations are available for download from www.ablongman.com/levack2e and www.ablongman.com/irc.

Text-Specific Transparency Set
0-321-42732-7
Instructors can download files with which to make full-color transparency map acetates taken from the text at www.ablongman.com/irc.

History Video Program
Longman offers more than one hundred videos from which qualified adopters can choose. Restrictions apply.

History Digital Media Archive CD-ROM
0-321-14976-9
This CD-ROM contains electronic images, interactive and static maps, and media elements such as video. It is fully customizable and ready for classroom presentation. All images and maps are available in PowerPoint as well.

Discovering Western Civilization Through Maps and Views
0-673-53596-7
Created by Gerald Danzer, University of Illinois at Chicago, and David Buissert, this unique set of 140 full-color acetates contains an introduction to teaching history through maps and a detailed commentary on each transparency. The collection includes cartographic and pictorial maps, views and photos, urban plans, building diagrams, and works of art. Available to qualified college adopters on Longman's Instructor Resource Center (IRC) at www.ablongman.com/irc.

For Students

Study Guide
Volume I: 0-321-42733-5
Volume II: 0-321-42734-3
Containing activities and study aids for every chapter in the text, each chapter of the *Study Guide* written by Carron Fillingim, Louisiana State University, includes a thorough chapter outline; timeline; map exercises; identification, multiple-choice and thought questions; and critical-thinking questions based on primary source documents from the text.

Companion Website (www.ablongman.com/levack2e)

Providing a wealth of resources for students using *The West: Encounters & Transformations,* Second Edition, this Companion Website contains chapter summaries, interactive practice test questions, and Web links for every chapter in the text.

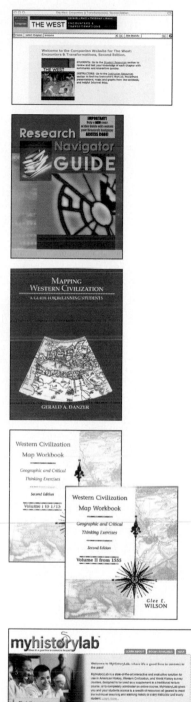

Research Navigator and Research Navigator Guide

0-205-40838-9

Research Navigator is a comprehensive Website comprising four exclusive databases of credible and reliable source material for research and for student assignments: EBSCO's ContentSelect Academic Journal & Abstract Database, the *New York Times* Search-by-Subject Archive, *Financial Times* Article Archive and Company Financials, and "Best of the Web" Link Library. The site also includes an extensive help section. The Research Navigator Guide provides your students with access to the Research Navigator website and includes reference material and hints about conducting online research. Available to qualified college adopters when packaged with the text.

Mapping Western Civilization: Student Activities

0-673-53774-9

Created by Gerald Danzer, University of Illinois at Chicago, this FREE map workbook for students is designed as an accompaniment to *Discovering Western Civilization Through Maps and Views.* It features exercises designed to teach students to interpret and analyze cartographic materials such as historical documents. Available to qualified college adopters when packaged with the text.

Western Civilization Map Workbook

Volume I: 0-321-01878-8
Volume II: 0-321-01877-X

The map exercises in these volumes, created by Glee Wilson at Kent State University, test and reinforce basic geography literacy while building critical-thinking skills. Available to qualified college adopters when packaged with the text.

Study Card for Western Civilization

0-321-29233-2

Colorful, affordable, and packed with useful information, Longman's Study Cards make studying easier, more efficient, and more enjoyable. Course information is distilled down to the basics, helping students quickly master the fundamentals, review a subject for understanding, or prepare for an exam. Because they're laminated for durability, they can be kept for years to come and used whenever necessary for a quick review. Available to qualified college adopters when packaged with the text.

MyHistoryLab (www.myhistorylab.com)

MyHistoryLab provides students with an online package complete with the entire electronic textbook, numerous study aids, primary sources, and chapter exams. With several hundred primary sources and images, as well as map workbook activities with gradable quizzes, the site offers students a unique, interactive experience that brings history to life. The comprehensive site also includes a History Bookshelf with fifty of the most commonly assigned books in history classes and a History Toolkit with tutorials and helpful links.

Longman Atlas of Western Civilization

0-321-21626-1

This fifty-two-page atlas features carefully selected historical maps that provide comprehensive coverage for the major historical periods. Each map has been designed to be colorful, easy to read, and informative, without sacrificing detailed accuracy. This atlas makes history—and geography—more comprehensible.

A Short Guide to Writing About History, Fifth Edition

0-321-22716-6

Written by Richard A. Marius, late of Harvard University, and Melvin E. Page, Eastern Tennessee State University, this engaging and practical text helps students get beyond merely compiling dates and facts; it teaches them how to incorporate their own ideas into their papers and to tell a story about history that interests them and their peers. Covering both brief essays and the documented resource paper, the text explores the writing and researching processes; identifies different modes of historical writing, including argument; and concludes with guidelines for improving style.

Penguin-Longman Partnership

The partnership between Penguin Books and Longman Publishers offers a discount on the following titles when bundled with any Longman history survey textbook. Visit www.ablongman.com/penguin for more information.

Available Titles

Peter Abelard, *The Letters of Abelard and Heloise*

Dante Alighieri, *Divine Comedy: Inferno*

Dante Alighieri, *The Portable Dante*

Anonymous, *Early Irish Myths & Sagas*

Anonymous, *The Epic of Gilgamesh*

Anonymous, *The Song of Roland*

Anonymous, *Vinland Sagas*

Hannah Arendt, *On Revolution*

Aristophanes, *The Birds and Other Plays*

Aristotle, *The Politics*

Louis Auchincloss, *Woodrow Wilson* (Penguin Lives Series)

St. Augustine, *The Confessions of St. Augustine*

Jane Austen, *Emma*

Jane Austen, *Persuasion*

Jane Austen, *Pride and Prejudice*

Jane Austen, *Sense and Sensibility*

Edward Bellamy, *Looking Backward*

Richard Bowring, *Diary of Lady Murasaki*

Charlotte Brontë, *Jane Eyre*

Charlotte Brontë, *Villette*

Emily Brontë, *Wuthering Heights*

Edmund Burke, *Reflection on the Revolution in France and on the Proceedings in Certain Societies in London Relative to that Event*

Benvenuto Cellini, *The Autobiography of Benvenuto Cellini*

Geoffrey Chaucer, *The Canterbury Tales*

Marcus Tullius Cicero, *Cicero: Selected Political Speeches*

Miguel de Cervantes, *The Adventures of Don Quixote*

Bartolome de las Casas, *A Short Account of the Destruction of the West Indies*

René Descartes, *Discourse on Method and Related Writings*

Charles Dickens, *Great Expectations*

Charles Dickens, *Hard Times*

John Dos Passos, *Three Soldiers*

Einhard, *Two Lives of Charlemagne*

Olaudah Equiano, *The Interesting Narrative and Other Writings*

M. Finley (ed.), *The Portable Greek Historians*

Benjamin Franklin, *The Autobiography and Other Writings*

Jeffrey Gantz (tr.), *Early Irish Myths and Sagas*

Peter Gay, *Mozart* (Penguin Lives Series)

William Golding, *Lord of the Flies*

Grimm & Grimm, *Grimms' Fairy Tales*

Thomas Hardy, *Jude the Obscure*

Herodotus, *The Histories*

Thomas Hobbes, *Leviathan*

Homer, *The Iliad*

Homer, *The Iliad* (Deluxe)

Homer, *Odyssey Deluxe*

Homer, *Odyssey: Revised Prose Translation*

The Koran

Deborah Lipstadt, *Denying the Holocaust*
Machiavelli, *The Prince*
Bill Manley, *The Penguin Historical Atlas of Ancient Egypt*
Karl Marx, *The Communist Manifesto*
Colin McEvedy, *The New Penguin Atlas of Ancient History*
Colin McEvedy, *The New Penguin Atlas of Medieval History*
John Stuart Mill, *On Liberty*
Jean-Baptiste Molière, *Tartuffe and Other Plays*
Sir Thomas More, *Utopia and Other Essential Writings*
Robert Morkot, *The Penguin Historical Atlas of Ancient Greece*
Sherwin Nuland, *Leonardo Da Vinci*
George Orwell, *1984*
George Orwell, *Animal Farm*
Plato, *Great Dialogues of Plato*
Plato, *The Last Days of Socrates*
Plato, *The Republic*
Plutarch, *Fall of the Roman Republic*
Marco Polo, *The Travels*
Procopius, *The Secret History*
Jean-Jacques Rousseau, *The Social Contract*
Sallust, *The Jugurthine Wars, The Conspiracy of Cataline*
Chris Scarre, *The Penguin Historical Atlas of Ancient Rome*
Desmond Seward, *The Hundred Years' War*
William Shakespeare, *Four Great Comedies: The Taming of the Shrew, A Midsummer's Night Dream, Twelfth Night, The Tempest*

William Shakespeare, *Four Great Tragedies: Hamlet, Macbeth, King Lear, Othello*
William Shakespeare, *Four Histories: Richard II, Henry IV: Part I, Henry IV: Part II, Henry V*
William Shakespeare, *Hamlet*
William Shakespeare, *King Lear*
William Shakespeare, *Macbeth*
William Shakespeare, *The Merchant of Venice*
William Shakespeare, *Othello*
William Shakespeare, *The Taming of the Shrew*
William Shakespeare, *The Tempest*
William Shakespeare, *Twelfth Night*
Mary Shelley, *Frankenstein*
Aleksandr Solzhenitsyn, *One Day in the Life of Ivan Denisovich*
Sophocles, *The Three Theban Plays*
Robert Louis Stevenson, *The Strange Case of Dr. Jekyll and Mr. Hyde*
Suetonius, *The Twelve Caesars*
Jonathan Swift, *Gulliver's Travels*
Tacitus, *The Histories*
Various, *The Penguin Book of Historical Speeches*
Voltaire, *Candide, Zadig and Selected Stories*
Carl von Clausewitz, *On War*
von Goethe, *Faust, Part 1*
von Goethe, *Faust, Part 2*
Edith Wharton, *Ethan Frome*
Willet, *The Signet World Atlas*
Gary Wills, *Saint Augustine* (Penguin Lives Series)
Virginia Woolf, *Jacob's Room*

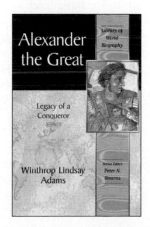

Longman Library of World Biography Series

Each interpretive biography in the new Library of World Biography series focuses on a figure whose actions and ideas significantly influenced the course of world history. Pocket-sized and brief, each book relates the life of its subject to the broader themes and developments of the time. Longman Publishers offers your students a discount on the titles below when instructors request that they be bundled with any Longman history survey textbook. Series titles include:

Ahmad al-Mansur: Islamic Visionary by Richard Smith (Ferrum College)
Alexander the Great: Legacy of a Conqueror by Winthrop Lindsay Adams (University of Utah)
Benito Mussolini: The First Fascist by Anthony L. Cardoza (Loyola University)
Fukuzawa Yūkichi: From Samurai to Capitalist by Helen M. Hopper (University of Pittsburgh)
Ignatius of Loyola: Founder of the Jesuits by John Patrick Donnelly (Marquette University)

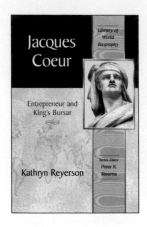

Jacques Coeur: Entrepreneur and King's Bursar by Kathryn L. Reyerson
  (University of Minnesota)
Katô Shidzue: A Japanese Feminist by Helen M. Hopper (University of Pittsburgh)
Simón Bolívar: Liberation and Disappointment by David Bushnell (University of Florida)
Vasco da Gama: Renaissance Crusader by Glenn J. Ames (University of Toledo)
Zheng He: China and the Oceans in the Early Ming, 1405–1433 by Edward Dreyer
  (University of Miami)

Acknowledgments

In writing this book we have benefited from the guidance of many members of the superb editorial staff at Longman. We would like to thank our acquisitions editor Janet Lanphier for helping us refine and develop this second edition. David Kear, our development editor, gave us valuable criticisms and helped us keep our audience in mind. Heather Johnson superintended the copyediting and proofreading with skill and efficiency, while Christine Buese helped us locate the most appropriate illustrations. Sue Westmoreland, the executive marketing manager for history, offered many creative ideas for promoting the book.

The authors wish to thank the following friends and colleagues for their assistance: Kenneth Alder, Joseph Alehermes, Karl Appuhn, Sharon Arnoult, Nicholas Baker, Paula Baskovits, Paul-Alain Beaulieu, Kamilia Bergen, Timothy Breen, Peter Brown, Peter Carroll, Shawn Clybor, Jauabeth Condie-Pugh, Patricia Crone, Tracey Cullen, Arthur Eckstein, Susanna Elm, Benjamin Frommer, Cynthia Gladstone, Dena Goodman, Stefka Hadjiandonova, Matthias Henze, Stanley Hilton, Kenneth Holum, Mark Jurdjevic, Werner Kelber, Cathleen Keller, Anne Kilmer, Jacob Lassner, Robert Lerner, Nancy Levack, Richard Lim, David Lindenfeld, Brian Maxson, Sarah Maza, Peter Mazur, Laura McGough, Roderick McIntosh, Susan K. McIntosh, Glenn Markoe, William Monter, Randy Nichols, Scott Noegel, Monique O'Connell, Carl Petry, Michael Rogers, Karl Roider, Sarah Ross, Michele Salzman, Paula Sanders, Regina Schwartz, Ethan Shagan, Julia M. H. Smith, James Sidbury, and Rachel Wahlig.

We would also like to thank the many historians who gave generously of their time to review during the various stages of development of our second edition. Their comments and suggestions helped to improve the book. Thank you:

Melanie A. Bailey, *South Dakota State University*
Brett Berliner, *Morgan State University*
Alfred S. Bradford, *University of Oklahoma*
Linda Charmaine Powell, *Amarillo College*
Daniel Christensen, *California State University, Fullerton*
William L. Cumiford, *Chapman University*
Rebecca Durrer, *Columbia College*
Steven Fanning, *University of Illinois at Chicago*
Sean Farrell, *Northern Illinois University*
Judy E. Gaughan, *Colorado State University*
Jennifer Hedda, *Simpson College*
David Hudson, *California State University, Fresno*
Rebecca Huston, *Hinds Community College*
Barbara A. Klemm, *Broward Community College*
Molly McClain, *University of San Diego*
Randall McGowen, *University of Oregon*

John A. Nichols, *Slippery Rock University*
James T. Owens, *Oakton Community College*
Elizabeth Propes, *Mesa State College*
Miriam Raub Vivian, *California State University, Bakersfield*
Anne Rodrick, *Wofford College*
Jarbel Rodriguez, *San Francisco State University*
Jacquelyn A. Royal, *Lee University*
Jutta Scott, *South Carolina University*
Susan O. Shapiro, *Utah State University*
Steven E. Sidebotham, *University of Delaware*
David Stone, *Kansas State University*
Charles R. Sullivan, *University of Dallas*
Mary C. Swilling, *University of Mississippi*
Larissa Juliet Taylor, *Colby College*
Jonathan Ziskind, *University of Louisville*

We would also like to thank the historians whose careful reviews and comments on the first edition helped us revise the book for its second edition. Our thanks for your contributions:

Henry Abramson, *Florida Atlantic University*

Patricia Ali, *Morris College*

Joseph Appiah, *J. Sergeant Reynolds Community College*

Sharon L. Arnoult, *Midwestern State University*

Arthur H. Auten, *University of Hartford*

Clifford Backman, *Boston University*

Suzanne Balch-Lindsay, *Eastern New Mexico University*

Wayne C. Bartee, *Southwest Miami State University*

Brandon Beck, *Shenandoah University*

James R. Belpedio, *Becker College*

Richard Berthold, *University of New Mexico*

Cynthia S. Bisson, *Belmont University*

Richard Bodek, *College of Charleston*

Melissa Bokovoy, *University of New Mexico*

William H. Brennan, *University of the Pacific*

Morgan R. Broadhead, *Jefferson Community College*

Theodore Bromund, *Yale University*

April A. Brooks, *South Dakota State University*

Nathan M. Brooks, *New Mexico State University*

Michael Burger, *Mississippi University for Women*

Susan Carrafiello, *Wright State University*

Kathleen S. Carter, *High Point University*

William L. Combs, *Western Illinois University*

Joseph Coohill, *Pennsylvania State University–New Kensington*

Richard A. Cosgrove, *University of Arizona*

Leonard Curtis, *Mississippi College*

Miriam Davis, *Delta State University*

Alexander DeGrand, *North Carolina State University*

Marion Deshmukh, *George Mason University*

Janusz Duzinkiewicz, *Purdue University, North Central*

Mary Beth Emmerichs, *University of Wisconsin, Sheboygan*

Steven Fanning, *University of Illinois at Chicago*

Bryan Ganaway, *University of Illinois at Urbana–Champaign*

Frank Garosi, *California State University–Sacramento*

Christina Gold, *Loyola Marymount University*

Ignacio Götz, *Hofstra University*

Louis Haas, *Duquesne University*

Linda Jones Hall, *Saint Mary's College of Maryland*

Paul Halsall, *University of North Florida*

Donald J. Harreld, *Brigham Young University*

Carmen V. Harris, *University of South Carolina at Spartanburg*

James C. Harrison, *Siena College*

Mark C. Herman, *Edison Community College*

Curry A. Herring, *University of Southern Alabama*

Patrick Holt, *Fordham University*

W. Robert Houston, *University of South Alabama*

Lester Hutton, *Westfield State College*

Jeffrey Hyson, *Saint Joseph's University*

Paul Jankowski, *Brandeis University*

Padraic Kennedy, *McNeese State University*

Joanne Klein, *Boise State University*

Theodore Kluz, *Troy State University*

Skip Knox, *Boise State University*

Cynthia Kosso, *Northern Arizona University*

Ann Kuzdale, *Chicago State University*

Lawrence Langer, *University of Connecticut*

Oscar E. Lansen, *University of North Carolina at Charlotte*

Michael V. Leggiere, *Louisiana State University at Shreveport*

Rhett Leverett, *Marymount University*

Alison Williams Lewin, *Saint Joseph's University*

Wendy Liu, *Miami University, Middletown*

Elizabeth Makowski, *Southwest Texas State University*

Daniel Meissner, *Marquette University*

Isabel Moreira, *University of Utah*

Kenneth Moure, *University of California–Santa Barbara*

Melva E. Newsom, *Clark State Community College*

John A. Nichols, *Slippery Rock University*

Susannah R. Ottaway, *Carleton College*

James H. Overfield, *University of Vermont*

Brian L. Peterson, *Florida International University*

Hugh Phillips, *Western Kentucky University*

Jeff Plaks, *University of Central Oklahoma*

Thomas L. Powers, *University of South Carolina, Sumter*

Carole Putko, *San Diego State University*

Barbara Ranieri, *University of Alabama at Birmingham*

Elsa M. E. Rapp, *Montgomery County Community College*

Marlette Rebhorn, *Austin Community College*

Roger Reese, *Texas A&M University*

Travis Ricketts, *Bryan College*

Thomas Robisheaux, *Duke University*

Bill Robison, *Southeastern Louisiana University*

Mark Ruff, *Concordia University*

Frank Russell, *Transylvania University*

Marylou Ruud, *The University of West Florida*

Michael Saler, *University of California–Davis*

Timothy D. Saxon, *Charleston Southern University*

Daniel A. Scalberg, *Multnomah Bible College*

Ronald Schechter, *College of William and Mary*

Philip Skaggs, *Grand Valley State University*

Helmut Walser Smith, *Vanderbilt University*

Eileen Solwedel, *Edmonds Community College*

Sister Maria Consuelo Sparks, *Immaculata University*

Ilicia J. Sprey, *Saint Joseph's College*

Charles R. Sullivan, *University of Dallas*

Frederick Suppe, *Ball State University*

Frank W. Thackery, *Indiana University Southeast*
Frances B. Titchener, *Utah State University*
Katherine Tosa, *Muskegon Community College*
Lawrence A. Tritle, *Loyola Marymount University*

Clifford F. Wargelin, *Georgetown College*
Theodore R. Weeks, *Southern Illinois University*
Elizabeth A. Williams, *Oklahoma State University*
Mary E. Zamon, *Marymount University*

BRIAN LEVACK
EDWARD MUIR
MEREDITH VELDMAN
MICHAEL MAAS

Meet the Authors

Brian Levack grew up in a family of teachers in the New York metropolitan area. From his father, a professor of French history, he acquired a love for studying the past, and he knew from an early age that he too would become a historian. He received his B.A. from Fordham University in 1965 and his Ph.D. from Yale in 1970. In graduate school he became fascinated by the history of the law and the interaction between law and politics, interests that he has maintained throughout his career. In 1969 he joined the history department of the University of Texas at Austin, where he is now the John Green Regents Professor in History. The winner of several teaching awards, Levack teaches a wide variety of courses on British and European history, legal history, and the history of witchcraft. For eight years he served as the chair of his department, a rewarding but challenging assignment that made it difficult for him to devote as much time as he wished to his teaching and scholarship. His books include *The Civil Lawyers in England, 1603–1641: A Political Study* (1973), *The Formation of the British State: England, Scotland and the Union, 1603–1707* (1987), and *The Witch-Hunt in Early Modern Europe* (1987 and 1995), which has been translated into eight languages.

His study of the development of beliefs about witchcraft in Europe over the course of many centuries gave him the idea of writing a textbook on Western civilization that would illustrate a broader set of encounters between different cultures, societies, and ideologies. While writing the book, Levack and his two sons built a house on property that he and his wife, Nancy, own in the Texas hill country. He found that the two projects presented similar challenges: It was easy to draw up the design, but far more difficult to execute it. When not teaching, writing, or doing carpentry work, Levack runs along the jogging trails of Austin, and he has recently discovered the pleasures of scuba diving.

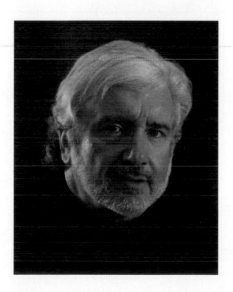

Edward Muir grew up in the foothills of the Wasatch Mountains in Utah, close to the Emigration Trail along which wagon trains of Mormon pioneers and California-bound settlers made their way westward. As a child he loved to explore the broken-down wagons and abandoned household goods left at the side of the trail and from that acquired a fascination with the past. Besides the material remains of the past, he grew up with stories of his Mormon pioneer ancestors and an appreciation for how the past continued to influence the present. During the turbulent 1960s, he became interested in Renaissance Italy as a period and a place that had been formative for Western civilization. His biggest challenge is finding the time to explore yet another new corner of Italy and its restaurants.

Muir received his Ph.D. from Rutgers University, where he specialized in the Italian Renaissance and did archival research in Venice and Florence, Italy. He is now the Clarence L. Ver Steeg Professor in the Arts and Sciences at Northwestern University and former chair of the history department. At Northwestern he has won several teaching awards. His books include *Civic Ritual in Renaissance Venice* (1981), *Mad Blood Stirring: Vendetta in Renaissance Italy* (1993 and 1998), and *Ritual in Early Modern Europe* (1997 and 2005).

Some years ago Muir began to experiment with the use of historical trials in teaching and discovered that students loved them. From that experience he decided to write this textbook, which employs trials as a central feature. He lives beside Lake Michigan in Evanston, Illinois. His twin passions are skiing in the Rocky Mountains and rooting for the Chicago Cubs, who manage every summer to demonstrate that winning isn't everything.

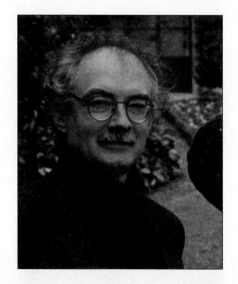

Meredith Veldman grew up in the western suburbs of Chicago in a close-knit, closed-in Dutch Calvinist community. In this immigrant society, history mattered: the "Reformed tradition" structured not only religious beliefs but also social identity and political practice. This influence certainly played some role in shaping Veldman's early fascination with history. But probably just as important were the countless World War II reenactment games she played with her five older brothers. Whatever the cause, Veldman majored in history at Calvin College in Grand Rapids, Michigan, and then earned a Ph.D. in modern European history, with a concentration in nineteenth- and twentieth-century Britain, from Northwestern University in 1988.

As associate professor of history at Louisiana State University, Veldman teaches courses in nineteenth- and twentieth-century British history and twentieth-century Europe, as well as the second half of "Western Civ." In her many semesters in the Western Civ. classroom, Veldman tried a number of different textbooks but found herself increasingly dissatisfied. She wanted a text that would convey to beginning students at least some of the complexities and ambiguities of historical interpretation, introduce them to the exciting work being done now in cultural history, and, most important, tell a good story. The search for this textbook led her to accept the offer made by Levack, Maas, and Muir to join them in writing *The West: Encounters & Transformations*.

The author of *Fantasy, the Bomb, and the Greening of Britain: Romantic Protest, 1945–1980* (1994), Veldman is also the wife of a Methodist minister and the mother of two young sons. They reside in Baton Rouge, Louisiana, where Veldman finds coping with the steamy climate a constant challenge. She and her family recently returned from Manchester, England, where they lived for three years and astonished the natives by their enthusiastic appreciation of English weather.

Michael Maas was born in the Ohio River Valley, in a community that had been a frontier outpost during the late eighteenth century. He grew up reading the stories of the early settlers and their struggles with the native peoples, and seeing in the urban fabric how the city had subsequently developed into a prosperous coal and steel town with immigrants from all over the world. As a boy he developed a lifetime interest in the archaeology and history of the ancient Mediterranean world and began to study Latin. At Cornell University he combined his interests in cultural history and the classical world by majoring in classics and anthropology. A semester in Rome clinched his commitment to these fields—and to Italian cooking. Maas went on to get his Ph.D. in the graduate program in ancient history and Mediterranean archaeology at the University of California at Berkeley.

He has traveled widely in the Mediterranean and the Middle East and participated in several archaeological excavations, including an underwater dig in Greece. Since 1985 he has taught ancient history at Rice University in Houston, Texas, where he founded and directs the interdisciplinary B.A. program in ancient Mediterranean civilizations. He has won several teaching awards.

Maas's special area of research is late antiquity, the period of transition from the classical to the medieval worlds, which saw the collapse of the Roman Empire in western Europe and the development of the Byzantine state in the East. During his last sabbatical, he was a member of the Institute for Advanced Study in Princeton, New Jersey, where he worked on his current book, *The Conqueror's Gift: Ethnography, Identity, and Imperial Power at the End of Antiquity* (forthcoming). His other books include *John Lydus and the Roman Past: Antiquarianism and Politics in the Age of Justinian* (1992), *Readings in Late Antiquity: A Sourcebook* (2000), and *Exegesis and Empire in the Early Byzantine Mediterranean* (2003).

Maas has always been interested in interdisciplinary teaching and the encounters among different cultures. He sees *The West: Encounters & Transformations* as an opportunity to explain how the modern civilization that we call "the West" had its origins in the diverse interactions among many peoples of antiquity.

THE WEST

What Is the West?

ANY OF THE PEOPLE WHO INFLUENCE PUBLIC OPINION—POLITI-cians, teachers, clergy, journalists, and television commenta-tors—refer to "Western values," "the West," and "Western civilization." They often use these terms as if they do not re-quire explanation. But what *do* these terms mean? The West has always been an arena within which different cultures, religions, values, and philosophies have interacted, and any definition of the West will inevitably arouse controversy.

The most basic definition of the West is of a place. Western civilization is now typically thought to comprise the regions of Europe, the Americas, Australia, and New Zealand. However, this is a contemporary definition of the West. The inclusion of these places in the West is the result of a long history of European expansion through colonization. In addition to being a place, Western civilization also encompasses a cultural history—a tradition stretching back thousands of years to the ancient world. Over this long period the civilization we now identify as Western gradually took shape. The many characteristics that identify any civilization emerged over this time: forms of government, economic systems, and methods of scientific inquiry, as well as religions, languages, literature, and art.

Throughout the development of Western civilization, the ways in which people identified themselves changed as well. People in the ancient world had no such idea of the common identity of the West, only of being mem-bers of a tribe, citizens of a town, or subjects of an empire. But with the spread of Christianity and Islam between the first and seventh centuries, the notion of a distinct civilization in these "Western" lands subtly changed. People came to identify themselves less as subjects of a particular empire and more as members of a community of faith—whether that community com-prised followers of Christianity, Judaism, or Islam. These communities of faith drew lines of inclusion and exclusion that still exist today. Starting

The Temple of Hera at Paestum, Italy Greek colonists in Italy built this temple in the sixth century B.C.E. Greek ideas and artistic styles spread throughout the ancient world both from Greek colonists, such as those at Paestum, and from other peoples who imi-tated the Greeks.

about 1,600 years ago, Christian monarchs and clergy began to obliterate polytheism (the worship of many gods) and marginalize Jews. From a thousand to 500 years ago, Christian authorities strove to expel Muslims from Europe. Europeans developed definitions of the West that did not include Islamic communities, even though Muslims continued to live in Europe and Europeans traded and interacted with the Muslim world. The Islamic countries themselves erected their own barriers, seeing themselves in opposition to the Christian West, even as they continued to look back to the common cultural origins in the ancient world that they shared with Jews and Christians. During the Renaissance in the fifteenth century, these ancient cultural origins became an alternative to religious affiliation for thinking about the identity of the West. From this Renaissance historical perspective Jews, Christians, and Muslims descended from the cultures of the ancient Hebrews, Greeks, and Romans. Despite all their differences, the followers of these religions shared a history. In fact, in the late Renaissance a number of thinkers imagined the possibility of rediscovering the single universal religion that they thought must have once been practiced in the ancient world. If they could just recapture that religion they could restore the unity they imagined had once prevailed in the West.

A Satellite View of Europe
What is the West? Western civilization has undergone numerous transformations throughout history, but it has always included Europe.

The definition of the West has also changed as a result of European colonialism, which began about 500 years ago. When European powers assembled large overseas empires, they introduced Western languages, religions, technology, and culture to many distant places in the world, making Western identity a transportable concept. In some of these colonized areas—such as North America, Argentina, Australia, and New Zealand—the European newcomers so outnumbered the indigenous people that these regions became as much a part of the West as Britain, France, and Spain. In other European colonies, especially in European trading outposts on the Asian continent, Western culture failed to exercise similar levels of influence.

As a result of colonialism Western culture sometimes merged with other cultures, and in the process both were changed. Brazil, a South American country inhabited by large numbers of indigenous peoples, the descendants of African slaves, and European settlers, epitomizes the complexity of what defines the West. In Brazil, almost everyone speaks a Western language (Portuguese), practices a Western religion (Christianity), and participates in Western political and economic institutions (democracy and capitalism). Yet in Brazil all of these features of Western civilization have become part of a distinctive culture, in which in-

digenous, African, and European elements have been blended. During Carnival, for example, Brazilians dressed in indigenous costumes dance in African rhythms to the accompaniment of music played on European instruments.

For many people today, the most important definition of the West involves adherence to a certain set of values, the "Western" values. The values typically identified as Western today include universal human rights, toleration of religious diversity, equality before the law, democracy, and freedom of inquiry and expression. However, these values have not always been part of Western civilization. They came to be fully appreciated only very recently as the consequence of a long and bloody history. In fact, there is nothing inevitable about these values, and Western history at various stages exhibited quite different ones. For example, the rulers of ancient Rome did not extend the privileges of citizenship to all the inhabitants of the empire until a century after it had reached its greatest size. The extent to which women could participate in public life was limited by law. Rich and powerful people enjoyed more protection under the law than did slaves or humble people. Most medieval Christians were completely convinced that their greatest contribution to society would be to make war against Muslims and heretics and to curtail as much as possible the actions of Jews. Western societies seldom valued equality until quite recently. Before the end of the eighteenth century, few Westerners questioned the practice of slavery; a social hierarchy of birth remained powerful in the West through the entire nineteenth century; most Western women were excluded from equal economic and educational opportunities until well into the twentieth century. Swiss women did not get the vote until 1971 (and in one canton not until 1990). Also in the twentieth century, Nazi Germany and the Soviet Union demonstrated that history could have turned out very differently in the West. These totalitarian regimes in Europe rejected most of the Western values so prized today and terrorized their own populations and millions of others beyond their borders through massive abuses of human rights. The history of the West is riddled with examples of leaders who stifled free inquiry and who censored authors and journalists. These examples testify to the fact that the values of Western societies have always been contended, disputed, and fought over. In other words, they have a history. This text highlights and examines that history, demonstrating how hard values were to formulate in the first place and how difficult they have been to preserve.

The Shifting Borders of the West

The geographical setting of the West also has a history. This textbook begins about 10,000 years ago in what is now Iraq and it ends in Iraq, but in the meantime the Mesopotamian region is only occasionally a concern for Western history. The West begins with the domestication of animals, the cultivation of the first crops, and the establishment of long-distance trading networks in the Tigris, Euphrates, and Nile River valleys. Cities, kingdoms, and empires in those valleys gave birth to the first civilizations. By about 500 B.C.E., the civilizations that are the cultural ancestors of the modern West had spread from southwestern Asia and North Africa to include the entire Mediterranean basin—areas influenced by Egyptian, Hebrew, Greek, and Roman thought, art, law, and religion. By the first century C.E. the Roman Empire drew the map of what historians consider the heartland of the West: most of western and southern Europe, the coastlands of the Mediterranean Sea, and the Middle East.

The West is now usually thought to include Europe and the Americas. However, the borders of the West have in recent decades come to be less about geography than culture, identity, and technology. When Japan, an Asian country, accepted human rights, democracy, and industrial capitalism after World War II, did it become part of the West? Most Japanese might not think they have adopted "Western" values, but the industrial power and stable democracy of a traditional Asian country that had never been colonized by a European power complicates the idea of what is the West. Or consider the Republic of South Africa, which until 1994 was ruled by the white minority, people descended from European immigrants. The oppressive regime violated human rights, rejected full legal equality for all citizens, and jailed or murdered those who questioned the government. Only when that government was replaced through democratic elections and a black man became president did South Africa fully embrace what the rest of the West would consider Western values. To what degree was South Africa part of the West before and after these developments?

Russia long saw itself as a Christian country with a tradition of cultural, economic, and political ties with the rest of Europe. The Russians have intermittently identified with their Western neighbors, but their neighbors were not always sure about the Russians. After the Mongol invasions of the thirteenth and fourteenth centuries much of Russia was isolated from the rest of the West; during the Cold War from 1949 to 1989, Russian communism and the Western democracies were polarized. When was Russia "Western" and when not?

Thus, when we talk about where the West is, we are almost always talking about the Mediterranean basin and much of Europe (and later, the Americas). But we will also show that countries that border "the West," and even countries far from it, might be considered Western in many aspects as well.

The Astrolabe
The mariner's astrolabe was a navigational device intended for use primarily at sea. The astrolabe originated in the Islamic world and was adopted by Europeans in the twelfth century—a cultural encounter that enabled Europeans to embark on long ocean voyages around the world.

Asking the Right Questions

So how can we make sense of the West as a place and an identity, the shifting borders of the West, and Western civilization in general? In short, what has Western civilization been over the course of its long history—and what is it today?

Answering these questions is the challenge this book poses. There are no simple answers to any of these questions, but there is a method for finding answers. The method is straightforward. Always ask the *what, when, where, who, how,* and *why* questions of the text.

The *What* Question

What is Western civilization? The answer to this question will vary according to time and place. In fact, for much of the early history covered in this book, Western civilization as we know it today did not exist as a single cultural entity. Rather, a number of distinctive civilizations were taking shape in the Middle East, northern Africa, and Europe, each of which contributed to what later became Western civilization. But throughout time the idea of Western civilization slowly began to form. Thus the understanding of Western civilization will change from chapter to chapter. The most extensive change in the place of the West was through the colonial expansion of the European nations between the fifteenth and twentieth centuries. Perhaps the most significant cultural change in the West came with acceptance of the values of scientific inquiry for solving human and philosophical problems, an approach that did not exist before the seventeenth century but became one of the distinguishing characteristics of Western civilization. During the late eighteenth and nineteenth centuries, industrialization became the engine that drove economic development in the West, and during the twentieth century industrialization in both its capitalist and communist forms dramatically gave the West a level of economic prosperity unmatched in the non-industrialized parts of the world.

The *When* Question

When did the defining characteristics of Western civilization first emerge, and for how long did they prevail? Dates frame and organize each chapter, and there are numerous short chronologies offered. These resources make it possible to keep track of what happened when. Dates have no meaning by themselves, but the connections *between* them can be very revealing. For example, dates show that the agricultural revolution that permitted the birth of the first civiliza-

tions unfolded over a span of about 10,000 years—which is more time than was taken by all the other events and developments covered in this textbook. Wars of religion plagued Europe for nearly 200 years before Enlightenment thinkers articulated the ideals of religious toleration. The American Civil War—the war to preserve the union, as President Abraham Lincoln termed it—took place at exactly the same time as other wars were being fought to achieve national unity in Germany and Italy. In other words, by paying attention to other contemporaneous wars for national unity the American experience seems less peculiarly an American event.

By learning when things happened, one can identify the major causes and consequences of events and thus see the transformations of Western civilization. For instance, the ability to produce a surplus of food through agriculture and the domestication of animals was a prerequisite for the emergence of civilizations. The violent collapse of religious unity after the Protestant Reformation in the sixteenth century led some Europeans to propose the separation of church and state two centuries later. And during the nineteenth century many Western states—in response to the enormous diversity among their own peoples—became preoccupied with maintaining or establishing national unity.

The *Where* Question

Where has Western civilization been located? Geography, of course, does not change very rapidly, but the idea of where the West is does. The location of the West is not so much a matter of changing borders but of how people identify themselves. The key to understanding the shifting borders of the West is to study how the peoples within the West thought of themselves. These groups include Muslims and the peoples of eastern Europe (such as the Soviet Union during the Cold War), which some people have wanted to exclude from the West. In addition, the chapters trace the relationships between the West (as it was constituted in different periods) and other, more distant civilizations with which it interacted. Those civilizations include not only those of East Asia and South Asia but also the indigenous peoples of sub-Saharan Africa, the Americas, and the Pacific islands.

The *Who* Question

Who were the people responsible for making Western civilization? Sometimes they were anonymous, such as the unknown geniuses who invented the mathematical systems of ancient Mesopotamia. At other times the makers of the

West were famous—saints such as Joan of Arc, creative thinkers such as Galileo Galilei, or generals such as Napoleon. But history is not made only by great and famous people. Humble people, such as the many millions who migrated from Europe to North America or the unfortunate millions who suffered and died in the trenches of World War I, can also influence the course of events.

Perhaps most often this book encounters people who were less the shapers of their own destinies than the subjects of forces that conditioned the kinds of choices they could make, often with unanticipated results. When during the eleventh century farmers throughout Europe began to employ a new kind of plow to till their fields, they were merely trying to do their work more efficiently. They certainly did not recognize that the increase in food they produced would stimulate the enormous population growth that made possible the medieval civilization of thriving cities and magnificent cathedrals. Answering the who question requires an evaluation of how much individuals and groups of people were in control of events and how much events controlled them.

The *How* Question

How did Western civilization develop? This is a question about processes—about how things change or stay the same over time. This book identifies these processes in several ways. First, the theme of encounters and transformations has been woven throughout the story. What is meant by encounters? When the Spanish *conquistadores* arrived in the Americas some 500 years ago, they came into contact with the cultures of the Caribs, the Aztecs, the Incas, and other peoples who had lived in the Americas for thousands of years. As the Spanish fought, traded with, and intermarried with the natives, each culture changed. The Spanish, for their part, borrowed from the Americas new plants for cultivation and responded to what they considered serious threats to their worldview. Many native Americans, in turn, adopted European religious practices and learned to speak European languages. At the same time, they were decimated by European diseases to which they had never before been exposed. They also witnessed the destruction of their own civilizations and governments at the hands of the colonial

Map 1 Core Lands of the West

The geographical borders of the West have changed substantially throughout history.

Cortés Meets Montezuma
As the Spanish fought, traded, and intermarried with the native peoples of the
Americas during the fifteenth and sixteenth centuries, each culture changed.

powers. Through centuries of interaction and mutual influence, both sides became something other than what they
had been.

The European encounter with the Americas is an obvious example of what was, in fact, a continuous process of
encounters with other cultures. These encounters often occurred between peoples from different civilizations, such
as the struggles between Greeks and Persians in the ancient
world or between Europeans and Chinese in the nineteenth century. Other encounters took place among people
living in the same civilization. These include interactions
between lords and peasants, men and women, Christians
and Jews, Catholics and Protestants, factory owners and
workers, and capitalists and communists. Western civilization developed and changed through a series of external
and internal encounters.

Second, features in the chapters formulate answers to the
question of how Western civilization developed. For example, each chapter contains an essay titled "Justice in
History." These essays discuss a trial or some other episode
involving questions of justice. Some "Justice in History" essays illustrate how Western civilization was forged in struggles over conflicting values, such as the discussion of the
trial of Galileo, which examines the conflict between religious and scientific concepts of truth. Others show how efforts to resolve internal cultural, political, and religious tensions helped shape Western ideas about justice, such as the

essay on the *auto-da-fé,* which illustrates how authorities
attempted to enforce religious conformity. At the end of
each "Justice in History" feature are several questions tying
that essay to the theme of the chapter.

Some chapters include two other features as well. Essays
titled "The Human Body in History" demonstrate that even
the body, which is typically understood as a product of ge-
netics and biology, has a history. These essays show that the
ways in which Western people understand their bodies, how
they cure them, how they cover and uncover them, and how
they adorn them tell us a great deal about the history of
Western culture. For example, the book explores how the
bodies of World War I soldiers afflicted with shell shock
were treated differently from women experiencing similar
symptoms of hysteria. Shell-shocked soldiers gave people a
sense of the horrors of war and stimulated powerful movements in Europe to outlaw war as an instrument of government policy.

The "Encounters and Transformations" features show
how encounters between different groups of people, tech-
nologies, and ideas were not abstract historical processes
but events that brought people together in a way that transformed history. For example, when the Arabs encountered
the camel as an instrument of war, they adopted it for their
own purposes and were able to conquer their neighbors
very quickly and spread Islam far beyond its original home
in Arabia.

The *Why* Question

Why did things happen in the way they did in history? This is the hardest question of all, one that engenders the most debate among historians. To take one persistent example, why did Hitler initiate a plan to exterminate the Jews of Europe? Can it be explained by something that happened to him in his childhood? Was he full of self-loathing that he projected onto the Jews? Was it a way of creating an enemy so that he could better unify Germany? Did he really believe that the Jews were the cause of all of Germany's problems? Did he merely act on the deeply seated anti-Semitic tendencies of the German people? Historians still debate the answers to these questions. These questions raise issues about human motivation and the role of human agency in historical events. Can historians ever really know what motivated a particular individual in the past, especially when it is so notoriously difficult to understand what motivates other people in the present? Can any individual determine the course of history? The *what, when, where, who,* and *how* questions are much easier to answer, but the *why* question, of course, is the most interesting one, the one that cries out for an answer.

This book does not always offer definitive answers to the *why* question, but it attempts to lay out the most likely possibilities. For example, historians do not really know what disease caused the Black Death in the fourteenth century, which killed about one-third of the population in a matter of months. But they can answer many questions about the consequences of that great catastrophe. Why were there so many new universities in the fourteenth and fifteenth centuries? It was because so many priests had died in the Black Death, creating a huge demand for replacements. The answers to the *why* questions are not always obvious, but they are always intriguing, and finding them is the joy of studying history.

The Medieval West in Crisis

10

THE FOURTEENTH CENTURY DAWNED WITH A CHILL. IN 1303 AND THEN again during 1306–1307, the Baltic Sea froze over. No one had ever heard of that happening before, and the freezings foretold worse disasters. The cold spread beyond its normal winter season, arriving earlier in the autumn and staying later into the summer. Then it started to rain and did not let up. The Caspian Sea began to rise, flooding villages along its shores. In the summer of 1314 all across Europe, crops rotted in sodden fields. The meager harvest came late, precipitating a surge in prices for farm produce and forcing King Edward II of England to impose price controls. But capping prices did not grow more food.

In 1315 the situation got worse. In England during that year, the price of wheat rose 800 percent. Preachers compared the ceaseless rains to the great flood in the Bible, and floods did come, overwhelming dikes in the Netherlands and England, washing away entire towns in Germany, turning fields into lakes in France. Everywhere crops failed.

Things got much worse. Torrential rains fell again in 1316, and for the third straight year the crops failed, creating the most severe famine in recorded European history. The effects were most dramatic in the far north. In Scandinavia agriculture almost disappeared, in Iceland peasants abandoned farming and turned to fishing and herding sheep, and in Greenland the European settlers began to die out. Already malnourished, the people of Europe became susceptible to disease and starvation. Desperate people resorted to desperate options. They ate cats, rats, insects, reptiles, animal dung, and tree leaves. Stories spread that some ate their own children. In Poland the starving were said to cut down criminals from the gallows for food.

By the 1340s, nearly all of Europe was gripped by a seemingly endless cycle of disease and famine. Then came the deadliest epidemic in European history, the Black Death, which killed at least one-third of the total population.

The Mongol Threat This detail from the "Martyrdom of the Franciscans at Ceuta" shows a stereotypical Mongol, the man in the middle with a tall peaked hat. Ceuta is in North Africa, far from Mongol lands, but the depiction of a Mongol among the Muslims who executed Franciscan missionaries illustrates how Christians felt as threatened by the distant Mongols as by the nearby Muslims. The fresco is in the Franciscan church in Siena, Italy.

The economy collapsed. Trade disappeared. Industry shriveled. Hopeless peasants and urban workers revolted against their masters, demanding relief for their families. Neither state nor church could provide it. The two great medieval kingdoms of France and England became locked in a struggle that depleted royal treasuries and wasted the aristocracy in a series of clashes that historians call the Hundred Years' War. The popes left the dangerous streets of Rome for Avignon, France, where they were obliged to extort money to survive. After the pope returned to Rome, a group of French cardinals refused to go and elected a second pope, leading to the Great Schism when Europe was divided by allegiances to two different popes.

Of all the frightening elements of these disasters, perhaps most frightening was that their causes were hidden or completely unknowable given the technology and medical understanding that became available only a century ago. In many respects, the West was held captive by the climate, economic forces that no one completely understood, and microbes that would not be identified for another 550 years. During the twelfth and thirteenth centuries the West had asserted itself against Islam through the Crusades and spread Catholic Christianity to the far corners of Europe. During the fourteenth and early fifteenth centuries, however, the West drew into itself due to war, epidemics, and conflicts with the Mongol and Ottoman Empires. Western European contact with Russia became more intermittent, and the Byzantine Empire, once the bastion of Orthodox Christianity, fell to the Muslim armies of the Ottomans. The contact during the fourteenth and fifteenth centuries between Europe and the powerful Asian empires and between Europe and epidemic diseases raises the question of how such encounters could so profoundly transform the identity of the West.

- What caused the deaths of so many Europeans?
- How did forces outside Europe, in particular the Mongol and Ottoman Empires, influence conditions in the West?
- How did disturbances in the rudimentary global economy of the Middle Ages precipitate almost complete financial collapse and widespread social discontent in Europe?
- How did incessant warfare transform the most powerful medieval states?
- Why did the church fail to provide leadership and spiritual guidance during these difficult times?
- How did European culture offer explanations and solace for the otherwise inexplicable calamities of the times?

A Time of Death

- What caused the deaths of so many Europeans?

Because of demographic research, we know a great deal about life and death during the fourteenth century. The magnitude of Europe's demographic crisis is evident from the raw numbers. In 1300 the population of Europe was about 74 million—roughly 15 percent of its current population. Population size can be an elementary measure of the success of a subsistence economy to keep people alive, and by this measure Europe had been very successful up to about 1300. It had approximately doubled its population over the previous 300 years. After the 1340s, however, Europe's ability to sustain its population evaporated. Population fell to just 52 million.

The raw numbers, however, hardly touch the magnitude of human suffering, which fell disproportionately on the poor, the very young, and the old. Death by starvation and disease became the fate of uncomprehending millions. The demographic crisis of the fourteenth century was the greatest natural disaster in Western civilization since the epidemics of antiquity. How did it happen?

Mass Starvation

Widespread famine began during the decade of 1310–1320. During the famines in 1315 and 1316 alone, more than 10 percent of Europe's population probably died. One eyewitness described bands of people as thin as skeletons in 1315:

> We saw a large number of both sexes, not only from nearby places but from places as much as five leagues away, barefooted, and many even, except the women, in a completely nude condition, with their priests coming together in procession at the church of the holy martyrs, and they devoutly carried bodies of the saints and other relics to be adored.[1]

A crisis in agriculture produced the Great Famine.

The agricultural revolution of the eleventh century had made available more food and more nutritious food, triggering the growth of the population during the Middle Ages. During the twelfth and thirteenth centuries, vast tracks of virgin forests were cleared for farming, especially in eastern Europe. By the thirteenth century this region resembled the American frontier during the nineteenth century, as settlers flocked in, staked out farms, and established new towns. The additional land under the plow created an escape valve for population growth by preventing large numbers of people from going hungry. But by the fourteenth century no more virgin land was available for clearing, which meant that an ever-growing population tried to survive on a fixed amount of farming land. Because of the limitations of medieval agriculture, the ability of farmers to produce food could not keep up with unchecked population growth.

At the same time there was probably a change in climate, known as the "Little Ice Age." The mean annual temperatures dropped just enough to make it impossible to grow crops in the more northerly parts of Europe and at high elevations such as the Alps. Before the fourteenth century, for example, grapes were grown in England to produce wine, but with the decline in temperatures, the grape vineyards ceased to produce. Growing grapes in England became possible again only with global warming in the late twentieth century. The result of the Little Ice Age was twofold. First, there was less land available for cultivation as it became impossible to grow crops in marginal areas. Second, a harsher climate shortened the growing season, which meant that even where crops could still grow they were less abundant.

The imbalance between food production and population set off a dreadful cycle of famine and disease. Insufficient food resulted in either malnutrition or starvation. Those who suffered from prolonged malnutrition were particularly susceptible to epidemic diseases, such as typhus, cholera, and dysentery. By 1300, children of the poor faced the probability of extreme hunger once or twice during the course of their childhood. In Pistoia, Italy, priests kept the *Book of the Dead*, which recorded the pattern: famine in 1313, famine in 1328–1329, famine and epidemic in 1339–1340 that killed one-quarter of the population, famine in 1346, famine and epidemic in 1347, and then the killing hammer blow—the Black Death in 1348 (see Map 10.1).

The Black Death

Following on the heels of the Great Famine, the Black Death arrived in Europe in the spring of 1348 with brutal force. In the lovely hilltop city of Siena, Italy, all industry stopped, carters refused to bring produce and cooking oil in from the countryside, and on June 2 the daily records of the

Map 10.1 Spread of the Black Death
After the Black Death first appeared in the ports of Italy in 1348, it spread relentlessly throughout most of Europe, killing at least 20 million people in Europe alone.

Spread of the Black Death

- 1347
- 1348
- 1349
- 1350
- After 1350
- Area partially or totally spared

city council and civil courts abruptly ended, as if the city fathers and judges had all died or rushed home in panic. A local chronicler, Agnolo di Tura, wrote down his memories of those terrible days:

> Father abandoned child, wife husband, one brother another; for this illness seemed to strike through the breath and sight. And so they died. And none could be found to bury the dead for money or friendship. Members of a household brought their dead to a ditch as best they could, without priest, without divine offices. Nor did the [death] bell sound. And in many places in Siena great pits were dug and piled deep with the multitude of dead. . . . And I, Agnolo di Tura, called the Fat, buried my five children with my own hands. And there were also those who were so sparsely covered with earth that the dogs dragged them forth and devoured many bodies throughout the city.[2]

During the summer of 1348 more than half of the Sienese died. The construction of Siena's great cathedral, planned to be the largest in the world, stopped and was never resumed due to a lack of workers. In fact, Siena, once among the most prosperous cities in Europe, never fully recovered and lost its economic preeminence to other cities.

Experts still dispute the cause of the Black Death, but there is growing doubt about the validity of the traditional theory that the bubonic plague° was the most likely culprit. The dispute about the cause of the Black Death is a revealing example of the difficulty of interpreting evidence from the distant past. According to the traditional theory the bubonic plague can appear in two forms. In the classic form it is usually transmitted to humans by a flea that has bitten a rodent infected with the *Yersinia pestis* bacillus, usually a rat. The infected flea then bites a human victim. The infection enters the bloodstream, causing inflamed swellings called buboes (hence, "bubonic" plague) in the glands of the groin or armpit, internal bleeding, and discoloration of the skin, which is why some historians have thought that the "Black Death" was the bubonic plague. The symptoms of the Black Death were, indeed, exceptionally disgusting, according to one quite typical contemporary description: "all the matter which exuded from their bodies let off an unbearable stench; sweat, excrement, spittle, breath, so fetid as to be overpowering; urine turbid, thick, black or red. . . . "[3]

The second form of plague was the pneumonic type, which infected the lungs and spread by coughing and sneezing. Either form could be lethal, but the complex epidemiology of bubonic plague meant that the first form could not be transmitted directly from one person to another. According to the traditional theory, after being infected, many victims probably developed pneumonia as a secondary symptom, which then spread quickly to others. As one contemporary physician put it, one person could seemingly infect the entire world. In some cases, the doctor caught the illness and died before the patient did. The visitations of the bubonic plague in the late nineteenth and twentieth centuries, which have been observed by physicians trained in modern medicine, formed that basis for this theory. Alexandre Yersin discovered the bubonic plague bacillus in Hong Kong in 1894 and traced its spread through rats and fleas. For more than a century most historians and epidemiologists have thought that something similar to this must have happened in 1348.

However, there are problems with the traditional theory that the Black Death was caused by bubonic plague. The Black Death spread much more rapidly from person to person and place to place than the bubonic plague does in modern epidemics. For example, rats do not travel very fast, and in modern examples the bubonic plague has rarely spread more than twelve miles per year. In 1348, however, the Black Death traveled as far in a day as rat-borne bubonic plague does in a year. Many of the reported symptoms from the fourteenth century do not match the symptoms observed in modern plague victims. Moreover, the Black Death, unlike the bubonic plague, seems to have had a long incubation period before the first symptoms appeared. Because of the long incubation, those who had the disease transmitted it to others before they knew they were sick, which helps explain why the disease was so lethal despite attempts to quarantine those afflicted with it. The most recent revisionist research suggests that the Black Death may have been caused by an unidentified virus that produced bleeding similar to the Ebola virus that has appeared in Africa in recent years.

Why does it matter which theory for the cause of the Black Death is correct—the traditional one about bubonic plague or the revisionist one about a bleeding virus? In one sense it does not matter because it is clear that the effects of the Black Death were devastating no matter what the cause. In another sense, it does matter because if the Black Death was caused by a virus, it could reappear again at any time and kill many millions again. There is now medical treatment for bubonic plague, but if a virus caused the Black Death, then extensive research would need to take place to provide a cure in the event it reappeared. Thus, a debate about events that took place more than 650 years ago could have vital importance for the future.

Two summers before the Black Death's appearance in Europe, sailors returning from the East had told stories about a terrible pestilence in China and India. Entire regions of India, they said, were littered with corpses with no survivors to bury them. But the vague information that arrived in European seaports in 1346 caused no particular alarm. Asia was far away and the source of stories so baffling that most people could hardly credit them.

With the galley slaves dying at their oars, Genoese ships first brought the disease to ports in Italy, and by the spring of 1348 the Black Death began to spread throughout the Italian peninsula. Ironically, the very network of shipping that had connected the Mediterranean with northern European waters and propelled the great economic boom of the Middle Ages spread the deadly disease. By summer the pestilence had traveled as far north as Paris; by the end of the year it had crossed the English Channel, following William the Conqueror's old route from Normandy to England. From Italy the Black Death passed through the rugged Alpine passes into Switzerland and Hungary. In 1349 the relentless surge continued, passing from France into the Netherlands and from England to Scotland, Ireland, and Norway, where a ghost ship of dead men ran aground near Bergen. From Norway the deadly disease migrated to Sweden, Denmark, Prussia, Iceland, and Greenland. By 1351 it had arrived in Russia.

Modern estimates indicate that during the late 1340s and early 1350s from India to Iceland, about one-third of the population perished. In Europe this would have meant that about 20 million people died, with the deaths usually clustered in a matter of a few weeks or months after the disease first appeared in a particular locale. The death toll, however, varied erratically from place to place, ranging from about 20 to 90 percent. So great was the toll that entire villages were depopulated or abandoned. In Avignon 400 died daily, in Pisa 500, in Paris 800. Paris lost half its population, Florence as much as four fifths, and Venice two-thirds. In the seaport of Trapani, Italy, everyone apparently died or left. Living in enclosed spaces, monks and nuns were especially hard hit. All the Franciscans of Carcassonne and Marseille in France died. In Montpellier, France, only 7 of the 140 Dominicans survived. In isolated Kilkenny, Ireland, Brother John Clyn found himself left alone among his dead brothers, and he began to write a diary of what he had witnessed because he was afraid he might be the last person left alive in the world.

Civic and religious leaders had neither the knowledge nor the power to prevent or contain the disease. Following the biblical passages that prescribed ostracizing lepers, governments began to treat Black Death victims as temporary lepers and quarantined them for forty days. Because such measures were ineffective, the Black Death kept coming back. In the Mediterranean basin where the many port cities formed a network of contagion, the plague reappeared between 1348 and 1721 in one port or another about every fifteen to twenty years. Some of the later outbreaks were just as lethal as the initial 1348 catastrophe. Florence lost half its population in 1400; Venice lost a third in 1575–1577 and a third again in 1630–1631. Half a million people died in northern Spain from an epidemic in 1596–1602. Less exposed than the Mediterranean, northern Europe suffered less and saw the last of the dread disease in the Great Plague of London of 1665–1666.

No matter which theory of the cause of the Black Death is correct, both demonstrate how the fate of the West was largely in the hands of unknown forces that ensnared Eurasia and Africa in a unified biological web. If the revisionist theory is correct, then the disease came out of Africa, afflicting Europe via Italy, which had regular contacts with North Africa and where the disease first appeared. If the

Flagellants

During the Black Death many people believed God was punishing them for their sins. In order to expiate those sins some young men practiced flagellation, a practice once reserved for monks who whipped themselves as a form of penance. In order to control the practice among laymen, confraternities were formed in which collective flagellation was organized and carried out under the supervision of a priest. These confraternities took on a variety of charitable obligations, including succoring the sick, building hospitals and orphanages, and burying the dead.

The Black Death: The Signs of Disease

Infectious diseases are invisible. They are carried by viruses or bacteria that infect the body, but until the invention of the microscope in the seventeenth century and the development of epidemiology in the nineteenth the disease itself could not be directly observed. Diseases manifest themselves indirectly through symptoms: fevers, cold sweats, pain, coughing, vomiting, diarrhea, paleness, glandular swellings, skin lesions, and rashes. Through these symptoms, the disease leaves a distinctive sign on the body.

No disease left more distinctive and disturbing signs on the body than the Black Death. In the introduction to *The Decameron*, Giovanni Boccaccio described what he had witnessed of the symptoms:

> *In the year 1348 after the fruitful incarnation of the Son of God, that most beautiful of Italian cities, noble Florence, was attacked by deadly plague. . . . The symptoms . . . began both in men and women with certain swellings in the groin or under the armpit. They grew to the size of a small apple or an egg, more or less, and were vulgarly called tumors. In a short space of time these tumors spread from the two parts named [to] all over the body. Soon after this the symptoms changed and black or purple spots appeared on the arms or thighs or any other part of the body, sometimes a few large ones, sometimes many little ones. These spots were a certain sign of death, just as the original tumor had been and still remained.*[4]

The fear of the Black Death and the inability to discern its causes focused the attention of contemporaries on the bodies of the sick, and when someone fell ill there was intense concern to determine whether the signs of the Black Death were present. As a result, almost any discoloration of the skin or glandular swellings could be interpreted as a sign of its presence, and other diseases, such as smallpox, could be diagnosed as the Black Death. Physicians and surgeons, of course, were the experts in reading the signs of the body for disease. As victims and their distraught families soon discovered, however, physicians did not really know what the glandular swellings and discolorations of the skin meant. Boccaccio reported that "No doctor's advice, no medicine could overcome or alleviate this disease. . . . Either the disease was such that no treatment was possible or the doctors were so ignorant that they did not know what caused it, and consequently could not administer the proper remedy."[5]

On the advice of physicians, governmental authorities tried to stop the contagion by placing the houses of the sick and sometimes entire neighborhoods under quarantine when plague was suspected. Within the councils of city governments, greater attention began to be paid to the poor, largely because their bodies were more likely to manifest deformities and skin problems because of malnutrition and poor living conditions. The bodies of the poor became subject to systematic regulation. In general, the poor were much more likely to be quarantined than the rich. The deformed might even be driven out of town. Cities established hospitals to segregate the most wretched of the poor, and health officials set up border guards to prevent poor vagabonds from entering towns. To maintain quarantines and bury the dead, a public health bureaucracy was created, complete with its own staff physicians, grave diggers, and police force. The extraordinary powers granted to the public health authorities helped expand the authority of the state over its citizens in the name of pursuing the common good. The expansion of governmental bureaucracy that distinguished modern from medieval states was partly the result of the need to keep human bodies under surveillance and control—a need that began with the Black Death.

For Discussion

How did the government's need to control the Black Death contribute to the expansion of the state? How did it reveal the limits of the power of the state?

The Triumph of Death
A detail from Francesco Traini's fresco *The Triumph of Death,* in the Camposanto, Pisa, ca. 1350. Frescoes such as this reflect the horror of the Black Death.

traditional theory is correct then Europe was victimized by a disease from Asia. Modern research has suggested that the homeland of the *Yersinia pestis* bacillus is an extremely isolated area in Central Asia, from which the plague could have spread during the fourteenth century. The strongest strands in that web were those of merchant traders and armies who were responsible for accidentally disseminating microbes. Whether or not they were the means for transmitting the Black Death, no armies were as important for the fate of Europe as the mounted warriors of the distant Mongol tribes, whose relentless conquests drove them from Outer Mongolia across central Asia toward Europe.

A Cold Wind from the East

■ How did forces outside Europe, in particular the Mongol and Ottoman Empires, influence conditions in the West?

The Mongols and Turks were nomadic peoples from central Asia. Closely related culturally but speaking different languages, these peoples exerted an extraordinary influence on world history despite a rather small population. Map 10.2 shows the place of origin of the

Map 10.2 The Mongol Empire, 1206–1405

The Mongols and Turks were nomadic peoples who spread out across Asia and Europe from their homeland in the region of Mongolia. The Mongol armies eventually conquered vast territories from Korea to the borders of Hungary and from the Arctic Ocean to the Arabian Sea.

Mongols and Turks and where they spread across a wide belt of open, relatively flat steppe land stretching from the Yellow Sea between China and the Korean peninsula to the Baltic Sea and the Danube River basin in Europe. Virtually unwooded and interrupted only by a few easily traversed mountain ranges, the broad Eurasian steppes have been the great migration highway of world history from prehistoric times to the medieval caravans and the modern trans-Siberian railway.

As the Mongols and Turks charged westward out of central Asia on their fast ponies, they put pressure on the kingdoms of the West. Mongol armies hobbled Russia, and Turks conquered Constantinople. As a consequence the potential Orthodox allies in the East of the Catholic Christian West were weakened or eliminated. Under the Ottomans, adherents to Islam were reinserted into the West, this time in the Balkans. In contrast to the era of the twelfth-century Crusades, Catholic Europe found itself on the defensive against a powerful Muslim foe.

The Mongol Invasions

Whereas the Europeans became successful sailors because of their extensive coastlines and close proximity to the sea, the Mongols became roving horsemen because they needed to migrate several times a year in search of grass and water for their ponies and livestock. They also became highly skilled warriors because they competed persistently with other tribes for access to the grasslands.

Between 1206 and 1258, the Mongols transformed themselves from a collection of disunited tribes with a vague ethnic affinity to create the most extensive empire in the history of the world. The epic rise of the previously obscure Mongols was the work of a Mongol chief who succeeded in uniting the various quarreling tribes and transforming them into a world power. In 1206 he was proclaimed Genghis Khan (ca. 1162–1227) ("Very Mighty King"), the supreme ruler over all the Mongols. Genghis broke through the Great Wall of China, destroyed the Jin (Chin) empire in northern China, and occupied Beijing. His cavalry swept across Asia as far as Azerbaijan, Georgia, northern Persia, and Russia. Eventually, Mongol armies conquered territories that stretched from Korea to Hungary and from the Arctic Ocean to the Arabian Sea. They even attempted seaborne expeditions to overpower Japan, which ended in disaster, and Java, which they were able to hold only temporarily. These failures indicated that Mongol strength was in their army rather than their navy.

The Mongol success was accomplished through a highly disciplined military organization, tactics that relied on extremely mobile cavalry forces, and a sophisticated intelligence network. During the Russian campaign in the winter of 1223, the Mongol cavalry moved with lightning speed

Mongol Horseman
Unlike the fourteenth-century European representations of the Mongols, this contemporary Chinese illustration of a Mongol archer on horseback accurately depicts their appearance, dress, and equipment.

across frozen rivers to accomplish the only successful winter invasion of Russia in history. Although the Russian forces outnumbered the Mongol armies and had superior armor, they were crushed in every encounter with the Mongols.

The Mongol armies employed clever tactics. First they unnerved enemy soldiers with a hail of arrows. Then the Mongols would appear to retreat, only to draw the enemy into false confidence before the Mongol horsemen delivered a deadly final blow. European chroniclers at the time tried to explain their many defeats at the hands of the Mongols by reporting that the Mongol "hordes" had overwhelming numbers, but evidence clearly shows that their victories were the result not of superior numbers but of superior discipline and the sophistication of the Mongol intelligence network.

The Mongol invasions completely altered the composition of Asia and much of eastern Europe—economically, politically, and ethnically. Once they had conquered new territories, they established the Mongol Peace by reopening the caravan routes across the Asian steppes, making trans-Eurasian trade possible and merchants safe from robbers. The most famous of the many merchants who traversed this route were the Venetians from the Polo family, including Marco Polo, who arrived at the court of the Great Khan in China in 1275. Marco Polo's book about his travels offers a vivid and often remarkably perceptive account of the Mongol Empire during the Mongol Peace. It also illustrates better than any other source the cultural engagement of the Christian West with the Mongol East during the late thirteenth century, an encounter in which both sides demonstrated an abiding fascination with the other's religion and social mores.

Mongol power climaxed in 1260. In that year the Mongols suffered a crushing defeat in Syria at the hands of the Mamluk rulers of Egypt, an event that ended the Mongol reputation for invincibility. Conflicts and succession disputes among the various Mongol tribes made them vulnerable to rivals and to rebellion from their unhappy subjects. The Mongol Empire did not disappear overnight, but its various successor kingdoms never recaptured the dynamic unity forged by Genghis Khan. During the fourteenth century the Mongol Peace fitfully sputtered to an end.

In the wake of these upheavals, a warrior of Mongol descent known as Tamerlane (r. 1369–1405) created an army composed of Mongols, Turks, and Persians, which challenged the established Mongol khanates. Tamerlane's conquests rivaled those of Genghis Khan, but with very different results. His armies pillaged the rich cities that supplied the caravan routes. Thus, in his attempt to monopolize the lucrative trans-Eurasian trade, Tamerlane largely destroyed it. The collapse of the Mongol Peace broke the thread of commerce across Eurasia and stimulated the European search for alternative routes to China that ultimately resulted in the voyages of Christopher Columbus in 1492.

CHRONOLOGY

The Mongols

1206–1227	Reign of Genghis Khan
1206–1258	Mongol armies advance undefeated across Eurasia
1260	Defeat in Syria of Mongols by Mamluks of Egypt
1369–1405	Reign of Tamerlane

The Rise of the Ottoman Turks

The Mongol armies were never very large, so the Mongols had always augmented their numbers with Turkish tribes. The result was that outside Mongolia, Turks gradually absorbed the Mongols. Turkish replaced Mongolian as the dominant language, and the Turks took over the government of the central Asian empires that had been scraped together by the Mongol conquests. In contrast to the Mongols, many of whom remained Buddhists, the Turks became Muslims and created an exceptionally dynamic, expansionist society of their own (see Map 10.3).

Among the Turkish peoples, the most successful state builders were the Ottomans. Named for Osman I (r. 1281–1326), who brought it to prominence, the Ottoman dynasty endured for more than 600 years, until 1924. The nucleus of the Ottoman state was a small principality in Anatolia (a portion of present-day Turkey), which in the early fourteenth century began to expand at the expense of its weaker neighbors, including the Byzantine Empire. The Ottoman state was built not on national, linguistic, or ethnic unity, but on a purely dynastic network of personal and military loyalties to the Ottoman prince, called the sultan. Thus the vitality of the empire depended on the energy of the individual sultans. The Ottomans thought of themselves as *ghazis,* warriors for Islam devoted to destroying polytheists, including Christians. (To some Muslims in this period the Christian belief in the Trinity and veneration of numerous saints demonstrated that Christians were not true monotheists.) During the fourteenth century, incessant Ottoman guerilla actions gradually chipped away at the Byzantine frontier.

The Byzantine Empire in the middle of the thirteenth century was emerging from a period of domination by Frankish knights and Venetian merchants who had conquered Constantinople during the Fourth Crusade in 1204. In 1261, the Byzantine emperor Michael VIII Palaeologus (r. 1260–1282) recaptured the great city. The revived Byzantine Empire, however, was a pale vestige of what it once had been, and the Palaeologi emperors desperately sought military assistance from western Europe to defend themselves from the Ottomans. Dependent on mercenary armies and divided by civil wars, the Byzantines offered only pathetic resistance to the all-conquering Ottomans.

Map 10.3 The Ottoman Empire

The Ottoman state expanded from a small principality in Anatolia, which is south of the Black Sea. From there the Ottomans spread eastward into Kurdistan and Armenia. In the West they captured all of Greece and much of the Balkan peninsula.

From their base in Anatolia, the Ottomans raided far and wide, launching pirate fleets into the Aegean and gradually encircling Constantinople after they crossed over into Europe in 1308. By 1402 Ottoman territory had grown to forty times its size a century earlier. During that century of conquests, the frontier between Christianity and Islam shifted. The former subjects of the Byzantines in the Balkans fell to the Ottoman Turks. Fragile Serbia, a bastion of Orthodox Christianity in the Balkans, broke under Ottoman pressure. First unified in the late twelfth century, Serbia established political independence from Byzantium and autonomy for the Serbian church. Although the Serbs had taken control over a number of former Byzantine provinces, they fell to the invincible Ottomans at the Battle of Kosovo in 1389. Lamenting the Battle of Kosovo has remained the bedrock of Serbian national identity to this day.

Serbia's western neighbors, the kingdoms of Bosnia and Herzegovina, deflated under Ottoman pressure during the late fifteenth century. Unlike Serbia, where most of the population remained loyal to the Serbian Orthodox Church, Bosnia and Herzegovina had long been divided by religious schisms. The dominant, educated classes were Serbian-speaking Muslims; the subjugated peasants, also Serbian-speaking, were Orthodox Christians who turned over one-third of everything they raised to their Muslim lords. The parallel divisions along religious and class lines long enfeebled Bosnian unity.

When Mehmed II, "The Conqueror" (r. 1451–1481), became the Ottoman sultan, he began to obliterate the last remnants of the Byzantine Empire. During the winter of 1451–1452, the sultan ordered the encirclement of Constantinople, a city that had

DOCUMENT

Mehmed II

once been the largest in the world but now was reduced from perhaps a million people to fewer than 50,000. The Ottoman siege strategy was to bombard Constantinople into submission with daily rounds from enormous cannons. The largest was a monster cannon, twenty-nine feet long, that could shoot 1,200-pound stones. It required a crew of 200 soldiers and sixty oxen to handle it, and each firing generated so much heat that it took hours to cool off before it could be fired again. The siege was a gargantuan task because the walls of Constantinople, which had been built, repaired, and improved over a period of a thousand years, were formidable. However, the new weapon of gunpowder artillery had rendered city walls a military anachronism. Brought from China by the Mongols, gunpowder had gradually revolutionized warfare, and breaching city walls in sieges was merely a matter of time as long as the heavy metal cannons could be dragged into position. Quarrels among the Christians also hampered the defense of the walls. Toward the end, the Byzantine emperor was forced to melt down church treasures so "that from them coins should be struck and given to the soldiers, the sappers and the builders, who selfishly cared so little for the public welfare that they were refusing to go to their work unless they were first paid."[6]

The final assault came in May 1453 and lasted less than a day. When the city fell, the Ottoman army spent the day plundering, raping, and enslaving the populace. The last Byzantine emperor, Constantine XI, was never found amid the multitude of the dead. The fall of Constantinople ended the Christian Byzantine Empire, the continuous remnant of the ancient Roman Empire. But the idea of Rome was not so easily snuffed out. The first Ottoman sultans residing in Constantinople continued to be called "Roman emperors."

DOCUMENT

Nestor-Iskander on the Fall of Constantinople

Although the western European princes had done little to save Byzantium, its demise was a profound shock, rendering them vulnerable to the Ottoman onslaught. For the next 200 years the Ottomans used Constantinople as a base to threaten Christian Europe. Hungary and the eastern Mediterranean empire of Venice remained the last lines of defense for the West, and at various times in succeeding

---

DOCUMENT

The Ottoman Conquest of Constantinople

The Turkish sultan Mehmed II led the Ottoman army and navy in the final siege of Constantinople. A brilliant leader and strategist, he succeeded in taking the capital of Byzantium, which had been unsuccessfully attacked so many times before. This account of what he said to inspire his troops before the final assault on the walls on Constantinople is by a Greek named Kritovoulos who began to work for Mehmed shortly after the conquest. He gathered this account from many eyewitnesses. Notice how Mehmed emphasizes the various rewards promised by the conquest of the city.

My friends and my comrades in the present struggle! I have called you together here . . . to show you how many and how great [are the rewards] and what great glory and honor accompany the winning. And I also wish that you may know well how to carry on the struggle for the very highest rewards.

First, then, there is a great wealth of all sorts in this city, some in the royal palaces and some in the houses of the mighty, some in the homes of the common people and still other, finer and more abundant, laid up in the churches as votive offerings and treasures of all sorts, constructed of gold and silver and precious stones and costly pearls.

Then too, there are very many noble and distinguished men, some of whom will be your slaves, and the rest will be put up for sale; also very many and very beautiful women, young and good-looking, and virgins lovely for marriage, noble, and of noble families, and even till now unseen by masculine eyes, some of them, evidently intended for the weddings of great men. . . .

And you will have boys, too, very many and very beautiful and of noble families.

Further, you will enjoy the beauty of the churches and public buildings and splendid houses and gardens, and many such things, suited to look at and enjoy and take pleasure in and profit by.

And the greatest of all is this, that you will capture a city whose renown has gone out to all parts of the world. It is evident that to whatever extent the leadership and glory of this city has spread, to a like extent the renown of your valor and bravery will spread for having captured by assault a city such as this. . . .

And, best of all, we shall demolish a city that has been hostile to use from the beginning and is constantly growing at our expense and in every way plotting against our rule. . . .

I myself will be in the van of the attack [applause by all the gathering]. Yes, I myself will lead the attack, and will be fighting by your side and will watch to see what each one of you does."

Source: From Kritovoulos, *History of Mehmed the Conqueror*, translated by Charles T. Riggs (Westport, Conn.: Greenwood Press, 1970), 61–64.

CHRONOLOGY

The Conquests of the Ottoman Turks

1281–1326	Reign of Osman I
1308	Ottoman Empire advances into Europe
1389	Battle of Kosovo; Serbia becomes vassal state of the Ottomans
1451–1481	Reign of Mehmed II, "The Conqueror"
1453	Fall of Constantinople and death of last Byzantine emperor

centuries the Ottomans launched expeditions against Europe, including two sieges of Vienna (1529 and 1683) and several invasions of Italy.

Hundreds of years of attacks by the Mongol and Ottoman Empires redrew the map of the West. Events in western Europe did not and could not take place in isolation from the eastern pressures and influences. For more than 200 years Christian Russia was isolated from cultural influences in the rest of the Christian world. The experience made the Russians much more aware of their eastern neighbors, and when they did recover from the Mongol conquests in the fifteenth century, much of their energy and military might was directed toward expanding eastward into the void left by the collapse of the Mongol Empire. The Ottoman conquests also created a lasting Muslim presence within the borders of Europe, especially in Bosnia and Albania. In succeeding centuries Christian Europe and the Muslim Ottoman Empire would be locked in a deadly competitive embrace, but they also benefited from innumerable cultural exchanges and regular trade. Hostility between the two sides was recurrent but never inevitable and was broken by long periods of peaceful engagement. In fact, the Christian kingdoms of western Europe went to war far more often with one another than with the Turks.

Economic Depression and Social Turmoil

■ How did disturbances in the rudimentary global economy of the Middle Ages precipitate almost complete financial collapse and widespread social discontent in Europe?

Adding insult to injury in this time of famine, plague, and conquest, the West began to suffer a major economic depression during the fourteenth century. The economic boom fueled by the agricultural revolution and the revitalization of European cities during the eleventh century and the commercial prosperity of the twelfth and thirteenth centuries petered out in the fourteenth. The causes of this economic catastrophe were complex, but the consequences were obvious. Businesses went bust, banks collapsed, guilds were in turmoil, and workers rebelled.

At the same time, the effects of the depression were unevenly felt. The economic conditions for many peasants actually improved because there was a labor shortage in the countryside due to the loss of population. Forced to pay their peasants more for their labor and crops, landlords saw their own fortunes decline. Finding it harder to pay the higher prices for food, urban workers probably suffered the most because their wages did not keep up with the cost of living.

The Collapse of International Trade and Banking

The Mongol Peace during the thirteenth century had stimulated vast, lucrative trade in exotic luxury items between Europe and Asia. When the Mongol Empire began to break up in the fourteenth century, the trade routes were cut off or displaced. Later in the century, Tamerlane's forcible channeling of the caravan trade through his own territory created a narrow trade corridor with outlets on the coast of the Middle East. Rulers along this path, such as the Mamluks in Egypt, took advantage of the situation to levy heavy tolls on trade, raising the price of goods beyond what the market could bear. As a result, trade dwindled. Alternative routes would have taken merchants through Constantinople, but Ottoman pressure on Byzantium endangered these routes.

The financial infrastructure of medieval Europe was tied to international trade in luxury goods. The successful, entrepreneurial Italian merchants who dominated the luxury trade deposited their enormous profits in Italian banks. The Italian bankers lent money to the aristocracy and royalty of northern Europe to finance the purchases of exotic luxuries and to fight wars. The whole system was mutually reinforcing, but it was very fragile. With the disruption of supply sources for luxury goods, the financial networks of Europe collapsed, precipitating a major depression.

For most of the thirteenth century the Italian city of Siena had been one of the principal banking centers of the world, the equivalent of New York or Tokyo today. In 1298, however, panic caused a run on its largest bank, which failed. Soon the lesser Sienese banks were forced to close, and the entire city fell into a deep economic depression. Siena never recovered its economic stature and is a major tourist attraction today simply because it is largely unchanged from the time when the banks went broke.

In nearby Florence, several local banks took advantage of Siena's collapse and became even bigger than the Sienese banks had been. Through these banks, the coinage of Florence, the florin, became the common currency of Europe. By 1346, however, all of these banks crashed due to a series of bad loans to several kings of Europe. With the bank crash, virtually all sources of credit dried up all across Europe. At the same time, wars between France and England deprived their aristocracies of the money to buy luxuries from the Italian merchants whose deposits had been the principal source of capital for the banks. With disruptions in the supply of Asian luxury goods, a catastrophic loss of capital by Italian bankers, and a decline in demand for luxuries in France and England, Europe entered a major depression.

Rebellions from Below

The luxury trade that brought exotic items from Asia to Europe represented only half of the economic equation. The other half was the raw materials and manufactured goods that Europeans sold in exchange, principally woolen cloth. The production of woolen cloth depended on a highly sophisticated economic system that connected shepherds in England, the Netherlands, and Spain with woolen cloth manufacturers in cities. The manufacture of cloth and other commodities was organized by guilds. The collapse of the luxury trade reduced the demand for the goods produced by the guilds, depriving guildsmen and urban workers of employment at a time when the cost of food to feed their children was rising. The situation must have seemed ironic. Workers knew that the population decline from famine and pestilence had created a labor shortage, which according to the elementary laws of supply and demand should have produced higher wages for the workers who survived. However, wages stagnated because of the decline in business. Royal and local governments made matters worse by trying to control wages and raise taxes in a period of declining revenues. Frustrated and enraged, workers rebelled.

An Economy of Monopolies: Guilds

Central to the political and economic control of medieval cities were the guilds°. Guilds were professional associations devoted to protecting the special interests of a particular trade or craft and to monopolizing production and trade in the goods the guild produced. There were two dominant types of guilds. The first type, merchant guilds, attempted to monopolize the local market for a particular commodity. There were spice guilds, fruit and vegetable guilds, and apothecary guilds. The second type, craft guilds, regulated the manufacturing processes of artisans, such as carpenters, bricklayers, woolen-cloth manufacturers, glass blowers, and painters. These guilds were dominated by master craftsmen, who ran their own shops. Working for wages in these shops

were the journeymen, who knew the craft but could not yet afford to open their own shops. Under the masters and journeymen were apprentices, who worked usually without pay for a specific number of years to learn the trade.

Guild regulations governed virtually all aspects of guildsmen's lives. In fact, until a youth passed from apprenticeship to become a journeyman, he could not marry or own property. Craft guilds functioned like a modern professional association by guaranteeing that producers met certain standards of training and competence before they could practice a trade. Like merchant guilds, they also regulated competition and prices in an attempt to protect the masters' local monopoly in the craft.

In many cities the guilds expanded far beyond the economic regulation of trade and manufacturing to become the backbone of urban society and politics. The masters of the guilds constituted part of the urban elite, and guild membership was often a prerequisite for holding public office. One of the obligations of city government was to protect the interests of the guildsmen, who in turn helped stabilize the economy through their influence in city hall. The guilds were often at the center of a city's social life as well, countering the anonymity of city life by offering fellowship and a sense of belonging. Medieval festivals were often organized by the guilds, whose members engaged in sports competitions with other guilds. In Nuremberg, for example, the butchers' guild organized and financed the elaborate carnival festivities that absorbed the energies of the entire city for days on end. In many places guilds supplied the actors for the Corpus Christi plays that acted out stories from the Bible or the lives of the saints for the entertainment and edification of their fellow citizens. In Florence the church of the guildsmen became a display case for works of sculpture by the city's most prominent artists, each work sponsored by a specific guild. The guilds endowed magnificent chapels and provided funeral insurance for their members and welfare for the injured and widows of masters.

When the economy declined during the fourteenth century, the urban guilds became lightning rods for mounting social tension. Guild monopolies produced considerable conflict, provoking anger among those who were blocked from joining guilds, young journeymen who earned low wages, and those who found themselves unemployed due to the depression. These tensions exploded into dangerous revolts.

"Long Live the People, Long Live Liberty"

Economic pressures erupted into rebellion most dramatically among woolen-cloth workers in the urban centers in Italy, the Netherlands, and France. The most famous revolt involved the Ciompi, the laborers in the woolen-cloth industry of Florence, Italy, where guilds were the most powerful force in city government. The Ciompi, who performed the heaviest jobs such as carting and the most noxious tasks such as dyeing, had not been allowed to have their own guild and were therefore deprived of the political and economic rights of guild membership.

Fueling the Ciompi's frustration was the fact that by the middle of the fourteenth century woolen-cloth production in Florence dropped by two-thirds, leaving many workers unemployed. In 1378 the desperate Ciompi rebelled. A crowd chanting, "Long live the people, long live liberty," broke into the houses of prominent citizens, released political prisoners from the city jails, and sacked the rich convents that housed the pampered daughters of the wealthy. Over the course of a few months, the rebels managed to force their way onto the city council, where they demanded tax and economic reforms and the right to form their own guild. The Ciompi revolt is one of the earliest cases of workers demanding political rights. The disenfranchised workers did not want to eliminate the guilds' monopoly on political power; they merely wanted a guild of their own so that they could join the regime. That was not to be, however. After a few weeks of success, the Ciompi were divided and defeated.

Shortly after the Ciompi revolt faded, troubles broke out in the woolen-cloth centers of Ghent and Bruges in Flanders and in Paris and Rouen in France. In these cases, however, the revolt spread beyond woolen-cloth workers to voice the more generalized grievances of urban workers. In Ghent and Bruges the weavers attempted to wrest control of their cities from the local leaders who dominated politics and the economy. In Paris and Rouen in 1380, social unrest erupted in resistance to high taxes and attacks by the poor on the rich. The pinnacle of the violence involved the *Maillotins* ("people who fight with mallets") in Paris during March 1382, when the houses of tax collectors were sacked and the inhabitants murdered. Although the violence in Flanders and France was precipitated by local issues, such as control of the town council and taxes, both cases were symptomatic of the widespread social conflicts that followed in the wake of the great depression of the fourteenth century that profoundly affected the crucial woolen-cloth industry.

Like urban workers, many rural peasants also rebelled during the troubled fourteenth century. In France in 1358 a peasant revolt broke out that came to be called the *Jacquerie,* a term derived from "Jacques Bonhomme" ("James Goodfellow"), the traditional name for the typical peasant. Jacquerie became synonymous with extreme, seemingly mindless violence. Filled with hatred for the aristocracy, the peasants indulged in pillaging, murder, and rape, but they offered no plan for an alternative social system or even for their own participation in the political order, so their movement had no lasting effects. They were quickly defeated by a force of nobles.

Unlike the French Jacquerie, the peasants who revolted in England in 1381 had a clear political vision for an alternative society, a fact that makes their revolt far more significant. In England the rebels' motives stemmed from the frustration of rising expectations that were never realized.

DOCUMENT

Worker Rebellions in Flanders and France

A Florentine businessman, Buonaccorso Pitti, who had witnessed the Ciompi revolt in Florence in 1378, found himself in Paris when the Maillotins *revolt broke out. Like his contemporaries, he concluded that the violence in Bruges and Ghent was somehow connected to the outbreak of violence in Rouen and Paris. This was a reasonable assumption, because the count of Flanders and the French royal court had many intimate ties. Thus, rebellion in one place had political implications elsewhere. Here is what Pitti reported.*

In 1381 the people of Ghent rebelled against their overlord, the count of Flanders, who was the father of the duchess of Burgundy. They marched in great numbers to Bruges, took the city, deposed the Count, robbed and killed all his officers, and dealt in the same way with all the other Flemish towns which fell into their hands. Their leader was Philip van Artevelde. As the number of Flemings rebelling against their overlords increased, they sent secret embassies to the populace of Paris and Rouen, urging them to do the like with their own lords, and promising them aid and succor in this undertaking. Accordingly, these two cities rebelled against the King of France. The first insurrection was that of the Paris mob, and was sparked off by a costermonger [someone who sells produce from a cart] who, when an official tried to levy a tax on the fruit and vegetables he was selling, began to roar "Down with the *gabelle* [a food tax]." At this cry the whole populace rose, ran to the tax-collectors' houses and robbed and murdered them. Then, since the mob was unarmed, one of their number led them to the Chatelet where Bertrand du Guesclin, a former High Constable, had stored 3000 lead-tipped cudgels in preparation for a battle which was to have been fought against the English. The rabble used axes to break their way into the tower where these cudgels or mallets (in French, *maillets*) were kept and, arming themselves, set forth in all directions to rob the houses of the King's representatives and in many cases to murder them. The . . . men of substance who in French are called *bourgeois,* fearing lest the mob (who were later called *Maillotins* and were of much the same kidney [nature] as the *Ciompi* in Florence) might rob them too, took arms and managed to subdue them. They then proceeded to take government into their own hands, and together with the *Maillotins,* continued the war against their royal lords.

Source: Reprinted by permission of Waveland Press, Inc. from Gene Brucker, ed., *Two Memoirs of Renaissance Florence: The Diaries of Buonaccorso Pitti and Gregorio Dati,* translated by Julia Martines (Prospect Heights, IL: Waveland Press, Inc., 1967, reissued 1991). All rights reserved.

Jacquerie
A leader of the Jacquerie is beheaded while the king looks on.

CHRONOLOGY

Economic Depression and Social Turmoil

1298	Collapse of Sienese banks
1310–1320	Famines begin
1342–1346	Collapse of Florentine banks
1348	Arrival of Black Death in Europe
1358	Jacquerie revolt in France
1378	Ciompi revolt in Florence
1379–1385	Urban revolts in Flanders and France
1381	Peasants revolt in England

The peasants believed that the labor shortage caused by the Black Death should have improved their condition, but the exact opposite was happening. Landlords clung to the old system that defined peasants as serfs who were tied to the land and unable to bargain for the price of their labor. Although the English peasants were probably better off than their fathers and grandfathers had been, their expectations of an even better life were blocked by the land-holding aristocracy. The clashing interests of the peasants and the aristocrats needed only a spark to ignite a conflagration. That spark came from the Poll Tax controversy.

The traditional means of raising revenue in England had been a levy on the more well-to-do landowners, who were taxed according to the size and value of their holdings. In 1381, however, the crown attempted to levy a Poll Tax, which taxed with little concern for the ability of each person to pay. The Poll Tax, in effect, shifted the burden of taxation to a lower social level, and the peasants bitterly resented it. As agents came to collect the Poll Tax in June 1381, riots broke out throughout eastern England, and rioters burned local tax records. The rebels briefly occupied London, where they lynched the lord chancellor and treasurer of the kingdom. The rebels demanded lower rents, higher wages, and the abolition of serfdom—all typical peasant demands—but to these they added a class-based argument against the aristocracy. They had been influenced by popular preachers who told them that in the Garden of Eden there had been no aristocracy. Following these preachers, the English rebels imagined a classless society, a utopian vision of an alternative to medieval society that was entirely structured around distinctive classes.

The 15-year-old English king, Richard II (r. 1377–1399), promised the rebels that their demands would be met. Satisfied that they had gotten what they wanted, including the abolition of serfdom, the peasants disbanded. The king then rescinded his promises and ordered that the peasant leaders be hunted down and executed. Thus, the greatest peasant rebellion in medieval English history ended with broken promises and no tangible achievements.

None of the worker or peasant revolts of the fourteenth century met with lasting success. The universal failure of lower-class rebellion was due, in part, to the lack of any clear alternative to the existing economic and political system. The Ciompi wanted to join the existing guild system. The weavers of Ghent and Bruges were as much competing with one another as rebelling against the Flanders establishment. The extreme violence of the Jacquerie frightened away potential allies. Only the English rebels had precise revolutionary demands, but they were betrayed by King Richard. However, the rebellions revealed for the first time in the West a widespread impulse among the lower classes to question and protest the existing social and economic order. The tradition of worker protest became common and recurrent during subsequent centuries.

An Age of Warfare

■ How did incessant warfare transform the most powerful medieval states?

Western Europe was further weakened during the fourteenth century by prolonged war between its two largest and previously most stable kingdoms, England and France. The Hundred Years' War° (1337–1453) was a struggle over England's attempts to assert its claims to territories in France. The prolonged conflict drained resources from the aristocracies of both kingdoms, deepening and lengthening the economic depression. The Hundred Years' War sowed the seeds of a military revolution that by the sixteenth century transformed the kingdoms of western Europe. In that transformation monarchies, ruled by relatively weak kings and strong aristocracies, evolved into modern states, ruled by strong monarchs who usurped many of the traditional privileges of the aristocracy in order to centralize authority and strengthen military prowess.

The Fragility of Monarchies

The most dangerous threat to the kings of France and England during the fourteenth and fifteenth centuries came less from worker and peasant rebellions than from members of the aristocracy, who were fiercely protective of their jurisdictional privileges over their lands. The privilege of jurisdiction allowed aristocrats to act as judges for crimes committed in their territories, a privilege that was a crucial source of their power. In both kingdoms, royal officials asserted the legal principle that aristocratic jurisdictions originated with the crown and were subordinate to it. The problem in enforcing this principle, however, was that there were overlapping, conflicting, and sometimes contradictory jurisdictions and loyalties, which were produced by many generations of inheritance. The system bred strife and limited the power of the monarch. Thus the Hundred Years' War was both a conflict between two kingdoms and a series of civil wars between aristocratic factions and imperiled monarchs.

Medieval monarchies depended on the king to maintain stability. Despite the remarkable legal reforms and bureaucratic centralization of monarchies in England and France during the twelfth and thirteenth centuries (see Chapter 9), weak or incompetent kings were all too common during the fourteenth. Weak kings created a perilous situation made worse by disputed successions. The career of Edward II (r. 1307–1327) of England illustrates the peril. Edward was unable to control the vital judicial and financial sinews of royal power. He continued the policy of his father, Edward I, by introducing resident justices of the peace who had replaced the inadequate system of itinerant judges who traveled from village to village to hear cases. In theory, these justices of the peace should have prevented the abuses of justice typical of aristocratic jurisdictions, but even though they were royal officials who answered to the king, most of those appointed were also local landowners who were deeply implicated in many of the disputes that came before them. As a result, justice in England became notoriously corrupt and the cause of discontent. Edward II was so incompetent to deal with the consequences of corrupted justice that he provoked a civil war in which his own queen joined his aristocratic enemies to depose him.

The French monarchy was no better. In fact, the French king was in an even weaker constitutional position than the

Royal Justice
English kings were preoccupied with extending their prerogatives over the judiciary as a way to express royal power. Despite the corruption of the many lower courts, the Court of the King's Bench attempted to assert a level of uniform procedures and royal control of justice.

English monarch. In France the king had effective jurisdiction over only a small part of his realm. Many of the duchies and counties of France were quasi-independent principalities, paying only nominal allegiance to the king, whose will was ignored with impunity. In these regions the administration of justice, the collection of taxes, and the recruitment of soldiers all remained in the hands of local lords. To explain why he needed to raise taxes, Philip IV, "The Fair" (r. 1285–1314), created a representative assembly, the Estates General, which met for the first time in 1302, but he still had to negotiate with each region and town individually to collect the taxes. Given the difficulty of raising taxes, the French kings resorted to makeshift solutions that hurt the economy, such as confiscating the property of vulnerable Jewish and Italian merchants and debasing the coinage to increase the value of scarce silver. Such a system made the finances of the kingdom of France especially shaky because the king lacked a dependable flow of revenue.

The Hundred Years' War

The Hundred Years' War revealed the fragility of the medieval monarchies. The initial cause of the war involved disputes over the duchy of Aquitaine. The king of England also held the title of duke of Aquitaine, who was a vassal of the French crown, which meant that the English kings technically owed military assistance to the French kings whenever they asked for it. A long succession of English kings had reluctantly paid homage as dukes of Aquitaine to the king of France, but the unusual status of the duchy was a continuing source of contention.

The second cause of the war derived from a dispute over the succession to the French crown. When King Charles IV died in 1328, his closest surviving relative was none other than the archenemy of France, Edward III (r. 1327–1377), king of England. To the barons of France, the possibility of Edward's succession to the throne was unthinkable, and they excluded him because his relation to the French royal family was through his mother. Instead the barons elected to the throne a member of the Valois family, King Philip VI (r. 1328–1350), and at first Edward reluctantly accepted the decision. However, when Philip started to hear judicial appeals from the duchy of Aquitaine, Edward changed his mind. He claimed the title of king of France for himself, sparking the beginning of more than a century of warfare (see Map 10.4).

The Hundred Years' War (1337–1453) was not a continuous formal war but a series of occasional pitched battles, punctuated by long truces and periods of general exhaustion. The term *Hundred Years' War* was invented by nineteenth-century historians to describe the prolonged time of troubles between the two countries. In terms of its potential for warfare, France, far richer and with three times the population, held the advantage over sparsely populated England. In nearly every battle the French outnumbered the English, but the English were usually victorious because of superior discipline and the ability of their longbows to break up cavalry charges. As a rule, the English avoided open battle, preferring raids, sieges of isolated castles, and capturing French knights for ransom. For many Englishmen the objective of fighting in France was to get rich by looting. Because all the fighting took place on French soil, France suffered extensive destruction and significant civilian casualties from repeated English raids.

From English Victories to French Salvation
In the early phases of the war, the English enjoyed a stunning series of victories. At the Battle of Sluys in 1340, a

Siege Warfare
English soldiers pillaging and burning a French town.

small English fleet of 150 ships carrying the English invasion forces ran into a French blockade of more than 200 ships. In the heavy hand-to-hand combat, the English captured 166 French ships and killed some 20,000 men, so many that it was later said, "If fish could talk, they would speak French." At Crécy in 1346, the English longbowmen shot thousands of arrows "like thunderbolts" into the flanks of the charging French knights, killing men and horses in shocking numbers. The French knights mounted one disorderly, hopeless charge after another, until the piles of dead blocked further charges. Though wounded, King Philip escaped, leaving 3,000 of his men dead on the field, including 1,500 knights. The aristocracy of France was decimated. At Poitiers in 1356, King John of France (r. 1350–1364) encircled 6,000 English with a vastly superior royal army of 15,000, but—as at Crécy—the English archers broke up the overly hasty French cavalry charge, and the English counterassault crushed the French. Two thousand French knights died and another 2,000 were captured, including King John himself. With its king imprisoned in England, France was forced to pay a huge ransom and grant formal sovereignty over a third of France to the king of England.

At Agincourt in 1415, King Henry V (r. 1413–1422) and England's disease-racked army of 6,000 were cut off by a French force of about 20,000. In the ensuing battle the English archers repelled a hasty French cavalry charge and

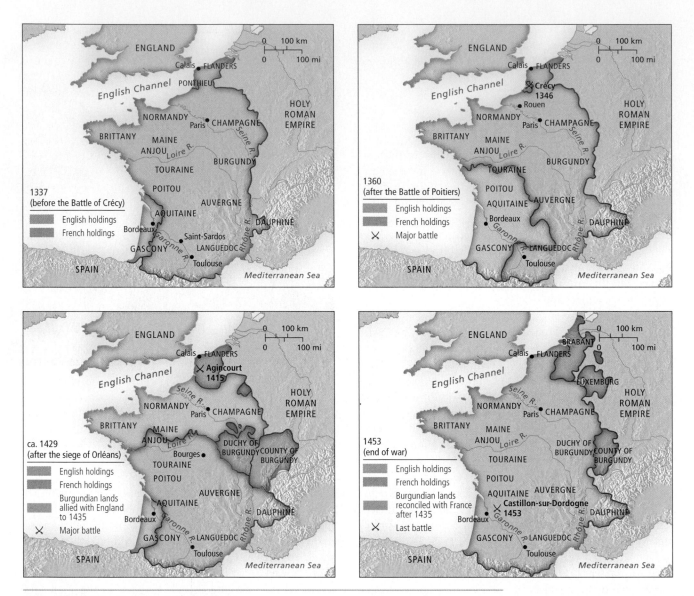

Map 10.4 The Hundred Years' War

This map illustrates four phases of the Hundred Years' War. In the first phase (1337), England maintained a small foothold in the southwest of France. In the second phase (1360), England considerably expanded the territory around Aquitaine and gained a vital base in the north of France. In the third phase (ca. 1429), England occupied much of the north of France, and England's ally Burgundy established effective independence from French authority. In the fourth phase at the end of the war (1453), England had been driven from French soil except at Calais, and Burgundy maintained control over its scattered territories.

the fleeing, terrified horses trampled the French men-at-arms as they advanced. The English lost only a few hundred, but the French suffered nearly 10,000 casualties. After Agincourt, the French never again dared challenge King Henry in open battle, and were forced to recognize him as the heir to the French throne. By 1420 the English victory appeared complete. Now with the responsibility of ruling rather than conquering France, the English could no longer

rely on their old strategy of mounted raiding and had to hold the French cities, which proved exceedingly difficult. By 1422, however, Henry V was dead, leaving two claimants to the French throne. The English asserted the rights of the infant King Henry VI of England, son of King Henry V, the victor at Agincourt. Most of the French defended the claim of the Dauphin (the title of the heir to the throne) Charles, the only surviving son of the late King Charles VI of France.

English Archers

English archers practicing the longbow. Note that the unpulled bows are the height of a man.

The Hundred Years' War entered a new phase with factions of the French aristocracy supporting the two rivals in a bloody series of engagements.

By 1429 the English were on the verge of final victory. They occupied Paris and Rheims, and their army was besieging Orleans. The Dauphin Charles was penniless and indecisive. Even his own mother denied his legitimacy as the future king. At this point a 17-year-old illiterate peasant from Burgundy, Joan of Arc (Jeanne d'Arc, ca. 1412–1431), following "divine voices," went to Orleans to lead the French armies. Under her inspiration Orleans was relieved, French forces began to defeat the English, much of the occupied territory was regained, and the Dauphin was crowned King Charles VII (r. 1429–1461) in the cathedral of Rheims. After Joan failed to recapture Paris, however, her successes ceased. The final success of the French came from the leadership of King Charles and the general exhaustion of the English forces.

Charles VII reorganized the French army and gradually chipped away at the English holdings in France, eventually taking away Aquitaine in 1453. The English lost all their possessions in France except Calais, which was finally surrendered in 1558. There was no peace treaty, just a fading away of war in France, especially after England stumbled into civil war—the War of the Roses (1455–1485).

The Hundred Years' War in Perspective

The Hundred Years' War had broad consequences. First, nearly continuous warfare between the two most powerful kingdoms in the West exacerbated other conflicts as well. Scotland, the German princes, Aragon, Castile, and most importantly Burgundy were drawn into the conflict, making the English-French brawl a European-wide war at certain stages. The squabble between France and England made it much more difficult to settle the Great Schism that split the Church during the same period. Second, the war devastated France, which eventually regained control of most of its territory but still suffered the most from the fighting. During the century of the war, the population dropped by half, due to the ravages of combat, pillage, and plague. Agriculture languished after the English repeatedly mounted raids that destroyed crops and sacked peasant villages. Third, the deaths of so many nobles and destruction of their fortunes diminished the international luxury trade; merchants and banks as far away as Italy went broke; and the Flemish woolen industry was disrupted, causing further economic damage. Finally, the war helped make England more English. Before the war the Plantagenet dynasty in England was more French than English. The monarchs possessed extensive territories in France and were embroiled in French affairs. English aristocrats also had business in France, spoke French, and married their French cousins. After 1450 the English abandoned the many French connections that had stretched across the English Channel since William the Conqueror sailed from Normandy to England in 1066. Henceforth, the English upper classes cultivated English rather than French language and culture.

CHRONOLOGY

An Age of Warfare

1285–1314	Reign of Philip IV, "The Fair," of France
1307–1327	Reign of Edward II of England
1327–1377	Reign of Edward III of England
1328–1350	Reign of Philip VI of France
1337–1453	Hundred Years' War
1340	Battle of Sluys
1346	Battle of Crécy
1356	Battle of Poitiers
1377–1399	Reign of Richard II of England
ca. 1412–1431	Life of Joan of Arc
1413–1422	Reign of Henry V of England
1415	Battle of Agincourt
1429–1461	Reign of Charles VII of France
1455–1485	War of the Roses in England

The Trial of Joan of Arc

After only fifteen months as the inspiration of the French army, Joan of Arc fell into the hands of the English, who brought her to trial for witchcraft. The English needed to stage a kind of show trial to demonstrate to their own demoralized forces that Joan's remarkable victories had been the result not of military superiority but rather of witchcraft. In the English trial, conducted at Rouen in 1431, Joan testified that her mission to save France was in response to voices she heard that commanded her to wear men's clothing. On the basis of this evidence of a confused or double gender identity, the ecclesiastical tribunal declared her a witch and a relapsed heretic. The court sentenced her to be burned at the stake.

Political motivations governed the 1431 English trial for witchcraft, but Joan's testimony provides some clues to her own identity conflicts. The two pieces of evidence against Joan ultimately resulted in her condemnation: the spiritual "voices" she claimed to hear and her cross-dressing in men's clothing.

From the beginning of her emergence onto the political scene, Joan's voices intrigued all who came into contact with her. Joan claimed that she was guided by the voices of St. Catherine, St. Margaret, and the Archangel Michael. To Joan, these voices had the authority of divine commands. The problem the English judges faced was to demonstrate that the voices came not from God but from the Devil. If they could prove that, then they had evidence of witchcraft and sorcery. Following standard inquisitorial guidelines, the judges knew that authentic messages from God would always conform to church dogma. Any deviation from official doctrines would constitute evidence of demonic influence. Thus, during Joan's trial the judges demanded that she make theological distinctions that were alien to her. When they wanted to know if the voices were those of angels or saints, Joan seemed perplexed and responded, "This voice comes from God . . . I am more afraid of failing the voices by saying what is displeasing to them than answering you."[7] The judges kept pushing, asking if the saints or angels had heads, eyes, and hair. Exasperated, Joan simply replied, "I have told you often enough, believe me if you will."

The judges reformulated Joan's words to reflect their own rigid scholastic categories and concluded that her "veneration of the saints seems to partake of idolatry and to proceed from a pact made with devils. These are less divine revelations than lies invented by Joan, suggested or shown to her by the demon in illusive apparitions, in order to mock at her imagination while she meddled with things that are beyond her and superior to the faculty of her condition."[8] In other words, Joan was just too naive and uneducated to have authentic visions. But the English judges were on dangerous ground because during the previous fifty years there had been a number of notable female mystics, including St. Catherine of Siena and St. Bridget of Sweden, whose visions had been accepted as authentic by the pope. The English could not take the chance that they were executing a real saint. They had to prove Joan was a witch by showing that her visions were theologically unsound. But that they could not do.

If they could not convict her for bad theology, the English needed evidence for superstitious practices. In an attempt to do that, they drew up seventy charges against her. Many of these consisted of allegations of performing magic, such as chanting spells, visiting a magical tree at night, and invoking demons. They attempted to prove bad behavior by insinuating that a young man had refused to marry her on account of her immoral life. They asserted that her godmother was a notorious witch who had taught her sorcery. None of these ploys worked, however, because Joan consistently denied these charges. She did, however, admit to one allegation: she cross-dressed as a man.

Some of the charges against her and many of the questions she was asked concerned how she dressed:

The said Joan put off and entirely abandoned women's clothes, with her hair cropped short and round in the fashion of young men, she wore shirt, breeches, doublet, with hose joined together, long and fastened to the said doublet by twenty points, long leggings laced on the outside, a short mantle reaching to the knee, or thereabouts, a close-cut cap, tight-fitting boots or buskins, long spurs, sword, dagger, breastplate, lance and other arms in the style of a man-at-arms.[9]

The judges explained to her that "according to canon law and the Holy Scriptures" a woman dressing as a man or a man as a woman is "an abomination before God."[10] She replied simply and consistently that "everything that I have done, I did by command of the voices" and that wearing male dress "would be for the great good of France."[11] When they asked her to put on a woman's dress in order to take the Eucharist on Easter Sunday, she refused, saying the miracle of the Eucharist did not depend on whether she wore a man's or a woman's clothing. On many occasions she had been asked to put on a woman's dress and refused. "And as for womanly duties, she said there were enough other women to do them."[12]

After a long imprisonment and psychological pressure from her in-

The Execution of Joan of Arc
There are no contemporary portraits of Joan, and this image is clearly a generalized one of a young woman rather than a portrait taken from the real Joan.

The bundle of stakes will be used for the fire that will consume her.

Joan of Arc is tied to the stake before her execution.

These onlookers are holding sticks for the fire.

quisitors, Joan confessed to charges of witchcraft, signed a recantation of her heresy, and agreed to put on a dress. She was sentenced to life imprisonment on bread and water. Why did she confess? Some historians have argued that she was tricked into confessing because the inquisitors really wanted to execute her but could not do so unless she was a *relapsed* heretic. To be relapsed she had to confess and then somehow return to her heretical ways. If that was the inquisitors' intention, Joan soon obliged them. After a few days in prison, Joan threw off the women's clothes she had been given and resumed dressing as a man. As a witness put it, "The said Catherine and Margaret [instructed] this woman in the name of God to take and wear a man's clothes, and she had worn them and still wears them, stubbornly obeying the said command, to such an extent that this woman had declared she would rather die than relinquish these clothes."[13]

Joan was willing to be burned at the stake rather than disobey her voices. Why? Historians will never know for sure, but dressing as a man may have been necessary for her to fulfill her role as a military leader. The men who followed her into battle and trusted her voices accepted the necessity of this mutation of gender. In her military career, Joan had adopted the masculine qualities of chivalry: bravery, steadfastness, loyalty, and a willingness to accept pain and death. She made herself believable by dressing as a knight. A number

of soldiers who had served with her testified that although they knew Joan was a woman, they had never felt any sexual desire for her, which suggests that she seemed androgynous to them. It was precisely Joan's gender ambiguity that the inquisitors found a dangerous sign of Satan's hand. And it was Joan's refusal to abandon her ambiguous gender identity that provided the inquisitors with the evidence they needed.

Joan's condemnation was much more than another example of men's attempt to control women. The inquisitors needed evidence of demonic influence, which to their minds Joan's transgressive gender behavior supplied. Joan's confused gender identity threatened the whole system of neat hierarchical distinctions upon which scholastic theology rested. To the theologians, everything in God's Creation had its own proper place and anyone who changed his or her divinely ordained position in society presented a direct affront to God.

The English verdict and Joan's tragic fate greatly wounded French pride. In 1456 at her mother's instigation the French clergy reopened her case in a posthumous trial that sought to rehabilitate her

in the eyes of the church. To these churchmen, she was an authentic visionary and a saint who listened to a direct command from God. To the French people ever since, she has become a national symbol of pride and of French unity against a foreign invader. In our own time, Joan has been characterized as many things—a saint, a madwoman, a female warrior, a woman exercising power in a male world, and a woman openly transgressing gender categories by dressing in men's clothes.

Questions of Justice

1. In medieval ecclesiastical trials such as this one, what kinds of evidence were presented and what kind of justice was sought?
2. What did Joan's claim that she heard voices reveal about her understanding of what constituted the proper authority over her life?

Taking It Further

Joan of Arc. *In Her Own Words,* trans. Willard Trask. 1996. The record of what Joan reputedly said at her trials.

Warner, Marina. *Joan of Arc: The Image of Female Heroism.* 1981. A highly readable feminist reading of the Joan of Arc story.

The Military Revolution

The "military revolution," whose effects first became evident during the Hundred Years' War, refers to changes in warfare that marked the transition from the late medieval to the early modern state. The heavily armored mounted knights, who had dominated European warfare and society since the Carolingian period, were gradually supplanted by foot soldiers as the most effective fighting unit in battle. Infantry units were composed of men who fought on foot in disciplined ranks, which allowed them to break up cavalry charges by concentrating firepower in deadly volleys. Infantry soldiers could fight on a greater variety of terrains than mounted knights, who needed even ground and plenty of space for their horses to maneuver. The effectiveness of infantry units made battles more ferocious but also more decisive, which was why governments favored them. Infantry, however, put new requirements on the governments that recruited them. Armies now demanded large numbers of well-drilled foot soldiers who could move in disciplined ranks around a battlefield. Recruiting, training, and drilling soldiers made armies much more complex organizations than they had been, and officers needed to possess a wide range of management skills. Governments faced added expenses as they needed to arrange and pay for the logistical support necessary to feed and transport those large numbers. The creation of the highly centralized modern state resulted in part from the necessity to maintain a large army in which infantry played the crucial role.

Infantry used a variety of weapons. The English demonstrated the effectiveness of longbowmen during the Hundred Years' War. Capable of shooting at a much more rapid rate than the French crossbowmen, the English longbowmen at Agincourt protected themselves behind a hurriedly erected stockade of stakes and rained a shower of deadly arrows on the French cavalry to break up charges. In the narrow battlefield, which was wedged between two forests, the French cavalry had insufficient room to maneuver, and when some of them dismounted to create more room, their heavy armor made them easy to topple over and spear through the underarm seam in their armor. Some English infantry units deployed ranks of pikemen who created an impenetrable wall of sharp spikes.

The military revolution of the fourteenth and fifteenth centuries also introduced gunpowder to European warfare. Arriving from China with the Mongol invasions, gunpowder was first used in the West in artillery. Beginning in the 1320s huge wrought-iron cannons were used to shoot stone or iron against fortifications during sieges. By the early sixteenth century bronze muzzle-loading cannons were used in field battles. With the introduction during the late fifteenth century of the first handgun and the harquebus (a matchlock shoulder gun), properly drilled and disciplined infantrymen could deliver very destructive firepower.

Gunshot pierced plate armor, whereas arrows bounced off. The slow rate of fire of these guns, however, necessitated carefully planned battle tactics. Around 1500 the Spanish introduced mixed infantry formations that pursued "shock" and "shot" tactics. Spanish pikemen provided the shock, which was quickly followed up by gunshot or missile fire. Spanish infantry formations were capable of defeating cavalry even in the open field without defensive fortifications, an unprecedented feat. By the end of the fifteenth century, trained infantry were necessary in every army.

The chivalric aristocrats, who made up the heavily armored cavalry forces and whose fighting ability justified their social privileges, tried to adapt to the changes by improving plate armor, employing longer lances, and drilling their horses for greater maneuverability. They were successful enough and retained enough political influence that heavy cavalry remained necessary in the professional armies that began to appear in the fifteenth century. However, the military revolution precipitated a major shift in European society as well as in battlefield tactics. The successful states were those that created the financial base and bureaucratic structures necessary to put into the field a well-trained professional army composed of infantry units and artillery. Armies now required officers who were capable of drilling infantry or understanding the science of warfare in order to serve as an artillery officer. The traditional landed aristocrats, accustomed to commanding armored knights, found that noble lineage was not as important as technical skills and talents.

A Troubled Church and the Demand for Religious Comfort

■ Why did the church fail to provide leadership and spiritual guidance during these difficult times?

In reaction to the suffering and widespread death during the fourteenth century, many people naturally turned to religion for spiritual consolation and for explanations of what had gone wrong. But the spiritual authority of the Church was so dangerously weakened during this period that it failed to satisfy the popular craving for solace. The moral leadership that had made the papacy such a powerful force for reform during the eleventh through thirteenth centuries was completely lacking in the fourteenth. Many laypeople gave up looking to the pope for guidance and found their own means of religious expression, making the Later Middle Ages one of the most religiously creative epochs in Christian history. Some of the new religious movements, especially in England and Bohemia, veered onto the dangerous shoals of heresy, breaking the fragile unity of the Church.

The Babylonian Captivity of the Church and the Great Schism

Faced with anarchy in the streets of Rome as local aristocrats engaged in incessant feuding, a succession of seven consecutive popes chose to reside in the relative calm of Avignon, France. This period of voluntary papal exile is known as the Babylonian Captivity of the Church° (1305–1378), a biblical reference recalling the captivity of the Jews in Babylonia (587–539 B.C.E.). The popes' presumed subservience to the kings of France during this period dangerously politicized the papacy, destroying its ability to rise above the petty squabbles of the European princes. Even though these popes were never the French kings' lackeys, the enemies of the kings of France did not trust popes who were residing in France and who were themselves French. The loss of revenues from papal lands in Italy lured several popes into questionable financial schemes, which included accepting kickbacks from appointees to church offices, taking bribes for judicial decisions, and selling indulgences°. Indulgences were certificates that allowed penitents to atone for their sins and reduce their time in Purgatory.

When Pope Urban VI (r. 1378–1389) was elevated to the papacy in 1378 and announced his intention to reside in Rome, a group of disgruntled French cardinals returned to Avignon and elected a rival French pope. The Church was then divided over allegiance to Italian and French claimants to the papal throne, a period called the Great Schism° (1378–1417). Toward the end of the schism there were actually four rival popes. Some of these antipopes completely lacked spiritual qualities. The most infamous was Baldassare Cossa, whom a faction of cardinals elected Pope

John XXIII (r. 1410–1415) because he had been an effective commander of the papal troops. The cardinals who supported rival popes charged Pope John with the crimes of piracy, murder, rape, sodomy, and incest—charges without much substance—but the publication of the allegations further undermined the moral reputation of the papacy. During the Great Schism the kings, princes, and cities of Europe divided their allegiances between the rival candidates. The Church was split not because of doctrinal differences but because competing systems of political alliances sustained the schism. The French king and the allies of France supported the French pope. The enemies of France gave aid and comfort to the Italian pope.

Urban VI's decision to return the papacy to Rome and attempt to end the Babylonian Captivity of the Church resulted from an intense demand for his presence in Italy. Part of the reason was the growing influence of a young woman mystic. Catherine Benincasa (1347–1380), now known as St. Catherine of Siena, demonstrated her mystic tendencies at an early age by locking herself in a room of her parents' house for a year to devote herself to prayer and fasting. She soon became famous for her holiness and severe asceticism, which during the troubled times of the Babylonian Captivity gave her a powerful moral authority. She went to Avignon, and although the pope ignored her, she attracted the attention of others in the papal court. Catherine became the most important advocate for encouraging the return of the pope from Avignon to Rome and launching a new crusade against the Muslims. She helped Pope Urban VI reorganize the Church after he returned to Rome, and she sent out letters and pleas to the kings and queens of Europe to gain support for him during the schism. Catherine dictated an influential body of letters,

The Babylonian Captivity of the Church
From 1303 to 1378 the popes lived in exile from Rome in this fortress-like Palace of the Popes in Avignon, France. The French claimants to the papal throne continued to live here during the Great Schism until 1417.

prayers, and treatises that attempted to remind the popes and kings of Europe of their religious responsibilities.

The Great Schism created the need for a mechanism to sort out the competing claims of rival popes. That need led to the Conciliar Movement°. The conciliarists argued that a general meeting or council of the bishops of the Church had authority over the pope, it could be called to order by a king, and it could pass judgment on a standing pope or order a conclave to elect a new one. Several general councils were held during the early fifteenth century to resolve the schism and initiate reforms, but solutions were difficult to achieve because politics and the affairs of the Church were so closely intertwined. The Council of Constance (1414–1417) finally succeeded in restoring unity to the Church and also in formally asserting the principle that a general council is superior to the pope and should be called frequently. The Council of Basel (1431–1449) approved a series of necessary reforms, although these were never implemented due to the hostility to conciliarism by Pope Eugene IV (r. 1431–1447). The failure of even the timid reforms of the Council of Basel opened the way for the more radical rejection of papal authority during the Protestant Reformation of the sixteenth century. The Conciliar Movement, however, was not a complete failure because it provided a model for how reform could take place. This model would later become central to the Catholic Reformation and the foundation of modern Catholicism (see Chapter 13).

The Search for Religious Alternatives

The popes' loss of moral authority during the Babylonian Captivity and the Great Schism opened the way for a remarkable variety of reformers, mystics, and preachers, who appealed to lay believers crying out for a direct experience of God and a return to the message of the original apostles of Christ. Most of these movements were quite traditional in their doctrines, but some were heretical, and the weakened papacy was unable to control them, as it had successfully done during the thirteenth-century crusade against the Albigensians.

Protests Against the Papacy: New Heresies

For most Catholic Christians during the fourteenth century, religious life consisted of witnessing or participating in the seven sacraments, which were formal rituals celebrated by duly consecrated priests usually within the confines of churches. After baptism, which was universally performed on infants, the most common sacraments for lay adults were penance and communion. Both of these sacraments emphasized the authority of the clergy over the laity and therefore were potential sources for resentment. The sacrament of penance required the layperson to confess his or her sins to a priest, who then prescribed certain penalties to satisfy

the sin. At communion, it was believed, the priest changed the substance of an unleavened wafer of bread, called the Eucharist, into the body of Christ and a chalice of wine into his blood, a miraculous process called transubstantiation. Priests and lay recipients of communion both ate the wafer, but the chalice was reserved for the priest alone. More than anything else, the reservation of the chalice for priests profoundly symbolized the privileges of the clergy. Because medieval Catholicism was primarily a sacramental religion, reformers and heretics tended to concentrate their criticism on sacramental rituals, especially of their spiritual value compared to other kinds of worship such as prayer.

The most serious discontent about the authority of the popes, the privileges of the clergy, and the efficacy of the sacraments appeared in England and Bohemia (a region in the modern Czech Republic). An Oxford professor, John Wycliffe (1320–1384), criticized the power and wealth of the clergy, played down the value of the sacraments for encouraging ethical behavior, and exalted the benefits of preaching, which promoted a sense of personal responsibility. During the Great Schism, Wycliffe rejected the authority of the rival popes and asserted instead the absolute authority of the Bible, which he wanted to make available to the laity in English rather than in Latin, which most laypeople could not understand.

The Execution of Jan Hus
Despite a safe-conduct from the emperor, Jan Hus was arrested and convicted as a heretic at the Council of Constance in 1415. This miniature from later in the fifteenth century depicts his burning.

Outside England Wycliffe's ideas found their most sympathetic audience among a group of reformist professors at the University of Prague in Bohemia, where Jan Hus (1369–1415) regularly preached to a large popular following. Hus's most revolutionary act was to offer the chalice of consecrated communion wine to the laity, thus symbolically diminishing the special status of the clergy. When Hus also preached against indulgences, which he said converted the sacrament of penance into a cash transaction, Pope John XXIII excommunicated him. Hus attended the Council of Constance to defend his ideas. Despite the promise of a safe-conduct from the Holy Roman emperor (whose jurisdiction included Bohemia and Constance) that would have made him immune from arrest, Hus was imprisoned, his writings were condemned, and he was burned alive as a heretic.

Imitating Christ: The Modern Devotion

In the climate of religious turmoil of the fourteenth and fifteenth centuries, many Christians sought deeper spiritual solace than the institutionalized Church could provide. Most of these people pursued deeply traditional forms of piety, exhibiting how medieval spirituality was capable of seemingly infinite renewal and vitality. By stressing individual piety, ethical behavior, and intense religious education, a movement called the Modern Devotion° built on the existing traditions of spirituality and became highly influential. Promoted by the Brothers of the Common Life, a religious order established in the Netherlands, the Modern Devotion was especially popular throughout northern Europe. In the houses for the Brothers, clerics and laity lived together without monastic vows, shared household tasks, joined in regular prayers, and engaged in religious studies. (A similar structure was devised for women.) The lay brothers continued their occupations in the outside world, thus influencing their neighbors through their pious example. The houses established schools that prepared boys for church careers through constant prayer and rigorous training in Latin. Many of the leading figures behind the Protestant Reformation in the sixteenth century had attended schools run by the Brothers of the Common Life.

The Modern Devotion was also spread by the best-seller of the late fifteenth century, the *Imitation of Christ,* written about 1441 by a Common Life brother, probably Thomas à Kempis. By emphasizing frequent private prayer and moral introspection, the *Imitation* provided a manual to guide laypeople in the path toward spiritual renewal that had traditionally been reserved for monks and nuns. There was nothing especially reformist or antisacramental about the *Imitation of Christ,* which emphasized the need for regular confession and communion. However, its popularity helped prepare the way for a broad-based reform of the Church by turning the walls of the monastery inside out, spilling out a large number of lay believers who were dedicated to becoming living examples of moral purity for their neighbors.

The moral and financial degradation of the papacy during the fourteenth and early fifteenth centuries was countered by the persistent spirituality of the laity, manifest in the Modern Devotion. As a result, throughout Europe laypeople took responsibility not only for their own behavior but for the spiritual and material welfare of their entire community and of the Church itself. Lay spirituality remained deeply traditional rather than innovative. These pious people founded hospitals for the sick and dying, orphanages for abandoned children, and confraternities that engaged in a wide range of charitable good works—from providing dowries for poor women to accompanying condemned criminals to the gallows.

The Culture of Loss

■ How did European culture offer explanations and solace for the otherwise inexplicable calamities of the times?

During the fourteenth and early fifteenth centuries, the omnipresence of violence and death made suffering a common theme in the arts and strangely the subject matter for jokes, fancy-dress masquerades, and wild dances. The preoccupation with death revealed an anxious attachment to fleeting life.

This widespread anxiety had many manifestations. Some aristocrats sought escape from the terror by indulging in a beautiful fantasy life of gallant knights and beautiful ladies. Others went on long penitential pilgrimages to the shrines of saints or to the Holy Land. During the fourteenth century the tribulations of the pilgrim's travels became a metaphor for the journey of life itself, stimulating creative literature. Still others tried to find someone to blame for calamities. When no other explanation could be found, alleged witches became handy scapegoats. The search for scapegoats also focused on minority groups, especially Jews and Muslims.

Reminders of Death

In no other period of Western civilization has the idea of death constituted such a pervasive cultural force as during the fourteenth and fifteenth centuries. The religious justification for this preoccupation was the Reminder of Death, a theme found in religious books, literary works, and the visual arts. A contemporary book of moral guidance advised the reader that "when he goes to bed, he should imagine not that he is putting himself to bed, but that others are laying him in his grave."[14] Reminders of Death became the everyday theme of preachers, and popular woodcuts represented death in simple but disturbing images. These representations emphasized the transitory nature of life, admonishing that every created thing perishes. The Reminder of Death tried to encourage ethical behavior in this life by showing that in everyone's future was neither riches, nor fame, nor love, nor pleasure, but only the decay of death.

The most famous Reminder of Death was the Dance of Death. First appearing in a poem of 1376, the Dance of Death evolved into a street play, performed to illustrate sermons that called for repentance. It also appeared in church murals, depicting a procession led by a skeleton that included representatives of the social orders, from children and peasants to pope and emperor. All were being led to their inevitable deaths. At the Church of the Innocents in Paris, the mural depicting the Dance of Death is accompanied by an inscription that reads:

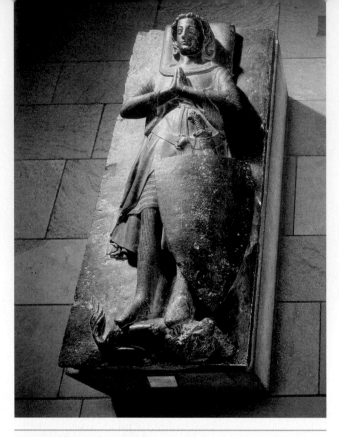

Tomb Effigy of a Knight
This effigy above the tomb of Jean d'Alluy shows the deceased as if he were serenely sleeping, still dressed in the armor of his worldly profession.

Advance, see yourselves in us, dead, naked, rotten and stinking. So will you be. . . . To live without thinking of this risks damnation. . . . Power, honor, riches are nothing; at the hour of death only good works count. . . . Everyone should think at least once a day of his loathsome end [in order to escape] the dreadful pain of hell without end which is unspeakable.[15]

In earlier centuries, tombs had depicted death as serene: On top of the tomb was an effigy of the deceased, dressed in the finest clothes with hands piously folded and eyes open to the promise of eternal life. In contrast, during the fourteenth century tomb effigies began to depict putrefying bodies or naked skeletons, symbols of the futility of human status and achievements. These tombs were disturbingly graphic Reminders of Death. Likewise, poems spoke of the disgusting smell of rotting flesh, the livid color of plague victims, the cold touch of the dead. Preachers loved to personalize death. They would point to the most beautiful young woman in the congregation and describe how she would look while rotting in the grave, how worms would crawl through the empty sockets that once held her alluring eyes.

In reminding people of the need to repent their sins in the face of their inevitable deaths, no sin was more condemned than pride, the high opinion

Decomposing Cadaver
The tomb effigy of Jean de Lagrange.

The Art of Dying

In this death scene, the dying man receives extreme unction (last rites) from a priest. A friar holds a crucifixion for him to contemplate. Above his head an devil and angel compete for his soul while behind him Death lurks waiting for his moment.

of one's own qualities and conduct. In contrast to modern times, when pride is often understood as a virtue, late medieval moralists saw pride as an affront to God, a rejection of God's will that humanity should concentrate on spiritual rather than worldly things. Pride, in fact, was often discussed as the ultimate source of all the other deadly sins: lust, gluttony, avarice, sloth, wrath, and covetousness. The theme was encapsulated by the inscription on the tomb of a cardinal who died in 1402: "So, miserable one, what cause for pride?"[16]

Late medieval society was completely frank about the unpleasant process of dying, unlike modern societies that hide the dying in hospitals and segregate mourning to funeral homes. Dying was a public event, almost a theatrical performance. The last rites of the Catholic Church and the Art of Dying served to assist souls in their final test before God and to separate the departed from their kin. According to the Art of Dying, which was prescribed in numerous advice books and illustrations, the sick or injured person should die in bed, surrounded by a room full of people, including children. It was believed that a dying person watched a supernatural spectacle visible to him or her alone as the heavenly host fought with Satan and his demon minions for the soul. The Art of Dying compared the deathbed contest to a horrific game of chess in which the Devil did all he could to trap the dying person into a checkmate just at the moment of death. In the best of circumstances, a priest arrived in time to hear a confession, offer words of consolation, encourage the dying individual to forgive his or her enemies and redress any wrongs, and perform the last rites.

Illusions of a Noble Life

Eventually death arrived for everyone, peasant and noble alike, a fact that the Reminders of Death were designed to keep foremost in the minds of all Christians. Some people, especially among the nobility, sought to ignore this fundamental truth through escapist fantasies. These fantasies shielded nobles not only from the inevitability of death but also from all the other perils of the age—the worker and peasant rebellions, the economic depression that depleted their wealth, and the military revolution that challenged their monopoly on soldierly valor. During the Later Middle Ages, many nobles indulged in chivalric escapism and idealized their class as the remedy for evil times. They thought God had placed them on Earth to purify the world.

Much of the attraction of chivalry derived from its fanciful vision of the virtues of the ascetic life, the life that practices severe self-discipline and abstains from physical pleasures. The ideal medieval knight was as much a self-denying ascetic as the ideal medieval monk. The highest expression of the chivalric ideal was the knight-errant, a warrior who roamed in search of adventure. He was poor and free of ties to home and family, a man who lived a life of perfect freedom but whose virtue led him to do the right thing. In reality most knights were hardly ascetics but rich, propertied men who were completely involved in the world and who indulged in all of its pleasures.

The ideal of the ascetic knight-errant was pursued in an elaborately developed fantasy culture that occupied much of the time and cultural energy of the aristocracy. The French nobleman Philippe de Mézières (ca. 1327–1405), whose chivalric imagination knew no bounds, dreamed of establishing a new order of knights, the Order of the Passion, whose members would be spiritually removed from worldly affairs and devoted to reconquering the Holy Land. He drew up a plan for the order, but it never became a reality. He imagined that the knights in the Order of the Passion would peacefully end all wars among Christians and bind themselves together in a great Crusade against the Mongols, Jews, Turks, and other Muslims. Several kings actually did establish new crusading orders, which aristocrats joined with unbridled enthusiasm—the Order of the Garter in England, the Order of the Stars and Order of St. Michael in France, and the most fantastic of all, the Order of the Golden Fleece in Burgundy. Members of these orders indulged in extravagant acts of self-deprivation—for example, wearing fur coats in summer but refusing to wear a

A Sumptuous Aristocratic Banquet
An aristocratic banquet with scenes of fighting in the background. Dining was the principal occasion at which nobles displayed refined manners showing their commitment to the beautiful life.

coat, hat, or gloves in freezing temperatures. They loved to take vows: One knight swore he would not sleep in a bed on Sundays until he had fought the Muslims; another took an oath that he would keep his right arm bare of any armor during battle with the Turks. None of these would-be crusaders came close to fighting Turks.

Many vows were taken in the name of ladies, revealing that the chivalric ideal also included a heavy dose of erotic desire. Besides ascetic self-denial, the most persistent chivalric fantasy was the motif of the young hero who liberates a virgin, either from a dragon or from a rioting mob of peasants. The myth of the noble knight suffering to save his beloved was the product of the male imagination, revealing how men wished to be admired in the eyes of women, but the myth has had a profound and lasting influence on Western culture.

The fantasy world of the noble life especially animated the duchy of Burgundy, a quasi-independent principality that paid nominal allegiance to the French king. Burgundy set the chivalric standards for all of Europe during the fifteenth century. Famous for his lavish lifestyle, Duke Philip the Good (r. 1419–1467) was a notorious rake who seduced numerous noble ladies and produced many illegitimate children, but he also epitomized the ideals of chivalry in his love of horses, hunting, and court ceremonies. He was an extravagant patron of the arts, which made him famous throughout Europe. Musicians, manuscript illuminators, painters, tapestry makers, and historians thrived with his support and made Burgundy the center of European aristocratic fashion.

The dukes of Burgundy sustained their power through their personal ties to the nobility and elites of the cities of their dominions. They were constantly on the move, visiting palaces, castles, and towns. They created a kind of theater state, staging elaborate entry ceremonies to the towns they visited; celebrating with fantastic splendor every event in the ducal family, such as marriages and births; entertaining the nobles with tournaments and the people with elaborate processions; and guaranteeing the loyalty of the nobles by inviting them to join the Order of the Golden Fleece, which occupied its members by training for a crusade.

Pilgrims of the Imagination

During the Middle Ages, a pilgrimage offered a religiously sanctioned form of escape from the omnipresent suffering and peril. Pious Christians could go on a pilgrimage to the Holy Land, Rome, or the shrine of a saint, such as Santiago de Compostela in Spain or Canterbury in England. The usual motive for a pilgrimage was to fulfill a vow or promise made to God, or to obtain an indulgence, which exempted the pilgrim from some of the time spent in punishment in Purgatory after death. The pilgrimage became the instrument for spiritual liberation and escape from difficulties. As a result, going on a pilgrimage became a compelling model for creative literature, especially during the fourteenth century. Not all of these great works of literature were fictional pilgrimages, but many evoked the pilgrim's impulse to find a refuge from the difficulties of daily life or to find solace in the promise of a better life to come.

Dante Alighieri and *The Divine Comedy*

In *The Divine Comedy* an Italian poet from Florence, Dante Alighieri (1265–1321), imagined the most fantastic pilgrimage ever attempted, a journey through Hell, Purgatory, and Paradise. A work of astounding originality, *The Divine Comedy* remains the greatest masterpiece of medieval literature. Little is known about Dante's early life except that somehow he acquired an encyclopedic education that gave him

DOCUMENT

Dante, *Divine Comedy* (1321)

Dante and the Plague Victims

The ancient poet Virgil and Dante come across victims of the plague in their journey through Hell. This depiction, which comes from a sixteenth-century manuscript, is anachronistic because the Black Death arrived after Dante wrote *The Divine Comedy,* but he does describe victims of epidemic diseases in his poem.

expertise in Greek philosophy, scholastic theology (the application of logic to the understanding of Christianity), Latin literature, and the newly fashionable poetic forms in Provençal, the language of southern France. Dante was involved in the dangerous politics of Florence, which led to his exile under pain of death if he ever returned. During his exile Dante wandered for years, suffering grievously the loss of his home: "bitter is the taste of another man's bread and . . . heavy the way up and down another man's stair" (*Paradiso,* canto 17). While in exile, Dante sustained himself by writing his great poetic vision of human destiny and God's plan for redemption.

In the poem Dante himself travels into the Christian version of the afterlife, but the poetic journey displays numerous non-Christian influences. The passage through Hell, for example, derived from a long Muslim poem reconstructing Muhammad's *miraj,* a night journey to Jerusalem and ascent to heaven. Dante's poem can be read on many levels—personal, historical, spiritual, moral, theological—as it recounts an allegorical pilgrimage to visit the souls of the departed. Dante connects his personal suffering with the historical problems of Italy, the warnings of the dead who had sinned in life, and the promise of rewards to those who had been virtuous. Dante's trip, initially guided by the Latin poet Virgil, the epitome of ancient wisdom, starts in Hell. While traveling deeper into its harsh depths, Dante is

DOCUMENT

Dante Describes Hell

In The Divine Comedy, *Dante imagined a series of circles in Hell into which were cast those guilty of a certain class of sin. In the eighth circle Dante and his guide Virgil came upon those guilty of fraud. They suffered for all eternity in the depths of stinking, filthy caverns in the ground. Dante and Virgil followed a path through Hell, and at this point the path led to a series of arches that spanned over the caverns.*

Here we heard people whine in the next chasm,
and knock and thump themselves with open palms, and
blubber through their snouts as if in a spasm.

Steaming from that pit, a vapor rose
over the banks, crusting them with a slime
that sickened my eyes and hammered at my nose.

That chasm sinks so deep we could not sight
its bottom anywhere until we climbed
along the rock arch to its greatest height.

Once there, I peered down; and I saw long lines
of people in a river of excrement
that seemed the overflow of the world's latrines.

I saw among the felons of that pit
one wraith who might or might not have been tonsured—
one could not tell, he was so smeared with shit.

He bellowed: "You there, why do you stare at me
more than at all the others in this stew?"
And I to him: "Because if memory

serves me, I knew you when your hair was dry.
You are Alessio Interminelli da Lucca.
That's why I pick you from this filthy fry."

And he then, beating himself on his clown's head:
"Down to this have the flatteries I sold
the living sunk me here among the dead."

And my Guide prompted then: "Lean forward a bit
and look beyond them, there—do you see that one
scratching herself with dungy nails, the strumpet

who fidgets to her feet, then to a crouch?
It is the whore Thais . . ."

Source: From *The Divine Comedy* by Dante Alighieri, translated by John Ciardi. Copyright 1954, 1957, 1960, 1961, 1965, 1967, 1970 by the Ciardi Family Publishing Trust. Used by permission of W. W. Norton & Company, Inc.

warned of the harmful values of this world by meeting a cast of sinful characters who inhabit the world of the damned. In Purgatory his guide becomes Beatrice, Dante's deceased beloved, who stands for the Christian virtues. In this section of the poem, he begins the painful process of spiritual rehabilitation in which he comes to accept the Christian image of life as a pilgrimage. In Paradise he achieves spiritual fulfillment by speaking with figures from the past who have defied death.

The lasting appeal of this long, complex, and difficult poem is a wonder. Underlying the appeal of *The Divine Comedy* is perhaps its optimism, which expresses Dante's own cure to his depressing condition as an exile. The power of Dante's poetry established the form of the modern Italian language. Even in translation the images and stories can intrigue and fascinate.

Giovanni Boccaccio and *The Decameron*

Like Dante, Giovanni Boccaccio (1313–1375) was a Florentine. He grew up in a prosperous merchant banking family that was bankrupted during the Florentine financial crisis of the 1340s. Losing the shelter of economic and social privilege, Boccaccio's life became one of poverty and endless adversity. In the freedom from business responsibilities created by enforced poverty, Boccaccio turned to writing tales of chivalry and love, which were immediately very popular and had lasting influence on other writers.

After witnessing the ravages of the Black Death in Florence in 1348 and 1349, Boccaccio turned to polishing his masterpiece, *The Decameron*, a collection of 100 humorous, satirical, majestic, and sometimes pornographic stories. The book begins with a somber description of the social chaos created by the plague and tells how ten young people (seven women and three men) escaped the plague in Florence for a refuge in the country. *The Decameron* is less a story of a pilgrimage than the depiction of a refuge, but it is no less an escape from the cruel realities of the world. In their luxurious fantasy world of the country, each of the ten tells a story every night for ten nights. Displaying an open-minded attitude toward human weaknesses, *The Decameron* represents Boccaccio's initial response to the Black Death. Believing there was no future other than death, Boccaccio responded with a celebration of life in stories full of heroism, romance, unhappy love, wit, trickery, sexual license, and laughter. Although *The Decameron* was often read as escapist fantasy literature designed to lift the gloom of events, it was also a literary masterpiece that created a vivid, swift moving narrative.

Geoffrey Chaucer and *The Canterbury Tales*

Boccaccio profoundly influenced Geoffrey Chaucer (ca. 1342–1400), the most outstanding English poet prior to William Shakespeare. As a courtier and diplomat, Chaucer was a trusted adviser to three successive English kings. But he is best known for his literary output, including *The Canterbury Tales,* which exhibit some of the same earthy humor and tolerance for human folly as *The Decameron.*

In *The Canterbury Tales* a group of thirty pilgrims tell stories as they travel on horseback to the shrine at Canterbury. By employing the pilgrimage as a framing device for telling the stories, Chaucer was able to bring together a collection of people from across the social spectrum, including a wife, indulgence hawker, miller, town magistrate, clerk, landowner, lawyer, merchant, knight, abbess, and monk. The variety of characters who told the tales allowed Chaucer to experiment with many kinds of literary forms, from a chivalric romance to a sermon. The pilgrimage combined the considerations of religious morality with the fun of a spring vacation more concerned with the pleasures of this world than preparing for the next, which was the avowed purpose of going on a pilgrimage. In this intertwining of the worldly and the spiritual, Chaucer brought the abstract principles of Christian morality down to a level of common understanding.

Margery Kempe and the Autobiographical Pilgrimage

As the daughter of a town mayor, Margery Kempe (1373–1440) was destined for a comfortable life as a middle-class wife in provincial England. After her first child was born, however, she experienced a bout of depression during which she had a vision of Christ. She began to experience more visions and felt a calling to lead a more spiritual life. As a married woman she could not become a nun, which would have been the normal course for a woman with her spiritual inclinations. Instead, she accepted her marital duties and bore fourteen children.

At the age of about 40 she persuaded her husband to join her in a mutual vow of chastity and embarked on her own religious vocation. Always a bit of an eccentric, Kempe became a fervent vegetarian at a time when meat was scarce but highly desired. She also developed an insatiable wanderlust, undertaking a series of pilgrimages to Jerusalem, Rome, Germany, Norway, Spain, and numerous places in England. On these pilgrimages she sought out mystics and recluses for their spiritual advice. Her own devotions took the form of loud weeping and crying, which alienated many people who feared she might be a heretic or a madwoman. Toward the end of her life she dictated an account of her difficult dealings with her husband, her spells of madness, her ecstatic visions, and her widespread travels as a pilgrim. For Kempe the actual experience of undertaking pilgrimages made it possible for her to examine the course of her own life, which she understood as a spiritual pilgrimage. Her *Book* (1436) was the earliest autobiography in English.

Christine de Pisan and the Defense of Female Virtue

The work of the poet Christine de Pisan (1364–1430) was neither escapist like Giovanni Boccaccio's nor a spiritual pilgrimage like Dante's, Chaucer's, or Kempe's but was a thoughtful and passionate commentary on the tumultuous issues of her day. At age 15 Pisan married a notary of King Charles V of France, but by age 25 she was a widow with three young children. In order to support her family, she turned to writing and relied on the patronage of the royalty and wealthy aristocrats of France, Burgundy, Germany, and England.

Christine de Pisan championed the cause of women in a male-dominated society that was often overtly hostile to them. Following the fashion of the times, she invented a new chivalric order, the Order of the Rose, whose members took a vow to defend the honor of women. She wrote a defense of women for a male readership and an allegorical autobiography. But she is most famous for the two books she wrote for women readers, *The Book of the City of Ladies* and *The Book of Three Virtues* (both about 1407). In these she recounted tales of the heroism and virtue of women and offered moral instruction for women in different social roles. In 1415 she retired to a convent where in the last year of her life she wrote a masterpiece of ecstatic lyricism that celebrated the early victories of Joan of Arc. Pisan's book turned the martyred Joan into the heroine of France.

Defining Cultural Boundaries

During the Later Middle Ages, systematic discrimination against certain ethnic and religious groups increased markedly in Europe. As European society enforced ever-higher levels of religious uniformity, intolerance spread in the ethnically mixed societies of the European periphery. Intolerance was marked in three especially troubled areas: Spain with its mixture of Muslim, Jewish, and Christian cultures; the German borderlands in east-central Europe, where Germans mingled with Slavs; and Ireland and Wales, where Celts came under the domination of the English. Within the heartland of Europe were other areas of clashing cultures—for example, Switzerland where the folk culture of peasants and shepherds living in the isolated mountains collided with the intense Christian religiosity of the cities.

During the eleventh and twelfth centuries, ethnic diversity had been more widely accepted. A Hungarian cleric wrote in an undated work from this period, "As immigrants come from various lands, so they bring with them various languages and customs, various skills and forms of armament, which adorn and glorify the royal household and quell the pride of external powers. A kingdom of one race and custom is weak and fragile."[17] By the fourteenth and fifteenth centuries, however, this optimistic celebration of

---

DOCUMENT

Why Women Deserve an Education as Much as Men

In the Book of the City of the Ladies *Christine de Pisan addresses the reasons offered by some men who opposed the education of women. These men did not want their daughters, wives, or sisters to receive an education because it would compromise their morals. Christine forcefully answers that objection.*

Here you can clearly see that not all opinions of men are based on reason and that these men are wrong. For it must not be presumed that mores necessarily grow worse from knowing the moral sciences, which teach the virtues, indeed, there is not the slightest doubt that moral education amends and ennobles them. How could anyone think or believe that whoever follows good teaching or doctrine is the worse for it? Such an opinion cannot be expressed or maintained. . . .

Thus, not all men (and especially the wisest) share the opinion that is it bad for women to be educated. But it is very true that many foolish men have claimed this because it displeased them that women knew more than they did. . . .

If it were customary to send little girls to school and to teach them the same subjects as are taught to boys, they would learn just as fully and would understand the subtleties of all arts and sciences. Indeed maybe they would understand them better . . . for just as women's bodies are more soft than men's, so too their understanding is more sharp. . . . If they understand less it is because they do not go out and see so many different places and things but stay home and mind their own work. For there is nothing which teaches a reasonable creature so much as the experience of many different things.

Source: Christine de Pisan, *The Book of the City of Ladies*, translated by Earl Jeffrey Richards. Copyright © 1982 by Persea Books, Inc.

---

diversity had faded. Ethnic discrimination and residential segregation created the first ghettos for ethnic and religious minorities.

Spain: Religious Communities in Tension

The Iberian peninsula was home to thriving communities of Muslims, Jews, and Christians. Since the eleventh century the aggressive northern Christian kingdoms of Castile and Aragon had engaged in a protracted program of Reconquest (*Reconquista*) against the Muslim states of the peninsula. By 1248 the Reconquest was largely completed, with only a small Muslim enclave in Granada holding out until 1492. The Spanish Reconquest placed former enemies in close proximity to one another. Hostilities between Christians and Muslims ranged from active warfare to tense stalemate, with Jews working as cultural intermediaries between the two larger communities.

During the twelfth and thirteenth centuries Muslims, called the Mudejars, who capitulated to the conquering Christians, received guarantees that they could continue to practice their own religion and laws. During the fourteenth century, however, Christian kings gradually reneged on these promises. In 1301 the king of Castile decreed that the testimony of any two Christian witnesses could convict a Jew or Muslim, notwithstanding any previously granted privileges that allowed them to be tried in their own courts. The Arabic language began to disappear in Spain as the Mudejars suffered discrimination on many levels. By the sixteenth century, the practice of Islam became illegal, and the Spanish state adopted a systematic policy to destroy Mudejar culture by prohibiting Muslim dress, customs, and marriage practices.

The Jews also began to feel the pain of organized, official discrimination. Christian preachers accused Jews of poisonings, stealing Christian babies, and cannibalism. When the Black Death arrived in 1348, the Jews of Aragon were accused of having poisoned the wells, even though Jews were dying just like Christians. Beginning in 1378, a Catholic prelate in Seville, Ferrant Martínez, commenced an anti-Jewish preaching campaign by calling for the destruction of all twenty-three of the city's synagogues, the confinement of Jews to a ghetto, the dislodging of all Jews from public positions, and the prohibition of any social contact between Christians and Jews. His campaign led to an attack on the Jews of Seville in 1391. Violence spread to other cities throughout the peninsula and the nearby Balearic Islands. Jews were given a stark choice: conversion or death. After a year of mob violence, about 100,000 Jews had been murdered and an equal number had gone into hiding or fled to more tolerant Muslim countries. The 1391 pogroms led to the first significant forced conversions of Jews in Spain. A century later in 1492, on the heels of the final Christian victory of the Reconquest, all remaining Jews in Spain were compelled to either leave or convert.

German and Celtic Borderlands: Ethnic Communities in Tension

Other regions with diverse populations also witnessed discrimination and its brutal consequences. During the population boom of the twelfth and thirteenth centuries, German-speaking immigrants had established colonial towns in the Baltic and penetrated eastward, creating isolated pockets of German culture in Bohemia, Poland, and Hungary. During the fourteenth and fifteenth centuries, the bias of native populations against the colonizing Germans was manifest in various ways. One Czech prince offered 100 silver marks to anyone who brought him 100 German noses. The German settlers exhibited a similar intolerance

of the natives. The Teutonic Knights, who had been the vanguard of the German migrations in the Baltic, began to require German ancestry for membership. In German-speaking towns along the colonized borderlands of east-central Europe, city councils and guilds began to restrict by ethnicity the qualification for holding certain offices or joining a guild. The most famous example was the "German Paragraph" in guild statutes, which required candidates for admission to a guild to prove German descent. As the statutes of a bakers' guild put it, "Whoever wishes to be a member must bring proof to the councilors and the guildsmen that he is born of legitimate, upright German folk." Others required members to be "of German blood and tongue," as if language were a matter of biological inheritance.[18] German guildsmen were also forbidden to marry non-Germans.

A similar process of exclusion occurred in the Celtic fringe of the British Isles. In Ireland the ruling English promulgated laws that attempted to protect the cultural identity of the English colonists. The English prohibited native Irish from citizenship in town or guild membership. The Statutes of Kilkenny of 1366 attempted to legislate ethnic purity: They prohibited intermarriage between English and Irish; they required English colonists to speak English, use English names, wear English clothes, and ride horses in the English way; and they forbade the English to play Irish games or listen to Irish music. The aggressive legislation of the English in Ireland was essentially defensive. The tiny English community was attempting to prevent its absorption into the majority culture. A similar pattern appeared in Wales, where the lines dividing the Welsh and English communities hardened during the fourteenth century.

Enemies Within

The Black Death and its aftermath transformed many segments of Europe into a persecuting society. The year 1348 represented a watershed; in the period that followed, vague biases and dislikes sharpened into systematic violence against minorities. The plague sparked assaults against lepers, people with handicaps and physical deformities, beggars, vagabonds, foreigners, priests, pilgrims, Muslims, and Jews. Anyone who looked strange, dressed differently, spoke with an accent, practiced a minority religion, or did not fit in was vulnerable to becoming a scapegoat for the miseries of others. Minorities took the blame for calamities that could not be otherwise explained.

Violence against minorities occurred in many places, but it was most systematic in German-speaking lands. Between November 1348 and August 1350, violence against Jews occurred in more than eighty German towns. Like the allegations in Aragon, the fear that Jews poisoned the wells led to massacres in German lands even *before* plague had arrived in these communities. The frequent occurrence of violence on Sundays or feast days suggests that preachers consciously or unconsciously encouraged the rioting mobs.

The troubles caused by the Great Schism (1378–1417, when there was more than one pope) also contributed to a heightened sensitivity to cultural differences. During the Council of Basel (1431–1449), German bishops and theologians in attendance began to exchange information about cases of alleged witchcraft they had heard about in the nearby Swiss Alps. What these learned priests and friars thought of as witchcraft was probably nothing more than harmless folk magic, but to them the strange details of peasant behavior seemed evidence of a vast Satanic conspiracy to destroy Christianity. For most of its history, the Catholic Church had denied that witchcraft existed, but the terrible events of the fourteenth century cried out for explanation. In 1484 Pope Innocent VIII changed official Catholic policy by calling on two Dominican professors of theology to examine the alleged spread of witchcraft in Germany. As a guide to witch hunters, they wrote a detailed handbook on witchcraft, *The Hammer of Witches*, which went through twenty-eight editions between 1486 and 1600, evidence of its enormous success and influence.

The Hammer of Witches codified the folklore of the Alpine peasants as the basis for witchcraft practices. The book condemned as heretics those who disbelieved in the power of witches and established legal procedures for the prosecution of witches. It sanctioned torture as the most effective means for obtaining confessions, and it established much lower standards of evidence than in other kinds of cases. As an anthology of mythical stories about the activities of supposed witches, *The Hammer* summed up the worst of prevailing attitudes about women: "all witchcraft comes from carnal lust, which in women is insatiable." Most witchcraft persecutions came later in the sixteenth and seventeenth centuries, but the publication of *The Hammer of Witches* represented the culmination of the frenzied search to find enemies within European society, which was quickened by the events of the fourteenth and fifteenth centuries. With the dissemination of the idea of the reality of witchcraft, virtually anyone could be hauled before a court on charges of maintaining a secret liaison with Satan.

Conclusion

Looking Inward

Unlike the more dynamic, outward-looking thirteenth century, Europeans during the fourteenth and early fifteenth centuries turned their attention inward to their own communities and their own problems. Europe faced one calamity after another, each crisis compounding the misery. In the process the identity of the West became more defensive and the fragility of Christianity itself was laid bare. The process of changing Western identities can be seen in two ways. First, as a result of the Western encounters with the Mongol and Ottoman Empires, the political and religious frontiers of the West shifted. These two empires redrew the map of the West by ending the Christian Byzantine Empire and by leaving Christian Russia on the margins of the West. With the Mongol invasions, the eastward spread of Christianity into Asia ended. The Ottoman conquests left a lasting Muslim influence inside eastern Europe, particularly in Bosnia and Albania. Peoples who were predominantly Christian and whose political institutions were a heritage of the ancient Roman Empire now survived under the domination of Asian or Muslim empires and in a tenuous relationship with the rest of the Christian West. Most of the new subjects of these empires remained Christian, but their Mongol and Ottoman masters destroyed their political autonomy. The Ottoman Empire remained hostile to and frequently at war with the Christian West for more than 200 years.

Second, most Europeans reinforced their identity as Christians and became more self-conscious of the country in which they lived. At the same time Christian civilization was becoming eclipsed in parts of eastern Europe, it revived in the Iberian peninsula, where the Muslim population, once the most extensive in the West, suffered discrimination and defeat. The northern Spanish kingdoms, for example, began to unify their subjects around a militant form of Christianity that was overtly hostile to Muslims and Jews. In many places in the West, religious and ethnic discrimination against minorities increased. A stronger sense of self-identification by country can be most dramatically seen in France and England as a consequence of the Hundred Years' War. The French rallied around a saintly national heroine, Joan of Arc. After dropping claims to France after the Hundred Years' War, the English aristocracy stopped speaking French and adopting the customs of the French court. They became less international and more English. The Western countries became more self-consciously characterized by an attitude of "us versus them."

Except for the very visible military conquests of the Mongols and the Ottomans, the causes of most of the calamities of the fourteenth century were invisible or unknown. No one recognized a climate change or understood the dynamics of the population crisis. No one understood the cause of the epidemics. No one grasped the role of the Mongol Empire in the world economy or the causes for the collapse of banking and trade. Unable to distinguish how these forces were changing their lives, western Europeans only witnessed their consequences. In the face of these calamities, European culture became obsessed with death and with finding scapegoats to blame for events that could not be otherwise explained. However, calamity also bred creativity. The search for answers to the question, "Why did this happen to us?" produced a new spiritual sensibility and a rich literature. Following the travails of the fourteenth century, moreover, there arose in the fifteenth a new, more optimistic cultural movement—the Renaissance. Gloom and doom was not the only response to troubles. During the Renaissance some people began to search for new answers to human problems in a fashion that would transform the West anew.

Suggestions for Further Reading

For a comprehensive listing of suggested readings, please go to www.ablongman.com/levack2e/chapter10

Carmichael, Ann G. *Plague and the Poor in Renaissance Florence.* 1986. An innovative study that both questions the traditional theory of the bubonic plague as the cause of the Black Death and examines how fear of the disease led to regulation of the poor.

Cohn, Samuel. *The Black Death Transformed: Disease and Culture in Early Renaissance Europe.* 2003. A well-argued case that the Black Death was not caused by the bubonic plague.

Duby, Georges. *France in the Middle Ages, 987–1460: From Hugh Capet to Joan of Arc.* 1991. Traces the emergence of the French state.

Gordon, Bruce, and Peter Marshall, eds. *The Place of the Dead: Death and Remembrance in Late Medieval and Early Modern Europe.* 2000. A collection of essays that shows how the placing of the dead in society was an important activity that engendered considerable conflict and negotiation.

Herlihy, David. *The Black Death and the Transformation of the West.* 1997. A pithy, readable analysis of the epidemiological and historical issues surrounding the Black Death.

Holmes, George. *Europe: Hierarchy and Revolt, 1320–1450.* 1975. Excellent examination of rebellions.

Huizinga, Johan. *The Autumn of the Middle Ages,* trans. Rodney J. Payton and Urlich Mammitzsch. 1996. A new translation of the classic study of France and the Low Countries during the fourteenth and fifteenth centuries. Dated and perhaps too pessimistic, Huizinga's lucid prose and broad vision still make this an engaging reading experience.

Imber, Colin. *The Ottoman Empire, 1300–1481.* 1990. The basic work that establishes a chronology for the early Ottomans.

Jordan, William C. *The Great Famine: Northern Europe in the Early Fourteenth Century.* 1996. The most comprehensive book on the famine.

Lambert, Malcolm. *Medieval Heresy: Popular Movements from the Gregorian Reform to the Reformation.* 1992. Excellent general study of the Hussite and Lollard movements.

Le Roy Ladurie, Emmanuel. *Times of Feast, Times of Famine: A History of Climate Since the Year 1000,* trans. Barbara Bray. 1971. The book that introduced the idea of the Little Ice Age and promoted the study of the influence of climate on history.

Lynch, Joseph H. *The Medieval Church: A Brief History.* 1992. A pithy, elegant survey of ecclesiastical institutions and developments.

Morgan, David O. *The Mongols.* 1986. Best introduction to Mongol history.

Nirenberg, David. *Communities of Violence: Persecution of Minorities in the Middle Ages.* 1996. An important analysis of the persecution of minorities that is deeply rooted in Spanish evidence.

Scott, Susan, and Christopher Duncan. *Biology of Plagues: Evidence from Historical Populations.* 2001. An analysis by two epidemiologists who argue that the Black Death was not the bubonic plague but probably a virus similar to Ebola.

Sumption, Jonathan. *The Hundred Years' War: Trial by Battle.* 1991. First volume goes only to 1347. When it is completed, it will be the best comprehensive study.

Swanson, R. N. *Religion and Devotion in Europe, c. 1215–c. 1515.* 1995. The best up-to-date textbook account of late medieval religious practice.

Notes

1. Quoted in Emmanuel Le Roy Ladurie, *Times of Feast, Times of Famine: A History of Climate Since the Year 1000,* trans. Barbara Bray (1971), 47.

2. Quoted in William Bowsky, "The Impact of the Black Death," in Anthony Molho, ed., *Social and Economic Foundations of the Italian Renaissance* (1969), 92.

3. Cited in Philip Ziegler, *The Black Death* (1969), 20.

4. Giovanni Boccaccio, *The Decameron,* trans. Richard Aldington (1962), 30.

5. Ibid.

6. Quoted in Mark C. Bartusis, *The Late Byzantine Army: Arms and Society, 1204–1453* (1992), 133.

7. Trial record as quoted in Marina Warner, *Joan of Arc* (1981), 122.

8. Ibid., 127.

9. Ibid., 143.

10. *The Trial of Joan of Arc,* trans. W. S. Scott (1956), 134.

11. Ibid., 106.

12. Ibid., 135.

13. Warner, *Joan of Arc,* 145.

14. Johan Huizinga, *The Autumn of the Middle Ages,* trans. Rodney J. Payton and Ulrich Mammitzsch (1996), 156.

15. Quoted in Barbara W. Tuchman, *A Distant Mirror: The Calamitous 14th Century* (1978), 505–506. Translation has been slightly modified by the authors.

16. Ibid., 506.

17. *Libellus de institutione morum,* ed. J. Balogh, *Scriptores rerum Hungaricarum 2* (1938), 625. Quoted in Robert Bartlett, *The Making of Europe: Conquest, Colonization and Cultural Change 950–1350* (1993), 239.

18. *Codex diplomaticus Brandenburgensis,* ed. Adolph Friedrich Riedel (41 vols., 1838–1869), 365–367. Cited in Bartlett, *The Making of Europe,* 238.

The Italian Renaissance and Beyond: The Politics of Culture

11

OR FIFTEEN YEARS NICCOLÒ MACHIAVELLI WORKED AS A DIPLOMAT AND political adviser, a man always at the center of the action in his hometown of Florence. But in 1512 there was a change of regimes in the city-state of Florence. Distrusted by the new rulers and suspected of involvement in an assassination plot, he was abruptly fired from his job, imprisoned, tortured, and finally ordered to stay out of town. Exiled to his suburban farm, impoverished, and utterly miserable, Machiavelli survived by selling lumber from his woodlot to his former colleagues, who regularly cheated him. To help feed his family he snared birds; to entertain himself he played cards in a local inn with the innkeeper, a butcher, a miller, and two bakers. As he put it, "caught this way among these lice I wipe the mold from my brain [by playing cards] and release my feeling of being ill-treated by Fate."

In the evenings, however, Machiavelli transformed himself into an entirely different person. He entered his study, removed his mud-splattered clothes, and put on the elegant robes he had once worn as a government official. And then, "dressed in a more appropriate manner I enter into the ancient courts of ancient men and am welcomed by them kindly." Machiavelli was actually reading the works of the ancient Greek and Latin historians, but he described his evening reading as a conversation: He asked the ancients about the reasons for their actions, and in reading their books he found answers. For four hours, "I feel no boredom, I dismiss every affliction, I no longer fear poverty nor do I tremble at the thought of death: I become completely part of them."[1]

Machiavelli's evening conversations with the long-dead ancients perfectly expressed the sensibility of the Italian Renaissance. This wretched man, disillusioned with his own times and bored by his empty-headed neighbors, found in the ancients the stimulating companions he could not find in life. For him the ancient past was more alive than the present. In this sense Machiavelli was very much a Renaissance man, because feeling part of antiquity is what the Renaissance is all about. For those who were captivated

---

The Mona Lisa Leonardo da Vinci's portrait of a Florentine woman with her enigmatic smile testifies to the Renaissance fascination with portraits of individuals who appear completely natural.

by it, the ancient past and the examples of leadership and beauty it offered seemed to be a cure for the ills of a decidedly troubled time.

As discussed in Chapter 10, during the fourteenth and fifteenth centuries Europeans experienced a prevailing sense of loss, a morbid preoccupation with death, and a widespread pessimism about the human capacity for good. Yet in Florence during this same period a cultural movement began to express a different view of life that emphasized the responsibilities of humans to better their communities through social welfare, to beautify their cities, and to devote themselves to the duties of citizenship. We now call that movement the Renaissance. The movement emerged from the desire to improve the human condition during times of trouble, and that desire was first manifest in the intellectually free environment of the independent city-states of Italy. Machiavelli—despite the bleak circumstances of his later life—was one of the Renaissance thinkers who thought the world could be set right through concerted political action. Like the medieval thinkers he was pessimistic about the frailties of human nature, but he firmly believed that the weakness of most humans could be counteracted by strong leadership and strong laws. In this respect he differed from the medieval writers who thought the contemplative life of the monk was the highest calling to which a man could aspire. The Renaissance was born and developed because the political structures of the Italian city-states encouraged cultural experimentation and fostered the idea that society could be reengineered according to the principles that made ancient Greece and Rome great.

The word Renaissance°, which means "rebirth," is a term historians invented to describe a movement that sought to imitate and understand the culture of antiquity. The fundamental Renaissance principle was the need to keep everything in balance and proportion, an aesthetic ideal derived from ancient literature. In political theory, this meant building a stable society upon the foundations of well-balanced individuals who conformed to a rigorous code of conduct. In the arts it meant searching for the underlying harmonies in nature, which typically meant employing geometry and the mathematics of proportion in drawing, painting, sculpting, and designing buildings. Renaissance artists thought geometry unlocked the secrets of nature and revealed the hidden hand of God in creation.

The Italian Renaissance was not the first time the West experienced a revival of ancient learning and thought. In the Carolingian Renaissance of the ninth century, members of the emperor Charlemagne's court reinvigorated education in Latin. And the European-wide Renaissance of the twelfth century led to the foundation of the universities, the reintroduction of Roman law, and the spread of scholastic philosophy and theology. The Renaissance considered in this chapter refers to a diffuse cultural movement that occurred at different times in different regions, and as a result its dates are very approximate. Most historians date the Italian Renaissance from about 1350 to 1550. By 1500 the cultural movement that began in Italy had spread to much of western Europe.

The Renaissance helped refashion the concept of Western civilization. From the fifth to the fourteenth centuries, the West identified itself primarily through conformity to Latin Christianity or Roman Catholicism, which meant the celebration of uniform religious rituals in Latin and obedience to the pope. The Renaissance added a new element to this identity. Although by no means anti-Christian, Renaissance thinkers began to think of themselves as the heirs of pre-Christian cultures—Hebrew, Greek, and Roman. In this sense, they began to imagine a Western civilization that was more than just Christianity but as the history of a common culture dating back to Antiquity. Through reading the texts and viewing the works of art of the long-dead ancients, people during the Italian Renaissance gained historical and visual perspective on their own world and cultivated a critical attitude about both the past and their own culture. How then did the cultural encounter during the Renaissance with the philosophy, literature, and art of the Ancient world transform the way Europeans thought?

■ In what ways did the political and social climate peculiar to the Italian city-states help create Renaissance culture?

■ How did Renaissance thinkers create historical perspective and devise methods of criticism for interpreting texts?

■ How did various attempts to imitate antiquity in the arts alter perceptions of nature?

■ How did the monarchies of western Europe gather the strength to become more assertive and more effective during the last half of the fifteenth and early sixteenth centuries?

The Cradle of the Renaissance: The Italian City-States

■ In what ways did the political and social climate peculiar to the Italian city-states help create Renaissance culture?

In comparison with the rest of Europe and other world civilizations, Renaissance Italy was distinguished by the large number and political autonomy of its thriving city-states. The Netherlands and parts of the Rhine Valley were as thoroughly urbanized, but only in Italy did cities have so much political power. The evolution of the Italian city-states can be encapsulated into two distinct phases.

The first phase in the evolution of the Italian city-states occurred during the eleventh and twelfth centuries.

During this period about one hundred Italian towns became independent republics, also known as communes, and developed the laws and institutions of self-government. The male citizens of these tiny republics gathered on a regular basis in the town square to debate important issues such as assessing new taxes, improving the city walls, or going to war. To conduct the day-to-day business of government, they elected city officials from among themselves.

The governmental practices of these city-states produced the political theory of republicanism°, which described a state in which government officials were elected by the people or a portion of the people. The theory of republicanism was first articulated by Marsilius of Padua (1270–1342) in *The Defender of the Peace*, a book that relied on the precedents established by the ancient Roman republic. Marsilius recognized two kinds of government—principalities and republics. Principalities relied upon the descending principle that political authority came directly from God and trickled down through kings and princes to the rest of humanity. According to this principle, the responsibility of government was to enforce God's laws. Marsilius, however, rejected the idea that the task of the political world was to express the will of God. His ascending principle of republicanism suggested that laws derive not from God but from the will of the people, who freely choose their own form of government and who are equally free to change it. In Marsilius's theory, citizens regularly expressed their will through voting. The first phase in the evolution of the Italian city-states established the institutions of self-government, the procedures for electing officials, and the theory of republicanism.

In the second phase of evolution, which occurred during the fourteenth century, most city-states abandoned or lost their republican institutions and came to be ruled by princes. The reasons for the transformation of these republics into principalities were related to the economic and demographic turmoil created by the international economic collapse and the Black Death. Two of the largest republics, however, did not go through this second phase and survived without losing their liberty to a prince. The Renaissance began in these two city-states, Florence and Venice (see Map 11.1). Their survival as republics, which made them exceptions to the rule by the fifteenth century, helps explain the origins of the Renaissance.

The Renaissance Republics: Florence and Venice

In an age of despotic princes, Florence and Venice were keenly aware of how different they were from other cities, and they feared they might suffer the same fate as their neighbors if they did not defend their republican institutions and liberty. In keeping alive the traditions of republican self-government, these two cities created an environment of competition and freedom that stimulated creative ingenuity. Although neither of these cities were democracies, nor were they particularly egalitarian, they were certainly more open to new ideas than cities ruled by princes. In both Florence and Venice, citizens prized discussion and debate, the skills necessary for success in business and politics. By contrast, in the principalities all cultural activity tended to revolve around and express the tastes of the prince, who monopolized much of the wealth. In Florence and Venice a few great families called the *patriciate* controlled most of the property, but these patricians competed among themselves to gain recognition

Map 11.1 Northern Italy in the Mid-Fifteenth Century

During the Renaissance the largest city-states, such as Milan, Venice, and Florence, gained control of the surrounding countryside and smaller cities in the vicinity, establishing regional territorial states. Only Venice and Florence remained republics. Milan and Savoy were ruled by dukes. The Gonzaga family ruled Mantua and the Este family Modena and Ferrara. The states of the Church were ruled by the pope in Rome.

Northern Italy in the Mid-Fifteenth Century

and fame by patronizing great artists and scholars. This patronage by wealthy men and women made the Renaissance possible. Because the tastes of these patricians dictated what writers and artists could do, understanding who they were helps explain Renaissance culture.

Florence Under the Medici

The greatest patron during the early Renaissance was the fabulously rich Florentine banker Cosimo de' Medici (1389–1464). Based on his financial power, Cosimo effectively took control of the Florentine republic in 1434, ushering in a period of unprecedented domestic peace and artistic splendor called the Medicean Age (1434–1494). Cosimo's style of rule was exceedingly clever. Instead of making himself a prince, which the citizens of Florence would have opposed, he managed the policies of the republic from behind the scenes. He seldom held public office, but he made himself the center of Florentine affairs through shrewd negotiating, quiet fixing of elections, and generous distribution of bribes, gifts, and jobs. Cosimo's behind-the-scenes rule illustrated a fundamental value of Renaissance culture—the desire to maintain appearances. In this case, the appearance of the Florentine republic was saved, even as the reality of Florentine liberty was subverted.

Cosimo's brilliant patronage of intellectuals and artists mirrored a similar ambition to maintain appearances. It helped make Cosimo appear a pious, generous man who modeled himself after the great statesmen of the ancient Roman republic. Cosimo appreciated intelligence and merit wherever he found it. He frequented the discussions of prominent scholars, some of whom became his lasting friends. Intrigued by what he learned from them, he personally financed the search for and acquisition of manuscripts of ancient Latin and Greek literature and philosophy for new libraries he helped establish. In return for his financial support, many Florentine scholars dedicated their works to Cosimo. He took particular interest in the revival of the ancient Greek philosopher Plato, and he set up the

The Medici as Magi

During the fifteenth century the Medici had the power but lacked the legitimacy to rule Florence because they neither had been elected nor were the princes of the city. To compensate for their lack of legal authority, they created the image of themselves as "wise men" similar to the three wise men or magi who first recognized the divinity of Christ. In this fresco in the Medici Palace, the artist Benozzo Gozzoli depicted Lorenzo the Magnificent as one of the magi. He is the young man wearing a crown and gold robe riding on a white horse. His father, grandfather, and other senior members of the Medici family follow, wearing the red hats of common Florentine citizens.

neo-Platonic philosopher Marsilio Ficino (1433–1499) with a house and steady income.

Cosimo's most significant patronage of the arts clustered in the neighborhood where he lived. He rebuilt the nearby monastery of San Marco. He personally selected Fra Angelico, a monk, to paint the austere yet deeply emotive frescoes throughout the monastery. As the centerpiece of his neighborhood beautification plans, Cosimo built for his own family a magnificent new palace, which he filled with innumerable objects of beauty and exquisite paintings.

Cosimo's artistic patronage helped create the image of a man who was an open-handed and benevolent godfather for his community. Because Cosimo had not been elected to rule Florence, his political influence was illegitimate and he needed to find a way to create a proper image that would justify his power. To do that he decorated the private chapel in his palace with frescoes that depicted him accompanying the magi, the wise men or kings who brought gifts to the baby Jesus. Thus Cosimo made himself appear similar to those ancient kings who first recognized the divinity of Christ. By having himself depicted with the magi, Cosimo created an image that helped justify the fact that he controlled elections and dictated policies.

Cosimo's grandson Lorenzo the Magnificent (r. 1469–1492) expanded the family's dominance in Florentine politics through what has been called "veiled lordship." Lorenzo never took the title of prince but behaved very much like one by intervening publicly in the affairs of the state. In contrast to his grandfather's commitment to public patronage, Lorenzo's interest in the arts concentrated on building private villas, collecting precious gems, and commissioning small bronze statues, the kinds of things that gave him private pleasure rather than a public reputation. A fine poet and an intellectual companion of the most renowned scholars of his age, Lorenzo created a lasting reputation as a well-rounded, accomplished Renaissance man, but his princely style of rule, which ignored the republican sensibilities of the Florentines, created discontent and undermined public support for the Medicis. There were several conspiracies against him; during an attempted assassination of Lorenzo, his brother Giuliano was killed.

During the fifteenth century Florence became the first society that dedicated itself to the production and appreciation of what we now call Renaissance culture. As a republic on the perilous edge of financial survival, Florence had surrendered to the behind-the-scenes rule of the Medici family, who supported a movement in philosophy and the arts that, as we shall see, imitated and celebrated the heritage of pre-Christian antiquity, especially the culture of Greece and Rome.

Venice, the Cosmopolitan Republic

Venice resembled Florence in that it survived into the Renaissance period with its republican institutions intact,

Map 11.2 Venetian Colonial Empire
The Venetian colonies included the Greek-speaking islands in the Adriatic and a number of important islands in the Aegean. Between the fifteenth and seventeenth centuries these colonies were repeatedly threatened by the Ottoman Empire, with its capital in Constantinople.

but it was far more politically stable. Situated in the midst of a vast lagoon, Venice's streets consisted of broad channels in which great seagoing merchant ships were moored and small canals choked with private gondolas for local transportation. To protect their fragile city from flooding, the Venetians recognized that they had to cooperate among themselves, and thus the imperative for survival helped create a republic that became a model of stability and ecological awareness. The Venetians, for example, created the world's first environmental regulatory agencies, which were responsible for hydrological projects, such as building dikes and dredging canals, and for forestry management to prevent soil erosion and the consequent silting up of the lagoon.

Venice was among the first European powers to have colonies abroad. To guarantee its merchant ships access to the eastern Mediterranean and Constantinople, Venice conquered a series of ports, including a significant number in Greece (see Map 11.2). Its involvement in international trade and governing distant colonies made Venice unusually cosmopolitan. Many Venetian merchants spent years living abroad and some settled in the colonies. Moreover, people from all over Europe flocked to the city of Venice— Germans, Turks, Armenians, Albanians, Greeks, Slovenes,

Croats, and Jews—each creating their own neighborhood communities and institutions. Venetian households owned Russian, Asian, Turkish, and African slaves, all of whom contributed to the remarkable diversity of the city.

Of the many foreign groups in Venice, the most influential were the Greeks. Venice had long maintained close commercial and cultural ties with the Greek world. Its churches were modeled after the huge basilicas of Constantinople, and many Venetian merchants spoke Greek. After the fall of the Byzantine Empire to the Ottoman Turks in 1453, many Greek Christian refugees found a new home in Venice and other Italian cities, including influential scholars who helped reintroduce Greek philosophy and literature to an eager Italian readership. One of these scholars was John Bessarion (1403–1472), a Byzantine archbishop who compiled a magnificent library of Greek manuscripts that he bequeathed to the republic of Venice. Venice also became the leading center in western Europe for the publication of Greek books, printing the important texts in Greek philosophy and science, and making them widely available for the first time in western Europe.

The defining characteristic of Venetian government was its social stability, a trait that made it the envy of other more troubled cities and the source of imitation by republican-minded reformers throughout Europe. Whereas the Florentine republic was notoriously unstable and subject to quiet subversion by the Medicis, Venice boasted a largely unchanging republican constitution that lasted from 1297 to 1797. Thus Venice is the longest-surviving republic in history. It was, however, a very exclusive republic. Out of a total population of nearly 150,000, only a small political elite consisting of 2,500 nobles enjoyed voting privileges. From this elite and from Venice's many wealthy religious institutions came the resources to patronize Renaissance artists.

At the top of Venetian society was the *doge,* a member of the nobility who was elected to the job for life. The most notable Renaissance doge was Andrea Gritti (r. 1523–1538), whose reputation derived from his brilliant early career as a military administrator and diplomat. Gritti sometimes bent the laws in his favor, but he never manipulated elections or managed Venice's affairs as completely as Cosimo de' Medici did in Florence a century before. Like the Medicis, however, he used his own financial resources and his personal influence to transform his city into a major center of Renaissance culture.

Gritti hired some of the most prominent European artists, musicians, and poets to come to Venice. These included Pietro Aretino (1492–1556), the greatest master of satire of the sixteenth century, and the architect and sculptor Jacopo Sansovino (1486–1570). As official architect of the city, Sansovino transformed its appearance with his sculptures, palaces, and churches that imitated the styles of classical Greece and Rome. One of his most notable buildings is the Marciana Library, which was begun in 1537 to house Bessarion's collection of Greek manuscripts.

Artistic and scholarly creativity in Florence and Venice thrived on the competition among many different patrons. Neither the Medicis in Florence nor Gritti in Venice entirely dominated the cultural scene. Artistic patronage in these republics mirrored the dynamic political life that engaged many people. The diversity of patronage gave extensive employment to painters, sculptors, and architects, thereby attracting the best artists to these two cities. Later sections of the chapter will examine the works they produced.

Princes and Courtiers

Although the Renaissance began in the relative freedom of republics, such as Florence, it soon spread to principalities, those states ruled by one man, the prince. In contrast to the multiple sources of support for the arts and learning in the republics, patronage in the principalities was more constricted, confined to the prince and members of his court. The terms *lord* and *prince* refer to rulers who possessed formal aristocratic titles, such as the Marquis of Mantua, the Duke of Milan, or the King of Naples. Most Renaissance princes came from local aristocratic families who seized control of the government by force. Some, however, had been soldiers of fortune who had held on to a city as a spoil of war or had even overthrown a government that had once employed them to defend the city. Regardless of how a prince originally obtained power, his goal was to establish a dynasty, that is, to guarantee the rights of his descendants to continue to rule the city. Some dynasties—such as that of the D'Este family, which ruled Ferrara from 1240 to 1597—were well established and quite popular.

The Ideal Prince, the Ideal Princess

Federico II da Montefeltro (1422–1482), Duke of Urbino, succeeded in achieving the lasting fame and glorious reputation that so many princes craved. Although he was illegitimate, his father gave him the best possible education by sending him to study at the most fashionable school in Italy and to apprentice as a soldier under a renowned mercenary captain. In Renaissance Italy, an illegitimate boy could not inherit his father's property. Thus he usually had two career options: He could become a priest to obtain a living from the church, or he could become a mercenary and take his chances at war. Federico became a mercenary. From among the peasants of the duchy he recruited an army, which he hired out to the highest bidder. He soon earned a European-wide reputation for his many victories and enriched the duchy with the income from mercenary contracts and plunder. When his half-brother was assassinated in 1444, Federico became the ruler of Urbino, and by 1474 he obtained from the pope the title of duke. Federico epitomized the ideal Renaissance prince—a father figure to his subjects, astute diplomat, brilliant soldier, generous patron, avid collector, and man of learning. He was a prince who combined the insights of contempla-

Federico da Montefeltro as the Ideal Prince

The papal tiara in the upper left alludes to the pope's authorization of his title as duke. Federico is shown studying a book while dressed in armor, reflecting his two sides as scholar and soldier. His dynastic ambitions are represented by the presence of his son and potential successor standing at his feet.

tive study with active involvement in the affairs of the world.

Federico's rule was paternalistic. He was concerned for the welfare of his subjects and personally listened to their complaints and adjudicated their disputes. His military adventures tripled the size of his duchy. Conquests brought the prosperity that financed his expensive building projects and his collection of Latin manuscripts. Federico's personal library surpassed that of any contemporary university library in Europe, and his wide-ranging reading interests

showed his openness to the latest developments in learning. Federico's greatest achievement, however, was the building of a vast palace. At one stage the project was supervised by the architect Luciano Laurana (ca. 1420–1479), but it was Federico who clearly deserves most of the credit for what remains the single best example of Renaissance architectural ideals in a palace. Because of Federico, the small mountainous duchy of Urbino acquired a cultural importance far greater than its size warranted.

The best candidate for the ideal princess was Isabella d'Este (1474–1539), the Marchioness of Mantua. Such was her fame as a patron that she was known during her lifetime as "the first lady of the world." Enjoying an education that was exceptional for a girl in the fifteenth century, she grew up in the court at Ferrara, where she was surrounded by famous painters and poets and where she cultivated foreign ambassadors and leading intellectuals of the time. But her influence went far beyond that. When her husband was absent and after his death, she ruled Mantua by herself, earning a reputation for her just decisions and witty charm. She gained renown for her ability as a tenacious negotiator and behind-the-scenes diplomat. An avid reader and collector, she personally knew virtually all the great artists and writers of her age. Her influence spread far beyond Mantua, in part through her voluminous correspondence, which is estimated to include 12,000 letters.

The Ideal Courtier

The Renaissance republics developed a code of conduct for the ideal citizen. The code encouraged citizens to devote their time and energies to public service. The code insisted that the most valuable services of the citizen were to hold public office, to pay taxes honestly, and to help beautify the city through patronage of the arts. In similar fashion the Renaissance principalities created a code for the ideal courtier. A courtier was a man or woman who lived in or regularly visited the palace of a prince. Courtiers helped the prince's household function by performing all kinds of services, such as taking care of the family's wardrobe, managing servants, educating children, providing entertainment, keeping accounts, administering estates, going on diplomatic missions, and fighting battles. To best serve the princely family in whatever was needed, a courtier needed to cultivate a wide range of skills. Men trained in horsemanship, swordplay, and all kinds of sports, which were useful for keeping in shape for war. Women learned to draw, dance, play musical instruments, and engage in witty conversation. Both men and women needed to be adept at foreign languages so that they could converse with visitors and diplomats. According to the ideal, men should also know Latin and Greek, which were the foundations of a formal education. Some of the women in the courts also learned these ancient languages.

The stability and efficiency of the princely states depended on the abilities of the courtiers, who performed many of the functions that elected officials did in the republics. It was also extremely important to prevent conflicts among the courtiers; otherwise the peace of the state would be compromised. The most influential guide to how a courtier should behave was *The Book of the Courtier* (composed between 1508 and 1528) by the cultivated diplomat Baldassare Castiglione (1478–1529). Underlying the behavior and conversation of the ideal courtier described in this book were two general principles that governed all courtly manners—nonchalance and ease:

> I have found quite a universal rule which . . . seems to me valid above all others, and in all human affairs whether in word or deed: and that is to avoid affectation in every way possible as though it were some very rough and dangerous reef; and (to pronounce a new word perhaps) to practice in all things a certain nonchalance, so as to conceal all art and make whatever is done or said appear to be without effort and almost without any thought about it. . . .
>
> Therefore we may call that art true art which does not seem to be art; nor must one be more careful of anything than of concealing it, because if it is discovered, this robs a man of all credit and causes him to be held in slight esteem.[2]

In other words, nonchalance is the ability to do something that requires considerable training and effort while making it appear to be natural and without effort. The need to maintain appearances, which we first saw in the disguised rulership of Cosimo de' Medici in Florence, became one of the distinguishing traits of Italian Renaissance culture. According to Castiglione, all human action and communication should be moderate and balanced, creating the effect of ease. In effect, *The Book of the Courtier* translated the ideals of harmony and proportion so admired in Renaissance culture into a plan for human comportment. By using courtly manners, human beings governed the movements of the body according to an almost mathematical ideal of proportion.

Through *The Book of the Courtier* and its many imitators, the Renaissance ideal of courtly manners began to be widely disseminated during the sixteenth century due to the capacity of the newly invented printing press to produce inexpensive copies of the same text. Written in a lucid Italian that made for lively reading, the book was translated into Latin, English, French, and Spanish and absorbed into the literature of Europe. By studying these books, any young man or woman of talent and ambition could aspire to act and speak like a great aristocrat. The courtly ideal was completely accessible to anyone who could read, and many of its precepts were incorporated into the educational curriculum of schools, where it has survived to the present in the institution of the prom.

The Papal Prince

The Renaissance popes were the heads of the Church; they also had jurisdiction over the Papal State in central Italy. Thus they combined the roles of priest and prince. The Papal State was supposed to supply the pope with the in-

Courtiers Waiting on a Princely Family
Male courtiers pose while waiting around in the court of the Gonzaga in Mantua. These elegant gentlemen epitomized the nonchalance and ease idealized in Baldassare Castiglione's *The Book of the Courtier.*

come to run the affairs of the Church, but during the period when the popes left Rome and resided in Avignon (France) and during the Great Schism of 1305–1417, the popes lost control of the Papal State. After 1418 the popes saw that they had two main tasks—regain the revenues of the Papal State and rebuild the city of Rome, which had become a neglected ruin. To collect the taxes and revenues due them, many popes were obliged to use military force to bring the rebellious lords and cities into obedience. The popes also squabbled with the neighboring states that had taken advantage of the weakness of the papacy during the schism.

These military and diplomatic adventures thrust the popes into some very nasty quarrels—a situation that undermined the popes' ability to provide moral leadership. Pope Alexander VI (r. 1492–1503) financed his son Cesare Borgia's attempts to carve out a principality for himself along the northern fringe of the Papal State. He also married off his daughter, Lucrezia Borgia, in succession to several different Italian princes who were useful allies in the pope's military ambitions. The members of the Borgia family made many enemies who accused them of all kinds of evil deeds, including the poisoning of one of Lucrezia's husbands, brother-sister and father-daughter incest, and conducting orgies in the Vatican. Even though many of these allegations were false or exaggerated, the reputation of the papacy suffered. Alexander's successor, Pope Julius II (r. 1503–1513), continued to pursue a military strategy for regaining control of the Papal State. He took his princely role so seriously that he donned armor, personally led troops during the siege of Bologna, and rather presumptuously rewarded himself with a triumphal procession, an honor that had been granted in ancient Rome to victorious generals such as Julius Caesar.

Many of the Renaissance popes were embarrassed by the squalor of the city of Rome, an unfit place to serve as the capital of the Church. A number of popes sought to create a capital they felt worthy for Christendom. The most clear-sighted of the builders of Rome was Pope Leo X (r. 1513–1521), the second son of Lorenzo the Magnificent. Educated by the circle of scholars who surrounded the Medicis, Leo was destined for a clerical career at a young age. He received a doctorate in canon law and was made a cardinal at age 17. During Leo's pontificate, Rome was transformed into one of the centers of Renaissance culture. Leo made the University of Rome a distinguished institution through the appointment of famous professors. For his own private secretaries he chose intellectuals who had already gained an international reputation for their scholarship and learning. Leo's ambition can best be measured in his project to rebuild St. Peter's Basilica as the largest church in the world. He tore down the old basilica, which had been a major pilgrimage destination for more than a thousand years, and planned the great church that still dominates Rome today.

The Contradictions of the Patriarchal Family

The contradiction between the theory of the patriarchal family and realities of family life produced much of the creative energy of the Italian Renaissance. When theory dramatically departed from actual experience, many people began to distrust the theory and seek alternative ways of looking at society and the world. That is what happened in Renaissance Italy.

Advice books on family management, such as Leon Battista Alberti's *Four Books on the Family* (written in the 1430s), provide evidence for the widespread concern for better understanding the family. Such books propounded the theory that husbands and fathers ruled. These patriarchs were the sources of social order and discipline, and not just within the family but of all of society. Groups of male relatives

DOCUMENT

Juan Luis Vives, *The Office and Dutie of an Husband* (1529)

CHRONOLOGY

The Cradle of the Renaissance: The Italian City-States

after 1070	Founding of first city republics or communes
1270–1342	Marsilius of Padua, author of *The Defender of the Peace*
1434–1464	Rule of Cosimo de' Medici in Florence
1444–1482	Rule of Federico II da Montefeltro, Duke of Urbino
1469–1492	Rule of Lorenzo, the Magnificent, de' Medici in Florence
1474–1539	Life of Isabella d'Este, Marchioness of Mantua
1492–1503	Pontificate of Alexander VI
1508	Baldassare Castiglione begins writing *The Book of the Courtier*
1503–1513	Pontificate of Julius II
1513–1521	Pontificate of Leo X
1523–1538	Rule of Andrea Gritti, Doge of Venice

were responsible for rectifying injuries and especially for avenging any assault on a family member. Nearly all marriages were arranged by fathers or male guardians who sought beneficial financial and political alliances with other families, a situation that gave older men an advantage in the marriage market, as they were usually better off financially than younger ones. As a result, husbands tended to be much older than wives. In Florence in 1427, for example, the typical first marriage was between a 30-year-old man and an 18-year-old woman. Husbands were encouraged to treat their spouses with a kindly but distant paternalism. All women were supposed to be kept under strict male supervision, and the only honorable role for an unmarried woman was as a nun.

However, the reality of family life often departed from theory. A number of factors explain the disparity. First, a variety of circumstances made family life insecure and the very survival of families tenuous—death from epidemic diseases, especially the Black Death, and separations due to marital strife, which were common enough even though divorce was not possible. Second, the wide age gap between husbands and wives meant that husbands were likely to die long before their wives, and thus many women became widows at a relatively young age with children still to raise. Third, many men, especially international merchants and migrant workers, were away from their families for long periods of time. Regardless of the patriarchal assertion that

Vendetta as Private Justice

During the fourteenth and fifteenth centuries, the official justice provided by the law courts competed with the private justice of revenge. Private justice was based on the principle of retaliation. When someone was murdered or assaulted, it became the obligation of the victim's closest male relatives to avenge the injury by harming the perpetrator or one of his relatives to a similar degree. A son was obliged to avenge the death of his father, a brother the injury of his brother. Given the weakness of most governments, the only effective justice was often private justice or, as the Italians called it, *vendetta*. As the most significant source of disorder during the Renaissance, vendetta was a practice that all governments struggled to eradicate.

One of the attributes that distinguished an act of private justice from a simple violent crime was that avengers committed their acts openly and even bragged about what they had done. A criminal covered his tracks. An avenger did not. Therefore, the violence of an act of revenge was carried out in public so there would be witnesses, and often it was performed in a highly symbolic way in order to humiliate the victim as much as possible.

In Renaissance Italy private justice took many forms, but always such acts sought to do more than create another victim. They sought to deliver a message. After a period of disorder in 1342, the Florentines granted extraordinary judicial powers to a soldier of fortune, Walter of Brienne, known as the Duke of Athens. But Walter offended many Florentines by arresting and executing members of prominent families. In September of that year a crowd led by these families besieged the government palace and captured the duke's most hated henchmen, the "conservator" and his son.

Even though the conservator had been the highest judge of Florence, the Florentines repudiated his authority by obtaining revenge. An eyewitness reported what happened next:

> The son was pushed out in front, and they cut him up and dismembered him. This done, they shoved out the conservator himself and did the same to him. Some carried a piece of him on a lance or sword throughout the city, and there were those so cruel, so bestial in their anger, and full of such hatred that they ate the raw flesh.[3]

This story of revenge in the most sophisticated city in Europe on the eve of the Renaissance illustrates the brutality of private justice, especially the need to make a public example of the victim.

Another account from nearly 200 years later tells of the murder of Antonio Savorgnan, a nobleman from Friuli who had killed a number of his enemies the previous year. Rather than attempting to have Antonio arrested as they could have, the murderers avenged their dead relatives through private justice. One eyewitness recounted that Antonio was attacked while leaving church, and then, "It was by divine miracle that Antonio Savorgnan was wounded: his head opened, he fell down, and he never spoke another word. But before he died, a giant dog came there and ate all his brains, and one cannot possibly deny that his brains were eaten."[4] This time a dog did the avengers' work for them. Perhaps the strangest detail in both of these accounts is that the writers wanted readers to believe that the victim had been eaten, either by humans or by a dog. Why was this an important message to get across?

The eating of a victim was one way avengers signaled that they were killing as an act of private justice. In both of the killings just described, the killers were retaliating for the murder of one of their close relatives and symbolically announcing to others that the attack was not an unjustifiable crime but a legitimate act of revenge. To convey that message, avengers could not ambush their opponent in the dark of night but were obliged to confront him openly in broad daylight before witnesses. There had to be the appearance, at least, of a fair fight. Murderers symbolized their revenge in several ways: They butchered the corpse as if it were the prey of a hunt or fed the remains to hunting dogs or even ate it themselves in what appeared to be a frenzy of revenge.

One of the major objectives of any government, whether a tiny city-state or a great monarchy, was to substitute public justice for private justice; but the persistence of tradition was strong. During the sixteenth century as governments sought to control violence and as the Renaissance values of moderation spread, a different kind of private justice appeared—the duel. Traditionally, the duel had been a means of solving disputes among medieval knights, but during the sixteenth century duels became much more common, even among men who had never been soldiers. Dueling required potential combatants to conform to an elaborate set of rules: The legitimate causes for a challenge to a duel were few, the combatants had to recognize each other as honorable men, the actual fight took place only after extensive preparations, judges who were experts on honor had to serve as witnesses, and the combatants had to swear to accept the outcome and abstain from fighting one another in the future.

The very complexity of the rules of dueling limited the vio-

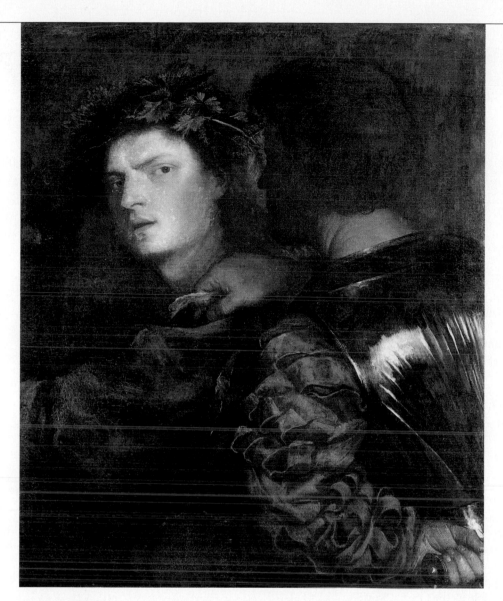

Private Justice

In Titian's painting *The Bravo* (ca. 1515/1520), a man wearing a breastplate and hiding a drawn sword behind his back grabs the collar of his enemy before assaulting him. To enact honorable revenge the attacker could not stab his enemy in the back but had to give him a chance in a fair fight.

lence of private justice, and that meant that fewer fights actually took place. Dueling, in effect, civilized private justice. Although dueling was always against the law, princes tended to wink at duels because they kept conflicts among their own courtiers under control. At the same time, governments became far less tolerant of other forms of private justice, especially among the lower classes. They at-

tempted to abolish feuds and vendettas and insisted that all disputes be submitted to the courts.

Questions of Justice

1. How did the persistence of private justice present a challenge to the emerging states of the Renaissance?
2. In what ways did private justice reflect Renaissance values, such as the value of keeping appearances?

Taking It Further

Muir, Edward. *Mad Blood Stirring: Vendetta in Renaissance Italy.* 1998. A study of the most extensive and long-lasting vendetta in Renaissance Italy. It traces the evolution of vendetta violence into dueling.

Weinstein, Donald. *The Captain's Concubine: Love, Honor, and Violence in Renaissance Tuscany.* 2000. A delightfully engaging account of an ambush and fight among two nobles over a woman who was the concubine of the father of one of the fighters and the lover of the other. It reveals the disturbing relationship between love and violence in Renaissance society.

The Age Gap Between Husbands and Wives

In Renaissance Italy older men typically married much younger women. In the middle of this fresco, *Marriage of the Virgin* by Fra Angelico, the young Mary holds out her hands to a rabbi who joins her in marriage to the gray-bearded Joseph. Behind Joseph young men hold up their fists as if to strike him. Fra Angelico dramatically conveys the anger of the young men about a marriage system that made it impossible for them to compete for brides with the older men.

fathers should be in control, in reality they were often absent or dead.

The contradiction between the theory of patriarchy and the fragile reality of family life had far-reaching consequences. Instead of wielding a strong hand over their families, most fathers were remote figures who had little direct influence. Mothers who were supposed to be modest, obedient to their husbands, and invisible to the outside world not only had to raise children alone but often had to manage their dead or absent husband's business and political affairs. By necessity, many resilient, strong, and active women were deeply involved in the management of worldly affairs, and mothers had much more direct influence on children than fathers. Despite the theory of patriarchy, the families of Renaissance Italy were in fact matriarchies in which mothers ruled.

The contradictions of family life became one of the most discussed problems in the Renaissance. Making fun of impotent old husbands married to beautiful but unfulfilled young wives became a major theme in comic drama. Given the demographic ravages of the Black Death, concern for the care of babies preoccupied preachers, while the many Renaissance paintings in which little cherubs seem to fall from the sky manifested a widespread craving for healthy children. A deep anxiety produced by the contradictions of family life and by the tenuous hold many families had on survival stimulated the distinctive family theme in the culture of Renaissance Italy.

The Influence of Ancient Culture

■ How did Renaissance thinkers create historical perspective and devise methods of criticism for interpreting texts?

The need in Renaissance Italy to provide effective models for how citizens, courtiers, and families should behave stimulated a reexamination of ancient culture. The civilizations of ancient Greece and Rome had long fascinated the educated classes in the West. In Italy, where most cities were built around or on top of the ruins of the ancient past, the seduction of antiquity was particularly pronounced. During the fourteenth and fifteenth centuries many Italian thinkers and artists attempted to foster a rebirth of ancient cultures. At first they merely attempted to imitate the Latin style of the best Roman writers. Then scholars tried to do the same thing with Greek, stimulated in part by direct contact with Greek-speaking refugees from Byzantium. Artists trekked to Rome to fill their notebooks with sketches of ancient ruins, sculptures, and medallions. Wealthy collectors hoarded manuscripts of ancient philosophy, built libraries to house them, bought up every piece of ancient sculpture they could find, and dug up ruins to find more antiquities to adorn their palaces. Patrons demanded that artists produce new works that imitated the styles of the ancients and that displayed a similar concern for rendering natural forms. Especially prized were lifelike representations of the human body.

Patrons, artists, and scholars during the Renaissance not only appreciated the achievements of the past but began to understand the enormous cultural distance between themselves and the ancients. That insight made their perspective historical. They also developed techniques of literary analysis to determine when a particular text had been written and to differentiate authentic texts from ones that had been corrupted by the mistakes of copyists. That ability made their perspective critical.

Petrarch and the Illustrious Ancients

The founder of the historical critical perspective that characterized the Renaissance was Francesco Petrarca (1304–1374), known in English as Petrarch. In contrast to the medieval thinkers who admired the ancients and treated their words as repositories of eternal wisdom, Petrarch discovered that the ancients were mere men much like himself. More than anything else, that insight might distinguish what was new about the Italian Renaissance, and Petrarch was the first to explore its implications.

Petrarch's early fame came from his poetry, in both his native Italian and Latin. In an attempt to improve his Latin style, Petrarch engaged in a detailed study of the best ancient Roman writers and searched to find old manuscripts that were the least corrupted by copyists. In that search he was always watching for anything by the Roman orator Cicero (106–43 B.C.E.), who was the Latinist most revered for literary style. In 1345 Petrarch briefly visited Verona to see what he could find in the library of a local monastery. While thumbing through the dusty volumes, he excitedly happened upon a previously unknown collection of letters Cicero had written to his friend Atticus.

As Petrarch began to read the letters, however, he suffered a profound shock. Cicero had a reputation as the greatest sage of the Romans, a model of good Latin style, of philosophical sophistication, and most of all of high ethical standards. But in the letters Petrarch found not sage moral advice but gossip, rumors, and crude political calculations. Cicero looked like a scheming politician, a man of crass ambition rather than grand philosophical wisdom. Although Petrarch could never forgive Cicero for being less than what he had avowed in his philosophical writings, he had discovered the human Cicero rather than just the idealized Cicero, a man so human you could imagine having a conversation with him.

And having a conversation was precisely what Petrarch set out to do. Cicero, however, had been dead for 1,388 years. So Petrarch wrote a letter to Cicero's ghost. Adopting Cicero's own elegant Latin style, Petrarch lambasted the Roman for going against the moral advice he had given

others. Petrarch quoted Cicero back to Cicero, asking him how he could be such a hypocrite:

DOCUMENT

Petrarch, Letters to Cicero (14th c.)

Your letters I sought for long and diligently; and finally, where I least expected it, I found them. At once I read them, over and over, with the utmost eagerness. And as I read I seemed to hear your bodily voice, O Marcus Tullius [Cicero's given names], saying many things, uttering many lamentations, ranging through many phases of thought and feeling. I long had known how excellent a guide you have proved for others; at last I was to learn what sort of guidance you gave yourself.... Now it is your turn to be the listener.[5]

Petrarch went on to lecture Cicero for his false dealings, his corruption, and his moral failures. The point of the exercise of writing a letter to a dead man was to compare the ideals Cicero had avowed in his philosophical work and the reality he seemed to have lived. Making comparisons is one of the elementary techniques of a critical method, and it became the hallmark of Petrarch's mode of analysis. Petrarch's letter reduced the stature of the ancients a bit, making them less like gods and more like other men who made mistakes and told lies. Petrarch ended this remarkable, unprecedented letter with a specific date, given in both the Roman and Christian ways, and a description of Verona's location in a way an ancient Roman would understand—as if he were making it possible for Cicero to find and answer him. This concern for historical precision typified the aspect that was most revolutionary about Petrarch's approach. No longer a repository of timeless truths, the ancient world became a specific time and place that Petrarch perceived to be at a great distance from himself. The ancients had ceased to be godlike; they had become historical figures. After his letter to Cicero, Petrarch wrote a series of letters to other illustrious ancients in which he revealed the human qualities and shortcomings of each.

Petrarch and his follower Lorenzo Valla (1407–1457) developed critical methods by editing classical texts, including parts of Livy's history of Rome, which was written about the time of Jesus. Petrarch compared different manuscript versions of Livy's work in an attempt to establish exactly the original words, a method very different from the medieval scribe's temptation to alter or improve a text as he saw fit. Petrarch strived to get the words right because he wanted to understand exactly what Livy had meant, a method now called the philological approach. Philology° is the comparative study of language, devoted to understanding the meaning of a word in a particular historical context. Valla elaborated on Petrarch's insights into philology to demonstrate that words do not have fixed meanings but take on different meanings depending on who is using them and when they were written. It was obvious, for example, that the word *virtue* had meant something quite different to the polytheist Livy than it did to readers in the fourteenth and fifteenth centuries, who understood virtue in Christian terms. A concern for philology gave Petrarch and his followers access to the individuality of a writer. In the particularity of words, Petrarch discovered the particularity of actual individuals who lived and wrote many centuries before.

An interest in the meaning of words led Petrarch to study the rhetoric° of language. Rhetoric refers to the art of persuasive or emotive speaking and writing. From his studies of rhetoric, Petrarch became less confident about the ability of language to represent truth than he was about its capacity to motivate readers and listeners to action. He came to think that rhetoric was superior to philosophy because he preferred a good man over a wise one, and rhetoric offered examples worthy of emulation rather than abstract principles subject to debate. Petrarch wanted people to behave morally, not just talk or write about morality. And he believed that the most efficient way to inspire his readers to do the right thing was to write moving rhetoric.

The Humanists: The Latin Point of View

Those who followed Petrarch's approach to the classical authors were the Renaissance humanists°. The Renaissance humanists studied Latin and sometimes Greek texts on grammar, rhetoric, poetry, history, and ethics. (The term *humanist* in the Renaissance meant something very different from what it means today—someone concerned with human welfare and dignity.) The humanists sought to resurrect a form of Latin that had been dead for more than a thousand years and was distinct from the living Latin used by the Church, law courts, and universities—which they thought was mediocre compared to ancient Latin. In this effort, humanists acquired a difficult but functional skill that opened a wide variety of employment opportunities to them and gave them great public influence. They worked as schoolmasters, secretaries, bureaucrats, official court or civic historians, and ambassadors. Many other humanists were wealthy men who did not need a job but were fascinated with the rhetorical capabilities of the new learning to persuade other people to do what they wanted them to do.

Because humanists could be found on different sides of almost all important questions of the day, the significance of their work lies less in what they said than in how they said it. They wrote about practically everything: painting pictures, designing buildings, planting crops, draining swamps, raising children, managing a household, and educating women. They debated the nature of human liberty, the virtues of famous men, the vices of infamous ones, the meaning of Egyptian hieroglyphics, and the cosmology of the universe.

How did the humanists' use of Latin words and grammar influence the understanding of this vast range of subjects? Their approach was entirely literary. When they wanted to design a building, they read ancient books on architecture instead of consulting masons and builders. By studying the ancients, humanists organized experience into new categories that changed people's perceptions of themselves, the society they lived in, and the universe they inhabited. Humanist writing revealed what might be called the *Latin point of view*. Each language organizes experience according to the needs of the people who speak it, and all languages make arbitrary distinctions, dividing up the world into different categories. People who study a foreign language run across these arbitrary distinctions when they learn that some expressions can never be translated exactly.

The humanists' recovery of the Latin point of view contributed new words, new sentence patterns, and new rhetorical models that often altered their own perceptions in very subtle ways. For example, when a fifteenth-century humanist examined what the ancient Romans had written about painting, he found the phrase *ars et ingenium*. *Ars* referred to skills that can be learned by following established rules and adhering to models provided by the best painters. Thus, the ability of a painter to draw a straight line, to mix colors properly, and to identify a saint with the correct symbol are examples of *ars* or what we would call craftsmanship. The meaning of *ingenium* was more difficult to pin down, however. It referred to the inventive capacity of the painter, to his or her ingenuity. The humanists discovered that the ancients had made a distinction between the craftsmanship and the ingenuity of a painter. As a result, when humanists and their pupils looked at paintings, they began to make the same distinction and began to admire the genius of artists whose work showed ingenuity as well as craftsmanship. Ingenuity came to refer to the ability of the painter to arrange figures in a novel way, to employ unusual colors, or to create emotionally exciting effects that conveyed piety, sorrow, or joy as the subject demanded. So widespread was the influence of the humanists that the most ingenious artists demanded higher prices and became the most sought after. In this way, creative innovation was encouraged in the arts, but it all started very simply with the introduction of new words into the Latin vocabulary of the people who paid for paintings. A similar process of establishing new categories altered every subject the humanists touched.

The humanist movement spread rapidly during the fifteenth century. Leonardo Bruni (ca. 1370–1444), who became the chancellor of Florence (the head of the government's bureaucracy), employed humanist techniques to defend the republican institutions and values of the city. Bruni's defense of republican government is called civic humanism°. He argued that the truly ethical man should devote himself to active service to his city rather than to passive contemplation in scholarly retreat or monastic seclusion. Thus Bruni formulated the ethic of responsible citizenship that remains today as necessary to sustain a free society. Given the supreme value Christianity had long placed on the passive contemplation of divine truth, Bruni's assertion that active public service constituted an even higher vocation was radical indeed.

Lorenzo Valla employed philological criticism to undermine papal claims to authority over secular rulers, such as

DOCUMENT

A Humanist Laments the Ruins of Rome

In 1430 the distinguished humanist Poggio Bracciolini (1380–1459) was working in Rome as a papal secretary. In this account he describes his and a friend's response to seeing the ruins of the once-great city of Rome. Poggio's lament and those of other humanists stimulated popes to commit themselves to the rebuilding of the city, but the enthusiasm to return Rome to its ancient splendor had some unfortunate side effects. Many of the building materials for the new Rome were pillaged from the ruins of the old Rome. As a result, much of the destruction of the ancient city of Rome occurred during the Renaissance.

Not long ago, after Pope Martin left Rome shortly before his death for a farewell visit to the Tuscan countryside, and when Antonio Lusco, a very distinguished man, and I were free of business and public duties, we used to contemplate the desert places of the city with wonder in our hearts as we reflected on the former greatness of the broken buildings and the vast ruins of the ancient city, and again on the truly prodigious and astounding fall of its great empire and the deplorable inconstancy of fortune. And once when we had climbed the Capitoline hill, and Antonio, who was a little weary from riding, wanted to rest, we dismounted from our horses and sat down together within the very enclosures of the Tarpeian ruins, behind the great marble threshold of its very doors, as I believe, and the numerous broken columns lying here and there, whence a view of a large part of the city opens out.

Here, after he had looked about for some time, sighing and as if struck dumb, Antonio declared, "Oh, Poggio, how remote are these ruins from the Capitol that our Vergil celebrated: 'Golden now, once bristling with thorn bushes.' How justly one can transpose this verse and say: 'Golden once, now rough with thorns and overgrown with briars.'

Source: "The Ruins of Rome" by Poggio Bracciolini, translated by Mary Martin McLaughlin, from *The Portable Renaissance Reader* by James B. Ross and Mary Martin McLaughlin, editors, copyright 1953, renewed © 1981 by Viking Penguin Inc. Used by permission of Viking Penguin, a division of Penguin Group (USA) Inc.

the princes and republics of Italy. He did so by proving that a famous document, the Donation of Constantine, was a forgery. The Donation recorded that during the fourth century the emperor Constantine had transferred his imperial authority in Italy to the pope, and although Renaissance popes could not get what they wanted just by citing this document, it was part of the legal arsenal popes used against secular rulers. Valla demonstrated that the Donation had actually been forged in the ninth century, a work of detection that showed how the historical analysis of documents could be immensely useful for resolving contemporary political disputes. The controversy between defenders and enemies of the papacy that followed Valla's discovery stimulated the demand for humanist learning because it became clear that humanist methods were necessary for political debate and propaganda.

The intellectual curiosity of the humanists led them to master many fields of endeavor. This breadth of accomplishment contributed to the ideal of the "Renaissance Man," a person who sought excellence in everything he did. No one came closer to this ideal than Leon Battista Alberti (1404–1472). As a young man, Alberti wrote Latin comedies and satirical works that drew on Greek and Roman models, but as he matured he tackled more serious subjects. Although he was a bachelor and thus knew nothing firsthand about marriage, he drew upon the ancient writers to create the most influential Renaissance book on the family, which included sections on relations between husbands and wives, raising children, and estate management. He composed the first grammar of the Italian language. He dabbled in mathematics and wrote on painting, law, the duties of bishops, love, horsemanship, dogs, agriculture, and flies. He mapped the city of Rome and wrote the most important fifteenth-century work on the theory and practice of architecture. His interest in architecture, moreover, was not just theoretical. In the last decades of his life, he dedicated much of his spare time to architectural projects that included restoring an ancient church in Rome, designing Renaissance façades for medieval churches, and building a palace for his most important patron. One of his last projects was the first significant work for making and deciphering secret codes in the West.

The humanists guaranteed their lasting influence through their innovations in the educational curriculum. The objective of humanist education was to create well-rounded male pupils (girls were not usually accepted in humanist schools) who were not specialists or professionals, such as the theologians, lawyers, and physicians trained in universities, but critical thinkers who could tackle any problems that life presented. It was a curriculum well suited for the active life of civic leaders, courtiers, princes, and churchmen. The influence of the humanist curriculum persists in the general-education requirements of modern universities, which require students, now of both sexes, to obtain intellectual breadth before they specialize in narrow professional training.

Historians have identified a few female humanists from the Renaissance. Because they were so unusual, learned humanist women were often ridiculed. Jealous men accused the humanist Isotta Nogarola (1418–1466) of promiscuity and incest, and other women insulted her in public. A famous male schoolmaster said that Isotta was too feminine in her writings and should learn how to find "a man within the woman."[6] Laura Cereta (1475–1506), who knew Greek as well as Latin and was adept at mathematics, answered the scorn of a male critic with rhetorical insult worthy of Petrarch himself:

> *I would have been silent, believe me, if that savage old enmity of yours had attacked me alone. . . . But I cannot tolerate your having attacked my entire sex. For this reason my thirsty soul seeks revenge, my sleeping pen is aroused to literary struggle, raging anger stirs mental passions long chained by silence. With just cause I am moved to demonstrate how great a reputation for learning and virtue women have won by their inborn excellence, manifested in every age as knowledge, the [purveyor] of honor. Certain, indeed, and legitimate is our possession of this inheritance, come to us from a long eternity of ages past.[7]*

These few humanist women can be seen as among the first feminists. They advocated female equality and female education but also urged women to take control of their own lives. Nogarola answered her critics in a typical humanist fashion by reinterpreting the past. Thinking at this time suggested that all women were the daughters of Eve, who in her weakness had submitted to the temptation of the serpent, which led to the exile of humanity from the Garden of Eden. Nogarola pointed out that Eve had been no weaker than Adam, who also ate of the forbidden fruit, and therefore women should not be blamed for the Fall from God's grace. Cereta was the most optimistic of the female humanists. She maintained that if women paid as much attention to learning as they did to their appearances, they would achieve equality. Despite the efforts of Cereta and other female humanists, progress in women's education was extremely slow. The universities remained closed to talented women. The first woman to earn a degree from a university did so in 1678, and it took another 200 years before very many others could follow her example.

Through the influence of the humanists, the Latin point of view permeated Renaissance culture. They educated generations of wealthy young gentlemen whose appreciation of antiquity led them to pay to collect manuscripts of ancient literature, philosophy, and science. These patrons were also responsible for encouraging artists to imitate the ancients. What began as a narrow literary movement became the stimulus to see human society and nature through entirely new eyes. Some humanists, especially in northern Europe, applied these techniques with revolutionary results to the study of the Bible and the sources of Christianity.

Understanding Nature: Moving Beyond the Science of the Ancients

The humanists' initial concern was to emulate the language of the ancients. Most of them preferred to spend time reading a book rather than observing the world around them. In fact, their methods were ill-suited to understanding nature, and when they wanted to explain some natural phenomenon such as the movement of blood through the body or the apparent movements of the planets and stars, they looked to ancient authorities for answers rather than to nature itself. The Renaissance humanists' most prominent contributions to science consisted of recovering classical texts and translating the work of ancient Greek scientists into the more widely understood Latin. This is in contrast to the scientific method of today, in which scientists form a hypothesis and then determine whether it is correct by observing the natural world as directly as possible. In contrast, Renaissance scientists searched for ancient texts about nature, and then debated about which ancient author had been correct.

These translated texts broadened the discussion of two subjects crucial to the scientific revolution of the late sixteenth and seventeenth centuries—astronomy and anatomy. In 1543 the Polish humanist Nicolaus Copernicus (1473–1543) resolved the complications in the cosmological system of the second-century astronomer Ptolemy. Whereas Ptolemy's writings had placed Earth at the center of the universe, Copernicus cited other ancient writers who put the sun in the center. Thus the first breakthrough in theoretical astronomy was achieved not by making new observations but by comparing ancient texts. Nothing was proven, however, until Galileo Galilei (1564–1642) turned his telescope to the heavens in 1610 to observe the stars through his own eyes rather than through an ancient text.

Andreas Vesalius (1514–1564) built upon recently published studies in anatomy from ancient Greece to write a survey of human anatomy, *On the Fabric of the Human Body* (1543), a book that encouraged dissection and anatomical observations. With Vesalius, anatomy moved away from relying exclusively on the authority of ancient books to encouraging medical students and physicians to examine the human body with their own eyes. Building upon Vesalius's work, Gabriele Falloppio (ca. 1523–1562) made many original observations of muscles, nerves, kidneys, bones, and most famously the "Fallopian tubes," which he described for the first time. By the late sixteenth century, astronomy and anatomy had surpassed what the ancients had known.

Besides recovering ancient scientific texts, the most important Renaissance contributions to science came secondhand from developments in the visual arts and technology. A number of Florentine artists experimented during the early fifteenth century with the application of mathematics to the preliminary design of paintings. The goal was to make paintings more accurately represent reality by creating the visual illusion of the third dimension of depth on a two-dimensional rectangular surface, a technique known as linear perspective (see next section). These artists contributed to a more refined understanding of how the eye perceives objects, and their understanding of how the eye worked led to experiments with glass lenses. A more thorough knowledge of optics made possible the invention of the telescope and microscope.

Of all the developments in the fifteenth century, however, none matched the long-term significance of a pair of rather simple inventions—cheap manufactured paper and the printing press. Paper made from rags created an inexpensive alternative to sheepskins, which had been the preferred medium for medieval scribes. And just as paper replaced sheepskin, the printing press replaced the scribe. Several Dutch and German craftsmen had experimented with printing during the 1440s, but credit for the essential innovation of movable metal type has traditionally been accredited to Johannes Gutenberg (ca. 1398–1468) of Mainz in the 1450s. German immigrants brought printing to Italy, which rapidly became the publishing center of Europe, largely because it boasted a large, literate urban population who bought books.

Scientific books accounted for only about 10 percent of the titles of the first printed books, but the significance of printing for science was greater than the sales figures would indicate. In addition to making ancient scientific texts more readily available, print meant that new discoveries and new ideas reached a wider audience, duplication of scientific investigation could be avoided, illustrations were standardized, and scientists built upon each other's work. With the invention of the printing press, scientific work became closely intertwined with publishing, so that published scientific work advanced science, and scientific work that was not published went largely unnoticed. It is revealing that Leonardo da Vinci (1452–1519), the greatest Renaissance observer of nature, contributed nothing to science because he failed to publish his findings. The fundamental principle of modern science and, in fact, of all modern scholarship is that research must be made available to everyone through publication.

Antiquity and Nature in the Arts

■ How did various attempts to imitate antiquity in the arts alter perceptions of nature?

More than any other age in Western history, the Italian Renaissance is identified with the visual arts. The unprecedented clusters of brilliant artists active in a handful of Italian cities during the fifteenth and sixteenth centuries overshadow any other contribution of Renaissance culture. Under the influence of the humanists, Renaissance artists began to imitate the sculpture, architecture, and painting of the ancients. At first they concerned themselves with merely copying ancient styles and poses. But soon they attempted a more sophisticated form of imitation. They wanted to understand the principles that made

CHRONOLOGY

The Influence of Ancient Culture

106–43 B.C.E.	Marcus Tullius Cicero, Latin rhetorician
1304–1374	Francesco Petrarca (Petrarch), first humanist
ca. 1370–1444	Leonardo Bruni, chancellor of Florence
1404–1472	Leon Battista Alberti, humanist and architect
1407–1457	Lorenzo Valla, humanist
1418–1466	Isotta Nogarola, first female humanist
ca. 1454	Johannes Gutenberg begins printing books
1473–1543	Nicolaus Copernicus, humanist and cosmological theorist
1475–1506	Laura Cereta, humanist
1514–1564	Andreas Vesalius, writer on anatomy
ca. 1523–1562	Gabriele Falloppio, conducted anatomical dissections
1564–1642	Galileo Galilei, astronomer

it possible for the artists from classical Greece and Rome to make their figures so lifelike. That led them to observe more directly nature itself, especially the anatomy of the human body. Renaissance art was driven by the passionate desire of artists and their patrons both to imitate ancient models and to imitate nature. These twin desires produced a certain creative tension in their work because the ancients, whose works of art often depicted gods and goddesses, had idealized and improved on what they observed in nature. Renaissance artists sought to depict simultaneously the ideal and the real—an impossible goal, but one that sparked remarkable creativity.

All of the Renaissance arts displayed the mark of patrons, the discriminating and wealthy people who controlled the city-states and who had been educated in humanist schools. Until the end of the sixteenth century, all painters, sculptors, and even poets worked for a patron. An individual patron would commission a particular work of art, such as an altar painting, portrait bust, or palace. The patron and artist would agree to the terms of the work through a contract, which might spell out in considerable detail exactly what the artist was to do, what kinds of materials he was to use, how much they could cost, how much he was allowed to rely on assistants, how much he had to do himself, and even how he was to arrange figures. The same sort of contract was used when work was commissioned by a group—for example, a guild, lay religious society (called a confraternity), convent, or government. Michelangelo Buonarroti (1475–1564) sculpted *David*, which has become the most famous work of Renaissance art, to fulfill a

The Tribute Money: Combining Natural and Idealized Representations

In this detail of a fresco of Christ and his apostles, Masaccio mixed naturalism and idealized beauty. The figure on the right with his back turned to the viewer is a tax collector, who is depicted as a normal human being. The head of the fourth figure to the left of him, who represents one of the apostles, was copied from an ancient statue that represents ancient ideals of beauty.

pictorial space. In *The Tribute Money*, he drew the spectator's eye to the head of Jesus, who is the figure in the middle pointing with his right hand. In addition, Masaccio recognized that the human eye perceives an object when light shines on it to form lighted surfaces and shadows. He used this understanding in creating a painting technique called *chiaroscuro* ("light and shade"). There is a single source of light in the painting coming from the same direction as the light in the room. That light defines figures and objects in the painting through the play of light and shadow. The strokes of Masaccio's paintbrush tried to duplicate the way natural light plays upon surfaces.

The techniques developed by Masaccio came to complete fulfillment in the career of Leonardo da Vinci (1452–1519). So compelling was Leonardo's curiosity and desire to tackle new problems that many of his paintings remained unfinished. He was a restless experimenter, never settling on simple solutions. Because of experiments Leonardo made with paint, his *Last Supper* fresco in Milan has seriously deteriorated. His mature works, such as *Mona Lisa*, completely reconciled the technical problems of representing human figures with realistic accuracy and the spiritual goal of evoking deep emotions. Unlike some of his predecessors, who grouped figures in a painting as if they were statues, Leonardo managed to make his figures appear to interact and communicate with one another.

The technique of painting with oils achieved new levels among painters in the Netherlands and in Flanders (in present-day Belgium, but at the time a province in the Duchy of Burgundy). By carefully layering numerous coats of tinted oil glazes over the surface of the painting, these painters created

DOCUMENT

Vasari on Leonardo da Vinci

IMAGE

Leonardo da Vinci, *Madonna with the Carnation*, c. 1435

Leonardo Invents an Airplane

Leonardo da Vinci's notebooks are filled with numerous examples of his unprecedented inventions. In this drawing he designed the fuselage of a flying machine. However, Leonardo had no influence at all on science or technology because he kept his inventions in his secret notebooks, and no one knew about them until they were discovered centuries later.

Northern Renaissance Art
In this fifteenth-century Flemish painting by Jan van Eyck, the use of oil paint and glazes made it possible to convey the shimmering surfaces of the brass chandelier and mirror hanging in the background. Shown in the mirror are the backs of the posing couple and the artist at his easel. Northern European artists delighted in using oils and glazes to create visual tricks, such as mirrored images. This is a portrait of Giovanni Arnolfini and Giovanna Cenami, who were married in 1434. Arnolfini was an Italian banker residing in the Flemish city of Bruges.

a luminous surface that gave the illusion of depth. The use of glazes enabled painters to blend brushstrokes in a way that made them virtually imperceptible. As a result Flemish and Dutch painters excelled in painting meticulous details, such as the textures of textiles, the reflections of gems, and the features of distant landscapes. Jan van Eyck (ca. 1395–1441) was the most famous Flemish painter. He worked as a court painter for the Duke of Burgundy, for whom he undertook many kinds of projects including decorating his palaces and designing stage sets and ornaments for festivals. His oil paintings were so famous that he was much praised by the Italian humanists, and numerous Italian patrons, including the Medicis, bought his works.

Most humanist theorists of painting linked artistic creativity with masculinity. By the sixteenth century, however, these theorists were proved wrong, as a number of female painters rose to prominence. The most notable was Sofonisba Anguissola (ca. 1532–1625). Born into an aristocratic family in Cremona, Italy, she received a humanist education along with her five sisters and brother. Because she was a woman, she was prohibited from studying anatomy or drawing male models. As a result she specialized in portraits, often of members of her family, and self-portraits. She developed a distinctive style of depicting animated faces. Her example inspired other aristocratic women to take up painting.

Music of the Emotions

Renaissance humanists' fascination with the visual arts of the ancients led them to assume that composers should imitate ancient music. But in attempting to turn humanist theories about music into real music, fifteenth-century composers faced a formidable problem—no one had the slightest clue what ancient Greek music actually sounded like. As a result, musical innovations lagged behind the other arts until the late sixteenth century, when a musical Renaissance finally took hold.

During the fourteenth and fifteenth centuries the principal composers came from France and the Netherlands. The greatest of them, Josquin de Prez (ca. 1440–1521), was born

CHRONOLOGY

Antiquity and Nature in the Arts

1377–1446	Filippo Brunelleschi, Florentine sculptor and architect
1378–1455	Lorenzo Ghiberti, Florentine sculptor who created the "Gates of Paradise"
1386–1466	Donatello, Florentine sculptor
ca. 1395–1441	Jan van Eyck, Flemish painter
1401–ca. 1428	Masaccio, Florentine fresco painter
ca. 1440–1521	Josquin de Prez, composer
1452–1519	Leonardo da Vinci, Florentine painter and inventor
1475–1564	Michelangelo Buonarroti, Florentine sculptor, painter, architect, poet
ca. 1532–1625	Sofonisba Anguissola, painter
1567–1643	Claudio Monteverdi, opera composer

and trained in the Netherlands and later found patrons in Milan, Rome, and Ferrara. His finest talent as a composer consisted of his ability to enhance musically the meaning of lyrics. In contrast to Josquin's sensitivity to matching music and lyric, most other composers relied on stereotypical rhythmic patterns and a simple melodic line that had no connection to the text. In fact, almost any lyric could be sung to the same music.

Recognizing that the music of their time did not measure up to what ancient writers had reported about the emotional intensity of their music, several prominent musician-humanists conducted extensive discussions about how to combine music and words in a way that would create a fuller aesthetic and emotional experience. The initial consequence of these discussions was the Renaissance madrigal, a type of song in which the music closely followed a poetic lyric to accentuate the shades of textual meaning. For example, when the text described a happy mood, the music would rise up the scale. A somber text would be lower-pitched. When the lyric described agitation or fear, the rhythm would quicken in imitation of the heart beating faster.

The most important consequence of the discussions about the need for a richer musical experience was the invention of opera° during the final decades of the sixteenth century. A group of humanist thinkers called the *Camerata* thought the power of ancient Greek music could be recovered by writing continuous music to accompany a full drama. The drama was performed as a kind of speech-song with the range of pitch and rhythms closely following those of natural speech. Singers were accompanied by a small ensemble of musicians. The first operas composed in this vein were by Jacopo Peri (1561–1633) and Giulio Caccini (ca. 1550–1618) and were performed in Florence

at the Grand Duke's court around 1600. These lengthy, bloated works attracted little attention among audiences, and opera likely would have sunk under its own weight had it not been for Claudio Monteverdi (1567–1643), who discovered its dramatic and lyrical potential. His sumptuous productions employed large ensembles of singers and instrumentalists, punctuated speech-song with arias (long sung solos) and dances, and included magnificent stage machines that simulated earthquakes, fires, and battles. Under Monteverdi's masterful hand, opera became the first complete multimedia art form. Arias from his productions became popular hits sung on every street corner, and opera moved from being a private amusement for princely courtiers to mass entertainment. The first public opera house opened in Venice in 1637. By the end of the seventeenth century, Venice boasted seventeen opera houses for a population of only 140,000. With the rise of opera houses and theaters for plays, the close bond between patrons and artists began to break down. Until then, artists were bound by the wishes of patrons. Now they began to serve the much larger marketplace for popular entertainment.

The Early Modern European State System

■ How did the monarchies of western Europe gather the strength to become more assertive and more effective during the last half of the fifteenth and early sixteenth centuries?

The civic independence that had made the Italian Renaissance possible was profoundly challenged during the Italian Wars (1494–1530). During these wars France, Spain, and the Holy Roman Empire attempted to carve up the peninsula for themselves, and the Italian city-states were thrown into turmoil. By 1530 the Italian city-states, with the exception of Venice, had lost their independence to the triumphant king of Spain. The surrender of the rich city-states of Italy was the first and most prominent sign of a major transformation in the European system of states. The age of city-states was over because they could never muster the level of materiel and manpower necessary to put and keep a large army in the field. Only the large monarchies of the West could do that. The Italian Wars revealed the outlines of the early modern European state system, which was built on the power of large countries that had been brought under control by their own kings. These kings amassed an unprecedented level of resources that not only crushed Italy but made possible the European domination of much of the globe through establishment of colonies in the Americas, Asia, and eventually Africa.

Monarchies: The Foundation of the State System

During the last half of the fifteenth century, the monarchies of western Europe began to show signs of recovery from the turmoil of the fourteenth and early fifteenth centuries, which had been marked by famine, plague, revolts, and the Hundred Years' War. France and England ended the Hundred Years' War, which had bled both kingdoms of men and resources during the century before 1453. England escaped from its civil war, the War of the Roses, in 1485. The kingdoms of Castile and Aragon joined in 1479 to create the new kingdom of Spain, which in 1492 completed the reconquest of territories from the Muslims that had been underway since the eleventh century. The Holy Roman Empire, which became allied to Spain through marriage, pursued a grand new vision for unifying the diverse principalities of Germany.

The early modern European state system was the consequence of five developments. First, governments established standing armies. As a result of the military revolution that brought large numbers of infantrymen to the field of battle and gunpowder cannons to besiege cities and castles, governments were obliged to modernize their armies or face defeat. Since the ninth century, kings had relied on feudal levies, in which soldiers were recruited to fulfill their personal obligation to a lord, but by the late fifteenth century governments began to organize standing armies. These armies enjoyed high levels of professionalism and skill, but they were very expensive to maintain because the soldiers had to be regularly paid. Moreover, the new artillery was costly, and improvements in the effectiveness of artillery bombardments necessitated extensive improvements in the walls of castles, fortresses, and cities. As a result, kings were desperate for new revenues.

The need for revenues led to the second development, the systematic expansion of taxation. Every European state struggled with the problem of taxation. The need to tax efficiently produced the beginnings of a bureaucracy of tax assessors and collectors in many states.

People naturally resisted the burden of new taxes, and monarchs naturally responded to the resistance. This tension led to the third development. Monarchs attempted to weaken the institutional seats of resistance by abolishing the tax-exempt privileges of local communities and ignoring regional assemblies and parliaments that were supposed to approve new taxes. During the twelfth and thirteenth centuries, effective government was local government, and kings seldom had the power to interfere in the affairs of towns and regions. During the fifteenth century, however,

kings everywhere attempted to eliminate or erode the independence of towns and regional parliaments in order to raise taxes more effectively and to express the royal will throughout the realm.

The fourth development, closely linked to the third, can be seen in monarchs' attempts to constrain the independence of the aristocracy and the Church. In virtually every kingdom, the most significant threats to the power of the king were the powerful aristocrats. In England a civil war among aristocrats almost tore the kingdom apart. Kings everywhere struggled to co-opt or force submission from these aristocrats. Likewise, the autonomy of the Church threatened monarchical authority, and most monarchs took measures to oblige churchmen to act as agents of government policy.

The fifth development in the evolution of the European state system was the institution of resident ambassadors. During the Italian Wars, the kings of Europe began to exchange permanent, resident ambassadors who were responsible for informing their sovereign about conditions in the host country and representing the interests of their country abroad. Resident ambassadors became the linchpins in a sophisticated information network that provided intelligence about the intentions and capabilities of other kings, princes, and cities. These ambassadors typically enjoyed a humanist education, which helped them adapt to many strange and unpredictable situations, understand foreign languages, negotiate effectively, and speak persuasively. Ambassadors cultivated courtly manners, which smoothed over personal conflicts. For the development of the new state system, gathering reliable information became just as important as maintaining armies and collecting taxes.

France: Consolidating Power and Cultivating Renaissance Values

With the largest territory in western Europe and a population of more than 16 million, France had the potential to become the most powerful state in Europe if the king could figure out how to take advantage of the kingdom's size and resources. By 1453 the Hundred Years' War between France and England had come to an end. With the inspiration of Joan of Arc and with the reform of royal finances by the merchant-banker Jacques Coeur, King Charles VII (r. 1422–1461) expelled the English and regained control of his kingdom. Under Charles, France created its first professional army. Equally important, during the Hundred Years' War the Pragmatic Sanction of Bourges° (1438) guaranteed the virtual autonomy of the French Church from papal control, giving the French king unparalleled opportunities to interfere in religious affairs and to exploit Church revenues for government purposes.

Louis XI (r. 1461–1483), called the "Spider King" because of his fondness for secret intrigue, took up the challenge of consolidating power over the great nobles of his kingdom, who thwarted his state building and threatened his throne. When Louis came to power, the Duchy of

Brittany was virtually independent; one great aristocrat, René of Anjou, controlled more territory and was richer than the king himself; and, most dangerous of all, the dukes of Burgundy had carved out their own splendid principality, which celebrated extravagant forms of courtly ritual and threatened to eclipse the prestige of France itself.

Against these powerful rivals, Louis turned to an equally powerful new weapon—the *taille*. During the final years of the Hundred Years' War, in order to support the army, the Estates General (France's parliament) granted the king the *taille*, the right to collect an annual direct tax. After the war, the tax continued and Louis turned it into a permanent source of revenue for himself and his successors. Armed with the financial resources of the *taille*, Louis took on his most rebellious vassal, Charles the Bold, the Duke of Burgundy, and in 1477 professional Swiss infantrymen in the pay of Louis defeated the plumed knights of Burgundy. Charles was killed in battle, and only his daughter Mary's hurried marriage to the Habsburg Archduke Maximilian bought the protection Burgundy needed to prevent France from seizing all of the duchy.

The monarch most responsible for the spread of Renaissance culture in France was Francis I (r. 1515–1547), a sportsman and warrior who thrilled to the frenzy of battle. Much of his early career was devoted to pursuing French interests in the Italian Wars, until he was captured in battle in 1525 in Italy. Thereafter he focused more on patronizing Italian artists and humanists at his court and importing Italian Renaissance styles. He had the first Renaissance-style chateau built in the Loire Valley and hired artists, including Leonardo da Vinci. As a result of Francis's patronage, Italy was no longer the exclusive center of Renaissance culture.

Spain: Unification by Marriage

In the early fifteenth century the Iberian peninsula was a diverse place, lacking political unity. It was home to several different kingdoms—Portugal, Castile, Navarre, and Aragon, which were all Christian, and Granada, which was Muslim. Each kingdom had its own laws, political institutions, customs, and languages. Unlike France, the Christian kingdoms of medieval Iberia were poor, underpopulated, and preoccupied with the reconquest, the attempt to drive

---

DOCUMENT

The Expulsion of the Jews from Spain

In 1492 after the conquest of Granada, the last Muslim kingdom on the Iberian peninsula, Ferdinand and Isabella ordered the expulsion of all Jews, who were given three months to leave Spain. Some sought an agreement to remain in the country in return for the payment of a large sum of money. However, the Jews soon discovered that was impossible. This account was written by a Jew living in Italy in 1495 who assembled his information from the reports of Jewish refugees.

Then they saw that there was evil determined against them by the King, and they gave up the hope of remaining. But the time had become short, and they had to hasten their exodus from Spain. They sold their houses, their landed estates, and their cattle for very small prices to save themselves. The King did not allow them to carry silver and gold out of his country, so that they were compelled to exchange their silver and gold for merchandise of cloths and skins and other things. . . .

One hundred and twenty thousand of them went to Portugal, according to a compact which a prominent man, Don Vidal bar Benveniste del Cavalleria, had made with the King of Portugal, and they paid one ducat for every soul, and the fourth part of all the merchandise they had carried thither; and he allowed them to stay in his country six months. This King acted much worse toward them than the King of Spain, and after the six months had elapsed he made

slaves of all those that remained in his country, and banished seven hundred children to a remote island to settle it, and all of them died. Some say that there were double as many. . . .

Many of the exiled Spaniards went to Mohammedan countries. . . . On account of their large numbers the Moors did not allow them into their cities, and many of them died in the fields from hunger, thirst, and lack of everything. The lions and bears, which are numerous in this country, killed some of them while they lay starving outside of the cities.

When the edict of expulsion became known in the other countries, vessels came from Genoa to the Spanish harbors to carry away the Jews. The crews of these vessels, too, acted maliciously and meanly toward the Jews, robbed them, and delivered some of them to the famous pirate of that time who was called the Corsair of Genoa. To those who escaped and arrived at Genoa the people of the city showed themselves merciless, and oppressed and robbed them, and the cruelty of their wicked hearts went so far that they took the infants from their mothers' breasts.

Many ships with Jews, especially from Sicily, went to the city of Naples on the coast. The King of this country was friendly to the Jews, received them all, and was merciful towards them, and he helped them with money. The Jews that were at Naples supplied them with food as much as they could, and sent around to the other parts of Italy to collect money to sustain them. . . . Even the Dominican Brotherhood acted mercifully toward them. . . .

Source: Jacob R. Marcus, ed., *The Jew in the Medieval World: A Source Book, 315–1791* (Cincinnati: Sinai Press, 1938), 51–55.

Map 11.3 The Dynastic Marriages That Encircled France

Through skillfully arranging the marriages of their sons and daughters, Ferdinand of Aragon and Isabella of Castile managed to completely surround the rival kingdom of France with a network of alliances.

the Muslims from the peninsula. There was little reason to assume that this region would become one of the greatest powers in Europe, the rival of France.

That rise to power began with a wedding. In 1469 Isabella, who later would become queen of Castile (r. 1474–1504), married Ferdinand, who later would be king of Aragon (r. 1479–1516). The objective of this arranged marriage was to solidify an alliance between the two kingdoms, not to unify them, but in 1479 Castile and Aragon were combined into the kingdom of Spain. Of the two, Castile was the larger, with a population of perhaps six million, and the richer because of the government-supported sheep-raising industry called the *Mesta*. Aragon had less than a million people and was a hybrid of three very distinct regions that had nothing in common except that they shared the same king. Together Isabella and Ferdinand, each still ruling their own kingdoms, at least partially subdued the rebellious aristocracy and built up a bureaucracy of well-educated middle-class lawyers and priests to manage the administration of the government.

The Christian kings of Iberia had long aspired to making the entire peninsula Christian. In 1492 the armies of Isabella and Ferdinand defeated the last remaining Iberian

Muslim kingdom of Granada. While celebrating the victory over Islam, the monarchs made two momentous decisions. The first was to rid Spain of Jews as well as Muslims. Isabella and Ferdinand decreed that within six months all Jews must either convert to Christianity or leave. To enforce conformity to Christianity among the converted Jews who did not leave, the king and queen authorized an ecclesiastical tribunal, the Spanish Inquisition, to investigate the sincerity of conversions. The second decision was Isabella's alone. She financed a voyage by a Genoese sea captain, Christopher Columbus, to sail west into the Atlantic in an attempt to reach India and China. Isabella's intention seems to have been to outflank the Muslim kingdoms of the Middle East and find allies in Asia. As we shall see in the next chapter, Columbus's voyage had consequences more far-reaching than Isabella's intentions, adding to the crown of Castile immense lands in the Americas.

Despite the diversity of their kingdoms, Isabella and Ferdinand made Spain a great power. The clever dynastic marriages they arranged for their children allowed Spain to encircle rival France and established the framework for the diplomatic relations among European states for the next century and a half (see Map 11.3). Their eldest daughter and, after her death, her sister were married to the king of Portugal. Their son and another daughter, Joanna, married offspring of Mary of Burgundy and the Emperor Maximilian I of the Holy Roman Empire. Joanna's marriage produced a son, Charles V, who amassed extraordinary power. He succeeded to the Habsburg lands of Burgundy, inherited the crowns of Castile and Aragon (r. 1516–1556), was elected Holy Roman Emperor (r. 1519–1558), ruled over the Spanish conquests in Italy, and was the emperor of the Indies, which included all of Spanish Central and South America. This was the greatest accumulation of territories by a European ruler since Charlemagne. The encirclement of France was completed with the wedding of Isabella and Ferdinand's daughter Catherine of Aragon to the Prince of Wales and, after his death, to his brother, King Henry VIII (r. 1509–1547) of England.

The Holy Roman Empire: The Costs of Decentralization

Like Spain, the Holy Roman Empire saw powerful France as its most dangerous enemy. And when the French king's invasion of Italy initiated the Italian Wars, it launched a struggle that pitted the empire and Spain against France for the next 200 years. Members of the Habsburg family had been elected to the throne of the Holy Roman Empire since 1438. Emperor Maximilian I (r. 1493–1519) wed Mary, the daughter of Charles the Bold of Burgundy, and although they were not able to preserve all of Burgundy from the French, they did keep substantial parts, including the extremely rich Netherlands.

In an era of coolly calculating monarchs, Maximilian cut an odd figure. Like his father-in-law, Charles the Bold, he loved chivalry and enjoyed nothing more than to play the role of a knight leading his men into battle. The problem was that he was not very good in that role. His military adventures led to a series of disasters, often at the hands of the rough Swiss mercenaries who were experts in using the pike (a long pole with a metal spearhead) to cut up aristocratic cavalrymen and who passionately hated everything about the autocratic Habsburgs who had once ruled their lands. Maximilian also came under the influence of Italian Renaissance culture and imagined himself another Caesar with a special mission to reconquer Italy for the Holy Roman Empire. The French invasion of Italy in 1494 drew him into the quagmire of Italian affairs as he attempted to counter French influence there. His erratic military policies, however, could not quite keep pace with these imperial ambitions.

Maximilian's inability to execute a consistent military policy in Italy was a consequence of the highly decentralized nature of the empire. Unlike the other European monarchs who inherited their thrones at the death of their predecessors, the emperor was selected by seven electors, who even after an election exercised considerable independent power. The German part of the Holy Roman Empire, home

to 15 to 20 million people, was composed of some 300 sovereign and quasi-sovereign principalities and free cities (legally exempt from direct imperial rule). Besides the emperor, only a few institutions served to unify the empire. Most important was the imperial diet, an assembly that included the seven electors, other princes, and representatives of the imperial free cities. The imperial diet was established during the fifteenth century to control the relentless feuding among the German princes, but it often became instead a forum for resisting the emperor.

Maximilian's reign produced some limited reforms. These included a moratorium on feuds, a Supreme Court to impose ancient Roman law throughout the German-speaking portions of the empire, a graduated property and income tax, and eventually an imperial council to exercise executive functions in the absence of the emperor. In practice, however, these institutions worked only to the degree that the emperor and German princes cooperated. The empire remained a fractured, dissent-ridden jumble with no real unity. Compared to the centralizing monarchies in France, Spain, and England, or even to the better managed among the Italian city-states such as tiny Venice, which recurrently defeated Maximilian in battle, the empire under Maximilian was little more than a glorious-sounding name.

England: From Civil War to Stability Under the Tudors

At the end of the Hundred Years' War in 1453, the English crown was defeated. Thousands of disbanded mercenaries were let loose in England and enlisted with one quarreling side or the other in feuds among aristocratic families. The mercenaries brought to England the evil habits of pillage, murder, and violence they had previously practiced in the wars with France. King Henry VI (r. 1422–1461) suffered from bouts of madness that made him unfit to rule and unable to control the disorder. Under the tensions caused by defeat and revolt, the royal family fractured into the two houses of Lancaster and York, which fought a vicious civil war, now known as the Wars of the Roses (1455–1485) from the red and white roses used to identify members of the two opposing sides.

After decades of bloody conflict, the cynical but able Richard III (r. 1483–1485) usurped the throne from his 12-year-old nephew Edward V and had Edward and his brother imprisoned in the Tower of London, where they were murdered, perhaps on Richard's orders. Richard's apparent cruelty and his scandalous intent to marry Edward's young sister, now heir to the throne, precipitated open defections against him.

The Tower of London

When Henry Tudor challenged Richard, many nobles flocked to Henry's banner. At the Battle of Bosworth Field (1485), Richard was slain and his crown discovered on the field of battle. His naked corpse was dragged off and buried in an unmarked grave.

When Henry Tudor became King Henry VII (r. 1485–1509), there was little reason to believe that exhausted England could again become a major force in European events. It took years of patient effort for Henry to become safe on his own throne. He revived the Court of Star Chamber as an instrument of royal will to punish unruly nobles who had long bribed and intimidated their way out of trouble with the courts. Because the king's own hand-picked councilors served as judges, Henry could guarantee that the court system became more equitable and obedient to his wishes. Henry confiscated the lands of the rebellious lords, thereby increasing his own income, and he prohibited all private armies except those that served his interests. By managing his administration efficiently, eliminating unnecessary expenses, and staying out of war, Henry governed without the need to call on Parliament for increased revenues.

England was still a backward country and, with fewer than three million people, a fraction of the size of France. By nourishing an alliance with newly unified Spain, Henry was able to bring England back into European affairs. When his son Henry VIII succeeded to the throne, the Tudor dynasty was more secure than any of its predecessors and England more stable than it had ever been before. By the reign of Henry VII's granddaughter, Elizabeth I (r. 1558–1603), England could boast of a splendid Renaissance court and a fleet that would make it a world power.

CHRONOLOGY

The Early Modern European State System

1422–1461	Reign of Charles VII of France
1455–1485	Wars of the Roses in England
1461–1483	Reign of Louis XI of France
1474–1504	Reign of Isabella of Castile
1479–1516	Reign of Ferdinand of Aragon
1479	Unification of Spain
1483–1485	Reign of Richard III of England
1485–1509	Reign of Henry VII of England
1492	Conquest of Granada; expulsion of the Jews from Spain; voyage of Christopher Columbus
1493–1519	Reign of Maximilian I, Holy Roman Emperor
1494–1530	The Italian Wars
1515–1547	Reign of Francis I of France
1516–1556	Reign of Charles I, king of Spain, who also became Charles V, Holy Roman Emperor (1519–1558)

The Origins of Modern Historical and Political Thought

The revival of the monarchies of western Europe and the loss of the independence of the Italian city-states forced a rethinking of politics. As in so many other fields, the Florentines led the way. In an attempt to understand their own troubled city-state, they analyzed politics by making historical comparisons between one kind of government and another and by carefully observing current events. Two crucial figures in these developments, Francesco Guicciardini and Niccolò Machiavelli, had both served Florence as diplomats, an experience that was crucial in forming their views.

History: The Search for Causes

During the fifteenth century there were two kinds of historians. The first kind consisted of chroniclers who kept records of the important events in their city or principality. The chroniclers recorded a great deal of factual information in the simple form of one-occurrence-after-another. In so doing they established chronologies, which meant they arranged history according to a sequence of dates. But they lacked any sense of how one event caused another, and they failed to interpret the meaning and consequences of the decisions leaders and other people had made.

The second kind of historians consisted of the humanists. Petrarch established that the fundamental principle for writing humanist history was to maintain historical distance—the sense that the past was past and had to be reconstructed in its own terms. The most dangerous historical error in writing history became anachronism, that is, imposing present sensibilities and understandings on the past. Before the Renaissance the most common version of anachronism was for historians to interpret pre-Christian history in the light of Christian understandings of God's plan for humanity. In contrast to that approach, humanist historians attempted to offer explanations for why things had happened in human terms. When they interpreted past events, they tried to respect the limitations people had faced. For example, they understood that the moral code of the Roman orator and senator Cicero, who died two generations before Jesus was born, derived from Greek philosophy and Roman ethics rather than a premonition of Christianity. The humanists' interest in rhetoric, however, led them to make moral judgments about the past in an attempt to encourage morality among their readers. Thus, they were prone to pull especially compelling instances of good or bad conduct out of the historical context in which it had taken place and to compare it with other cases. For example, they might compare the behavior of the citizens in fifth-century-B.C.E. Athens with the actions of citizens in fifteenth-century Florence.

The shock of the Italian Wars that began in 1494 stimulated a quest for understanding the causes of Italy's fall and prompted a new kind of history writing. The first person to write a successful history in the new vein was Francesco Guicciardini (1483–1540). Born to a well-placed Florentine family, educated in a humanist school, and experienced as a diplomat, governor, and adviser to the Medicis, Guicciardini combined literary skill and practical political experience. Besides collecting information about contemporary events, Guicciardini kept a record of how his own thoughts and values evolved in response to what he observed. One of the hallmarks of his work was that as he analyzed the motives of others, he engaged in self-scrutiny and self-criticism.

From this habit of criticizing himself and others, Guicciardini developed a strong interpretive framework for his histories. His masterpiece, *The History of Italy* (1536–1540), was the first account of events that occurred across the entire Italian peninsula. In many respects, this book originated the idea that Italy is more than just a geographical term and has had a common historical experience. Like the humanist historians, Guicciardini saw human causes for historical events rather than the hidden hand of God, but he refined the understanding of causation through his psychological insights. He suggested, for example, that emotions mattered more than rational calculation and noted that nothing ever turns out quite as anticipated.

Political Thought: Considering the End Result

Guicciardini's contemporary and Florentine compatriot Niccolò Machiavelli (1469–1527) also wrote histories, but he is best known as a political theorist. Trained as a humanist, he lacked the personal wealth and family connections that allowed Guicciardini to move as a matter of birthright in high social and political circles. As seen in the story that opened this chapter, Machiavelli had worked as a diplomat and military official but was exiled for complicity in a plot against the Medici family, who had retaken Florence in 1512. While in exile he wrote a book of advice for the Medicis in the vain hope that they would give him back his job. They probably never read his little book, *The Prince* (1513), but it became a classic in political thought. In it he encouraged rulers to understand the underlying principles of political power, which differed from the personal morality expected of those who were not rulers. He thought it was important for a prince to appear to be a moral person, but Machiavelli pointed out that the successful prince might sometimes be obliged to be immoral in order to protect the interests of the state. How would the prince know when this might be the case?

DOCUMENT

Machiavelli's *The Prince*

DOCUMENT

Machiavelli on the Source of Liberty

Niccolò Machiavelli is best known for his book, The Prince, *which offers advice to princes on how to rule. His more important study, however, was* The Discourses of the First Decade of Livy *(1516–1519), which discussed how a republic should be governed. In this book he asked how the ancient Roman Republic managed to be both free and powerful. His startling answer was that all liberty and greatness in republics comes from class conflict.*

It seems to me that those who criticize the conflicts between the nobles and the plebeians [the lower classes of ancient Rome] condemn those very things which were the primary cause of Roman liberty, and that they pay more attention to the noises and cries raised by such quarrels than to the good effects that they brought forth; nor do they consider that in every republic there are two different inclinations: that of the people and that of the upper class, and that all the laws which are made in favor of liberty are born of the conflict between the two, as one can easily see from what happened in Rome. . . .

And the desires of free peoples are very rarely pernicious to liberty, for they arise from being oppressed or from the suspicion of future oppression. And should these opinions prove to be mistaken, there is the remedy of public meetings, in which some good man of influence may rise up and make a speech showing them that they are mistaken.

Source: *The Portable Machiavelli,* translated by Peter Bondanella and Mark Musa (Penguin Books, 1970), 183–84.

Machiavelli's answer was that "necessity" forced political decisions to go against normal morality. The prince "must consider the end result," which meant that his highest obligation was preserving the very existence of the state, which had been entrusted to him and which provided security for all citizens of the state. This obligation was higher even than his obligation to religion.

Machiavelli's *The Prince* has sometimes been considered a blueprint for tyrants. However, as his more learned and serious work, *The Discourses of the First Decade of Livy* (1516–1519), makes clear, Machiavelli himself preferred a free republic over a despotic princely government. In some ways, *The Discourses* is an even more radical work than *The Prince* because it suggests that class conflict is the source of political liberty: "In every republic there are two different inclinations: that of the people and that of the upper class, and . . . all the laws which are made in favor of liberty are born of the conflict between the two."[8] In this passage,

Machiavelli suggested that political turmoil was not necessarily a bad thing, because it was by provoking conflict that the lower classes prevented the upper classes from acting like tyrants.

In all his works, Machiavelli sought to understand the dynamics behind political events. To do this, he theorized that human events were the product of the interaction between two forces. One force was fortune, a term derived from the name of the ancient Roman goddess Fortuna. Fortune stood for all things beyond human control and could be equated with luck or chance. Machiavelli depicted fortune as extremely powerful, like an irresistible flood that swept all before it or like the headstrong goddess who determined the fate of men. Fortune controlled perhaps half of all human events. The problem with fortune was its changeability and unpredictability: "since Fortune changes and men remain set in their ways, men will succeed when the two are in harmony and fail when they are not in accord." How could rulers or even simple citizens put themselves in harmony with fortune and predict its shifts? The answer could be found in the characteristics of the second force, virtue, which he understood as deriving from the Roman concept of *virtus,* literally "manliness." The best description of virtue could be found in the code expected of an ancient Roman warrior: strength, loyalty, and courage. If a man possessed these traits he was most likely to be able to confront the unpredictable. As Machiavelli put it, "I am certainly convinced of this: that it is better to be impetuous than cautious."[9] The man possessing virtue, therefore, looked for opportunities to take control of events before they took control of him. In that way he put himself in harmony with fortune.

Through Guicciardini's analysis of human motivations and Machiavelli's attempt to discover the hidden forces behind events, history and political thought moved in a new direction. The key to understanding history and politics was in the details of human events. To Guicciardini these details provided clues to the psychology of leaders. To Machiavelli they revealed the hidden mechanisms of chance and planning that governed not just political decisions but all human events.

Conclusion

The Politics of Culture

The Renaissance began simply enough as an attempt to imitate the Latin style of the best ancient Latin authors and orators. Within a generation, however, humanists and artists pushed this narrowly technical literary project into a full-scale attempt to refashion human society on the model of ancient cultures. Reading about the ancients and looking at their works of art provoked comparisons with contemporary Renaissance society. The result was the development of a critical approach to the past and present. The critical approach was accompanied by an enhanced historical sensibility, which transformed the idea of the West from one defined primarily by religious identification with Christianity to one forged by a common historical experience.

During the sixteenth century, western Europeans absorbed the critical-historical methods of the Renaissance and turned them in new directions. As shown in the next chapter, Spanish and Portuguese sailors encountered previously unknown cultures in the Americas and only vaguely known ones in Africa and Asia. Because of the Renaissance, those who thought and wrote about these strange new cultures did so with the perspective of antiquity in mind. As shown in Chapter 13, in northern Europe the critical historical methods of the humanists were used to better understand the historical sources of Christianity, especially the Bible. With that development, Christianity began to take on new shades of meaning, and many thoughtful Christians attempted to make the practices of the Church conform more closely to the Bible. The humanist approach to religion led down a path that permanently divided Christians into contending camps over the interpretation of Scripture, breaking apart the hard-won unity of the Roman Catholic West.

Suggestions for Further Reading

For a comprehensive listing of suggested readings, please go to www.ablongman.com/levack2e/chapter11

Baxandall, Michael. *Painting and Experience in Fifteenth Century Italy: A Primer in the Social History of Pictorial Style.* 1988. A fascinating study of how the daily social experiences of Florentine bankers and churchgoers influenced how these individuals saw Renaissance paintings and how painters responded to the viewers' experience. One of the best books on Italian painting.

Brown, Howard M. *Music in the Renaissance.* 1976. Dated but still the best general study of Renaissance music.

Brown, Patricia Fortini. *Art and Life in Renaissance Venice.* 1997. A delightful study about how art fit into the daily lives and homes of the Venetian upper classes.

Brucker, Gene. *Florence: The Golden Age, 1138–1737.* 1998. A brilliant, beautifully illustrated history by the most prominent American historian of Florence.

Burke, Peter. *The Italian Renaissance.* 1999. A concise and readable synthesis of the most recent research.

Hale, J. R. *Renaissance Europe, 1480–1520.* 2000. A witty, engaging, and enlightening study of Europe during the formation of the early modern state system. Strong on establishing the material and social limitations of Renaissance society.

King, Margaret L. *Women of the Renaissance.* 1991. The best general study of women in Renaissance Europe. It is especially strong on female intellectuals and women's education.

Kohl, Benjamin G., and Alison Andrews Smith, eds. *Major Problems in the History of the Italian Renaissance.* 1995. A useful collection of articles and short studies of major historical problems in the study of the Renaissance.

Martines, Lauro. *Power and Imagination: City-States in Renaissance Italy.* 1988. An excellent general survey that is strong on class conflicts and patronage.

Nauert, Charles G., Jr. *Humanism and the Culture of Renaissance Europe.* 1995. The best survey of humanism for students new to the subject. It is clear and comprehensive.

Skinner, Quentin. *Machiavelli: A Very Short Introduction.* 2000. This is the place to begin in the study of Machiavelli. Always clear and precise, this is a beautiful little book.

Stephens, John. *The Italian Renaissance: The Origins of Intellectual and Artistic Change Before the Reformation.* 1990. A stimulating analysis of how cultural change took place.

Vasari, Giorgio. *The Lives of the Artists.* 1998. Written by a sixteenth-century Florentine who was himself a prominent artist, this series of artistic biographies captures the spirit of Renaissance society.

Notes

1. *The Portable Machiavelli,* trans. and ed. Peter Bondanella and Mark Musa (1979), 67–69.

2. Baldesar Castiglione, *The Book of the Courtier,* trans. Charles S. Singleton (1959), 43.

3. Giovanni Villani, *Cronica,* vol. 7 (1823), p. 52. Translation by the authors.

4. Agostino di Colloredo, "Chroniche friulane, 1508–18," *Pagine friulane* 2 (1889), 6. Translation by the authors.

5. Francesco Petrarca, "Letter to the Shade of Cicero," in Kenneth R. Bartlett, ed., *The Civilization of the Italian Renaissance: A Sourcebook* (1992), 31.

6. Quoted in Margaret L. King, *Women of the Renaissance* (1991), 197.

7. "Laura Cereta to Bibulus Sempronius: Defense of the Liberal Instruction of Women," in Margaret King and Alfred Rabil, eds., *Her Immaculate Hand: Selected Words by and About the Women Humanists of Quattrocento Italy* (1983), 82.

8. *The Portable Machiavelli,* 183.

9. Ibid., 161–162.

The West and the World: The Significance of Global Encounters, 1450–1650

Ｏn a hot October day in 1492, Christopher Columbus and his men, dressed in heavy armor, clanked onto the beach of an island in the Bahamas. The captain and his crew had been at sea sailing west from the Canary Islands for five weeks, propelled by winds they thought would take them straight to Asia. As the ships under Columbus's command vainly searched among the islands of the Caribbean for the rich ports of Asia, Columbus thought he must be in India and thus called the natives he met "Indians." At another point he thought he might be among the Mongols of central Asia, which he described in his journal as the "people of the Great Khan." Both of Columbus's guesses about his location were incorrect, but they have left a revealing linguistic legacy in terms still in use: "Indians" for the native Americans, and both "cannibals" and "Caribbean" from Columbus's inconsistent spellings of Khan. Columbus believed that the people he called the Cannibals or Caribs ate human flesh. But he got that information—also incorrect—from their enemies. Thus began one of the most lasting misunderstandings from Columbus's first voyage.

Historians know very little about the natives' first thoughts of the arrival of their foreign visitors, but they know that the effects of the arrival were catastrophic. Within a few generations the Caribs almost completely died out, replaced by African slaves who worked the plantations of European masters.

Western civilization at the end of the fifteenth century hardly seemed on the verge of encircling the globe with outposts and colonies. Its kingdoms had barely been able to reorganize themselves sufficiently for self-defense, let alone world exploration and foreign conquest. The Venetian and Genoese colonies in the Mediterranean were retreating from the advancing Ottoman Turks, who would continue to occupy the Balkans for at least four more centuries. The Ottoman threat was so great that all of southern Europe was

CHAPTER OUTLINE

- Europeans in Africa

- Europeans in the Americas

- Europeans in Asia

- The Beginnings of the Global System

The Encounter of Three Cultures On this wooden bottle painted in the Incan style about 1650, an African drummer leads a procession, followed by a Spanish trumpeter and an Incan official. The mixing of cultures that occurred after the arrival of the Spanish and Portuguese distinguished the Americas from other civilizations.

on the defensive. And the hostilities had blocked the traditional trade routes to Asia, which had stimulated the great medieval economic expansion of Europe. Scandinavian voyages to North America had ceased in the fourteenth century, and the isolated Western outpost of Christianity in Greenland vanished under the onslaught of advancing ice by the middle of the fifteenth. In comparison with the Ottoman Empire or Ming China, Europe's puny, impoverished states seemed more prone to quarreling among themselves than to seeking expanded horizons.

Nevertheless, by 1500 Europeans could be found fighting and trading in Africa, the Americas, and Asia. A mere fifty years later, Europeans had destroyed the two greatest civilizations in the Americas, had begun the forced migration of Africans to the Americas through the slave trade, and had opened trading posts throughout South and East Asia.

Before 1500 the West, identified by its languages, religions, agricultural technology, literature, folklore, music, art, and common intellectual tradition that stretched back to pre-Christian antiquity, was largely confined to Europe and the Middle East. After 1500, European travelers and missionaries began to export Western culture and technology to the rest of the world and to be greatly influenced themselves by the cultures they encountered abroad, especially after large numbers of European settlers moved to the Americas.

After the sixteenth century, European culture could be found in many distant lands, and western European languages and forms of Christianity were adopted by or forced upon other peoples. The West was now more of an idea than a place, a certain kind of culture that thrived in many different environments. As western Europeans came under the influence of the far-flung cultures they visited, Europe itself was transformed into a much more cosmopolitan region than it had ever been before. The European voyages integrated the globe biologically and economically. Microbes, animals, and plants that had once been isolated were now transported throughout the world. Because the Europeans possessed the ships for transport and the guns for coercion, they became the dominant players in international trade, even in places thousands of miles from the European homeland. The question raised by this first phase of the European global encounters is, how were both the West and the rest of the world transformed?

- Why did the European incursions into sub-Saharan Africa lead to the vast migration of Africans to the Americas as slaves?
- How did the arrival of Europeans in the Americas transform native cultures and life?
- Why was the European encounter with Asian civilizations far less disruptive than those in Africa and the Americas?
- How was the world tied together in a global biological and economic system?

Europeans in Africa

- Why did the European incursions into sub-Saharan Africa lead to the vast migration of Africans to the Americas as slaves?

Geographers of the ancient world, writing in Greek and Latin, had accumulated a substantial knowledge about all of North Africa, but they were almost completely ignorant of the region south of the Sahara desert. Medieval writers remained equally ill-informed, reporting that sub-Saharan Africa was populated by man-eaters, "great giants of twenty-eight foot long . . . and they eat more gladly man's flesh than any other flesh," and Amazons, warrior women who cut off one breast to facilitate archery.

In fact, the interior of sub-Saharan Africa had been governed for centuries by highly developed kingdoms and boasted numerous wealthy cities. By the fifteenth century, Muslim contacts with sub-Saharan Africa made it clear that the region was a rich source of gold and slaves. In search of these, Europeans, especially the Portuguese, began to journey down the west coast of Africa. Enabled by new developments in ship technology, the Europeans were capable of making long sea voyages. European settlers founded colonies in the Atlantic islands off the west coast of Africa, establishing precedents for colonies that would later be installed in the Americas.

Sub-Saharan Africa Before the Europeans Arrived

During the Middle Ages a number of kingdoms that emulated ancient Egyptian forms of rulership arose south of the Sahara desert. Some kingdoms boasted large cities and consisted of as many as a million inhabitants who were subjects of strongly centralized regimes. The kingdoms were administered by public officials who could be transferred, demoted, or promoted according to the king's will in a bureaucratic system that paralleled what the European states had achieved.

For Europeans, the principal attraction to Africa were reports of its rich deposits of gold. These reports came from the Muslim kingdom of Mali, a landlocked empire between the Upper Senegal and Niger Rivers, to the north of the Guinea coast. The source of Mali's wealth was its monopoly of the gold caravans that carried the coveted metal from the fabled city of Timbuktu across the Sahara to the gold-greedy Mediterranean. The king of Mali, known as the Mansa, never owned the gold mines, the location of which was a closely kept secret, but he controlled the gold market. The

IMAGE

The Catalan Map

Map 12.1   The Maghreb and West Africa, Fourteenth Century

Long before the arrival of the Portuguese via sea routes, caravans of camels crisscrossed the Sahara desert during the fourteenth century, linking the sources of gold in Mali with the Maghreb (the coast of northwest Africa) and the seaports of the Mediterranean. The greatest medieval Arabic traveler, Ibn Battuta (1304–1368/69), crossed the Sahara and spent more than a year in Mali. He left the most extensive account of medieval West Africa.

gold from the mines went to the Mansa, whose agents traded it in distant lands for luxury goods. The Mansa's power rested on his cavalry, which by the middle of the fourteenth century had spread the rule of Mali from the Gambia and lower Senegal Rivers to the West through the Niger valley to the south.

The wealth of the Mansa became legendary after Mansa Musa (r. 1312–1337) conducted a spectacular pilgrimage to the Muslim holy city of Mecca in 1324. Mansa Musa made a magnificently opulent impression. A gold bird sat above the parasol that shaded him from the sun, and he carried a gilded staff, wore a goldskull cap, strung a gold quiver over his shoulder, and affixed a gold scabbard to his waist. The pilgrimage took more than a year, and Mansa Musa was so generous that his trip was remembered for centuries in Egypt, where he stayed for three months. He gave out so much gold that Egypt suffered a disastrous inflation of prices. Traveling with as many as a hundred camels, each loaded with 300 pounds of gold, the Mansa gave whole ingots of gold to officials along the way and to religious shrines he visited.

By 1400, however, the kingdom of Mali was in decline. Internal power struggles had split apart the once-vast empire. In 1482, when the Portuguese founded a gold-trading post at Elmina, some sixty miles west of the mouth of the Volta, they had to negotiate with a ruler called the Karamansa, whose title echoed the past glories of the Mansa of Mali but whose power was a mere shadow of what the rulers of Mali exercised during the fourteenth century (see Map 12.1).

Influenced by Mali, the forest kingdoms of Guinea were built on a prosperous urban society and extensive trading networks. Benin was a particularly great city, which European travelers compared favorably with the principal European cities of the time. The towns of Guinea held regu-

lar markets, similar to the periodic fairs of Europe, and carefully scheduled them so they would not compete with each other. The staples of the long-distance trade routes in this region were high-value luxury goods, especially imported cloth, kola nuts (a mild stimulant popular in Muslim countries), metalwork such as cutlasses, ivory, and of course gold. For money, African traders used cowrie shells, brought all the way from the Indian Ocean.

Unlike the kingdoms of the western sub-Sahara, which tended to be Muslim, mountainous Ethiopia was predominantly Christian. In fact, Europeans saw Ethiopians as potential allies against Islam. The Roman Catholic pope sent a delegation to Ethiopia in 1316, and Ethiopian embassies occasionally appeared in Italy and Portugal during the fifteenth century. Diplomatic contacts between Rome and Ethiopia intensified at the time of the Council of Florence in 1439, which attempted to unify Christianity in defense against the onslaught of the Muslim Ottoman Turks. Learned Ethiopian churchmen became known in western Europe and created the impression that Ethiopia was an abundant land peopled by pious Christians.

Conditions during the later Middle Ages tended to confirm this image of Ethiopia. Threatened by Muslim invaders in 1270, the Ethiopian kingdom created a powerful army, rumors of which tantalized European Christians who sought allies against Islam. As the armies expanded Ethiopian power to the south and east, missionaries proselytized among the conquered peoples and helped unify the kingdom. Ethiopian expansion greatly enriched the kingdom through the control of trade in ivory, gold, slaves, and

379

DOCUMENT

The Kings of West Africa

During the late sixteenth century a Dutch merchant, Pieter de Mareers, traveled to the kingdom of Guinea. During the sixteenth century what was known as the Gold Coast, now modern Ghana, was divided into more than a dozen states, some monarchies, some governed by collective councils. In this account Mareers described one of the more powerful kings.

The Kings are elected by the common people and by the highest vote; for the Kingdom does not devolve on friends or descendants, and even someone's children do not inherit. So, when the King is dead, they elect another to govern them and possess the Kingdom, and he takes possession of the Court, together with all that is in it. For his inauguration he must in the first place buy many Cows and much Palm wine and give these to his Subjects as a present; for they very much love a King who often fetes them, but hate a King who is frugal and keen on accumulating Gold. They will not respect such a King and he is not loved by the common people: they bear him great hatred and jealousy, seeking every means of taking action against him, in order to drive him out and choose a better person who is to their liking. . . .

His wives live with him in his Palace, and some also outside the Court; but these are the oldest wives, whom he does not love all that much and who can no longer please him. To each of the young and beautiful wives he normally gives separate living quarters, within his Palace, in order that they may serve him the better and [he] may have his comfort. These women do their husband the King great service and each fetes him as best she can in order to be loved by him; so he does not lack any services or comfort. Each woman has her own goods and wealth, and each also maintains and brings up her own children. Those who are the favourites of the King [do not] stand in want of anything. Whenever these women go out they lean on the shoulders of other women who serve them and are their Slaves; likewise the children are carried on the shoulders of other blacks or Slaves of the King.

Source: *Pieter de Mareers: Description and Historical Account of the Gold Kingdom of Guines* (1602), edited by A. Van Dantzig and A. Jones (1987), pp. 94–97. British Academy.

civet, a highly prized musky perfume. Portuguese visitors were duly impressed by the splendor of the emperor of Ethiopia, the Negus, who traveled with 2,000 attendants and 50,000 mules to carry provisions and tents.

By the early sixteenth century, the Ethiopian kingdom had become overextended. In the 1520s and 1530s Muslims attacked deep into the Ethiopian heartland, raiding and burning the wealthy Ethiopian monasteries. The raids severely weakened the power of the Negus. By destroying relics and religious images, the Muslims eradicated much of the great artistic heritage of Ethiopia. Ethiopia survived with the help of a Portuguese expeditionary force, but it was hobbled by competing Christian warlords and a weak central power, and it never regained its previous strength.

During the fifteenth and sixteenth centuries when European contacts with the sub-Sahara dramatically expanded, the once-strong kingdoms were either in decline or engaged in protracted struggles with regional rivals. The Europeans arrived at precisely the moment when they could take advantage of the weaknesses produced by internal African conflicts.

European Voyages Along the African Coast

Although sub-Saharan Africa represented something of a mystery to Europeans, merchants from Italy, Catalonia, Castile, and Portugal had long shown interest in the ports of the Maghreb, the collective name for the present-day regions of Morocco, Algeria, and Tunisia on the Mediterranean coast of North Africa. There they brought wool and woolen textiles, wine, dye stuffs, and clandestine items such as weapons, which they traded for various commodities, most significantly gold. Since at least the mid-thirteenth century, the Maghreb had been famous as the northern terminus of the gold caravans from Mali. In the thirteenth and fourteenth centuries, European traders obtained gold in the Maghreb in exchange for silver mined in Europe. They then resold the gold in the ports along the northern shore of the Mediterranean for more silver than they had originally paid to buy the gold. With the handsome silver profits made in the gold trade, merchants provided a steady supply that encouraged the general adoption of gold coinage throughout much of southern Europe. Gold was highly prized in Europe largely because it was rare in comparison to silver, and by the laws of supply and demand the commodity that is scarce is more valuable.

To gain more direct access to the sources of gold, European traders occasionally crossed the Sahara with camel caravans—the "ships of the desert." For example, the Florentine merchant Benedetto Dei told of traveling in 1470 as far as Timbuktu, where he saw many examples of European textiles on the local market. The efficient camel caravans created a vast trading network that stretched from Mali and Morocco in the west of Africa into central Asia,

The Lure of Gold

From the first Portuguese expeditions along the coast of West Africa to the extensive European explorations of the Americas, a persistent lure was finding gold. Columbus and the conquistadores seemed obsessed with finding gold. This illustration from the sixteenth century depicts North American native techniques for collecting gold, which involved digging in the mud of river bottoms and then sifting the soil to look for gold nuggets. Similar techniques were employed in Africa.

completely bypassing the Mediterranean. But Europeans had little hope of regularly using the "sea of sand" routes across North Africa because of the hostility of Muslim inhabitants who were wary about foreign interlopers, especially Christian ones.

The alternative for Europeans was to outflank the Muslims by crossing the sea of water. As early as the thirteenth century, European voyagers ventured down the west coast of Africa into uncharted waters. In 1291 the Vivaldi brothers left Genoa with the goal of circumnavigating Africa to reach the Indies. But their galleys were adapted to the relatively calm waters of the Mediterranean and were ill-suited for the voyage on the heavy seas of the Atlantic. Such ships, which required large crews of oarsmen, were easily swamped in the Atlantic, and the long coastline of West Africa lacked protective harbors for refuge from storms. The Vivaldi expedition disappeared without a trace.

New Maritime Technology

The disadvantages of Mediterranean galleys were surmounted during the fifteenth century through changes in the technology of ocean sailing. The Iberian peninsula (the land of present-day Portugal and Spain), situated between the Mediterranean and the Atlantic, was uniquely located to develop a hybrid ship that combined features of Mediterranean and Atlantic designs. The initial impulse for developing the shipping technology was to facilitate trade between the Mediterranean and northern Europe via the Atlantic. The resulting changes, however, also made possible much more ambitious voyages into the unknown southern regions.

The Iberians modified the cog design, the dominant ship in the Atlantic, by adding extra masts and creating a new kind of rigging that combined the square sails of Atlantic ships, suitable for sailing in the same direction as the wind was blowing, with the triangular "lateen" sails of Mediterranean galleys, which permitted sailing into the wind. The result was a ship that could sail in a variety of winds, carry large cargoes, be managed by a small crew, and be defended by guns mounted in the castle superstructure. These hybrid three-mast ships, called caravels°, appeared about 1450, and for the next 200 years Europeans sailed ships of this same basic design on long ocean voyages to the very ends of the Earth.

Also assisting European navigators were other technological innovations, the fruit of late medieval Mediterranean seafaring. The compass provided an approximate indicator of direction, and the astrolabe and naked-eye celestial navigation made it possible to estimate latitudes. Books of sailing directions, called portolanos°, included charts and descriptions of ports and recorded the location of dangerous shoals and safe harbors for future voyages. The advances in maritime technology made it possible for Europeans motivated by economic need and religious fervor to sail wherever they wanted.

Technology alone, however, does not explain the extent of the European voyages because there had been great ocean navigating efforts before. For centuries Polynesians had successfully navigated their way across the Pacific Ocean. The Vikings had regularly crossed the North Atlantic from the tenth to fourteenth centuries, and the Chinese had engaged in extensive exploratory voyages throughout the Indian Ocean earlier in the fifteenth century. The explanation for

Early Caravels
The caravel was typical of the hybrid ship developed during the fifteenth century on the Iberian peninsula. The ship on the lower right is rigged with a lateen sail on its main mast.

the voyages must be sought in the European Christian imperative to profit from an expanded trade network and to outflank the Muslims who blocked the eastern trade routes.

New Colonialism

During the fifteenth century, European colonialism departed from the patterns of the past. Mediterranean colonies established during the Crusades of the twelfth and thirteenth centuries had relied on native inhabitants to produce commodities that could be expropriated by the colonizers. These were either aristocratic colonies in which a few warriors occupied castles to dominate the native population or mercantile colonies built around a trading post for foreign merchants.

As Europeans ventured into the Atlantic more frequently and expanded their contacts with sub-Saharan Africa, they established new patterns of colonization. In search of fertile lands for agriculture, Castile and Portugal founded colonies in the Canary Islands, the Madeira archipelago, the Azores, and the Cape Verde Islands. The climate of these islands was similar to that of the Mediterranean and invited the cultivation of typical Mediterranean crops, such as grains and

sugar cane, but the islands lacked a native labor force. When Europeans arrived, the Canaries had few inhabitants and the other islands were uninhabited. In response to the labor shortage, two new types of colonies emerged, both of which were later introduced into the Americas.

The first new type of colony during this period was the settler colony°. The settler colony derived from the medieval, feudal model of government, in which a private person obtained a license from a king to seize an island or some part of an island. The king supplied financial support and legal authority for the expedition. In return the settler promised to recognize the king as his lord and occasionally to pay a fee after the settlement was successful. The kings of Castile and Portugal issued such licenses for the exploitation of Atlantic islands. The actual expeditions to colonize these islands were private enterprises, and adventurers from various parts of Europe vied for a license from any king who would grant them one. For example, the first European settlement in the Canary Islands was led by a Norman knight, Jean de Béthencourt, who could not obtain sufficient support from the king of France and thus switched loyalties to the king of Castile.

After the arrival of the Europeans, all the natives of the Canaries, called the Guanches, were killed or died off from European diseases, creating the need for settler families from Europe to till the land and maintain the Castilian claim on the islands. These peasants and artisans, rather than living like islanders and adapting to the native culture, imported their own culture. They brought with them their traditional family structures, customs, language, religion, seeds, livestock, and patterns of cultivation. Wherever settler colonies were found, whether in the Atlantic islands or the Americas, which the Europeans called the New World, they Europeanized the landscape and remade the lands they cultivated in the image of the Old World.

The second new type of colony was the plantation colony°. Until the occupation of the Cape Verde Islands in the 1460s, the Atlantic island colonies had relied on European settlers for labor. However, the Cape Verdes attracted few immigrants because of the rigors of the tropical climate, and yet the islands seemed especially well-suited for growing the lucrative sugar cane crop. The few permanent European colonists there tended to be exiled criminals, and the Cape Verdes became a haven for lawless ruffians who were disinclined to work. Because there was no indigenous population to exploit on the Cape Verdes, the few European colonizers began to look elsewhere for laborers and voyaged to the African coast, where they bought slaves who had been captured from inland villages. These slaves worked as agricultural laborers in the Cape Verdes sugar cane fields. Thus in the Cape Verdes began the tragic conjunction between African slavery and the European demand for sugar. When sugar began to replace honey as the sweetener of choice for Europeans, the almost insatiable demand was supplied by sugar cultivated by slaves in plantation colonies, first in the Atlantic islands and later in the

West Indies and American mainland. Over the next 300 years, this pattern for plantation colonies was repeated for other valuable agricultural commodities, such as indigo for dyes, coffee, and cotton, which were grown to sell in European markets. The first loop of what would eventually become a global trading circuit was now completed.

The Portuguese in Africa

The first European voyages along the African coast during the fifteenth century were launched by the Portuguese. The sponsor of these voyages was Prince Henry the Navigator (1394–1460). As governor of Algarve, the southernmost province of Portugal, Henry established a headquarters at Sagres and financed numerous exploratory voyages. Driven by the quest for fame and a profound faith in astrology, Henry had two objectives above all else: In order to enhance his reputation, he wanted to steal the Canary Islands from his archrival, the king of Castile, and to reward the men who sailed his ships, he desperately needed to get his hands on more gold.

The first Portuguese expeditions along the African coast were prompted by Henry's desire to capture the Canaries. He tried armed force, negotiations with the inhabitants, and entreaties to the pope, all with no success. He even purchased phony titles to the Canaries in a transparent attempt to fool the Castilians into believing that he was really the lord of the islands. In the mid-1450s, however, Henry's disappointment over the Canaries subsided as it became evident that gold from Mali could be obtained farther south from bases near the Senegal and Gambia Rivers. Although the many voyages of Henry's sailors did not fulfill his dreams of conquest and enormous riches, he and other members of his family did help colonize Madeira and the Azores. As a source of sugar, Madeira became a valuable colony (see Maps 12.1 and 12.2).

After Henry's death, Portuguese exploration of the African coast accelerated. In only six years, a private merchant of Lisbon commissioned voyages that added 2,000 miles of coastline to what was known to the Portuguese. In 1482 the exploration policy that had been a loose and

Map 12.2   Europeans in the World, Fifteenth and Sixteenth Centuries
During the fifteenth and sixteenth centuries European sailors opened sea lanes for commerce across the Atlantic, Pacific, and Indian Oceans. Dates indicate first arrival of Europeans.

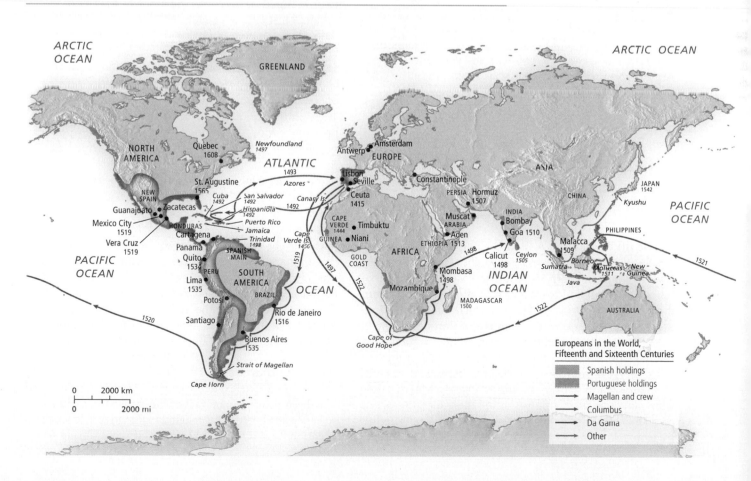

haphazard enterprise under private contractors was transformed. That year the Portuguese royal family took control of trade with Africa; they required that all sailings be authorized and all cargoes inventoried, and they built a permanent fortress at Elmina near the mouth of the Volta River in modern Ghana in West Africa. At Elmina, Portuguese traders found local sources of gold and opportunities to obtain more upriver. Rather than establishing new settler or plantation colonies, the Portuguese on the African coast relied on trading posts that supplied gold, ivory, pepper, and slaves.

Europeans in the Americas

■ How did the arrival of Europeans in the Americas transform native cultures and life?

Like the Europeans who sailed along the African coast, the first European voyagers to the Americas coveted gold and an alternative route to India and China. The European impulse to reach Asia by sailing west came from the fact that the Ottoman Empire, which was pushing into the Mediterranean after the conquest of Constantinople in 1453, blocked the traditional trade routes through the Middle East and across the Black and Red Seas. Europeans relied on Asian sources for medicines, spices, and all kinds of luxury goods that were unavailable elsewhere. Those who gained access to the source of these lucrative goods could make enormous profits. The desire to profit from this trade impelled men to take great risks to find an alternative

route to East Asia. In the short run, the Americas proved to be an impediment to achieving these goals because the two continents stood in the way of getting to Asia. But in the long run, the European voyages to the Americas brought consequences unimaginable to those who first began to sail west from Europe.

The Americas Before the Conquistadores

Prior to their contact with Europeans, the peoples of the Americas displayed remarkable cultural variety. Nomadic hunters spread across the sub-Arctic regions, western North America, and the Amazon jungles, while farming settlements prevailed in much of South America and eastern North America. Some of these North American cultures, such as the Anasazi and Iroquois, developed highly sophisticated forms of political organization, but none matched the advanced civilizations of Mesoamerica and the central Andes to the south. On the eve of the arrival of Europeans, two great civilizations, the Aztecs of central Mexico and the Incas of highland Peru, had built extensive empires that dominated their neighbors.

The Aztec Empire of Mexico

Mesoamerica (the region known today as Mexico and Central America) had been the home of a series of highly urbanized, politically centralized cultures: the Mayas (300–900), the Toltecs (900–1325), and finally the Aztecs (1325 to the Spanish conquest in 1522). The Aztecs found safety from incessant warfare with neighboring tribes on an island in Lake Texcoco, where they established the city of Tenochtitlán, now Mexico City. From their base at Tenochtitlán the Aztecs followed a brilliantly successful policy of divide and conquer, first allying with powerful neighbors to attack weaker groups, then turning against former allies.

The Aztec king Montezuma I (r. 1440–1469) consolidated an empire that stretched across most of central Mexico. In order to provide food for his people during a severe famine between 1450 and 1454, Montezuma first conquered the breadbasket of Mexico, the rich coastal region of the Totonacs. In repeated attacks, swarms of Aztec warriors took city after city, captured the local chief whenever possible, burned the temple, and extorted tribute payments from the population. With the riches gained from conquest, Montezuma transformed Tenochtitlán from a dusty town of mud houses to a great imperial capital built of stone with a grand botanical garden that displayed plants taken from various climates.

The Aztecs excelled in the perpetual state of war that had long been the dominant fact of life in Mexico, and as a result they attributed great religious value to war. They practiced the "flowery war," a staged occurrence during which states agreed to a predetermined time and place for a battle, the only objective of which was to take prisoners for temple sacrifice. Sustaining the gods' hunger for human sacrifices became the most notorious feature of Aztec religion. The Aztecs attributed their military successes to their tribal god, Huitzilpochti, the giver of light and all things necessary for life, but Huitzilpochti could be nourished only with human blood, creating the need among the Aztec faithful to acquire human captives.

The rituals of sacrifice permeated Aztec society. It has been estimated that 10,000 victims were sacrificed each year, with the number rising to 50,000 on the eve of the Spanish conquest. From the very first encounters, Europeans have been baffled by the paradox of Aztec culture. Despite their apparent practice of human sacrifice, the Aztecs displayed refined manners, a sensitivity to beauty, and a highly developed religion.

The Incan Empire of the Andes

At about the same time the Aztecs were thriving in Mexico, the Incas expanded their empire in Peru and developed a comprehensive imperial ideal. Whereas the Aztecs created a loosely linked empire based on tribute payments, the Incas employed a more direct form of rulership. As they pushed out from their base in the south Andes during the fifteenth century, they imposed their authority on conquered peoples.

The first Incan emperor, Pachacuti Inca Yupanqui (r. 1438–1471), founded the empire around 1438 when he spread Incan rule beyond the valley of Cuzco. By the end of the fifteenth century, the Incas had begun to integrate by

Incan Expansion

force the distinctive cultures of the various conquered regions. In this way, they created a mountain empire 200 miles wide and 2,000 miles long, stretching from modern Chile to Ecuador and comprising a population of about ten million. From his capital at Cuzco, the Incan emperor lived in luxury and established an elaborately hierarchic political structure. His authority was carried through layers of aristocrats down to officials who were responsible for every ten families in every village. These families supplied food and tribute for the empire, worked on roads and bridges, and served in the army. State-owned warehouses of food guaranteed the peasants freedom from starvation and provided for the sick and elderly.

Emperor Huayna Capac (r. 1493–1525) founded a second capital further south at Quito, established to decentralize the overextended empire, but at his death a bitter civil war broke out between the northern and southern halves of the empire, led respectively by his rival sons. This war weakened Incan unity on the eve of the Spanish conquest.

The Incas were impressive in creating a strong imperial administration, and as rulers they were as severe as the Aztecs. Huayna Capac slaughtered 20,000 recalcitrant Caranqui and poisoned Lake Yahuar-Cocha with their corpses. After conquering a region, the Incas killed the native population or removed them to a secure area and replaced the inhabitants with loyal colonists. During the early sixteenth century, for example, Huayna Capac brought in 14,000 colonists from all over the empire to settle the Cochabamba valley. A superb network of roads and bridges covered more than 18,000 miles and made it possible to

The Aztec Rite of Human Sacrifice
Human victims had their hearts cut out by a priest at the top of the stairs to a temple.

communicate with relays of runners who could cover as much as 140 miles a day. Troops could also be quickly dispatched to trouble spots via these roads. Despite this well-organized imperial system, the Incan Empire became overly centralized because decisions could only be made by the emperor himself, a fatal flaw that allowed the Spanish invaders to crush it very quickly.

The Mission of the European Voyagers

The European arrival in the Americas was the result of a mistake suggested by Christopher Columbus's (1451–1506) ardent sense of Christian mission. Born in Genoa to an artisan family, Columbus followed the destiny of so many of his compatriots by becoming a sailor. "From my earliest youth," he reported late in life, "I went to sea and I have remained at sea until this day. It has occupied me for more than forty years. Wherever men have sailed, I too have sailed." Columbus certainly had extensive experience as a seaman, but more crucial to understanding his stubborn sense of mission was his personality, which remains an enigma that has allowed a wide variety of interpretations. Historians once depicted Columbus as a practical-minded experimenter, who was opposed by ignorant fools, but now he is understood as a more complex figure whose defining characteristic was his religious devotion. Columbus believed that he had been predestined to fulfill biblical prophecies. If he could reach China, he could outflank the Ottoman Turks and recapture Jerusalem from the Muslims who had held it since 1187, an achievement that he believed would usher in the Second Coming of Christ. In trying to persuade Queen Isabella of Castile to finance his voyage to China by sailing west, he later admitted that to make his case he ignored navigational data and, instead, relied "entirely on holy, sacred Scripture and certain prophetic texts by certain saintly persons, who by divine revelation have had something to say on this matter."[1]

It had long been recognized that it was theoretically possible to reach China by sailing west. Most educated people, and certainly all those influenced by the Renaissance humanists, agreed the world was round. The problem was not a theoretical one about the shape of the Earth but a practical one about getting around it. During Columbus's life the most widely accepted authority on the circumference of the Earth was the ancient Greek geographer Ptolemy, who had estimated that the distance across the Atlantic Ocean from Europe to Asia was more than 10,000 miles. The practical problem was that no ship in Columbus's day could hope to sail that far without landfalls along the way for finding provisions and making repairs. In fact, Ptolemy had underestimated the size of the Earth by 25 percent, but Columbus decided that Ptolemy had overestimated the distance. Columbus also imagined that the wealthy island of Japan lay farther east of the Asian continent than it actually does,

DOCUMENT

Columbus's Christian Mission

One of the most common features of Christopher Columbus's writings is the prevalence of Christian images and themes. Expectations of Christian salvation and the second coming of Christ motivated Columbus in his attempts to reach Asia by sailing west. The Introduction to the journal of his first voyage offers a glimpse of Columbus's militant Christianity. It depicts the stirring moment of Christian triumph when the Muslim king of Granada surrendered to Ferdinand and Isabella in 1492.

I saw your Highnesses' banners victoriously raised on the towers of the Alhambra, the citadel of that city [of Granada], and the Moorish king come out of the city gates and kiss the hands of your Highnesses [Ferdinand and Isabella] . . . And later in that same month, on the grounds of information I had given your royal Highnesses concerning the lands of India and a prince who is called the Great Khan—which means in Spanish "King of Kings"—and of his and his ancestors' frequent and vain applications to Rome for men learned in the holy faith who should instruct them in it, your Highnesses decided to send me, Christopher Columbus, to see these parts of India and the princes and peoples of those lands and consider the best means for their conversion. For, by the neglect of the Popes to send instructors, many nations had fallen to idolatory and adopted doctrines of perdition, and your Highnesses as Catholic princes and devoted propagators of the holy Christian faith have always been enemies of the sect of Mahomet and of all idolatries and heresies.

Your Highnesses ordained that I should not go eastward by land in the usual manner but by the western way which no one about whom we have positive information has ever followed. Therefore having expelled all the Jews from your dominions in that same month of January, your Highnesses commanded me to go with an adequate fleet to those parts of India.

Source: From *The Four Voyages of Christopher Columbus*, translated by J. M. Cohen (London: Penguin Classics, 1969). Copyright © 1969 by J. M. Cohen. Reproduced by permission of Penguin Books Ltd.

thus further minimizing the distance of the voyage. When he first proposed sailing west to Asia, King John II of Portugal consulted a committee of experts who quite correctly pointed out how seriously Columbus had miscalculated the distance. His extremely inaccurate estimate of how close China was seems to have been more the result of wishful thinking and religious fervor than geographical expertise. King John's rejection led Columbus to seek patronage elsewhere. Columbus applied to Queen Isabella of newly unified Spain, whose own advisers at first recommended against the voyage for the same reasons the Portuguese experts had rejected his plan. When the Spanish defeated the Muslim kingdom of Granada in 1492, which completed the Christian reconquest of the Iberian peninsula, Isabella succumbed to the religious enthusiasm of the moment and relented. She offered Columbus a commission for the voyage in the hope that it would ensure a final Christian victory over Islam.

On August 3, 1492, Columbus set sail with three small ships—the Niña, Pinta, and Santa Maria—and a crew of ninety men and boys. After refitting in the Canary Islands, the modest convoy entered unknown waters guided only by Columbus's faith in finding China, which was, in fact, thousands of miles farther west than he thought it would be. At two in the morning on the moonlit night of October 12, a lookout spied land, probably Watling Island in the Bahamas.

In all, Columbus made four voyages across the Atlantic (1492, 1493, 1498, 1502), exploring the Caribbean Islands, the coast of Central America, and part of the coast of South America. He never abandoned the belief that he had arrived in Asia. His four voyages were filled with adventures. On the third voyage, he was arrested by the newly appointed Spanish governor of Hispaniola on false charges and sent home in chains for trial; on the fourth he was marooned for nearly a year on Jamaica after worms weakened the timbers of his ships. He garnered considerable wealth in gold found on his voyages, but he never received the ti-tles and offices that Queen Isabella had promised him before his first voyage.

Soon after Columbus returned to Spain from his first voyage, the Spanish monarchs who had sponsored him tried to obtain a monopoly to explore the western Atlantic. They appealed to Pope Alexander VI, who was himself a Spaniard and sympathetic to their request. In an effort to give the Spanish a firm legal monopoly to the lands across the Atlantic, the pope confirmed in 1493 the right of Spanish sailors to explore all lands to the west as long as they did not infringe upon the rights of another Christian ruler. Since all involved still thought Columbus had arrived in China, the obvious other Christian ruler was the king of Portugal, whose sailors had already pushed far enough south down the African coast to realize that they could eventually reach China by sailing east. The pope ordered a line of demarcation drawn along a north-south line 100 leagues (about 300 miles) west of the Azores and Cape Verde Islands. Spain received all lands to the west of the line; Portugal obtained the lands to the east. This line of demarcation seemed to limit the Portuguese to Africa, which alarmed them and led to direct negotiations between the Portuguese and the Spaniards. The result of the negotiations was the Treaty of Tordesillas in 1494, which moved the line of demarcation to 370 leagues (about 1,110 miles) west of the Cape Verde Islands, a decision that granted to Portugal all of Africa, India, and Brazil.

Spanish Conquistadores Land on an Island in the New World

The armored Spaniards are met by the naked inhabitants who offer them jewels and gold. As one of their first acts, the Spaniards erect a cross, symbolizing the Christian conquest of the New World.

Despite Columbus's persistent faith that he had found a route to the East Indies, other voyagers began to suspect, even before Columbus's death, that he had not found Asia at all and that other routes had to be explored. Another Italian, the Florentine Amerigo Vespucci (1454–1512), met Columbus, helped him prepare for the third voyage, and later made at least two voyages of his own across the Atlantic. From his voyages, Vespucci recognized something of the immensity of the South American continent and was the first to use the term "New World." Because he coined the term and because the account of his voyages got into print before Columbus's, Vespucci's given name, Amerigo (America), came to be attached to the New World rather than Columbus's. By the 1520s, Europeans had explored the Americas extensively enough to recognize that the New World was nowhere near India or China.

After the Treaty of Tordesillas, explorers followed two distinct strategies for finding a sea route to East Asia. The first strategy was the Portuguese continued pursuit of routes to the south and east around Africa. Between 1487 and 1488, Bartholomew Dias (ca. 1450–1500) reached the Cape of Good Hope at the southern tip of the African continent. This discovery made it evident that passage to India could be achieved by sailing south, rounding the tip of Africa, and crossing the Indian Ocean. Political and financial problems in Portugal, however, prevented a followup to Dias's voyage for ten years. Between 1497 and 1499, Vasco da Gama (ca. 1460–1524) finally succeeded in sailing from Lisbon to India around the Cape of Good Hope. This celebrated voyage included a great looping westward course far out into the Atlantic to escape the doldrums, an area in the ocean where the winds died. As a consequence of the route opened by da Gama, the Portuguese were the first Europeans to establish trading posts in Asia. They reached the Malabar coast of India in 1498 and soon found their way to the Spice Islands and China. By the middle of the sixteenth century, the Portuguese had assembled a string of more than fifty trading posts° and forts from Sofala on the east coast of Africa to Nagasaki in Japan.

The second strategy for reaching Asia consisted of Spanish attempts to pursue Columbus's proposed route west. The problem faced by those sailing under the Spanish flag was to find a way around the barrier presented by the American continents. A Portuguese sailor named Ferdinand Magellan (ca. 1480–1521), who had previously sailed to Asia aboard Portuguese ships, persuaded the king of Spain to sponsor a voyage to Asia sailing west around South America. That venture (1519–1522), which began under Magellan's command, passed through the strait named after him at the tip of South America and crossed the Pacific in a voyage of extreme hardship as his men suffered from thirst and hunger and died of scurvy. Magellan himself was killed by natives in the Philippines. After three years at sea, 18 survivors from the original 240 in Magellan's fleet reached Seville, Spain, having sailed around the world for the first time. Contemporaries immediately recognized the epic significance of the voyage, but the route opened by Magellan was too long and arduous for the Spanish to employ as a reliable alternative to the Portuguese route around Africa.

In the course of three centuries (about 1480–1780), European navigators linked the previously isolated routes of seaborne commerce, opened all the seas of the world to trade, and encountered many of the cultures and peoples of the world. Within the Indian Ocean and the western Pacific, the Europeans faced stiff competition from Arab and Chinese merchant sailors. But for the first hundred years or so, the Portuguese and Spanish effectively maintained a monopoly over the global trade routes back to Europe. Gradually English, Dutch, and French sailors also made their way around the globe. In the Americas, inadvertently made known to Europeans by Christopher Columbus, the Spanish immediately began settlements and attempted to subdue the indigenous populations.

European Empires in Latin American 1660

The Fall of the Aztec and Incan Empires

Following the seafaring captains, such as Columbus and Magellan, came the conquistadores°. They were Spanish adventurers, usually from impoverished minor noble families, who sought fortune and royal recognition through explorations and conquests of indigenous peoples. Spain was a poor land with few opportunities for advancement, a bleak situation that made the lands of the New World a powerful lure to many men seeking a fortune. Embroiled in almost continuous warfare in Europe, the Spanish crown was also perennially strapped for cash, which meant the king of Spain was highly motivated to encourage profitable foreign conquests. Many of the conquistadores launched their own expeditions with little or no legal authority, hoping to acquire sufficient riches to impress the king to give them official sanction for additional conquests. Those who did acquire legal authority from the crown received the privilege to conquer new lands in the name of the king of Spain and to keep a portion of those territories for themselves. In return they were obliged to turn over to the king one fifth—the "royal fifth"—of everything of value they acquired, an obligation enforced by a notary sent along with the conquistadores to keep a record of valuables that were found. The conquistadores also extended Spanish sovereignty over new lands and opened the way for missionaries to bring millions, at least nominally, into the Christian fold.

All conquistadores were required to read a document, called the *requerimiento*°, to the natives before making war on them. Derived from the Muslim declaration of *jihad* or holy war, this Spanish Christian document briefly explained the principles of Christianity and commanded the natives to accept them immediately along with the authority of the pope and the sovereignty of the king of Spain. If the natives refused, they were warned that they would be forced through war to subject themselves "to the yoke and obedience of the Church and of Their Highnesses. We shall take you and your wives and your children, and shall make slaves of them, and as such shall sell and dispose of them as Their Highnesses may command. And we shall take your goods, and shall do you all the mischief and damage that we can."[2] The *requerimiento* revealed the conflicting motives behind the Spanish conquest. On the one hand, the Spanish were sincerely interested in converting the natives to Christianity. On the other, the conquistadores were trying to justify the immorality of their actions by suggesting that the natives had brought the attack on themselves by refusing to obey the Spanish king.

Hernán Cortés and the Conquest of Mexico

Among the first and most successful of the conquistadores was Hernán Cortés (1485–1547). Cortés arrived on the Yucatán peninsula of present-day Mexico in February 1519, beginning a conquest that culminated in the collapse of the Aztec Empire and the Spanish colonization of Mexico. He followed a policy of divide and conquer with the natives, making alliances with peoples who hated the Aztecs and then using their warriors on the front lines of his battles where they absorbed most of the losses. If after a

reading of the *requerimiento* the native chieftains did not immediately surrender, Cortés's men attacked them, breaking through their lines on horses, which the natives had never seen before.

After a number of bloody battles, Cortés set off with 450 Spanish troops, 15 horses, and 4,000 native allies to conquer the great capital of the Aztec Empire, Tenochtitlán, a city of at least 300,000 and defended by thousands of warriors. As Cortés approached, Montezuma II was slow to set up a strong defense, because he suspected Cortés might be the white god, Quetzalcóatl, who according to prophecies would arrive one day from the east. The result was disastrous for the Aztecs. Montezuma knew his reign was doomed unless he could gain the assistance of other gods to drive Quetzalcóatl away. Thus, rather than an ardent military campaign, the king's defense primarily took the form of human sacrifices made to please the gods. Cortés captured Montezuma, who continued to rule for several months as a puppet of the conquistadores. The city revolted, however, killing Montezuma and driving out the Spanish. Cortés then gathered new troops and additional allies, built ships for use on the lake that surrounded Tenochtitlán, and besieged the city. By the time Tenochtitlán finally surrendered, the shiny jewel that had so impressed the Spanish when they first glimpsed it from the surrounding mountains lay in smoldering ruins.

By 1522 Cortés controlled a territory in New Spain—as Mexico was renamed—larger than Old Spain itself. Aztec culture and its religion of human sacrifice disappeared as Franciscan friars arrived to evangelize the surviving population.

Cortés Arrives in Mexico
The figure on the right is the native woman La Malinche, who served as Cortés's mistress and translator, a position often occupied by native women who served as mediators between the indigenous and Spanish cultures. Cortés is the bearded man in breeches. Following him is an African servant, Spanish soldiers dressed in full armor, and finally three native porters, bent over from their heavy burdens.

DOCUMENT

Why the Aztecs Lost to the Spanish Conquerors

A Spaniard named Diego Munoz Camargo married into the nobility of one of the native groups that allied with Cortés against the Aztecs. He had access to local knowledge that suggests the Aztecs feared the Spanish, not because of their technology of horses and guns, but because of portents that their world was coming to an end.

Ten years before the Spaniards came to this land, the people saw a strange wonder and took it to be an evil sign and portent. This wonder was a great column of flame which burned in the night, shooting out such brilliant sparks and flashes that it seemed to rain fire on the earth and to blaze like daybreak. It seemed to be fastened against the sky in the shape of a pyramid, its base set against the ground, where it was of vast width, and its bulk narrowing to a peak that reached up and touched the heavens. It appeared at midnight and could still be seen at dawn, but in the daytime it was quelled by the force and brilliance of the sun. This portent burned for a year, beginning in the year which the natives called 12-House—that is, 1517 in our Spanish reckoning. . . .

To the natives, these marvels augured their death and ruin, signifying that the end of the world was coming and that other peoples would be created to inhabit the earth. They were so frightened and grief-stricken that they could form no judgment about these things, so new and strange and never before seen or reported.

Source: Miguel Leon-Portilla, *The Broken Spears: The Aztec Account of the Conquest of Mexico* (Boston, Beacon Press, 1962), pp. 7, 11.

Quetzalcóatl, Aztec God of Life and Death

Quetzalcóatl took the form of a feathered snake, which in this Aztec image can be seen coiled beneath its head. According to myth, another god had expelled Quetzalcóatl, who embarked on a raft of snakes into the Atlantic and disappeared to the east. The prophecy that he would return from the east led Montezuma II to assume that Cortés was the god returned.

Francisco Pizarro and the Conquest of Peru

Like other conquistadores, Francisco Pizarro (ca. 1478–1541) was poor, but he bore the additional social liabilities of illegitimacy and illiteracy. With no prospects at home, Pizarro found his way to Panama, where he accompanied Vasco Núñez de Balboa (1475–1519) on an expedition in 1513 across the Isthmus of Panama during which Europeans got their first look at the Pacific Ocean.

In 1531 Pizarro left Panama with a small expedition of 180 men and 30 horses. Pizarro's goal was to conquer Peru, known to be a land rich with gold. Gathering additional recruits along the way, he sailed to northern Peru and sent out spies who discovered that the Incan emperor, Atahuallpa, could be found in the highland city of Cajamarca. When Pizarro and his forces arrived there, the central square was empty, but Atahuallpa was encamped nearby with a large army. Pizarro treacherously invited Atahuallpa to come for a parlay, but instead took him captive. The news of the capture plunged the overly centralized Incan Empire into a crisis because no one dared take action without the emperor's orders. In an attempt to satisfy the Spaniards' hunger for gold and to win his freedom, Atahuallpa had a room filled with gold and silver for the conquistadores, but the treasure merely stimulated their appetite for more. In July 1533 Pizarro executed the emperor, and by the following November he had captured the demoralized Incan capital of Cuzco.

The conquest of Peru vastly increased the size of the Spanish Empire and began to satisfy the craving for gold that had impelled Columbus and the conquistadores in the first place. Through the collection of the royal fifth, gold and silver flowed into the royal coffers in Spain. The discovery in 1545 of the fabulous Peruvian silver mine of Potosí (in what is now southern Bolivia) coincided with the introduction of the mercury amalgamation process that separated silver from ore. Mercury amalgamation enabled the Spaniards to replace surface gathering of silver ore with tunneling for ore, a procedure that led to greatly elevated yields of precious metals. For a century the silver of Peru helped provide otherwise impoverished Spain with the resources to become the most powerful kingdom in Europe.

Spanish America: The Transplanting of a European Culture

With the defeat of the Aztec and Incan Empires, the process of transplanting Spanish society to the Americas began in earnest. The arrival of Europeans was a catastrophe for most native peoples, some of whom—in the Caribbean, northern Argentina, and central Chile—completely disappeared through the ravages of conquest and diseases. Whereas Spanish became the language of government and education, some native traditions survived and a mixed-blood immigrant and native population called *mestizos* gradually appeared. Through this process, Spanish America became the first lasting outpost of Western civilization outside of Europe.

The basic form of economic and social organization in Spanish America was the encomienda° system, which was created as an instrument to exploit native labor. An encomienda was a royal grant awarded for military or other services that gave the conquistadores and their successors the right to gather tribute from the Indians in a defined area. In return, the encomendero (the receiver of the royal grant and native tribute) was theoretically obliged to protect the natives and teach them the rudiments of the Christian faith. Because the encomiendas were very large, only a small number of Spanish settlers were actually encomenderos. In greater Peru, which included modern Peru, Ecuador, and Bolivia, there were never more than 500 encomenderos. By the seventeenth century these encomiendas had evolved to become great landed estates called haciendas°.

There were only a few prosperous encomenderos, but the stories about those who rose from rags to riches in the New World were so compelling that during the sixteenth century alone more than 200,000 Spaniards migrated there. They came from every part of the Iberian peninsula, from

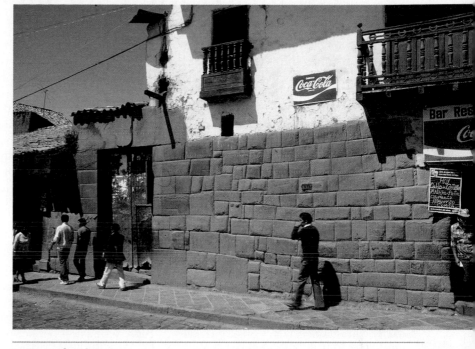

Layers of Cultures

Cuzco, Peru, was the capital of the Incan Empire before the Spanish Conquest in 1533. In this photo the heavy stone wall at the lower level was built by the Incas. Above it is a whitewashed wall built during the colonial period, and affixed to it is a sign of the contemporary global economy, Coca-Cola.

every class except the peasantry, and they practiced a wide variety of trades. There were nobles, notaries, lawyers, priests, physicians, merchants, artisans, and sailors; there were also vagabonds prone to crime and rebellion. In effect, these immigrants duplicated Spanish Catholic society in the New World, complete with its class divisions and tensions, except that the native population or African slaves substituted for the peasants as agricultural workers. Included among the immigrants were an unknown number of Jews who hid their faith and who escaped the rigors of the Spanish Inquisition by removing themselves to the Americas, where they were less likely to suffer persecution.

Only one in ten of Spanish immigrants were women, and for a long time the colonies suffered from a shortage of Spanish women. Although native Americans were usually excluded from Spanish society, many native women who were the mistresses or wives of Spaniards became partially assimilated to European culture and helped pass it on to their offspring. These native women learned Spanish and were converted to Christianity, and because of their origins they could mediate between the dominant Spanish and the subordinate native population. These women knew both languages, which made them valuable interpreters, and were familiar with both cultures, which enabled them to explain native customs to the Spanish. The progeny of

Between Indian and Christian: Creating Hybrid Religion in Mexico

As conquest passed into colonialism during the sixteenth century, Christian missionaries began to exert a profound influence on Indian moral and religious practices. However, as the Indians accepted Christianity they subtly adapted it to meet their needs and to fit into their culture. As a result native Americans created a new hybrid religion that combined both Christian and Indian elements.

No example of the hybrid nature of native Christianity is more revealing than the Indian uses of the cross. As his army marched across Mexico, Cortés had ordered the smashing of idols and their substitution with Christian crosses. Missionaries later placed crosses in churches, encouraged making the sign of the cross a ritual practice, and introduced the wearing of miniature crosses as a kind of personal talisman that offered protection from illness and evil influences.

Mayas adapted to the Christian cross so readily because Maya culture already had a symbol similar to the Christian cross. However, the Maya at first misunderstood what the missionaries meant when they preached about the cross and took the example of Christ's sacrifice on the cross too literally. Some Maya actually performed crucifixions, usually of children, whose hands were nailed or tied to the cross and whose hearts were torn out in a vestige of pre-Christian practices. There are also reports of pigs and dogs sacrificed on crosses. Needless to say, the Christian missionaries were horrified at these crucifixions. Even though the Maya had missed the point of Christ's singular sacrifice, they had understood the power behind the Christian symbol, which the Spaniards had used in their conquest of the Maya, and they wanted some of that power for themselves.

When the Franciscan friars arrived in Mexico City in 1524, they introduced the practice of flagellation, in which the missionaries whipped themselves to aid in the conversion of the recently conquered Aztec population. In Europe the ritual of self-flagellation was usually practiced by monks, friars, and small numbers of laymen who joined "confraternities of the discipline," which carefully supervised the whippings. The practice imitated the flagellation of Christ under the whips of Roman soldiers and served as a means of mortification for the penance of sins.

The friars first employed self-flagellation as a tool for impressing the natives. Fray Antonio de Roa encouraged conversions through dramatic flagellations, called "a general discipline," which was attended by everyone in the village. After a collective flagellation in which the Indians who had converted to Christianity imitated Fray Roa, he proceeded out of the church, naked from the waist up with a cord around his neck and shoeless. He walked over hot coals, and then delivered a sermon about how much greater the pains of Hell would be than those from the burning coals. After the sermon he doused his whole body with boiling water. During the sixteenth century the Indians themselves began to practice flagellation, especially during processions conducted during Holy Week. The natives flogged themselves with such evident enthusiasm that the friars had to intervene to prevent the Indians from seriously harming themselves. On many occasions during the colonial period, the Indians used self-flagellation as a means of rousing their fellows in protest against Spanish domination. Even now flagellation remains the most distinctive feature of the Mexican passion plays. By adapting European Christian rituals for their own purposes, the natives created a new hybrid religious culture that was distinctively Mexican.

Hybrid Religion
Here a priest flagellates a naked Incan in Peru. Introduced by Christian missionaries, flagellation became one of the more extreme forms of religious practice among the newly converted Indians.

Question for Discussion

Why do you think the natives of Mexico changed the practices of Christianity?

European men and Indian women constituted the mestizo, or genetically mixed, population.

Wherever they went in the Americas, the Spaniards brought African slaves with them. Most of the slaves remembered little about their original African cultures, however, because many had been born in Spain, the Caribbean, or the Cape Verde Islands, and Spanish had become their native language. At every stage from initial explorations to the building of new cities, Africans participated in helping make the Americas Spanish. In 1533, while Pizarro held the Incan emperor captive at Cajamarca, he sent to Cuzco an advance party of five men, including a black man who was entrusted to bring back a huge fortune in gold and silver. Unlike in the West Indies and the coastal regions where they became plantation workers, blacks in the interior of South America often fought and worked as partners with the Spanish, not as full equals but as necessary auxiliaries for and beneficiaries of the conquest.

The king of Spain was represented in the Americas by the two viceroys, who were the highest colonial officials. One in Mexico City governed the West Indies, the mainland north of Panama, Venezuela, and the Philippines; the other in Lima, Peru, had authority over all of Spanish South America, excluding Venezuela. However, the vast territory of Spanish America and the enormous cultural diversity within it precluded any rigorous centralized control either from Spain or from the viceregal capitals.

In Spanish America the church was a more effective presence than the state. Driven by the same religious fervor as Columbus, Catholic missionaries trekked into the farthest reaches of Spanish America, converting the native populations to Christianity with much more success than in Africa or Asia. Greed had enticed the conquistadores, but an ardent desire to spread the gospel of Christianity spurred the missionaries. As heirs to the long Christian struggle against Islam and, in particular, the reconquest of the Iberian peninsula from the Muslims, the missionaries found in the Americas an exceptional opportunity to expand Christianity. The most zealous missionaries were members of religious orders—Franciscans, Dominicans, and Jesuits—who were distinguished from the parish priests by their autonomy and special training for missionary work. Instead of answering to a bishop who had authority over a defined region, members of religious orders were organized like an army, followed the commands of the head of their order in Rome, and were willing to travel anywhere in the world.

The Spanish colonization of South America meant that missionaries did not have to contend with the opposition of local governments, as they did in Africa and Asia. Church officials generally assumed that it took ten years for the transition to a settled Christian society, a policy that meant that Christianity arrived in two stages. First, members of a religious order evangelized the population by learning the native language, then preaching and teaching in it. They also introduced the celebration of the Catholic sacraments. Once churches were built and Christianity was accepted by the local elite, the missionaries moved on to be replaced, in the second stage, by parish priests who expected to stay in one place for their entire lives. In the border regions, evangelizing never ceased and members of the missionary orders stayed on until the end of colonial times. In California, New Mexico, and Texas, missions formed outposts of Spanish society in regions that were otherwise often lawless borderlands. In Paraguay, the members of the Jesuit Order gathered the Guaraní peoples into *reductions*, highly disciplined and closed communities where the natives were subjected to a rigorous regime of labor and prayer, and even the smallest details of their daily lives were regulated.

Portuguese Brazil: The Tenuous Colony

In 1500 Pedro Cabral sighted the Brazilian coast, claiming it for Portugal under the Treaty of Tordesillas. While the Spaniards busied themselves with the conquest of Mexico and Peru, the Portuguese largely ignored Brazil, which lacked any obvious source of gold or temptingly rich civilizations to conquer. Instead, the Portuguese concentrated on developing their lucrative empire in Asia.

Brazil became a haven for pirates and castaways, especially French. In 1532 the Portuguese crown finally answered the French threat by devising a plan for Portuguese settlement and government of Brazil. Brazil was divided into fifteen captaincies, which were passed out to court favorites as compensation for services rendered or just to get them out of the way. The captains turned out to be tyrannical, incompetent, or absent, and they so completely failed to govern effectively that in 1549 the crown was forced to appoint a governor-general and to establish a capital city at Salvador in eastern Brazil.

The impetus for the further colonization of Brazil was the growing European demand for sugar. The Brazilian climate was perfectly suited for cultivating sugar cane. Between 1575 and 1600, Brazil became the Western world's leading producer of sugar, luring thousands of poor young men from Portugal and the Azores who took native women as wives, thereby producing a distinctive mestizo population. In the coastal regions, the land was cleared for vast sugar cane plantations. Sugar cane production required back-breaking, dangerous labor to weed and especially to cut the cane. To help work the plantations the Portuguese attempted to enslave the Tupí-Guaraní natives, but European diseases soon killed them off.

The Portuguese increasingly looked to Africans to perform the hard labor they were unwilling to do themselves. As a result, the Brazilian demand for slaves intensified the Portuguese presence in West Africa and the African presence in Brazil. In the search for ever more slaves, Portuguese

The Difficulties of a Transatlantic Marriage

In 1557 Francisco Noguerol de Ulloa, a Spanish conquistador who had fought in Peru, returned home to Spain. During his nearly two decades in the New World, he had amassed a sizable fortune and earned a great reputation for himself. He expected to enjoy his wealth and fame in a peaceful retirement, but instead almost immediately upon his return he was arrested on the charge of bigamy. During his long stay in Peru, he had neither seen nor heard from the Spanish woman he had married before he left, and when his sisters wrote to him that she had died he thought he was free to marry again. So he did. But when he returned to Spain, his first wife, Dona Beatriz, who was alive and well, heard about his second marriage and filed suit against him for bigamy.

The chance to escape Beatriz had impelled Francisco across the Atlantic in the first place. Many Spanish conquistadores were trying to flee troubles at home, such as a bad marriage. Francisco had married Beatriz under pressure from his widowed mother for the usual reasons parents forced their children into arranged marriages. Beatriz came with a large dowry and provided useful alliances for Francisco's mother and sisters, who felt vulnerable because of Francisco's father's untimely death.

But the marriage was a failure from the beginning. According to Francisco, they had never slept together, and in the eyes of the Church, at least, an unconsummated marriage was not a real marriage. Certainly Francisco and Beatriz never lived together, and she bore him no children. However, his lack of affection for his wife did not prevent him from accepting large payments for her dowry or from writing to his in-laws to ask for money when in his early years abroad he ran into difficulties in Peru. Even a letter of consolation on the death of his wife's sister included a request for more money. Francisco may never have had an affectionate or sexual relationship with Beatriz, but he certainly had a financial one.

Peru eventually rewarded Francisco with a great fortune. For his military prowess and devotion to the Spanish crown, he was granted one of the largest and most productive encomiendas in Peru, a vast tract of land that included the labor of thousands of Incas and a retinue of personal slaves, including a harem of female domestics. Once the false news of Beatriz's death spread throughout Peru, Francisco came to be regarded as the most eligible bachelor in the entire colony. Although many women were eager to become his wife, Francisco did not remarry for years after the news of his first wife's death.

Francisco's second wife, Dona Catalina, shared at least two attributes with his first wife: wealth and social prominence. Born into a respectable Castilian family, she was herself the widow of one of the most powerful Spaniards in Peru. She controlled her own vast fortune in property and other assets, which meant that she could bring a substantial dowry to her new husband. Her reputation as a woman of modesty and virtue was impeccable; she also possessed one vital asset that Beatriz apparently lacked—great beauty. Catalina was known as the "crown jewel of all the women of those parts." It is no wonder that Francisco chose her as his new wife. This time he consummated the marriage.

This case reveals much about the nature of marriage in imperial Spain and the relative power of men and women in Spanish and colonial society. Marriage was the union of two families, not just two people. Social standing counted for more than affection in the choice of a spouse. Francisco, in fact, had to defend himself against the charge that he had fallen in love with Catalina and had, therefore, abandoned Beatriz so that he could marry Catalina. Love was not an acceptable reason for marriage, let alone an acceptable reason for leaving one marriage for another. In his trial and subsequent litigation, he never claimed to love his new wife and in fact denied that he knew her well at all before the wedding. As an honorable and respectable widow, she had lived a secluded life that would have made it impossible for Francisco to have had much contact with her at all, or so he said.

To escape Beatriz, Francisco had to prove that the marriage had never been a real marriage. To this end, he and his lawyers highlighted the fact that he had never consummated his first marriage, a fact that would have automatically invalidated it as a legal marriage according to the canon law of the Church. To keep Francisco as her husband, Beatriz had to prove that they had had sex together at least once. Francisco's belief that Beatriz was dead had no legal bearing on the case because she was not.

Despite Francisco's arguments that the marriage had never been valid, the judges initially decided in favor of Beatriz. Francisco was sentenced to pay a heavy fine to Beatriz, to serve time in jail, and to separate from his second wife, whom he was forbidden to ever see again. Perhaps most galling of all, he was obliged to resume marital relations with Beatriz, with whom he had certainly never lived before. Beatriz won the case

A Spanish Couple
Francisco Noguerol de Ulloa and Catalina would have dressed much like this aristocratic couple out for a stroll.

his heirs but only to her. Beatriz supplied the court with extensive evidence of receipts for dowry payments, signed by Francisco himself. The judges respected the legal protections for women and would not allow Francisco to squander the dowry or relegate it entirely for himself. Francisco's repeated requests to his in-laws for more money made him look like an opportunistic fortune hunter rather than a valuable family ally. The court's judgment in favor of Beatriz had less to do with the emotions of love than the defense of the dowry system and its role in maintaining social stability.

Catalina did not accept lightly the loss of the man she considered her husband. She needed to protect her own dowry from Beatriz's claims. Catalina filed a countersuit to assert that much of Francisco's assets were profits earned from her own dowry, which could not, therefore, be transferred to Beatriz. Catalina was fighting not just for her dowry but for her good name

and her marriage, and the courts eventually found a way to recognize the rights of both women—Beatriz to her dowry portion and Catalina to her honorable marriage to Francisco.

In the end, it was the women who resolved the legal struggle that surrounded Francisco. For both women, the courts and the dowry system served as a powerful form of protection for their financial well-being and their honor. Despite the overwhelming authority of men in Spanish society, women were not passive pawns. They found ways to assert control over their own lives. It is revealing that the distance between the Old and New Worlds had little bearing on the status of or legal protections for these women. Far from becoming a lawless frontier, early colonial Peru was for Spaniards at least, an extension of Spanish society.

Questions of Justice

1. In what ways did the sixteenth-century Spanish legal system protect the rights of women?
2. What does this case reveal about how Spanish society was transported to the New World?

Taking It Further

Cook, Alexandra Parma, and Noble David Cook. *Good Faith and Truthful Ignorance: A Case of Transatlantic Bigamy*. 1991. A detailed study of the Noguerol de Ulloa case.

largely because of the legal protection women enjoyed in sixteenth-century Spain. Husbands had obligations toward their wives that the courts consistently enforced.

One of the most important protections women had was the dowry itself. A man could enjoy the income from his wife's dowry, but legally she still had certain claims to it. If he died before she did—which was quite likely given the difference in age between men and women at first marriage—she had a claim on his estate to have the entire sum of her dowry restored to her, not to his family or slave buyers enlarged their area of operations in Africa south to Angola, where in 1575 they founded a trading post. This post became the embarkation point for slave traders who sailed directly to Brazil and sold slaves in exchange for low-grade Brazilian tobacco, which they exchanged for more slaves when they returned to Angola.

As in Spanish America, Portuguese authorities felt responsible for converting the natives to Christianity. In Brazil, the Jesuits took the lead during the last half of the sixteenth century by establishing a school for the training of missionaries on the site of the present city of São Paulo. São Paulo became the headquarters for the "Apostle of Brazil," José de Anchieta, who worked among the indigenous peoples. In the seventeenth century, Father Antonio Vieira established a string of missions in the Amazon valley. Once converted, natives were resettled into villages called aldeias°, which were similar to Spanish missions. The Jesuits attempted to protect the natives against the white colonists who wanted to enslave them, creating a lasting conflict between the Jesuit fathers and local landowners. Both Jesuits and colonists appealed to the king to settle their dispute; finally the king gave the Jesuits complete responsibility for all Indians in aldeias but allowed colonists to enslave Indians who had not been converted or who were captured in war. The Portuguese connected Christian conversion with settlement in aldeias, which meant that any unsettled native was, by definition, a heathen. Nevertheless, these restrictions on enslaving Indians created a perceived labor shortage and further stimulated the demand for African slaves.

More rural, more African, and less centrally governed than Spanish America, Brazil during its colonial history remained a plantation economy in which the few dominant white European landowners were vastly outnumbered by their African slaves. In certain areas a racially mixed population created its own vibrantly hybrid culture that combined native, African, and European elements, especially in the eclectic religious life that combined Catholic with polytheistic forms of worship. Although Brazil occupied nearly half of the South American continent, until the twentieth century most of the vast interior was unexplored by Europeans and unsettled except by the small native population.

North America: The Land of Lesser Interest

Compared with Central and South America, North America outside Mexico held little attraction for Europeans during the sixteenth century. European experience in North America consisted of a number of exploratory missions and several failed attempts at colonization. By 1600, when hundreds of thousands of Europeans and Africans had settled in the Caribbean, Central and South America, the only European settlements in North America (except for New Spain) consisted of a tiny Spanish garrison at St. Augustine,

Florida, a doomed Spanish colony on the upper Rio Grande in New Mexico, and a few marooned Frenchmen on Sable Island far off the coast of Nova Scotia. Even by 1700, when English, French, and Spanish colonies were finally thriving in North America, they still played a very minor role in the global picture of European economic interests.

At first the principal attraction of North America was the cod fisheries in the waters off Newfoundland, which every spring lured ships from England, France, Spain, and Portugal and which may have been frequented by Europeans even before Columbus. An Italian captain in the employ of England, John Cabot (ca. 1450–ca. 1498), landed in North America in 1497 and established the basis for an English claim in the New World, but after he disappeared on a return trip the following year no one else bothered to follow up on the claim. Occasionally fishermen dropped anchor at the harbors at St. John's, Newfoundland, and came to know the coasts of Maine and the Gulf of St. Lawrence. In 1521 some Portuguese families founded a settlement on Nova Scotia, but they soon disappeared.

The second attraction of North America lay in the vain hope of a Northwest Passage to China and India through or around the continent to the north. After Magellan's voyage (1519–1522), the Spanish knew how to sail around South America, but they preferred overland transportation from Vera Cruz, Mexico, to reach the Pacific coast at Acapulco, which became an embarkation port for Spanish trade with Asia. In 1524 the French king sent the Italian Giovanni da Verrazano (ca. 1485–1528) to find a passage around North America, which resulted in the first geographical description of the coast from North Carolina to Newfoundland. Following up on Verrazano's voyage, Jacques Cartier (1491–1557) discovered the St. Lawrence River in 1534. Hard winters defeated two French attempts to found a colony in the St. Lawrence Valley between 1541 and 1543. The English explored further north in a series of voyages that led to the discovery of Hudson Bay, which was thought for some time to be part of the Pacific Ocean. Only in 1616 did William Baffin (ca. 1584–1622) determine that there was no ice-free passage around North America.

In the competition over North America, the English arrived late, devoting themselves at first to preying on Spanish shipping rather than building their own colonies. During most of the sixteenth century England was considerably less well prepared than Spain or Portugal to sustain a campaign of conquest and colonization in the Americas. At this time the English monarchy had a fragile hold on power, its naval fleet was tiny, and it lacked the financial backing for risky expeditions. In contrast to the great convoys of Spanish and Portuguese ships that plied the Atlantic, the English were represented by a few "privateers," which was a polite word for pirates. These men sought quick, easy profits rather than the rigors of settling and pacifying the country. John Hawkins, the most famous of the early English privateers, and his nephew, Francis Drake (ca. 1543–1596), specialized in harassing the Spanish fleet, both to steal the gold and silver that was being transported back to Spain and to sustain an intermittent war against England's most powerful enemy.

During the reign of Queen Elizabeth I (r. 1558–1603), English efforts finally turned to establishing colonies in the Americas. Two prominent courtiers, Humphrey Gilbert and his stepbrother, Walter Raleigh, sponsored a series of voyages intended to establish an English colony called Virginia in honor of Elizabeth, "The Virgin Queen." The shift of English interest from piracy to colonization was made possible by Elizabeth's success in strengthening the monarchy, building up the fleet, and encouraging investments in New World colonies. In 1585 the first English colonists in the Americas landed on Roanoke Island off the coast of North Carolina, but they were so poorly prepared that their attempt and a second one in 1587 failed. The inexperienced and naive English settlers did not even make provisions for planting crops.

The successful English colonies came a generation later. Learning from past mistakes, the colonists of Jamestown in Virginia, who landed in 1607, brought seeds for planting, built fortifications for protection, and established a successful form of self-government. From these modest beginnings, the English gradually established vast plantations along the rivers of Virginia. There they raised tobacco to supply the new European habit of smoking, which had been picked up from native Americans. In 1620 religious refugees from England settled in Massachusetts Bay, but in contrast to Central and South America, most of North America by 1650 remained only marginally touched by Europeans.

Europeans in Asia

■ Why was the European encounter with Asian civilizations far less disruptive than those in Africa and the Americas?

India, the Malay peninsula, Indonesia, the Spice Islands, and China were the ultimate goal of the European explorers during the fifteenth and sixteenth centuries. They were eventually reached by many routes—by the Portuguese sailing around Africa, by the Spanish sailing around South America, and by the Russians trekking across the vastness of Siberia. Trade between Europe and Asia was very lucra-

CHRONOLOGY

Europeans in the Americas

ca. 1438	Founding of Incan Empire in Peru by Pachacuti Inca Yupanqui
1440–1469	Reign of Montezuma I of the Aztec Empire
1492–1493	First two voyages of Christopher Columbus
1497	John Cabot lands in North America
1498	Third voyage of Columbus
1500	Cabral sights Brazil
1502	Fourth voyage of Columbus
1519–1522	Spanish conquer Mexico
1524	Giovanni da Verrazano explores North American coast for France
1534	Jacques Cartier discovers St. Lawrence River
1549	Portuguese establish a governor-general at Salvador, Brazil
1585	English establish colony on Roanoke Island, North Carolina
1607	English establish colony at Jamestown, Virginia
1616	William Baffin fails to discover Northwest Passage around North America
1620	English establish colony at Massachusetts Bay

tive. Europeans were especially dependent on Asian sources for luxury goods such as silk, spices for cooking and preserving food, and medicines for pain relief and healing.

Asia Before the European Empires

After the collapse of the Mongol Empire in the fourteenth century, direct access for European merchants to China and the Indian Ocean was blocked. Plague, political unrest, and Muslim hostility to Christians reduced trade to a mere trickle of what it had been. The elaborate trade networks that had helped drive the expansion of the economy of the West during the thirteenth century were in disarray.

The greatest potential rival to the Europeans who sought access to Asian trade was Ming China (1368–1644), a highly advanced civilization with maritime technology and organizational capability to launch exploratory voyages far superior to Europe's. Even before the Portuguese began their slow progress down the west coast of Africa, the Chinese organized a series of huge maritime expeditions into the Indian Ocean that reached far down the east coast of Africa. Between 1405 and 1433 the Chinese established diplomatic contacts and demanded tribute in dozens of kingdoms in

DOCUMENT

A Ming Naval Expedition (15th c.)

India and Africa. The size and ambition of these fleets far surpassed anything that sailed from Europe at this time, and the massive crews of as many as 27,500 men (compared to Columbus's crew of 90) included a complement of scholars to communicate with foreign kings and highly skilled technicians to make repairs to the fleet. The Chinese fleets took trade goods, such as silk, tea, and porcelains, and brought back to China strange animals, hostage kings, and possible trade items. After nearly thirty years of searching the Indian Ocean ports, the Ming emperors concluded that China already possessed all the goods that were available abroad, that China was indeed the center of civilization, and that further investments in oceangoing expeditions were unwarranted.

The European and Chinese voyages of the fifteenth century differed in their objectives and in the motives of the governments that sponsored them. The Europeans were mostly privateers seeking personal profit or captains who enjoyed official government backing in return for a portion of the profits. The economic motive behind the European voyages made them self-sustaining because the Europeans sailed only to places where they could make money. In contrast, the imperial Chinese expeditions were only partially motivated by the desire for economic gain. The official purpose of the Chinese voyages was to learn about the world, and once the Chinese found out what they wanted, they ceased the official voyages. Chinese merchant traders continued to ply the seas on their own, however, and when the Europeans arrived in East Asia, they simply inserted themselves into this already developed Chinese-dominated trade network.

In contrast to the trade in Africa and America, Europeans failed to monopolize trade in Asia. The Europeans were just one among many trading groups, some working under government sponsorship, such as the Portuguese, and others working alone, such as the Chinese.

The Trading Post Empires

In 1497–1499 Vasco da Gama opened the most promising route for the Portuguese around Africa to South and East Asia. But the sailing distances were long, limiting the number of people who could be transported to Asia, and the Asian empires were well equipped to defend themselves against European conquest. As a result, European engagement with Asia was slight for 300 years. Because Europeans lacked the support system provided by colonial conquest, few Europeans settled in Asia, and even missionary work proved much more difficult than in the Americas.

Unlike Brazil, where the Portuguese established colonial plantations, in Asia they established trading posts along the coasts of India, China, and the Spice Islands. When the Portuguese first arrived at a location with a safe harbor and easy access to the hinterland, they built a fort and forced, bribed, or tricked the local political authority, usually a chieftain, to cede the land around the post to Portugal. The agents sent to trade in Asia were called factors and their trading posts were called factories. But they were not factories in the modern sense of sites for manufacturing; they were safe places where merchants could trade and store their merchandise. The factors lived in the factories with a few other Portuguese traders, a small detachment of troops, and servants recruited from the local population. Nowhere did Portuguese authority extend very far into the hinterland. The traditional political structures of local chieftains remained, and the local elites usually went along with the arrangement because they profited by reselling European wares, such as cloth, guns, knives, and many kinds of cheap gadgets. The factors acquired silks, gold, silver, raw cotton, pepper, spices, and medicines. Some of these outposts of the Portuguese Empire survived until late in the twentieth century, but their roots remained exceedingly shallow. Even in places such as East Timor, an island in Indonesia, and Macao on the south China coast, which were Portuguese outposts for more than four centuries, only a small native elite ever learned the Portuguese language or adapted to European culture.

The Portuguese and later other Europeans were motivated to establish colonies in Asia primarily by commercial considerations. Consider the search for the spice nutmeg, which illustrates something of the enticement of the Asia trade. In an account published in 1510, an Italian traveler, Ludovico di Varthema, described for the first time in a European language nutmeg trees, which he found growing in the Banda Islands, a small archipelago some thousand miles east of Java. These were the only places in the world where nutmeg grew. Besides adding flavor to foods, nutmeg was believed to possess powers to cure all kinds of diseases and to induce a hallucinatory euphoria. The demand for nutmeg was so great and the supply so limited that exporting it yielded enormous profits. At one time, nutmeg was the most valuable commodity in the world after gold and silver. In the early seventeenth century the markup on a pound of nutmeg transported from the Banda Islands to Europe was 60,000 percent. It is no wonder European traders were willing to risk their lives on long, dangerous sea voyages to obtain nutmeg and other spices.

In return for raw materials such as nutmeg, European merchants typically traded manufactured goods, and they made every effort to ensure that other European powers were excluded from competing in this trade in Asia. Given the high profit potential, there was a great temptation to break a European rival's trading monopoly on a rare commodity such as nutmeg. Crucial to enforcing the system was a network of factories and a strong navy, which was primarily used against other European and occasionally Muslim interlopers. Through the trading post empires, commercial rivalries among European states extended abroad to Asia. Competition over these trading posts foreshadowed the beginnings of a global economy dominated by Europeans. It also demonstrated the Europeans' propensity to transform European wars into world wars.

In addition to trade, the Portuguese and other European powers sought to spread Christianity among the local Asian populations. Franciscan, Dominican, and later Jesuit missionaries preached to the indigenous peoples. To accomplish conversions, they tried persuasion, because without the backing of a full-scale conquest as in the Americas, resorting to force was usually not an option. The missionaries frequently drew the ire of local rulers, who viewed the converts as traitors—a situation that led to the persecution of some of the new Christians. To accomplish their task of conversion, Christian missionaries had to learn the native languages and something of the native culture and religion. In this effort, the Jesuits were particularly dedicated; they sent members of their order to the Chinese imperial court, where they lived incognito for decades, although they made few converts. Jesuits also traveled to Japan, where they established an outpost of Christianity at Nagasaki. With the exception of the Spanish Philippines, which was nominally converted to Catholicism by 1600, Christian missionaries in Asia were far less successful than in the Americas. Perhaps one million Asians outside the Philippines had been converted during this period, but many of these conversions did not last. Christians were most successful in converting Buddhists and least effective among Muslims, who almost never abandoned their faith.

DOCUMENT

St. Francis Xavier, Jesuit in India (1530s–1550s)

By the end of the sixteenth century, Portuguese and Spanish shipping in Asian waters faced recurrent harassment from the English, French, and Dutch. The Dutch drove the Portuguese from their possessions in Ceylon, India, and the Spice Islands, except for East Timor. But none of these sixteenth-century European empires was particularly effective at imposing European culture on Asia in a way comparable with the Americas. In the Spanish Philippines, for example, few natives spoke Spanish, and there were fewer than 5,000 Spanish inhabitants as late as 1850. European states competed among themselves for trade and tried to enforce monopolies, but the Europeans remained peripheral to Asian culture until the late eighteenth and early nineteenth centuries, when the British expanded their power in India and colonized Australia and New Zealand.

The expansion of the Russian Empire into Asia depended not on naval power but on cross-country expeditions. The heartland of the Russian Empire was Muscovy, the area around Moscow, but the empire would eventually spread from the Baltic Sea to the Pacific Ocean. After 1552 Russians began to push across the Ural mountains into Siberia, lured by the trade in exotic furs, which were in great demand among the upper classes of northern Europe, both to keep warm and as fashion statements. The Russians' search for furs was equivalent to the Spanish search for

gold; like gold, fur attracted adventurous and desperate men. Following the navigable rivers and building strategic forts along the way, expeditions collected furs locally and then advanced deeper into the frozen wilds of Siberia. Several of the great aristocratic families of Russia acquired enormous wealth from the Siberian fur trade, which was so lucrative that Russian trappers kept pushing farther and farther east. In this quest for furs, expeditions reached the Pacific coast in 1649, by which time Russia had established a network of trading posts over all of northern Asia.

The significance of the European trading post empires lies less in the influence of Europe on Asia than in the influence of Asia on Europe. Asian products from spices and opium to silk cloth and oriental rugs became commonplace items in middle- and upper-class European households. European collectors became fascinated with Chinese porcelains, lacquered boxes, and screen paintings. At the same time, Asians began to visit Europe, a tradition begun when four Japanese converts to Christianity arrived in Lisbon in 1586 and made a celebrated tour of Europe.

CHRONOLOGY

Europeans in Asia

1487–1488	Bartholomew Dias reaches Cape of Good Hope
1497–1499	Vasco da Gama reaches India via Cape of Good Hope
1498	Portuguese reach Malabar coast of India
1514	Portuguese reach China
1519–1522	Ferdinand Magellan's crew circumnavigate the globe

The Beginnings of the Global System

■ How was the world tied together in a global biological and economic system?

As a result of the European voyages of the fifteenth and sixteenth centuries, a network of cultural, biological, and economic connections formed along intercontinental trading routes. These connections created a global system that has been sustained ever since. Today's global economy, based on cellular telephones, the World Wide Web, air transportation, and free trade, operates much more efficiently and quickly than its predecessors, but it is merely an extension and elaboration of a system

Coming to terms with the variety of world cultures became a persistent and absorbing problem in Western civilization. Most Europeans retained confidence in the inherent superiority of their civilization, but the realities of the world began to chip away at that confidence, and economic globalization profoundly altered Western civilization itself. Westerners began to confront the problem of understanding "other" cultures and in so doing changed themselves. The West came to mean less a place in Europe than a certain kind of culture that was exported throughout the world through conversion to Christianity, the acquisition of Western languages, and the spread of Western technology.

Suggestions for Further Reading

For a comprehensive listing of suggested readings, please go to www.ablongman.com/levack2e/chapter12

Chaudhuri, K. N. *Trade and Civilization in the Indian Ocean: An Economic History from the Rise of Islam to 1750.* 1985. Arguing for the long-term unity of trade routes, the book lays out the importance of Asian merchants to maritime trade networks from the South China Sea to the Mediterranean.

Clendinnen, Inga. *Aztecs: An Interpretation.* 1991. A provocative, sometimes disturbing book that directly confronts the implications of human sacrifice and cannibalism among the Aztecs and offers an explanation for it by analyzing Aztec religion.

Crosby, Alfred W., Jr. *The Columbian Exchange: Biological and Cultural Consequences of 1492.* 1973. The most significant study on the implications of the biological exchanges for the cultural history of both the Old and New Worlds. It has the benefit of being an exciting book to read.

Curtin, Philip D. *African History: From Earliest Times to Independence.* 1995. An excellent survey by one of the most distinguished comparative historians.

Elvin, Mark. *The Pattern of the Chinese Past: A Social and Economic Interpretation.* 1973. An excellent overview of Chinese history that covers Chinese responses to Western encounters.

Fernández-Armesto, Felipe. *Before Columbus: Exploration and Colonization from the Mediterranean to the Atlantic, 1229–1492.* 1987. Engagingly written and original in scope, this is the best single account of early European colonization efforts.

Fernández-Armesto, Felipe. *Columbus.* 1991. The 500th anniversary of Columbus's voyage in 1492 provoked a wide-ranging reappraisal of his motives and career. This pithy, engaging book is by far the most convincing in revising Columbus's image, but it deflated much of the Columbus myth and caused considerable controversy.

Oliver, Roland. *The African Experience from Olduvai Gorge to the 21st Century.* 2000. A highly readable general survey.

Pagden, Anthony. *European Encounters with the New World: From Renaissance to Romanticism.* 1993. A fascinating examination of how Europeans interpreted their encounters with America.

Parry, J. H. *The Age of Reconnaissance.* 1982. An analysis of European shipping technology and the causes behind European explorations. It covers all the major voyages.

Parry, J. H. *The Spanish Seaborne Empire.* 1990. The standard study on the subject. It brings together an enormous range of material and presents it clearly and cogently.

Phillips, William D., Jr., and Carla Rahn Phillips. *The Worlds of Christopher Columbus.* 1992. A balanced analysis of Columbus's attempts to find financing for his voyage that pays equal attention to his personal ambition, Christian zeal, and navigational skills.

Notes

1. Christopher Columbus, quoted in Felipe Fernández-Armesto, *Columbus* (1991), 154.

2. Sir Arthur Helps, *The Spanish Conquest in America,* Vol. 1 (1900), 1, 264–267.

3. Alfred W. Crosby, Jr., *The Columbian Exchange: Biological and Cultural Consequences of 1492* (1973), 3.

4. *The Book of Chilam Balam of Chumayel,* ed. and trans. Ralph L. Roy (1933), 83.

5. *The Conquistadores: First-Person Accounts of the Conquest of Mexico,* ed. and trans. Patricia de Fuentes (1963), 159.

6. *The Annals of the Cakchiquels and Title of the Lords of Totnicapán,* trans. Adrian Recinos, Dioniscio José Chonay, and Delia Goetz (1953), 116.

7. Quoted in Margaret T. Hodgen, *Early Anthropology in the Sixteenth and Seventeenth Centuries* (1964), 9.

8. Quoted in ibid., 207. Spelling has been modernized.

9. Quoted in ibid., 369.

10. Quoted in ibid., 373–374. Spelling and syntax have been modernized.

The Reformations of Religion

13

O N OCTOBER 31, 1517, AN OBSCURE MONK-TURNED-UNIVERSITY-professor was reported to have nailed on the door of the cathedral in Wittenberg, Germany, an announcement containing ninety-five theses or debating propositions. Martin Luther had no hint of the ramifications of this simple act—as common then as posting an announcement for a lecture or concert on a university bulletin board now. But Luther's seemingly harmless deed would spark a revolution. Within weeks all Germany was ablaze over what was widely seen as Luther's daring attack on the pope. Within a few short years Wittenberg became the European center for a movement to reform the Church. As the pope and high churchmen resisted Martin Luther's call for reform, much of Germany and eventually most of northern Europe and Britain broke away from the Catholic Church in a movement called the Protestant Reformation, which dominated European affairs from 1517 until 1560.

Martin Luther was successful because he expressed in print what many felt in their hearts—that the Church was failing in its most fundamental obligation to help Christians achieve salvation. In contrast, many Catholics considered the Protestants dangerous heretics who offended God with their errors and whose heresies made salvation impossible. Moreover, many Catholics had long recognized the need for reforms in the Church and had been diligently working on achieving them. To them the intemperate Martin Luther only made matters worse.

The division between Protestants and Catholics split the West into two distinctive religious cultures. The result was that the hard-won unity of the West, which had been achieved during the Middle Ages through the expansion of Christianity to the most distant corners of the European continent and through the leadership of the papacy, was lost. Catholics and Protestants continued to share a great deal of the Christian tradition, but fateful issues

CHAPTER OUTLINE

- Causes of the Reformation

- The Lutheran Reformation

- The Diversity of Protestantism

- The Catholic Reformation

- The Reformation in the Arts

The Imitation of Christ In Albrecht Dürer's self-portrait at age 28, he literally shows himself imitating Christ's appearance. The initials AD are prominently displayed in the upper left-hand corner. They stand for Albrecht Dürer but also for *anno domini*, "the year of our Lord."

divided them: their understanding of salvation, the function of the sacraments in promoting pious behavior, the celebration of the liturgy in Latin, and obedience to the pope. After the Reformation of the sixteenth century, the common Christian culture was permanently severed by the Protestants' refusal to accept the authority of the pope on these issues.

Throughout western Europe, countries officially became either Catholic or Protestant—a situation that enforced obedience to the official faith through the police powers of the state and caused considerable suffering among adherents to unofficial religions. The fundamental conflict during the Reformation was about religion, but religion can never be entirely separated from politics or society. The competition among the kingdoms and the social tensions within the cities of central and northern Europe magnified the religious controversies, making the Reformation a broad cultural movement that seeped into all aspects of life. The Reformation raises the question, how did encounters between Catholics and Protestants permanently transform religious unity into religious division in the West?

- What caused the religious rebellion that began in German-speaking lands and spread to much of northern Europe?
- How did the Lutheran Reformation create a new kind of religious culture?
- How and why did Protestant denominations multiply to such an extent in northern Europe and Britain?
- How did the Catholic Church respond to the unprecedented threat to its dominance of religious authority in the West?
- How did the religious turmoil of the sixteenth century transform the role of the visual arts and music in public life?

Causes of the Reformation

- What caused the religious rebellion that began in German-speaking lands and spread to much of northern Europe?

The Protestant Reformation was the culmination of nearly 200 years of turmoil within the Church. During the fourteenth and fifteenth centuries the Church was especially hampered by the contradiction between its divine mission and its obligations in this world. On the one hand, the Church taught that its mission was otherworldly, as the source of spiritual solace and the guide to eternal salvation. On the other hand, the Church was thoroughly of this world. It owned vast amounts of property, maintained a far-reaching judicial bureaucracy to enforce canon

(Church) law, and was headed by the pope, who was also the territorial prince of the Papal State in central Italy. Whereas from the eleventh to the thirteenth centuries the popes had been the source of moral reform and spiritual renewal in the Church, by the fifteenth century they had become part of the problem. The problem was not so much that they had become corrupt but that they were unable to respond effectively to the demands of ordinary people who were increasingly concerned with their own salvation and the effective government of their communities.

Three developments, in particular, contributed to the demand for religious reform: the search for the freedom of private religious expression; the print revolution; and the northern Renaissance interest in the Bible and sources of Christianity.

The Search for Spiritual and Fiscal Freedom

A series of events during the fourteenth century had weakened the authority of the popes and driven the Church to the point of splitting apart, more for political than theological reasons (see Chapter 10). Between 1305 and 1378 seven popes in a row abandoned Rome, which was plagued by dangerous feuds among its aristocratic families, and chose to reside in the relative calm of Avignon, France. The period came to be called the Babylonian Captivity of the Church, a pejorative term that reflected the widespread opinion outside France that the popes had become subservient to the kings of France. The loss of revenues from the Papal State in Italy forced the financial advisers of the popes into various shady financial schemes, which undermined the moral reputation of the papacy. The Babylonian Captivity was followed by an equally contentious period between 1378 and 1417, the Great Schism, when the Church was divided over allegiance to rival Italian and French popes, and eventually to three and four competing popes.

The degradation of the papacy during the Babylonian Captivity and the Great Schism led to the Conciliar Movement, an attempt by a group of bishops to solve the schism and to liberate the Church from the abuses of papal authority. The conciliarists argued that at a general meeting or council (hence, "conciliar") the bishops would have authority over the pope and could depose him and arrange for the election of a new pope. Accordingly, the Council of Constance (1414–1417) ended the Great Schism, and the Council of Basel (1431–1449) voted for reforms. But the reforms were never implemented because of the uncompromising attitude of Pope Eugeneus IV (1431–1447). The failure of the moderate reforms of the Council of Basel opened the way for the more radical rejection of papal authority during the Protestant Reformation of the sixteenth century.

While the papacy's moral authority precipitously declined, lay Christians were drawn to new forms of worship.

Vision of the Other World

Hieronymus Bosch (ca. 1450–1516) attempted to visualize in this painting the concern of all Christians for transcendence. In the panel on the left, angels offer those who have been saved a vision of Heaven. In the panel on the right, the angels assist the saved on their ascension through a tunnel that divides this world from the pure light of God.

tion the moral authority of the papacy. They began to see the pope as a thieving foreigner who extorted money that could be better spent locally. German communities, in particular, protested against the financial demands and the questionable practices of the pope and higher clergy. Some bishops neglected their duties regarding the spiritual guidance of their flock. Some never resided in their dioceses (the district under the bishop's care), knew nothing of the problems of their people, and were concerned only with retaining their incomes and lavish living standards. Living amid the pleasures of Rome, these high clergymen were in no position to discipline parish priests, some of whom also ignored their moral responsibilities by living openly with concubines and even selling the sacraments. Although immorality of this sort was probably not widespread, a few notorious examples bred enormous resentment among the laity.

In an effort to assert control over the church in their own communities, city officials known as magistrates attempted to stem the financial drain and end clerical abuses. They restricted the amount of property ecclesiastical institutions could own, tried to tax the clergy, made priests subject to the town's courts of law, and eliminated the churchmen's exemption from burdensome duties, such as serving in the town militia or providing labor for public works. On the eve of the Reformation—especially in the cities of Germany and the Netherlands—magistrates had already begun to assert local control over the church, a tendency that prepared the way for the Protestants' efforts. For many laypeople, the overriding desire was to obtain greater spiritual and fiscal freedom from the Church.

Particularly influential were the Modern Devotion, which was promoted by the Brothers of the Common Life, and the *Imitation of Christ,* written by a Common Life brother about 1441. By emphasizing frequent private prayer and moral introspection, the *Imitation* provided a kind of spiritual manual that helped laypeople follow the same path toward spiritual renewal that traditionally had been reserved for monks and nuns. The goal was to imitate Christ so thoroughly that Christ entered the believer's soul. For example, the 1500 self-portrait of Albrecht Dürer (1471–1528), a work influenced by the Modern Devotion, portrayed the artist as if he were Christ himself. This portrait is the opening image in this chapter.

The religious fervor that drew many Christians to such profound forms of religious expression led them to ques-

The Print Revolution

Until the mid-fifteenth century, the only way in the West to reproduce any kind of text—a short business record or a long philosophical book—was to copy it laboriously by hand. As medieval scribes made copies on parchment, however, they often introduced errors or "improved" the original text as they saw fit. Thus, two different copies of the same text could read differently. Parchment books were also very expensive; a book as long as the Bible might require the skins of 300 sheep to make the parchment sheets and hundreds of hours of labor to copy the text. The high cost meant that books were limited to churchmen and to the very rich. Few Christians ever actually read the Bible simply because Bibles—like all books—were so rare.

Gutenberg
Bible

Two fifteenth-century inventions revolutionized the availability of books. First, movable metal type was introduced around 1450, and after that time printed books first began to appear. Perhaps the very first was a Bible printed by Johannes Gutenberg in Mainz, Germany. Equally important, cheap manufactured paper replaced expensive sheepskins. These two developments reduced the cost of books to a level that made them available even to artisans of modest incomes.

The demand for inexpensive printed books was astounding. During the first forty years of print, more books were produced than had been copied by scribes during the previous thousand years. By 1500, presses in more than 200 cities and towns had printed six million books. Half of the titles were on religious subjects, and because the publishing industry (then as now) produced only what people wanted to buy, the predominance of religion is a telling indication of what was on the minds of the reading public.

The buyers of printed books included, of course, the traditionally literate classes of university students, churchmen, professionals, and aristocratic intellectuals. Remarkably, however, there was also an enormous demand among people for whom books had previously been an unimaginable luxury. During the fourteenth and fifteenth centuries literacy rates had steadily risen and the power of literate culture was strongly felt even by those who could not write. For example, an illiterate farmer near Siena, Italy, had someone else keep a farming diary for him because he recognized that a written record would give him greater power over his own affairs. Literacy rates varied enormously across Europe. They were highest in the cities, especially in northern Italy, Germany, and the Netherlands. In the rural areas,

literacy was still rare, probably limited to the village priest, the notary, and perhaps the local nobility. Everywhere men were more often literate than women. However, the knowledge of what was in books spread widely beyond the literate few. The reason was that reading for most people in the fifteenth and sixteenth centuries was an oral, public activity rather than a silent, private one. In parish churches, taverns, and private houses the literate read books out loud to others for their entertainment and edification.

The expansion of the university system during this period also created more demand for books. Between 1300 and 1500 the number of European universities grew from twenty to seventy. The universities also developed a new way of reading. During the fifteenth century the Sorbonne in Paris and Oxford University decreed that libraries were to be quiet places, an indication of the spread of silent reading among the most highly educated classes. Compared to the tradition of reading aloud, silent reading was faster and more private. The silent reader learned more quickly and also decided independently the meaning of what had been read. Once many cheap books were available to the silent readers among the best educated, the interpretation of texts, especially the notoriously difficult text of the Bible, could no longer be easily regulated.

Would the Reformation have succeeded without the print revolution? It is impossible to imagine that it could have. Print culture radically changed how information was disseminated and gave people new ways to interpret their experiences. Between 1517 and 1520, Martin Luther wrote some thirty tracts, mostly in a riveting colloquial German; 300,000 copies were printed and distributed throughout Europe. No other author's ideas had ever spread so fast to so many.

The First Printing Press

The first printing press, invented by Johannes Gutenberg in Mainz, Germany, probably looked very much like this reconstructed model. The metal blocks with interchangeable letters were inked and then pressed onto each sheet of paper. Then the sheets were hung up while the ink dried.

The Northern Renaissance and the Christian Humanists

As discussed in Chapter 11, the humanists were writers devoted to rediscovering the lost works of antiquity and imitating the style of the best Greek and Latin authors of the ancient world. As the humanists examined these ancient texts, they developed the study of philology, of how the meanings of words change over time. These endeavors stimulated a new kind of approach to the sources of Christianity. The humanist Lorenzo Valla (ca. 1407–1457), for example, evaluated the historical sources of papal authority, including the Donation of Constantine—a document that provided the legal justification for the Papal State and papal assertions of supreme authority in Italy. Because the Donation of Constantine used words that were not current during the time when it was supposedly written, Valla argued that it was a forgery. He went on to question the accuracy of the Vulgate, the Latin translation of the Bible accepted by the Church.

The humanists who specialized in subjecting the Bible to philological study are called the Christian humanists°. In examining the sources of Christianity, their goal was not to criticize Christianity or the Church but to understand the precise meaning of its founding texts, especially the Bible and the writings of the Church fathers, who wrote in Greek and Latin and commented on the Bible during the early centuries of Christianity. The Christian humanists sought to correct what they saw as mistakes in interpreting Christian doctrine and by making the proper interpretations they tried to improve the morals of all. They believed that the path to personal morality and to Church reform lay in imitating "the primitive church," which meant the practices of Christianity at the time of Jesus and the apostles. Most of the Christian humanists came from northern Europe. They constituted the most influential wing of the northern Renaissance, a movement that built on the foundations of the Italian Renaissance. Through their efforts, the foundations of Christianity came under intense scrutiny during the early sixteenth century.

By far the most influential of the Christian humanists was a Dutchman, Desiderius Erasmus (ca. 1469–1536). To remedy the evils of the world, Erasmus became an ardent advocate of education, especially for future priests, whom he wanted to learn "the philosophy of Christ." As a guide to that philosophy, he published an annotated text of the Greek New Testament, which he opened with the optimistic preface: "If the Gospel were truly preached, the Christian people would be spared many wars." He later translated the

Albrecht Dürer, *The Knight, Death, and the Devil*
This engraving of 1513 illustrates Erasmus's *Handbook for the Militant Christian* by depicting a knight steadfastly advancing through a frightening landscape. A figure of death holds an hourglass, indicating that the knight's time on Earth is limited. A devil follows behind him threateningly. His valiant horse and loyal dog represent the virtues that a pious Christian must acquire.

Greek New Testament into a new Latin version. His critical studies were the basis of many translations of the Hebrew and Greek Bible into vernacular languages, including the popular English translation, the King James Bible. His lasting fame rests on his perceptive philological analysis of the Bible and other early Christian texts.

Exploiting the potential of the relatively new printing industry, Erasmus became the most inspiring moral critic of his times. During times of war he eloquently called for peace; he published a practical manual for helping children develop a sense of morality; and he laid out easy-to-follow guidelines for spiritual renewal in the *Handbook for the Militant Christian*. He was most popular for his biting criticisms of the Church that revealed a genuine spiritual sorrow shared by many of his readers:

I could see that the common body of Christians was corrupt not only in its affections but in its ideas. I pondered on the fact that those who profess themselves pastors and doctors for the most part misuse these titles, which belong to Christ, for their own advantage. . . . Is there any religious man who does not see with sorrow that this generation is far the most corrupt there has ever been?[1]

Erasmus's penchant for moral criticism reached the level of high satire in his masterpiece, *The Praise of Folly* (1514). In it he attacked theologians preoccupied by silly questions, such as whether the Resurrection could take place at night; he lampooned corrupt priests who took money from dying men to read the last rites; he ridiculed gullible pilgrims who bought phony relics as tourist souvenirs; and he parodied the vanity of monks who thought the color of their robes more important than helping the poor. He saved some of his most biting sarcasm for the monks by pointing out "their filthiness, their ignorance, their bawdiness, and their insolence."[2]

Despite these criticisms Erasmus refused to abandon Catholicism and engaged in a very public conflict with Luther and the Protestants. He thought the militants on both sides were driven more by egotism than by Christian humility. In the combative age of the Reformation, Erasmus stood virtually alone as a voice of peace and moderation, and like many nonviolent people since that time, he was deeply hated. Erasmus was an eloquent popularizer, some-

one who demonstrated to a large public how individuals could apply to their daily lives previously obscure trends in humanist learning and how a better understanding of the Bible could purify faith and combat corruption within the Church.

Erasmus's friend, the Englishman Thomas More (1478–1535), is best known for his book *Utopia* (1516). More's little book established the genre of utopian fiction, which describes imaginary, idealized worlds. It depicted a fantasy island in the New World, "Utopia," which in Greek means "nowhere." Utopia was inhabited by monotheists who, although not Christians, intuitively understood pure religion, lived a highly regulated life, and shared their property in common. Utopia represented More's understanding of what a society based on the primitive church might look like. In particular he took the idea of abolishing all private property from Scripture, which states that the believers in Christ "were of one heart and soul, and no one claimed private ownership of any possessions, but everything they owned was held in common" (Acts 4:32). More shared some of Erasmus's ideas about the critical study of Scripture and a purer Church, but unlike Erasmus he was no pacifist. In his capacity as chancellor of England, he ruthlessly persecuted Protestants.

Erasmus and More remained loyal Catholics, and More even sacrificed his own life to the faith. Nevertheless, their

DOCUMENT

Thomas More's Argument Against Capital Punishment

In sixteenth-century England, there were hundreds of offenses, including simple theft, that could lead to capital punishment. Among the many aspects of contemporary society that Thomas More criticized in Utopia *(1516), capital punishment especially offended him because it was so clearly prohibited in the Bible. More combined moral precepts derived from Scripture and reasoned argument, a combination that is especially characteristic of the Christian humanists. Thomas More was himself a victim of capital punishment, executed by the courts of King Henry VIII.*

God said, "Thou shalt not kill"—does the theft of a little money make it quite all right for us to do so? If it's said that this commandment applies only to illegal killing, what's to prevent human beings from similarly agreeing among themselves to legalize certain types of rape, adultery, or perjury? Considering that God has forbidden us even to kill ourselves, can we really believe that purely human arrangements for the regulation of mutual slaughter are enough, without any divine authority, to exempt execu-

tioners from the sixth commandment? Isn't that rather like saying that this particular commandment has no more validity than human laws allow it?—in which case the principle can be extended indefinitely, until in all spheres of life human beings decide just how far God's commandments may conveniently be observed.

. . .

Well, those are my objections on moral grounds. From a practical point of view, surely it's obvious that to punish thieves and murderers in precisely the same way is not only absurd but also highly dangerous for the public. If a thief knows that a conviction for murder will get him into no more trouble than a conviction for theft, he's naturally impelled to kill the person that he'd otherwise merely have robbed. It's no worse to him if he's caught, and it gives him a better chance of not being caught, and of concealing the crime altogether by eliminating the only witness. So in our efforts to terrorize thieves we're actually encouraging them to murder innocent people.

Source: From *Utopia*, by Thomas More, translated by Paul Turner (Penguin Classics, 1961). Copyright © 1961 by Paul Turner. Reproduced by permission of Penguin Books Ltd.

work helped popularize some of the principles that came to be associated with the Protestant reformers. To them, the test for the legitimacy of any religious practice was twofold: First, could it be found in the Bible; second, did it promote moral behavior? The Christian humanists' preoccupation with textual criticism focused attention on the sources of Christianity, and some readers were profoundly shaken by the deep disparity they perceived between the Christianity of the New Testament and the state of the Church in their own time.

The Lutheran Reformation

■ How did the Lutheran Reformation create a new kind of religious culture?

The Protestant Reformation began with the protests of Martin Luther against the pope and certain Church practices. Like Erasmus and More, Luther used the Bible as the litmus test of what the Church should do. If a practice could not be found in the Bible, Luther thought, then it should not be considered Christian. But unlike Erasmus and More, he also introduced theological innovations that made compromise with the papacy impossible.

Luther and his followers would not have succeeded without the support of local political authorities, who had their own grievances against the pope and the Holy Roman Emperor, a devout defender of the Catholic faith. The Lutheran Reformation first spread in Germany with the assistance and encouragement of those local authorities: the town magistrates and the territorial princes. Luther's ideas had a magnetic appeal to a wide spectrum of the population, especially women and peasants. When the peasants thought that Luther's ideas about the freedom of the Christian also meant economic freedom, they revolted against their feudal lords. The violence of that revolt forced Luther to retreat and to back the forces of order, the lords and princes. In so doing he made it clear that the Reformation was not to be a social revolution but a religious reform. Lutheranism would not threaten the established political order. Under the sponsorship of princes and kings, Lutheranism spread from Germany into Scandinavia.

Martin Luther and the Break with Rome

Martin Luther (1483–1546) suffered a grim childhood and uneasy relationship with his father, a miner who wanted his son to become a lawyer. During a break from the University of Erfurt, where he was studying law, Luther was thrown from his horse in a storm and nearly died. That frightening experience impelled him to become a monk, a decision that infuriated his father because it meant young Luther abandoned a promising professional career. By becoming a monk, Luther replaced the control of his father with obedience to his superiors in the Augustinian Order. They sent him back to the University of Erfurt for advanced study in theology and then transferred him from the lovely garden city of Erfurt to Wittenberg in Saxony, a scruffy town "on the edge of beyond," as Luther described it. At Wittenberg Luther began to teach at an undistinguished university, far from the intellectual action. Instead of lamenting his isolation, Luther brought the world to his university by making it the center of the religious reform movement.

As a monk, Luther had been haunted by a deep lack of self-worth: "In the monastery, I did not think about women, or gold, or goods, but my heart trembled, and doubted how God could be gracious to me. Then I fell away from faith, and let myself think nothing less than that I had come under the Wrath of God, whom I must reconcile with my good works."[3] Obsessed by the fear that no amount of charitable good works, prayers, or religious ceremonies would compensate for God's contempt of him, Luther suffered from anxiety attacks and prolonged periods of depression. He understood his psychic turmoil and shaky faith as any monk would—the temptations of the Devil, who was a very powerful figure in Luther's imagination.

Over several years, while preparing and revising his university lectures on St. Paul, Luther gradually worked out a solution to his own spiritual crisis by reexamining the theology of penance. The sacrament of penance provided a way to confess sins and receive absolution for them. If a penitent had lied, for example, he could seek forgiveness for the sin by feeling sorry about it, confessing it to a priest, and receiving a penalty, usually a specified number of prayers. Penance took care of only those penalties the Church could inflict on sinners; God's punishment for sins would take place in Purgatory (a place of temporary suffering for dead souls) and at the Last Judgment. But Catholic theology held that penance in this world would reduce punishment in the next. In wrestling with the concept of penance, Luther long meditated on the meaning of a difficult passage in St. Paul's epistle to the Romans (1:17): "The just shall live by faith." Luther came to understand this passage to mean that eternal salvation came not from performing the religious good works of penance but as a gift from God. That gift was called "grace" and was completely unmerited. Luther called this process of receiving God's grace "justification by faith alone°," because the ability to have faith in Christ was a sign that one had received grace.

Luther's emphasis on justification by faith alone left no room for human free will in obtaining salvation, because Luther believed that faith could come only from God's grace. This did not mean that God controlled every human action, but it did mean that humans could not will to do good. They needed God's help. Those blessed with God's grace would naturally perform good works. This way of thinking about God's grace had a long tradition going back to St. Augustine, the Church father whose work profoundly influenced Luther's own thought. In fact, many Catholic thinkers had embraced a similar position, but they did not draw the same conclusions about free will that Luther did. In the turmoil of the Reformation Luther's interpretation of St. Augustine separated Lutheran from Catholic theology. The issue of free will became one of the most crucial differences between Protestants and Catholics. Based on his rejection of free will, Luther eventually concluded that the sacraments of the Church could work only if the person receiving them had received God's grace. One could not will for them to work. He abandoned all but two of the sacraments because sacraments were examples of vain works that deluded people into thinking they could earn salvation by performing them. He was obliged to retain communion and baptism because they were clearly authorized by the Bible, but disputes over the meaning of these two sacraments created divisions within the Protestant Reformation movement itself.

Communion in Both Kinds

In this woodcut by Lucas Cranach the Elder, Lutheran ministers offer both the communion wine and bread to the laity. Catholics reserved the wine for the priests, which set them apart from the laity. Changes in the rituals of the Eucharist or communion were among the most divisive issues separating Catholic from Protestant.

For Luther this seemingly bleak doctrine of denying the human will to do good liberated him from his persistent fears of damnation. He no longer had to worry whether he was doing enough to please God or could muster enough energy to fight the Devil. All he had to do was trust in God's grace. After this breakthrough, Luther reported that "I felt myself to be born anew, and to enter through open gates into paradise itself. From here, the whole face of the Scriptures was altered."[4]

The Ninety-Five Theses

In 1517 Luther became embroiled in a controversy that led to his and his followers' separation from the Roman Catholic Church. In order to finance the building of a new St. Peter's Basilica in Rome, Pope Leo X had issued a special new indulgence. An indulgence was a particular form of penance whereby a sinner could remove years of punishment in Purgatory after death by performing a good work here on Earth. For example, pilgrims to Rome or Jerusalem were often in search of indulgences, which were concrete measures of the value of their penances. Indulgences formed one of the most intimate bonds between the Church and the laity because they offered a means for the forgiveness of specific sins.

During the fourteenth century popes in need of ready cash had begun to sell indulgences. But Pope Leo's new indulgence went far beyond the promise of earlier indulgences by offering a one-time-only opportunity to escape penalties in Purgatory for all sins. Moreover, the special indulgence could apply not only to the purchaser but to the dead already in Purgatory. The new indulgence immediately made all other indulgences worthless because it removed all penalties for sin whereas others removed only some.

Frederick the Wise, the Elector of Saxony (a princely title indicating that he was one of those who elected the emperors of the Holy Roman Empire) and the patron of Martin Luther's university, prohibited the sale of Pope Leo's special indulgence in Electoral Saxony, but it was sold just a few miles away from Wittenberg, across the border in the domain of Archbishop Albrecht of Mainz. Albrecht needed the revenues that the sale of indulgences would bring because he was in debt. He had borrowed enormous sums to bribe Pope Leo to allow him to hold simultaneously three ecclesiastical offices—a practice that was against Church law. To help Albrecht repay his debts, the pope allowed Albrecht to keep half of the revenue from the indulgence sale in his territories. Wittenbergers began to trek over the border to Albrecht's lands to listen to the sales pitch of a shameless indulgence hawker, the Dominican John Tetzel (1470–1519). Tetzel staged an ecclesiastical version of a carnival barker's act in which he harangued the crowd about their dead parents who could be immediately released from the flames of Purgatory for the sacrifice of a few coins. He allegedly ended his sermons with the notorious jingle,

*As soon as gold in the basin rings,
Right then the soul to heaven springs.*[5]

A group of the Wittenbergers who heard Tetzel asked Martin Luther for his advice about buying the indulgence. Luther responded less as a pastor offering comforting advice to his flock than as a university professor keen for debate. He prepared in Latin ninety-five theses—arguments or talking points—about indulgences that he announced he was willing to defend in an academic disputation. Luther had a few copies printed and, according to Lutheran tradition, dramatically posted one on the door of Wittenberg Cathedral. In fact, his posting of the theses makes a good story, but there is no evidence that he actually did so. It was just standard practice for debates. The Ninety-Five Theses were hardly revolutionary in themselves. They argued a simple point that salvation could not be bought and sold, a proposition that was sound, conservative theology, and they explicitly accepted the authority of the pope even as they set limits on that authority. On that point, Luther was merely following what the Church councils of the fifteenth century had decreed. Luther's tone was moderate. He simply suggested that Pope Leo may have been misled in issuing the new indulgence. No one showed up to debate Luther, but someone translated the Ninety-Five Theses into German and printed them, and within a few weeks, a previously unknown professor from an obscure university was the talk of the German-speaking lands.

The Dominicans counterattacked. Tetzel himself drew up opposing theses, which provoked a public clamor that Luther had tried to avoid. In 1519 at Leipzig before a raucous crowd of university students, Luther finally debated the theses and other issues with Johann Eck, a professor from the University of Ingolstadt. When Eck cleverly backed him into a logical corner, Luther refused to retreat; he insisted that the Bible was the sole guide to human conscience, and he questioned the authority of both popes and councils. This was the very teaching for which earlier heretics had been burned at the stake. At this point Luther had no choice but to abandon his allegiance to the Church to which he had dedicated his life. By this time, Luther also had a large following in Wittenberg and beyond. The core of this group, who called themselves "evangelicals," were university students, younger humanists, and the well-educated, reform-minded priests and monks.

The Path to the Diet of Worms

In the wake of the Leipzig debate and Pope Leo's rejection of Luther's objections to indulgences, Luther abandoned his moderate tone and launched an inflammatory pamphlet campaign. Some pamphlets were first written in Latin, for learned readers, but all soon became available in Luther's acerbic German prose, which delighted readers. *Freedom of a Christian* (1520) argued that the Church's emphasis on good works had distracted Christians from the only source of salvation—God's grace, which was manifest in the faith of the Christian. It proclaimed the revolutionary doctrine of the "priesthood of all believers°," which reasoned that all those of pure faith were themselves priests, a doctrine that undermined the authority of the Catholic clergy over the laity. The most inspirational pamphlet, *To the Christian Nobility of the German Nation* (1520), called upon the German princes to reform the Church and to defend Germany from exploitation by the corrupt Italians who ran the Church in Rome. When Pope Leo ordered Luther to retract his writings, Luther responded with a defiant demonstration in which he and his students burned the pope's decree and all of the university library's books of Church law. The die was cast.

The pope demanded that Luther be arrested, but Luther's patron, the Elector Frederick, answered by defending the professor. Frederick refused to make the arrest without first giving Luther a hearing at the Imperial Diet (parliament), which was set to meet at the town of Worms in 1521. Assembled at the Diet of Worms were haughty princes, grave bishops, and the resplendent young emperor Charles V (r. 1519–1558), who was presiding over his first Imperial Diet. The emperor ordered Luther to disavow his writings, but Luther refused to do so. For several days the diet was in an uproar, divided by friends and foes of Luther's doctrines. Just before he was to be condemned by the emperor, Luther disappeared, and rumors flew that he had been assassinated. For days no one knew the truth. Frederick the Wise had kidnapped Luther for his own safety and hidden him in the castle at Wartburg, where for nearly a year he labored in quiet seclusion translating the New Testament into German.

The Lutheran Reformation in the Cities and Principalities

Luther had escaped arrest and execution at the hands of the emperor, but he could not control his own followers and allies. The Reformation quickly became a vast, sprawling movement far beyond the control of any individual, even in Luther's own Wittenberg. One of the characteristics of the Protestant Reformation was that once reformers rejected the supreme authority of the papacy, differences about forms of worship or biblical interpretation led to division within the movement and eventually to the formation of separate churches.

DOCUMENT

Martin Luther, *The German Mass* (1526)

In its early phases the Reformation spread most rapidly among the educated urban classes. During the sixteenth century, fifty of the sixty-five German imperial cities, at one time or another, officially accepted the Protestant Reformation. Besides these large imperial cities, most of the 200 smaller German towns with a population of more than

DOCUMENT

Martin Luther's Powers of Persuasion

Part of Martin Luther's appeal derived from his polemical style. The Freedom of a Christian (1520) was probably Luther's last serious attempt to reconcile himself with Pope Leo X. In the open letter to Pope Leo that introduces the tract, Luther asserts that he is criticizing corrupt advisers in the papal curia rather than the pope himself, but Luther's language seems more designed to embolden his own followers than to persuade the pope.

Living among the monsters of this age with whom I am now for the third year waging war, I am compelled occasionally to look up to you, Leo, most blessed father, and to think of you. Indeed, since you are occasionally regarded as the sole cause of my warfare, I cannot help thinking of you. To be sure, the undeserved raging of your godless flatterers against me has compelled me to appeal from your see [officials] to a future council [of all the bishops of the Church], despite the decrees of your predecessors Pius and Julius, who with a foolish tyranny forbade such an appeal.

. . .

I have truly despised your see, the Roman Curia, which, however, neither you nor anyone else can deny is more corrupt than any Babylon or Sodom [places condemned for sinfulness in the Bible] ever was, and which, as far as I can see, is characterized by a completely depraved, hopeless, and notorious godlessness. I have been thoroughly incensed over the fact that good Christians are mocked in your name and under the cloak of the Roman church. I have resisted and will continue to resist your see as long as the spirit of faith lives in me.

. . .

I never intended to attack the Roman Curia or to raise any controversy concerning it. But when I saw all efforts to save it were hopeless, I despised it, gave it a bill of divorce, and said, "let the evildoer still do evil, and the filthy still be filthy" [Revelations 22:11]. Then I turned to the quiet and peaceful study of the Holy Scriptures so that I might be helpful to my brothers around me. When I had made some progress in these studies, Satan opened his eyes and then filled his servant Johann Eck, a notable enemy of Christ, with an insatiable lust for glory and thus aroused him to drag me unawares to a debate, seizing me by means of one little word which I had let slip concerning the primacy of the Roman church. Then that boastful braggart, frothing and gnashing his teeth, declared that he would risk everything for the glory of God and the honor of the Apostolic See. Puffed up with the prospect of abusing your authority, he looked forward with great confidence to a victory over me. . . . When the debate ended badly for the sophist, an unbelievable madness overcame the man, for he believed that it was his fault alone which was responsible for my disclosing all the infamy of Rome.

Source: Excerpt from *Luther's Works, vol. 31, Career of the Reformer: I,* edited by Harold J. Grimm (Philadelphia: Muhlenberg Press, 1957). Translated by W. A. Lambert and revised by Harold J. Grimm.

1,000 experienced some form of the Protestant movement. During the 1520s and 1530s, the magistrates (mayors and other office holders) of these towns took command of the Reformation movement by seizing control of the local churches. The magistrates implemented Luther's reform of worship, disciplined the clergy, and stopped the drain of revenues to irresponsible bishops and the distant pope.

The German princes of the Holy Roman Empire had their own reasons to resent the Church. They wanted to appoint their own nominees to ecclesiastical offices and to diminish the legal privileges of the clergy. During the 1520s Luther's enormous popularity gave many German princes the opportunity they had been waiting for. Despite his steadfast Catholicism, Emperor Charles V was in no position to resist their demands. During most of his reign, Charles faced a two-front war—against France and against the Ottoman Turks. Charles could ill afford additional trouble with the German princes because he desperately needed their military assistance. At the first Imperial Diet of Speyer in 1526, Charles granted the princes territorial sovereignty in religion by allowing them to decide whether they would enforce the imperial edict of the Diet of Worms against Luther and his followers. To preserve the empire from external enemies, Charles was forced to allow its internal division along religious lines.

The Appeal of the Reformation to Women

As divisive as Reformist theology was to imperial politics, it had a particular appeal to people who were habitually excluded from the political world and governance of the Church, especially women and peasants. In the early days of the movement, women felt that Luther's description of "the priesthood of all believers" meant that women as well as men could participate fully in the religious life of the Church. Women understood Luther's phrase "the freedom of a Christian" as freeing them from the restrictive roles that had traditionally kept them silent and at home. Moreover, Luther and the other major reformers saw positive religious value in the role of wife and mother. Abandoning the Catholic Church's view that celibate monks and nuns were morally superior to married people, Luther declared marriage holy and set an example by taking a wife, the ex-nun Katherine von Bora. The wives of the reformers often became partners in the Reformation, taking particular responsibility for organizing charities and administering to the poor.

In the early phases of the Reformation, women preached and published on religious matters. These women demanded to be heard in churches and delivered inspiring sermons. They asked that their writings be accepted as authentic products of the Holy Spirit. In some cases, female rulers brought their entire land over to the Reformation. Elisabeth of Brunswick-Calenburg reformed the local church and invited Protestant preachers into her lands. The noblewoman Argula von Grumbach argued that even though St. Paul had warned that women should be silent in church, she felt driven by the word of God to profess her faith publicly. Marie Dentière, a former abbess of a French convent who joined the Reformation cause, asked, "Do we have two Gospels, one for men and the other for women? . . . For we [women] ought not, any more than men, hide and bury within the earth that which God has . . . revealed to us women?"[6]

Most women were soon disappointed. Women's preaching and writing threatened the male religious and political authorities. They ordered Argula von Grumbach's husband to make her stop writing. Other women who defended the Reformation were silenced by the reformers themselves, and women who spoke up in church were widely condemned. In some places laws were passed that prohibited groups of women from discussing religious questions. In England, noblewomen were even prevented from reading the Bible aloud to others. One kind of writing could not be controlled, however—the private diary. The Protestant imperative to discover the workings of faith within oneself helped promote writing private diaries. The practice spread rapidly with Protestantism, and many women used diaries as an outlet for personal expression and a way to develop a sense of their own personal identities.

The few women who were able to speak and act openly in public were either from the upper classes or the wives of prominent reformers. No man could silence Marguerite of Navarre and her daughter Jeanne d'Albret, who used their authority as queens to promote the Reformation. A body of religious literature developed that held up as models more

Martin Luther and Katherine von Bora
For many pious Lutherans the images of Luther and his wife, herself a former nun, replaced the images of the Virgin Mary and the saints favored by the Catholics.

humble women such as Katherine Zell, the wife of one of Strasbourg's reformers.

For most women participation in the Reformation was confined to the domestic sphere, where they instructed children, quietly read the Bible, and led prayer circles. Protestant authorities also allowed divorce, which was prohibited by Catholic Church law. However, the reform leaders were quite reluctant to grant women the same rights as their husbands in obtaining a divorce. During the early years of the Reformation, there were many marriages in which one spouse followed the old faith and the other the new. But if the woman converted and her husband did not, the Protestant reformers counseled that she obey her husband even if he forced her to act contrary to God's will. She could pray for his conversion but could not leave or divorce him. Most women were forced to remain married regardless of their feelings. A few exceptional women left their husbands anyway and continued to proclaim their religious convictions to the world. One such woman, Anne Askew from England, was tortured and executed for her beliefs.

The German Peasants' Revolt

The Reformation also appealed to many peasants simply because it offered them a simplified, purified religion and, most important, local control of their churches. The peasants of Wendelstein, a typical South German village, had been complaining about the conduct of its priests for some time. In 1523, they hired a "Christian teacher" and told him in no uncertain terms: "We will not recognize you as a lord, but only as a servant of the community. We will command you, not you us, and we order you to preach the gospel and the word of God purely, clearly, and truthfully—without any human teachings—faithfully and conscientiously."[7] These villagers understood the Reformation to mean that they could take control of their local church and demand responsible conduct from the minister they hired. However, other peasants understood the Reformation in more radical terms as licensing social reforms that Luther himself never supported.

In June 1524 a seemingly minor event sparked a revolt of peasants in many parts of Germany. When an aristocratic lady demanded that the peasants in her village abandon their grain harvest to gather snails for her, they rebelled and set her castle on fire. Over the next two years, the rebellion spread as peasants rose up against their feudal lords to demand the adoption of Lutheran reforms in the Church, a reduction of feudal privileges, the abolition of serfdom, and the self-government of their communities. Their rebellion was unprecedented: the largest and best-organized peasant movement up to that time in European history, a measure of the powerful effect of the Protestant reform message. Like the Reformation, the revolt was the culmination of a long period of discontent, but unlike the Reformation, it was a tragic failure.

These peasants were doing exactly what they thought Luther had advocated when he wrote about the "freedom of the Christian." They interpreted his words to mean complete social as well as religious freedom. However, Luther had not meant anything of the sort. To him the freedom of the Christian referred to inner, spiritual freedom, not liberation from economic or political bondage. Instead of supporting the rebellion begun in his name, Luther and nearly all the other reformers backed the feudal lords and condemned in uncompromising terms the violence of the peasant armies. In *Against the Thieving, Murderous Hordes of Peasants* (1525), Luther expressed his own fear of the lower classes and revealed that despite his acid-tongued attacks on the pope, he was fundamentally a conservative thinker who was committed to law and order. He urged that the peasants be hunted down and killed like rabid dogs. And so they were. Between 70,000 and 100,000 peasants died, a slaughter far greater than the Roman persecutions of the early Christians. To the peasants, Luther's conservative position on social and economic issues felt like betrayal, but it enabled the Lutheran Reformation to retain the support of the princes, which was essential for its survival.

Lutheran Success

Soon after the crushing of the Peasants' Revolt, the Lutheran Reformation faced a renewed threat from its Catholic opponents. In 1530 Emperor Charles V bluntly commanded all Lutherans to return to the Catholic fold or face arrest. Enraged, the Lutherans refused to comply. The following year the Protestant princes formed a military alliance, the Schmalkaldic League, against the emperor. Renewed trouble with France and the Turks prevented a military confrontation between the league and the emperor for fifteen years, giving the Lutherans enough breathing space to put the Reformation on a firmer basis in Germany by training ministers and educating the laity in the new religion. In place of the Catholic bishops, Lutherans established regional consistories (boards of clerics) to supervise the new Protestant churches. Educational reforms introduced a humanist curriculum, established schools for girls, and organized religious instruction for the laity. In the meantime Lutheranism spread beyond Germany into Scandinavia, where it received support from the kings of Denmark and Sweden as it had among the princes of northern Germany.

After freeing himself yet again from foreign wars and failing to effect a compromise solution in Germany, Charles V turned his armies against the Protestants. However, in 1552 the Protestant armies defeated in battle the Catholic forces of the emperor, and Charles was forced to relent. In 1555 the Religious Peace of Augsburg° established the principle of *cuius regio, eius religio*, which means "he who rules determines the religion of the land." Protestant princes were permitted to retain all church lands seized before 1552 and to enforce Protestant worship, but Catholic princes were also allowed to enforce Catholic worship in their territories. Those who disagreed with the religion of their ruler would not be tolerated; their options were to change religious affiliations or to emigrate elsewhere. With the Peace of Augsburg the religious division of the Holy Roman Empire became permanent, and the legal foundations were in place for the development of the two distinctive religious cultures—Protestant and Catholic.

The following year, Emperor Charles, worn out from ceaseless warfare, the anxieties of holding his vast territories together, and nearly forty years of trying to stamp out Protestantism, abdicated and retired to a monastery, where he died in 1558.

CHRONOLOGY

The Lutheran Reformation

1517	Luther posts the Ninety-Five Theses
1519	Luther debates Johann Eck at Leipzig; election of Charles V as Holy Roman Emperor
1521	Diet of Worms
1524–1525	German peasants revolt
1531	Formation of the Schmalkaldic League
1555	The Religious Peace of Augsburg

The Diversity of Protestantism

■ How and why did Protestant denominations multiply to such an extent in northern Europe and Britain?

The term *Protestant* originally applied only to the followers of Luther who *protested* the decisions of the second Imperial Diet of Speyer in 1529, which attempted to force them back into the Catholic fold, but the term came to describe much more than that small group. It designated all western European Christians who refused to accept the authority of the pope. Protestantism encompassed innumerable churches and sects. Many of these have survived since the Reformation; some disappeared in the violence of the sixteenth century; others have sprung up since, especially in North America, where Protestantism has thrived.

The varieties of Protestantism can be divided into two types. The first type was the product of the Magisterial Reformation°, which refers to the churches that received official government sanction. These included the Lutheran churches (Germany and Scandinavia); the Reformed and Calvinist churches (Switzerland, Scotland, the Netherlands, and a few places in Germany); and the Anglican church (England, Wales, parts of Ireland, and later in England's colonies). The second type was the product of the Radical Reformation° and includes the movements that failed to gain official recognition and were at best tolerated, at worst persecuted. This strict division into Magisterial and Radical Protestantism broke down in eastern Europe, where the states were too weak to enforce religious conformity. In eastern Europe religious variety prevailed over rigid conformity, at least for the sixteenth century (see Map 13.1).

The Reformation in Switzerland

The governmental independence of Switzerland from the Holy Roman Empire meant that from the beginning of the Reformation local authorities could cooperate with the re-

formers without opposition from the emperor. The Swiss Confederation bound together thirteen fiercely proud regions, called cantons, which had established their independence from the Habsburg dynasty of the Holy Roman Empire. Except for the leading cities of Zürich, Basel, and Geneva, Switzerland remained an impoverished land of peasants who could not fully support themselves from the barren mountainous land. To supplement their meager incomes, young Swiss men fought as mercenaries in foreign armies, often those of the pope. Each spring, mercenary captains recruited able-bodied Swiss men from the mountain villages. The Swiss men left the women behind to tend the animals and farms. By summer, the villages were emptied of all men except the old and invalid. Each fall at the end of the fighting season, the survivors of that season's campaign trudged home, always bringing bad news to a fresh group of widows. The strain created by the mercenary's life stimulated the desire for sweeping reforms in Switzerland.

Zwingli's Zürich

Ulrich Zwingli (1484–1531) had served as a chaplain with the Swiss mercenaries serving the pope in Italy. In 1520, after being named the People's Priest of Zürich, Zwingli criticized his superior bishop for recruiting local young men to die in the papal armies. That same year he began to call for reform of the Church, advocating the abolition of the Roman Catholic mass, the marriage of priests, and the closing of monasteries. One of the novel features of Zwingli's reform was the strict emphasis on preaching the Word of Scripture during Church services, in contrast to the emphasis on ritual in the traditional Catholic liturgy. He ordered the removal of all paintings and statues from churches because they were too powerful a distraction from concentrating on the preaching. Zwingli was certainly influenced by the writings of Erasmus, but he denied that Luther had any effect on him at all. The Zwinglian Reformation began independently of the Lutheran Reformation and created a separate reform center from

Map 13.1 The Division of Western Christianity by 1555
The West, which had been culturally unified by Christianity for more than a thousand years, split apart during the sixteenth century. These religious divisions persist to this day.

The Division of Western Christianity by 1555

- Lutheran
- Anglican
- Calvinist control or influence
- Anabaptist
- Roman Catholic
- ■ Eastern border of Western Christianity

which initiatives spread throughout Switzerland, southern Germany, and England.

Two features distinguished the Zwinglian from the Lutheran Reformation. One was Zwingli's desire to have reformed ministers participate in governmental decisions. In Lutheran Germany, church and state supported each other, but they remained legally separate, and the prince alone had the authority to determine the religion of the land. In Zürich, the moral Christian and the good citizen were one and the same, and Zwingli worked with the magistrates of the city council, who step-by-step legalized the Reformation and enforced conformity through its police powers.

Luther and Zwingli also differed in their understanding of the nature of the Eucharist, the communion sacrament that reenacted Christ's Last Supper with his apostles. Luther believed that Christ's body was spiritually present in the communion bread. "You will receive," as he put it, "as much as you believe you receive."[8] This emphasis on the inner, spiritual state of the believer was very characteristic of Luther's introspective piety. In contrast to Luther, Zwingli could not accept the idea of Almighty God making himself present in a humble piece of bread. To Zwingli the Eucharistic bread was just a symbol that stood for the body of Christ. The problem with the symbolic interpretation of the Eucharist was that the various reformers could not agree with Zwingli on exactly what the Eucharist symbol-

ized. As early as 1524, it became evident that each reformer was committed to a different interpretation, and these different interpretations became the basis for different Protestant churches.

In 1529 Count Philip of Hesse (1504–1567) tried to forge a military alliance between the Protestants of Germany and Switzerland against the Catholics. The theological disputes over the Eucharist blocked full cooperation, however. Philip brought together Luther, Zwingli, and the other principal reformers for a formal discussion at the new Protestant University of Marburg. But Luther adamantly refused to compromise and shrugged off Zwingli's tearful pleas for cooperation. The failure of the Marburg Colloquy marked the permanent rupture of the Reformation movement.

Calvin's Geneva

In the next generation the momentum of the Reformation shifted to Geneva, Switzerland, under the leadership of John Calvin (1509–1564). Calvin arrived in French-speaking Geneva as a religious refugee in 1536 and came to support the city's long struggle for independence from the Duke of Savoy, who had been rejected as the city's lord a few years before. Calvin worked with the Genevan magistrates who attempted to build a holy community that was independent of the dictates of the city's Catholic bishop. But Calvinism spread far beyond its Swiss home, becoming the dominant form of Protestantism in France, the Netherlands, Scotland, and New England.

Trained as a lawyer and exiled from his home in France in 1533 for his reformist views, Calvin spent several years wandering, searching for a quiet retreat and collaborating with other reformers. After he settled in Geneva, Calvin spent the rest of his life transforming the town into the City of God. The linchpin of the Genevan reform was the close cooperation between the magistrates of the city council and the clergy in enforcing the moral discipline of the citizens. To achieve this goal, Calvin persuaded the magistrates in 1555 to grant the clergy the right to excommunicate sinners as well as those who disagreed with Calvinist theology. And in the Calvinist construction, excommunication meant more than banishment from church. Excommunicated people were completely shunned; no one could talk to them, including members of their own family; they effectively lost their property and ability to conduct business. Excommunication became a form of exile. The financial and psychological consequences of excommunication were deeply feared because the excommunicated were, in effect, socially dead.

Calvin's theology extended the insights of Luther and Zwingli to their logical conclusion. This pattern was most obvious in Calvin's understanding of justification by faith. Luther had argued that the Christian could not earn salvation through good works and that faith came only from God. Calvin reasoned that if an all-knowing, all-powerful God knew everything in advance and caused everything to happen, then the salvation of any individual was predetermined or, as Calvin put it, "predestined." Calvin's doctrine of predestination° was not new. In fact, it had long been discussed among Christian theologians. But for Calvin two considerations made it crucial. First was Calvin's certainty that God was above any influence from humanity. The "majesty of God," as Calvin put it, was the principle from which everything else followed. Second, Calvin and other preachers had noticed that in a congregation attending a sermon, only a few paid attention to what was preached, while the vast majority seemed unable or unwilling to understand. The reason for this disparity seemed to be that only the Elect could truly follow God's Word. The Elect were those who had received God's grace and would be saved. The Elect were known only to God, but Calvin's theology encouraged the converted to feel the assurance of salvation and to accept a "calling" from God to perform his will on Earth. God's calling° gave Calvinists a powerful sense of personal direction, which committed them to a life of moral activity, whether as preacher, wife, or shoemaker.

Calvin composed an elegant theological treatise, the *Institutes of the Christian Religion,* first published in six chapters in 1535 but constantly revised and expanded until it reached eighty chapters in the definitive 1559 edition.

DOCUMENT

Calvin on Predestination (16th c.)

Calvin the lawyer wrote a tightly argued and reasoned work, like a trial attorney preparing a case. In Calvin's theology the parts fit neatly together like a vast, intricate puzzle. Calvin's work aspired to be a comprehensive reformed theology that would convince through reasoned deliberation, and it became the first systematic presentation of Protestant doctrine. Whereas Luther spun out his sometimes contradictory ideas in a series of often polemical pamphlets, Calvin devoted himself to perfecting his comprehensive theology of Protestantism.

Given its emphasis on building a holy community, Calvinism helped transform the nuclear family into a social unit for training and disciplining children, a family in which women had a vital educational function that in turn encouraged women's literacy. Calvinist communities also began to allow divorce for women who had been abused by their husbands. Calvinist women and men were both disciplined and liberated—disciplined to avoid physical and material pleasures, liberated from the necessity to do good works but guided by God's grace to do them anyway.

The Reformation in Britain

Great Britain, as the island kingdom is known today, did not exist in the sixteenth century. The Tudor dynasty, which began in 1485 with Henry VII (see Chapter 11), ruled over England, Wales, and Ireland, but Scotland was still a separate kingdom with its own monarch and church institutions. These countries had distinctive political traditions, culture, and language, and as a result their Reformation experiences differed considerably. The Tudors imposed the Reformation as a matter of royal policy, and they were mostly successful in England and Wales. But they hardly made a dent in the religious culture of Ireland, which was a remarkable exception to the European pattern of conformity to the religion of the ruler. There the vast majority of the population were Catholics, a faith different from that of their Protestant monarch. Scotland, also an exception to the rule, wholeheartedly accepted the Protestant Reformation against the will of its Catholic queen and most of the clergy.

The Tudors and the English Reformation

In 1527 the rotund, self-absorbed, but crafty King Henry VIII (r. 1509–1547) announced that he had come to the pious conclusion that he had gravely sinned by marrying his brother's widow, Catherine of Aragon. By this time the couple had been married for eighteen years, their only living child was the princess Mary, and at age 42 Catherine was unlikely to give birth to more children. Henry let it be known that he wanted a son to secure the English throne for the Tudor dynasty. He also had his eye on the most engaging woman of the court, Anne Boleyn, who was less than half Catherine's age. In the past popes had usually been cooperative when a powerful king needed an annulment, but Pope Clement VII (r. 1523–1534) was in no position to oblige Henry. At the time of the marriage, the papal curia had issued a dispensation for Henry to marry his brother's widow, a practice that is prohibited in the Bible. In effect, Henry was asking the papacy to admit it had made a mistake. In addition, at the moment when Henry's petition for divorce arrived, Clement was under the control of Catherine's nephew, the Emperor Charles V, whose armies had recently captured and sacked the city of Rome. In 1531 Henry gave up trying to obtain papal approval and definitively separated from Catherine. Eighteen months later he secretly married Anne Boleyn. England's compliant Archbishop Thomas Cranmer (1489–1556) pronounced the marriage to Catherine void and the one to Anne valid. But the marriage to Anne did not last. When she began to displease him, Henry had her arrested, charged with incest with her brother and adultery with other men. She was convicted and beheaded.

The English separation from the Roman Catholic Church, which took place in 1534 through the Acts of Supremacy and Succession, passed at Henry's request by the English Parliament, has often been understood as a by-product of Henry's capricious lust and the plots of his brilliant minister, Thomas Cromwell (ca. 1485–1540). It is certainly true that Henry's desire to rid himself of Catherine led him to reject papal authority and to establish himself as the head of the Church of England. It is also certainly true that Henry was an inconstant husband: Of his six wives, two were divorced and two beheaded. However, the English Reformation cannot be explained simply as the consequence of royal whim or the machinations of a single minister.

The English Reformation began as a declaration of royal independence from papal supervision rather than an attempt to reform the practices of the Church. Under Henry VIII the English Reformation could be described as Catholicism without the pope. Protestant doctrine, at first, had little role in the English Reformation, and Henry had himself been one of the most vociferous critics of Martin Luther. Royal supremacy established control over the Church by granting to the king supervising authority over liturgical rituals and religious doctrines. Thomas Cromwell, who worked out the practical details for parliamentary legislation, was himself a Protestant, and no doubt his religious views emboldened him to reject papal authority. But the principal theorist of royal supremacy was a Catholic, Thomas Starkey (ca. 1499–1538). A sojourn in Italy had acquainted Starkey with Italian Renaissance political theory, which emphasized concepts of civic liberty. In fact, even many English Catholics found the change acceptable as long as it meant only abandoning submission to the pope in distant Rome. Those who opposed cutting the connection to Rome suffered for their opposition, however. Bishop John Fisher (ca. 1469–1535) and Sir Thomas More, the humanist author of *Utopia* and former chancellor of England,

were both executed for their refusal to go along with the king's decision.

With this display of despotic power, Henry seized personal control of the English church and then closed and confiscated the lands of the monasteries. He redistributed the monastic lands to the nobility in an effort to purchase their support and to make money for the crown. Henry's officials briefly flirted with some Protestant reforms, but theological innovations were largely avoided. The Reformation of Henry VIII was more significant for consolidating the dynastic power of the Tudors than for initiating wide-ranging religious reform. On the local level many people embraced the Reformation for their own reasons, often because it gave them a sense of control over the affairs of their community. Others went along simply because the power of the king was too strong to resist.

Henry's six wives bore three surviving children. As each succeeded to the throne, the official religion of England gyrated wildly. Because his youngest child, Edward, was male, Henry designed him successor to the throne. His two daughters, Mary and Elizabeth, were to succeed only if Edward died without an heir, which he did. Only 10 years old when he followed his father to the throne, King Edward VI (r. 1547–1553) was the pawn of his Protestant guardians, some of whom pushed for a more thorough Protestant Reformation in England than Henry had espoused. After Edward's premature death, his half-sister, Queen Mary I (r. 1553–1558), daughter of Henry and Catherine of Aragon, attempted to bring England back to obedience to the pope. Her unpopular marriage to the king of Spain and her failure to retain the support of the nobles, who were the foundation of Tudor government, damaged the Catholic cause in England.

Mary's successor and half-sister, Elizabeth Tudor, the daughter of Henry and Anne Boleyn, was an entirely different sort. Queen Elizabeth I (r. 1558–1603), raised as a Protestant, kept her enemies off balance and her quarrelsome subjects firmly in hand with her tremendous charisma and shrewd political judgments. Elizabeth became one of the most successful monarchs to ever reign anywhere. Without the considerable talents of Elizabeth, England could easily have fallen into civil war over religion—as the Holy Roman Empire and France did and as England itself did some forty years after her death.

Between 1559 and 1563, Elizabeth repealed the Catholic legislation of Mary and promulgated her own Protestant laws, collectively known as the Elizabethan Settlement, which established the Church of England, known as the Anglican Church (Episcopalian in the United States). Her principal adviser, William Cecil (1520–1598), implemented the details of the reform through reasonable debate and compromise rather than by insisting on doctrinal purity and rigid conformity. The touchstone of the Elizabethan Settlement was the Thirty-Nine Articles (finally approved by Parliament in 1571), which articulated a moderate version of Protestantism. It retained the ecclesiastical hierarchy of bishops as well as an essentially Catholic liturgy translated into English. This "middle way" between Roman Catholicism and militant Calvinism was ably defended by the Calvinist Richard Hooker (1553–1600), whose *Laws of Ecclesiastical Polity* emphasized how the law as promulgated by the royal government manifested the divine order.

The Church of England under Elizabeth permitted a wide latitude of beliefs, but it did not tolerate "recusants," those who as a matter of principle refused to attend Church of England services. These were mostly Catholics who set up a secret network of priests to serve their sacramental needs and whom the government considered dangerous agents of foreign powers. Many others were militant Protestants who thought the Elizabethan Settlement did not go far enough in reforming religion. The most vocal and influential of the Protestant dissenters were the Puritans, who were influenced by Calvinism and demanded a church purified of what they thought were remnants of Roman Catholicism.

Scotland: The Citadel of Calvinism

While England groped its way toward moderate Protestantism, neighboring Scotland became one of the most thoroughly Calvinist countries in Europe. In 1560 the parliament of Scotland, with encouragement from Queen Elizabeth of England, overthrew Roman Catholicism against the will of Mary Stuart, Queen of Scots (1542–1587). The wife of the French king, Francis II, Mary was absent in France during the crucial early phases of the Reformation and returned to Scotland only after her husband's death in 1561. Despite her Catholicism, Mary proved remarkably conciliatory toward the Protestants by putting royal funds at the disposal of the new Reformed Kirk (Church) of Scotland. But the Scottish Calvinists never trusted her, and their mistrust would bring about her doom when they rebelled against her and drove her into exile in England, where Queen Elizabeth had her imprisoned and eventually executed for treason against the English crown.

The Scots Confession of 1560, written by a panel of six reformers, established the new church. John Knox (ca. 1514–1572) breathed a strongly Calvinist air into the church through his many polemical writings and the official liturgy he composed in 1564, the *Book of Common Order*. Knox emphasized faith and individual Christian conscience over ecclesiastical authority, a priority that discouraged compromise among the Scots. Instead of the episcopal structure in England, which granted bishops the authority over doctrine and discipline, the Scots Kirk established a Presbyterian form of organization, which gave organizational authority to the pastors and elders of the congregations, all of whom had equal rank. As a result the Presbyterian congregations were more independent and subject to local variations than the episcopal structure allowed in the Anglican Church.

The Radical Reformation

The magisterial reformers in Germany, Switzerland, England, and Scotland managed to obtain official sanction for their religious reforms, often at the cost of some compromise with governmental authorities. As a result of those compromises, the magisterial reformers were challenged by radicals from among their own followers who demanded faster, more thorough reform. In most places the radicals represented a small minority, perhaps never more than 2 percent of all Protestants. But their significance outstripped their small numbers, in part because they forced the magisterial reformers to respond to their arguments and because their enemies attempted to eradicate them through extreme violence.

The radicals can be divided into three categories: Anabaptists, who attempted to construct a holy community on the basis of literal readings of the Bible; Spiritualists, who abandoned all forms of organized religion to allow individuals to follow the inner voice of the Holy Spirit; and Unitarians, who advocated a rational religion that emphasized ethical behavior over ceremonies.

Anabaptists: The Holy Community

For Anabaptists, the Bible was a blueprint for reforming not just the church but all of society. Because the Bible reported that Jesus was an adult when he was baptized, the Anabaptists rejected infant baptism and adopted adult baptism (Anabaptism° means to rebaptize). An adult, they believed, could accept baptism as an act of faith, unlike an oblivious infant. Anabaptists saw the sacraments of baptism and communion as symbols of faith, which had no purpose or meaning unless the recipient was already a person of faith. Adult baptism reserved for the faithful allowed the creation of a pure church, isolated from the sinfulness of the world.

Because they did not want the faithful to be tainted by contact with the sinful, Anabaptists advocated the complete separation of Church and state. Anabaptists sought to obey only God and completely rejected all established religious and political authorities; they required adherents to refuse to serve in government offices, swear oaths, pay taxes, or serve as soldiers. Anabaptists sought to live in highly disciplined "holy communities," which excommunicated errant members and practiced simple services based on scriptural readings. Because the Anabaptist communities consisted largely of uneducated peasants, artisans, and miners, a dimension of economic radicalism colored the early Anabaptist movement. For example, some Anabaptist radicals advocated the elimination of all private property and the sharing of wealth. On the position of women, however, Anabaptists were staunchly conservative, denying women any public role in religious affairs and insisting that they remain under the strict control of their fathers and husbands.

The Trial of Anne Boleyn: The Dynastic Crime

Anne Boleyn, the first of Henry VIII's wives to be executed, was beheaded in the Tower of London's courtyard in May 1536, just a few hundred feet from the hall in which she had celebrated her coronation three years earlier. She had been tried by a court of peers and unanimously convicted of high treason. The evidence against her was for adultery, but the alleged adultery of a queen was considered treason because it put in question the paternity of potential heirs to the throne. Queen Anne insisted on her innocence until the end, but her final address to the crowd did not protest her execution. Instead, she said, "According to the law and by the law I am judged to die, and therefore I will speak nothing against it."[9] To twenty-first-century observers, Anne seems to accept her unjust fate passively. To sixteenth-century observers, however, she died "boldly," and her refusal to admit guilt and to accept the law was one of the best indicators of her innocence.

To understand Anne Boleyn's scaffold statement, it is necessary to look at the idea of a "fair trial" in sixteenth-century England. She was condemned for high treason because of her supposed adultery with five men, including her own brother. But her supposed lovers were in other places when the adulteries were alleged to take place—evidence that casts doubt on their truth. She was unable to present this evidence, which today would serve as an alibi for the defendant, because she heard the charges against her for the first time at the actual trial. The queen enjoyed no counsel for the defense, had no opportunity to call witnesses on her own behalf, and had no protection against self-incrimination. Because she was

the queen of England, her trial was unusual, but these procedures were standard in the sixteenth century.

It was widely known that the king wished her death, but because her trial followed the accepted legal procedures, it was considered a fair trial by the standards of the sixteenth century. When Anne married Henry, who had recently divorced Catherine of Aragon, Anne's most important role was to provide the king with a male heir. Anne soon gave birth to a daughter, Elizabeth, but she then suffered two miscarriages. Some historians argue that Henry wanted to get rid of Anne in favor of her younger rival, Jane Seymour, but others have suggested that because the fetus of Anne's second miscarriage was deformed, she was suspected of witchcraft. Henry himself stated that he had been seduced by witchcraft, which was why God had not permitted him to have a son. He considered the marriage null and void because Anne's witchery had coerced him into the liaison. As far as Henry was concerned, Anne's failure to bear him a son was evidence of some sort of wrongdoing on her part. It remained only to construct a case against her.

The king and his prosecutors assembled a large number of statements about Anne's infidelity, which shocked observers of the trial. John Husee wrote, "I think

Portrait of King Henry VIII
This portrait by Hans Holbein the Younger depicts Henry as he looked shortly after Queen Anne's execution.

ANNA · BOLINA · VXOR ·   HENRI · OCTA

Portrait Sketch of Anne Boleyn
This portrait of Anne Boleyn may be by Hans Holbein the Younger. It was probably painted while Anne was queen of England.

same."[11] Most telling was the opinion of Chapuys, the ambassador of Emperor Charles V to Henry's court. Chapuys had previously been hostile to Anne, but he considered the whole trial a sham. After the jury returned a guilty verdict, Anne herself shrewdly observed, "I believe you have reasons . . . upon which you have condemned me: but they must be other than those that have been produced in court."[12]

The trial of Anne Boleyn was a classic example of the triumph of judicial form over the substance of evidence. Because Henry and the prosecutors had followed the proper trial procedures, they believed they were above reproach on legal grounds. Anne had been justly condemned even if the evidence against her had been faked.

Questions of Justice

1. Assuming that the evidence against Anne was false, why was her alleged treason defined as adultery rather than something else, such as witchcraft or heresy?
2. What do these charges tell us about the nature of early modern conceptions of kingship?

Taking It Further

Guy, John. *Tudor England*. 1990. Taking account of recent scholarship, this is the best general history of the period. It includes illuminating portraits of the principal figures.

Warnicke, Retha M. *The Rise and Fall of Anne Boleyn: Family Politics at the Court of Henry VIII*. 1991. Based on a careful examination of all the available evidence, Warnicke shows how the trial was a consequence of Henry VIII's desire to preserve his dynasty.

verily, if all the books and chronicles . . . which against woman hath been penned, contrived, and written since Adam and Eve, those same were, I think, verily nothing in comparison of that which hath been done and committed by Anne the Queen." James Spelman commented, "All the evidence was of bawdery and lechery, so that there was no such whore in all the realm."[10]

The quantity and offensive nature of the evidence was part of a propaganda campaign Henry orchestrated to convince the members of the nobility and the English people that Anne's execution was justified.

Despite the careful orchestration of the trial, the preponderance of the evidence, and the procedures that denied her systematic defense, Anne Boleyn managed to convince a number of observers that she was innocent. Charles Wriothesley recounted, "She made so wise and discreet answers to all things laid against her, excusing herself through her words so clearly as though she had never been faulty to the

Because the Anabaptists promoted such a radical reorganization of society along biblical lines, they provoked a violent reaction. In Zürich the city council decreed that the appropriate punishment for all Anabaptists was to be drowned in the local river where they had been rebaptizing themselves. By 1529 it became a capital offense in the Holy Roman Empire to be rebaptized, and during the sixteenth century perhaps as many as 5,000 Anabaptists were executed for the offense, a persecution that tended to fragment the Anabaptists into isolated, secretive rural communities.

During a brief period in 1534 and 1535, Anabaptists managed to seize control of the city of Münster in northern Germany. An immigrant Dutch tailor, John of Leiden, set up a despotic regime in Münster that punished with death any sin, even gossiping or complaining. John of Leiden introduced polygamy and collective ownership of property. John set an example by taking sixteen wives, one of whom he beheaded for talking back, stomping on her body in front of the other frightened wives. As the besieging armies closed in, John forced his followers to crown him king and worship him. After his capture, John was subjected to an excruciating torture, and as a warning to others his corpse was displayed for many years hanging in an iron cage.

"God opened the eyes of the governments by the revolt at Münster," as the Protestant reformer Heinrich Bullinger put it, "and thereafter no one would trust even those Anabaptists who claimed to be innocent."[13] The surviving Anabaptists abandoned the radicalism of the Münster community, embracing pacifism and nonviolent resistance. A Dutchman, Menno Simons (1496–1561), tirelessly traveled about the Netherlands and Germany, providing solace and guidance to the isolated survivors of the Münster disaster. His followers, the Mennonites, preserved the noblest features of the Anabaptist tradition of quiet resistance to persecution. Both the Mennonites and the Amish in North America are direct descendants of sixteenth- and seventeenth-century Anabaptist groups. Under Mennonite influence, Thomas Helwys founded the first Baptist church in England in 1612. As the leader of the English Baptists, Helwys wrote an unprecedented appeal for the absolute freedom of religion. In it he defended the religious rights of Jews, Muslims, and even atheists as well as all varieties of Christians. He was almost immediately put in prison, where he died.

The most significant measure of the influence of the Anabaptists is the fact that the largest number of Protestants in the United States are Baptists. The modern Baptist movement has lost the social radicalism of its Anabaptist forebearers and no longer advocates the communal ownership of property as the Anabaptists did in the sixteenth century. Baptists no longer refuse to pay taxes or accept the authority of the government. Most Baptists have also forsaken pacifism and will serve in the military, but during the civil rights movement of the 1950s and 1960s, it was a Baptist

Cages for the Anabapist Leaders of Münster
The bodies of John of Leiden and two other Anabaptist leaders were displayed after their execution in these three cages, hanging on the tower of St. Lambert Church in Münster, Germany. The slaughter of the Anabaptists after the fall of Münster was one of the most violent episodes in the Reformation.

preacher, Dr. Martin Luther King, Jr., who reintroduced the principle of nonviolent resistance to persecution.

Spiritualists: The Holy Individual

Whereas the Anabaptists radicalized the Swiss Reformation's emphasis on building a godly community, the Spiritualists° radicalized Luther's commitment to personal introspection. Perhaps the greatest Spiritualist was the aristocratic Caspar Schwenckfeld (1490–1561), who was a friend of Luther's until he broke with the reformer over what he considered the weak spirituality of established Lutheranism. Schwenckfeld believed that depraved humanity was incapable of casting off the bonds of sin, which only a supernatural act of God could achieve. This separation from sinfulness was revealed through an intense conversion experience, after which the believer gained spiritual illumination. Schwenckfeld called this illumination the "inner Word," which he understood as a living form of the Scriptures written directly on the believer's soul by the hand of God. Schwenckfeld also prized the "outer Word," that is, the Scriptures, but he found the emotional experience of the inner Word more powerful than the intellectual experience that came from reading the Bible. Spiritualists reflected an inner peace evident in their calm physical appearance, lack of anxiety, and mastery of bodily appetites—a state Schwenckfeld called the "castle of peace."

The most prominent example of the Spiritualist tendency in the English-speaking world is the Quakers, who first appeared in England a century after the Lutheran Reformation. The Quakers, or Society of Friends, interpreted the priesthood of all believers to mean that God's spirit, which they called the Light of Christ, was given equally to all men and women. This belief led them to abandon entirely a separately ordained ministry and to replace organized worship with meetings in which any man, woman, or child could speak, read Scripture, pray, or sing, as the spirit moved them. The Quakers' belief in the sacredness of all human beings also inclined them toward pacifism and egalitarianism.

In no other religious tradition have women played such a prominent role for so long. From the very beginning of the movement, female Friends were prominent in preaching the Quaker gospel. In Quaker marriages, wives were completely equal to their husbands—at least in religious matters. Quakers long played a prominent role in various social reform movements as well. In the eighteenth century, they were the first to campaign for the abolition of slavery; in the nineteenth century, Quaker women were prominent in the movement to establish women's rights; and in the twentieth century they led antiwar movements and the campaign for nuclear disarmament.

Unitarians: A Rationalist Approach

The universal acceptance of the Trinity among Christians changed in the middle of the sixteenth century with the emergence of numerous radical sects that rejected the divinity of Christ. They were called Arians, Socinians, Anti-Trinitarians, or Unitarians°. Distinctive to Christian theology—in comparison to other monotheistic religions, such as Judaism and Islam—is the doctrine of the Trinity, which posits that the one God has three identities: God the Father, God the Son, and God the Holy Spirit. The doctrine of the Trinity made it possible for Christians to believe that God the Son "took on flesh" in what is called the *incarnation*. At a particular moment in history, God became the human being Jesus Christ. The doctrine of the Trinity was officially established as Christian dogma at the Council of Nicaea in

325, in response to the Arians who accepted Jesus as a religious leader but denied that he was "co-eternal" with God the Father. The Trinitarian Christians denounced the Arian doctrine because they thought it rejected Christ's full divinity.

During the sixteenth-century Reformation various forms of the Arian doctrine were revived. The Italian Faustus Socinus (1539–1604) taught a rationalist interpretation of the Scriptures and argued that Jesus was a divinely inspired man, not God-become-man. Socinus's followers thus rejected the doctrine of the Trinity, which they found contrary to simple common sense and without support in Scripture. Socinus's ideas remain central to Unitarianism—the specific rejection of Trinitarian doctrine and the general emphasis on rationality.

Catholics and magisterial Protestants alike were extremely hostile to Unitarians, who tended to be well-educated humanists and men of letters. Unitarian views thrived in advanced intellectual circles in northern Italy and eastern Europe, but the most famous critic of the Trinity was the brilliant, if eccentric, Spaniard Michael Servetus (1511–1553). Trained as a physician and widely read in the literature of the occult, Servetus published influential Anti-Trinitarian works and daringly sent his provocative works to the major Protestant reformers. Based on a tip from the Protestants in Geneva, the Catholic inquisitor-general in Lyons, France, arrested Servetus, but he escaped from prison during his trial. While passing through Protestant Geneva on his way to refuge in Italy, he was recognized while attending a church service and again imprisoned. Although no law in Geneva allowed capital punishment, Servetus was convicted of heresy and burned alive.

The Anabaptists and Unitarians shared some early connections and similarities, but the two groups soon parted ways. Both Anabaptists and Unitarians followed the logic of their own beliefs and were unwilling to compromise with other Protestants. Anabaptists isolated themselves in their own communities and avoided contact with outsiders to avoid pollution from sinners and persecution from the authorities. Unitarians were more open to public debate, and in eastern Europe they attracted support from the powerful.

The Free World of Eastern Europe

During the sixteenth century eastern Europe offered a measure of religious freedom and toleration unknown elsewhere in Europe. As a result, eastern Europe was open to considerable religious experimentation and attracted refugees from the oppressive princes of western Europe, none of whom tolerated more than one religion in their territories if they could help it. Such religious toleration was made possible by the relative weakness of the monarchs in Bohemia, Hungary, Transylvania, and especially Poland-Lithuania, where the great land-owning aristocrats exercised nearly complete freedom on their estates. All of these kingdoms had Catholic monarchs, but the Reformation radicalized the aristocrats who dominated the parliaments, enabling Protestantism to take hold even against the wishes of the monarch.

In Bohemia (now in the Czech Republic), the Hussite movement in the fourteenth century had rejected papal authority and some of the sacramental authority of the priesthood long before the Protestant Reformation. After the Lutherans and Calvinists attracted adherents in Bohemia, the few surviving old Hussites and the new Protestants formed an alliance in 1575, which made common cause against the Catholics. In addition to this formal alliance, substantial numbers of Anabaptists found refuge from persecution in Bohemia and lived in complete freedom on the estates of tolerant landlords who were desperate for settlers to farm their lands.

The religious diversity of Hungary was also remarkable by the standards of the time. By the end of the sixteenth century, much of Hungary's diverse population had accepted some form of Protestantism. Among the German-speaking city dwellers and the Hungarian peasants in western Hungary, Lutheranism prevailed, whereas in eastern Hungary Calvinism was dominant.

No other country was as tolerant of religious diversity as Transylvania (now in Romania), largely because of the weak monarchy, which could not have enforced religious uniformity even if the king had wanted to do so. In Transylvania, Unitarianism took hold more firmly than anywhere else. In 1572 the tolerant ruler Prince István Báthory (r. 1571–1586) granted the Unitarians complete legal equality to establish their own churches along with Catholics, Lutherans, and Calvinists—the only place in Europe where equality of religions was achieved. Transylvania was also

home to significant communities of Jews, Armenian Christians, and Orthodox Christians.

The sixteenth century was the golden age of the Polish-Lithuanian Commonwealth, which was the largest state in the size of its territory in Europe. It escaped both the Ottoman invasions and the religious wars that plagued the Holy Roman Empire. From the Lutheran cities in the German-speaking north to the vast open plains of Great Poland, where Calvinism took hold among the independent-minded nobility, religious lines often had been drawn along ethnic or class divisions. When Sigismund August (r. 1548–1572) became king, he declared, "I am not king of men's conscience," and inaugurated extensive toleration of Protestant churches, even while the vast majority of peasants remained loyal to Orthodoxy or Catholicism. Fleeing persecution in other countries, various Anabaptist groups and Unitarians found refuge in Poland. This extensive religious diversity in Poland was later snuffed out during the Catholic Reformation.

The Catholic Reformation

■ How did the Catholic Church respond to the unprecedented threat to its dominance of religious authority in the West?

The Catholic Reformation, also known as the Counter Reformation, profoundly revitalized the Catholic Church and established an institutional and doctrinal framework that persisted into the late twentieth century. The Catholic Reformation° was a series of efforts to purify the Church; these efforts were not necessarily just a reaction to the Protestant Reformation but evolved out of late medieval spirituality, driven by many of the same impulses that stimulated the Protestants. The most important of these efforts was the creation of new religious orders, especially the Society of Jesus, whose members are known as the Jesuits. They promoted a vast educational program that improved understanding of the faith and a missionary effort that spread Christianity throughout the world. However, the Church also responded to the challenge of the Protestant Reformation by establishing the Holy Office of the Inquisition, promulgating the *Index of Forbidden Books*, and implementing the decrees of the Council of Trent (1545–1563).

The Catholic Reformation came both from the religious enthusiasm that welled up from the laity and lower clergy and the leadership of a series of influential popes who gave the movement a strongly international character. Catholicism retained Latin, in contrast to Protestantism, which conducted services in vernacular languages such as German or English. The success of the Catholic

CHRONOLOGY

The Diversity of Protestantism

1520	Zwingli declared the People's Priest in Zürich
1529	Marburg Colloquy
1534	Parliament in England passes the Acts of Supremacy and Succession
1534–1535	Anabaptist control of Münster, Germany
1535	Execution of John Fisher and Thomas More; first edition of John Calvin's *Institutes of the Christian Religion*
1559–1563	The Elizabethan Settlement of the Anglican Church
1560	Scots Confession

Reformation tended to obliterate differences in religious culture from one Catholic country to another, creating greater uniformity in Catholic practice and doctrine than had been the case in the medieval period. The international spread of the Catholic Reformation was a source of tremendous strength in revitalizing the Church and in creating a distinctively Catholic culture. For 400 years after the Catholic Reformation, Catholics who found themselves in a foreign land could experience something very familiar merely by attending a mass, spoken or chanted in the ancient Latin of the Church.

The Religious Orders in the Catholic Reformation

The most dramatic and effective manifestation of the Catholic Reformation was the founding of new religious orders. These orders exhibited a religious vitality that had little to do with the Protestant threat. In fact, none of the new orders began near the centers of Protestantism, such as Germany. Italy, which remained strongly Catholic, produced the largest number of new orders, followed by Spain and France. All of the new orders remained committed to a very traditional Catholic theology, but they differed from the prayerful isolation of the traditional monastic orders by their commitment to an active ministry in the world.

Jesuits: The Soldiers of God

By far the most influential new order was the Society of Jesus, also known as the Jesuits. In 1534 a group of seven students at the University of Paris took a vow to go on a pilgrimage to Jerusalem after graduation. They were an international lot—a Portuguese, a Savoyard, an Aragonese, two Basques, and two Castilians. When the original seven plus some French companions gathered in Venice to take a ship to Palestine, they found their way blocked by a war, a turn of events that led them to place themselves at the disposal of the pope. This loosely organized group of kindred spirits became the core of a new order. In 1540 they officially organized the Society of Jesus and elected Ignatius Loyola (1491–1556) the first General of the Society.

Loyola's dynamic personality and intense spirituality gave the new order its distinctive commitment to moral action in the world. Loyola began his career as a courtier to King Ferdinand of Aragon and a soldier. In 1521 during a French attack on the Spanish garrison at Pamplona, Loyola's leg was shattered by a cannonball. Driven by vanity to keep his leg from looking deformed, he insisted on having his leg rebroken and reset several times despite the excruciating pain of the procedure. During the boredom of his convalescence, he turned to reading a life of Christ and the lives of the saints. From these he discovered tales of heroism superior to anything he had read of medieval knights. These revelations converted Loyola to Christ.

Loyola's background as a courtier and soldier deeply influenced his religiosity. The Society of Jesus that he helped found preserved some of the values Loyola had acquired as a courtier-soldier—social refinement, loyalty to authority, sense of duty, and high-minded chivalry.

Loyola's most impressive personal contribution to religious literature was the *Spiritual Exercises* (1548), which became the foundation of Jesuit practice. Republished in more than 5,000 editions in hundreds of languages, the *Exercises* prescribe a month-long retreat devoted to a series of meditations in which the participant mentally reexperiences the spiritual life, physical death, and miraculous resurrection of Christ. Much of the power of the *Exercises* derives from the systematic employment of each of the five senses to produce a defined emotional, spiritual, and even physical response. Participants in the *Exercises* seem to hear the blasphemous cries of the soldiers at Christ's crucifixion, feel the terrible agony of his suffering on the cross, and experience the blinding illumination of his resurrection from the dead. Those who participated in the *Exercises* considered the experience life-transforming and usually made a steadfast commitment to serve the Church.

The Jesuits distinguished themselves from other religious orders by extending their personal spirituality to minister to others. They did not wear clerical clothing, and on foreign missions they devoted themselves to learning the language and culture of the peoples they hoped to convert. Jesuits became famous for their loyalty to the pope, and some took a special fourth vow (in addition to the three traditional vows of poverty, chastity, and obedience) to go on a mission if the pope requested it. Many traveled as missionaries to distant parts of the globe, such as China and Japan. In Europe and the Americas the Jesuits established a vast network of colleges, most similar to modern high schools but some became universities. These colleges offered free tuition, which made them open to the poor who had few other opportunities for education. The Jesuit colleges combined a thorough training in languages, humanities, and sciences with religious instruction and moral guidance. They became especially popular because the Jesuit fathers were much more likely to pay personal attention to their students than professors in the established universities. In Europe the Jesuit college system transformed the culture of the Catholic elite. These colleges attracted the sons of the aristocrats and the wealthy who absorbed from the Jesuit instructors the values of Renaissance humanism and the Catholic Reformation. By 1615 there were 372 Jesuit colleges in Europe, and the demand for new colleges was so great that the Jesuits could not recruit and train enough qualified instructors. With the success of these colleges, education gradually replaced missionary work as the most important Jesuit activity.

The Jesuit order grew rapidly. At Loyola's death in 1556 there were about a thousand Jesuits, but by 1700 there were nearly 20,000, and many young men who wished to join

The Ecstasy of Teresa of Avila: The Body and the Soul

Teresa of Avila (1515–1582, canonized St. Teresa in 1622) eloquently expressed the intimate connection between physical and spiritual experiences that was a common feature of Catholic mysticism. She was a Spanish Carmelite nun whose accounts of her own mystical experiences made her a model for other nuns throughout the world. Filled with religious ardor, she devoted herself to an ascetic regime of self-deprivations so intense that she fell ill and suffered paralysis.

Often afflicted by an intense pain in her side, Teresa reported that an angel had stuck a lance tipped with fire into her heart. This "seraphic vision," which became the subject of Gianlorenzo Bernini's famous sculpture in Santa Maria della Vittoria in Rome (1645–1652), epitomized the Catholic Reformation sensibility of understanding spiritual states through physical feelings. In Teresa's case, her extreme bodily deprivations, paralysis, and intense pain conditioned how she experienced the spiritual side of her nature. Many have seen an erotic character to the vision, which may be true, but the vision best demonstrates a profound psychological awareness that bodily and spiritual sensations cannot be precisely distinguished. As Teresa put it, "it is not bodily pain, but spiritual, though the body has a share in it—indeed, a great share." She described the paralysis of her soul and her body as interconnected: "The soul is unable to do either this or anything else. The entire body contracts and neither arm nor foot can be moved." She then described, in remarkably graphic terms, her repeated vision:

It pleased the Lord that I should sometimes see the following vision. I would see beside me, on my left hand, an angel in bodily form—a type of vision which I am not in the habit of seeing, except very rarely. . . . I pleased the Lord that I should see this angel in the following way. He was not tall, but short, and very beautiful, his face so aflame that he appeared to be one of the highest types of angel who seem to be all afire. . . . In his hands I saw a long golden spear and at the end of the iron tip I seemed to see a point of fire. With this he seemed to pierce my heart several times so that it penetrated to my entrails. When he drew it out, I thought he was drawing them out with it and he left me completely afire with a great love for God. The pain was so sharp that it made me utter several moans; and so excessive was the sweetness caused me by this intense pain that one can never wish to lose it, nor will one's soul be content with anything less than God. . . . So sweet are the colloquies of love which pass between the soul and God that if anyone thinks I am lying I beseech God, in His goodness, to give him the same experience.[14]

Visions such as this one were difficult to interpret. Exactly what was going on in those sweet colloquies between Teresa's soul and God? Teresa associated these visions with intense physical pain, as if she had to suffer in order to receive divine illumination, which she described as a sweet conversation between her soul and God. Her sensibility about the necessary relationship between physical pain and spiritual experiences was especially pronounced among sixteenth-century Catholics. Pain and suffering were understood as a form of penance, and thus the body could play a positive and redemptive role in enabling spirituality. The best way to transcend this world was in bodily pain, because through pain the Christian escaped the temptations of the flesh and renounced the attractions of the world.

For Discussion

How was pain understood to have religious value? What was happening around Teresa that might explain her preoccupation with pain?

An angel is about to pierce her side with an arrow.

St. Teresa lies suspended in the air in a swoon induced by a vision.

The Ecstasy of St. Teresa

DOCUMENT

The Constitution of the Society of Jesus

In 1540, Pope Paul III approved the Constitution of the Society of Jesus. This excerpt includes some of the characteristics of the society that help explain its success, including to go on a mission to distant lands if the pope so orders.

He who desires to fight for God under the banner of the cross in our society—which we wish to distinguish by the name of Jesus—and to serve God alone and the Roman pontiff, his vicar on earth, after a solemn vow of perpetual chastity, shall set this thought before his mind, that he is a part of a society founded for the especial purpose of providing for the advancement of souls in Christian life and doctrine and for the propagation of faith through public preaching and the ministry of the word of God, spiritual exercises and deeds of charity, and in particular through the training of the young and ignorant in Christianity and through the spiritual consolation of the faithful of Christ in hearing confessions; and he shall take care to keep first God and next the purpose of this organization always before his eyes . . .

All members shall realize, and shall recall daily, as long as they live, that this society as a whole and in every part is fighting for God under faithful obedience to one most holy lord, the pope, and to the other Roman pontiffs who succeed him. And although we are taught in the gospel and through the orthodox faith to recognize and steadfastly profess that all the faithful of Christ are subject to the Roman pontiff as their head and as the vicar of Jesus Christ, yet we have adjudged that, for the special promotion of greater humility in our society and the perfect mortification of every individual and the sacrifice of our own wills, we should each be bound by a peculiar vow, in addition to the general obligation, that whatever the present Roman pontiff, or any future one, may from time to time decree regarding the welfare of souls and the propagation of the faith, we are pledged to obey without evasion or excuse, instantly, so far as in us lies, whether he send us to the Turks or any other infidels, even to those who inhabit the regions men call the Indies; whether to heretics or schismatics, or, on the other hand, to certain of the faithful.

Source: From James Harvey Robinson, ed. *Readings in European History*, vol. 2 (Boston: Ginn, 1904), pp. 162–63.

had to be turned away because there were insufficient funds to train them. The influence of the Jesuits was even greater than their numbers would indicate, however. Besides their success in education, which shaped the values of the upper classes and guided intellectual life throughout Catholic Europe, Jesuits often served as the personal confessors to powerful figures, including several kings of France and Holy Roman Emperors. By giving private advice on spiritual matters, confessors had many opportunities to influence royal policy, an influence the Jesuits were not shy to exercise.

Women's Orders: In But Not of the World

Creating a ministry that was active in the world was much more difficult for the female orders than for the Jesuits and the other male orders. Women who sought to reinvigorate old orders or found new ones faced hostility from ecclesiastical and civic authorities, who thought women had to be protected by either a husband or the cloister wall. Women in convents were supposed to be entirely separated from the world, "as if they were dead," but this principle was at odds with the desires of many devout women who wanted to help make the world a better place.

The cloistering of women was a highly controversial issue during the sixteenth century. Because it was cheaper to place a daughter in a convent than to provide her with a dowry for marriage, about one-third of the women of aristocratic families in Catholic countries found themselves in convents rather than on the marriage market. In some places, such as Venice during the late sixteenth century, more than three-quarters of the noblewomen were cloistered. In many convents, aristocratic women tried to live much as they would have in secular society, enjoying private apartments, servants, regular visits with relatives, musical entertainments, and even vacations. Many of these women felt like involuntary inmates living in a "Convent Hell," to quote the title of Arcangela Tarabotti's famous exposé of the nun's life (1654). The dreary experience of these reluctant nuns, however, contrasted with the genuine enthusiasm for convent life of many other women who were caught up in the religious enthusiasm of the Catholic Reformation.

The first task of those who were ardently religious was to reform convent life. The most famous model was provided by Teresa of Avila (1515–1582), who wrote a strict new rule for the Carmelites, who had been established in 1452. The new rule required mortifications of the flesh and complete withdrawal from the world. Teresa described her own mystical experiences in her *Autobiography* (1611) and in the *Interior Castle* (1588), a compelling masterpiece in the literature of mysticism. Teresa advocated a very cautious brand of mysticism, which was checked by regular confession and skepticism about extreme acts of self-deprivation. For example, she recognized that a nun who fell into an apparent rapture after extensive fasting was probably just having hallucinations from the hunger.

The many orders of nuns during the sixteenth century presented many contradictions. On the one hand, they housed some women who had no special religious vocation, who did not want to be locked away from family and friends, and who suffered from the stifling boredom of living without apparent purpose. On the other hand, many women who willingly chose the religious life thrived in a community of women, were liberated from the rigors of childbearing, and were freed from direct male supervision. These women could devote themselves to cultivating musical or literary talents to a degree that would have been impossible in the outside world. Nuns created their own distinctly female culture, producing a number of learned women and social reformers who had considerable influence in the arts, education, and charitable work such as nursing.

Paul III, The First Catholic Reformation Pope

Despite the many earlier attempts at reform and the Protestant threat, the Church was slow to initiate its own reforms because of resistance among bishops and cardinals of the Church hierarchy who worried that reform would threaten their income. More than twenty years after Luther's defiant stand at the Diet of Worms in 1521, Pope Paul III (r. 1534–1549) finally launched a systematic counterattack. As a member of the powerful Farnese family, who had long treated church offices as their private property, Paul seemed an unlikely reformer. But more than any other pope, Paul understood the necessity to respond to the political winds of change. It was Pope Paul, for example, who formally approved the Jesuits and began to employ them as missionary soldiers for the Church.

In 1541, in an attempt to resolve the dangerous religious disputes provoked by the Lutherans, Paul sent a representative to a discussion between Catholic and Protestant theologians held in conjunction with the Imperial Diet of Regensburg. Despite the best efforts of the pope's reform-minded representative, the meeting failed, making it stunningly clear how wide the gap had become between Protestant and Catholic theology. The failure of Regensburg shifted Pope Paul's efforts from a plan of hesitant accommodation to a defensive strategy devoted to building a Catholic bulwark against Protestant ideas.

The following year, on the advice of an archconservative faction of cardinals, Paul III reorganized the Roman Inquisition, called the Holy Office. The function of the Inquisition was to inquire into the beliefs of all Catholics primarily to discover indications of heresies such as those of the Protestants. Jews, for example, were exempt from its authority, although Jews who had converted or been forced to convert to Christianity did fall under the jurisdiction of the Inquisition. There had been other inquisitions, but most had been local or national. The Spanish Inquisition was controlled by the Spanish monarchs, for example. In contrast, the Holy Office came under the direct control of the pope and cardinals and termed itself the Universal Roman Inquisition. Its effective authority did not reach beyond northern and central Italy, but it set the tone for the entire Catholic Reformation Church.

The Inquisition immediately began to crack down on suspected heretics. One of the first to be investigated was Bernardino Ochino (1487–1563), the most popular preacher in Rome and the Minister General of the Capuchin order. When summoned to answer questions before the Holy Office, he fled to Geneva. His defection to Calvin's Geneva caused an enormous sensation and fueled the clamor for more extensive investigations. Any form of criticism of the Church within earshot of an informant of the Inquisition became very dangerous. The Inquisition could subject defendants to lengthy interrogations and stiff penalties, including prison sentences and even execution in exceptional cases.

A second effort to stop the spread of Protestant and other ideas deemed heretical led to the first *Index of Forbidden Books,* drawn up in 1549 in Venice, the capital of the publishing industry in Italy. The *Index* censored or banned many books that the Church considered detrimental to the faith and the authority of the Church. Most affected by the strictures were books about theology and philosophy, but books of moral guidance were also prohibited or butchered by the censors, such as the works of Erasmus, and classics of literature, such as Giovanni Boccaccio's *The Decameron.* The official papal *Index* of 1559 prohibited translations of the Bible into vernacular languages such as Italian. The prohibition of vernacular Bibles was especially important because the Church insisted that laypeople required a trained intermediary in the person of a priest to interpret and explain the Bible. The Church's protective attitude about biblical interpretation clearly distinguished the Catholic from the Protestant attitude of encouraging widespread Bible reading. It remained possible to buy certain heretical theological books "under the counter," much as people today find ways to obtain illegal drugs, but possessing such books could be dangerous if agents of the Inquisition conducted a raid.

The Council of Trent

By far the most significant of Pope Paul III's contributions to the Catholic Reformation was his call for a general council of the Church, which began to meet in 1545 in Trent on the border between Italy and Germany. The Council of Trent established principles that guided the Catholic Church for the next 400 years.

DOCUMENT

Council of Trent (1545–1563)

Between 1545 and 1563 the council met under the auspices of three different popes in three separate sessions, with long intervals of as much as ten years between sessions. The objective of these sessions was to find a way to respond to the Protestant criticisms of the Church, to reassert the authority of the pope, and to launch reforms that would guarantee a well-educated and honest clergy. The decrees of the Council of Trent, which had the force of legislation for the entire Church, defied the Protestants by refusing to yield any ground on the traditional doctrines of the Church. The decrees confirmed the efficacy of all seven of the traditional sacraments, the reality of Purgatory, and the spiritual value of indulgences. In order to provide better supervision of the Church, bishops were ordered to reside in their dioceses or regions. Trent decreed that every diocese should have a seminary to train priests, providing a practical solution to the problem of clerical ignorance.

The Council of Trent represented a dramatic reassertion of the authority of the papacy, the bishops, and the priesthood. The actual implementation of the decrees varied considerably from country to country and from diocese to diocese, however. The model for enforcing the decrees was Archbishop Carlo Borromeo (r. 1565–1584) of Milan. His energetic visitations of his diocese and attention to administrative detail became an example for others. Despite the hopes of some of the participants in the council, it had no effect whatsoever in luring Protestants back into the Catholic fold.

The Reformation in the Arts

■ How did the religious turmoil of the sixteenth century transform the role of the visual arts and music in public life?

Most of the paintings, sculptures, and musical compositions created before and during the sixteenth century were destined for churches or had some kind of religious function. But with the tensions brought about during the Reformation, one of the major issues dividing Protestants and Catholics was defining the proper role of the arts in Christian worship. Except among the most radical Protestants, who entirely rejected any role for the arts in religious worship, the difference between the two was more one of degree than of kind. Catholics considered religious images, properly regulated, vital for devotion. Protestants, however, were uneasy about religious art because they worried about confining divine truths within any kind of visual representation.

Protestant Iconoclasm

Protestants sometimes initiated reform by vandalizing churches through acts of iconoclasm—the removing,

CHRONOLOGY

The Catholic Reformation

1534–1549	Pontificate of Pope Paul III
1540	Founding of the Society of Jesus
1541	Imperial Diet of Regensburg
1542	Reorganization of the Roman Inquisition or Holy Office
1545–1563	Meetings of the Council of Trent
1548	*Spiritual Exercises* of Ignatius Loyola
1549	*Index of Forbidden Books*

breaking, or defacing of religious statues, paintings, and symbols such as crucifixes. The destruction of religious works of art more often than not took place even when the reformers themselves discouraged or denounced it. Nevertheless, in town after town in the thrall of reform enthusiasm, laypeople destroyed religious art, including some of the greatest masterpieces of the Middle Ages and Renaissance. Their violence against property was seldom matched by violence against people. Protestant mobs were much more likely to rip down an altar painting than to attack a priest.

Three factors likely explain iconoclasm. One was that people feared the power of such images. Guillaume Farel, the reformer of Geneva before Calvin, told how his parents had taken him as a child to the shrine of the Holy Cross at Tallard in southern France. A priest stationed at the shrine told the pilgrims that the cross shook violently during storms. What Farel remembered most about the cross was his fear, reinforced by the apprehension of his parents. The implication was that images possessed great powers that could be used both to protect and to destroy. The problem with religious images, therefore, was not that they were idols, which were by definition without power. They were dangerous because they were perceived to be *too* powerful.

A second reason for iconoclasm was that religious images devoured financial resources that could be better spent on the poor. Ulrich Zwingli was especially articulate on this point. He hoped that the assets devoted to paying for paintings and statues could be transformed into "food of the poor." In this sense iconoclasm was part of a pious project to redirect the energy of Christians toward solving the social problems of the community. Great paintings were given to hospitals to serve as fuel, and crucifixes were sold as lumber with the proceeds going to the indigent.

Many reformers spoke of a third concern about images. They worried that a church filled with works of art distracted worshipers from paying attention to the Word of

Iconoclasm in the Netherlands
This engraving shows statues being hauled down by the men on the left of the church pulling ropes. Note that one statue is already lying on the ground. On the right side of the church, men are breaking the stained glass windows with clubs.

Scripture. They found the meaning of images too ambiguous, too subject to misinterpretation. Instead they wanted to ensure that their preaching provided the interpretation of Scripture. In effect, they wanted to substitute the Word of God for the image of God. In many reformed Dutch churches, for example, the walls were stripped bare of images and whitewashed. Passages of Scripture were then painted on the walls in place of the images.

Although skeptical of the role of images in churches, propagandists for the Reformation had no such reservation about woodcuts and engravings, which could be reproduced in multiple copies and cheaply sold to thousands of people. These images, the visual by-product of the printing revolution, promoted the Reformation to the masses in a simple graphic way by lampooning the pope and ridiculing the wealth of the clergy. These images were the prototype for modern political cartoons. Also popular were portraits of the reformers. Many a pious Lutheran household replaced an image of the Madonna with an engraving of Martin Luther and his wife, Katherine von Bora.

Anti-Catholic Propaganda
This woodcut, titled *I Am the Pope*, satirizes the papacy by depicting Pope Alexander VI as a monster. Alexander was infamous for allegedly conducting orgies in the Vatican. This kind of visual propaganda was an effective way to undermine support for the papacy.

Catholic Reformation Art

The Catholic Church retained a strong commitment to the religious value of the arts. However, the Catholic Reformation recognized that abuses had taken place in works of art that depicted events that did not appear in Scripture. The Church placed artists under much closer surveillance than before. The Council of Trent enjoined artists to avoid representing impieties of any sort and to use their art to teach correct doctrine and to move believers to true piety. Religious art had to convey a message simply, directly, and in terms that unlettered viewers could understand. The best Catholic art employed dramatic theatrical effects in lighting and the arrangement of figures to represent deep emotional and spiritual experiences. Through contemplating these pictures, viewers were supposed to create similar experiences within themselves. In this sense an aesthetic and a spiritual appreciation of art were inseparable.

The Council of Trent forced a reevaluation of previous trends in the arts and a number of existing works of art. The Italian Renaissance, in particular, had glorified the human body, often represented in the nude. In earlier generations churchmen and popes had not objected to the display of naked figures in churches and chapels because after all, the human body was God's finest creation. However, after the Council of Trent many influential ecclesiastics disapproved this practice in the strongest terms. Michelangelo's *The Last Judgment*, a fresco painted in the Sistine Chapel in the Vatican in Rome between 1534 and 1541, came under severe attack the year after the last session of Trent. The

The Last Judgment
In this fresco by Michelangelo, the figure with the raised hand in the upper center is Christ. On his right sits the Virgin Mary. Both figures were painted over with clothing to hide their nudity.

The Inquisition Criticizes a Work of Art

This painting was originally intended to represent the Last Supper when Christ introduced the mass to his apostles. Because there are many figures in it who are not mentioned in the biblical account and the supper appears as if it were a Renaissance banquet, the artist, Paolo Veronese, was obliged to answer questions from the Inquisition. Ordered to remove the offending figures, Veronese instead changed the name of the painting to depict the less theologically controversial supper in the house of Levi.

polemical *Dialogue on the Errors of Painters* criticized Michelangelo for subordinating the representation of Christian truths to his own stylistic interests in the human nude. Genitals and bare breasts in *The Last Judgment* were painted over, disfiguring one of the greatest masterpieces of the Renaissance. The crude overpainting was not removed until the fresco was cleaned during the 1990s.

Everywhere in Catholic Europe, offending body parts were painted over and paintings of indecorous subject matter removed from churches. In the Catholic parts of the Netherlands, paintings and statues deemed indecent were even destroyed, in an odd echo of Protestant iconoclasm. In Venice the Inquisition got involved. In a celebrated inquiry in 1573, the inquisitor called in the painter, Paolo Veronese, to answer why he put into a painting of the Last Supper various figures that did not appear in the Bible. The inquisitor noticed a figure dressed like a German and badgered Veronese with the allegation that this might indicate Lutheran sympathies. Ordered to change the painting, Veronese quietly changed its title instead.

Because artists' livelihoods depended on the patronage of aristocrats and high ecclesiastical officials, most quickly fell into line with the new requirements. Artistic rebels were unknown in the late sixteenth-century Catholic world. In 1577 the pope founded a new academy in Rome to create guidelines for artists in promoting Christianity, and the Jesuits proved very influential in defining a new path for artists. Many prominent artists across Europe enthusiastically embraced the Catholic Reformation. Some became friends of Jesuits, undertook commissions for Jesuits, and practiced the *Spiritual Exercises*, thereby suffusing a Jesuit sensibility throughout Catholic culture.

IMAGE

Ignatius of Loyola

Sacred Music: Praising God

The Protestants' concern that the Word of God be intelligible to ordinary believers also influenced their attitude toward music. Luther, in particular, recognized the power of music to move the souls of the congregation. In the Lutheran mass he retained much of the traditional chant, but he translated the words into German and encouraged congregational singing so that believers sang the text themselves rather than passively listened to a choir. A number of new hymns were composed for the Lutheran service, some by Luther himself. One of the lasting masterpieces of the Reformation is Luther's great hymn "A Mighty Fortress Is

Our God." The Lutheran hymnbook laid the foundations for the magnificent tradition of Protestant church music that culminated in the compositions of Johann Sebastian Bach (1685–1750).

Zwingli, less certain about the value of music, banished organs from churches because he thought they obscured the clarity of the biblical text. Some radicals eliminated all music from churches, creating an austere form of worship practiced in houses or bare chapels, in which nothing was allowed to distract from the preaching of God's Word and the direct influence of the Holy Spirit. In these radical sects, the intimate connection between Western Christianity and the arts, which had been so pronounced for centuries, came to an abrupt end. Radical Protestants such as Anabaptists left a lasting legacy of hostility toward creative artists.

The Council of Trent spent more than a year debating the reform of sacred music. The Council decreed that the purpose of liturgical music was to encourage a sense of worship in the congregation. This meant that unlike Protestant music, which appealed to the laity by employing folk tunes, Catholic compositions should not borrow from secular music, but like Protestant music, the style of composition must allow for the words to be clearly heard. The Catholics did not follow the Protestant emphasis on congregational singing and rejected virtuoso vocal or instrumental displays. Catholic liturgical performances consisted only of the organ either accompanying voices or playing solos.

The new music of the Catholic Reformation remained firmly rooted in the innovations of Renaissance music and consisted of compositions for various forms of the Latin mass. The most important Catholic composer of church music in the later sixteenth century was Giovanni Pierluigi da Palestrina (ca. 1525–1594). Palestrina spent most of his career in Rome, where he worked as an organist and choir master. His more than 100 masses demonstrated to the often skeptical prelates, who wanted to abolish all elaborate compositions, that music could reflect the meaning of the words while not obscuring their audibility. Palestrina amplified the sumptuous effects of the unaccompanied choir, employing an exotic mixture of harmonic and melodic purity, carefully controlled dissonance, and a sensuous sound. For many generations his music served as the model for Catholic composers.

Conclusion

Competing Understandings

During the Reformation the West was permanently divided into two discordant religious cultures of Protestant and Catholic. The religious unity of the West achieved during the Middle Ages had been fruit of many centuries of diligent effort by missionaries, monks, popes, and crusading knights. That unity was lost through the conflicts between, on the one hand, reformers, city magistrates, princes, and kings who wanted to control their own affairs and, on the other, popes who continued to cling to the medieval concept of the papal monarchy. In the West, Christians no longer saw themselves as dedicated to serving the same God as all other Christians. Instead, Catholics and Protestants emphasized their differences.

The differences between these two cultures had lasting implications for how people understood and accepted the authority of the Church and the state, how they conducted their family life, and how they formed their own identities as individuals and as members of a larger community. The next chapter will explore all of these themes.

As the result of intransigence on the part of both confessional cultures, the division had tragic consequences. From the late sixteenth century to the late seventeenth century, European states tended to create diplomatic alliances along this ideological and religious divide, allowed disputes about doctrine to prevent peaceful reconciliation, and conducted wars as if they were a fulfillment of God's plan. Even after the era of religious warfare ended, Protestant and Catholic confessional cultures remained ingrained in all aspects of life, influencing not just government policy but painting, music, literature, and education. This division completely reshaped the West into a place of intense religious and ideological conflict, which by the eighteenth century drove many thoughtful people to reject the traditional forms of Christianity altogether and to advocate religious toleration and the separation of Church and state, ideas that were barely conceivable in the sixteenth century.

Suggestions for Further Reading

For a comprehensive listing of suggested readings, please go to www.ablongman.com/levack2e/chapter13

Bireley, Robert. *The Refashioning of Catholicism, 1450–1700: A Reassessment of the Counter Reformation.* 1999. A fair reappraisal of the major events by one of the most prominent historians of Catholicism in this period.

Bossy, John. *Christianity in the West, 1400–1700.* 1985. A short study not of the institutions of the Church but of Christianity itself, this book explores the Christian people, their beliefs, and their way of life. The book demonstrates considerable continuities before and after the Reformation and is especially useful in understanding the attitudes of common lay believers as opposed to the major reformers and Church officials.

Cameron, Euan. *The European Reformation.* 1995. The most comprehensive general survey, this bulky book covers all the major topics in considerable detail. It is excellent in explaining theological issues.

Hsia, R. Po-chia. *The World of Catholic Renewal, 1540–1770.* 1998. An excellent survey of the most recent research.

Koenigsberger, H. G., George L. Mosse, and G. Q. Bowler. *Europe in the Sixteenth Century,* 2nd ed. 1989. A good beginner's survey. Strong on political events.

McGrath, Alister E. *Reformation Thought: An Introduction,* 3rd rev. ed. 1999. Indispensable introduction for anyone seeking to understand the ideas of the European Reformation. Drawing on the most up-to-date scholarship, McGrath offers a clear explanation of these ideas, set firmly in their historical contexts.

Muir, Edward. *Ritual in Early Modern Europe.* 2nd ed. 2005. A broad survey of the debates about ritual during the Reformation and the implementation of ritual reforms.

Oberman, Heiko A. *Luther: Man Between God and the Devil,* trans. Eileen Walliser-Schwarzbart. 1992. First published to great acclaim in Germany, this book argues that Luther was more the medieval monk than history has usually regarded him. Oberman claims that Luther was haunted by the Devil and saw the world as a cosmic battleground between God and Satan. A brilliant, intellectual biography that is sometimes challenging but always clear and precise.

O'Malley, John. *Trent and All That: Renaming Catholicism in the Early Modern Era.* 2000. O'Malley works out a remarkable guide to the intellectual and historical developments behind the concepts of Catholic reform and, in his useful term, Early Modern Catholicism. The result is the single best overview of scholarship on Catholicism in early modern Europe, delivered in a pithy, lucid, and entertaining style.

Ozment, Steven. *The Age of Reform, 1250–1550: An Intellectual and Religious History of Late Medieval and Reformation Europe.* 1986. Firmly places the Protestant Reformation in the context of late medieval spirituality and theology; particularly strong on pre-Reformation developments.

Reardon, Bernard M. G. *Religious Thought in the Reformation.* 2nd ed. 1995. A good beginner's survey of the intellectual dimensions of the Reformation.

Scribner, R. W. *For the Sake of the Simple Folk: Popular Propaganda for the German Reformation.* 1994. An innovative and fascinating study of the Lutheran use of visual images.

Scribner, R. W. *The German Reformation.* 1996. A short and very clear analysis of the appeal of the Reformation by the leading social historian of the period. Pays attention to what people actually did rather than just what reformers said they should do.

Notes

1. *Correspondence of Erasmus*, trans. R. A. B. Mynors and D. F. S. Thomson, annotated by Wallace K. Ferguson (1974–1994), no. 858, 167–177.

2. *Desiderius Erasmus, The Essential Erasmus*, ed. John P. Dolan (1964), 148.

3. Quoted in Gordon Rupp, *Luther's Progress to the Diet of Worms* (1964), 29.

4. Ibid., 33.

5. Quote from an anonymous caricature reproduced in A. G. Dickens, *Reformation and Society in Sixteenth-Century Europe* (1966), Figure 46, 61.

6. Translated and quoted in Thomas Head, "Marie Dentière: A Propagandist for the Reform," in Katharina M. Wilson, ed., *Women Writers of the Renaissance and Reformation* (1987), 260.

7. Quoted in Peter Blickle, "The Popular Reformation," in *Handbook of European History 1400–1600: Late Middle Ages, Renaissance and Reformation*, Vol. 2: *Visions, Programs and Outcomes*, eds. Thomas A. Brady, Jr., Heiko A. Oberman, and James D. Tracy (1995), 171.

8. Quoted in Heiko A. Oberman, *Luther: Man Between God and the Devil*, trans. Eileen Walliser-Schwarzbart (1989), 240.

9. E. W. Ives, *Anne Boleyn* (1986), 398.

10. Quoted in Margery Stone Schauer and Frederick Schauer, "Law as the Engine of State: The Trial of Anne Boleyn," *William and Mary Law Review* 22 (1992): 68.

11. Quoted in Ives, "Anne Boleyn," 387.

12. Quoted in Schauer and Schauer, "Law as the Engine of State," 70.

13. Quoted in Dickens, *Reformation and Society*, 134.

14. Quoted in Irving Lavin, *Bernini and the Unity of the Visual Arts* (1980), 107.

The Age of Confessional Division

O N JULY 10, 1584, CATHOLIC EXTREMIST FRANÇOIS GUION, WITH A brace of pistols hidden under his cloak, surprised William the Silent, the Prince of Orange, as he was leaving the dining hall of his palace and shot him at point-blank range. William had been the leader of the Protestant nobility in the Netherlands, which was in revolt against the Catholic king of Spain. Guion masqueraded as a Protestant for seven years in order to ingratiate himself with William's party, and before the assassination he had consulted three Catholic priests who had confirmed the religious merit of his plan. Spain's representative in the Netherlands, the Duke of Parma, had offered a reward of 25,000 crowns to anyone who killed William, and at the moment of the assassination four other fanatics were in Delft trying to gain access to the Prince of Orange.

The murder of William the Silent exemplified an ominous figure in Western civilization—the religiously motivated assassin. There had been many assassinations before the late sixteenth century, but the assassins tended to be motivated by the desire to gain political power or to avenge a personal or family injury and less often by religious differences. In the wake of the Reformation the idea that killing a political leader of the opposing faith would serve God's plan became all too common. The assassination of William illustrated patterns of violence that have become the modus operandi of the political assassin—the use of deception to gain access to the victim, the vulnerability of leaders who wish to mingle with the public, the lethal potential of easily concealed pistols (a new weapon at that time), the corruption of politics through vast sums of money, and the obsessive hostility of zealots against their perceived enemies. The widespread acrimony among the varieties of Christian faith created a climate of religious extremism during the late sixteenth and early seventeenth centuries. After the Protestant and Catholic Reformations, the various forms of Christianity

Procession of the Catholic League During the last half of the sixteenth century, Catholics and Protestants in France formed armed militias or leagues. Bloody confrontations between these militias led to prolonged civil wars. In this 1590 procession of the French Catholic League, armed monks joined soldiers and common citizens in a demonstration of force.

came to be called confessions° because their adherents believed in a particular confession of faith, or statement of religious doctrine.

Religious extremism was just one manifestation of an anxiety that pervaded European society at the time—a fear of hidden forces controlling human events. In an attempt to curb that anxiety, the European monarchs created confessional states. The combined effort of state and church sought to discipline common people, persecute deviants of all sorts, and combat enemies through a religiously driven foreign policy. During this age of confessional division, European countries polarized along confessional lines, and governments persecuted followers of minority religions, whom they saw as threats to public security. Anxious believers everywhere were consumed with pleasing an angry God, but when they tried to find God within themselves many Christians seemed only to find the Devil in others. The bloody history of confessional conflicts during the sixteenth and seventeenth centuries, in fact, eventually stimulated the formation of the modern ethical principles of religious toleration, separation of church and state, and human rights during the eighteenth.

By attempting to discipline the people of Europe and make them better Christians, educated and elite society directly confronted a thriving popular culture. In many respects, the culture they encountered was nearly as alien as the native cultures in the newly discovered America. Certainly, the peoples of early modern Europe considered themselves Christian, but what they meant by Christianity was quite at odds with that of the Protestant and Catholic reformers. In a confused, haphazard, and sometimes violent fashion, members of the elite attempted to blot out many elements of popular culture that they suspected might be remnants of pre-Christian beliefs and practices. One of the most curious consequences of the Reformations during the sixteenth and seventeenth centuries was a dramatic conflict between two cultures, that of the educated elite and that of the ordinary people. However, the disciplining of the people was primarily confined to western Europe. In eastern Europe religious diversity and popular culture thrived largely due to the relative weakness of the monarchs.

The religious controversies of the age of confessional division redefined the West. During the Middle Ages, the West came to be identified with the practice of Roman Catholic Christianity. The Reformation of the early sixteenth century broke up the unity of medieval Christian Europe by dividing westerners into Catholic and Protestant camps. During the late sixteenth and seventeenth centuries, governments reinforced religious divisions and attempted to unify their peoples around a common set of beliefs. By the end of the eighteenth century, these confessional religious identities changed in some places into more secular political ideologies, such as the belief in the superiority of a republic over a monarchy, but the assumption that all citizens of a state should believe in some common ideology re-

mained. The period from about 1500 to 1750—the Early Modern period in European history—produced the lasting division of the West into national camps that were based on either religious confessions or ideological commitments. How did the encounter between the confessions and the state transform Europe into religiously driven camps?

- How did the expanding population and price revolution exacerbate religious and political tensions?
- How did religious and political authorities attempt to discipline the people?
- How did religious differences provoke violence and start wars?
- How did the countries of eastern Europe during the late sixteenth century become enmeshed in the religious controversies that began in western Europe during the early part of the century?

The Peoples of Early Modern Europe

- How did the expanding population and price revolution exacerbate religious and political tensions?

During the tenth century if a Russian had wanted to see the sights of Paris—assuming he had even heard of Paris—he could have left Kiev and walked under the shade of trees all the way to France, so extensive were the forests and so sparse the human settlements of northern Europe. By the end of the thirteenth century, the nomadic Russian would have needed a hat to protect him on the shadeless journey. Instead of human settlements forming little islands in a sea of forests, the forests were by then islands in a sea of villages and farms, and from any church tower the sharp-eyed traveler could have seen other church towers, each marking a nearby village or town. At the end of the thirteenth century, the European continent had become completely settled by a dynamic, growing population, which had cleared the forests for farms.

During the fourteenth century all of that changed. A series of crises—periodic famines, the catastrophic Black Death, and a general economic collapse—left the villages and towns of Europe intact, but a third or more of the population was gone. In that period of desolation, many villages looked like abandoned movie sets, and the cities did not have enough people to fill in the empty spaces between the central market square and the city walls. Fields that had once been put to the plow to feed the hungry children of the thirteenth century were neglected and overrun with bristles and brambles. During the fifteenth century a general European depression and recurrent epidemics kept the population stagnant.

In the sixteenth century the population began to re-bound, but the sudden swell brought dramatic and destabilizing consequences that contributed to pervasive anxiety. An important factor in the population growth was the transformation of European agriculture from subsistence to commercial farming, an uneven transformation that impoverished some villages while it enriched others. Moreover, the expanded population transformed the balance of power, as northern Europe recovered its population more successfully than southern Europe. As the population grew, young men and women flocked to the cities, creating enormous social strains and demands on local governments. Perhaps most disruptive was the price revolution, which brought inflation that ate away at the buying power of everyone from working families to kings and queens. The anxiety produced by these circumstances lasted into the seventeenth century.

The Population Recovery

During a period that historical demographers call the "long sixteenth century" (ca. 1480–1640), the population of Europe began to grow consistently again for the first time since the late thirteenth century. In 1340, on the brink of the Black Death, Europe had about 74 million inhabitants, or 17 percent of the world's total. By 1400 the population of all of Europe had dropped to 52 million (less than one-fifth of the population of the United States today), or 14 percent of the world's total. Over the course of the long sixteenth century, Europe's population grew from 60.9 million to 77.9 million, just barely surpassing the pre–Black Death level.

The table to the right shows some representative population figures for the larger European countries during the sixteenth century. Two stunning facts emerge from these data. The first is the much greater rate of growth in northern Europe compared to southern Europe. England grew by 83 percent, Poland grew by 76 percent, and even the tiny, war-torn Netherlands gained 58 percent. During the same period Italy grew by only 25 percent and Spain by 19. These trends signal a massive, permanent shift of demographic and economic power from the Mediterranean countries of Italy and Spain to northern, especially northwestern, Europe. The second fact to note from these data is the overwhelming size of France, which was home to about a quarter of Europe's population. Once France recovered from its long wars of religion, its demographic superiority overwhelmed competing countries and made it the dominant power in Europe, permanently eclipsing its chief rival, Spain. Because the Holy Roman Empire and especially its core regions in the German-speaking lands lacked political unity, it was unable to take advantage of its position as the second-largest state.

What explains the growth in the population and the economy? To a large extent, it was made possible by the

European Population, 1500–1600 (in millions)			
	1500	**1550**	**1600**
England	2.30	3.10	4.20
Germany	12.00	14.00	16.00
France	16.40	19.00	20.00
Netherlands	0.95	1.25	1.50
Belgium	1.25	1.65	1.30
Italy	10.50	11.40	13.10
Spain	6.80	7.50	8.10
Austria-Bohemia	3.50	3.60	4.30
Poland	2.50	3.00	3.40

Source: Jan de Vries, "Population," in *Handbook of European History 1400–1600: Late Middle Ages, Renaissance and Reformation,* Vol. 1: *Structures and Assertions,* eds. Thomas A. Brady, Jr., Heiko A. Oberman, and James D. Tracy (1994), Table 1, 13.

transformation from subsistence to commercial agriculture in certain regions of Europe. Subsistence farmers, called peasants, had worked the land year in and year out, raising grains for the coarse black bread that fed their families, supplemented only by beer, grain porridge, and occasionally vegetables. Meat was rare and expensive. Peasants consumed about 80 percent of everything they raised, and what little was left over went almost entirely to the landlord as feudal dues and to the church as tithing—the obligation to give to God one-tenth of everything earned or produced. Peasant families lived on the edge of existence. In a bad year some starved to death, usually the vulnerable children and old people. But during the sixteenth century, in areas with access to big cities, subsistence agriculture gave way to commercial crops, especially wheat, which was hauled to be sold in town markets. Profits from this market agriculture stimulated farmers to raise even greater surpluses in the agricultural regions around the great cities—London, Antwerp, Amsterdam, Paris, Milan, Venice, Barcelona, and scattered places in Germany. Commercial crops and the cash income they produced meant fewer starving children and a higher standard of living for those who were able to take advantage of the new opportunities. As commercial agriculture spread, the population grew because the rural population was better fed and more prosperous.

The Prosperous Villages

Success in commercializing agriculture could make an enormous difference in the lives of peasants. The village of Buia tells the story of many similarly prosperous hamlets.

Situated in Friuli, a region in the northeast corner of Italy, it served as part of the agricultural hinterland of the great metropolis of Venice. For centuries the peasants of hilly and pleasant Buia had lived in thatched hovels surviving at the subsistence level. But during the fourteenth and fifteenth centuries serfdom disappeared in the region and the peasants' legal status changed. Now free to sell their labor to the highest bidder, peasant families contracted with a landlord to lease a plot of land for a certain number of years in exchange for annual rent payments in kind. A typical yearly rent might include two bushels of wheat, two of oats, one of beans, one of millet, three barrels of wine, two chickens, one ham, three guinea hens, thirty eggs, two cartloads of firewood, and two days' work mowing hay. In contrast to the servitude of serfdom, which tied peasants to the land, agricultural leases created a measure of economic freedom. They allowed landlords to find labor at a time when laborers were scarce, and they enabled peasants to negotiate for a better reward for their labor.

Unlike some neighboring villages that were still under the heel of their lords, Buia had incorporated as a town, a status that provided it with more autonomy from its lords, the Savorgnan family. Moreover, Buia had diversified its economy, branching out into cattle raising and marketing its fierce pear brandy and smooth white wine. But Buia's crucial economic advantage derived from its access to capital. The Savorgnan lords liberally lent money to their tenants in Buia, which enabled them to survive hard times and to invest in commercial profit-making enterprises. Unlike other families, the Savorgnans were willing to invest in their tenants, because they had established political and economic ties with the nearby commercial metropolis of Venice, whose bankers were more than happy to bankroll the Savorgnan family. From the commercial banks of Venice, money flowed through the hands of the Savorgnan to the peasants of the little village of Buia, who in turn produced crops that could be sold in the markets of Venice, a flow of money and goods that enriched, although unequally, everyone involved—the peasants, their Savorgnan landlords, and the Venetian bankers. With the increased income from commercial agriculture, Buia even began to look more affluent during the sixteenth century, boasting a substantial church, a tavern, and a simple one-room town hall where citizens could gather to debate their affairs.

The success of commercial agriculture during the sixteenth century depended on a free and mobile labor supply, access to capital for investment, and proximity to the markets of the big cities. What happened in Buia happened in many places throughout Europe, but overall the amount of

The Rise of Commercial Agriculture

During the sixteenth century commercial agriculture began to produce significant surpluses for the expanding population of the cities. This scene depicts a windmill for grinding grain and a train of wagons hauling produce from the country to be marketed in a city.

land available could not provide enough work for the growing farm population. As a result, the growth of the rural population created a new class of landless, impoverished men and women, who were forced to take to the road to find their fortunes. These vagabonds, as they were called, exemplified the social problems that emerged from the uneven distribution of wealth created by the new commerce.

The Regulated Cities

By the 1480s cities began to grow, largely through migration from the more prosperous countryside, but the growth was uneven with the most dramatic growth occurring in the cities of the North, especially London, Antwerp, and Amsterdam (see Map 14.1). The surpluses of the countryside, both human and agricultural, flowed into the cities during the sixteenth century. Compared to even the prosperous rural villages, such as Buia, the cities must have seemed incomparably rich. Half-starved vagabonds from the countryside would have marveled at shops piled high with food (white bread, fancy pies, fruit, casks of wine, roasting meats); they would have wistfully passed taverns full of drunken, laughing citizens; and they would have begged for alms in front of magnificent, marble-faced churches.

Every aspect of the cities exhibited dramatic contrasts between the rich and poor, who lived on the same streets and often in different parts of the same houses. Around 1580 Christian missionaries brought a Native American chief to the French city of Rouen. Through an interpreter he was asked what impressed him the most about European cities, so unlike the villages of North America. He replied that he was astonished that the rag-clad, emaciated men and women who crowded the streets did not grab the plump, well-dressed rich people by the throat.

The wretched human surplus from the farms continuously replenished and swelled the populations of the cities, which were frequently depleted by high urban death rates. As wealthy as the cities were, they were unhealthy places: human waste overflowed from open latrines because there were no sewage systems; garbage, manure, dead animals, and roaming pigs and dogs made the streets putrid and dangerous; and water came from polluted rivers or sat stale in cisterns for months. Under such conditions, entire neighborhoods could be wiped out in epidemics. Both ends of the life span were vulnerable: one in three babies died in the first year of life; old people did not last long in cold, drafty houses. When the epidemics appeared, which they continued to do about every twenty years until 1721, the rich escaped to their country retreats while the poor died in the streets or in houses locked up and under quarantine.

Despite the danger from disease in the cities, rural immigrants were less likely to starve than those who remained in small villages where they lacked land. Every city maintained storehouses of grain and regulated the price of bread and the size of a loaf so that the poor could be fed. The impulse to feed the poor was less the result of humanitarian motives than a recognition that nothing was more dangerous than a hungry mob. Given the contrasts in wealth among its inhabitants, cities guarded carefully against revolts and crime. Even for petty crime, punishment was

Map 14.1 Population Distribution in the Sixteenth Century

The population of Europe concentrated around the cities of northern Italy, the Danube and Rhine River valleys, Flanders and northern France, and southeastern England. During the late sixteenth century, northwestern Europe began to grow significantly more rapidly than southern Europe.

swift, sure, and gruesome. The beggar who stole a loaf of bread from a baker's cart would have his hand amputated on a chopping block in the market square. A shabbily dressed girl who grabbed a lady's glittering trinket would have her nose cut off so that she could never attract a man. A burglar would be tortured, drawn, and quartered, and have his severed head impaled on an iron spike at the town gate as a warning to others.

To deal with the consequences of commerce and massive immigration, European cities attempted to regulate the lives of their inhabitants. Ringing bells measured each working day, and during the sixteenth century many cities erected a large mechanical clock in a prominent place so that busy citizens could keep to their schedules. Municipal officers inspected the weights and measures in the city market, regulated the distribution of produce to guarantee an abundant food supply, and repaired the streets and city walls. However talented or enterprising, new arrivals to the city had very limited opportunities. They could hardly start up their own business because all production was strictly controlled by the guilds, which were associations of merchants or artisans organized to protect their interests. Guilds rigidly regulated their membership; they required an apprenticeship of many years, prohibited technological innovations, guaranteed certain standards of workmanship, and did not allow branching out into new lines. A member of the goldsmiths' guild could not make mirrors; a baker could not sell fruit on the side; a house carpenter could not lay bricks. Given the limited opportunities for new arrivals, immigrant men and women begged on the streets or took charity from the public dole. The men picked up any heavy-labor jobs they could find. Both men and women became servants, a job that paid poorly but at least guaranteed regular meals.

Among the important social achievements of both Protestant and Catholic Reformations were efforts to address the problems of the destitute urban poor, who constituted at least a quarter of the population, even in the best of times. In Catholic countries such as Italy, Spain, southern Germany, and France, there was an enormous expansion of credit banks, which were financed by charitable contributions in order to provide small loans to the poor. Catholic cities established convents for poor young women who were at risk of falling into prostitution and for other women who had retired from the sex trade. Catholic and Protestant cities established orphanages, hospitals for the sick, hospices for the dying, and apartments lent out for a modest rent to poor widows. Both Catholic and Protestant cities attempted to distinguish between the "honest" poor—those who were disabled and truly deserving—and the "dishonest" poor who were thought to be malingerers. Protestant cities established poorhouses, which segregated the poor, subjected them to prisonlike discipline, and forced the able-bodied to work.

The more comfortable classes of the cities enjoyed large palaces and luxurious lifestyles. They hired extensive staffs of servants, feasted on meat and fine wines, and purchased exotic imports such as silk cloth, spices from the East, and, in the Mediterranean cities, slaves from eastern Europe, the Middle East, or Africa. The merchants whose fortunes came from cloth manufacturing, banking, and regional or international trade maintained their status by marrying within their own class, providing municipal offices to those whose fortunes had fallen, and educating their children in the newly fashionable humanist schools. The wealthy of the cities were the bastions of social stability. They possessed the financial resources and economic skills to protect themselves from the worst consequences of economic instability, especially the corrosive wave of price inflation that struck the West after about 1540.

The Price Revolution

Price inflation became so pervasive during the last half of the sixteenth century that it contributed to the widespread fear that events were being controlled by hidden forces. The effects of inflation are illustrated by the experience of the students at Winchester College in England. These young men were the privileged sons of English aristocrats and country gentlemen, destined for leisured wealth and public responsibility. The curriculum of Winchester emphasized the unchanging values of aristocratic privilege and Christian rectitude, but the dusty account books, kept in meticulous detail by generations of college stewards, reveal that change was very much a fact of college life during the sixteenth century. For example, in 1500 a piece of cloth large enough to make a student's uniform cost forty shillings. By 1580 the cost had doubled, and by 1630 it had tripled. During the sixteenth century the cost of a dozen sheets of parchment doubled, the cost of a dozen candles quadrupled, and the cost of a twelve-gallon barrel of wine (yes, the college served wine to its teenaged students) rose from eight to sixty-four shillings. English masons' experience of price inflation during this period was far more painful. Over the course of the century their wages doubled, but the price of bread increased four- or fivefold, and because the survival of their families depended on the cost of bread, price inflation seriously threatened their lives.

The finances of English college students and masons reveal the phenomenon that historians call the Price Revolution°. After a long period of falling or stable prices that stretched back to the fourteenth century, Europe experienced sustained price increases, beginning around 1540. The inflation lasted a century, forcing major economic and social changes that permanently altered the face of Western society. During this period overall prices across Europe multiplied five- or sixfold.

? population

What caused the inflation? The basic principle is simple. The price paid for goods and services is fundamentally the result of the relationship between *supply* and *demand.* If the number of children who need to be fed grows faster than the supply of grain, the price of bread goes up. This happens simply because mothers who can afford it will be willing to pay a higher price to save their children from hunger. If good harvests allow the supply of grain to increase at a greater rate than the demand for bread, then prices go down. The equation gets somewhat more complicated when taking into account two other factors that can influence price. One factor is the *amount of money in circulation.* If the amount of gold or silver available to make coins increases, there is more money in circulation. When more money is circulating, people have more money to buy more things, which creates the same effect as an increase in demand—prices go up. The other factor is called the *velocity of money in circulation,* which refers to the number of times money changes hands to buy things. When people buy commodities with greater frequency, it has the same effect as increasing the amount of money in circulation or of increasing demand—again, prices go up.

The precise combination of these factors in causing the great Price Revolution of the sixteenth century has long been a matter of considerable debate. Most historians would now agree that the primary cause of inflation was population growth, which increased demand for all kinds of basic commodities, such as bread and woolen cloth for clothing. As Europe's population finally began to recover, it meant that more people needed and desired to buy more things. This explanation is most obvious for commodities that people need to survive, such as grain to make bread. These commodities have what economists call *inelastic demand,* that is, consumers do not have a great deal of discretion in purchasing them. Everybody has to eat. The commodities that people could survive without if the price is too high are said to have *elastic demand,* such as dancing shoes and lace collars. In England between 1540 and 1640 overall prices rose by 490 percent. More telling, however, is that the price of grain (inelastic demand) rose by a stunning 670 percent, whereas the price of luxury goods (elastic demand) rose much less, by 204 percent. Thus, inflation hurt the poor, who needed to feed their children, more than the rich, whose desires were more elastic.

Monetary factors also contributed to inflation. The Portuguese brought in significant amounts of gold from Africa, and newly opened mines in central Europe increased the amount of silver by fivefold as early as the 1520s. The discovery in 1545 of the fabulous silver mine of Potosí (in present-day Bolivia) brought to Europe a flood of silver, which Spain used to finance its costly wars. As inflation began to eat away at royal incomes, financially strapped monarchs all across western Europe debased their money because they believed, mistakenly, that producing more coins

containing less silver would buy more. In fact, the minting of more coins meant each coin was worth less and would buy less. In England, for example, debasement was the major source of inflation during the 1540s and 1550s.

During the sixteenth century, no one understood these causes, however. People only experienced the effects of inflation, and then only gradually. The real wages of workers declined, causing widespread suffering and discontent. Incomes eroded for those dependent on fixed incomes—clergymen, pensioners, government clerks, and landlords who rented out land on long leases. Landlords who were willing to be ruthless and enterprising survived and even prospered. Those who were more paternalistic or conservative in managing their estates often lost their land to creditors.

The Price Revolution severely weakened governments. Most monarchs derived their incomes from their own private lands and from taxes on property. As inflation took hold, property taxes proved dangerously inadequate to cover royal expenses. Even frugal monarchs such as England's Elizabeth I were forced to take extraordinary measures, in her case to sell off royal lands. Spendthrift monarchs faced disaster. Spain was involved in the costly enterprise of nearly continuous war during the sixteenth century. To pay for the wars, Charles V resorted to a form of deficit financing in which he borrowed money by issuing *juros,* which provided lenders an annuity yielding between 3 and 7 percent on the amount of the principal. By the 1550s, however, the annuity payments of the *juros* consumed half of the royal revenues. Charles's son, Philip II, inherited such an alarming situation that in 1557, the year after he assumed the throne, he was forced to declare bankruptcy. Philip continued to fight expensive wars and borrow wildly, and thus failed to get his financial house in order. He declared bankruptcy again in 1575 and 1596. Philip squandered Spain's wealth, impoverishing his own subjects through burdensome taxes and contributing to inflation by borrowing at high rates of interest and debasing the coinage. Although the greatest power of the sixteenth century, Spain sowed the seeds of its own decline by fighting on borrowed money.

Probably the most serious consequence of the Price Revolution was that the hidden force of inflation caused widespread human suffering. During the late sixteenth and early seventeenth centuries, people felt their lives threatened, but they did not know the source and so they imagined all kinds of secret powers at work, especially supernatural ones. The suspicion of religious differences created by the Reformation provided handy, if utterly false, explanations for what had gone wrong. Catholics suspected Protestants, Protestants suspected Catholics, both suspected Jews, and they all worried about witches. Authorities sought to relieve this widespread anxiety by looking in all the wrong

DOCUMENT

Michel de Montaigne, *Essays* (1575)

places, disciplining the populace, hunting for witches, and battling against enemies from the opposite side of the confessional divide.

Disciplining the People

■ How did religious and political authorities attempt to discipline the people?

The first generation of the Protestant and Catholic Reformations had been devoted to doctrinal disputes and to either rejecting or defending papal authority. Subsequent generations of reformers in the last half of the sixteenth and the early seventeenth centuries faced the formidable task of building the institutions that would firmly establish a Protestant or Catholic religious culture. Leaders of all religious confessions attempted to revitalize the Christian community by disciplining nonconformists and enforcing moral rigor. Members of the community came to identify responsible citizenship with conformity to a specific Christian confession.

Whether Lutheran, Calvinist, Catholic, or Anglican, godly reformers sought to bring order to society, which meant they often felt obliged to attack popular culture. They reformed or abolished wild festivals, imprisoned town drunks, decreased the number of holidays, and tried to regulate sexual behavior. Many activities that had once been accepted as normal came to be considered deviant or criminal. The process of better ordering society required that the common people accept a certain measure of discipline. Discipline required cooperation between church and secular authorities, but it was not entirely imposed from above. Many people wholeheartedly cooperated with moral correction and even encouraged reformers to go further. Others passively, actively, or resentfully resisted it.

Establishing Confessional Identities

Between 1560 and 1650 religious confessions reshaped European culture, and loyalty to a single confession governed the relationships between states. A confession consisted of the adherents to a particular statement of religious doctrine—the Confession of Augsburg for Lutherans, the Helvetic Confessions for Calvinists, the Thirty-Nine Articles for Anglicans, and the decrees of the Council of Trent for Catholics. Based on these confessions of faith, the clergy disciplined the laity, exiled nonconformists, and promoted distinct religious institutions, beliefs, and culture.

The process of establishing confessional identities did not happen overnight; it lasted for centuries and had far-reaching consequences. During the second half of the sixteenth century, Lutherans turned from the struggle to survive within the hostile Holy Roman Empire to establishing a confessional identity in the parts of the empire where Lutheranism was the chosen religion of the local prince. They had to recruit Lutheran clergy and provide each clergyman with a university education, which was made possible by scholarship endowments from the Lutheran princes of the empire. Once established, the Lutheran clergy became a branch of the civil bureaucracy, received a government stipend, and enforced the will of the prince. Calvinist states followed a similar process, but where they were in a minority, as in France, Calvinists had to go it alone, and the state often discriminated against them. In those places confessional identities were established in opposition to the state and the dominant confession.

Catholics responded with their own aggressive plan of training new clergymen, educating the laity, and reinforcing the bond between church and state. Just as with the Lutheran princes, Catholic princes in the Holy Roman Empire associated conformity to Catholicism with loyalty to themselves, making religion a pillar of the state. Everywhere in western Europe (except for Ireland, a few places in the Holy Roman Empire, and for a time France) the only openly practiced religion was the religion of the state.

The authorities primarily formed confessional identities among the laity by promoting distinctive ritual systems. These ritual systems embodied ways of acting and even of gesturing that transformed the way people moved their bodies so that a Catholic and a Protestant might be instantly recognized by certain telltale signs of posture, speech, and comportment.

The Catholic and Protestant ritual systems differed primarily in their attitude toward the sacred. Whereas Catholic ritual behavior depended on a repertoire of gestures that indicated reverence in the presence of the sacred, Protestant ritual depended on a demonstration of sociability that identified people as members of a certain congregation or church. For example, until the late sixteenth century Europeans greeted one another either by raising a hand, palm outward, which meant "welcome," or with a bow by which someone of lower status recognized the superiority of another. Some radical Protestants, however, insisted that all gestures of deference, such as bows and curtsies, were an affront to God and introduced a new form of greeting, the handshake. Shaking hands was completely egalitarian, and one could identify English Quakers or Scottish Calvinists, for example, simply by the fact that they shook hands with one another.

A particularly revealing ritual difference can be seen in the contrasting ways that Scottish Calvinists and Spanish Catholics reintegrated repentant sinners into the Church. In Calvinism disciplinary authority rested with the presbytery, a board of pastors and elders elected by the community. If a Scottish Calvinist blasphemed God, the presbytery could discipline him, shun him, or banish him from the community. If he wished to be reinstated and the presbytery agreed, he would be obliged to come before the entire congregation to confess sincerely his wrongs and beg forgiveness. The congregation would make a collective judgment about his acceptability for renewed membership. The pain inflicted on the Calvinist sinner was the social pain of having his transgression openly discussed and evaluated by his friends and neighbors.

If a Spanish Catholic blasphemed, he would be subjected to an extended ritual of penance, the auto-da-fé°, which meant a theater of faith. The auto-da-fé was designed to promote fear and to cause physical pain because, according to Catholic doctrine, bodily suffering in this world was necessary in order to free the soul from worse suffering in the next. An *auto* was a public performance in which dozens or sometimes hundreds of sinners and criminals were paraded through the streets in a theatrical demonstration of the authority of the Church and the power of penance. The *auto* culminated in a mass confirmation of faith in which the repentant sinners utterly subjected themselves to the authority of the clergy, while those who refused to repent or were relapsed heretics were strangled and their corpses burned.

Whereas the punishment of the Calvinist community was primarily a rite of social humiliation, the auto-da-fé involved physical torture as well as social degradation. The nub of the difference was that Calvinists had to demonstrate the sincerity of their social conformity; Catholics had to go through a performance that emphasized the authority of the clergy and that purified sin with physical pain.

Regulating the Family

One matter on which Calvinists, Lutherans, and Catholics agreed was that the foundation of society should be the authority fathers had over their families. This principle, known as patriarchy, was very traditional. The confessions that emerged from the Reformation further strengthened patriarchy because it so usefully served the needs of church and state to establish social order and encourage morality. According to an anonymous treatise published in 1586 in Calvinist Nassau, the three pillars of Christian society were the church, the state, and the household. This proposition made the father's authority parallel to the authority of clergy and king—a position that all the confessions would have accepted. Enforcing patriarchy led to regulating sexuality and the behavior of children.

Marriage and Sexuality: The Self-Restrained Couple

However, regional differences in the structure of the family itself meant that despite the near universal acceptance of the theory of patriarchy, the reality of the father's authority varied a great deal. Since the early Middle Ages in northwestern Europe—in Britain, Scandinavia, the Netherlands, northern France, and western Germany—couples tended to

wait to marry until their mid- or late twenties, well beyond the age of sexual maturity. When these couples married, they established their own household separate from either of their parents. Husbands were usually only two or three years older than their wives, and that proximity of age tended to make those relationships more cooperative and less authoritarian than the theory of patriarchy might suggest. In northwestern European the couple had to be economically independent before they married, which meant both had to accumulate savings or the husband needed to inherit from his deceased father before he could marry. By contrast, in southern Europe, men in their late twenties or thirties married teenaged women over whom they exercised authority by virtue of their age. In the South patriarchy meant husbands ruled over wives. In eastern Europe, both spouses married in their teens and resided in one of the parental households for many years, which placed both spouses for extended periods under the authority of the husband's parents.

The marriage pattern in northwestern Europe required prolonged sexual restraint by young men and women until they were economically self-sufficient. In addition to individual self-control, sexual restraint required social control by church and secular authorities, who seem to have been more vigilant about regulating sexual behavior than in southern and eastern Europe. Their efforts seem to have been generally successful. For example, in sixteenth-century Geneva, where the elders were especially wary about sexual sins, the rates of illegitimate births were extremely low. The elders were particularly vigilant about disciplining women and keeping them subservient, often making and enforcing highly minute regulations. In 1584 Calvinist elders in another Swiss town excommunicated Charlotte Arbaleste and her entire household because she wore her hair in curls, which the elders thought were too alluring.

Northwestern European families also tended to be smaller. Married couples in northwestern Europe began to space their children through birth control and family planning. These self-restrained couples practiced withdrawal, the rhythm method, or abstinence. When mothers no longer relied on wet nurses and nursed their own infants, often for long periods, they also reduced their chances of becoming pregnant. Thus, limiting family size became the social norm in northwestern Europe, especially among the educated and urban middle classes. Protestant families tended to have fewer children than Catholic families, but Catholics in this region also practiced some form of birth control, even though Church law prohibited all forms except abstinence.

For prospective couples, parental approval remained more important than romantic love. In fact, a romantic attachment between a husband and wife was frowned upon as unseemly and even dangerous. More highly prized in a marriage partner were trust, dependability, and the willingness to work. Many married couples certainly exhibited

The *Auto-da-Fé:* The Power of Penance

Performed in Spain and Portugal from the sixteenth to eighteenth centuries, the auto-da-fé merged the judicial processes of the state with the sacramental rituals of the Catholic Church. An *auto* took place at the end of a judicial investigation conducted by the inquisitors of the Church after the defendants had been found guilty of a sin or crime. The term *auto-da-fé* means "theater of faith," and the goal was to persuade or force a person who had been judged guilty to repent and confess. Organized through the cooperation of ecclesiastical and secular authorities, autos-da-fé brought together an assortment of sinners, criminals, and heretics for a vast public rite that dramatized the essential elements of the sacrament of penance: contrition, by which the sinner recognized and felt sorry for the sin; confession, which required the sinner to admit the sin to a priest; and satisfaction or punishment, by which the priest absolved the sinner and enacted some kind of penalty. The auto-da-fé transformed penance, especially confession and satisfaction, into a spectacular affirmation of the faith and a manifestation of divine justice.

The *auto* symbolically anticipated the Last Judgment, and it provoked deep anxiety among those who witnessed it about how God would judge them. By suffering bodily pain in this life the soul might be relieved from worse punishments in the next. The sinners, convicts, and heretics, now considered penitents, were forced to march in a procession that went through the streets of the city from the cathedral to the town hall or place of punishment. These processions would typically include some thirty or forty penitents, but in moments of crisis they could be

far larger. In Toledo in 1486 there were three *autos*—one parading 750 penitents and two displaying some 900 each.

A 1655 *auto* in Córdoba illustrates the symbolic character of the rites. Soldiers bearing torches that would light the pyre for those to be burnt led the procession. Following them came three bigamists who wore on their heads conical miters or hats painted with representations of their sin, four witches whose miters depicted devils, and three criminals with harnesses around their necks to demonstrate their status as captives. The sinners carried unlit candles to represent their lack of faith. Criminals who had escaped arrest were represented in the procession by effigies made in their likeness, and those who had died before punishment were carried in their coffins. The marching sinners appeared before their neighbors and fellow citizens stripped of the normal indicators of status, dressed only in the emblems of their sins. Among them walked a few who wore the infamous *sanbenitos,* a kind of tunic or vest with a yellow strip down the back, and a conical hat painted with flames. These were the *relajados,* the unrepentant or relapsed sinners who were going to be "relaxed" (released into the hands of the secular authorities) at the culminating moment of the *auto* when they were strangled and burned.

The procession ended in the town square at a platform from which penances were performed as on the stage of a theater. Forced to their knees, the penitents were asked to confess and to plead for readmission into the bosom of the church. For those who did confess, a sentence was an-

nounced that would rescue them from the pains of Purgatory and the flames of the *auto.* The sentence required them to join a penitential procession for a certain number of Fridays, perform self-flagellation in public, or wear a badge of shame for a prescribed period of time. Those who failed to confess faced a more immediate sentence.

The most horrendous scenes of suffering awaited those who refused to confess or who had relapsed into sin or heresy, which meant their confession was not considered sincere. If holdouts confessed prior to the reading of the sentence, then the *auto* was a success, a triumph of the Christian faith over its enemies, and everything that could possibly elicit confessions was attempted, including haranguing, humiliating, and torturing the accused until their stubborn will broke. If the accused finally confessed after the sentence was read, then they would be strangled before burning, but if they held out to the very end, they would be burned alive. From the ecclesiastics' point of view, the refusal to confess was a disaster for the entire Church because the flames of the pyre opened a window into Hell. They would certainly prefer to see the Church's authority acknowledged through confession than to see the power of Satan manifest in such a public fashion.

It is reported that crowds witnessed the violence of the autos-da-fé with silent attention in a mood of deep dread, not so much of the inquisitors, it seems, as for the inevitability of the final day of divine judgment that would arrive for them all. The core assumption of the auto-da-fé was that bodily pain could save a soul from damnation. As one contemporary

Relapsed heretics were burned on a pyre.

The conical hats were painted with the representation of the sinner's sin.

Sinners wearing the sanbenitos.

A procession conducted the sinners to the town square.

Auto da fé in Lisbon

witness put it, the inquisitors removed "through external ritual [the sinners'] internal crimes." It was assumed that the public ritual framework for the sacrament of penance would have a salutary effect on those who witnessed the *auto* by encouraging them to repent before they too faced divine judgment.

Questions of Justice

1. How did the auto-da-fé contribute to the formation of an individual and collective sense of being a Catholic?
2. In the auto da fé, inflicting physical pain was more than punishment. How was pain understood to have been socially and religiously useful?

Taking It Further

Flynn, Maureen. "Mimesis of the Last Judgment: The Spanish *Auto da fe*," *Sixteenth Century Journal* 22 (1991): 281–97. The best analysis of the religious significance of the auto-da-fé.

Flynn, Maureen. "The Spectacle of Suffering in Spanish Streets," in Barbara A. Hanawalt and Kathryn L. Reyerson, eds., *City and Spectacle in Medieval Europe*. 1994. In this fascinating article Flynn analyzes the spiritual value of physical pain.

signs of affection—addressing one another lovingly in letters, nursing a sick mate, mourning a dead one—but overly sentimental attachments were discouraged as contrary to the patriarchal authority that ideally characterized family life. Most husbands and wives seem to have treated one another with a certain coolness and emotional detachment.

The moral status of marriage also demonstrated regional variations during the early modern period. Protestants no longer considered husbands and wives morally inferior to celibate monks and nuns, and the wives of preachers in Protestant communities certainly had a respected social role never granted to the concubines of priests. But the favorable Protestant attitude toward marriage did not necessarily translate into a positive attitude toward women. In Germany the numerous books of advice, called the Father of the House literature, encouraged families to subordinate the individual interests of servants, children, and the mother to the dictates of the father, who was encouraged to be just but who must be obeyed. Even if a wife was brutally treated by her husband, she could neither find help from authorities nor expect a divorce.

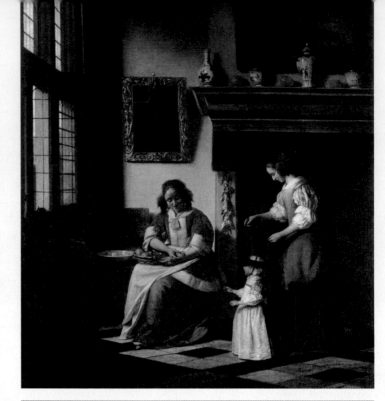

The Domestic Ideal

During the late sixteenth and seventeenth centuries, idealized depictions of harmonious family life became very popular, especially in the Netherlands. In this painting by Pieter De Hooch a young child is learning to walk.

Children: Naturally Evil?

Although families had always cherished their children, during the Reformation both Protestant and Catholic preachers placed even greater emphasis on the welfare, education, and moral upbringing of children. Protestants contributed to this process by emphasizing the family's responsibility for their children's moral guidance and religious education. One of the obligations of Protestant fathers was to read and teach the Bible in the home. This directive may have been more a theoretical ideal than a practical reality, but the rise in literacy among both boys and girls in Protestant countries attests to the increased importance of education.

Discipline also played a large role in the sixteenth-century family. Parents had always demonstrated love toward their children by indulging them with sweets and toys and protecting them from danger. But during the sixteenth century some authors of advice books and many preachers began to emphasize that parental love must be tempered by strict discipline. In effect, the clergy attempted to impose their own authoritarian impulses on the emotional lives of the family. The Protestant emphasis on the majesty of God and a belief in original sin translated into a negative view of human nature. Calvinist theologians who held such a view placed a special emphasis on family discipline. The *Disquisition on the Spiritual Condition of Infants* (1618) pointed out that from a theological point of view, babies were naturally evil. The godly responsibility of the father was to break the will of his evil offspring, taming them so that they could be turned away

from sin toward virtue. The very title of a 1591 Calvinist treatise revealed the strength of the evil-child argument: *On Disciplining Children: How the Disobedient, Evil, and Corrupted Youth of These Anxious Last Days Can Be Bettered.* The treatise also advised that the mother's role should be limited to her biological function of giving birth. It directed fathers to be vigilant so that their wives did not corrupt the children, because women "love to accept strange, false beliefs, and go about with benedictions and witches' handiwork. When they are not firm in faith and the Devil comes to tempt them . . . they follow him and go about with supernatural fantasies."[1]

In order to break the will of their infants, mothers were encouraged to wean them early and turn them over for a strict upbringing by their fathers. The ideal father was to cultivate both love and fear in his children by remaining unemotional and firm. He was to be vigilant to prevent masturbation, to discourage frivolity, and to toughen little children by not allowing them to eat too much, sleep too long, or stay too comfortably warm. Although discouraged from being unnecessarily brutal, the godly father was never to spare the rod on either his children or his wife.

It is clear that disciplining children was an important theoretical guideline in sixteenth- and seventeenth-century Europe. It is less clear whether this was as true in practice as in theory. Historians disagree on the issue. It is likely that then, as now, there were many different ways of raising children, and each family exhibited its own emotional chemistry. And it is also likely that sixteenth-century parents did considered firm discipline loving.

Suppressing Popular Culture

The family was not the only institution that sixteenth-century educated reformers sought to discipline. Their efforts also targeted many manifestations of traditional popular culture. The reformers or puritans, as they came to be called in England, wanted to purify both the church and society, to transform them into a "godly community" by encouraging and even enforcing moral behavior, particularly in rowdy youths and members of the lower classes. The suppression of popular culture had two aspects. One was a policing effort, aimed at ridding society of presumably un-Christian practices. The other was a missionary enterprise, an attempt to bring the Protestant and Catholic Reformations to the people through instruction and popular preaching.

Overall the reformers sought to encourage an ethic of moderation, which valued thrift, modesty, chastity, and above all self-control. This ethic was neither Protestant nor Catholic but was promoted by clerics of all religious confessions. The traditional popular culture they so distrusted stressed other values such as spontaneity and emotional freedom, values that were hardly subject to control and could have dangerous, often violent consequences.

Once the reformers had cleaned up the churches by eliminating idolatry, unnecessary holidays, and superfluous rituals, they turned to the secular world, and they found much to criticize. The reformers saw impiety in comedians, dancing, loud music, rough sports, dice and card games, public drinking, dressing up in costumes, puppets, and above all actors. The Catholic Bishop of Verona condemned preachers who told stories that made the congregations laugh. To the reformers, these things were despicable because they seemed to be vestiges of pre-Christian practices and because they led people into sin.

The festival of Carnival° came under particularly virulent attack. The most popular annual festival, Carnival took place for several days or even weeks before the beginning of Lent and included all kinds of fun and games—silly pantomimes, bear baiting, bullfights, masquerades, dances, lots of eating and drinking, and illicit sex. The *Discourse Against Carnival* (1607) complained about the temptations to sin and the money wasted in Carnival play. Catholics attempted to reform Carnival by eliminating the most offensive forms of behavior, especially those that led to violence or vice. Other popular festivals and entertainments suffered a similar fate of scornful criticism, regulation, or even abolition.

Pieter Brueghel the Elder's painting *The Battle Between Carnival and Lent* (1559) illustrates the role of festivals in the popular culture. In the painting, a fat man riding on a wine barrel engages in a mock joust with an emaciated, stooped figure of uncertain gender who rides a wheeled cart pulled by a monk and nun. The two figures in the painting symbolize the two festival seasons. The fat man represents Carnival, a time of joyous, gluttonous, drunken feasting; the lean one represents Lent, a period of sexual abstinence and fasting that precedes Easter. During the

The Battle Between Carnival and Lent

In this allegory, called *The Battle Between Carnival and Lent* (1559) by Pieter Brueghel the Elder, the festive season of Carnival is represented on the left by a fat man riding a wine barrel wielding as a lance a roasted pig on a spit. He is engaged in a mock joust with an emaciated figure holding a paddle of fish representing Lent, the season for fasting and giving up meat. On the Carnival side are cards, dice, and people dressed in the funny costumes of Carnival. On the Lent side are pretzels and flatbread, the unleavened breads of the fasting season.

The Introduction of the Table Fork: The New Sign of Western Civilization

Sometime in the sixteenth century, western Europeans encountered a new tool that would initiate a profound and lasting transformation in Western society: the table fork. Before people used the table fork and practiced the refined dining manners that accompanied its use, they dined in a way that, to our modern sensibilities, would seem disgusting. Meat was a luxury available only to people in the upper classes, who indulged themselves by devouring it in enormous quantities. Whole rabbits, lambs, and pigs roasted on a spit would be placed before diners. A quarter of veal or venison or even an entire roast beef, complete with its head, might be heaved onto the table. Diners would use knives to cut off a piece of meat that they would then eat with their hands, allowing the juices to drip down their arms. The long sleeves of their shirts were used to wipe meat juices, sweat, and spittle from their mouths and faces. These banquets celebrated the direct physical contact between the body of the dead animal and the bodies of the diners themselves who touched, handled, chewed, and swallowed it.

During the sixteenth century, reformers who were trying to abolish the cruder aspects of popular culture also promoted new table manners that treated the eating of meat as discomforting, if not shameful. Well-mannered people increasingly felt the need to distance themselves from the fact that they were consuming a dead animal. To accomplish this, new implements made certain that diners did not come into direct physical contact with their food before they placed it in their mouths. In addition to napkins—which came into widespread use to replace shirt sleeves for wiping the mouth—table forks appeared on upper-class tables. It became impolite to transfer food directly from the table or common serving plate to the mouth. Food first had to go onto each individual's plate and then be cut into small portions and raised to the mouth. A French treatise of 1672 warns that "meat must never be touched . . . by hand, not even while eating."[2] This prohibition had nothing to do with cleanliness, because bacteria were not discovered until the end of the nineteenth century. The fear was not of disease, but of direct contact with the bodies of dead animals. The fear, it seems, derived from a growing sense of revulsion with the more physical aspects of human nature, including sexuality, which was regulated by church authorities, and the killing of animals in order to survive, which was regulated by table manners. The table fork made it possible to eat meat without ever touching it. Forks enabled diners to avoid their growing sense of discomfort with the textures and juices of meats that perhaps reminded them of the flesh and blood of the dead animal.

The use of the table fork, therefore, has more to do with civility than hygiene, which can be demonstrated by the fact that certain foods, such as bread, cherries, or chocolates, are always eaten with the hands, even by the Queen of England. In determining when to use a fork it is not cleanliness that matters but the kind of food consumed. Moreover, the civility that resulted from use of the table fork promoted individualism, because everyone—regardless of their social origins—could learn how to use it. A clerk or governess could disguise a humble background simply by learning how to eat properly. In the end, the transformations that occurred in Western society because of its encounter with the table fork—the blurring of class distinctions and creation of a universal code of manners—were so gradual and subtle that few of us who use a table fork daily are even aware of its profound significance.

For Discussion

How do manners, both good and bad, communicate messages to other people? Does it matter to have good manners?

The Introduction of the Table Fork
During the late sixteenth century the refinement of manners among the upper classes focused on dining. No innovation was more revolutionary than the spread of the use of the table fork. Pictured here are the travel cutlery, including two table forks, of Queen Elizabeth I.

sixteenth century contemporaries understood the contrast between Carnival, which was devoted to bodily pleasure, and Lent, during which the bodily desires were ignored to enable repentance, as the battle between two divergent ideas of society. The battle was not just a symbol but a reality that took place through the attempts to suppress popular culture.

What Catholics reformed, Protestants abolished. Martin Luther had been relatively tolerant of popular culture, but later reformers were not. The most famous German Carnival, the *Schembartlauf* of Nuremberg, was abolished; in England the great medieval pageants of York, Coventry, Chester, Norwich, and Worcester disappeared; in Calvinist Holland, the Christmas tradition of giving children gifts was strongly denounced.

The Carnival festival was highly resilient, however. Along with many other forms of popular culture, it persisted, even if less openly public. The moralist attack on popular culture meant that some activities retreated from outside to inside—into sports arenas, taverns, theaters, and opera houses. And some were professionalized by athletes, entertainers, actors, and singers. The attempts of mayors and clerics to abolish fun also provoked open resistance. In 1539 in Nuremberg the Lutheran pastor Andreas Osiander, who had preached against Carnival, found himself lampooned by a float in the shape of a ship of fools, in which he was depicted as the captain.

The attempts to suppress popular culture produced a confrontation between the educated elites of Europe and the workers, peasants, servants, and artisans who surrounded them and served them. Although not entirely successful, by the late sixteenth century the suppression had the effect of broadening the cultural gap between the educated few and the masses. Practices that previously had been broadly accepted forms of public entertainment, in which even members of the clergy participated, came to be seen as unworthy of educated people.

Hunting Witches

The most catastrophic manifestation of the widespread anxiety of the late sixteenth and seventeenth centuries was the great witch-hunt°. The judicial prosecution of alleged witches in either church or secular courts dramatically increased about the middle of the sixteenth century and lasted until the late seventeenth, when the number of witchcraft trials rapidly diminished and stopped entirely in western Europe.

Throughout this period, people accepted the reality of two kinds of magic°. The first kind was natural magic, such as the practice of alchemy or astrology, which involved the manipulation of occult forces believed to exist in nature. The fundamental assumption of natural magic was that everything in nature is alive. The trained magician could coerce the occult forces in nature to do his bidding. During the Renaissance many humanists and scientific thinkers were drawn to natural magic because of its promise of power over nature. Natural magic, in fact, had some practical uses. Alchemists, for example, devoted themselves to discovering what they called the "philosopher's stone," the secret of transmuting base metals into gold. In practice this meant that they learned how to imitate the appearance of gold, a very useful skill for counterfeiting coins or reducing the content of precious metals in legal coins. Natural magic was practiced by educated men and involved the human manipulation of the occult, but it did not imply any kind of contact with devils. Most practitioners of natural magic desired to achieve good, and many considered it the highest form of curative medicine.

Many people of the sixteenth and seventeenth centuries also believed in a second kind of magic—demonic magic. The practitioner of this kind of magic—usually but not always a female witch—called upon evil spirits to gain access to power. Demonic magic was generally understood as a way to work harm by ritual means. Belief in the reality of harmful magic and of witches had been widespread for centuries, and there had been occasional witch trials throughout the Middle Ages. Systematic witch-hunts, however, began only when ecclesiastical and secular authorities showed a willingness to employ the law to discover and punish accused witches. The Reformation controversies of the late sixteenth century and the authorities' willingness to discipline deviants of all sorts certainly intensified the hunt for witches. Thousands of people were accused of and tried for practicing witchcraft. About half of these alleged witches were executed, most often by burning. Cases of alleged witchcraft rarely occurred in a steady flow, as one would find for other crimes. Typically, witchcraft trials took place during localized hunts when a flare-up of paranoia and torture multiplied allegations against vulnerable members of the community. Most allegations were against women, in particular young unmarried women and older widows, but men and even young children could be accused of witchcraft as well.

People in many different places—from shepherds in the mountains of Switzerland to Calvinist ministers in the lowlands of Scotland—thought they perceived the work of witches in human and natural events. The alleged demonic magic of witchcraft appeared in two forms: *maleficia* (doing harm) and *diabolism* (worshiping the devil). The rituals of *maleficia* consisted of a simple sign or a complex incantation, but what made them *maleficia* was the belief that the person who performed them intended to cause harm to someone or something. There were many kinds of *maleficia*, including coercing an unwilling lover by sprinkling dried menstrual blood in his food, sickening a pig by cursing it, burning a barn by marking it with a hex sign, bringing wasting diarrhea to a child by reciting a spell, and killing an enemy by stabbing a wax statue of him. Midwives and women who specialized in healing were especially vulnerable to accusations of witchcraft. The intention behind a particular action they might have performed was often obscure, making it difficult to distinguish between magic designed to bring beneficial results, such as the cure of a child, and *maleficia* designed to bring harmful ones. With the high infant mortality rates of the sixteenth and seventeenth centuries, performing magical rituals for a sick baby could be very risky. The logic of witchcraft beliefs implied that a bad ending must have been caused by bad intentions.

While some people certainly attempted to practice *maleficia*, the second and far more serious kind of ritual practice associated with demonic magic, diabolism, almost certainly never took place. Diabolism was a fantasy that helped explain events that could not otherwise be explained. The theory behind diabolism asserted that the witch had sold her soul to the Devil, whom she worshiped as her god. These witches had made a pact with the Devil, worshiped the Devil in the ritual of the witches' sabbath, flew around at night, and sometimes changed themselves into animals. The two core beliefs of the pact with the Devil and the witches' sabbath created the intellectual and legal conditions for the great witch-hunts of the sixteenth and seventeenth centuries.

A pact with the Devil was believed to give the witch the ability to accomplish *maleficia,* in exchange for which she was obliged to serve and worship Satan. The most influential witchcraft treatise, *The Hammer of Witches* (1486), had an extensive discussion of the ceremony of the pact. After the prospective witch had declared her intention to enter his service, Satan appeared to her, often in the alluring form of a handsome young man who offered her rewards, including a demonic lover, called an *incubus.* To obtain these inducements, the witch was obliged to renounce her allegiance to Christ, usually signified by stomping on the cross. The Devil rebaptized her in a disgusting substance, guaranteeing that her soul belonged to him. To signify that she was one of his own, the Devil marked her body in a hidden place, creating a sign, which could easily be confused with a birthmark or blemish. To an inquisitor or judge almost any mark on the skin might confirm guilt.

One of the fullest accounts of beliefs in the witches' sabbath comes from the tragic trial of the Pappenheimer family in Bavaria in 1600. The Pappenheimers, consisting of a mother, a father, and their sons, were vagrants arrested for killing babies and cutting off their hands for the purposes of witchcraft. In her confession under torture, Anna Pappenheimer gave a full account of her participation in a fantastic witches' sabbath that supposedly took place at night on a hill outside of the village of Tettenwang. She claimed that witches arrived from near and far flying in on broomsticks and pitchforks. The assembled company largely consisted of women, young and old and most of them naked, but there were a few male witches (known as warlocks) and even some children. With a clap of thunder

DOCUMENT

How Women Came to Be Accused of Witchcraft: A Witch's Confession

Walpurga Hausmännin, an elderly widow and midwife from a small town near Augsburg in the Holy Roman Empire, was accused in 1587 of killing more than forty children. Her confession, extracted out of her through fear and torture, is tragic but typical, complete with lurid details of sexual intercourse with the Devil, the Devil's mark, a pact with the Devil, and riding on a broomstick to a witches' sabbath. This excerpt from her confession, which lists some of her alleged victims, illustrates how the collective fears of the community were channeled into imagined crimes against children.

[The Devil] also compelled her to do away with and to kill young infants at birth, even before they had been taken to Holy Baptism. This she did, whenever possible. These as follows:

1 and 2. About ten years ago, she had rubbed Anna Hämännin, who dwelt far from Dursteigel, with her salve on the occasion of her first childbirth and also otherwise damaged her so that mother and child remained together and died.

3. Dorothea, the stepdaughter of Christian Wachter, bore her first child ten years before; at its birth she made press on its little brain so that it died. The Devil had specially bidden her destroy the first-born.

5. When, four years ago, the organist's wife was awaiting her confinement, she touched her naked body with her salve whereby the child promptly died and came stillborn.

8. Three years ago when she was called to a mill to the miller's wife there she had let the child fall into the water and drown.

11. When six years ago, she partook of food with Magdalena Seilerin, called *Kammerschreiberin* (wife of the chamber scribe), she had put a salve in her drink, so that she was delivered prematurely. This child she, Walpurga, secretly buried under the doorway of the said wife of the scribe on the pretext that then she would have no other miscarriage. The same she also did with many others. When she was questioned under torture for the reasons of this burial, she admitted that it was done in order to cause disunion between two spouses. This her Devil-Paramour had taught her.

15. She had also rubbed a salve on a beautiful son of the late Chancellor, Jacob by name: this child had lovely fair hair and she had given him a hobby-horse so that he might ride on it till he lost his senses. He died likewise.

Source: From George T. Matthews, ed., *News and Rumor in Renaissance Europe: The Fugger Newsletters,* pp. 137–143. Copyright © 1959 by G. P. Putnam's Sons.

The Witches' Kitchen
During the sixteenth and seventeenth centuries it was widely believed that witches were women
who practiced *maleficia* and worshiped Satan. Both attractive
young and wrinkled old women
appear here as witches. From the
right an old witch embraces her
naked demon lover, a young
woman opens her blouse for her
approaching lover, another young
woman points to the witch's mark
on her leg, a hag reads spells from
a book in front of a human skull,
a witch brews noxious substances
in a large kettle, and a kneeling
woman worships a satanic idol. In
the background is a house fire, the
product of the witches' evil work.

and a profusion of smoke, Satan himself suddenly appeared
with his eyes glowing, dressed in black and smelling horri-
bly. The assembled witches and warlocks bowed low before
him, praying in a travesty of the Lord's Prayer, "Our Satan
which art in Hell. . . ." There followed an infernal banquet of
disgusting foods, including horse meat, ravens, crows, toads,
frogs, and boiled and roasted infants. After the feast, an or-
chestra of demons played tuneless, screeching dance music
that aroused a mad lust in the witches and their demon
lovers, who began a wild spinning dance that finally broke

down into a indiscriminate orgy. The family and some other
drifters were grotesquely tortured and burned alive.

Between about 1550 and 1650, approximately 100,000
people in Europe were tried for witchcraft. About 50,000 of
these were executed. Approximately half of the trials were in
the German-speaking lands of the Holy Roman Empire.
Prosecutions were also extensive in Switzerland, France,
Scotland, Poland, Hungary, Transylvania, and Russia.
10,000 people were tried in Spain and Italy, but these were
mostly for minor offenses of *maleficia*, and very few people

**Burning of Witches at
Dernberg in 1555**
One of the witches is being
taken away by a flying demon to
whom she had sold her soul.

were executed, probably none in Italy. As the product of collective beliefs and collective paranoia, witchcraft beliefs could be applied to all kinds of people, but allegations were most commonly lodged against poor, older women in small rural villages. Perhaps most tragic is the fact that these women were the members of the community most dependent on their neighbors for kindness and charity.

The Confessional States

■ How did religious differences provoke violence and start wars?

The Religious Peace of Augsburg of 1555 provided the model for a solution to the religious divisions produced by the Reformation. According to the principle of *cuius regio, eius religio* (he who rules determines the religion of the land), each prince in the Holy Roman Empire determined the religion to be followed by his subjects, and those who disagreed were obliged to convert or emigrate elsewhere. Certainly, forced exile was economically and personally traumatic for those who emigrated, but it preserved what was almost universally believed to be the fundamental principle of successful rulership—one king, one faith, one law. In other words, each state should have only one church. Except in the notoriously weak states of eastern Europe and a few small troubled principalities in the Holy Roman Empire, few thought it desirable to allow more than one confession in the same state.

The problem with this political theory of religious unity, of course, was the reality of religious divisions created by the Reformation. In some places there were as many as three active confessions—Catholic, Lutheran, and Calvinist—in addition to the minority sects, such as the Anabaptists and the Jewish communities. The alternative to religious unity would have been religious toleration, but hardly anyone in a position of authority was willing to advocate that. Calvin had expelled advocates of religious toleration, and Luther had been aggressively hostile to those who disagreed with him on seemingly minor theological points. After 1542 with the establishment of the Universal Inquisition, the Catholic Church was committed to exposing and punishing anyone who professed a different faith, with the exception of Jews in Italy, who were under papal protection. Geneva and Rome became competing missionary centers, each flooding the world with polemical tracts and specially trained missionaries willing to risk their lives by going behind the enemy lines to console their co-religionists and evangelize for converts.

Wherever there were significant religious minorities within a state, the best that could be hoped for was a condition of anxious tension, omnipresent suspicion, and periodic hysteria (see Map 14.2). The worst possibility was civil war in which religious affiliations and political rivalries were intertwined in such complicated ways that finding peaceful solutions was especially difficult. Between 1560 and 1648 several religious civil wars broke out, including the French Wars of Religion, the Dutch revolt against Spain, the Thirty Years' War in Germany, and the English Civil War. (The latter two will be discussed in Chapter 15.)

During the late sixteenth century a new word appeared to describe a personality type that may not have been entirely new but was certainly much more common—the fanatic°. Originally referring to someone possessed by a demon, *fanatic* came to mean a person who expressed immoderate enthusiasm in religious matters, a person who pursued a supposedly divine mission, often to violent ends. Fanatics from all sides of the religious divide initiated waves of political assassinations and engaged in grotesque massacres of their opponents. François Guion, the assassin of William the Silent, whose story began this chapter, was in many ways typical of fanatics in his steadfast pursuit of his victim and his willingness to masquerade for years under a false identity. During the sixteenth and seventeenth centuries, no religious community had a monopoly on fanatics. They presented themselves as serving the pope as well as the Protestant churches.

The sharp confessional divisions that produced fanatics and assassins also stimulated writers, poets, and dramatists to examine the human condition. Perhaps no period in the history of the West produced so many great works of literature as the late sixteenth and early seventeenth centuries.

The French Wars of Religion

When King Henry II (r. 1547–1559) of France died unexpectedly from a jousting accident, he left behind his widow, the formidable Catherine de Médicis (1519–1589), and a brood of young children—including his heir, Francis II (r. 1559–1560), who was only 15. Henry II had been a peacemaker. He succeeded in keeping France from civil war by carefully pacifying the quarrelsome nobles of the realm, and at the Peace of Cateau-Cambrésis (1559) he finally ended more than sixty years of war with Spain. In contrast, Catherine and her children, including three sons who successively ascended to the throne, utterly failed to keep the peace, and for some forty years France was torn apart by a series of desperate civil wars.

The Huguenots:
The French Calvinist Community

By 1560 Calvinism had made significant inroads into predominantly Catholic France. Pastors sent from Geneva had been especially successful in the larger provincial towns, where their evangelical message appealed to enterprising

Map 14.2 Religious Divisions in Europe About 1600
After 1555 the religious borders of Europe became relatively fixed, with only minor changes in confessional affiliations to this day.

merchants, professionals, and skilled artisans. One in ten of the French had become Calvinists, or Huguenots° as French Protestants were called. The political strength of the Huguenots was greater than their numbers might indicate, because between one-third and one-half of the lower nobility professed Calvinism. Calvinism was popular among the French nobility for two reasons. One involved the imitation of social superiors. The financial well-being of any noble depended on his patron, an aristocrat of higher rank who had access to the king and who could distribute jobs and lands to his clients. When a high aristocrat converted to Protestantism, he tended to bring into the new faith as well his noble clientele, who converted through loyalty to their patron or through the patron's ability to persuade those who were financially dependent on him. As a result of a few aristocratic conversions in southwest France, Calvinism spread through "a veritable religious spider's web,"[3] as one contemporary put it.

Even more important than networks of male patrons was the influence of aristocratic women. The sister of King Francis I of France (r. 1515–1547), Marguerite of Angoulême (1492–1549), married the King of Navarre (an independent kingdom situated between France and Spain) and created a haven in Navarre for Huguenot preachers and theologians. Her example drew other aristocratic ladies to the Huguenot cause, and many of the Huguenot leaders during the French Wars of Religion were the sons and grandsons of these early female converts. Marguerite's daughter, Jeanne d'Albret, sponsored Calvinist preachers for several years before she publicly announced her own conversion in 1560, and her son, Henry Bourbon, became the principal leader of the Huguenot cause during the French Wars of Religion° and the person responsible for eventually bringing the wars to an end.

The Origins of the Religious Wars

Like all civil wars, the French Wars of Religion exhibited a bewildering pattern of intrigue, betrayal, and treachery. Three distinct groups constituted the principal players. The first group was the royal family, consisting of Queen Catherine de Médicis and her four sons by Henry II—King Francis II (r. 1559–1560), King Charles IX (r. 1560–1574),

King Henry III (r. 1574–1589), and Duke Francis of Alençon (1554–1584)—and her daughter, Marguerite Valois (1553–1615). The royal family remained Catholic but on occasion reconciled themselves with the Huguenot opposition, and Marguerite married into it. The second group was the Huguenot faction of nobles led by the Châtillon family and the Bourbon family who ruled Navarre. The third group was the hard-line Catholic faction led by the implacable Guise family. These three groups vied for supremacy during the successive reigns of Catherine de Médicis's three sons, none of whom proved to be effective monarchs.

During the reign of the sickly and immature Francis II, the Catholic Guise family dominated the government and raised the persecution of the Huguenots to a new level. In response to that persecution, a group of Protestant nobles plotted in 1560 against the Guises, and some Calvinist ministers provided scriptural justifications for vengeance against tyrants. The Guises got wind of a conspiracy to kill them and surprised the plotters as they arrived in small groups at the royal chateau of Amboise. Some were ambushed, some drowned in the Loire River, and some hanged from the balconies of the chateau's courtyard. A tense two years later in 1562, the Duke of Guise was passing through the village of Vassy just as a large congregation of Protestants was holding services in a barn. The duke's men attacked the worshipers, killing some 740 of them and wounding hundreds of others.

Following the massacre at Vassy, civil war broke out in earnest. For nearly forty years a series of religious wars sapped the strength of France. Most of the battles were indecisive, which meant neither side sustained military superiority for long. Both sides relied for support on their regional bases: The Protestant strength was in the southwest, the Catholic in Paris and the north. Besides military engagements, the French Wars of Religion were characterized by political assassinations and massacres.

Massacre of St. Bartholomew's Day

After a decade of bloody yet inconclusive combat, the royal family tried to resolve the conflict by making peace with the Protestants, a shift of policy signified by the announcement of the engagement of Marguerite Valois, daughter of Henry II and Catherine de Médicis, to Henry Bourbon, the son of the Huguenot King of Navarre. At age 19, Marguerite—or Queen Margot, as she was known—was already renowned for her brilliant intelligence. But she was renowned also for her wanton morals, and to complicate the situation further, on the eve of the wedding she was having an affair with another Henry, the young new Duke of Guise who was the leader of the intransigent Catholic faction. The marriage between Marguerite and Henry of Navarre was to take place in Paris in August 1572, an event that brought all the Huguenot leaders to the heavily armed Catholic capital for the first time in many years. The gathering of all their enemies in one place presented too great a temptation for the Guises, who hatched a plot to assassinate the Huguenot leaders. Perhaps because she had become jealous of the Huguenots' growing influence on her son, King Charles IX, the mercurial Catherine suddenly switched sides and became implicated in the plot.

Catherine somehow convinced the weak-willed king to order the massacre of the Huguenot nobles gathered in Paris. On August 14, 1572, St. Bartholomew's Day, the people of Paris began a slaughter. Between 3,000 and 4,000 Huguenots were butchered in Paris and more than 20,000 were put to death throughout the rest of France. Henry of Navarre saved his life by pretending to convert to Catholicism, while most of his companions were murdered.

DOCUMENT

St. Bartholomew's Day Massacre (1572)

DOCUMENT

The St. Bartholomew's Day Massacre: Painful Memories

The Duke of Sully (1560–1641) became an ambassador and finance minister for French King Henry IV and was the principal architect of the Edict of Nantes, which provided a measure of religious toleration for Protestants in France after 1589. During the St. Bartholomew's Day massacre he was 12 years old, but he never forgot what he witnessed. Sully was one of the few members of Henry of Navarre's personal entourage to survive the massacre.

Intending on that day to wait upon the king my master [Henry of Navarre, later King Henry IV of France], I went to bed early on the preceding evening; about three in the morning I was awakened by the cries of people, and; the alarm-bells, which were everywhere ringing. . . . I was determined to escape to the College de Bourgogne, and to effect this I put on my scholar's gown, and taking a book under my arm, I set out. In the streets I met three parties of the Life-guards; the first of these, after handling me very roughly, seized my book, and, most fortunately for me, seeing it was a Roman Catholic prayer-book, suffered me to proceed, and this served me as a passport with the two other parties. As I went along I saw the houses broken open and plundered, and men, women, and children butchered, while a constant cry was kept up of, "Kill! Kill! O you Huguenots! O you Huguenots!" This made me very impatient to gain the college, where, through God's assistance, I at length arrived, without suffering any other injury than a most dreadful fright.

Source: From "The Saint Bartholomew's Day Massacre" in Bayle St. John, ed., *Memoirs of the Duke of Sully, Vol. 1* (London: George Bell and Sons, 1877).

St. Bartholomew's Day Massacre
This Protestant painter, François Dubois, depicted the merciless slaughter of Protestant men, women, and children in the streets of Paris in 1572. The massacre was the most bloody and infamous in the French Wars of Religion and created a lasting memory of atrocity.

After the massacre of St. Bartholomew's Day, both sides tried to interpret the events to their own advantage. Catholics celebrated. The pope marked the occasion by having a medal struck and frescoes painted in the Vatican. King Philip II of Spain wrote that the massacre "was indeed of such value and prudence and of such service, glory, and honor to God and universal benefit to all Christendom that to hear of it was for me the best and most cheerful news which at present could come to me."[4] For Catholics the massacre was a great service to God. Protestants had a very different reaction, and presented it as a great affront to God.

Catherine's attempted solution for the Huguenot problem failed to solve anything, however. Henry of Navarre escaped his virtual imprisonment in the royal household, set Marguerite up in an isolated castle, returned to Navarre and his faith, and reinvigorated Huguenot resistance. Two Huguenot political thinkers laid out a theory justifying political revolution: François Hotman in *Francogallia* (1573) and Théodore de Bèze in *Right of Magistrates* (1579). They argued that because the authority of all magistrates, including even low-ranking nobles, came directly from God, the Huguenot nobles had the right and obligation to resist a tyrannical Catholic king. During the same period, Catholic moderates known as the *politiques* rejected the excesses of the Guises and argued for an accommodation with the Huguenots.

The wars of religion continued until the assassination of King Henry III, brother of the late Charles IX. Both Charles and Henry had been childless, a situation that made Henry Bourbon of Navarre the rightful heir to the throne, even though he was a Huguenot. Henry Bourbon became King Henry IV (r. 1589–1610) and recognized that predominantly Catholic France would never accept a Huguenot king, and so in 1593 with his famous quip, "Paris is worth a mass," Henry reconverted to the ancient faith, and most opposition to him among Catholics collapsed. Once he returned to Catholicism he managed to have the pope annul his childless marriage to Marguerite so that he could marry Marie de' Medici and obtain her huge dowry. Affable, witty, generous, and exceedingly tolerant, "Henry the Great" became the most popular king in French history, reuniting the war-torn country by ruling with a very firm hand. With the Edict of Nantes° of 1598, he allowed the Huguenots to build a quasi state within the state, giving them the right to have their own troops, church organization, and political autonomy within their walled towns, but they were banned from the royal court and the city of Paris.

Henry encouraged economic development under his minister the Duke of Sully, who retired the crushing state debt and built up a fiscal surplus by reforming finances and eliminating corruption. Henry declared that his ambition was for even the poorest peasant to be able to afford a chicken in his pot every Sunday, and even though he did not achieve this laudatory goal, his public works included the beautification of Paris and an impressive canal system to facilitate transportation.

Despite his enormous popularity, Henry too fell victim to fanaticism. After surviving eighteen attempts on his life, in 1610 the king was fatally stabbed by a Catholic fanatic, who took advantage of the opportunity presented when the royal coach unexpectedly stopped behind a cart loading hay. Unlike the aftermath of the St. Bartholomew's Day massacre, Catholics all over France mourned Henry's death and considered the assassin mad. Henry's brilliant conciliatory nature and the horrors of the religious wars had tempered public opinion.

The French Wars of Religion

1559	Peace of Cateau-Cambrésis between France and Spain
1560	Protestant conspiracy of Amboise
1572	Massacre of St. Bartholomew's Day
1573	François Hotman publishes *Francogallia*
1579	Théodore de Bèze publishes *Right of Magistrates*
1593	King Henry IV of France converts to Catholicism
1598	Edict of Nantes granting Protestants religious toleration

Philip II, His Most Catholic Majesty

France's greatest rivals were the Habsburgs, who possessed vast territories in the Holy Roman Empire, controlled the elections for emperor, and had dynastic rights to the throne of Spain. As archenemies of the Protestant Reformation, they had regularly helped finance the Catholic cause during the French Wars of Religion. During the late sixteenth century, Habsburg Spain took advantage of French weakness to establish itself as the dominant power in Europe. When Emperor Charles V (who had been both Holy Roman Emperor and king of Spain) abdicated his thrones in 1556, the Habsburg possessions in the Holy Roman Empire and the emperorship went to his brother, Ferdinand I, and the balance of his vast domain to his son, Philip II (r. 1556–1598). Philip's inheritance included Milan, Naples, Sicily, the Netherlands, scattered outposts on the north coast of Africa, colonies in the Caribbean, Central America, Mexico, Peru, the Philippines, and most important of all, Spain. In 1580 he also inherited Portugal and its far-flung overseas empire, which included a line of trading posts from West Africa to the Spice Islands and the vast colony of unexplored Brazil.

Ruling over these enormous territories was a gargantuan task that Philip undertook with obsessive seriousness. From the rambling palace of El Escorial, which was also a mausoleum for his father and a monastery, Philip lived in semimonastic seclusion and ruled as the "King of Paper," an office-bound bureaucrat rather than the rule-from-the-saddle warrior his father had been and many of his contemporary monarchs remained. Philip kept himself to a rigid daily work discipline that included endless committee meetings and long hours devoted to poring over as many as 400 documents a day, which he annotated extensively in his crabbed hand. Because of his inability to delegate authority and his immersion in minutiae, Philip tended to lose his grasp of the larger picture, especially the shaky finances of Spain.

This grave, distrustful, rigid man saw himself as the great protector of the Catholic cause and committed Spain to perpetual hostility toward Muslims and Protestants. On the Muslim front he first bullied the Moriscos, the descendants of the Spanish Muslims. The Moriscos had received Christian baptism, but they were suspected of secretly practicing Islam, and in 1568 Philip issued an edict that banned all manifestations of Muslim culture and ordered the Moriscos to turn over their children to Christian priests to educate. The outraged Moriscos of Granada rebelled but were soundly defeated. At first dispersed throughout Spain, the surviving Moriscos were eventually expelled from the country in 1609. Philip hardened his policy toward the Moriscos because he feared, not unreasonably, that they would become secret agents on Spanish soil for his great Mediterranean rivals, the Ottoman Turks. To counter the Turkish threat, Philip maintained expensive fortresses on the North African coast. In 1571 he joined the Venetians and the pope to check Turkish advances after the Ottomans captured Cyprus, Venice's richest colony. The Christian victory at Lepanto in the Gulf of Corinth, which destroyed more than one-third of the enemy's fleet, was heralded as one of the greatest events of the sixteenth century, proving that the Turks could be beaten. Lepanto renewed the crusading spirit in the Catholic world. Although the victory at Lepanto was a valuable propaganda tool, it had slight military significance because the Turks quickly rebuilt their fleet and forced Venice to cede Cyprus to them. The island remains divided between Christian and Muslim populations to this day.

Philip once said he would rather lose all his possessions and die a hundred times than be the king of heretics. His attitude toward Protestants showed that he meant what he said. Through his marriage to Queen Mary I of England (r. 1553–1558), Philip encouraged her persecutions of Protestants, but they got their revenge. After Mary's death her half-sister, Queen Elizabeth I, refused his marriage proposal and in 1577 signed a treaty to assist the Protestant Netherlands, which was in rebellion against Spain. To add insult to injury, the English privateer Sir Francis Drake (ca. 1540–1596) conducted a personal war against Catholic Spain by raiding the Spanish convoys bringing silver from the New World. In 1587 Drake's embarrassing successes culminated with a daring raid on the great Spanish port city of Cadiz, where, "singeing the king of Spain's beard," he destroyed the anchored Spanish fleet and many thousands of tons of vital supplies. Philip retaliated by building a huge fleet of 132 ships armed with 3,165 cannons, which sailed from Portugal to rendezvous with the Spanish army stationed in the Netherlands and launch an invasion of England in 1588. As the Invincible Armada, as it was called, passed through the English Channel, it was met by a much smaller English fleet, assembled out of merchant ships refit for battle. Unable to maneuver as effectively as the English in the fluky winds of the channel and mauled by the rapid-firing

DOCUMENT

John Hawkins Reports on the Spanish Armada (1588)

Defeat of the Spanish Armada

The smaller English ships on the left outmaneuvered the Spanish Armada arrayed in the formal curved line of galleons in the middle.

English guns, the Spanish Armada° suffered heavy losses and was forced to retreat to the north, where it sustained further losses in storms off the coast of Scotland and Ireland. Barely more than half of the fleet finally straggled home. The defeat severely shook Philip's sense of invincibility.

The reign of Philip II illustrated better than any other the contradictions and tensions of the era. No monarch had at his grasp as many resources and territories as Philip, and yet defending them proved extremely costly. The creaky governmental machinery of Spain put a tremendous burden on a conscientious king such as Philip, but even his unflagging energy and dedication to his duties could not prevent military defeat and financial disaster. Economic historians remember Philip's reign for its series of state bankruptcies and for the loss of the Dutch provinces in the Netherlands, the most precious jewel in the crown of Spain.

The Dutch Revolt

The Netherlands boasted some of Europe's richest cities, situated amid a vast network of lakes, rivers, channels, estuaries, and tidal basins that periodically replenished the exceptionally productive soil through flooding. The Netherlands consisted of seventeen provinces, each with its own distinctive identity, traditions, and even language. The southern provinces were primarily French-speaking; those in the north spoke a bewildering variety of Flemish dialects. In 1548 Emperor Charles V annexed the northern provinces that had been part of the Holy Roman Empire to the southern provinces he had inherited from his father. His decision meant that when his son, Philip II, became king of Spain, all of the Netherlands was included with the Spanish crown. With his characteristic bureaucratic mentality, Philip treated Dutch affairs as a management problem rather than a political sore spot, an attitude that subordinated the Netherlands to Spanish interests. Foreign rule irritated the Dutch, who had long enjoyed ancient privileges including the right to raise their own taxes and muster their own troops.

Consolidating the Netherlands under the Spanish crown deprived the Dutch princes of the right to chose the official religion of their lands, a right they would have enjoyed had the provinces remained in the Holy Roman Empire, where the Religious Peace of Augsburg granted princes religious freedom. Philip's harsh attitude toward Protestants upset the Netherlands' delicate balance among Catholic, Lutheran, Calvinist, and Anabaptist communities. Huguenot refugees from the French Wars of Religion heightened the anti-Catholic fanaticism of the local Calvinists, who in 1566 occupied many Catholic churches and destroyed paintings and statues.

In response to the rapidly deteriorating situation in the Netherlands, Philip issued edicts against the heretics and strengthened the Spanish Inquisition. The Inquisition in Spain was an arm of the monarchy charged with ensuring religious conformity among the extremely diverse cultures of the Iberian peninsula. The Spanish Inquisition had been preoccupied with investigating the Christian sincerity of former Jews, who after the expulsions of 1492 had converted to Christianity in order to stay in Spain. When introduced in the Netherlands, the Inquisition became an investigating agency devoted to finding, interrogating, and, if necessary, punishing Protestants. Philip also dispatched 20,000 Spanish troops under the command of the Duke of Alba (1508–1582), a veteran of the Turkish campaigns in North Africa and victories over the Lutheran princes in the Holy Roman Empire. Alba directly attacked the Protestants. He personally presided over the military court, the Council of Troubles, which became so notoriously tyrannical that the people called it the Council of Blood. As an example to others, he systematically razed several small villages where there had been incidents of desecrating Catholic images, slaughtering every inhabitant. Alba himself boasted that during the campaign against the rebels, he had 18,000 people executed, in addition to those who died in battle or were massacred by soldiers. The Prince of Orange, William the

Silent (1533–1584), accompanied into exile some 60,000 refugees, who constituted about 2 percent of the population. While abroad William began to organize resistance to Alba.

Alba's cruelty backfired by steeling Protestant opposition to the Spanish. Alba also lost support among otherwise loyal Catholics when he attempted to introduce a 10 percent tax on trade. His policies a failure, Alba was recalled to Spain in 1573. Meanwhile the sea-beggars, as the Dutch Calvinist privateers were called, had begun to achieve some success against the Spanish. Within a few short years, William the Silent seized permanent control of the provinces of Holland and Zealand, which were then flooded by Calvinist refugees from the southern provinces. After Alba's departure, no one kept control of the unpaid Spanish soldiers, who in mutinous rage turned against cities loyal to Spain, including Brussels, Ghent, and most savagely Antwerp, the rich center of trade. Antwerp lost 7,000 citizens and one-third of its houses to the "Spanish fury," which permanently destroyed its prosperity. Alba's replacement, the shrewd statesman and general the Duke of Parma (r. 1578–1592), ultimately subdued the southern provinces, which remained a Spanish colony. The seven northern provinces, however, united in 1579 and declared independence from Spain in 1581 (see Map 14.3). William the Silent became the *stadholder* (governor) of the new United Provinces, and after his assassination his 17-year-old son, Maurice of Nassau, inherited the same title.

The Netherlands' struggle for independence transformed the population of the northern provinces from mixed religions to staunch Calvinism. The Dutch Revolt°

Map 14.3   The Netherlands During the Dutch Revolt, ca. 1580

During the late sixteenth century the northern United Provinces separated from the Spanish Netherlands. The independence of the United Provinces was not recognized by the other European powers until 1648.

CHRONOLOGY

Spain and the Netherlands

1548	Annexation of the northern provinces of the Netherlands to the Spanish crown
1568	Edict against Morisco culture
1571	Christian victory over Ottoman Turks at Lepanto
1580	King Philip II inherits Portugal and the Portuguese Empire
1581	Seven northern provinces of the Netherlands declare independence from Spain
1584	Assassination of William the Silent
1588	Defeat of the Spanish Armada
1609	Expulsion of the Moriscos from Spain
1648	Treaty of Westphalia recognizes independence of the Netherlands

became ensnared in the French Wars of Religion through Huguenot refugees, and the alliance with England, which provided much-needed financial and moral support, reinforced the Protestant identity of the Dutch. The international Protestant alliance created by the Dutch Revolt and centered in the Netherlands withstood both Philip's fury and Parma's calm generalship. The failure of the Spanish Armada to land Parma's men in England guaranteed the survival of an independent Netherlands. The Dutch carried on a sporadic and inconclusive war against Spain until the end of the Thirty Years' War in 1648, when the international community recognized the independent Republic of the United Provinces.

Literature in the Age of Confessional Division

Churches and monarchs everywhere demanded religious conformity in word and deed, a situation that would seem to stifle creativity, and yet the late sixteenth and early seventeenth centuries were one of the most remarkable periods in the history of creative literature. During this period the native or vernacular languages of western Europe became literary languages, replacing Latin as the dominant form of expression, even for the educated elite. Italian was the first vernacular to be prized for its literary qualities and considered a worthy alternative to Latin. The availability of cheap printed books and the Bible reading encouraged by the Protestant Reformation stimulated literature in other vernacular languages so that by the late sixteenth century great literary figures were writing in French, Portuguese, Spanish, and English.

French Literature During the Religious Turmoil

In France royal decrees in 1520 and 1539 substituted French for Latin in official legal and government documents. A century later with the founding of the Académie Française, it became government policy to promote, protect, and refine the French language. The greatest masters of French prose during this crucial period were François Rabelais (ca. 1483–1553) and Michel de Montaigne (1533–1592). Trained as a lawyer, Rabelais became a friar and priest but left the Church under a cloud of heresy to become a physician. Rabelais's satirical masterpiece, a series of novels recounting the fantastic and grotesque adventures of the giants Gargantua and Pantagruel, combined an encyclopedic command of humanist thought with stunning verbal invention that has had a lasting influence on humorous writers to this day. One of Rabelais's most remarkable creations was the imaginary Abbey of Thélème, inhabited by a kind of antimonastic community of monks and nuns for whom "all their life was regulated not by laws, statutes, or rules, but according to their free will and pleasure." This was an abbey for hedonists who lived by the motto, "DO WHAT YOU WILL, because people who are free, well-born, well-bred, and easy in honest company have a natural spur and instinct which drives them to virtuous deeds and deflects them from vice."[5] Rabelais's optimistic vision of human nature represented a startling contrast to the growing anxiety provoked by the religious controversies of his time. Rabelais's controversial work was banned, and he was briefly forced into exile.

It is ironic that Montaigne became a master of French prose. His mother was a Catholic of Spanish-Jewish origins, and the young Michel spoke only Latin for the first six years of his life because his German tutor knew no French. After a modestly successful legal career, Montaigne retired to the family chateau to discover himself by writing essays, a literary form well suited to reflective introspection. In his essays, Montaigne struggled with his lasting grief over the premature death from dysentery of a close friend, reflected on his own experience of the intense physical pain of illness, and diagnosed the absurd causes of the French Wars of Religion. Montaigne's essays are a profound series of

DOCUMENT

Men Are the Source of the Epidemic of Violence

Lucrezia Marinella (1571–1653) was a brilliant, well-educated intellectual who wrote passionately on moral issues of the day. Her masterpiece was The Nobility and Excellence of Women, and the Defects and Vices of Men, *first published in 1600. The book was an answer to the alleged defects of women in which she argued that morally and in many other ways women are superior to men. Marinella depicts violence as the product of male swagger and feelings of insecurity. She contrasts male bluster with women's use of cosmetics. If women were in charge, she implies, the civil wars and violence of the age would be quickly resolved.*

Since beauty is women's special gift from the Supreme Hand, should she not seek to guard it with all diligence? And when she is endowed with but a small amount of that excellent quality, should she not seek to embellish it by every means possible, provided it is not ignoble? I certainly believe that it is so. When man has some special gift such as physical strength, which enables him to perform as a gladiator or swagger around, as is the common usage, does he not seek to conserve it? If he were born courageous, would he not seek to augment his natural courage with the art of defense? But if he were born with little courage would he not practice the martial arts and cover himself with plate and mail and constantly seek out duels and fights in order to demonstrate his courage rather than reveal his true timidity and cowardice?

I have used this example because of the impossibility of finding a man who does not swagger and play the daredevil. If there is such a one people call him effeminate, which is why we always see men dressed up like soldiers with weapons at their belts, bearded and menacing, and walking in a way that they think will frighten everyone. Often they wear gloves of mail and contrive for their weapons to clink under their clothing so people realize they are armed and ready for combat and feel intimidated by them.

What are all these things but artifice and tinsel? Under these trappings of courage and valor hide the cowardly souls of rabbits or hunted hares, and it is the same with all their other artifices. Since men behave in this way, why should not those women who are born less beautiful than the rest hide their less fortunate attributes and seek to augment the little beauty they possess through artifice, provided it is not offensive?

Source: From Lucrezia Marinella, *The Nobility and Excellence of Women, and the Defects and Vices of Men,* edited and translated by Anne Dunhill, Chicago: University of Chicago Press, 1999, pp. 166–67.

meditations on the meaning of life and death, presented in a calm voice of reason to an age of violent fanaticism. In one essay, for example, he exposed the presumption of human beings: "The most vulnerable and frail of all creatures is man, and at the same time the most arrogant." Montaigne thought it presumptuous that human beings picked themselves out as God's favorite creatures. How did they know they were superior to other animals? "When I play with my cat, who knows if I am not a pastime to her more than she is to me?"[6] His own skepticism about religion insulated him from the sometimes violent passions of his era.

Stirrings of the Golden Age in Iberia

The literary tradition in the Iberian peninsula differed from that of other regions in Europe in that Iberia is a polyglot region in which several languages are spoken—Basque, Galician, Portuguese, Castilian, and Catalan. The greatest lyric poet of the peninsula, Luís Vaz de Camões (1524–1580), lost an eye in battle and was sent to the Portuguese East Indies after he killed a royal official in a street brawl. When he returned years later, he completed his epic poem *The Lusiads* (1572), which became the national poem of Portugal by celebrating Vasco da Gama's discovery of the sea route to India. This great work was modeled on the ancient epics, especially the *Aeneid*, the greatest Latin epic of ancient Rome, and even included the gods of Olympus as commentators on the human events of Camões's time. In the opening lines, Jupiter spoke of contemporary Portugal:

> *Eternal dwellers in the starry heavens, you will not have forgotten the great valor of that brave people the Portuguese. You cannot therefore be unaware that it is the fixed resolve of destiny that before their achievements those of Assyrians, Persians, Greeks and Romans shall fade into oblivion. Already with negligible forces— you were witnesses—they have expelled the Moslem, for all his strength and numbers . . . while against the redoubtable Castilians they have invariably had heaven on their side. Always, in a word, they have known victory in battle and have reaped, with its trophies, fame and glory too.[7]*

By connecting Portugal directly to the glories of the ancient empires, Camões managed to elevate the adventures of his fellow Portuguese in Asia to an important moment in the history of the world.

Because Spain was unified around the crown of Castile, the Castilian language became the language we now call Spanish. The period when Spain was the dominant power in Europe coincided with the Golden Age of Spanish literature. The greatest literary figure was Miguel de Cervantes Saavedra (1547–1616), an impoverished son of an unsuccessful doctor with little formal education. Like Camões, Cervantes survived many adventures, losing the use of his left hand at the naval battle of Lepanto and spending five years languishing in a Turkish prison after he was captured by Algerian pirates. In order to survive, the disabled veteran was forced to write plays for the Madrid theater and to work as a tax collector, but he was still imprisoned several times for debts. Desperate to make money, Cervantes published a serial novel in installments between 1605 and 1615. It became the greatest masterpiece in Spanish literature, *Don Quixote*.

The prototype of the modern novel form, *Don Quixote* was a satire of chivalric romances. Cervantes presented reality on two levels, the "poetic truth" of the master and dreamer Don Quixote and the "historic truth" of his squire and realist Sancho Panza. Don Quixote's imagination persistently ran away with him as he tilted at windmills, believing they were fierce dragons. It remained to Sancho Panza to point out the unheroic truth. Cervantes pursued the interaction between these two incongruous views of truth as a philosophical commentary on existence. For Cervantes there was no single, objective truth, only psychological truths revealed through the interaction of the characters, an idea that contrasted with the notion of dogmatic religious truth that dominated the time. Despite the extensive popularity of *Don Quixote*, Cervantes died a pauper, buried in an unmarked grave in Madrid.

The Elizabethan Renaissance

During the reign of Elizabeth I (r. 1558–1603), the Renaissance truly arrived in England. The daughter of Henry VIII and Anne Boleyn, Elizabeth faced terrible insecurity as a girl. Her father had her mother beheaded, she was declared illegitimate, and her sister Mary imprisoned her for treason in the Tower of London. After she ascended to the throne in 1558, however, she proved to be a brilliant leader. She prevented the kind of religious civil wars that broke out in France by establishing a moderate form of Protestantism as the official religion. She presided over the beginnings of England's rise as a major European power. Perhaps most remarkably, she became the patron and inspiration for England's greatest age of literature. Never married, Elizabeth used her eligibility for marriage as a lure in diplomacy, and even though she may have had real lovers, she addressed her subjects as if they were her only love. Her "golden speech" delivered before a troublesome House of Commons in 1601 exemplifies her ability to inspire exuberant loyalty:

> *Though God hath raised me high, yet this I account the glory of my crown, that I have reigned with your loves. . . . It is not my desire to live or reign longer than my life and reign shall be for your good. And though you have had, and may have, many mightier and wiser princes sitting in this seat, yet you never had, nor shall have any that will love you better.[8]*

Among Elizabeth's courtiers were major literary figures, including the adventurer-poet Sir Walter Raleigh (ca. 1552–1618), the soldier-poet Sir Philip Sidney (1554–1586), and Edmund Spenser (ca. 1552–1599), whose great poem *The Faerie Queen* was a personal tribute to Elizabeth.

Queen Elizabeth I of England
Elizabeth presided over the greatest age of English literature.

The principal figure of the Elizabethan Renaissance, however, was not a courtier but a professional dramatist, William Shakespeare (1564–1616). In a series of theaters, including the famous Globe on the south side of the Thames in London, Shakespeare wrote, produced, and acted in comedies, tragedies, and history plays. Shakespeare's enormous output of plays, some of which made veiled allusions to the politics of Elizabeth's court, established him not only as the most popular dramatist of his time but the greatest literary figure in the English language. The power of his plays derives from the subtle understanding of human psychology found in his characters and the stunning force of his language. For Shakespeare, as for Montaigne, the source of true knowledge was self-knowledge. One character advises,

> *Neither a borrower nor a lender be,*
> *For loan oft loses both itself and friend*
> *And borrowing dulls the edge of husbandry.*
> *This above all: To thine own self be true,*
> *And it must follow, as the night the day,*
> *Thou canst not then be false to any man.*
> (Hamlet I, iii, 75–80)

Unlike most contemporary authors, Shakespeare wrote for a broad audience of paying theatergoers that included common workers as well as highly educated members of Elizabeth's court. This need to appeal to a large audience who gave instant feedback helped him hone his skills as a dramatist.

Some of these literary figures found their works banned, as did Rabelais. Some had political or personal troubles with their monarch, as did Montaigne, Camões, Raleigh, and Sidney. But the controversies of the day seemed to have stimulated rather than inhibited these writers. Political and religious turmoil led them to ask penetrating questions about the meaning of life and to rise above the petty squabbles that preoccupied so many of their contemporaries.

States and Confessions in Eastern Europe

■ How did the countries of eastern Europe during the late sixteenth century become enmeshed in the religious controversies that began in western Europe during the early part of the century?

In contrast to the confessional states of western Europe where rulers demanded religious conformity, the weak states of eastern Europe during the early sixteenth century were less successful in linking religious conformity to political loyalty. Whereas in the West the religious controversies stimulated writers to investigate deeply the human condition but made them cautious about expressing nonconforming religious opinions, writers and creative people in the East during this period were able to explore a wide range of ideas in a relatively tolerant atmosphere. Bohemia and Poland, in particular, allowed levels of religious diversity unheard of in the West. During the last decades of the sixteenth century and early decades of the seventeenth, however, dynastic troubles compromised the relative openness of the eastern states, enmeshing them in conflicts among themselves that had an increasingly strong religious dimension. In the Holy Roman Empire, the weakness of the mad Emperor Rudolf permitted religious conflicts to fester, setting the stage for the disastrous Thirty Years' War (1618–1648) that pitted Catholic and Protestant princes against one another.

Around the Baltic Sea, rivalries among Lutheran Sweden, Catholic Poland-Lithuania, and Orthodox Russia created a state of almost permanent war in a tense standoff among three very different political and religious states. The enormous confederation of Poland-Lithuania struggled to sustain the most decentralized, religiously diverse state anywhere in Europe. By the end of the century, it remained politically decentralized but had become an active theater of the Catholic Reformation where dynastic policy firmly supported the Roman Church. Russia began to strengthen itself from obscurity under the authoritarian rule of the tsars, who began to transform it into a major European power.

The Dream World of Emperor Rudolf

In Goethe's *Faust*, set in sixteenth-century Germany, drinkers in a tavern sing:

> *The dear old Holy Roman Empire,*
> *How does it hang together?*[9]

Good question. How did this peculiarly decentralized state—neither holy, nor Roman, nor an empire—hang together? In the late sixteenth century the empire consisted of the following components: 1 emperor; 7 electors, comprising 4 secular princes and 3 archbishops; 50 other bishops and archbishops; 21 dukes, margraves, and landgraves; 88 independent abbots and assorted prelates of the Church; 178 counts and other sovereign lords; about 80 free imperial cities; and hundreds of free imperial knights. The emperor presided over all, and the Imperial Diet served as a parliament, but the Holy Roman Empire was, in fact, a very loose confederation of semi-independent, mostly German-speaking states, many of which ignored imperial decrees that did not suit them. During the first half of the sixteenth century the empire faced a number of challenges—the turmoil within the empire created by Lutheranism, endless French enmity on the western borders, and the tenacious Ottoman threat on the eastern frontier. Only the universal vision and firm hand of Emperor Charles V kept the empire together. The universal vision and firm hand disappeared in the succeeding generations of emperors, to be replaced by petty dynastic squabbles and infirm minds.

The crippling weakness of the imperial system became most evident during the reign of Rudolf II (r. 1576–1612).

The Habsburg line had a strain of insanity going back to Joanna "The Mad," the mother of Emperors Charles V (r. 1519–1558) and Ferdinand I (r. 1558–1564), who happened to be Rudolf's two grandfathers, giving him a double dose of Habsburg genes. Soon after his election to the imperial throne, Rudolf moved his court from bustling Vienna to the lovely quiet of Prague in Bohemia. Fearful of noisy crowds and impatient courtiers, standoffish toward foreign ambassadors who presented him with difficult decisions, paranoid about scheming relatives, and prone to wild emotional gyrations from deep depression to manic grandiosity, Rudolf was hardly suited for the imperial throne. In fact, many contemporaries, who had their own reasons to underrate him, described him as hopelessly insane. Rudolf certainly suffered from moments of profound melancholy and irrational fears that may have had genetic or organic causes, but he was probably unhinged by the conundrum of being the emperor, a position that trapped him between the glorious universal imperial ideal and the ignoble reality of unscrupulous relatives and petty rivalries.

Rudolf was not the only sixteenth-century prince in the Holy Roman Empire driven to distraction by the pressures of court life. At least twenty German princes and princesses were confined or deposed due to symptoms of serious mental disorder. Certainly inbreeding within a small pool of princely families contributed to the patterns of madness, but the most unhealthy emotional pressure was produced by the code of manners required of all courtiers, most particularly princes and princesses. This strictly maintained code demanded the repression of all spontaneous feelings, a repression that resulted in a prevailing sense of shame. When religious rigidity and extreme political conflict were mixed into this volatile psychological concoction, it is not surprising that some personalities shattered. Because the entire political system depended on the prince's guidance, a mad prince could seriously disrupt an entire society.

Incapable of governing, Rudolf transmuted the imperial ideal of universality into a strange dream world. In Prague he gathered around him a brilliant court of humanists, musicians, painters, physicians, astronomers, astrologers, alchemists, and magicians. These included an eclectic assortment of significant thinkers—the great astronomers Tycho Brahe and Johannes Kepler, the notorious occult philosopher Giordano Bruno, the theoretical mathematician and astrologer John Dee, and the remarkable inventor of surrealist painting Giuseppe Arcimboldo. Many of these figures are considered the immediate forerunners of the Scientific Revolution, but Rudolf also fell prey to fast-talking charlatans. These included the illusionist and opera-set designer Cornelius Drebber, who claimed to have invented a perpetual-motion machine. This weird court, however, was less the strange fruit of the emperor's hopeless dementia than the manifestation of a striving for universal empire. Rudolf sought to preserve the cultural and political unity of the

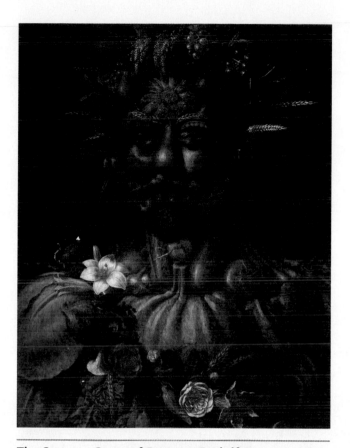

The Strange Court of Emperor Rudolf II

Among the many creative people in the Emperor Rudolf's court was the Italian surrealist painter Giuseppe Arcimboldo, who specialized in creating images out of fruits, vegetables, flowers, and animals. This is a portrait of the Emperor Rudolf.

empire, to eradicate religious divisions, and to achieve peace at home. Rudolf's court in Prague was perhaps the only place left during the late sixteenth century where Protestants, Catholics, Jews, and even radical heretics such as Bruno could gather together in a common intellectual enterprise. The goal of such gatherings was to discover the universal principles that governed nature, principles that would provide the foundations for a single unifying religion and a cure for all human maladies. It was a noble, if utterly improbable, dream.

While Rudolf and his favorite courtiers isolated themselves in their dream world, the religious conflicts within the empire reached a boiling point. Without a strong emperor, the Imperial Diets were paralyzed by confessional squabbles. In 1607 in the imperial free city of Donauworth in south Germany, a conflict between the Lutheran town council and the substantial Catholic minority gave the Catholic Duke of Bavaria the excuse to annex the city to his own territories. Despite the illegality of the duke's action,

Rudolf passively acquiesced, causing fear among German Protestants that the principles of the Religious Peace of Augsburg of 1555 might be ignored. In the following decade, more than 200 religious revolts or riots took place. In 1609 the insane Duke John William of Jülich-Cleves died without a direct heir, and the most suitable claimants to the Catholic duchy were two Lutheran princes. Were one of them to succeed to the dukedom, the balance between Catholics and Protestants in Germany would have been seriously disrupted. Religious tensions boiled over. As Chapter 15 will describe, in less than a decade the empire began to dissolve in what became the Thirty Years' War.

The Renaissance of Poland-Lithuania

During the late sixteenth and early seventeenth centuries, Poland-Lithuania experienced a remarkable cultural and political renaissance. It was inspired by influences from Renaissance Italy linked to strong commercial and diplomatic ties to the Republic of Venice and intellectual connections with the University of Padua. As the major power in eastern Europe, Poland-Lithuania engaged in a tug-of-war with Sweden over control of the eastern Baltic and virtually constant warfare against the expansionist ambitions of Russia (see Map 14.4). The most remarkable achievement of Poland-Lithuania during this contentious time was its unparalleled and still controversial experiments in government. Poland-Lithuania had an elected king but called itself a republic. The king was a figurehead, and Poland-Lithuania was a republic in the sense that it was effectively governed by assemblies of nobles.

Very loosely joined since 1336, Poland and Lithuania created a constitutional union in 1569, creating a confederation in which Poland supplied the king, but the Grand Duchy of Lithuania was considered an equal partner and allowed to retain its own laws, administration, and army. The novel feature of the confederation was how the nobles reserved power for themselves through their control of regional assemblies, which in turn dominated the central parliament called the Sejm. These nobles elected the king and treated him, at best, as a hired manager. They resisted all attempts to exert royal power by asserting the legal right to form local armed assemblies against the king and by exercising the principle of unanimity in the Sejm, which prevented the king or a strong faction from dominating affairs. In the last half of the seventeenth century Poland-Lithuania fell into chaos under this system, but for nearly three-quarters of a century it worked well enough—at least for the nobles.

The rule of the nobles in Poland-Lithuania came at a great cost to the Polish peasants, however, who were ruthlessly forced into serfdom and deprived of their legal rights.

Peasants were prohibited from leaving the land without permission from their landlords, and they were denied the ability to appeal the legal judgments of their local lords. In this regard, Poland-Lithuania moved in the opposite direction from western European states, which at this time were extending the right of judicial appeal and allowing serfdom to fade away. Moreover, the Polish kings could not stop the gradual erosion of their authority so that Poland-Lithuania, the greatest power in the East, enfeebled itself through the grasping hands of a notoriously self-interested and proud nobility.

Poland-Lithuania contained an incomparable religious mixture of Roman Catholics, Lutherans, Calvinists, Russian Orthodox, Anabaptists, Unitarians, and Jews, but these communities were strongly divided along geographic and class lines. Lutheranism was a phenomenon of the German-speaking towns, the peasants of Poland remained Catholic, those in Lithuania were Orthodox, and many of the nobles were attracted to Calvinism. During the late sixteenth century, however, Christians in Poland almost completely returned or converted to the Roman Catholic faith. The key to the transformation was the changing attitude of the Polish nobles, who had tolerated religious diversity because they believed that religious liberty was the cornerstone of political liberty. The return to Catholicism owed a great deal to Stanislas Hosius (1504–1579), who had studied in Italy before he returned to Poland to become successively a diplomat, bishop, and cardinal. Imbued with the zeal of the Italian Catholic Reformation, Hosius invited the Society of Jesus into Poland and worked closely with the papal *nuncios* (the diplomatic representatives of the pope), who organized a campaign to combat all forms of Protestantism.

Map 14.4 Poland-Lithuania and Russia

These countries were the largest in Europe in the size of their territories but were relatively underpopulated compared to the western European states.

Between 1565 and 1586, forty-four young Polish nobles studied at the Jesuit college in Rome and when they returned took up the most influential church and government offices in Poland. Jesuit colleges sprouted up in many Polish towns, attracting the brightest sons of the nobility and urban bourgeoisie. A close alliance between the kings of Poland and the Jesuits enhanced the social prestige of Catholicism.

The cultural appeal of all things Italian helped lure the Polish nobility back to Catholicism. Through the spread of elite education, Catholicism returned to Poland largely through persuasion rather than coercion. But the transformation did not occur without violent repercussions. Lutheran, Calvinist, and Bohemian Brethren churches were burned. In Cracow armed confrontations between Protestant and Catholic militants led to casualties. However, Poland did not degenerate into civil war, as did France or the Netherlands over much the same issues. As the monarchy progressively weakened, the Catholic Church became the only solid institutional pillar of Polish national identity and Polish culture.

The Troubled Legacy of Ivan the Terrible

While Poland experimented with a decentralized confederation dominated by nobles that severely restricted the king's initiative, Russia evolved in the opposite direction. During the late fifteenth and sixteenth centuries, the grand dukes of Moscow who became the tsars of Russia eclipsed the authority of the great landed nobles and snuffed out the independence of the towns. The authoritarian tendencies of the tsars harmed the Russian peasants, however, just as royal weakness harmed the Polish peasants. After 1454 Moscow's creation of military fiefs (*pomestye*) to supply soldiers against the Tartars (Mongol tribes) allowed the nobles to push the peasants back into serfdom. Refusing to accept enserfment, the peasants fled the fields in massive numbers, depopulating central Russia as they found refuge among the Cossack colonies along the borders to the southeast.

Russia was already well integrated into the European diplomatic community and engaged in trade with its western neighbors. But for more than 300 years Russia had been under the "Tartar Yoke," a term describing the Mongolian tribes that overran the country, pillaging and depopulating it. Ivan III, "The Great" (1462–1505), succeeded in gradually throwing off the Tartar Yoke by refusing to continue to pay tribute to the Mongols. Ivan married Zoë, the niece of the last Greek emperor of Constantinople. The marriage gave him the basis for claiming that the Russian rulers were the heirs of Byzantium and the exclusive protectors of Orthodox Christianity, the state religion of Russia. Following the Byzantine tradition of imperial pomp, Ivan practiced Byzantine court ceremonies, and his advisers developed the theory of the Three Romes. According to this theory, the authority of the ancient Roman Empire had passed first to the Byzantine Empire, which God had punished with the Turkish conquest, and then to Moscow as the third and last "Rome." Ivan celebrated this theory by assuming the title of tsar (or "Caesar"). With his wife's assistance, he hired Italian architects to rebuild the grand ducal palace, the Kremlin. Ivan captured the vast northern territories of the city-state of Novgorod, expanding the Russian state north to the White Sea and east to the Urals. Ivan's invasion of parts of Lithuania embroiled Russia in a protracted conflict with Poland that lasted more than a century. Like his fellow monarchs in western Europe, Ivan began to bring the aristocrats under control by incorporating them into the bureaucracy of the state.

Ivan III's grandson, Ivan IV, "The Terrible" (1533–1584), succeeded his father at age 3 and became the object of innumerable plots, attempted coups, and power struggles among his mother, uncles, and the boyars (the upper-level nobles who dominated Russian society). The trauma of his childhood years and a painful disease of the spine made him inordinately suspicious and prone to acts of impulsive violence. When at age 17 Ivan was crowned, he reduced the power of the dukes and the boyars by forcing them to exchange their hereditary estates for lands that obligated them to serve the tsar in war. In weakening the boyars, Ivan gained considerable support among the common people and was even remembered in popular songs as the people's tsar. Nevertheless, Ivan distrusted everyone. He often arrested people on charges of treason, just for taking a trip abroad. In a cruel revenge on his enemies among the boyars, he began a reign of terror in which he personally committed horrendous atrocities. His massacre in 1570 of the inhabitants of Novgorod, whom he suspected of harboring Polish sympathies, contributed to his reputation as a bloody tyrant. By setting aside half of the realm as his personal domain, he created a strong financial base for the army, which led to military successes in the prolonged wars against Poland-Lithuania and Sweden. During his reign, however, the Polish threat and boyar

CHRONOLOGY

States and Confessions in Eastern Europe

1480	Grand Duke and later Tsar Ivan III, "The Great," of Russia refuses to pay tribute to Tartars
1569	Constitutional Union of Poland and Lithuania
1604–1613	Time of Troubles in Russia
1613	Michael Romanov elected Tsar of Russia

The Kremlin

The Kremlin was the seat of government for the Russian tsars until 1712. Originally built in 1156, the present enclosure of the Kremlin dates from the sixteenth century and reflects the influence of Italian architects brought to Moscow as well as traditional Byzantine styles.

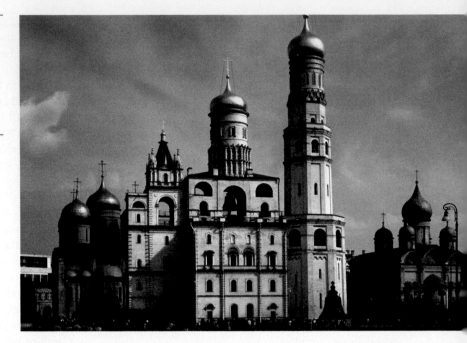

opposition to his rule revealed signs of the fragility of Russian unity.

During the "Time of Troubles°" (1604–1613), Russia fell into chaos. Boyar families struggled among themselves for supremacy, the Cossacks from the south led a popular revolt, and Poles and Swedes openly interfered in Russian affairs. Finally, the Time of Troubles ended when in 1613 the national assembly elected Tsar Michael Romanov, whose descendants ruled Russia until they were deposed in 1917. During the seventeenth century the Romanovs gradually restored order to Russia, eroded the independence of local governments, and strengthened the institution of serfdom. By the end of the seventeenth century Russia was strong enough to reenter European affairs as a major power.

Conclusion

The Divisions of the West

During the late sixteenth and early seventeenth centuries, hidden demographic and economic pressures eroded the confidence and security of many Europeans, creating a widespread sense of unease. Most people retreated like confused soldiers behind the barricades of a rigid confessional faith, which provided reassurance that was unavailable elsewhere. To compensate for the absence of predictability in daily life, societies everywhere imposed strict discipline—discipline of women, children, the poor, criminals, and alleged witches. The frenzy for social discipline displaced the fear of those things that could not be controlled onto the most easily controllable people, especially the weak, the subordinate, and those perceived to be different in some way.

The union between religion and political authority in the confessional states bolstered official religious faith with the threat of legal or military coercion. Where different religious confessions persisted within one state—most notably France and the Netherlands—the result was riots, assassinations, and civil war. The West had become divided along religious lines in two ways. The first kind of division was within countries with religiously mixed populations, where distinctive religious communities competed for political power and influence. In these countries religion became the cornerstone to justify patriotism or rebellion, loyalty or disloyalty to the monarch. The second kind of division was international. The confessional states formed alliances, crafted foreign policies, and went to war, with religion determining friend and foe. The West split into religiously driven camps. Over the subsequent centuries, religious differences mutated into ideological differences, but the sense that alliances among states should be linked together by a common set of beliefs has persisted to this day as a legacy from the sixteenth century.

During the period of the middle seventeenth to eighteenth centuries, confessional identity and the fear of religious turmoil led monarchs throughout Europe to build absolutist regimes, which attempted to enforce stability through a strengthened, centralized state. The principles of religious toleration and the separation of church and state were still far in the future. They were made possible only as a consequence of the hard lessons learned from the historical turmoil of the late sixteenth and seventeenth centuries.

Suggestions for Further Reading

For a comprehensive listing of suggested readings, please go to
www.ablongman.com/levack2e/chapter14

Anderson, M. S. *The Origins of the Modern European State System, 1494–1618.* 1998. The best short study for students new to the subject of the evolution of the confessional states in Europe. This book is very good at establishing common patterns among the various states.

Burke, Peter. *Popular Culture in Early Modern Europe.* 1994. This wide-ranging book includes considerable material from eastern Europe and Scandinavia, as well as the more extensively studied western European countries. Extraordinarily influential, it practically invented the subject of popular culture by showing how much could be learned from studying festivals and games.

Davies, Norman. *God's Playground: A History of Poland.* Rev. ed., 2 vols. 1982. By far the most comprehensive study of Polish history, this is particularly strong for the sixteenth and seventeenth centuries. Davies offers a Polish-centered view of European history that is marvelously stimulating even if he sometimes overstates his case for the importance of Poland.

Dukes, Paul. *A History of Russia: Medieval, Modern, Contemporary, ca. 882–1996.* 3rd ed. 1998. A comprehensive survey that synthesizes the most recent research.

Dunn, Richard S. *The Age of Religious Wars, 1559–1715.* 2nd ed. 1980. An excellent survey for students new to the subject.

Evans, R. J. W. *Rudolf II and His World: A Study in Intellectual History, 1576–1612.* 1973. A sympathetic examination of the intellectual world Rudolf created. Evans recognizes Rudolf's mental problems but lessens their significance for understanding the period.

Holt, Mack P. *The French Wars of Religion, 1562–1629.* 1996. A lucid short synthesis of the events and complex issues raised by these wars.

Hsia, R. Po-chia. *Social Discipline in the Reformation: Central Europe, 1550–1750.* 1989. An excellent, lucid, and short overview of the attempts to discipline the people in Germany.

Huppert, George. *After the Black Death: A Social History of Early Modern Europe.* 1986. Engaging, entertaining, and elegantly written, this is the best single study of European social life during the Early Modern period.

Levack, Brian P. *The Witch-Hunt in Early Modern Europe.* 2nd ed. 1995. The best and most up-to-date short examination of the complex problem of the witch-hunt. This is the place to begin for students new to the subject.

Ozment, Steven E. *Ancestors: The Loving Family in Old Europe.* 2001. This comprehensive study of family life demonstrates that families were actually far more loving than the theory of patriarchy would suggest.

Parker, Geoffrey. *The Dutch Revolt.* Rev. ed. 1990. The classic study of the revolt by one of the most masterful historians of the period. This study is especially adept at pointing to the larger European context of the revolt.

Parker, Geoffrey. *The Grand Strategy of Philip II.* 1998. Rehabilitates Philip as a significant strategic thinker.

Wiesner, Merry E. *Women and Gender in Early Modern Europe.* 1993. The best short study of the subject. This is the best book for students new to the subject.

Notes

1. Quoted in R. Po-Chia Hsia, *Social Discipline in the Reformation: Central Europe, 1550–1750* (1989), 147–148.

2. Quoted in Norbert Elias, *The Civilizing Process,* Vol. 1: *The History of Manners,* trans. Edmund Jephcott (1978), 119.

3. Quoted in R. J. Knecht, *The French Wars of Religion, 1559–1598,* 2nd ed. (1996), 13.

4. Quoted in John Neale, "The Massacre of St. Bartholomew," reprinted in Orest Ranum, ed., *Searching for Modern Times,* Vol. 1, *1500–1650* (1969), 176.

5. François Rabelais, *The Histories of Gargantua and Pantagruel,* trans. J. M. Cohen (1955), 159.

6. Michel de Montaigne, *Essays and Selected Writings,* trans. and ed. Donald M. Frame (1963), 219–221.

7. Luís Vaz de Camões, *The Lusiads,* trans. William C. Atkinson (1952), 42.

8. Quoted in "Elizabeth I," *Encyclopedia Britannica* 8 (1959), 364b.

9. Quoted in Norman Davies, *Europe: A History* (1996), 529.

Absolutism and State Building, 1618–1715

15

N 1651 THOMAS HOBBES, AN ENGLISH PHILOSOPHER LIVING IN EXILE IN France, was convinced that the West had descended into chaos. As he looked around him, Hobbes saw nothing but political instability, rebellion, and civil war. The turmoil had begun in the late sixteenth century, when the Reformation sparked the religious warfare described in the last chapter. In 1618 the situation deteriorated when another cycle of internal political strife and warfare erupted. The Thirty Years' War (1618–1648) began as a religious and political dispute in Germany but soon became an international conflict involving the armies of Spain, France, Sweden, and England as well as those of many German states. The war wreaked economic and social havoc in Germany, decimated its population, and forced governments throughout Europe to raise large armies and tax their subjects to pay for them. The entire European economy suffered as a result.

During the 1640s, partly as a result of that devastating conflict, the political order of Europe virtually collapsed. In England a series of bloody civil wars led to the destruction of the monarchy and the establishment of a republic. In France a civil war over constitutional issues drove the royal family from Paris. In Spain the king faced rebellions in no fewer than four of his territories, while in many European kingdoms peasants had risen in protest against the taxes their governments were collecting. Europe was in the midst of a profound and multifaceted crisis.

Hobbes, a man plagued by anxiety even since he was a child, proposed a solution to this crisis. In 1651 he published a book, *Leviathan*, about the origin and exercise of political power. He began by observing that people had a natural tendency to quarrel among themselves and seek power over each other. If left to their own devices in a hypothetical state of nature, in which government did not exist, they would find themselves in constant conflict. In these circumstances, which Hobbes referred to as a state of war, people would be unable to engage in trade or agriculture or pursue cultural

Louis XIV Portrait of Louis XIV in military armor, with his plumed helmet and his crown on the table to the right. The portrait was painted during the period of French warfare. In the background is a French ship.

interests. Life would soon become, in Hobbes's famous words, "solitary, poor nasty, brutish, and short."[1] The only way for people to find peace in this dangerous and unproductive world would be to agree with their neighbors to form a political society, or a state, by surrendering their independent power to a ruler who would make laws, administer justice, and maintain order. In this state the ruler would wield great power, and he would not share it with others. His subjects, having agreed to endow him with such extensive power, and having agreed to submit to his rule, could not resist or depose him.

Hobbes wrote *Leviathan* not simply as an abstract study of political philosophy but as a solution to the problems that plagued the West in the middle of the seventeenth century. He was suggesting that the best way to achieve peace and security was for people to submit themselves to the authority of a single ruler. The term used to designate this type of government is absolutism°. In the most general terms, absolutism means a political arrangement in which one ruler possesses complete and unrivaled power.

The political history of the West during the seventeenth and early eighteenth centuries can be written largely in terms of the efforts made by European monarchs to introduce absolutism. Those efforts were accompanied by policies intended to make the states they ruled wealthier and more powerful. Attempts to introduce absolutism and to strengthen the state took place in almost every country in Europe. In all these countries a succession of encounters took place between rulers who were trying to enlarge the power of the state and those who resisted their efforts. The outcome of these encounters varied from country to country, but for the most part the advocates of state building and absolutism prevailed. By the end of the seventeenth century the West comprised a number of large states, governed by rulers who had achieved unrivaled power and who commanded large, well-equipped armies. The West had entered the age of absolutism, which lasted until the outbreak of the French Revolution in 1789.

Not only did the West acquire a clear political identity during the seventeenth century, but its geographical boundaries also began to shift. Russia, which Europeans thought of as part of the East, began a program of imitating Western governments and became a major player in European diplomacy and warfare. At the same time Russia's southern neighbor, the Ottoman Empire, which had long straddled the boundary between East and West, was increasingly viewed by Europeans as part of a remote, Asian world.

The overarching question that this chapter addresses is: How did Western rulers strengthen the administrative and military capacities of the states they governed during this

The Frontispiece of Thomas Hobbes's Treatise
***Leviathan*, Published in London in 1651**
The ruler is depicted as incorporating the bodies of all his subjects, as they collectively authorized him to govern.

period? The individual sections of the chapter will answer the following questions:

- What did absolutism mean, both as a political theory and as a practical program, and how was absolutism related to the growth of the power of the state?
- How did the encounters that took place in France and Spain during the seventeenth century result in the establishment of absolutism, and how powerful did those two states become in the seventeenth century?
- What was the nature of royal absolutism in central and eastern Europe, and how did the policies of the Ottoman Empire and Russia help establish the boundaries of the West during this period?
- Why did absolutism fail to take root in England and the Dutch Republic during the seventeenth century?

The Nature of Absolutism

■ **What did absolutism mean, both as a political theory and as a practical program, and how was absolutism related to the growth of the power of the state?**

Seventeenth-century absolutism had both a theoretical and a practical dimension. Theoretical absolutists included writers like Hobbes who described the nature of power in the state and explained the conditions for its acquisition and continuation. Practical absolutists were the rulers who took concrete political steps to subordinate all other political authorities within the state to themselves. Efforts to introduce royal absolutism in Europe began in the late sixteenth and early seventeenth centuries, but only in the late seventeenth century, after the Thirty Years' War and the political turmoil of the 1640s, did many European rulers consolidate their political positions and actually achieve absolute power.

The word *absolutism* usually conjures up images of despotic kings terrorizing every segment of the population, ruling by whim and caprice, and executing their subjects at will. Nothing could be further from the truth. Absolute monarchs succeeded in establishing themselves as the highest political authorities within their kingdoms, but they never attained unlimited power. Nor could they exercise power in a completely arbitrary manner. Theoretical absolutists never sanctioned this type of arbitrary rule, and the laws of European states never permitted it. Even if European monarchs had wished to act in this way, they usually could not because they did not have the political or judicial resources to impose their will on the people. The exercise of royal power in the seventeenth century, even when it was considered absolute, depended on the tacit consent of noblemen, office holders, and the members of local political assemblies. Kings usually could not afford to risk losing the support of these prominent men by acting illegally or arbitrarily, and when they did, they found themselves faced with rebellion.

The Theory of Absolutism

When seventeenth-century political writers referred to the monarch as having absolute power, they usually meant that he possessed the highest legislative power in his kingdom. In particular, they meant that he did not share the power to make law with representative assemblies such as the English Parliament. The French magistrate Jean Bodin (1530?–1596), who was one of the earliest proponents of absolutist theory, argued in *Six Books of a Commonweal* (1576) that absolute power consisted of several attributes, the most important of which was the power to make law. In similar fashion Hobbes referred to the absolute ruler as

"sole legislator." Absolute monarchs, therefore, were rulers who could make law by themselves.

In order to bolster their authority, absolute monarchs frequently asserted that they received their power directly from God and therefore ruled by divine right. This idea was hardly new in the seventeenth century. The Bible proclaimed that all political authorities were "of God" and that people must therefore be obedient to them. In the fourteenth century European monarchs asserted that because God had given them the right to rule, the pope could not depose them. In the sixteenth century the idea of divine right was used to discourage rebellion, for to resist the king was to attack God's representative on Earth. In the seventeenth century many theorists of absolutism—although not Hobbes—used the idea of divine right to insist that kings were accountable only to God, rather than to their subjects.

Absolute rulers often claimed that they were above the law. This meant that when monarchs acted for reason of state, that is, for the benefit of the entire kingdom, they were not strictly bound by the law of their kingdoms. Being above the law also meant that they could not be held legally accountable for their actions, as they were the highest judges in the land. Being above the law did not mean kings or queens could act arbitrarily, illegally, or despotically, even though some of them did so from time to time. Absolute rulers, no less than those who shared power with representative assemblies, were always expected to observe the individual rights and liberties of their subjects as well as the moral law established by God. They were expected, for example, to try people in a court of law rather than execute them at will. The French preacher Jacques Bossuet (1627–1704), who wrote an absolutist treatise on the authority of kings in 1670, insisted that even though kings were not subject to the penalties of the law, they still were not freed from the obligation to observe that law. No less than their subjects, kings were subject to the "equity of the laws." This meant that they should not rule despotically or arbitrarily.

Theorists of absolutism distinguished between European monarchs and rulers in other parts of the world, such as Turkish sultans, Russian tsars, and the kings of Asian and African lands. In those so-called Eastern countries, according to Bodin, "the prince has become the lord of the goods and the persons of his subjects," by which Bodin meant that the rulers of those lands could seize the possessions of their subjects or execute them without due process of law.[2] Only in the West, wrote Bodin, did royal subjects live under a regime that abided by the rule of law. Bodin exaggerated the powers of both Turkish sultans and Russian tsars, who had much in common with the absolute rulers of western and central Europe. But by emphasizing the rule of law and the king's obligation to abide by it, Bodin identified one of the distinctive features of Western politics during the age of absolutism.

The Practice of Absolutism

What steps did the European monarchs who claimed absolute power take to establish and maintain themselves as the supreme authorities within the state? The first strategy they employed was the elimination or the weakening of national representative assemblies, such as Parliament in England, Diets in German states, and the Cortes in Spain and Portugal. In France, which is considered to have been the most absolutist state in seventeenth-century Europe, the monarchy stopped summoning its national assembly, the Estates General, in 1614. This assembly did not meet again until the late eighteenth century.

The second strategy of absolutist rulers was to subordinate the nobility to the king and make them dependent on his favor. The political and social power of the nobility often led them to participate in rebellions and conspiracies against the king. Monarchs who aspired to a position of unrivaled power in their kingdoms therefore took steps to keep the nobility in line, not only by suppressing challenges to their authority but also by appointing men from different social groups as their chief ministers, At the same time, however, the king could not afford to alienate these wealthy and high-ranking men, upon whom he still relied for running his government and maintaining order in the localities. Absolute monarchs, therefore, offered nobles special privileges, such as exemption from taxation, positions in the king's household, and freedom to exploit their peasants in exchange for their recognition of the king's superiority and their assistance in maintaining order in the localities. In this way nobles became junior partners in the management of the absolutist state.

The final strategy of absolute monarchs was to gain effective control of the administrative machinery of the state and to use it to enforce royal policy throughout their kingdoms. Absolute monarchs were by nature state builders. They established centralized bureaucracies that extended the reach of their governments down into the smallest towns and villages and out into the most remote regions of their kingdoms. The business conducted by these centrally controlled bureaucracies included collection of taxes, recruitment of soldiers, and operation of the judicial system. Some absolute monarchs used the central machinery of the state to impose and maintain religious conformity. As the seventeenth century advanced, they also used the same machinery to regulate the price of grain, stimulate the growth of industry, and relieve the plight of the poor. In these ways the policies pursued by absolute monarchs had an impact on the lives of all royal subjects, not just noblemen and royal councilors.

Warfare and the Absolutist State

Much of the growth of European states in the seventeenth century can be related in one way or another to the conduct of war. During the period from 1600 to 1721, European powers were almost constantly at war. The entire continent was at peace for only four of those years. To meet the demands of war, rulers kept men under arms at all times. By the middle of the seventeenth century, after the Thirty Years' War had come to an end, most European rulers had acquired such standing armies. These armies not only served their rulers in foreign wars but also helped them maintain order and enforce royal policy at home. Standing armies thus became one of the main props of royal absolutism.

During the seventeenth and early eighteenth centuries European armies became larger, in many cases tripling in size. In the 1590s Philip II of Spain had mastered Europe with an army of 40,000 men. By contrast, in the late seventeenth century Louis XIV of France needed an army of 400,000 men to become the dominant power on the continent. The increase in the size of these forces can be traced to the invention of gunpowder and its more frequent use in the fifteenth and sixteenth centuries. Gunpowder led to the widespread use of the musket, a heavy shoulder firearm carried by a foot soldier. The use of the musket placed a premium on the recruitment and equipment of large armies of infantry, who marched in square columns with men holding long pikes (long wooden shafts with pointed metal heads) to protect the musketeers from enemy attacks. As the size of these armies of foot soldiers grew, the role of mounted soldiers, who had dominated medieval warfare, was greatly reduced.

Changes in military technology and tactics also necessitated more intensive military training. In the Middle Ages mounted knights had acquired great individual skill, but they did not need to work in precise unison with other men under arms. Seventeenth-century foot soldiers, however, had to learn to march in formation, to coordinate their maneuvers, and to fire without harming their comrades in arms. Therefore they needed to be drilled. The introduction of volley fire, by which each successive line of soldiers stepped forward to fire while the others were reloading, placed an even greater premium on precise drilling. Drilling took place in peacetime as well as during war. The wearing of uniforms, which began when the state assumed the function of clothing its thousands of soldiers, gave further unity and cohesion to the trained fighting force.

The cost of recruiting, training, and equipping these mammoth armies was staggering. In the Middle Ages individual lords often had sufficient financial resources to assemble their own private armies. By the beginning of the seventeenth century the only institution capable of putting the new armies in the field was the state itself. The same was true for navies, which now consisted of heavily armed sailing ships, each of which carried as many as 400 sailors. To build these large armies and navies, as well as to pay the increasing cost of waging war itself (which rose 500 percent between 1530 and 1630), the state had to identify new methods of raising and collecting taxes. In times of war as much as 80 percent of the revenue taken in by the state went for military purposes.

The equipment and training of military forces and the collection and allocation of the revenue necessary to subsidize these efforts stimulated the expansion and refinement of the state bureaucracy. Governments found it necessary to employ thousands of new officials to supervise the collection of new taxes, and in order to make the system of tax collection more efficient, governments often introduced entirely new administrative systems. Some states completely reorganized their bureaucracies to meet the demands of war. New departments of state were created to supervise the recruitment of soldiers, the manufacture of equipment and uniforms, the building of fleets, and the provisioning of troops in time of war. Rulers of European states recognized that the exercise of absolute power greatly facilitated the utilization of state power for these purposes.

The Absolutist State in France and Spain

■ How did the encounters that took place in France and Spain during the seventeenth century result in the establishment of absolutism, and how powerful did those two states become in the seventeenth century?

The two European countries in which royal absolutism first became a political reality were France and Spain. The histories of these two monarchies in the seventeenth century followed very different courses. The kingdom of France, especially during the reign of Louis XIV (r. 1643–1715), became a model of state building and gradually emerged as the most powerful country in Europe. The Spanish monarchy, on the other hand, struggled to introduce absolutism at a time when the overall economic condition of the country was deteriorating and its military forces were suffering a series of defeats. Spain established the forms of absolutist rule, but the monarchy was not able to match the political or military achievements of France in the late seventeenth century.

The Foundations of French Absolutism

Efforts to make the French monarchy absolute began in response to the disorder that occurred during the wars of religion in the late sixteenth century. Bodin wrote his treatises during those wars, and the threat of renewed civil war between Protestants and Catholics affected French politics throughout the seventeenth century. The first steps toward the achievement of absolutism were taken during the reign of Henry IV (r. 1589–1610), the Huguenot who converted to Catholicism in 1594 and who ended the wars of religion by granting freedom of worship and full civil rights to French Protestants by the Edict of Nantes (1598). This decree brought internal religious peace to the kingdom, while the progressive financial and economic policies of Henry's brilliant minister, the Duke of Sully, helped restore the financial strength of the crown and involve the government in a process of commercial recovery and expansion. Despite this success, Henry could not prevent the great nobles from conspiring against him, and his policy of religious toleration encountered resistance from Catholics committed to the suppression of Protestantism. In 1610 a fanatical Catholic, François Ravaillac, stabbed the king to death in his carriage on a Parisian street.

On Henry's death the crown passed to his young son, Louis XIII (r. 1610–1643), while the queen mother, Marie de' Medici, assumed the leadership of a government acting in the king's name during his youth. This period of regency, in which aristocratic factions vied for supremacy at court, exposed the main weakness of the monarchy, which was the rival power of the great noble families of the realm. The statesman who addressed this problem most directly was Louis's main councilor, Cardinal Armand Jean du Plessis de Richelieu (1585–1642). A member of an old and wealthy family, Richelieu rose to power through the patronage of the queen mother and then, after losing her support, maintained his preeminent position with the support of the king himself. He became the king's chief minister in 1628. Richelieu was arguably the greatest state builder of the seventeenth century. He directed all his energies toward centralizing the power of the French state in the person of the king.

Richelieu's most immediate concern was bringing the independent nobility to heel and subordinating their local power to that of the state. This he accomplished by suppressing several conspiracies and rebellions led by noblemen and by restricting the independent power of the provincial assemblies and the eight regional parlements°, which were the highest courts in the country. His great administrative achievement was the strengthening of the system of the intendants°. These paid crown officials, who were recruited from the professional classes and the lower ranks of the nobility, became the main agents of French local administration. Responsible only to the royal council, they collected taxes, supervised local administration, and recruited soldiers for the army. Because they could not come from the districts to which they were assigned, they had no vested interest in maintaining local customs or privileges.

Richelieu also modified the religious policy embodied in the Edict of Nantes. According to that document, Huguenots not only had freedom of worship but could also fortify the towns in which they lived. Richelieu resented the maintenance of these citadels of local power, which represented a challenge to the type of absolutist state he envisioned. He also suspected that rivals of the king from the nobility were using the Huguenot towns as a means of maintaining their independent power. A series of military confrontations between the government and the

Cardinal Richelieu
Triple portrait of Cardinal Richelieu, who laid the foundations of French absolutism.

Protestants in the late 1610s and 1620s brought the country to the brink of civil war. Following the successful siege of the town of La Rochelle in 1627–1628, the government razed the fortifications of the Huguenot cities, melted down their cannons, and disarmed their Protestant citizens. A peace treaty signed in 1629 ratified the government's victory, but it did not deny the Huguenots their right to worship freely.

CHRONOLOGY

France in the Age of Absolutism

1598	The Edict of Nantes grants toleration to French Calvinists, known as Huguenots
1610	Assassination of Henry IV of France, who was succeeded by Louis XIII (r. 1610–1643)
1628	Cardinal Richelieu becomes chief minister of Louis XIII of France
1643	Death of Louis XIII of France and accession of Louis XIV; Louis's mother, Anne of Austria, becomes queen regent with Cardinal Mazarin as his minister
1648–1653	The Fronde
1661	Death of Cardinal Mazarin; Louis XIV assumes personal rule
1685	Revocation of the Edict of Nantes
1715	Death of Louis XIV of France; succeeded by his grandson, Louis XV

The most challenging task for Richelieu, as for all French ministers in the early modern period, was increasing the government's yield from taxation, a task that became more demanding during times of war. Levying taxes on the French population was always a delicate process, as the needs of the state conflicted with the privileges of various social groups, such as the nobles, who were exempt from taxation, and the estates of individual provinces such as Brittany that claimed the right to tax the people themselves. Using a variety of tactics, including negotiation and compromise, and relying heavily on the support of the provincial intendants, Richelieu managed to increase the yield from the *taille,* the direct tax on land, as much as threefold during the period 1635–1648. He supplemented the taille with taxes on office holding. Even then, the revenue was insufficient to meet the extraordinary demands of war.

Opposition to Richelieu's financial policies lay at the root of the main problem the government faced after the cardinal's death in 1642. The minister who succeeded him was his protégé Jules Mazarin (1602–1661), a diplomat of Italian birth who had entered French government service during Richelieu's administration. Mazarin dominated the government of Louis XIV when the king, who inherited the throne at age 5, was still a boy and while his mother was serving as regent. Mazarin continued the policies of his predecessor, but he was unable to prevent civil war from breaking out in 1648. This challenge to the French state, known as the *Fronde* (a pejorative reference to a Parisian game in which children flung mud at passing carriages), had two phases. The first, the Fronde of the Parlement (1648–1649), began when the members of the Parlement of Paris, the most important of all the provincial parlements, refused to register an edict of the king that had required them to surrender four years' salary. This act of resistance led to demands that the king sign a document limiting royal authority. Barricades went up in the streets of Paris, and the royal family was forced to flee the city. A blockade of the city by royal troops led to an uneasy compromise in 1649. Revolts in three other parlements, each of which had its own dynamic and which were not coordinated with that of Paris, came to a similar resolution. The second and more violent phase was the Fronde of the Princes (1650–1653), during which the Prince de Condé and his noble allies waged war on the government and even formed an alliance with

France's enemy, Spain. Only after Condé's military defeat did the entire rebellion collapse.

The Fronde stands as the great crisis of the seventeenth-century French state. It revealed the strength of the local, aristocratic, and legal forces with which the king and his ministers had to contend. These forces managed to disrupt the growth of the French state, drive the king from his capital, and challenge his authority throughout the kingdom. But in the long run they could not destroy the achievement of Richelieu and Mazarin. By the late 1650s the damage had been repaired and the state had resumed its growth.

Absolutism in the Reign of Louis XIV

The man who presided over the development of the French state for the next fifty years was the king himself, Louis XIV, who assumed direct control of his government after the death of Mazarin in 1661. In an age of absolute monarchs, Louis towered among his contemporaries. He is widely regarded as the most powerful king of the seventeenth century. This reputation comes as much from the image he conveyed as from the policies he pursued. Artists, architects, dramatists, and members of his immediate entourage helped the king project an image of incomparable majesty and authority. Paintings and sculptures of the king depicted him in sartorial splendor, holding the symbols of power and displaying expressions of regal superiority that bordered on arrogance. At Versailles, about ten miles from Paris, Louis constructed a lavishly furnished palace that be-

came his main residence and the center of the glittering court that surrounded him. The palace was built in the baroque° style, which emphasized the size and grandeur of the structure while also conveying a sense of unity and balance among its diverse parts. The sweeping façades of baroque buildings gave them a dynamic quality that evoked an emotional response from the viewer. The baroque style, criticized by contemporaries for its exuberance and pomposity, appealed to absolute monarchs who wished to emphasize their unrivaled position within society and their determination to impose order and stability on their kingdoms.

Court life at Versailles revolved entirely around the king. Court dramas depicted Louis, who styled himself "the sun king," as Apollo, the god of light. The paintings in the grand Hall of Mirrors at Versailles, which recorded the king's military victories, served as reminders of his unrivaled accomplishments. Louis's formal routine in receiving visitors created appropriate distance between him and his courtiers while keeping his subjects in a state of subservient anticipation of royal favor. His frequent bursts of anger achieved the same effect. When an untitled lady took the seat of a noblewoman at a dinner in his presence, he described the act as one of "incredible insolence" that "had thrown him into such a rage that he had been unable to eat." After rebuking the offending lady for her "impertinence," he became so angry that he left the room.[3]

The image of magnificence and power that Louis conveyed in art and ceremony mirrored and reinforced his more tangible political accomplishments. His greatest

Versailles Palace, Center of the Court of Louis XIV After 1682
The palace was constructed between 1669 and 1686. Its massiveness and grandeur and the order it imposed on the landscape made it a symbol of royal absolutism.

achievement was to solve the persistent problem of aristocratic independence and rebellion by securing the complete loyalty and dependence of the old nobility. This he achieved first by requiring the members of these ancient families to come to Versailles for a portion of every year, where they stayed in apartments within the royal palace itself. At Versailles Louis involved them in the elaborate cultural activities of court life and in ceremonial rituals that emphasized their subservience to the king. At the same time, he excluded the nobles from holding important offices in the government of the realm, a strategy designed to prevent them from building an independent power base within the bureaucracy. Instead he recruited men from the mercantile and professional classes to run his government. This policy of taming the nobility and depriving them of central administrative power could work only if they received something in return. Like all the absolute monarchs of western Europe, Louis used the patronage at his disposal to grant members of the nobility wealth and privileges in exchange for their loyalty to the crown. In this way the monarchy and the nobility served each other's interests.

In running the actual machinery of government Louis built upon and perfected the centralizing policies of Richelieu and Mazarin. After the death of Mazarin in 1661

the king, now 23 years old, became his own chief minister, presiding over a council of state that supervised the work of government. An elaborate set of councils at the highest levels of government set policy that was implemented by the department ministers. The provincial intendants became even more important than they had been under Richelieu and Mazarin, especially in providing food, arms, and equipment for royal troops. It was the intendants' job to secure the cooperation of the local judges, city councils, and parish priests as well as the compliance of the local population. If necessary they could call upon royal troops in order to enforce their will, but for the most part they preferred to rely on the more effective tactics of negotiation and compromise with local officials. The system, when it worked properly, allowed the king to make decisions that directly affected the lives and beliefs of his 20 million subjects.

A further manifestation of the newfound power of the French state in the late seventeenth century was the government's active involvement in the economic and financial life of the country. The minister who was most responsible for this series of undertakings was Jean Baptiste Colbert (1619–1683), a protégé of Mazarin who in 1661 became controller general of the realm. Born into a family of merchants, and despised by the old nobility, Colbert epitomized the type of government official Louis recruited into his service. Entrusted with the supervision of the entire system of royal taxation, Colbert managed to increase royal revenues dramatically simply by reducing the cut taken by the agents whom the government hired to collect taxes.

Even more beneficial to the French state was the determination of Colbert to use the country's economic resources for its benefit. The theory underlying this set of policies was mercantilism°, which held that the wealth of the state depended on its ability to import fewer commodities than it exported. Its goal was to secure the largest possible share of the world's monetary supply. In keeping with those objectives, Colbert increased the size of France's merchant fleet, founded overseas trading companies, and levied high tariffs on France's commercial rivals. To make France economically self-sufficient he encouraged the growth of the French textile industry, improved the condition of the roads, built canals throughout the kingdom, and reduced some of the burdensome tolls that impeded internal trade.

The most intrusive exercise of the power of the state during Louis XIV's reign was the decision to enforce religious uniformity. The king always considered the existence of a large Huguenot minority within his kingdom an affront to his sense of order. Toleration was divisive and dangerous, especially to someone who styled himself as "Most Christian King." Even after Richelieu had leveled the walls of the fortified Huguenot towns, the problem of religious pluralism remained. In 1685 Louis addressed this problem by revoking the entire Edict of Nantes, thereby denying freedom of religious worship to about one million of his subjects. The enforcement of this policy was violent and disruptive, with the army being called upon to enforce public conversions to Catholicism. Protestant churches were closed and often destroyed, while large numbers of Huguenots were forced to emigrate to the Netherlands, England, and Protestant German lands. Few exercises of absolute power in the seventeenth century caused more disruption in the lives of ordinary people than this attempt to realize the king's ideal of "one king, one law, one faith."

Louis XIV and the Culture of Absolutism

A further manifestation of the power of the French absolutist state was Louis's success in influencing and transforming French culture. Kings had often served as patrons of the arts by providing income for artists, writers, and musicians while endowing cultural and educational institutions. Louis took this type of royal patronage to a new level, making it possible for him to control the dissemination of ideas and the very production of culture itself. During Louis's reign royal patronage, emanating from the court, extended the king's influence over the entire cultural landscape. The architects of the palace at Versailles, the painters of historical scenes that hung in its hallways and galleries, the composers of the plays and operas that were performed in its theaters, the sculptors who created busts of the king to decorate its chambers, and the historians and pamphlet

DOCUMENT

Revocation of the Edict of Nantes, October 25, 1685

In 1685 King Louis XIV of France revoked the Edict of Nantes, the decree of King Henry IV that had granted freedom of worship to French Protestants in 1598. Before the revocation was published, the government sent dragoons (cavalry who arrived on horseback but fought on foot) to terrorize Protestant households and make them convert to Catholicism. The terms of the revocation were particularly harsh, and despite the prohibition against leaving the country, hundreds of thousands of Huguenots emigrated to England, the Dutch Republic, and North America.

. . . Therefore we decided that there was nothing better we could do to erase from memory the troubles, the confusion, and the evils that the growth of this false religion had caused in our kingdom and that gave rise to the said Edict and to so many other edicts and declarations that preceded it . . . than to revoke entirely the said Edict of Nantes and the detailed articles attached to it and everything that has been done since on behalf of the said Supposedly Reformed Religion [Calvinism].

1. We therefore for these reasons and in full knowledge, power, and Royal authority, by means of the present perpetual and irrevocable edict, do suppress and revoke the Edict of the king, our grandfather, issued at Nantes in April 1598. . . . As a result we desire and it is our pleasure that all the temples of the Supposedly Reformed Religion situated in our kingdom, county, lands and seigneuries within our obedience be immediately demolished. . . .
2. Our subjects of the Supposedly Reformed Religion are not to assemble for worship in any place or house for any reason.
3. Noble lords are not to hold worship services in their houses or fiefs of any sort on pain of confiscation of goods and property.
4. Ministers of the Supposedly Reformed Religion who have not converted are to leave the kingdom within fifteen days and are not to preach or perform any functions in the meantime, or they will be sent to the galleys.
5. Ministers who convert, and their widows after their death, are to enjoy the same exemptions from taxes and troop lodgings that they had as ministers. . . .
6. Converted ministers can become lawyers or doctors of law without the usual three years of study and for half the fees usually charged by the universities.
7. Special schools for the children of the Supposedly Reformed Religion are prohibited.
8. Children of [Huguenot] parents are to be baptized by the chief priests of their parishes and raised as Catholics, and local judges are to oversee this.
9. If Protestants who left the kingdom before this edict was issued return within four months, they can regain their property and resume their lives. If, however, they do not return within four months, their goods will be confiscated.
10. All subjects belonging to the Supposedly Reformed Religion and their wives and children are forbidden to leave the country or to send out their property and effects. The penalty for men is the galleys and women confiscation of their persons and property.
11. The declarations already issued concerning those who relapse are to be executed in full.

And, in addition, those who adhere to the Supposedly Reformed Religion, while waiting until it pleases God to enlighten them like the others, may continue to live in the cities and communities of our realm, continue their commerce, and enjoy their property without being bothered or hindered because of the Supposedly Reformed Religion, on condition, however, of not practicing their religion or assembling for prayers or worship or for any other pretext, with the penalties stated above.

Source: Copyright © 2000 by Bedford/St. Martin's. From *Louis XIV & Absolutism: A Brief Study with Documents* by William Beik. Reprinted with permission of Bedford/St. Martin's.

writers who celebrated the king's achievements in print all benefited from Louis's direct financial support.

Much of Louis's patronage went to cultural institutions, thereby enabling the king to influence a wider circle of artists and have a greater effect on the cultural life of the nation. He took over the Academy of Fine Arts in 1661, founded the Academy of Music in 1669, and chartered a theater company, the *Comédie Française*, in 1680. Two great French dramatists of the late seventeenth century, Jean Baptiste Molière (1622–1673), the creator of French high comedy, and Jean Racine (1639–1699), who wrote tragedies in the classical style, benefited from the king's patronage. Louis even subsidized the publication of a new journal, the *Journal des savants*, in which men of letters advanced their ideas. In 1666 Louis extended his patronage to the sciences with the founding of the *Académie des Sciences*, which had the twofold objective of advancing scientific knowledge and glorifying the king. It also benefited the state by devising improvements in ship design and navigation.

Of all the cultural institutions that benefited from Louis XIV's patronage, the *Académie Française* had the most enduring impact on French culture. This academy, a society of literary scholars, had been founded in 1635 with the support of Cardinal Richelieu. Its purpose was to standardize the French language and serve as the guardian of its integrity. In 1694, twenty-two years after Louis became the academy's patron, the first official French dictionary appeared in print. This achievement of linguistic uniformity, in which words received authorized spellings and definitions, reflected the pervasiveness of Louis's cultural influence as well as the search for order that became the defining characteristic of his reign.

Louis introduced order and uniformity into every aspect of his own life and that of his country. He followed a precise routine in ordering his daily life, created ceremonies that ordered the life of his court, and insisted on the court's adoption of table manners that followed strict rules of politeness. He created a bureaucracy that was organized along rational, orderly principles, and he sought to ensure that all his subjects would practice the same religion. The establishment of a clearly defined chain of command in the army, which Louis's minister the Marquis de Louvois introduced, gave organizational cohesion and hierarchical order to the large military force the king and his ministers assembled. Nearly all areas of French public life were transformed by the king's desire to establish order and uniformity and his use of the power of the state to enforce it.

One indication of the extent of Louis's achievement was the conspicuous attempt of other monarchs to imitate France, even in the eighteenth century. The absolute monarchs in Prussia, Austria, and Russia, as well as aspiring ones in England and Sweden, not only experimented selectively with French political methods but imported many of the features of French culture that Louis had supported. They built palaces in the same architectural style as that of Versailles, designed French gardens to surround them, imported the fashions and decorative styles of the French court, staged French ballets and operas in their capitals, and even spoke French, which had replaced Latin as the language of international diplomacy, when conducting official business. The power of the French monarchy had made French culture the dominant influence in the courts and capitals of Europe.

The Wars of Louis XIV, 1667–1714

The seventeenth-century French state was designed not only to maintain internal peace and order but also to wage war against other states. Colbert's financial and economic policies, coupled with the military reforms of the Marquis de Louvois, had laid the foundations for the creation of a

formidable military machine. In 1667 Louis XIV began unleashing its full potential. Having assembled an army that was twenty times larger than the French force that had invaded Italy in 1494, Louis deployed this armed force against an array of European powers in four separate wars between 1667 and 1714. His goal in all these wars, as it had been in all French international conflicts since 1635, was territorial acquisition (see Map 15.1). In this case Louis set his sights mainly on the German and Spanish territories in the Rhineland along the eastern borders of his kingdom. Contemporaries suggested, however, that he was thinking in grander terms than traditional French dynastic ambition. Propagandists for the king in the late 1660s claimed that Louis harbored visions of establishing a "universal monarchy" or an "absolute empire," reminiscent of the empires of ancient Rome, Charlemagne in the ninth century, and Charles V in the sixteenth century.

Louis never attained the empire of his dreams, but concerted action by almost all the other European powers was required to stop him. France's acquisition of new territories

---

Map 15.1 French Territorial Acquisitions, 1679–1714
The main acquisitions were lands in the Spanish Netherlands to the north and Franche Comté, Alsace, and Lorraine to the east. Louis thought of the Rhine River as France's natural eastern boundary, and territories acquired in 1659 and 1697 allowed it to reach that limit.

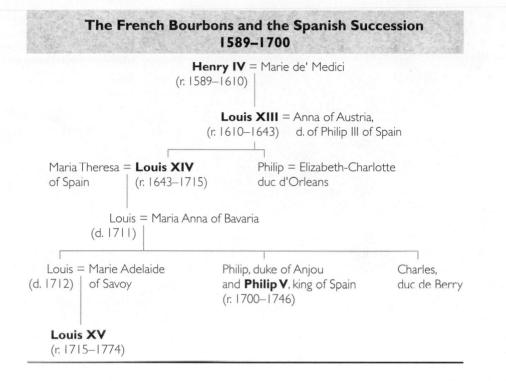

The French Bourbons and the Spanish Succession
1589–1700

Henry IV = Marie de' Medici
(r. 1589–1610)

Louis XIII = Anna of Austria,
(r. 1610–1643)   d. of Philip III of Spain

Maria Theresa = **Louis XIV**   Philip = Elizabeth-Charlotte
of Spain   (r. 1643–1715)   duc d'Orleans

Louis = Maria Anna of Bavaria
(d. 1711)

Louis = Marie Adelaide   Philip, duke of Anjou   Charles,
(d. 1712)   of Savoy   and **Philip V**, king of Spain   duc de Berry
                                (r. 1700–1746)

Louis XV
(r. 1715–1774)

---

along its eastern boundaries between 1668 and 1684 confirmed the fears of other European states that the king had imperial ambitions. After Louis had launched an offensive against German towns along the Rhine River in 1688, signaling the beginning of yet another round of European warfare, Great Britain, the Dutch Republic, Spain, and Austria formed a coalition against him. Finally matched by the combined military forces of these allies, forced to wage war on many different fronts (including North America), and unable to provide adequate funding of the war on the basis of its system of taxation, France felt compelled to conclude peace in 1697. The Treaty of Ryswick marked the turning point in the expansion of the French state and laid the groundwork for the establishment of a balance of power° in the next century, an arrangement whereby various countries form alliances to prevent any one state from dominating the others.

The Treaty of Ryswick, however, did not mark the end of French territorial ambition. In 1701 Louis went to war once again, this time as part of an effort to place a French Bourbon candidate, his grandson Duke Philip of Anjou, on the Spanish throne. The impending death of the mentally weak, sexually impotent, and chronically ill King Charles II of Spain (r. 1665–1700) without heirs had created a succession crisis. In 1698 the major European powers had agreed to a treaty in which Spanish lands would be divided between Louis himself and the Holy Roman Emperor, both of whom happened to be Charles's brothers-in-law. By his will, however, Charles left the Spanish crown and all its overseas possessions to Philip. This bequest offered France

more than it would have received on the basis of the treaty. If the will had been upheld, the Pyrenees mountains would have disappeared as a political barrier between France and Spain, and France, as the stronger of the two kingdoms, would have controlled unprecedented expanses of European and American territory.

Dreaming once again of universal monarchy, Louis rejected the treaty in favor of King Charles's will. The British, Dutch, and Austrians responded by forming a Grand Alliance against France and Spain. After a long and costly conflict, known as the War of the Spanish Succession (1701–1713), the members of this coalition were able to dictate the terms of the Treaty of Utrecht (1713). Philip, who suffered from fits of manic depression and went days without dressing or leaving his room, remained on the Spanish throne as Philip V (r. 1700–1746), but only on the condition that the French and Spanish crowns would never be united. Spain ceded its territories in the Netherlands and in Italy to the Austrian Habsburg Monarchy and its strategic port of Gibraltar at the entrance to the Mediterranean to the British. The treaty not only confirmed the new balance of power in Europe but also resulted in the transfer of large parts of French Canada, including Newfoundland and Nova Scotia, to Great Britain.

The loss of French territory in North America, the strains placed on the taxation system by the financial demands of war, and the weakening of France's commercial power as a result of this conflict made France a less potent state at the time of Louis's death in 1715 than it had been in the 1680s. Nevertheless the main effects of a century of

Map 15.2 The Decline of Spanish Power in Europe, 1640–1714
Revolts in the United Provinces of the Netherlands and Portugal account for two of the most significant losses of Spanish territory. Military defeat at the hands of the French in 1659 and Austria in 1714 account for the loss of most of the other territories.

French state building remained, including a large, well-integrated bureaucratic edifice that allowed the government to exercise unprecedented control over the population and a military establishment that remained the largest and best equipped in Europe.

Absolutism and State Building in Spain

The history of Spain in the seventeenth century is almost always written in terms of failure, as the country endured a long period of economic decline that began in the late sixteenth century with a precipitate drop in the size of its population and stretched well into the eighteenth century. The monarchy became progressively weaker during the seventeenth century, as it was occupied by a succession of ineffective kings who exercised far less power than their French counterparts. To make matters worse, Spain in the seventeenth century suffered a long series of military defeats, most of them at the hands of the French, and it lost the position it had held in the sixteenth century as the major

European power (see Map 15.2). By the early eighteenth century Spain was a shadow of its former self, and its culture reflected uncertainty, pessimism, and nostalgia for former imperial greatness. None of this failure, however, should obscure the fact that Spain, like France, underwent a period of state building during the seventeenth century, and that its government, like that of France, gravitated toward absolutism.

The Spanish monarchy in 1600 ruled more territory than did France, and the various kingdoms and principalities that it comprised possessed far more independence than even the most remote and peripheral French provinces. The center of the monarchy was the kingdom of Castile, with its capital at Madrid. This kingdom, the largest and wealthiest territory within the Iberian peninsula, had been united with the kingdom of Aragon in 1479 when King Ferdinand II of Aragon (r. 1479–1516), the husband of Queen Isabella of Castile (r. 1474–1504), ascended the throne. These two kingdoms, however, continued to exist as separate states after the union, each having its own representative institutions and administrative systems. Each of them, moreover, contained smaller, semiautonomous king-

The Absolutist State in France and Spain **489**

doms and provinces that retained their own distinctive political institutions. The kingdom of Valencia and the principality of Catalonia formed part of the Crown of Aragon, while in the sixteenth century the kingdoms of Navarre and Portugal had been annexed to the Crown of Castile. Outside the Iberian peninsula the Spanish monarchy ruled territories in the Netherlands, Italy, and the New World.

The only institution besides the monarchy itself that provided any kind of administrative unity to all these Spanish territories in the seventeenth century was the Spanish Inquisition, a centralized ecclesiastical court with a supreme council in Madrid and twenty-one regional tribunals in different parts of Spain, Italy, and America. Its function was to enforce religious uniformity and maintain the purity of the Catholic faith.

The great challenge for the Spanish monarchy in the seventeenth century was to integrate the various kingdoms and principalities of Spain into a more highly centralized state while at the same time making the machinery of that state more efficient and profitable. The statesman who made the most sustained efforts at realizing these goals was the energetic and authoritarian Count-Duke of Olivares (1587–1645), the contemporary and counterpart of Richelieu during the reign of the Spanish king Philip IV (1621–1665). The task Olivares faced was more daunting than anything the French cardinal had ever confronted. As a result of decades of warfare, the Spanish monarchy in the 1620s was penniless, the kingdom of Castile had gone bankrupt, and the entire country had already entered a period of protracted economic decline.

To deal with these deep structural problems Olivares proposed a reform of the entire financial system, the establishment of national banks, and the replacement of the main tax, the *millones*, which was levied on the consumption of basic commodities such as meat and wine, with proportional contributions from all the towns and villages in the kingdom. At the same time he tried to address the problem of ruling a disparate and far-flung empire, making all the kingdoms and principalities within the monarchy contribute to national defense on a proportionate basis. His ultimate goal was to unify the entire peninsula in a cohesive Spanish national state, similar to that of France. This policy involved suppression of the individual liberties of the various kingdoms and principalities and direct subordination of each area to the king himself. It was, in other words, a solution based on the principles of absolutism.

Olivares was unable to match the state-building achievement of Richelieu in France. His failure, which was complete by the time he fell from office in 1643, can be attributed to three factors. The first was the opposition he confronted within Castile itself, especially from the cities represented in the Cortes, over the question of taxation. The second, a problem facing Spain throughout the seventeenth century, was military failure, in this case the losses to France during the final phase of the Thirty Years' War. That failure aggravated the financial crisis and prevented the monarchy from capitalizing on the prestige that usually attends military victory. The third and most serious impediment was opposition to the policy of subordinating the outlying Spanish regions to the kingdom of Castile. The kingdoms and provinces on the periphery of the country were determined to maintain their individual laws and liberties, especially the powers of their own Cortes, in the face of the pressures to centralize power in Madrid. The problem became more serious as Olivares, in the wake of military defeat by the French and Dutch, put more pressure on these outlying kingdoms and provinces to contribute to the war effort.

Provincial resistance to a policy of Castilian centralization lay at the root of the Spanish crisis of the seventeenth

CHRONOLOGY

International Conflict in the Seventeenth Century

1609	Truce between the seven Dutch provinces and Spain
1618	Bohemian revolt against Habsburg rule; beginning of the Thirty Years' War
1620	Imperial forces defeat Bohemians at Battle of White Mountain
1648	Treaty of Westphalia, ending the Thirty Years' War; Treaty of Münster, ending the Dutch War of Independence
1667	Beginning of the wars of Louis XIV
1672	William III of Orange-Nassau becomes captain-general of Dutch; beginning of the war against France (1672–1678)
1688–1697	War of the League of Augsburg (Nine Years' War); England and Scotland join forces with Prussia, Austria, the Dutch Republic, and many German states against France
1697	Treaty of Ryswick
1700–1721	Great Northern War in which Russia eventually defeated Sweden; emergence of Russia as a major power
1701–1713	War of the Spanish Succession
1713	Treaty of Utrecht

century. This crisis did not throw Castile itself into a state of civil war. Unlike Paris during the Fronde, Madrid itself remained peaceful. Throughout the 1640s the crown managed to maintain order within its main kingdom, probably because it had learned the art of negotiating directly with the thousands of towns and villages that ran local government. Instead, the Spanish crisis took the form of separatist revolts in Portugal, Catalonia, Sicily, and Naples. With the exception of Portugal, which recovered its sovereignty in 1640, the monarchy met this test and managed to maintain control of its provincial and Italian territories. In the aftermath of the revolts, however, the monarchy failed to bring the areas within the sphere of effective central government control.

The relative weakness of the Spanish monarchy, especially in comparison with that of France, became most apparent in the late seventeenth century, the age of Louis XIV. In two important respects the Spanish government failed to match the achievement of the French. First, it could never escape the grip that the old noble families had on the central administration. The unwillingness of the nobility to recruit ministers and officials from the mercantile and professional groups within society (which were small to begin with in Spain) worked against the achievement of bureaucratic efficiency and made innovation virtually impossible. Second, unlike the French government during Colbert's ministry, the Spanish government failed to encourage economic growth. The hostility of the aristocratic ruling class to mercantile affairs, coupled with a traditional Spanish unwillingness to follow the example of foreigners (especially when they were Protestants) prevented the country from stemming its own economic decline and the government from solving the formidable financial problems facing it. To make matters worse, the Spanish government failed to make its system of tax collection more efficient.

The mood that prevailed within the upper levels of Castilian society in the seventeenth century reflected the failure of the government and the entire nation. The contrast between the glorious achievements of the monarchy during the reign of Philip II (r. 1555–1598) and the somber realities of the late seventeenth century led most members of the ruling class to retreat into that past, a nostalgia that only encouraged further economic and political stagnation. The work of Miguel de Cervantes (1547–1616), the greatest Spanish writer of the seventeenth century, reflected this change in the Spanish national mood. In 1605 and 1615 Cervantes published (in two parts) *Don Quixote*, the story of an idealistic wandering nobleman who pursued dreams of an elusive military glory. This work, which as we have seen in Chapter 14 explored the relationship between illusion and reality, served as a commentary on a nobility that had lost confidence in itself.

Spanish painting, which paradoxically entered its Golden Age at the time the country began to lose its economic, political, and military vitality, was less willing to accept the decline of Spain. There was very little in the paintings of the great Spanish artist Diego de Velázquez (1599–1660) that would suggest the malaise that was affecting Spain and its nobility at the time. Velázquez painted in the baroque style that was in favor at court throughout Europe, depicting his subjects in heroic poses and imbuing them with a sense of royal or aristocratic dignity. One of his historical paintings, *The Surrender of Breda* (1634), commemorated a rare Spanish military victory over the Dutch in 1625 and the magnanimity of the Spanish victors toward their captives. All this was intended to reinforce the prestige

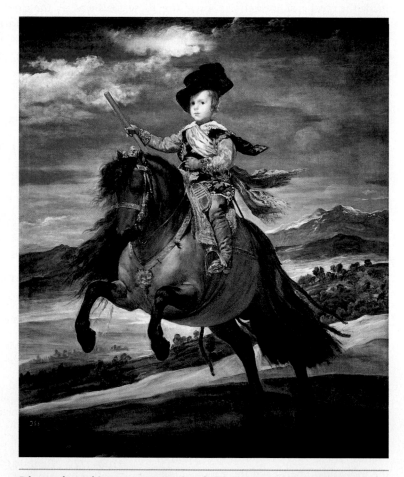

Diego de Velázquez, Portrait of the Prince Baltasar Carlos, Heir to the Spanish Throne
The depiction of the six-year-old prince on a rearing horse was intended to suggest military and political power at a time when the monarchy was losing both. The prince died in 1646, before he could succeed to the throne.

Diego de Velázquez, *The Surrender of Breda,* 1634
The Spanish victory over the Dutch in 1625 gave Velázquez a rare opportunity to depict Spanish soldiers in a role they had frequently played in the sixteenth century.

of the monarchy, the royal family, and the nation itself at a time when the imperial grandeur of the past had faded. Velázquez's painting reflected the ideals of absolutism but ignored the realities of Spanish political and military life.

ment followed a Western pattern in many respects, was increasingly dismissed by Europeans as part of a distant, non-Western world.

Absolutism and State Building in Central and Eastern Europe

- What was the nature of royal absolutism in central and eastern Europe, and how did the policies of the Ottoman Empire and Russia help establish the boundaries of the West during this period?

The forces that led to the establishment of absolutism and state building in France and Spain also made an impact on central and eastern Europe. In Germany the Thirty Years' War led to the establishment of two absolutist states, Prussia and the Austrian Habsburg Monarchy. Further to the East, the Ottoman and Russian Empires, both of them on the margins of the West, also developed absolutist political systems that shared many of the same characteristics as those in western and central Europe. Russia, previously thought of as belonging to an Eastern, Asian world, entered upon a program of westernization and staked a claim to be considered a Western power. At the same time the Ottoman Empire, whose political develop-

Germany and the Thirty Years' War, 1618–1648

Before 1648 the main political power within the geographical area known as Germany was the Holy Roman Empire. This large political formation was a loose confederation of kingdoms, principalities, duchies, ecclesiastical territories, and cities, each of which had its own laws and political institutions. The emperor, who was elected by a body of German princes, exercised immediate jurisdiction only in his own dynastic possessions and in the imperial cities. He also convened a legislative assembly known as the *Reichstag,* over which he exercised limited influence. But the emperor did not have a large administrative or judicial bureaucracy through which he could enforce imperial law in the localities. The empire was not in any sense a sovereign state, even though it had long been a major force in European diplomacy. It had acquired and maintained that international position by relying on the military and financial contributions of its imperial cities and the lands controlled directly by the Habsburg emperors.

The Thirty Years' War permanently altered the nature of this vast and intricate political structure. That war began as a conflict between Protestant German princes and the Catholic emperor over religious and constitutional issues. The incident that triggered it in 1618 was the so-called Defenestration of Prague, when members of the predominantly Protestant Bohemian legislature, known as the Diet, threw two imperial officials out a castle window as a protest against the religious policies of their recently elected king, the future emperor Ferdinand II. The Diet proceeded to depose Ferdinand, a Catholic, and elect a Protestant prince, Frederick V of the Palatinate, to replace him. The war soon broadened into a European-wide struggle over the possession of German and Spanish territory, as the Danes, Swedes, and French successively entered the conflict against the emperor and his Spanish Habsburg relatives. For a brief period in the late 1620s England also entered the conflict against Spain. The war, which was fought mainly on German soil, had a devastating effect on the country. More than one million soldiers marched across German lands, sacking towns and exploiting the resources of local communities. Germany lost up to one-third of its population, while the destruction of property retarded the economic development of the country for more than fifty years.

The political effects of the war were no less traumatic. By virtue of the Treaty of Westphalia, which ended the war in 1648, the empire was permanently weakened, although it continued to function until 1806 (see Map 15.3). The individual German territories within the empire developed more institutional autonomy than they had before the war.

They became sovereign states themselves, with their own armies, foreign policies, and central bureaucracies. Two of these German states soon surpassed all the others in size and military strength and became major European powers. The first was Brandenburg-Prussia, a collection of various territories in northern Germany that was transformed into the kingdom of Prussia at the beginning of the eighteenth century. In the nineteenth century Prussia would unify Germany under its leadership. The second state was the Austrian Habsburg Monarchy, which in the eighteenth century was usually identified simply as Austria. The Habsburgs had long dominated the Holy Roman Empire and continued to secure election as emperors after the Treaty of Westphalia. In the late seventeenth century, however, the Habsburg Monarchy acquired its own institutional identity, distinct from that of the empire. It consisted of the lands that the Habsburgs controlled directly in the southeastern part of the empire and other territories, including the kingdom of Hungary, which lay outside the territorial boundary of the empire. Both Prussia and Austria developed their own forms of absolutism during the second half of the seventeenth century.

The Growth of the Prussian State

In 1648, at the end of the Thirty Years' War, Prussia could barely have claimed the status of an independent state, much less that of an absolute monarchy. The core of the

Defenestration of Prague, May 23, 1618

The Thirty Years' War was touched off when Protestant nobles in the Bohemian legislature threw two Catholic imperial governors out the window of a castle in Prague.

Europe After the Treaty of Westphalia, 1648

- Spanish dominions
- Austrian dominions
- Brandenburg-Prussia
- Swedish dominions
- —— Boundary of Holy Roman Empire

Map 15.3 Europe After the Treaty of Westphalia, 1648

The Holy Roman Empire no longer included the Dutch Republic, which was now independent of Spain. Some of the lands of the Austrian Habsburg Monarchy and Brandenburg-Prussia lay outside the boundaries of the Holy Roman Empire. Italy was divided into a number of small states in the north, while Naples, Sicily, and Sardinia were ruled by Spain.

Prussian state was Brandenburg, which claimed the status of an electorate because its ruler cast one of the ballots to elect the Holy Roman Emperor. The lands that belonged to the elector of Brandenburg lay scattered throughout northern Germany and stretched into eastern Europe. As a result of the Thirty Years' War, the archbishoprics of Magdeburg and East Pomerania were annexed to Brandenburg. The Hohenzollern family, in whose line the electorate of Brandenburg passed, also owned or controlled various parcels of German territory in the Rhineland, near the borders of the Spanish Netherlands. In 1618 the Hohenzollerns had acquired the much larger but equally remote duchy of Prussia, a Baltic territory lying outside the boundaries of the Holy Roman Empire. As ruler of these disparate and noncontiguous lands, the elector of Brandenburg had virtually no state bureaucracy, collected few taxes, and commanded only a small army. Most of his territories, moreover, lay in ruins in 1648, having been devastated by Swedish and imperial troops at various times during the war.

The Great Elector Frederick William (r. 1640–1688) began the long process of turning this ramshackle structure into a powerful and cohesive German state (see Map 15.4). His son King Frederick I (r. 1688–1713) and grandson Frederick William I (r. 1713–1740) completed the transformation. The key to their success, as it was for all aspiring absolute monarchs in eastern Europe, was to secure the compliance of the traditional nobility, who in Prussia were known as Junkers°. The Great Elector Frederick William achieved this end by granting the Junkers a variety of privileges, including exemption from import duties and the excise tax. The most valuable concession was the legal confirmation of their rights over the serfs. During the previous 150 years Prussian peasants had lost their freedom, becoming permanently bound to the estates of their lords and completely subject to the Junkers' arbitrary brand of local justice. The Junkers had a deeply vested interest in perpetuating this oppressive system of serfdom, and the lawgiver Frederick was able to provide them with the legal guarantees they required.

DOCUMENT

A German Writer Describes the Horrors of the Thirty Years' War

In 1669 the German writer H. J. C. Grimmelshausen (1625–1676) published an imaginary account of the adventures of a German vagabond, to whom he gave the name Simplicissimus. The setting of the book was the Thirty Years' War in Germany, which Grimmelshausen had experienced firsthand. At age 10 Grimmelshausen, like the character Simplicissimus in the book, was captured by Hessian troops and later became a camp-follower. In this chapter Simplicissimus describes how the palace of his father was stormed, plundered, and ruined.

The first thing that these troops did was, that they stabbed their horses; thereafter each fell to his appointed task, which task was either more or less than ruin and destruction. For though some began to slaughter and to boil and to roast, so that it looked as if there should be a merry banquet forward, yet others there were who did but storm through the house above and below the stairs. . . . All that they had no mind to take with them they cut in pieces. Some thrust their swords through the hay and straw as if they had not enough sheep and swine to slaughter; and some shook the feathers out of the beds and in their stead stuffed in bacon and other dried meat and provisions as if such were better and softer to sleep upon. Others broke the stove and the windows as if they had a never-ending summer to promise. Housewares of copper and tin they beat flat, and packed such vessels, all bent and spoiled, in with the rest. Bedsteads, tables, chairs and benches they burned, though there lay many cords of dry wood in the yard. . . .

Our maid was so handled in the stable that she could not come out; which is a shame to tell of. Our man they laid bound upon the ground, thrust a gag into his mouth, and poured a pailful of filthy water into his body; and by this, which they called a Swedish draught, they forced him to lead a party of them to another place where they captured men and beasts, and brought them back to our farm, in which company were my dad, my mother, and our Ursula.

And now they began first to take the flints out of their pistols and in place of them to jam the peasants' thumbs in and so to torture the poor rogues as if they had been about the burning of witches. For one of them they had taken they thrust into the baking oven and there lit a fire under him, although he had as yet confessed no crime; as for another, they put a cord round his head and so twisted it tight with a piece of wood that the blood gushed from his mouth and nose and ears. In a word each had his own device to torture the peasants, and each peasant his several torture.

Source: Reprinted from The Adventurous Simplicissimus: Being the Description of the Life of a Strange Vagabond Named Melchior Sternfels Von Fuchshaim *by H. J. C. Grimmelshausen. Published by the University of Nebraska Press.*

With the loyalty of the Junkers secure, Frederick William went about the process of building a powerful Prussian state. A large administrative bureaucracy, centralized under a General Directory in Berlin, governed both financial and military affairs throughout the elector's lands. At first it was staffed by members of the nobility, but eventually educated commoners were recruited into the system. The taxes that the government collected, especially from the towns, went in large part to fund a standing army, which had come into being in the late 1650s.

The Prussian army grew rapidly, rising to 30,000 men in 1690 and 80,000 by 1740. It consisted of a combination of carefully recruited volunteers, foreign mercenaries, and, after 1713, conscripts from the general population. Its most famous regiment, known as the Blue Prussians or the Giants of Potsdam, consisted of 1,200 men, each of whom was at least six feet tall. Commanded by officers drawn from the nobility and reinforced by Europe's first system of military reserves, this army quickly became the best trained fighting force in Europe. Prussia became a model military state, symbolized by the transformation of the royal gardens into an army training ground during the reign of Frederick William I.

As this military state grew in size and complexity, its rulers acquired many of the attributes of absolute rule. Most significantly they became the sole legislators within the state. The main representative assembly in the electorate, the Diet of Brandenburg, met for the last time in 1652. Frederick William and his successors, however, continued to consult with smaller local assemblies, especially in the matter of taxation. The elevation of Frederick I's status to that of king of Prussia in 1701 marked a further consolidation of power in the person of the ruler. His son's style of rule, which included physical punishment of judges whose decisions displeased him, suggested that the Prussian monarchy not only had attained absolute power but could occasionally abuse it.

The Austrian Habsburg Monarchy

The Austrian Habsburgs were much less successful than the Hohenzollerns in building a centralized, consolidated state along absolutist lines. The various territories that made up the Austrian Habsburg Monarchy in the late seventeenth century were larger and more diverse than those that belonged to the king of Prussia. In addition to the collection of duchies that form present-day Austria and that then served as the core of the monarchy, it embraced two subordinate kingdoms, which were themselves composed of various semiautonomous principalities and duchies. The first of these, lying to the north, was the kingdom of Bohemia, which had struggled against Habsburg control for nearly a century and included Moravia and Silesia. The second, lying to the southeast, was the kingdom of Hungary, including the large semiautonomous principality of Transylvania. The Habsburgs regained Hungary from the Ottoman Empire in stages between 1664 and 1718. In 1713 the monarchy also acquired the former Spanish Netherlands and the Italian territories of Milan and Naples.

The Austrian Habsburg monarchs of the seventeenth and early eighteenth centuries never succeeded in integrating these ethnically, religiously, and politically diverse lands into a unified, cohesive state similar to that of France. The problem was a lack of a unified bureaucracy. The only centralized administrative institutions in this amalgam of kingdoms were the Court Chamber, which superintended the collection of taxes throughout the monarchy, and the Austrian army, which included troops from all Habsburg lands. Like many European military forces it had become a standing army in 1648, and by 1716 it had a troop strength of 165,000 men. Even these centralized institutions had difficulty operating smoothly. The council of the army had trouble integrating units drawn from separate kingdoms, while the Court Chamber never developed a uniform system of tax collection. For all practical purposes the Habsburgs had to rule their various kingdoms separately.

In governing its Austrian and Bohemian lands, this decentralized Habsburg Monarchy nonetheless acquired some of the characteristics of absolutist rule. This development toward absolutism began long before the Treaty of

Map 15.4 The Growth of Brandenburg-Prussia, 1618–1786

By acquiring lands throughout northern Germany, Prussia became a major European power. The process began during the early seventeenth century, but it continued well into the eighteenth century. The Prussian army, which was the best trained fighting force in Europe in the eighteenth century, greatly facilitated Prussia's growth.

The Growth of Brandenburg-Prussia, 1618–1786

- Brandenburg, 1440
- Acquisitions to 1618
- Acquisitions to 1740
- Acquisitions to 1786
- Holy Roman Empire boundary

Westphalia in 1648. After defeating the Bohemians at the Battle of White Mountain in 1620 during the Thirty Years' War, Emperor Ferdinand II (r. 1618–1637) had decided to strengthen his authority in the areas under his direct control. Bohemia, which had led the revolt against him, was the main target of this policy, but the emperor used this opportunity to increase his power throughout his territories. After punishing the rebels and exiling many of the Protestant nobility, he undertook a deliberate expansion of his legislative and judicial powers, and he secured direct control over all his administrative officials.

A policy of severe religious repression accompanied this increase in the emperor's authority. Like Cardinal Richelieu of France, Ferdinand assumed that Protestantism served as a justification for rebellion, and he therefore decided that its practice could not be tolerated. Protestants in all the emperor's territories were forced to take a Catholic loyalty oath, and Protestant education was banned. Protestant towns were destroyed at exactly the same time that Richelieu was razing the fortifications of the Huguenot town of La Rochelle. These efforts at reconversion continued right through the seventeenth century. They amounted to a policy of religious or "confessional" absolutism.

While the Habsburgs succeeded in imposing some elements of absolutist rule on the Austrians and the Bohemians in the early seventeenth century, they encountered much more resistance when they attempted to follow the same course of action with respect to Hungary in the late seventeenth and eighteenth centuries. Hungarians had a long tradition of limited, constitutional rule in which the national Diet had exercised powers of legislation and taxation, just as Parliament did in England. Habsburg emperors made some limited inroads on these traditions but they were never able to break them. They also were unable to achieve the same degree of religious uniformity that they had imposed on their other territories. In Hungary the Habsburgs encountered the limits of royal absolutism.

The Ottoman Empire: Between East and West

In the seventeenth and early eighteenth centuries the southeastern border of the Habsburg monarchy separated the kingdom of Hungary from the Ottoman Empire. This militarized frontier marked not only the political boundary between two empires but a deeper cultural boundary between East and West.

As we have seen in previous chapters, the West is not just a geographical but also a cultural realm, and the people who inhabit this realm, although distinct from one another, share many of the same religious, political, legal, and philosophical traditions. The Ottoman Turks, who posed a recurrent military threat to the Habsburg monarchy and who reached the gates of Vienna in 1683, were generally thought of as not belonging to this Western world. Because the Ottoman Turks were Muslims, Europeans considered them enemies of Christianity, infidels who were bent on the destruction of Christendom. In the sixteenth century Catholics and Protestants alike claimed that the military victories of the Turks over European forces were signs of divine punishment for the sins European Christians had committed. Ottoman emperors, known as sultans, were considered despots who ruled over their subjects as slaves. The sultans were also depicted in Western literature as cruel and brutal tyrants, the opposite of the ideal Christian prince of Europe. One French play of 1612 depicted the mother of the sultan Mehmed the Conquerer (r. 1451–1481) as drinking the blood of a victim.

These stereotypes of the Turks served the function of giving Europeans a sense of their own Western identity. Turks became a negative reference group with whom Europeans could favorably compare themselves. The realities of Ottoman politics and culture, however, were quite different from the ways in which they were represented in European literature. Turkish despotism, the name Europeans gave to the Ottoman system of government, existed only in theory. Ever since the fourteenth century Ottoman writers had claimed for the sultan extraordinary powers, including the right to seize the landed property of his subjects at will. In practice he never exercised unlimited power. His prerogatives were limited by the spirit of Muslim law, and he shared power with the grand vizier, who was his chief executive officer. In practice there was little difference between the rule of the sultans and that of European absolute monarchs. As far as religious policy is concerned, the Ottoman practice of tolerating non-Muslim religions within the empire made the sultans less absolutist than most of their seventeenth-century European counterparts.

DOCUMENT

Venetian Observations on the Ottoman Empire (late 16th c.)

Even the high degree of administrative centralization for which the Ottoman Empire was famous did not encompass all the regions under its control. Many of its provinces, especially those in the Balkans, enjoyed a considerable measure of autonomy, especially in the seventeenth century. The Balkans, which were geographically part of Europe, never experienced the full force of direct Turkish rule. In all the Ottoman provinces there was a complex pattern of negotiation between the central imperial administration and local officials. In this respect the Ottoman Empire was similar to the absolutist monarchies of western and central Europe. The Ottoman Empire bore the closest resemblance to the Spanish monarchy, which also ruled many far-flung territories in Europe. Like the Spanish monarchy, the Ottoman Empire declined in power during the seventeenth century and lost effective control of some of its outlying provinces.

Ottoman Turks and Europeans frequently went to war against each other, but there was a constant pattern of diplomatic, economic, and cultural interaction between them. The Turks had been involved in European warfare since the fifteenth century, and they had formed diplomatic alliances with the French against the Austrian Habsburgs on a number of occasions. Europeans and Ottomans often borrowed military technology from each other, and they also shared knowledge of administrative techniques. Trade between European countries and the Ottoman Empire remained brisk throughout this period. Europe supplied hardware and textiles to the Turks while they in turn shipped coffee, tobacco, and tulips to European ports. Communities of Turks and other Muslims lived in European cities, while numerous European merchants resided in territories under Ottoman control.

These encounters between Turks and Europeans suggest that the militarized boundary between the Habsburgs and the Ottoman Empire was much more porous than its fortifications would suggest. Military conflict and Western contempt for Muslim Turks disguised a much more complex process of political and cultural interaction between the two civilizations. Europeans tended to think of the Ottoman Empire as "oriental," but it is more accurate to view it as a region lying between the East and the West.

Russia and the West

The other seventeenth-century power that marked the boundary between East and West was the vast Russian Empire, which stretched from its boundary with Poland in the west all the way to the Pacific Ocean in the east. Until the end of the seventeenth century, the kingdom of Muscovy

DOCUMENT

Adan Olearius: A Foreign Traveler in Russia (early 17th c.)

and the lands attached to it seemed, at least to Europeans, part of the Asiatic world. Dominated by an Eastern Orthodox branch of Christianity, Russia drew very little upon the cultural traditions associated with western Europe. Unlike its neighboring Slavic kingdom of Poland, it had not absorbed large doses of German culture. It also appeared to Europeans to be another example of "oriental despotism," a state in which the ruler, known as the tsar, could rule his subjects at will, "not bound up by any law or custom."

During the reign of Tsar Peter I, known as Peter the Great (r. 1682–1725), Russia underwent a process

IMAGE

Peter the Great

of westernization, bringing it more into line with the culture of European countries and becoming a major European power. This policy began after Peter visited England, Holland, northern Germany, and Austria in 1697 and 1698. Upon his return he directed his officials and members of the upper levels of Russian society to adopt Western styles of dress and appearance, including the removal of men's beards. (Scissors were kept in the customs house for this purpose alone.) Beards symbolized the backward, Eastern, Orthodox culture from whose grip Peter hoped to extricate his country. Young Russian boys were sent abroad for their education. Women began to participate openly in the social

and cultural life of the cities, in violation of Orthodox custom. Smoking was permitted despite the Church's insistence that Scripture condemned it. The calendar was reformed and books were printed in modern Russian type. Peter's importation of Western art and the imitation of Western architecture complemented this policy of enforced cultural change. Westernization, however, involved more than a change of manners and appearance. It also involved military and political reforms that changed the character of the Russian state.

During the first twenty-five years of his reign Peter had found himself unable to achieve sustained military success against his two great enemies, the Ottoman Turks to the south and the Swedes to the west. During the Great Northern War with Sweden (1700–1721) Peter introduced a number of military reforms that eventually turned the tide against his enemy. These reforms were based on the knowledge he had acquired of military technology, organization, and tactics of western European states, especially Prussia and, ironically, Sweden itself. Having introduced a program of conscription, Peter assembled a large standing army of more than 200,000 men, which he trained and disciplined in the Prussian manner. All of this was supported by the imposition of new taxes on a variety of commodities, including beards, and the encouragement of Russian industry in much the same way that Colbert had encouraged French industry. A central council, established in 1711, not only directed financial administration but also levied and supplied troops, not unlike the General Directory of the electorate of Brandenburg.

This new military state also acquired many of the centralizing and absolutist features of western European

CHRONOLOGY

The Age of Absolutism in Central and Eastern Europe

1618	Ferdinand II becomes Holy Roman Emperor (r. 1618–1637)
1640	Beginning of the reign of Frederick William, the Great Elector of Brandenburg Prussia (r. 1640–1688)
1657	Leopold I becomes Holy Roman Emperor (r. 1657–1705)
1682	Accession of Tsar Peter the Great of Russia (r. 1682–1725)
1688	Accession of Frederick as elector of Prussia; becomes king of Prussia in 1701
1703	Foundation of St. Petersburg, Russia's new capital and "window on the West"
1705	Joseph I becomes Holy Roman Emperor (r. 1705–1711)
1711	Charles VI, brother of Joseph I, becomes Holy Roman Emperor (r. 1711–1740)

St. Petersburg and the West

The major encounter between Russia and the West during the reign of Peter the Great was the building of a new capital city, St. Petersburg, on the marshy delta of the Neva River, which empties into the Gulf of Finland. The land on which the city was located was seized from Sweden during the Northern War. The construction of the city, which first served as a fortress and then a naval base in that conflict, occurred at a tremendous cost in treasure and human life. Using the royal powers that he had significantly augmented earlier in his reign, Peter ordered more than 10,000 workers (and possibly twice that number) from throughout his kingdom to realize this ambitious and risky project. The harsh weather conditions, the ravages of malaria and other diseases, and the chronic shortages of provisions in a distant location resulted in the death of a few thousand workers—numbers that were often greatly exaggerated by foreigners. Beginning in 1710 Peter ordered the transfer of central governmental, commercial, and military functions to the new city. The city became the site for Peter's Winter Palace, the residences of Russia's foreign ambassadors, and the headquarters of the Russian Orthodox Church. The Academy of Fine Arts and the Academy of Sciences were built shortly thereafter. During the 1730s Russia's first bourse, or exchange, fulfilled the prophecy of a British observer in 1710 that the city, with its network of canals, "might one day prove a second Amsterdam or Venice." Thus St. Petersburg came to embody all the modernizing and westernizing achievements of Peter the Great.

Russia's encounter with the West at St. Petersburg was reflected both in the location of the new city and the styles in which the buildings were constructed. As a port with access to the Baltic Sea, the new city, often described as "a window on the West," looked toward the European ports with which Russia increased its commerce and the European powers that Russia engaged in battle and diplomacy. The architects, stonemasons, and interior decorators that Peter commissioned came from France, Italy, Germany and the Dutch Republic, and they constructed the buildings in contemporary European styles. The general plan of the city, drawn up by the French architect Le Blond, featured straight, paved streets with stone paths that are now called sidewalks. St. Petersburg thus became a port through which Western influences entered Russia. The contrast with the old capital, Moscow, which was situated in the center of the country and embodied the spirit of the old Russia that Peter strove to modernize, could not have been clearer.

The construction of St. Petersburg played a central role in transforming Russia from a medieval kingdom on the fringes of Europe into a modern, Western power. It did not, however, eliminate the conflict in Russia between those who held the West up as the cultural standard that Russia should strive to emulate and those who celebrated Russia's cultural superiority over the West. This conflict between westernizers and Slavophiles, which began in the eighteenth century, has continued to the present day. During the period of communism in the twentieth century, when St. Petersburg was renamed Leningrad and Moscow once again became the political capital of the country, the Slavophile tradition tended to prevail. It is no coincidence that the collapse of communism and the disintegration of the Union of Soviet Socialist Republics in 1989 has led to a renewed emphasis on Russia's ties with the West. The celebration of the 300th anniversary of St. Petersburg in 2003 and the restoration of its original name in 1991 constitute one more episode in the effort to integrate Russia more fully into the West.

For Discussion

How did the founding of St. Petersburg contribute to the growth of the Russian state?

How did Peter the Great's absolute power facilitate the growth of the city?

A Picture of St. Petersburg (1815)
This view of St. Petersburg from the quay in front of the Winter Palace reveals the city's Western character. The buildings lying across the Neva River, including the bourse, were designed by European architects. The gondolas, seen in the foreground docking at the quay, enhanced St. Petersburg's reputation as "Venice of the North."

monarchies. Efforts to introduce absolutism in Russia had begun during the reigns of Alexis (r. 1645–1676) and Fedor (r. 1676–1682), who had achieved limited success in strengthening the central administration, controlling the nobility, and brutally suppressing peasant rebellions. Peter built upon his predecessors' achievement. He created an entirely new structure for managing the empire, appointing twelve governors to superintend Russia's forty-three separate provinces. He brought the Church under state control. By establishing a finely graded hierarchy of official ranks in the armed forces, the civil administration, and the court, Peter not only improved administrative efficiency but also made it possible for men of nonaristocratic birth to attain the same privileged status as the old landowning nobility. At the same time he won the support of all landowners by introducing primogeniture (inheritance of the entire estate by the eldest son), which prevented their estates from being subdivided, and supporting the enserfment of the peasants. In dealing with his subjects Peter claimed more power than any other absolute monarch in Europe. During the trial of his own son, Alexis, for treason in 1718, he told the clergy that "we have a sufficient and absolute power to judge our son for his crimes according to our own pleasure."[4]

The most visible sign of Peter's policy of westernization was the construction of the port city of St. Petersburg on the Gulf of Finland, which became the new capital of the Russian Empire. One of the main objectives of Russian foreign policy during Peter's reign had been to secure access to the Baltic Sea, allowing Russia to open maritime trade with Europe and to become a Western naval power. By draining a swamp on the estuary of the Neva River, Peter laid the foundations of a city that became the new capital of his empire. Construction began in 1703, and within twenty years St. Petersburg had a population of 40,000 people. With his new capital city now looking westward, and an army and central administration reformed on the basis of Prussian and French example, Peter could enter the world of European diplomacy and warfare as both a Western and an absolute monarch.

Resistance to Absolutism in England and the Dutch Republic

■ Why did absolutism fail to take root in England and the Dutch Republic during the seventeenth century?

The kingdom of England and the northern provinces of the Netherlands stand out as the two great exceptions to the dominant pattern of political development in seventeenth-century Europe. Both of these countries successfully resisted the establishment of royal absolutism, and

neither underwent the rigorous centralization of power and the dynamic growth of the state that usually accompanied the establishment of absolutist rule. In England the encounter between the proponents and opponents of absolute monarchy was more pronounced than in any other European country. It resulted in the temporary destruction of the monarchy in 1649 and the establishment of parliamentary supremacy after the Glorious Revolution of 1688. In the northern provinces of the Netherlands, known as the Dutch Republic, an even more emphatic rejection of absolutism occurred. During their long struggle to win their independence from Spain, the Dutch established a republican, decentralized form of government, but that did not prevent them from acquiring considerable military strength and dominating the world's economy during the seventeenth century.

The English Monarchy

At various times in the seventeenth century English monarchs tried to introduce royal absolutism, but the political institutions and the political culture of the country stood as major obstacles to their designs. As early as the fifteenth century, the English writer and diplomat Sir John Fortescue (ca. 1395–1477) had celebrated England's parliamentary system of government by contrasting it with that of France, where he claimed the king could make laws by himself and impose his will on his subjects. Fortescue's treatise contributed to the pride Englishmen had in what they considered their distinctive set of political and legal traditions. The most important of these traditions was the making of law and the levying of taxes by the two Houses of Parliament, the House of Lords and the House of Commons, with the king holding the power to sign or veto the bills they passed.

In the early seventeenth century the perception began to arise, especially among certain members of the House of Commons, that this tradition of parliamentary government was under attack. The first Stuart king, James I (r. 1603–1625), who succeeded the last Tudor monarch, Elizabeth I, aroused some of these fears as early as 1604, when he called his first parliament. James thought of himself as an absolute monarch, and in a number of speeches and published works he emphasized the height of his independent royal power, which was known in England as the prerogative°. James also spoke often about his divine right to rule, and he claimed that the main function of Parliament was simply to give the king advice, rather than to make law. These statements had the effect of antagonizing members of Parliament, leading them to defend their privileges, including the right they claimed to discuss foreign policy and other affairs of state.

James believed that he was an absolute monarch, but he did not actually try to put his ideas into practice. For

DOCUMENT

James I on the Divine Right of Kings (1598)

example, he did not try to make laws or levy taxes without the consent of Parliament or deny men their legal rights, such as freedom from arbitrary imprisonment. The real political fireworks did not begin until James's son, Charles I (r. 1625–1649), succeeded him. Charles believed in absolutism every bit as much as his father, but unlike James, Charles actually put his theories into practice. His efforts to force his subjects to lend money to the government during a war with Spain (1625–1629) and his imprisonment of men who refused to make these loans led Parliament to pass the Petition of Right in 1628. This document declared boldly that subjects possessed fundamental rights that kings could not violate under any circumstances, even when the country was at war.

Charles consented to the Petition of Right, but when Parliament met again in 1629, further conflict between the king and certain members of the House of Commons developed over taxation and the king's religious policies. Charles had been collecting duties on exports without parliamentary approval since 1625. He had also begun to favor conservative clergymen known as Arminians, leading the more zealous English Protestants, the Puritans, to fear that the English Church was leaning in the direction of Catholicism or "popery." Faced with this opposition over constitutional and religious issues, Charles decided to dismiss this parliament and to rule indefinitely without calling another one.

This period of nonparliamentary government, known as the personal rule,° lasted until 1640. During these years Charles, unable to collect taxes by the authority of Parliament, used his prerogative to bring in new revenues, especially by asking all subjects to pay "ship-money" to support the outfitting of ships to defend the country against attack. During the personal rule the king's religious policy fell under the control of William Laud, who was named archbishop of Canterbury in 1633 and who became one of the king's main privy councilors. Laud's determination to restore many of the rituals associated with Roman Catholicism alienated large numbers of Puritans and led to a growing perception that members of the king's government were engaged in a conspiracy to destroy both England's ancient constitution and the Protestant religion.

This period of absolutism might have continued indefinitely if Charles had not once again been faced with the financial demands of war. In 1636 the king tried to introduce a new religious liturgy in his northern kingdom of Scotland. The liturgy included a number of rituals that the firmly Calvinist Scottish population considered popish. The new liturgy so angered a group of women in Edinburgh that they threw their chairs at the bishop when he introduced it. In response to this affront to their religion, the Scots signed a National Covenant (1638) pledging themselves to defend the integrity of their Church, abolished episcopacy (government of the church by bishops) in favor of a Presbyterian system of church government, and mobi-

The English House of Commons in 1604
The men elected to sit in the House of Commons were known as Members of Parliament or MPs. In the early seventeenth century many of these men claimed that King James I was denying them their ancient privileges and liberties, including freedom of speech. They also objected to the claims of James that he was an absolute monarch.

lized a large army. To secure the funds to fight the Scots, Charles was forced to summon his English Parliament, thereby ending the period of personal rule.

The English Civil Wars and Revolution

Tensions between the reconvened English Parliament and Charles led to the first revolution of modern times. The Short Parliament, called in April 1640, lasted only two months, but a Scottish military victory against the English in that year forced the king to call a second parliament. The Long Parliament, which met in November 1640, impeached many of the king's ministers and judges and dismantled the judicial apparatus of the eleven years of personal rule, including the courts that had been active in the prosecution of Puritans. Parliament declared the king's nonparliamentary taxes illegal and enacted a law limiting the time between the meetings of Parliament to three years.

This legislation did not satisfy the king's critics in Parliament. Their suspicion that the king was conspiring against them and their demand to approve all royal appointments created a poisoned political atmosphere in which neither side trusted the other. After the king and his armed guards forced their way into the House of Commons to arrest five members for treason, there was little hope of reconciliation. In August 1642 civil war began between the Parliamentarians, known as Roundheads because many of the artisans who supported them had close-cropped hair styles, and the Royalists or Cavaliers, who often wore their hair in long flowing locks. Parliament, which was supported by the Scots and which benefited from the creation in 1645 of a well-trained, efficient fighting force, the New Model Army, ultimately won this war in 1646 and took Charles prisoner. The king's subsequent negotiations with the Scots and the English Presbyterians, both of whom had originally fought against him, led to a second civil war in 1648. In this war, which lasted only a few months, the New Model Army once again defeated Royalist forces.

This military victory led to a series of revolutionary changes in the English system of government. Believing with some justification that Charles could never be trusted, and eager to bring about an end to years of political uncertainty, members of the army purged Parliament of its Presbyterian members, leaving only a small group of Independents. These men, who favored a form of church government in which the congregations had a high degree of autonomy, had broken off negotiations with Charles I. The remaining members of Parliament were known as the Rump, because they were all that was left of the Long Parliament elected in 1640. This small group of Independents in Parliament, following the wishes of the army, set up a court to try Charles in January 1649. The trial resulted in Charles's conviction and execution, and shortly thereafter the Rump destroyed the House of Lords and the monarchy itself. As Parliament had already abolished the episcopal structure of the English Church in 1646, these actions completed a genuine revolution, a political transformation that destroyed the very system of government and replaced it with new institutions.

The revolution resulted in the establishment of a republic, in which the House of Commons possessed supreme legislative power in the name of the people of England. This change in the system of government, however, did not lead to the introduction of a more democratic form of government. A government of this sort, in which a very large percentage of the adult male population would be allowed to vote, was the goal of a political party, the Levellers, which originated in the New Model Army and attracted consider-

CHRONOLOGY

A Century of Revolution in England and Scotland

1603	James VI of Scotland (r. 1567–1625) becomes James I of England (r. 1603–1625)
1625	Death of James I and accession of Charles I (r. 1625–1649)
1628	Parliament passes the Petition of Right
1629–1640	Personal rule of Charles I
1638	Scots sign the National Covenant
1640	Opening of the Long Parliament
1642–1646	Civil War in England, ending with the capture of King Charles I
1648	Second Civil War; New Model Army defeats English Presbyterians and Scots
1649	Execution of Charles I of England and the beginning of the Republic
1653	End of the Long Parliament; beginning and dissolution of Barebones Parliament; Oliver Cromwell becomes Protector of England, Scotland, and Ireland
1660	Restoration of the monarchy in the person of Charles II; House of Lords and the Church of England also restored
1685	Death of Charles II and accession of his brother, James II (r. 1685–1688)
1688–1689	Glorious Revolution in England and Scotland
1707	England and Scotland politically joined to form the United Kingdom of Great Britain

able support in London and the towns. In 1647 at Putney Bridge, near London, the Levellers participated in a debate with more conservative army officers concerning the future constitution of the country. The spokesmen for the Levellers called for annual parliaments, the separation of powers between the executive and legislative branches of government, and the introduction of universal suffrage for men. The army officers argued against this proposed constitution, arguing that the vote should be entrusted only to men who owned property. The officers made sure that the Leveller program would not be accepted. The Levellers eventually mutinied in the army, their leaders were imprisoned, and the party collapsed.

The fate of the Levellers and their program underlines the fact that the English revolution was brought about by men of property, especially by the gentry or lesser aristocracy who sat in the House of Commons and who served as officers in the New Model Army. Although these men defeated and executed the king and secured the right to participate regularly in the governance of the kingdom, they

The Trial of Charles I

In January 1649, after the New Model Army had defeated Royalist forces in England's second civil war and purged Parliament of its Presbyterian members, the few remaining members of the House of Commons voted by a narrow margin to erect a High Court of Justice to try King Charles I. This trial, which resulted in Charles's execution, marked the only time in European history that a monarch was tried and executed while still holding the office of king.

The decision to try the king formed part of a deliberate political strategy. The men who arranged the proceeding knew that they were embarking upon a revolutionary course by declaring that the House of Commons, as the elected representative of the people, was the highest power in the realm. They also knew that the republican regime they were establishing did not command a large body of popular support. By trying the king publicly in a court of law and by ensuring that the trial was reported in daily newspapers (the first such trial in history), they hoped to prove the legitimacy of their cause and win support for the new regime.

The decision to bring the king to justice created two legal problems. The first was to identify a crime upon which the trial would be based. For many years members of Parliament had insisted that the king had violated the ancient laws of the kingdom. The charge read that he had "wickedly designed to erect an unlimited and tyrannical power" and had waged war against his people in two civil wars. His prosecutors claimed that those activities amounted to the crime of treason. The problem was that treason in England was a crime committed by a subject against the king, not by the king against his subjects. In order to try the king for this crime, his accusers had to construct a new theory of treason, according to which the king had attacked his own political body, which they identified with the kingdom or the state.

The second problem was to make the court itself a legitimate tribunal. According to English constitutional law, the king possessed the highest legal authority in the land. He appointed his judges, and the courts represented his authority. Parliament could vote to erect a special court, but the bill authorizing it would become law only if the king agreed to it. In this case the House of Commons had set up the court by its own authority, and it had named 135 men, most of whom were army officers, to serve as its judges. The revolutionary nature of this tribunal was difficult to disguise, and Charles made its illegality the basis of his defense. When asked how he would plead, he challenged the legitimacy of the court.

"By what power am I called hither?" he asked. "I would know by what authority—I mean lawful authority. There are many unlawful authorities in the world—thieves and robbers by the highways. And when I know what lawful authority, I shall answer. Remember I am your king, your lawful king. . . . I have a trust committed to me by God by old and lawful descent; I will not betray it to answer to a new unlawful authority."

By taking this position Charles put himself on the side of the law, and by refusing to enter a plea he also prevented his prosecutors from presenting the evidence against him.

The arguments that King Charles and John Bradshawe, the president of the court, presented regarding the legitimacy of the court reflected the main constitutional conflict in seventeenth-century England. On the one hand was the doctrine of divine-right absolutism, according to which the king received his authority from God. He was therefore responsible to God alone, not to the people. His subjects could neither try him in a court of law nor fight him on the battlefield. "A king," said Charles, "cannot be tried by any superior jurisdiction on earth." On the other hand was the doctrine of popular sovereignty, which held that political power came from the people. As Bradshawe said in response to Charles's objection, "Sir, as the law is your superior, so truly Sir, there is something that is superior to the law, and that is indeed the parent or author of law, and that is the people of England." This trial, therefore, involved not only a confrontation between Charles and his revolutionary judges but an encounter between two incompatible political ideologies.

In 1649 the advocates of popular sovereignty triumphed over those of divine right. Charles was convicted as a "tyrant, traitor, murderer, and public enemy of the good people of this nation." The verdict was never in doubt, although only 67 of the 135 men originally appointed as judges voted to convict the king, and a mere 59 signed the death warrant. The trial succeeded only to the extent that it facilitated the establishment of the new regime. With Charles gone, the Rump could move ahead with the abolition of the monarchy and the establishment of a republic. But in dramatic terms the trial was a complete failure. Charles, a small shy man with a nervous stammer, was expected to make a poor impression, but he spoke eloquently when he refused to plead, and he won support from spectators in the gallery. In the greatest show trial of the seven-

Trial of Charles I at Westminster Hall, January 1649
The king is sitting in the prisoner's box in the foreground, facing the commissioners of the High Court of Justice. His refusal to plead meant that a full trial could not take place.

teenth century, the royal defendant stole the show.

When Charles's son, Charles II, was restored to the throne in 1660, Royalists finally had their revenge against the judges of this court. Those who could be found alive were hanged, disemboweled, and quartered. For those who were already dead, there was to be another type of justice. In 1661 Royalists exhumed the badly decomposed corpses of Bradshawe, Henry Ireton, and Oliver Cromwell, the three men who bore the largest responsibility for the execution of the king. The three cadavers were hanged and their skulls were placed on pikes on top of Westminster Hall. This macabre ritual served as the Royalists' way of vilifying the memory of the judges of this illegal and revolutionary trial, and their unpardonable sin of executing an anointed king.

Questions of Justice

1. The men who brought King Charles to trial often spoke about bringing him to "justice." How is justice best understood in this context?
2. How does this trial reveal the limitations of divine-right absolutism in England?

Taking It Further

Peacey, Jason, ed. *The Regicides and the Execution of Charles I*. 2001. A collection of essays on various aspects of this episode and the men who signed the death warrant.

Wedgewood, C. V. *The Trial of Charles I*. 1964. Presents a full account and analysis of the trial by one of the great historical stylists of the twentieth century.

were also determined to keep political power in the hands of their own class.

The republican government established in 1649 did not last. Tension between the army and the Rump, fueled by the belief that the Rump was not creating a godly society, resulted in the army's dissolution of the Long Parliament in 1653 and the selection of a small parliament of zealous Puritans, nominated by the army. Known as the Barebones Parliament for one of its members, Praise-God Barebones, this assembly soon became hopelessly divided between radicals who wished to eliminate state support of the Church, the Court of Chancery, and the universities, and the moderates who opposed these measures. Unable to overcome its divisions, it too was dissolved after sitting for only five months.

At that point Oliver Cromwell (1599–1658), the commander in chief of the army and the most prominent member of the Council of State after 1649, had himself proclaimed Protector of England, Scotland, and Ireland.

IMAGE

Allegorical View of Cromwell as Savior of England

Cromwell had been a leader of the revolution, a zealous Puritan who had provided crucial support for the execution of the king and the establishment of the republic. At the same time, however, Cromwell feared that the Levellers and now the radical Puritans of the Barebones Parliament would destroy the social order. The establishment of the Protectorate, in which Cromwell shared legislative power with Parliament, represented an effort to return to a more traditional system of government. Cromwell would not, however, go so far as to accept a petition of 1657 to make him king. After Cromwell's death in 1658 and the brief rule of his son Richard, the Protectorate collapsed. A period of political instability, in which there was renewed hostility between the army and the members of Parliament, led the army to restore the monarchy in 1660.

Later Stuart Absolutism and the Glorious Revolution

Charles II (r. 1660–1685) and his brother James II (r. 1685–1688) were both absolutists who admired the political achievement of their cousin, Louis XIV of France. At the same time, however, they realized that they could never return to the policies of their father, much less adopt those of Louis. Neither of them attempted to rule indefinitely without Parliament, as Charles I had. Their main objective was to destroy the independence of Parliament by packing it with their own supporters and use the prerogative to weaken the force of the parliamentary statutes to which they objected.

The main political crisis of Charles II's reign was the attempt by a group of members of Parliament, headed by the Earl of Shaftesbury (1621–1683) and known by their

---

DOCUMENT

John Locke Justifies the Glorious Revolution

John Locke wrote Two Treatises of Government *between 1679 and 1682, during the reign of Charles II. The main purpose of the book was to justify armed resistance against Charles, who was pursuing absolutist policies, including attacks on the freedom of the English Parliament. Locke did not publish the* Two Treatises, *however, until after the Glorious Revolution of 1688. In order to justify that revolution, Locke wrote two new paragraphs, claiming that when a king abandons his responsibility to enforce the law, as James II had when he fled to France in December 1688, the government was dissolved and the people had the right to form a new one, as they had when they offered the crown to William and Mary in February 1689.*

There is one more way whereby such a government may be dissolved, and that is when he who has the supreme executive power neglects and abandons that charge, so that the laws already made can no longer be put in execution. This is demonstrably to reduce all to anarchy, and so effectually to dissolve the government. For laws not being made for themselves, but to be by their execution the

bonds of the society, to keep every part of the body politic in its due place and function, when that totally ceases, the government visibly ceases, and the people become a confused multitude, without order or connection. Where there is no longer the administration of justice, for the securing of men's rights, nor any remaining power within the community to direct the force, or provide for the necessities of the public, there is certainly no government left. Where the laws cannot be executed, it is all one as if there were no laws, and a government without laws is, I suppose, a mystery in politics, unconceivable to human capacity, and inconsistent with human society.

In these and in the like cases, when the government is dissolved, the people are at liberty to provide for themselves, by erecting a new legislative, differing from the other by the change of persons or form, or both, as they shall find it most for their safety and good. For the society can never, by the fault of another, lose the native and original right it has to preserve itself, which can only be done by a settled legislative and a fair and impartial execution of the laws made by it.

Source: From *Two Treatises of Government* by John Locke, 1698.

The House of Stuart
1603–1714

James I = Anne of Denmark
(r. 1603–1625) | (d. 1619)

Henry (d.1612) **Charles I** = Henrietta Maria Frederick V = Elizabeth the Winter Queen
(r. 1625–1649) | (d.1669)

Sophia = Ernst of Hanover

George I (r. 1714–1727)

Charles II = Catherine Mary = William II Anne Hyde = **James II** = Mary of Modena Henrietta = Philippe
(r. 1660–1685) of Braganza (d. 1660) of Orange (d. 1671) (r. 1685–1688) (d. 1670) duc d'Orleans

James Scott, Duke of **William III** = **Mary II** **Anne** James Edward
Monmouth, illeg. of Orange and (r. 1689–1694) (r. 1702–1714) (James III)
(exec. 1685) England The Old Pretender
(r. 1689–1702) (d. 1766)

Charles Edward
(Bonnie Prince Charlie)
(d. 1788)

opponents as Whigs, to exclude the king's brother, James, from the throne on the grounds that he was a Catholic. Charles opposed this strategy because it violated the theory of hereditary divine right, according to which God sanctioned the right of the king's closest heir to succeed him. Those members of Parliament who supported Charles on this issue, whom the Whigs called Tories, thwarted the designs of the Whigs in three successive parliaments between 1679 and 1681.

An even more serious political crisis occurred after James II succeeded to the throne in 1685. James began to exempt his fellow Catholics from the penal laws, which prevented them from worshiping freely, and from the Test Act of 1673, which had denied them the right to hold office under the crown. Catholics began to secure appointments in the army, the court, and local government. These efforts by the monarchy to grant toleration and political power to Catholics revived the traditional English fears of absolutism and popery. Not only the Whigs but also the predominantly Anglican Tories became alarmed at the king's policies. The birth of a Catholic son to James by his second wife, the Italian princess Mary of Modena, in June 1688 created the fear that the king's religious policy might be continued indefinitely. A group of seven Whigs and Tories, including the Bishop of London, drafted an invitation to William III of Orange, the captain-general of the military forces of the

Dutch Republic and James's nephew, to come to England to defend their Protestant religion and their constitution. William was married to James's eldest daughter, the Protestant Princess Mary, and as the king's nephew he also had a claim to the throne himself.

Invading with an international force of 12,000 men, William gathered substantial support from the English population, and when James's army defected, he was forced to flee to France without ever engaging William's forces in battle. The Convention, a special parliament convened by William in 1689, offered the crown to William and Mary while at the same time securing their assent to the Declaration of Rights, a document that later became the parliamentary statute known as the Bill of Rights. This bill, which is considered a cornerstone of the English constitution, corrected many of the abuses of royal power at the hands of James and Charles, especially the practice of exempting individuals from the penalties of the laws made by Parliament. By proclaiming William king and by excluding Catholics from the throne, the Bill of Rights also destroyed the theory of hereditary divine right.

It would be difficult to argue that this sequence of events, which is known as the Glorious Revolution, amounted to a revolution in the full sense of the word, because it did not change the basic institutions of English government. The revolution simply replaced one monarch with a king and queen who were more acceptable to the nation's political elite. But the events of 1688–1689 were decisive in defeating once and for all the absolutist designs of the Stuart kings and in guaranteeing that Parliament would form a permanent and regular place in English government. That Parliament has in fact met every year since 1689, and its legislative power grew considerably when the crown vetoed a bill for the last time in 1707.

For the English aristocracy, the peers and gentry who sat in Parliament, the revolution guaranteed that they would occupy a paramount position within English politics and society for more than a hundred years. The revolution also had profound effects on British and European diplomacy, as it quickly brought England and Scotland into a war against Louis XIV of France, the great antagonist of William III. The main reason William had come to England and secured the crown in the first place was to secure British entry into the European alliance he was building against France.

Even if the Glorious Revolution has been misnamed, it prompted the publication of a genuinely revolutionary political manifesto, John Locke's *Two Treatises of Government* (1690). Locke was a radical Whig; he had written the *Treatises* in the early 1680s as a protest against the absolutist policies of Charles II, but only after the abdication and flight of James II could he safely publish his manuscript. Like Hobbes, Locke argued that men left the state of nature and agreed to form a political society in order to protect their property and prevent the chaos that characterized a state of war. But unlike Hobbes, Locke asserted that the government they formed was based on trust and that governments that acted against the interests of the people could be dissolved. In these circumstances the people, in whom sovereignty was always vested, could establish a new regime. Locke's treatises constituted an uncompromising attack on the system of royal absolutism, which he equated with slavery. His work gave the people permission to take up arms against an oppressive regime even before that regime had consolidated its power. Since its publication, the *Two Treatises of Government* has been pressed into the service of various revolutionary and radical causes, most notably in the Declaration of Independence by the United States of America in 1776.

The Glorious Revolution had a direct bearing on the growth of the English state. As long as Parliament had remained suspicious of the Stuart kings, it had been reluctant to facilitate the growth of the state, which until 1688 was under direct royal control. Once the king's power had been permanently restricted, however, and Parliament had begun to emerge as the highest power within the country, Members of Parliament had less to fear from the executive branch of government. The inauguration of a long period of warfare against France in 1689 required the development of a large army and navy, the expansion of the bureaucracy, government borrowing on an unprecedented scale, and an increase in taxes. Members of Parliament, especially those in the Whig party, which had formed the main opposition to the monarchy before the revolution and had long opposed standing armies as a threat to English liberty, supported this expansion of the state as well as the war effort itself. By 1720 the kingdom of Great Britain, which had been created by the parliamentary union of England and Scotland in 1707, could rival the French state in military power, wealth, and diplomatic prestige. In fact, with its system of parliamentary government, Great Britain proved to be more successful than absolutist France in tapping the wealth of the people in the form of taxation to support its military establishment.

The Dutch Republic

In many respects the United Provinces of the Netherlands, known as the Dutch Republic, forms the most striking exception to the pattern of state building in seventeenth-century Europe. Formally established in 1588 during its revolt against Spanish rule, the Dutch Republic was the only major European power to maintain a republican form of government throughout the entire seventeenth century. As a state it also failed to conform to the pattern of centralization and consolidation that became evident in virtually all European monarchies. Having successfully resisted the centralizing policies of a large multinational Spanish monarchy, the Dutch Republic never acquired much of a centralized bureaucracy of its own. The provinces formed little more than a loose confederation of sovereign republican states. Each of the provinces sent deputies to the States General, where unanimity was required on all important issues, such as the levying of taxes, the declaration of war, and the ratification of treaties. Executive power was vested in a Council of State, which likewise consisted of deputies from the provinces. Even the individual provinces, the most important of which was Holland, were themselves decentralized, with the cities and rural areas sending delegates to a provincial assembly known as the States. Only the province of Holland invested one official, known as the grand pensionary, with extraordinary executive power.

This system of decentralized republican rule was much better suited for domestic affairs than the conduct of foreign policy. During most of the seventeenth century the Dutch were at war. After finally securing Spanish recognition of their independence by the Treaty of Münster in 1648, the Republic engaged in three commercial naval wars against England (1652–1654, 1665–1667, 1672–1674) and a much longer struggle against the territorial ambitions and economic policies of Louis XIV of France (1672–1678, 1689–1697, 1701–1713). The conduct of Dutch foreign policy and the coordination of the military forces of the seven provinces required some kind of central direction. During the 1650s John de Witt, the grand pensionary of Holland, assumed an informal presidency of the republic and directed the state's foreign policy in the first two wars against England. After 1672 William III, a prince of the hereditary house of Orange-Nassau, gave further unity and coordination to Dutch state policy. William, who served as the stadholder or governor of each of the seven provinces, became the captain-general of the republic's military forces when war with France began in 1672.

The House of Orange, which had a permanent vote in the States General, represented the royal, centralizing force within the Dutch Republic, and it led a party within the republic that favored a modification of republican rule. These princes never acquired the same type of constitutional authority that monarchs exercised in other European states. William III of Orange, who became William III of England and Scotland in 1689, exercised far more power in his new British kingdoms than he did in the Dutch Republic. Nevertheless the House of Orange played a crucial role in the rise of this tiny republic to the status of a world power. During the period of its influence the size of the Dutch military forces increased dramatically, from 50,000 men in 1670 to 73,000 in 1690 and 130,000 in 1710. During the same period of time the size of the Dutch navy doubled. In this one respect the republican, decentralized United Provinces participated in the same process of state building as the other great powers of Europe. The main reason the government was able to support this large standing army was the enormous wealth it had accumulated by virtue of the country's thriving international trade.

Political power in the Dutch Republic lay mainly with the wealthy merchants and bankers who served as regents in the councils of the towns. These same men represented the towns in the States of each province. The rural areas, which predominated only in the eastern provinces, were represented by the aristocracy. The country was therefore ruled by an oligarchy, but the men who belonged to it represented a predominantly urban, mercantile elite rather than a rural nobility. The members of this bourgeois elite did not tend to seek admission to landed society in the way that successful English merchants often did. Nor were they lured into becoming part of an ostentatious court in the manner of the French nobility. As men completely immersed in the world of commerce, they remained part of mercantile society and used their political power to guarantee that the Dutch state would serve the interests of trade.

The political prominence of Dutch merchants reflected the highly commercial character of the Dutch economy. Shortly after its truce with Spain in 1609, the Dutch cities, especially the rapidly expanding port city of Amsterdam in Holland, began to dominate European and world trade. The Dutch served as middlemen and shippers for all the other powers of Europe, transporting grain from the Baltic, textiles from England, timber from Scandinavia, wine from Germany, sugar from Brazil and Ceylon, silk from Persia and China, and porcelain from Japan to markets throughout the world. The Dutch even served as middlemen for their archenemy Spain, providing food and manufactured goods to the Spanish colonies in the New World in exchange for silver from the mines of Peru and Mexico. As part of this process Dutch trading companies, such as the Dutch East India Company, began to establish permanent outposts in India, Indonesia, North America, the Caribbean, South America, and South Africa. Thus a relatively small country, with one-tenth the population of France and one-third that of Great Britain, became a colonial power.

The Amsterdam Stock Exchange in 1668
Known as the Bourse, this multi-purpose building served as a gathering point for merchants trading in different parts of the world. The main activity was the buying and selling of shares of stock in trading companies during trading sessions that lasted for two hours each day.

To support their dynamic mercantile economy, Dutch cities developed financial institutions favorable to trade. An Exchange Bank in Amsterdam, which had a monopoly on the exchange of foreign currencies, allowed merchants to make international transactions by adding sums to or deducting sums from their accounts whenever they imported or exported goods. The Dutch also developed rational and efficient methods of bookkeeping. A stock market, also situated in Amsterdam, facilitated the buying and selling of shares in commercial ventures. Even lawyers contributed to these commercial enterprises. In *The Freedom of the Sea* (1609), the great legal and political philosopher Hugo Grotius (1583–1645) defended the freedom of merchants to use the open seas for trade and fishing, thereby challenging the claims of European monarchs who wished to exclude foreigners from the waters surrounding their countries. Grotius, who also wrote *The Law of War and Peace* (1625), gained a reputation as the father of modern international law.

One of the most striking contrasts between the Dutch Republic and the kingdom of France in the seventeenth century lay in the area of religious policy. Whereas in France the revocation of the Edict of Nantes represented the culmination of a policy enforcing religious uniformity and the suppression of Protestant dissent, the predominantly Calvinist Dutch Republic gained a reputation for religious toleration. The Dutch Reformed Church did not always deserve this reputation, but secular authorities, especially in the cities, proved remarkably tolerant of different religious groups. Amsterdam, which attracted a diverse immigrant population during its period of rapid growth, contained a large community of Jews, including the

philosopher Baruch Spinoza (1632–1677). The country became the center for religious exiles and political dissidents, accommodating French Huguenots who fled their country after the repeal of the Edict of Nantes in 1685 as well as English Whigs (including the Earl of Shaftesbury and John Locke) who were being pursued by the Tory government in the 1680s. In keeping with this Dutch tradition of toleration, Dutch courts became the first to stop the prosecution of witches, executing the last person for this crime in 1608.

This tolerant bourgeois republic also made a distinct contribution to European culture during the seventeenth century, known as its Golden Age. The Dutch cultural achievement was greatest in the area of the visual arts, where Rembrandt van Rijn (1606–1669), Franz Hals (ca. 1580–1666) and Jan Steen (1626–1679) formed only part of an astonishing concentration of artistic genius in the cities of Amsterdam, Haarlem, and Leiden. Dutch painting of this era reflected the religious, social, and political climate in which painters worked. The Protestant Reformation had brought an end to the tradition of didactic and devotional religious painting that had flourished during the Middle Ages, leading many Dutch artists to adopt more secular themes for their work. At the same time the absence of a baroque court culture, such as that which still flourished in Spain and France as well as in the Spanish Netherlands, reduced the demand for royal and aristocratic portraiture as well as for paintings of heroic classical, mythological, and historical scenes. Instead the Dutch artists of the Golden Age produced intensely realistic portraits of merchants and financiers, such as Rembrandt's famous *Syndics of the Clothmakers of Amsterdam* (1662).

Rembrandt, *Syndics of the Clothmakers of Amsterdam* (1662)
Rembrandt's realistic portrait depicted wealthy Dutch bourgeoisie, who had great political as well as economic power in the Dutch Republic.

Realism became one of the defining features of Dutch painting, evident in the numerous street scenes, still lifes, and landscapes that Dutch artists painted and sold to a largely bourgeois clientele. At the same time Dutch engravers perfected the art of political printmaking, much of it highly satirical, an achievement that was encouraged by the political tolerance of the country.

In the early eighteenth century the Dutch Republic lost its position of economic superiority to Great Britain and France, which developed even larger mercantile empires of their own and began to dominate world commerce. The long period of war against France, which ended in 1713, took its toll on Dutch manpower and wealth, and the relatively small size of the country and its decentralized institutions made it more difficult for it to recover its position in European diplomacy and warfare. As a state it could no longer fight above its weight, and it became vulnerable to attacks by the French in the nineteenth century and the Germans in the twentieth. But in the seventeenth century this highly urbanized and commercial country showed that a small, decentralized republic could hold its own with the absolutist states of France and Spain as well as with the parliamentary monarchy of England.

and in two states, England and the Dutch Republic, they ended in failure. Nevertheless, during the seventeenth and eighteenth centuries the absolutist state became the main form of government in the West. For this reason historians refer to the period of Western history beginning in the seventeenth century as the age of absolutism.

The third change was the conduct of a new style of warfare by Western absolutist states. The West became the arena where large armies, funded, equipped, and trained by the state, engaged in long, costly, and bloody military campaigns. The conduct of war on this scale threatened to drain the state of its financial resources, destroy its economy, and decimate its civilian and military population. Western powers were not unaware of the dangers of this type of warfare. The development of international law and the attempt to achieve a balance of power among European powers represented efforts to place restrictions on the conduct of seventeenth-century warfare. These efforts, however, were not completely successful, and in the eighteenth and nineteenth centuries warfare in the West entered a new and even more dangerous phase, aided by the technological innovations that the Scientific and Industrial Revolutions made possible. To the first of those great transformations, the revolution in science, we now turn.

Conclusion

The Western State in the Age of Absolutism

Between 1600 and 1715 three fundamental political changes, all related to each other, helped redefine the West. The first was the dramatic and unprecedented growth of the state. During these years all Western states grew in size and strength. They became more cohesive as the outlying provinces of kingdoms were brought more firmly under central governmental control. The administrative machinery of the state became more complex and efficient. The armies of the state could be called upon at any time to take action against internal rebels and foreign enemies. The income of the state increased as royal officials collected higher taxes, and governments became involved in the promotion of trade and industry and in the regulation of the economy. By the beginning of the eighteenth century one of the most distinctive features of Western civilization was the prevalence of these large, powerful, bureaucratic states. There was nothing like them in the non-Western world.

The second change was the introduction of royal absolutism into these Western states. From one end of the European continent to the other, efforts were made to establish the monarch as a ruler with complete and unrivaled power. These efforts achieved varying degrees of success,

Suggestions for Further Reading

For a comprehensive listing of suggested readings, please go to www.ablongman.com/levack2e/chapter15

Aylmer, G. E. *Rebellion or Revolution.* 1986. A study of the nature of the political disturbances of the 1640s and 1650s.

Beik, William. *Louis XIV and Absolutism: A Brief Study with Documents.* 2000. An excellent collection of documents.

Collins, James B. *The State in Early Modern France.* 1995. The best general study of the French state.

Elliott, J. H. *Richelieu and Olivares.* 1984. A comparison of the two contemporary absolutist ministers and state builders in France and Spain.

Harris, Tim. *Politics Under the Later Stuarts.* 1993. The best study of Restoration politics, including the Glorious Revolution.

Hughes, Lindsey. *Russia in the Age of Peter the Great.* 1998. A comprehensive study of politics, diplomacy, society, and culture during the reign of the "Tsar Reformer."

Israel, Jonathan. *The Dutch Republic: Its Rise, Greatness and Fall, 1477–1806.* 1996. A massive and authoritative study of the Dutch Republic during the period of its greatest global influence.

Lincoln, W. Bruce. *Sunlight at Midnight: St. Petersburg and the Rise of Modern Russia.* 2000. The best study of the building of Peter the Great's new capital city.

Parker, David. *The Making of French Absolutism.* 1983. A particularly good treatment of the early seventeenth century.

Parker, Geoffrey. *The Military Revolution.* 1988. Deals with the impact of the military revolution on the world as well as European history.

Rabb, Theodore K. *The Struggle for Stability in Early Modern Europe.* 1975. Employs visual as well as political sources to illustrate the way in which Europeans responded to the general crisis of the seventeenth century.

Schama, Simon. *The Embarrassment of Riches: An Interpretation of Dutch Culture in the Golden Age.* 1987. Contains a wealth of commentary on Dutch art and culture during its most influential period.

Wilson, Peter H. *Absolutism in Central Europe.* 2000. Analyzes both the theory and the practice of absolutism in Prussia and Austria.

Notes

1. Thomas Hobbes, *Leviathan,* ed. C. B. Macpherson (1968), 186.

2. Jean Bodin, *The Six Books of the Commonweale* (1606), Book II, Chapter 2.

3. Louis de Rouvroy, duc de Saint-Simon, *Memoirs of Louis XIV and the Regency* trans. Bayle St. John (1901) vol. 2, p. 11.

4. Quoted in Lindsey Hughes, *Russia in the Age of Peter the Great* (1998), 92.

The Scientific Revolution

16

N 1609 GALILEO GALILEI, AN ITALIAN MATHEMATICIAN AT THE UNIVERSITY OF Padua, introduced a new scientific instrument, the telescope, which revealed a wealth of knowledge about the stars and planets that filled the night skies. Having heard that a Dutch artisan had put together two lenses in such a way that magnified distant objects, Galileo built his own such device and directed it toward the heavens. Anyone who has looked through a telescope or seen photographs taken from a satellite can appreciate Galileo's excitement at what he saw. Objects that appeared one way to the naked eye looked entirely different when magnified by his new "spyglass," as he called it. The Milky Way, the pale glow that was previously thought to be a reflection of diffused light, turned out to be composed of a multitude of previously unknown stars. The surface of the moon, long believed to be smooth, uniform, and perfectly spherical, now appeared to be full of mountains, craters, and other irregularities. The sun, which was also supposed to be perfect in shape and composed of matter that could not be altered, was marred by spots that appeared to move across its surface. When turned toward Jupiter, the telescope revealed four moons never seen before. Venus, viewed over the course of many months, appeared to change its shape, much in the way that the moon did in its various phases. This latter discovery provided evidence for the relatively new theory that the planets, including Earth, revolved around the sun rather than the sun and the planets around the Earth.

Galileo shared the discoveries he made not only with fellow scientists but with other Europeans. In 1610 he published *The Starry Messenger,* a treatise in which he described his discovery of the new moons of Jupiter. Twenty-two years later he included the evidence he had gained from his telescope in another book, *Dialogue Concerning the Two Chief World Systems,* to support the claim that the Earth orbited the sun. He also staged a number of public demonstrations of his new astronomical instrument, the first of which took place on top of one of the city gates of Rome in 1611. To convince those who doubted the reality of the images they saw, Galileo turned

CHAPTER OUTLINE

- The Discoveries and Achievements of the Scientific Revolution

- The Search for Scientific Knowledge

- The Causes of the Scientific Revolution

- The Intellectual Effects of the Scientific Revolution

- Humans and the Natural World

The Telescope The telescope was the most important of the new scientific instruments that facilitated discovery. This engraving depicts an astronomer using the telescope in 1647.

the telescope toward familiar landmarks in the city. Interest in the new scientific instrument ran so high that a number of amateur astronomers acquired telescopes of their own.

Galileo's observations and discoveries formed one facet of the development that historians call the Scientific Revolution. A series of remarkable achievements in astronomy, physics, chemistry, and biology formed the centerpieces of this revolution, but its effects reached far beyond the observatories and laboratories of seventeenth-century scientists. The Scientific Revolution brought about fundamental changes in Western thought, altering the way in which Europeans viewed the natural world, the supernatural realm, and themselves. It stimulated controversies in religion, philosophy, and politics and brought about changes in military technology, navigation, and economic enterprise. The revolution added a new dimension to Western culture and provided a basis for claims of Western superiority over people in other lands. For all these reasons the Scientific Revolution marked a decisive turning point in the history of Western civilization, and it set the West apart from contemporary civilizations in the Middle East, Africa, and Asia.

The scientific culture that emerged in the West by the end of the seventeenth century was the product of a series of cultural encounters. It resulted from a complex interaction among scholars proposing different accounts of how nature operated. In some cases the scientists who advanced the revolutionary ideas were themselves influenced by ideas drawn from different cultural traditions. Some of these ideas had originated in Greek philosophy, while others came from orthodox Christian sources. Still other ideas came from a tradition of late medieval science, which had in turn been heavily influenced by the scholarship of the Islamic Middle East. A skeptical refusal to rely on any inherited authority whatsoever had its own religious and philosophical sources.

The main question this chapter seeks to answer is how European scientists in the sixteenth and seventeenth centuries changed the way in which people in the West viewed the natural world. Five specific questions, each of which will be addressed in a separate section of the chapter, will structure our exploration of this subject:

- **What were the scientific achievements and discoveries of the late sixteenth and seventeenth centuries that historians refer to as the Scientific Revolution?**
- **What methods did scientists use during this period to investigate nature, and how did they think nature operated?**
- **Why did the Scientific Revolution take place in western Europe at this particular time?**
- **How did the Scientific Revolution influence the development of philosophical and religious thought in the seventeenth and early eighteenth centuries?**
- **How did the Scientific Revolution change the way in which seventeenth- and eighteenth-century Europeans thought of their relationship to the natural world?**

The Discoveries and Achievements of the Scientific Revolution

■ **What were the scientific achievements and discoveries of the late sixteenth and seventeenth centuries that historians refer to as the Scientific Revolution?**

Unlike political revolutions, such as the English Revolution of the 1640s discussed in the last chapter, the Scientific Revolution developed gradually and over a long period of time. It began in the middle and later decades of the sixteenth century and continued into the early years of the eighteenth century. Even though it took a relatively long time to unfold, it was revolutionary in the sense that it brought about a radical transformation of human thought, just as political revolutions have produced fundamental changes in systems of government. The most important changes in seventeenth-century science took place in the fields of astronomy, physics, chemistry, and biology.

Astronomy: A New Model of the Universe

The most significant change in astronomy was the acceptance of the view that the sun, not the Earth, was the center of the universe. Until the middle of the sixteenth century, most natural philosophers—as scientists were known at the time—subscribed to the writings of the Greek astronomer Claudius Ptolemy (100–170 C.E.). Ptolemy's observations and calculations had given considerable support to the cosmology° (a theory regarding the structure and nature of the universe) proposed by the Greek philosopher Aristotle (384–322 B.C.E.). According to Ptolemy and Aristotle, the center of the universe was a stationary Earth, around which the moon, the sun, and the other planets revolved in circular orbits. Beyond the planets a large sphere carried the stars, which stood in a fixed relationship to each other, around the Earth from east to west once every twenty-four hours, thus accounting for the rising and setting of the stars. Each of the four known elements—earth, water, air, and fire—had a natural place within this universe, with the heavy elements, earth and water, being pulled down toward the center of the Earth and the light ones, air and fire, hovering above it. All heavenly bodies, including the sun and the planets, were composed of a fifth element, called ether, which unlike matter on Earth was thought to be eternal and could not be altered, corrupted, or destroyed.

This traditional view of the cosmos had much to recommend it, and some educated people continued to subscribe to it well into the eighteenth century. The authority

(a)   (b)

Two Views of the Ptolemaic or Pre-Copernican Universe

(a) In this sixteenth-century engraving the Earth lies at the center of the universe and the elements of water, air, and fire are arranged in ascending order above the Earth. The orbit that is shaded in black is the firmament or stellar sphere. The presence of Christ and the saints at the top reflects the view that Heaven lay beyond the stellar sphere. (b) A medieval king representing Atlas holds a Ptolemaic cosmos. The Ptolemaic universe is often referred to as a two-sphere universe: The inner sphere of the Earth lies at the center and the outer sphere encompassing the entire universe rotates around the Earth.

of Aristotle, predominant in late medieval universities, was reinforced by the Bible, which in a few passages referred to the motion of the sun. The motion of the sun could be confirmed by simple human observation. We do, after all, see the sun "rise" and "set" every day, while the idea that the Earth rotates at a high speed and revolves around the sun contradicts the experience of our senses. Nevertheless, the Earth-centered model of the universe failed to provide an explanation for many patterns that astronomers observed in the sky, most notably the paths followed by planets. In the sixteenth century natural philosophers began to consider alternative models of the universe.

The first major challenge to the Ptolemaic system came from a Polish cleric, Nicolaus Copernicus (1473–1543), who in 1543 published *The Revolutions of the Heavenly Spheres,* in which he proposed that the center of the universe was not the Earth but the sun. The book was widely circulated, but it did not win much support for the sun-centered theory of the universe. The mathematical arguments Copernicus presented in the book were so abstruse

DOCUMENT

Nicolaus Copernicus, *On the Revolution of Heavenly Spheres* (1500s)

that only the most erudite astronomers could understand them. Even those who could appreciate his detailed plotting of planetary motion were not prepared to adopt the central thesis of his book. In the late sixteenth century the great Danish astronomer Tycho Brahe (1546–1601) accepted the argument of Copernicus that the planets revolved around the sun but still insisted that the sun continued to revolve around the Earth.

Significant support for the Copernican model of the universe among scientists began to materialize only in the seventeenth century. In 1609 a German astronomer, Johannes Kepler (1571–1630), using data that Brahe had collected, confirmed the central position of the sun in the universe. In his treatise *New Astronomy,* Kepler also demonstrated that the planets, including the Earth, followed elliptical rather than circular orbits and that the planets moved in accordance with a series of physical laws. Kepler's book, however, did not reach a large audience, and his achievement was not fully appreciated until many decades later.

Galileo Galilei (1564–1642) was far more successful than Kepler in gaining support for the sun-centered model of the universe. In some respects Galileo was more conservative than Kepler. For example, Galileo never took issue with the traditional idea that the planets followed circular orbits. But Galileo had the literary skill, lacking in Kepler, of being able to write for a broad audience. Using the evidence gained from his observations with the telescope, and presenting his views in the form of a dialogue between the advocates of the two competing worldviews,

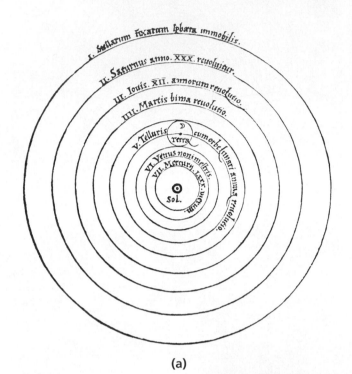

(a)

Two Early Modern Views of the Sun-Centered Universe

(a) The depiction by Copernicus. Note that all the orbits are circular, rather than elliptical, as Kepler was to show they were. The outermost sphere is that of the fixed stars. (b) A late-seventeenth-century depiction of the cosmos by Andreas Cellarius in which the planets follow elliptical orbits. It illustrates four different positions of the Earth as it orbits the sun.

(b)

he demonstrated the plausibility and superiority of Copernicus's theory.

The publication of Galileo's *Dialogue Concerning the Two Chief World Systems—Ptolemaic and Copernican* in 1632 won many converts to the sun-centered theory of the universe, but it lost him the support of Pope Urban VIII, who had been one of his patrons. Urban believed that by naming the character in *Dialogue* who defended the Ptolemaic system Simplicio (that is, a simple person), he was mocking the pope himself. In the following year Galileo was tried before the Roman Inquisition, an ecclesiastical court whose purpose was to maintain theological orthodoxy. The charge against him was that he had challenged the authority of Scripture and was therefore guilty of heresy, the denial of the theological truths of the Roman Catholic Church. (See "Justice in History: The Trial of Galileo" later in this chapter.)

As a result of this trial Galileo was forced to abandon his support for the Copernican model of the universe, and *Dialogue* was placed on the Index of Prohibited Books, a list compiled by the papacy of all printed works containing heretical ideas. Despite this setback, support for Copernicanism grew during the seventeenth century, and by 1700 it commanded widespread support among scientists and the educated public. *Dialogue*, however, was not removed from the Index until 1822.

Physics: The Laws of Motion and Gravitation

Galileo made his most significant contributions to the Scientific Revolution in the field of physics, which deals with matter and energy and the relationship between them. In the seventeenth century the main branches of physics were mechanics (the study of motion and its causes) and optics (the study of light). Galileo's most significant achievement in physics was to formulate a set of laws governing the motion of material objects. His work, which laid the foundation of modern physics, effectively challenged the theories of Aristotle regarding motion.

According to Aristotle, whose views dominated science in the late Middle Ages, the motion of every object except the natural motion of falling toward the center of the Earth required another object to move it. If the mover stopped, the object fell to the ground or simply stopped moving. One of the problems with this theory was that it could not account for the continued motion of a projectile, such as a discus or a javelin, after it left the hand of the person who threw it. Galileo's answer to that

question was a theory of inertia, which became the basis of a radical new theory of motion. According to Galileo, an object continues to move or to lie at rest until something external to it intervenes to change its motion. Thus motion is neither a quality inherent in an object nor a force that it acquires from another object; it is simply a state in which the object finds itself.

Galileo also discovered that the motion of an object occurs only in relation to things that do not move. A ship moves through the water, for example, but the goods carried by that ship do not move in relationship to the moving ship. This insight served the immediate purpose of explaining to the critics of Copernicus how the Earth can move even though we do not experience its motion. Galileo's most significant contribution to the study of mechanics was his formulation of a mathematical law of motion that explained how the speed and acceleration of a falling object are determined by the distance it travels during equal intervals of time.

The greatest achievements of the Scientific Revolution in physics belong to English scientist Sir Isaac Newton (1642–1727). Newton was one of those rare geniuses whose research changed the way future generations viewed the world. As a boy Newton found himself out of place while working on his mother's farm in a small hamlet in

CHRONOLOGY

Discoveries of the Scientific Revolution

1543	Andreas Vesalius publishes *On the Fabric of the Human Body,* the first realistic depiction of human anatomy; Copernicus publishes *The Revolutions of the Heavenly Spheres,* challenging the traditional Earth-centered cosmos
1609	Johannes Kepler publishes *New Astronomy,* identifying elliptical orbits of the planets
1628	William Harvey publishes *On the Motion of the Heart and Blood in Animals,* demonstrating the circulation of the blood
1632	Galileo publishes *Dialogue Concerning the Two Chief World Systems,* leading to his trial
1638	Galileo publishes *Discourses on the Two New Sciences of Motion and Mechanics,* proposing new laws of motion
1655	Evangelista Torricelli conducts experiments on atmospheric pressure
1659	Robert Boyle invents the air pump and conducts experiments on the elasticity and compressibility of air
1673	Christian Huygens publishes *On the Motion of Pendulums,* developing his theories of gravitation and centrifugal force
1687	Newton publishes his *Mathematical Principles of Natural Philosophy,* presenting a theory of universal gravitation

The Human Body in History

Dissecting the Human Corpse

As medical science developed in the sixteenth and seventeenth centuries, the dissection of human corpses became a standard practice in European universities and medical schools. Knowledge of the structure and composition of the human body, which was central to the advancement of physiology, could best be acquired by cutting open a corpse to reveal the organs, muscles, and bones of human beings. The practice reflected the emphasis scientists placed on observation and experimentation in conducting scientific research. In the sixteenth century the great Flemish physiologist Andreas Vesalius (1514–1564), who published the first realistic drawings of human anatomy in 1543, cut limbs and extracted organs in his lectures on anatomy at the University of Padua. A century later, the English physician William Harvey dissected human cadavers in his path-breaking study of the circulation of the blood.

The physicians who performed dissections had difficulty securing an adequate supply of corpses. A preference developed for the bodies of recently hanged criminals, mainly because rulers claimed jurisdiction over the bodies of the condemned and could dispose of them at will. Criminals, moreover, were generally young or middle-aged and in fairly good health, thus making them desirable specimens for dissection. Demand for corpses became so great in the late seventeenth and eighteenth centuries that surgeons were willing to pay a price for them, thus turning the dead human body into a commodity. In eighteenth-century England the demand for bodies of the hanged often resulted in brawls between the agents whom the surgeons paid to snatch the bodies from the scaffold and the relatives and friends of the deceased, who wanted to claim the corpses in order to guarantee a decent burial.

During the sixteenth and seventeenth centuries, dissection underwent two transformations. The first was the expansion of the audience from a small group of medical students to a large cross-section of scholars who attended in order to learn more about the relationship between human beings and the natural world. The audiences also began to include artists, who learned from these exercises how to depict the human body more accurately. The second change was the transformation of dissection into a public spectacle, controlled by municipal authorities. During the seventeenth century, the city of Bologna staged dissections every year before crowds of as many as 200 people.

To these public dissections, which took place in many other European cities, people from the lower classes were often admitted together with scholars, students, and artists. The uneducated men and women who attended were attracted by the entertaining aspects of the event and the eagerness to witness the violence done to the corpse, just as they were at public executions. They were particularly eager to see the dissection of the genital organs, so much so that some authorities restricted access to that part of the dissection in the interest of public decency.

The holding of public anatomy lessons had much less to do with the popularization of science than with the satisfaction of the popular taste for blood and sex. Only in the late eighteenth century, during the age of the Enlightenment, did a new sensitivity to blood and human torment and an unprecedented repugnance toward death bring about an end to public dissections, together with the public executions with which they were closely associated.

For Discussion

What interests were served by holding public dissections of human corpses in the seventeenth and eighteenth centuries?

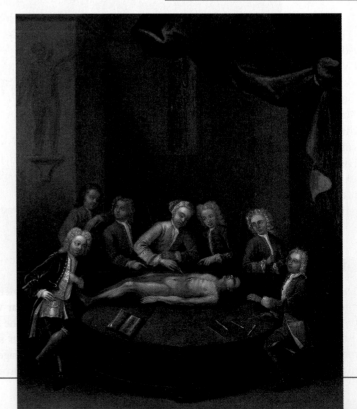

Dissection
The English surgeon William Cheselden giving an anatomical demonstration to spectators in London ca. 1735.

expressed their theories in mathematical terms, and argued that nature operated like a machine. Taken together, these common features of scientific research ultimately defined a distinctly Western approach to solving scientific problems.

Observation and Experimentation

The most prominent feature of scientific research in sixteenth- and seventeenth-century Europe was the extensive observation of nature, combined with the testing of hypotheses by means of rigorous experimentation. This was primarily a process of induction°, in which theories emerged only after the systematic accumulation and analysis of large amounts of data. It assumed a willingness to abandon all preconceived notions, whether they were those of Aristotle, Galen, or medieval philosophers, and to base scientific conclusions on experience and observation.

The English philosopher Francis Bacon (1561–1626) promoted this empirical, experimental approach in his book *New Organon* (1620), in which he complained that all previous scientific endeavors, especially those of ancient Greek philosophers, relied too little on experimentation. By contrast, Bacon's approach involved the thorough and systematic investigation of nature, a process that Bacon, who was a lawyer and judge, compared to the interrogation of a person suspected of committing a crime. Bacon claimed that scientific experimentation was "putting nature to the question" in order to obtain the truth, a phrase that referred to questioning a prisoner under torture to determine the facts of a case.

Francis Bacon, *Novum Organum* (1620)

All the great scientists of the sixteenth and seventeenth centuries abandoned preconceived notions and based their theories on the facts of nature, but the most enthusiastic practitioners of carefully planned and controlled experimentation came from England. Two of its most tireless advocates were Boyle, who performed a succession of experiments with an air pump to prove the existence of a vacuum, and Robert Hooke, whose experiments with a pendulum provided one of the foundations for Newton's theory of universal gravitation. Harvey belongs to the same English experimental tradition, although his commitment to this methodology originated at the University of Padua. Galileo and some other Italian scientists matched the English in their insistence on experimentation, but Galileo's experiments were designed more to demonstrate the validity of his theories than to help him establish them in the first place.

Deductive Reasoning

The second feature of sixteenth- and seventeenth-century scientific research was the application of deductive reasoning to scientific problems. Unlike the inductive experimental approach, which found its most enthusiastic practitioners in England, the deductive approach had its most zealous advocates on the European continent. The men who took this approach were just as determined as Bacon and Boyle to replace the testimony of human authorities with what they discovered from nature itself. Their main method, however, was to establish basic scientific truths or propositions from which other ideas or laws could be deduced logically. The French philosopher and mathematician René Descartes (1596–1650) became the champion of this methodology. In his *Discourse on the Method* (1637) he recommended that in solving any intellectual problem a person should first establish fundamental principles or truths and then proceed deductively from those ideas to more specific conclusions.

The model for deductive reasoning was mathematics, in which one also moves logically from certain premises to conclusions by means of equations. Rational deduction° proved to be an essential feature of scientific methodology, although some scientists relied too heavily on it at the expense of a more experimental approach. The limitations of an exclusively deductive approach became apparent when Descartes and his followers deduced a theory of gravitation from the principle that objects could influence each other only if they actually touched. The theory, as well as the principle upon which it was based, lacked an empirical foundation, which is one based on observation and experience, and eventually had to be abandoned.

Mathematics and Nature

The third feature of scientific research in the sixteenth and seventeenth centuries was the application of mathematics to the study of the physical world. The mathematical treatment of nature was undertaken by scientists working in both the experimental and the deductive traditions. Descartes shared with Galileo, Kepler, and Huygens the conviction that nature had a geometrical structure and that it could therefore be understood in mathematical terms. The physical dimensions of matter, which Descartes claimed were its only properties, could of course be expressed mathematically. Galileo claimed that mathematics was the language in which philosophy was written in "the book of the universe."

This mathematical way of looking at the physical world had a long history. The Greek philosophers Pythagoras (582–507 B.C.E.) and Plato (ca. 428–348 B.C.E.) had both emphasized the geometric structure of the cosmos and therefore considered numbers to hold the key to its secrets. In the fifteenth century Renaissance philosophers revived this ancient Greek emphasis on mathematics. Copernicus, who was influenced by Platonic thought, criticized the Islamic and western European medieval philosophers who had accepted an Earth-centered universe for their mathematical miscalculations. Copernicus advocated a rigorous application of mathematics to astronomical writing. One of the reasons his book *The Revolutions of the Heavenly Spheres* was so demanding was that he described planetary motion in technical, mathematical terms.

In the seventeenth century Isaac Newton's work provides the best illustration of the application of mathematics to scientific problems. Newton used observation and experimentation to confirm his theory of universal gravitation, but the work in which he presented his theory, *Mathematical Principles of Natural Philosophy,* was written in the language of mathematics. Just as Newton had synthesized previous work in physics to arrive at the law of universal gravitation, he also combined the experimental and deductive approaches to acquire scientific truth. His approach to solving scientific problems, which became a model for future scientific research, involved generalization on the basis of particular examples derived from experiments and the use of deductive, mathematical reasoning to discover the laws of nature.

The Mechanical Philosophy

Much of the scientific experimentation and deduction undertaken in the seventeenth century proceeded on the assumption that the natural world operated as if it were a machine made by a human being. This philosophy of nature, which is often referred to as the mechanical philosophy°, cannot be attributed to a single person, but its most comprehensive statement can be found in the work of Descartes. The scholastic philosophers of the fourteenth and fifteenth centuries insisted that nature was fundamentally different from a machine or any other object built by humans. According to the scholastics, natural bodies had an innate tendency to change, whereas artificial objects, that is, those constructed by humans, did not. Descartes, Kepler, Galileo, and Bacon all denied that assumption, arguing that nature operated in a mechanical way, just like a clock or some other piece of machinery. The only difference was that we cannot readily observe the structures of natural mechanisms, in the way that we can see the structure of a pump or a wagon.

According to mechanists—scientists who subscribed to the mechanical philosophy—nature consisted of many machines, some of them extremely small. The human body was itself a machine, and the center of that human machine, the heart, was in Harvey's words "a piece of machinery in which, though one wheel gives motion to another, yet all the wheels seem to move simultaneously." Because the human body was made by God, it was superior to any human-made machine, but it was still nothing more than a machine.

According to Descartes, the only part of a human being that was not a machine was the mind, which was completely different from the body and the rest of the material world. Unlike the body, the mind was an immaterial substance that could be neither extended in space nor divided. Nor could it

be measured mathematically, in the way one could record the dimensions of the human body. Because Descartes made this sharp distinction between the mind and the human body, we speak of his philosophy as being dualistic°.

The mechanical philosophy presented just as bold a challenge to the philosophers known as Neoplatonists° as it did to the scholastics. Neoplatonists were inspired by the work of Plotinus (205–270 C.E.), the last great philosopher of antiquity who had synthesized the work of Plato with that of other Greek philosophers. Plotinus also drew on many traditions of ancient Persian religion. Neoplatonic thought experienced a revival in the fifteenth and sixteenth centuries at the time of the Renaissance (see Chapter 11). Neoplatonists believed that the natural world was animistic—that is, it possessed a soul (known to them as a world soul) and was charged with various occult forces and spirits. The English natural philosopher William Gilbert (1544–1603), who wrote extensively on the phenomenon of magnetism, adopted a Neoplatonic worldview when he declared that the Earth and other planets were actually alive. Kepler clearly recognized the incompatibility of this outlook with that of the mechanical philosophy when he insisted that "the machine of the universe is not similar to a divine animated being but similar to a clock."[1]

René Descartes
Although Descartes was a scientist who made contributions to the study of biology and optics, he is best known for the method he proposed to attain certain knowledge and his articulation of the mechanical philosophy.

Descartes and other mechanists argued that matter was completely inert or dead. It had neither a soul nor any innate purpose. Its only property was extension, or the physical dimensions of length, width, and depth. Without a spirit or any other internal force directing its action, matter simply responded to the power of the other bodies with which it came in contact. According to Descartes, all physical phenomena could be explained by reference to the dimensions and the movement of particles of matter. He once claimed, "Give me extension and motion and I will construct the universe."[2] Even the human body contained no "vital spirits." It consisted only of flesh and the blood pumped by the mechanism of the heart. The only difference between the human body and other machines was that the mind (or soul) could move it, although how it did so was a matter of great controversy, as we shall see in a later section.

The view of nature as a machine implied that it operated in a regular, predictable way in accordance with unchanging laws of nature. Scientists could use reason to discover what those laws were and thus learn how nature performed under any circumstances. The scientific investigations of Galileo and Kepler were based on those assumptions, and Descartes made them explicit. The immutability of the laws of nature implied that the entire universe was uniform in structure, an assumption that underlay Newton's formulation of the laws of motion and of universal gravitation. Newton's theory of gravity denied Descartes's view of matter as inert, but he nonetheless accepted his view that the universe operated like a machine.

The Causes of the Scientific Revolution

■ Why did the Scientific Revolution take place in western Europe at this particular time?

Why did the Scientific Revolution take place at this particular time, and why did it originate in western European countries? What prompted natural philosophers in Italy, France, England, and the Dutch Republic to develop new ways of looking at the world? There are no simple answers to these questions. We can, however, identify a number of developments that inspired this remarkable set of scientific discoveries. Some of these developments were internal to science, in the sense that they arose out of earlier investigations conducted by natural philosophers in the late Middle Ages, the Renaissance, and the sixteenth century. Others were external to the development of science, arising out of the religious, political, social, and economic life of Europe during the early modern period.

Developments Within Science

The three internal causes of the Scientific Revolution were the research into motion conducted by scholastic natural philosophers in the fourteenth century, the scientific investigations conducted by humanists at the time of the Renaissance, and the collapse of the dominant conceptual frameworks that had governed scientific inquiry and research for centuries.

Late Medieval Science

Modern science can trace some of its origins to the fourteenth century, when the first significant modifications of Aristotle's scientific theories began to emerge. These challenges came not only from theologians, who objected that Aristotle was a pagan philosopher, but from natural philosophers, who refined some of the basic ideas of Aristotle's physics.

The most significant of these refinements was the theory of impetus. Aristotle, as we have seen, had argued that an object would stop as soon as it lost contact with the object that moved it. The scholastic philosophers who modified this principle claimed that objects in motion acquire a force that stays with them after they lose contact with the mover. The theory of impetus did not bring about a full-scale demolition of Aristotle's mechanics, but it did begin to call Aristotle's authority into question. The theory of impetus was known in Galileo's day, and it influenced some of his early thought on motion.

Scholastic philosophers of the fourteenth century also began to recommend direct, empirical observation in place of the traditional scholastic tendency to accept preconceived theories regarding the operation of nature. This approach to answering scientific questions did not result in the type of rigorous experimentation that Bacon demanded three centuries later, but it did encourage scientists to base their theories on the facts that emerged from an empirical study of nature.

The contribution of late medieval science to the Scientific Revolution should not be exaggerated. Scholastic natural philosophers continued to accept the cosmology of Ptolemy. They still perpetuated the anatomical theories of Galen. The restraints that theology exercised over scientific thought in the Middle Ages also prevented the emergence of new scientific ideas.

Renaissance Science

Natural philosophers during the Renaissance made more tangible contributions to the rise of modern science than the scholastics of the late Middle Ages. Renaissance natural philosophers made those contributions despite the fact that the Renaissance, the revival of classical antiquity in the fifteenth and sixteenth centuries, was not conducive to the type of scientific research that Galileo, Descartes, Boyle, and Newton conducted. Renaissance humanism was mainly a literary and artistic movement, and humanists were not particularly interested in scientific knowledge. Humanism also cultivated a tradition of deferring to the superior wisdom of classical authors, whereas the new science defined itself largely in opposition to the theories of the ancients, especially Aristotle, Ptolemy, and Galen. The main philosophical movement of the Renaissance, moreover, was Neoplatonism, which, as we have seen, promoted an animistic view of nature that mechanists such as Descartes and Kepler rejected.

The natural philosophers of the Renaissance did nonetheless make a number of important contributions to the birth of modern science. Many of the discoveries of the late sixteenth and seventeenth centuries drew their inspiration from Greek scientific works that had been recovered in their original form during the Renaissance. Copernicus found the original idea of his sun-centered universe in the writings of Aristarchus of Samos, a Greek astronomer of the third century B.C.E. whose work had been unknown during the Middle Ages. The theory that matter was divisible into small measurable particles known as atoms was inspired at least in part by the recovery of the texts of the ancient philosophers, most notably Democritus, who flourished around 480 B.C.E. Sixteenth-century editions of the works of Archimedes (287–212 B.C.E.), which had been virtually unknown in the Middle Ages, stimulated interest in the science of mechanics. The recovery and translation of previously unknown texts also made scientists aware that Greek scientists did not always agree with each other and thus provided a stimulus to independent observation and experimentation as a means of resolving their differences.

The Renaissance philosophy of Neoplatonism, despised by mechanists, also played an important role in the Scientific Revolution. In addition to the belief that the natural world had a soul, Neoplatonists adopted a geometric view of the universe and therefore encouraged the application of mathematics to the study of the natural world. Kepler developed his third law of planetary motion by applying to the cosmos the Neoplatonic idea of a harmony between numbers. The Neoplatonic tendency to think in terms of large, general categories also encouraged scientists such as Kepler, Galileo, and Newton to discover universal laws of nature. Even alchemy, which many Neoplatonists practiced during the Renaissance, involved natural philosophers in experiments that gave them a limited sense of control over the operations of nature. The followers of Paracelsus, whose alchemy was tinged with Neoplatonic mysticism, were firm advocates of the observation of nature and experimentation.

Some of the most prominent natural philosophers of the seventeenth century were influenced to some extent by the cultural traditions that we associate with the Renaissance. Kepler became involved in the study of magic at the court of the Holy Roman Emperor Rudolf II. From his reading in Neoplatonic sources, Kepler acquired his belief that the universe was constructed according to geometric principles.

DOCUMENT

Copernicus Proposes His Sun-Centered Theory of the Universe

In the dedication of his book On the Revolution of the Heavenly Spheres *(1543) to Pope Paul III, Copernicus explains that in his search for an orderly model of the universe he drew inspiration from a few ancient philosophers who had imagined that the Earth moved. He then explained how he had bolstered his theory through long and frequent observations. Anticipating condemnation from those who based their astronomical theories on the Bible, he appeals to the pope for protection while showing contempt for the theories of his opponents.*

. . . I began to chafe that philosophers could by no means agree on any one certain theory of the mechanism of the Universe, wrought for us by a supremely good and orderly Creator . . . I therefore took pains to read again the works of all the philosophers on whom I could lay my hand to seek out whether any of them had ever supposed that the motions of the spheres were other than those demanded by the mathematical schools. I found first in Cicero that Hicetas had realized that the Earth moved. Afterwards I found in Plutarch that certain others had held the like opinion. . . .

Taking advantage of this I too began to think of the mobility of the Earth; and though the opinion seemed absurd, yet knowing now that others before me had been granted freedom to imagine such circles as they chose to explain the phenomena of the stars, I considered that I also might easily be allowed to try whether, by assuming some motion of the Earth, sounder explanations than theirs for the revolution of the celestial spheres might so be discovered.

Thus assuming motions, which in my work I ascribe to the Earth, by long and frequent observations I have at last discovered that, if the motions of the rest of the planets be brought into relation with the circulation of the Earth and be reckoned in proportion to the circles of each planet . . . the orders and magnitudes of all stars and spheres, nay the heavens themselves, become so bound together that nothing in any part thereof could be moved from its place without producing confusion of all the other parts and of the Universe as a whole. . . .

It may fall out, too, that idle babblers, ignorant of mathematics, may claim a right to pronounce a judgment on my work, by reason of a certain passage of Scripture basely twisted to serve their purpose. Should any such venture to criticize and carp at my project, I make no account of them; I consider their judgment rash, and utterly despise it.

Source: From Nicolaus Copernicus, *De Revolutionibus Orbium Caelestium* (1543), translated by John F. Dobson and Selig Brodetsky in *Occasional Notes of the Royal Astronomical Society,* Vol. 2, No. 10, 1947. Reprinted by permission of Blackwell Publishing.

Bacon gained some of his enthusiasm for experimentation from his interest in natural magic°, which was the use of magical words and drawings to manipulate forces in the physical world without calling on supernatural beings for assistance. Newton was fascinated by the subject of magic and studied alchemy intensively. The original inspiration of Newton's theory of gravitation probably came from his professor at Cambridge, the Neoplatonist Henry More, who insisted on the presence of spiritual and immaterial forces in the physical world.

These contributions of the Renaissance to the new science were so important that some historians have identified the sixteenth century, when learned magic was in vogue and when the mechanical philosophy had not yet taken hold, as the first stage of the Scientific Revolution, to be followed by the mechanical phase when the discoveries of Galileo, Boyle, and Newton took center stage. Modern science resulted not so much from the victory of the mechanical philosophy over its Neoplatonic predecessor but from this encounter between these two worldviews.

The Collapse of Paradigms

The third internal cause of the Scientific Revolution was the collapse of the intellectual frameworks that had governed the conduct of scientific research since antiquity. The key to understanding this development is the recognition that scientists in all historical periods do not strive to introduce new theories but prefer to work within an established conceptual framework, or what the scholar Thomas Kuhn has referred to as a paradigm°. Scientists strive to solve puzzles that are presented by the paradigm. Every so often, however, the paradigm that has governed scientific research for an extended period of time collapses because it can no longer account for many different observable phenomena. A scientific revolution occurs when the old paradigm collapses and a new paradigm takes its place.[3]

The revolutionary developments we have studied in astronomy and biology can be explained at least in part by the collapse of old paradigms. In astronomy the paradigm that had governed scientific inquiry in antiquity and the Middle Ages was the Ptolemaic system, in which the sun and the planets revolved around the Earth. Whenever ancient or medieval astronomers confronted a new problem as a result of their observations, they tried to accommodate the results to the Ptolemaic model. In the process they had to refine the basic concept that Ptolemy had presented. By the sixteenth century the paradigm had been modified or adjusted so many times that it no longer made sense. As scientists gradually added numerous "epicycles" of planetary motion outside the prescribed spheres, and as they identified numerous "eccentric" or noncircular orbits around the Earth, Ptolemy's paradigm of a harmoniously functioning universe gradually became a confused collection of planets and stars following different motions. Faced with this situation, Copernicus began to look for a simpler and more plausible model of the universe. The sun-centered theory that he proposed became the new paradigm within which Kepler, Galileo, and Newton all worked.

In the field of biology a parallel development occurred when the old paradigm constructed by Galen, in which the blood originated in the liver and was drawn into the heart and from there traveled through the arteries to the brain and nerves, also collapsed. By the seventeenth century the paradigm of Galen could no longer satisfactorily explain the findings of medical scholars, such as the recognition that blood could not easily pass from one ventricle of the heart to the other. It was left to Harvey to introduce an entirely new paradigm, in which the blood circulated through the body. As in astronomy, the collapse of the old paradigm led to the Scientific Revolution, and Harvey's new paradigm served as a framework for subsequent biological research.

Developments Outside Science

A number of nonscientific developments also encouraged the development and acceptance of new scientific ideas. These developments outside science include the spread of Protestantism, the patronage of scientific research, the invention of the printing press, military and economic change, and voyages of exploration.

Protestantism

The growth of Protestantism in the sixteenth and seventeenth centuries encouraged the rise of modern science. Catholics as well as Protestants engaged in scientific research, and some of the most prominent European natural philosophers, including Galileo and Descartes, were devout Catholics. Protestantism, however, encouraged the emergence of modern science in three indirect ways.

First, Protestant countries proved to be more receptive than Catholic ones to new scientific ideas. Protestant churches, for example, did not prohibit the publication of books that promoted novel scientific ideas on the grounds that they were heretical, as the Papal Index did. The greater willingness of Protestant governments, especially those of England and the Dutch Republic, to tolerate the expression of unorthodox ideas helps to explain why the main geographical arena of scientific investigation shifted from the Catholic Mediterranean to the Protestant North Atlantic in the second half of the seventeenth century.

The second connection between Protestantism and the development of science was the emphasis Protestant writers placed on the idea that God revealed his intentions not only in the Bible but also in nature itself. Protestants claimed that individuals had a duty to discover what God had revealed to them in this way, just as it was their duty to read Scripture to gain knowledge of God's will. Kepler's claim that the astronomer was "as a priest of God to the book of nature," a reference to the Protestant idea of the priesthood governance. None of the great scientists of the seventeenth century actually adopted this position, but the acceptance of the mechanical philosophy made them vulnerable to the charge that they denied Christian doctrine. Because of his support for the mechanical philosophy, Descartes was suspected of atheism.

Although the new science and seventeenth-century Christianity appeared to be on a collision course, a number of scientists and theologians insisted that there was no conflict between them. One argument they made was that religion and science were separate disciplines that had very different concerns. Religion dealt with the relationship between humans and God, while science explained how nature operated. As Galileo wrote in a letter to the Grand Duchess Christina of Tuscany in 1615, "The intention of the Holy Ghost is to teach us how one goes to heaven, not how the heaven goes."[5] Scripture was not intended to explain natural phenomena, but to convey religious truths that could not be grasped by human reason. In making these points Galileo was pleading for the separation of religion and science by freeing scientific inquiry from the control of the

DOCUMENT

Galileo Galilei,
*Letter to the
Grand Duchess
Christina*

Church. To some extent, that separation has taken place over the course of the last three centuries. Theology and science have gradually become separate academic disciplines, each with its own objectives and methodology. Even the papacy eventually accepted the position of Galileo on this question in 1992. Nevertheless, conflicts between the claims of science and those who believe in the literal truth of the Bible have not disappeared, especially regarding the theory of evolution.

Another argument for the compatibility of science and religion was the claim that the mechanical philosophy, rather than relegating God to the role of a retired engineer, actually manifested his unlimited power. In a mechanistic universe God was still the creator of the entire physical world and the formulator of the laws of nature that guaranteed its regular operation. He was still all-powerful and present everywhere. According to Boyle and Newton, moreover, God played a supremely active role in governing the universe. Not only had he created the universe, but, in a theory developed by Boyle, he also continued to keep all matter constantly in motion. This theory served the purpose of redefining God's power without diminishing it in

---

DOCUMENT

Science and the Preternatural

Thomas Sprat (1635–1713), an English clergyman who rose to be bishop of Rochester, was elected a member of the Royal Society of London in 1663, and in 1667 he published a history of that society. Sprat praised the tradition of experimentation that became the hallmark of the society, and in this passage he claimed that the empiricism of modern science eliminated the imaginary creatures, such as fairies and ghosts, that classical writers had invented and medieval theologians had continued to claim were the causes of unusual phenomena. According to Sprat, all such phenomena can be explained by natural causes and effects, through which God governed the universe. Sprat claims that by showing these creatures to be mere phantasms, science has eliminated the fear that people have had of them from early childhood.

And as for the terrors and misapprehensions which commonly confound weaker minds and make men's minds to fail and boggle at trifles, there is so little hope of having them removed by speculation alone that it is evident they were first produced by the most contemplative men among the ancients and chiefly prevailed of late years, when that way of learning flourished. The poets began of old to impose the deceit. They to make all things look more venerable than they were devised a thousand false chimeras; on every field, river, grove and cove, they bestowed a phantasm of their own making. With these they amazed the

world; these they clothed with what shapes they pleased. By these they pretended that all wars and counsels and actions of men were administered. And in the modern ages these fantastical forms were revived and possessed Christendom in the very height of the schoolmen's time. An infinite number of fairies haunted every house; all churches were filled with apparitions; men began to be frightened from their cradles, which fright continued to their graves, and their names also were made the causes of scaring others. All which abuses if those acute philosophers did not promote, yet they were never able to overcome; nay, even not so much as King Oberon and his invisible army.

But from the time in which the real philosophy [science] appeared, there is scarce any whisper remaining of such horrors. Every man is unshaken at those tales at which his ancestors trembled. The course of things goes quietly along, in its own true channel of causes and effects. For this we are beholden to experiments, which though they have not yet completed the discovery of the true world, yet they have already vanquished those wild inhabitants of the false worlds that used to astonish the minds of men. A blessing for which we ought to be thankful, if we remember, that it is one of the greatest curses that God pronounces on the wicked, that they shall fear where no fear is.

Source: From *History of the Royal Society of London* by Thomas Sprat, 1702, pp. 339–341.

any way. Newton arrived at a similar position in his search for an immaterial agent who would cause gravity to operate. He proposed that God himself, who he believed "endures always and is present everywhere," made bodies move according to gravitational laws. Throughout the early eighteenth century this feature of Newtonian natural philosophy served as a powerful argument for the existence and immanence of God.

As the new science became more widely accepted, and as the regularity and immutability of the laws of nature became more apparent, religion itself began to undergo a transformation. Instead of denying the validity of the new science, many theologians, especially Protestants, accommodated scientific knowledge to their religious beliefs. Some Protestants welcomed the discoveries of science as an opportunity to purify the Christian religion by combating the superstition, magic, and ignorance that they claimed the Catholic Church had been promoting. Clerics who accepted the new science, including those who became members of the Royal Society, argued that because God worked through the processes of nature, human beings could acquire theological knowledge of him by engaging in scientific inquiry. For them religion and science were not so much separate but complementary forms of knowledge, each capable of illuminating the other.

The most widespread effect of the new science on religion was a new emphasis on the compatibility of reason and religion. In the Middle Ages scholastic theologians such as Thomas Aquinas had tried to reconcile the two, arguing that there was a body of knowledge about God, called natural theology, that could be obtained without the assistance of revelation. Now, however, with the benefit of the new science, theologians and philosophers began to expand the role that reason played in religion. In the religious writings of the English philosopher John Locke, the role of reason became dominant. In *The Reasonableness of Christianity* (1695), Locke argued that reason should be the final arbiter of the existence of the supernatural and it should also determine the true meaning of the Bible. This new emphasis on the role of reason in religion coincided with a rejection of the religious zeal that had characterized the era of the Reformation and the wars of religion. Political and ecclesiastical authorities looked down on religious enthusiasm not only as politically dangerous, as it had inspired revolution and rebellion throughout Europe, but as a form of behavior that had no rational basis.

The new emphasis on the reasonableness of religion and the decline of religious enthusiasm are often viewed as evidence of a broader trend toward the secularization of European life, a process in which religion gave way to more worldly concerns. In one sense this secular trend was undeniable. By the dawn of the eighteenth century, theology had lost its dominant position at the universities, the sciences had become autonomous academic disciplines, and religion had lost much of its intellectual authority. Religion also be-gan to exercise less influence on the conduct of politics and diplomacy and on the regulation of economic activity.

Religion had not, however, lost its relevance. Throughout the eighteenth century it remained a vital force in the lives of most European people. Religious books continued to be published in great numbers. Many of those who accepted the new science continued to believe in a providential God and the divinity of Christ. Moreover, a small but influential group of educated people, following the lead of the French mathematician, physicist, and religious philosopher Blaise Pascal (1623–1662), insisted that although reason and science have their place, they represent only one sphere of truth. In his widely circulated book *Reflections,* which lay unfinished at his death but was published in 1670, Pascal argued that religious faith occupied a higher sphere of knowledge that reason and science could not penetrate. Pascal, the inventor of a calculating machine and the promoter of a system of public coach service in Paris, had been an advocate of the new science. He endorsed the Copernican model of the universe and opposed the condemnation of Galileo. But on the question of the relationship between science and religion, Pascal presented arguments that could be used against Spinoza, Locke, and all those who considered reason the ultimate arbiter of truth.

Magic, Demons, and Witchcraft

The new science not only changed many patterns of religious thought but also led to a denial of the reality and effectiveness of magic. Magic is the use of a supernatural, occult, or mysterious power to achieve extraordinary effects in the physical world or to influence the course of human events. The effects can be beneficial or harmful. Magicians claimed to be able to use their special powers to cure a person or inflict disease, acquire political power, stimulate love or hatred in another individual, predict the future, or produce any number of natural "marvels," including changes in the weather. In the sixteenth and seventeenth centuries men and women believed in and practiced two forms of magic. Natural magic, such as the practice of alchemy, involved the manipulation of occult forces that were believed to exist in nature. As we have seen, many Neoplatonists believed in the possibility of this type of magic, and many of them actually practiced it. Demonic magic°, on the other hand, involved the invocation of evil spirits so that one might gain access to their supernatural power. The men who were most committed to the mechanical philosophy denied the effectiveness of both types of magic. By claiming that matter was inert, they challenged the central notion of natural magic, which is the belief that material objects are animated by occult forces, such as an innate attraction to another object. If matter was not alive, it contained no forces for a magician to manipulate.

The Trial of Galileo

The events leading to the trial of Galileo for heresy in 1633 began in 1616, when a committee of eleven theologians reported to the Roman Inquisition that the sun-centered theory of Copernicus was heretical. Those who accepted this theory were declared to be heretics not only because they called the authority of the Bible into question but because they denied the exclusive authority of the Catholic Church to determine how the Bible should be interpreted. The day after this report was submitted, Pope Paul V instructed Cardinal Robert Bellarmine, a theologian who was on good terms with Galileo, to warn him to abandon his Copernican views. Galileo had written extensively in support of the sun-centered thesis, especially in his *Letters on Sunspots* (1613) and his *Letter to the Grand Duchess Christina* (1615), although he had never admitted that the theory was proved conclusively. Now he was being told that he should not hold, teach, or defend in any way the opinion of the sun's stability or the Earth's mobility. If he were to ignore that warning, he would be prosecuted as a heretic.

During the next sixteen years Galileo published two books. The first, *The Assayer* (1623), was an attack upon the views of an Italian philosopher regarding comets. The book actually won Galileo considerable support, especially from the new pope, Urban VIII, who was eager to be associated with the most fashionable intellectual trends. Urban took Galileo under his wing and made him the intellectual star of his court. Urban even went so far as to declare that support for Copernicanism was not heretical but only rash.

The patronage of the pope may have emboldened Galileo to exercise less caution in writing his second book of this period, *Dialogue Concerning the Two Chief World Systems* (1632). This treatise was ostensibly an impartial presentation of the rival Ptolemaic and Copernican cosmologies, but in its own quiet way it served the purpose of promoting Copernicanism. Galileo sought proper authorization from ecclesiastical authorities to put the book in print, but he eventually allowed it to be published in Florence before it received official approval from Rome.

The publication of *Dialogue* precipitated Galileo's fall from the pope's favor. Urban, who at this time was coming under criticism for leniency with heretics, ordered the book taken out of circulation in the summer of 1632 and appointed a commission to investigate Galileo's activities. After receiving the report from the committee a few months later, he turned the matter over to the Roman Inquisition, which charged Galileo with heresy.

The Roman Inquisition had been established in 1542 to preserve the Catholic faith. Its main concern was the prosecution of heresy. Like the Spanish Inquisition, this Roman ecclesiastical court has acquired a reputation for being harsh and arbitrary, for administering torture, for proceeding in secrecy, and for denying the accused the right to know the charges in advance of the trial. There is some validity to these criticisms, although the Roman Inquisition did not torture Galileo or deny him the opportunity to present a defense. The most unfair aspect of the proceeding, and of inquisitorial justice in general, was the determination of the outcome of the trial by the same judges who had brought the charges against the accused and conducted the interrogation. This meant that in a politically motivated trial such as Galileo's, the verdict was a foregone conclusion. To accept Galileo's defense would have been a sign of weakness and a repudiation of the pope.

Although the underlying substantive issue in the trial was whether Galileo was guilty of heresy for denying the sun's motion and the Earth's immobility, the more technical question was whether by publishing *Dialogue* he had violated the prohibition of 1616. In his defense Galileo claimed that the only reason he had written *Dialogue* was to present "the physical and astronomical reasons that can be advanced for one side or the other." He denied holding Copernicus's opinion to be true.

In the end the court determined that by publishing *Dialogue,* Galileo had violated the injunction of 1616. He had disseminated "the false opinion of the Earth's motion and the sun's stability" and he had "defended the said opinion already condemned." Even Galileo's efforts "to give the impression of leaving it undecided and labeled as probable" was still a very serious error, because there was no way that "an opinion declared and defined contrary to divine Scripture may be probable." The court also declared that Galileo had obtained permission to publish the book in Florence without divulging to the authorities there that he was under the injunction of 1616.

Throughout the trial every effort was made to distance the pope from his former protégé. There was real fear among the members of the papal court that because the pope had been Galileo's patron and had given him considerable latitude in developing his ideas, he himself would be implicated in Galileo's heresy. Every step was taken to guarantee

The Trial of Galileo, 1633
Galileo is shown here presenting one of his four defenses to the Inquisition. He claimed that his book *Dialogue Concerning the Two Chief World Systems* did not endorse the Copernican model of the universe.

that information regarding the pope's support for Galileo did not surface. The court made sure, for example, that no one from the Medici court, which had provided support for Galileo, would testify on Galileo's behalf. The trial tells us as much about the efforts of Urban VIII to save face as about the Catholic Church's hostility to the new science.

Galileo was required to formally renounce his views and to avoid any further defense of Copernicanism. After making this humiliating submission to the court, he was sent to Siena and later that year was allowed to return to his villa in Arcetri near Florence, where he remained under house arrest until his death in 1642.

Questions of Justice

1. Galileo was silenced because of what he had put into print. Why had he published these works, and why did the Church consider his publications a serious threat?
2. Is a court of law an appropriate place to resolve disputes between science and religion? Why or why not?

Taking It Further

Finocchiaro, Maurice, ed. *The Galileo Affair: A Documentary History*. 1989. A collection of original documents regarding the controversy between Galileo and the Roman Catholic Church.

Sharratt, Michael. *Galileo: Decisive Innovator*. 1994. A study of Galileo's place in the history of science that provides full coverage of his trial and papal reconsiderations of it in the late twentieth century.

The denial of the reality of demonic magic was based on a rejection of the powers of demons. Seventeenth-century scientists did not necessarily deny the existence of angelic or demonic spirits, but the mechanical philosophy posed a serious challenge to the belief that those spirits could influence the operation of the physical world. The belief in demons experienced a slow death. Many scientists struggled to preserve a place for them in the physical world, arguing that the Devil, like God, could work through the processes of nature. Ultimately, however, the logic of the mechanical philosophy expelled demons from the worldview of the educated classes. By the beginning of the eighteenth century, scientists and even some theologians had labeled the belief in demons as superstition, which originally had meant false or erroneous religion but which was now redefined to mean ignorance of natural causes.

The denial of the power of magic, together with the rejection of the belief in the power of demonic spirits, also explains why many educated Europeans began to deny the reality of witchcraft in the second half of the seventeenth century. As we have seen in Chapter 14, witches were individuals, mostly women, who stood accused of using magic to harm their neighbors, their animals, or their crops. They were also accused of having made a pact with the Devil, the means by which they received their magical powers. In many cases it was claimed that witches worshiped the Devil collectively at nocturnal orgies known as sabbaths. To someone who subscribed to the mechanical philosophy, this entire set of beliefs about witches was highly questionable. Demons could not intervene in the operation of the physical world, nor could human beings perform magic with or without their assistance.

Science also played a major role in challenging the belief that demons could invade a human body and control the person's movements and behavior. During the seventeenth century Europe experienced a wave of such demonic possessions, in which individuals—often young girls—experienced fits and convulsions, spoke in deep, gruff voices, displayed preternatural strength, vomited foreign objects such as pins, and experienced temporary blindness and deafness. Believing that demons were the cause of these symptoms, clerics attempted to dispossess or exorcise them through either an elaborate ritual in Roman Catholic countries or a program of prayer and fasting in Protestant communities. By the end of the seventeenth century the belief that demons were responsible for such possessions had given way to the assumption that the behavior of the possessed person or demoniac had natural, medical causes. The range of possible maladies afflicting demoniacs included the disease known then as hysteria, in which the body of a person displayed such symptoms as a reaction to unbearable stress.

The most emphatic, comprehensive, and unequivocal attack on the entire body of beliefs regarding the Devil during the seventeenth century came from the pen of a Dutch minister and follower of Descartes, Balthasar Bekker. In his four-volume study, *The Enchanted World* (1691–1693), Bekker denied that the Devil could exercise any jurisdiction over the natural world. The mechanical philosophy was not the only basis for Bekker's skepticism. A biblical scholar, Bekker produced many passages from Scripture indicating that God exercised complete sovereignty over the Devil and had in fact chained him up in Hell. In this way the Devil had been rendered incapable of causing physical destruction in the world, either with or without the assistance of witches.

The skeptical views that many educated people acquired regarding demons and magic were usually not shared by people who remained illiterate. For them magic and witchcraft remained very real, and they continued to suspect and accuse their neighbors of engaging in diabolical practices until the early nineteenth century. In a number of instances they took the law into their own hands, stoning accused witches, drowning them, or burning them alive. All of this served to highlight a widening gap between the views of the educated and those of the common people. There had always been differences between learned and popular culture, but many aspects of culture were shared by educated and uneducated people. Both groups, for example, took part in the same religious services and rituals, and both groups also held some of the same beliefs about magic and witchcraft. In the late seventeenth century, however, this common cultural ground began to disappear, and members of the educated classes began to develop unprecedented contempt for the ignorance and superstition of the common people. The education of the upper classes in the new science and in Descartes's philosophy only aggravated what was already a noticeable trend.

The development of two separate realms of culture became one of the main themes of eighteenth-century history, and it contributed directly to the formation of class divisions. On the one side were the educated upper classes who prided themselves on their rational and enlightened views; on the other were the illiterate peasants who continued to believe in magic, witchcraft, and what the educated referred to as "vulgar superstition."

Humans and the Natural World

■ How did the Scientific Revolution change the way in which seventeenth- and eighteenth-century Europeans thought of their relationship to the natural world?

The spread of scientific knowledge not only redefined the views of educated people regarding the supernatural realm, but it also led them to reconsider their relationship to nature. This process involved three separate but related inquiries. The first was to determine the place of human beings in a sun-centered universe; the second to investigate how science and technology had given human beings greater control over nature; and the third to reconsider the relationship between men and women in light of new scientific knowledge regarding the human mind and body.

The Place of Human Beings in the Universe

The astronomical discoveries of Copernicus and Galileo offered a new outlook regarding the position of human beings in the universe. The Earth-centered Ptolemaic cosmos that dominated scientific thought during the Middle Ages was also human-centered. Not only was the planet that human beings inhabited situated at the center of the universe, but on Earth humans occupied a privileged position. This is not to say that the human condition was always viewed in positive terms. Trapped on a stationary Earth, which itself was corruptible, individuals were always vulnerable to the temptations of the demonic spirits that medieval clerics told them were constantly hovering in the atmosphere. But human beings nonetheless remained the absolute physical and moral center of this universe. They were, after all, created in the image of God, according to Christian belief. Renaissance Neoplatonism reinforced this medieval view. By describing human beings as having the characteristics of both angels and beasts, with the capacity to ascend toward God or descend to the level of animals, Neoplatonists accentuated the centrality and importance of humankind in the world.

The acceptance of a sun-centered model of the universe began to bring about a fundamental change in these views of humankind. Once it became apparent that the Earth was not the center of the universe, human beings began to lose their privileged position in nature. The Copernican universe was neither Earth-centered nor human-centered. Scientists such as Descartes continued to claim that human beings were the greatest of nature's creatures, but their habitation of a tiny planet circling the sun inevitably reduced the sense of their own importance. Moreover, as astronomers began to recognize the incomprehensible size of the cosmos, the possibility emerged that there were other habitable worlds in the universe, calling into further question the unique status of humankind.

In the late sixteenth and seventeenth centuries a number of literary works explored the possibility of other inhabited worlds and forms of life. In *The Infinite Universe and World* (1584), the Neoplatonist monk Giordano Bruno (1548–1600), who was eventually burned as a heretic, postulated the existence of other rational beings and suggested that they might be more intelligent than humans. Kepler's *Somnium,* or *Lunar Astronomy* (1634), a book that combined science and fiction, described various species of moon dwellers, some of whom were rational and superior to humans. This was followed by a number of works of fic-

tion on travel to the moon, including Francis Godwin's *The Man in the Moon* (1638) and Cyrano de Bergerac's *The Other World* (1657). The most ambitious and fascinating of all these books was a fictional work by the French dramatist and poet Bernard de Fontenelle, *Conversations on the Plurality of Worlds* (1686). This work, which became immensely popular throughout Europe, was more responsible than any purely scientific discovery of the seventeenth century for leading the general reading public to call into question the centrality of humankind in Creation.

The Control of Nature

The Scientific Revolution bolstered the confidence human beings had in their ability to control nature. By disclosing the laws governing the operation of the universe, the new science gave humans the tools they needed to make nature serve their own purposes more effectively than it had in the past. This confidence in human mastery over nature found its most articulate expression in the writings of Francis Bacon. Instead of accepting the traditional view that humans were either passively reconciled with nature or victimized by it, Bacon believed that knowledge of the laws of nature could restore the dominion over nature that humans had lost in the biblical Garden of Eden. Bacon believed that nature existed for human beings to control and exploit for their own benefit. His famous maxim, "knowledge is power," conveyed his confidence that science would give human beings this type of control over nature.

In the same spirit Descartes announced that as human beings we had the capacity "to turn ourselves into the masters and possessors of nature."[6] For him nature included animals or beasts, which, unlike human beings, did not have souls and were therefore merely corporal machines. (For this reason, he was not at all reluctant to dissect live animals.) Later in the seventeenth century the members of the Royal Society proclaimed their intention to make scientific knowledge "an instrument whereby mankind may obtain a dominion over things." This optimism regarding human control of nature found support in the belief that God permitted such mastery, first by creating a regular and uniform universe and then by giving people the rational faculties by which they could understand nature's laws.

Many scientists of the seventeenth century emphasized the practical applications of their research, just as scientists often do today. Descartes, who used his knowledge of optics to improve the grinding of lenses, contemplated ways in which scientific knowledge might improve the drainage of marshes, increase the velocity of bullets, and use bells to make clouds burst. In his celebration of the French Academy of Sciences in 1699, Fontenelle wrote that "the application of science to nature will constantly grow in scope and intensity and we shall go on from one marvel to the next; the day will come when man will be able to fly by

The Founding of the French Académie des Sciences
Like the Royal Society in England, the French Académie of Sciences was dependent upon royal patronage. Louis XIV, seen sitting in the middle of the painting, used the occasion to glorify himself as a patron of the sciences as well as the arts. The painting also commemorates the building of the Royal Observatory in Paris, which is shown in the background.

fitting on wings to keep him in the air . . . till one day we shall be able to fly to the moon."[7] As we mentioned earlier, members of the Royal Society discussed how their experiments would help miners, farmers, and merchants. They even discussed the possibility of making labor-saving machines. These efforts to apply scientific knowledge to practical problems encouraged the belief, which has persisted to the present day, that science could improve human life.

The hopes of seventeenth-century scientists for the improvement of human life by means of technology remained in large part unfulfilled until the eighteenth century. Only then did the technological promise of the Scientific Revolution begin to be realized, most notably with the innovations that preceded or accompanied the Industrial Revolution. The first steam engine, for example, which utilized the scientific study of atmospheric pressure conducted by a student of Galileo in the 1650s, was not invented until 1709. The great improvements in the construction of canals and the use of water power to drive machinery, which were based upon the study of Newtonian mechanics, likewise did not take place until the eighteenth century. In similar fashion, research on the internal structure of grains and the breeding of sheep did not significantly increase food production until the eighteenth century, at the time of the agricultural revolution.

By the middle of the eighteenth century, the belief that science would lead to an improvement of human life became an integral part of Western culture. Much less apparent at that time, however, was a recognition of the destructive potential of applied science. Governments supported scientific research on ballistics to gain military advantage, but it was not until the twentieth century, especially with the construction of engines of mass destruction, that people began to recognize technology's potential to cause permanent harm to the human race. In the seventeenth and eighteenth centuries, those who possessed scientific knowledge thought mainly in terms of the benefits that science and technology could confer. Their faith in human progress became one of the main themes of the Enlightenment, which will be discussed in Chapter 18.

Women, Men, and Nature

The new scientific and philosophical ideas of the seventeenth century challenged ancient and medieval notions regarding women's physical and mental inferiority to men. At the same time the new science left other traditional ideas about the roles of men and women unchallenged.

Until the seventeenth century, a woman's sexual organs were thought to be imperfect versions of a man's, an idea that made woman an inferior version of man and in some respects a freak of nature. During the sixteenth and seventeenth centuries, a body of scientific literature advanced the new idea that women had sexual organs that were perfect in their own right and served distinct functions in reproduction. Another traditional biological idea that came under attack during this period was Aristotle's view that men made a more important contribution to reproduction than did women. The man's semen was long believed to contain the form of the body as well as the soul, while the only contribution the woman was believed to make to the process

DOCUMENT

Elisabeth of Bohemia Challenges Descartes

Elisabeth of Bohemia, the daughter of King Frederick of Bohemia and granddaughter of King James I of England, engaged in a long correspondence with Descartes regarding his philosophy. Privately educated in Greek, Latin, and mathematics, Elisabeth was one of a small group of noblewomen who participated in the scientific and philosophical debates of the day. The letter concerns the relationship between the soul (or mind), which Descartes claimed was immaterial, and the body, which is entirely composed of matter. One of the problems for Descartes was to explain how the mind could move that body to perform certain functions. In the letter Elisabeth plays a deferential, self-effacing role but in the process exposes one of the weaknesses of Descartes's dualistic philosophy.

The Hague, 20 June 1643

Monsieur Descartes,

. . . The life I am forced to lead does not leave me the disposition of enough time to acquire a habit of meditation according to your rules. So many interests of my family that I must not neglect, so many interviews and civilities that I cannot avoid, batter my weak spirit with such anger and boredom that it is rendered for a long time afterward useless for anything else. All of which will excuse my stupidity, I hope, not to have been able to understand the idea by which we must judge how the soul (not extended and immaterial) can move the body by an idea we have in another regard of heaviness, nor why a power—which we have falsely attributed to things under the name of a quality—of carrying a body toward the center of the Earth when the demonstration of a contrary truth (which you promised in your Physics) confirms us in thinking it impossible. The idea of a separate independent quality of heaviness—given that we are not able to pretend to the perfection and objective reality of God—could be made up out of ignorance of that which truly propels bodies towards the center of the Earth. Because no material cause represents itself to the senses, one attributes heaviness to matter's contrary, the immaterial, which nevertheless I would never be able to conceive but as a negation of matter and which could have no communication with matter.

I confess that it is easier for me to concede the matter and the extension of the soul than to concede that a being that is immaterial has the capacity to move a body and to be moved by it. For if the former is done by giving information, it is necessary that the spirits which make the movement be intelligent, which you do not accord to anything corporal. And although, in your meditations, you show the possibility of the soul being moved by the body, it is nevertheless very difficult to comprehend how a soul, as you have described it, after having had the faculty and habit of good reasoning, would lose all that by some sort of vapors, or that being able to subsist without the body and having nothing in common with it, would allow itself to be so ruled by the body.

Source: From *The Princess and the Philosopher: Letters of Elisabeth of the Palatine to René Descartes* by Andrea Nye. Copyright © 1999 by Rowman & Littlefield Publishers, Inc. Reprinted by permission.

---

was the formless matter upon which the semen acted. By the beginning of the eighteenth century, a scholarly consensus had emerged that recognized equal contributions from both sexes to the process of reproduction.

Some seventeenth-century natural philosophers also called into question ancient and medieval ideas regarding women's mental inferiority to men. In this regard Descartes supplied a theory that presupposed intellectual equality between the sexes. In making a radical separation between the mind and the human body, Descartes found no difference between the minds of men and women. As one of his followers wrote in 1673, "The mind has no sex."[8] A few upper-class women provided solid evidence to support this revolutionary claim of female intellectual equality. Princess Elisabeth of Bohemia, for example, carried on a long correspondence with Descartes during the 1640s and challenged many of his ideas on the relationship between the body and the soul. The privately educated English noblewoman Margaret Cavendish (1623–1673) wrote scientific and philosophical treatises and conversed with the leading philosophers of the day. In early eighteenth-century France, small groups of women and men gathered in the salons or private sitting rooms of the nobility to discuss philosophical and scientific ideas. In Germany it was not uncommon for women to help their husbands run astronomical observatories.

Although seventeenth-century science laid the theoretical foundations for a theory of sexual equality, it did not challenge other traditional ideas that compared women unfavorably to men. Most educated people continued to ground female behavior in the humors, claiming that because women were cold and wet, as opposed to hot and dry, they were naturally more deceptive, unstable, and melancholic than men. They also continued to identify women with nature itself, which had always been depicted as female. Bacon's use of masculine metaphors to describe science and his references to "man's mastery over nature" therefore seemed to reinforce traditional ideas of male dominance

Eighteenth-Century Midwifery

Astronomers in Seventeenth-Century Germany
Elisabetha and Johannes Hevelius working together with a sextant in a German astronomical observatory. More than 14 percent of all German astronomers were female. Most of them cooperated with their husbands in their work.

over women. His language also reinforced traditional notions of men's superior rationality.[9] In 1664 the secretary of the Royal Society, which excluded women from membership, proclaimed that the mission of that institution was to develop a "masculine philosophy."[10] At the same time the tradition of depicting science as a female goddess, such as Minerva, began to disappear.

The new science provided the theoretical foundations for the male control of women at a time when many men expressed concern over the "disorderly" and "irrational" conduct of women. In a world populated with witches, rebels, and other women who refused to adhere to conventional standards of proper feminine behavior, the adoption of a masculine philosophy was associated with the reassertion of patriarchy.

Conclusion

Science and Western Culture

The Scientific Revolution was a uniquely Western phenomenon. It had no parallel in the Eastern world. During the Middle Ages the Islamic civilizations of the Middle East produced a rich body of scientific knowledge that had influenced the development of science in western Europe, but by the time of the Scientific Revolution Islamic science had entered a period of decline. Other civilizations, most notably in China and India, also possessed impressive scientific traditions, but they too failed to undergo a transformation similar to that which occurred in western Europe in the seventeenth century.

In all these non-Western civilizations, religious traditions had prevented philosophers from undertaking an objective study of the natural world. Either nature was viewed as an entirely secular (that is, not religious) entity and hence not worthy of study on its own terms, or it was viewed as something so heavily infused with spiritual value that it could not be subjected to rational analysis. Only in Europe did religious and cultural traditions allow the scientist to view nature as both a product of supernatural forces and something that was separate from the supernatural realm. Nature could therefore be studied objectively without losing its religious significance. Only when nature was viewed in this dual way, as both the creation of God and as something independent of the deity, could it be subjected to mathematical analysis and brought under human domination.

The Scientific Revolution gave the West a new source of identity. The West could be distinguished not only by its Christianity, its capitalist economic system, its large bureaucratic states, and its massive standing armies, but also by the scientific content of its education, its approach to the natural world, and its science-based technology. By the beginning of the eighteenth century, modern science became an essential component of Western culture. It also laid the foundations of the Enlightenment, another distinctively Western phenomenon, which will be discussed in Chapter 18.

The rise of Western science and technology had profound implications for the encounters that took place between Western and non-Western peoples in Africa, Asia, and the Americas. By the eighteenth century, European science provided explicit support for European empires, which will be discussed in Chapters 17 and 23. Science gave Western states the military and navigational technology that allowed them to establish their control over non-Europeans. Knowledge of botany and agriculture allowed Western powers to develop the resources of the areas they colonized and to use these resources for the improvement of their own societies. Most important, the possession of scientific knowledge and technology encouraged people in the West to think of themselves as superior to the people they subjugated or controlled. Scientific theories regarding biological and physiological differences between the people who inhabited the West and natives of other countries also contributed to those attitudes. Western imperialism had its roots in the Scientific Revolution of the seventeenth century.

Suggestions for Further Reading

For a comprehensive listing of suggested readings, please go to www.ablongman.com/levack2e/chapter16

Biagioli, Mario. *Galileo, Courtier: The Practice of Science in the Culture of Absolutism.* 1993. Argues that Galileo's desire for patronage determined the type of research he engaged in and the scientific questions he asked.

Cohen, H. Floris. *The Scientific Revolution: A Historiographical Inquiry.* 1995. A thorough account of all the different interpretations of the causes and significance of the Scientific Revolution.

Dear, Peter. *Discipline and Experience: The Mathematical Way in the Scientific Revolution.* 1995. Explains the importance of mathematics in the development of seventeenth-century science.

Debus, Allen G. *Man and Nature in the Renaissance.* 1978. Deals with the early history of the Scientific Revolution and develops many of its connections with the Renaissance.

Drake, Stillman, ed. *Discoveries and Opinions of Galileo.* 1957. Includes four of Galileo's most important writings, together with a detailed commentary.

Easlea, Brian. *Magic, Witch-Hunting and the New Philosophy.* 1980. Relates the end of witch hunting to the spread of the mechanical philosophy.

Feingold, Mordechai. *The Newtonian Moment: Isaac Newton and the Making of Modern Culture.* 2004. A richly illustrated volume that contains valuable material on the reception of Newtonian ideas in the eighteenth century as well as a chapter on Newtonian women.

Kuhn, Thomas S. *The Copernican Revolution.* 1957. The most comprehensive and authoritative study of the shift from an Earth-centered to a sun-centered model of the universe.

Popkin, Richard. *The History of Scepticism from Erasmus to Spinoza.* 1979. Discusses skepticism as a cause as well as an effect of the Scientific Revolution.

Schiebinger, Londa. *The Mind Has No Sex? Women in the Origins of Modern Science.* 1989. Explores the role of women in all aspects of scientific endeavor.

Shapin, Steven. *The Scientific Revolution.* 1996. A study of the origins of the modern scientific worldview that emphasizes the social influences on the production of knowledge and the social purposes for which scientific knowledge was intended.

Shapin, Steven, and Simon Schaffer. *Leviathan and the Air Pump.* 1989. Discusses the difference between Robert Boyle and Thomas Hobbes regarding the value of experimentation.

Thomas, Keith. *Man and the Natural World: A History of the Modern Sensibility.* 1983. A study of the shifting attitudes of human beings toward nature during the period from 1500 to 1800.

Webster, Charles. *The Great Instauration: Science, Medicine and Reform, 1626–1660.* 1975. Explores the relationship between Puritanism and the Scientific Revolution in England.

Westfall, Richard S. *Never at Rest: A Biography of Isaac Newton.* 1980. A superb biography of the most influential scientist in the history of the West.

Notes

1. Quoted in Steven Shapin, *The Scientific Revolution* (1996), 33.

2. René Descartes, *Le Monde,* Book VI.

3. Thomas S. Kuhn, *The Structure of Scientific Revolutions* (1970).

4. René Descartes, *Discourse on the Method and Meditations on First Philosophy,* ed. David Weissmann (1996), 21.

5. Galileo, "Letter to the Grand Duchess Christina," in *Discoveries and Opinions of Galileo,* ed. Stilman Drake (1957), 186.

6. Descartes, *Discourse on the Method,* 38.

7. Quoted in W. Hazard, *The European Mind, 1680–1715* (1964), 362.

8. François Poullain, *De l'égalite des deux sexes* (1673), 85.

9. Francis Bacon, *The Works of Francis Bacon,* ed. J. Spedding (1857–1874), vol. 3, 524–539.

10. Henry Oldenburg, "To the Reader," in Robert Boyle, *Experiments and Considerations in Touching Colours* (1664).

The West and the World: Empire, Trade, and War, 1650–1815

17

I N 1789 OLAUDAH EQUIANO, A FREED SLAVE LIVING IN GREAT BRITAIN, published an autobiographical account of his experiences in captivity. In this narrative Equiano recounted his seizure in the Gambia region of Africa and his transportation on a slave ship to the British Caribbean colony of Barbados. He described the unmerciful floggings to which the Africans on his ship were subjected, the unrelieved hunger they experienced, and the insufferable heat and smells they endured in the hold of the ship. He witnessed the suicide of those who threw themselves into the sea in order to avoid further misery. He was terrified that his white captors would eat him, and he wished for a merciful death.

Once the ship had reached its destination Equiano related how the Africans were herded into pens where white plantation owners examined, purchased, and branded them. The most moving part of Equiano's narrative is his account of the cries he heard as family members were sold to different masters. "O you nominal Christians," wrote Equiano, "might not an African ask you, learned you this from your God? Is it not enough that we are torn from our country and friends to toil for your luxury and lust of gain? Must every tender feeling be sacrificed to your avarice? Surely this is a new refinement in cruelty, which, while it has no advantage to atone for it, thus aggravates distress and adds fresh horrors to the wretchedness of slavery."[1]

The journey that Equiano was forced to take across the Atlantic Ocean and the emotions he described were experienced by millions of African men and women during the period from 1650 to 1815. The forced emigration of Africans from their homelands, their sale to white landlords, and their subjection to inhumane treatment number among the abiding horrors of Western civilization. To understand how these horrors could have occurred, especially at the hands of men who proclaimed a commitment to human freedom, we must study the growth of European empires during these centuries.

As European states grew in size, wealth, and military power in the sixteenth and seventeenth centuries, the most powerful of them acquired large

Samuel Scott, *A Thames Wharf* (1750s) British merchants conducted a brisk trade with Asia and the Americas in the eighteenth century.

overseas empires. By the end of the seventeenth century the British, French, and Dutch had joined the Portuguese and the Spanish as overseas imperial powers. As we discussed in Chapter 12, the first stage of empire building, which lasted from 1500 until about 1650, had many different motives. The search for gold and silver, the mission to Christianize the indigenous populations, the desire of some colonists to escape religious persecution, the urge to plunder, the efforts of monarchs to expand the size of their dominions, and the desire to profit from international trade all figured in the process. In 1625 the English government recognized many of these motives when it declared the purpose of the colony of Virginia to be "the propagation of the Christian religion, the increase of trade, and the enlarging of the royal empire."[2]

During the second stage of empire building, which lasted from roughly 1650 to 1815, the economic motive for acquiring overseas possessions became dominant. More than anything else, imperial policy was shaped by the desire for profit within a world economy. As far as the governments of western Europe were concerned, all colonies were economic enterprises. Whether these colonies were primarily involved in commerce or agriculture or mining was only a minor distinction. The main consideration was that they provided economic benefits to the European countries. They supplied the parent country, often referred to as the metropolis°, with agricultural products, raw materials, and minerals. Overseas colonies also provided the metropolis with markets for its manufactured goods.

The growth of these empires resulted in the expansion of the geographical boundaries of the West. It also resulted in the spread of Western ideas, political institutions, and economic systems to Asia and the Americas. At the same time, encounters between Europeans and non-Western peoples, especially those of Asia, brought about significant changes in the cultures of the West.

The main question that this chapter will address is how the growth of European empires in Asia and the Americas, the expansion of international trade, and the wars fought over empire and trade during the period 1650–1815 changed Western culture and politics. More specifically, the individual sections of the chapter will ask the following questions:

- How did the composition and organization of European empires change during the seventeenth and eighteenth centuries?
- In what ways did the wars waged by European powers during this period involve competition for overseas possessions and trading routes?
- How did European empires create an Atlantic economy in which the traffic in slaves was a major feature?
- What cultural encounters took place between European and Asian peoples during this period of empire building, and how did these encounters change Western attitudes toward outsiders?

- Why did European powers begin to lose control of some of their colonies, especially those in the Americas, between 1775 and 1825?

European Empires in the Americas and Asia

- How did the composition and organization of European empires change during the seventeenth and eighteenth centuries?

The main political units in Europe during this long period of history are usually referred to as states°. A state is a consolidated territorial area that has its own political institutions and recognizes no higher authority. Thus we refer to France, England (which became Great Britain after its union with Scotland in 1707), Prussia, the Dutch Republic, and Portugal as states. As we have discussed in Chapter 15, most of these states acquired larger armies and administrative bureaucracies during the sixteenth and seventeenth centuries, mainly to meet the demands of war. Consequently they became more highly integrated and cohesive political structures.

Many European states formed the center or core of much larger political formations known as empires°. The main characteristic of an empire in the seventeenth and eighteenth centuries was that it comprised many different kingdoms or territorial possessions outside the geographical boundaries of the state itself. These imperial territories were controlled by the metropolis, but they were not fully integrated into its administrative structure. Some of the territories that formed a part of these empires were located in Europe. The Austrian Habsburg monarchy, for example, had jurisdiction over a host of separate kingdoms and principalities in central and eastern Europe, including Hungary and Bohemia. This arrangement made Austria an empire, a designation it formally acquired in 1806. In like manner the Spanish monarchy, which also was an empire, controlled many different kingdoms and provinces in the Iberian peninsula as well as territories in southern Italy and the Netherlands. On the eastern and southeastern periphery of Europe lay two other empires: the Russian and the Ottoman, which controlled vast expanses of land not only in eastern Europe but also in the adjacent areas of Asia. As in previous centuries, the Russian and Ottoman empires marked the ever-shifting and often blurred boundaries between East and West.

Beginning in the fifteenth century, as the result of transoceanic voyages of exploration and the establishment of overseas colonies, western European states acquired, settled, or controlled territories in the Americas, Africa, and Asia. Mastery of these lands came much more quickly in the

New World than in Asia. The peoples of North and South America whom the Europeans encountered when they arrived were able fighters, but they were not organized politically, and diseases introduced by the Europeans drastically reduced their numbers. European settlers, who had the added advantage of superior military technology, were able to gain the upper hand in battle, seize or purchase their lands, and force those who survived to retreat into less inhabited areas.

When Europeans started to develop extensive trading routes in Asia, however, that continent was already highly developed politically and militarily. Three Muslim empires—the Ottoman, the Safavid (Persia), and the Mughal (India)—as well as the neighboring Chinese Empire in East Asia occupied the mass of land from the Balkans to the Pacific Ocean. Only when these Asian empires began to fall apart, giving greater autonomy to the smaller, subordinate states within their boundaries, were Europeans able to exploit the situation and secure favorable trading arrangements and ultimately control of Asian territory itself.

Until the late eighteenth century European governments usually allowed their colonies a considerable degree of political autonomy. Although monarchs claimed sovereignty over all their imperial possessions, the distance of these lands from the metropolis made direct rule difficult. The solution to this problem was to delegate the functions of government either to officials who represented royal authority in the colony or to some corporate body. In the British, Dutch, and French empires, trading companies that engaged in commerce with the East Indies assumed many of these functions. These companies could negotiate treaties, raise military forces, and govern the population of the colonies. In many ways the companies became small states themselves, operating under the authority of the Crown. In North America and the Caribbean, imperial governments usually granted charters to their colonies, authorizing them to establish their own legislative assemblies.

Colonists were granted considerable autonomy as long as they conducted trade exclusively with the metropolis. Metropolitan governments were determined to use the colonies to realize the objectives of gaining the largest possible share of world trade, acquiring a supply of gold and other precious metals, and collecting import and export duties on the colonial trade. To accomplish these ends they passed legislation forcing the colonists to trade exclusively with the metropolis. When colonists tried to break this monopoly by trading with other nations or colonies, they came into direct conflict with their own governments in Europe.

The earliest of the European overseas empires were established by the Spanish and the Portuguese. During the period under consideration, three rising European powers—Great Britain, France, and the Dutch Republic—began to rival the older empires. By the end of the period the British had emerged as the dominant imperial power. During the third period of imperial expansion in the late nineteenth and early twentieth centuries, the imperial rivalries that had developed in earlier years continued in different forms, and new European powers, most notably Germany and Italy, joined in the competition.

The Rise of the British Empire

The fastest-growing of these new European overseas empires during this period was that of Great Britain. England had begun its overseas empire in the late twelfth century, when it conquered the neighboring island of Ireland, but only in the seventeenth century did it begin to acquire lands in the New World and Asia. Attempts to establish colonies on the Atlantic coast of North America in the late sixteenth century had failed, most notably at Roanoke (in present-day North Carolina) in 1584. After Spain agreed not to contest English claims of territory north of Florida, the English succeed in settling a series of colonies along the Atlantic seaboard, the first of which was at Jamestown, Virginia, in 1607.

By 1700 this English empire in the New World included a number of colonies on the North American mainland, a vast territory in the northern part of Canada, and a cluster of islands in the Caribbean, most notably Barbados, Jamaica, and the Bahamas. These West Indian colonies developed an economy that used slave labor, and therefore blacks brought there from Africa soon outnumbered Europeans by a significant margin. In the colonies on the mainland of North America, however, most of the colonists were white. This was true even in the southern colonies, where slave labor was also introduced. Only in South Carolina, which was settled by Caribbean planters, did the black population exceed 50 percent.

A number of English colonists, especially in the northern colonies, had emigrated so that they might practice their religion without legal restraint. During the 1630s communities of English Protestants known as Puritans settled in New England. They objected to the control of the English Church by bishops, especially during the period from 1633 to 1641, when William Laud served as archbishop of Canterbury. Their main complaint was that the church services authorized by Laud too closely resembled those of Roman Catholicism. At the same time small groups of English Catholics, who often faced prosecution in English courts for practicing their religion, had taken refuge in Maryland. In the late seventeenth century a dissenting Protestant sect known as Quakers (so called because their founder, George Fox, told them to quake at the word of the Lord), smarting under legislation that denied them religious freedom and political power, emigrated to Pennsylvania.

Many other British colonists had come to America as indentured servants, usually serving for seven years in order to gain their freedom. By this time the size of the indigenous American population in the colonies had become negligible. The Indians of North America either had been pushed westward beyond the frontiers of these colonies, had died of diseases to which they were highly vulnerable, or had been killed in skirmishes with the English.

During the seventeenth century the English also established a number of trading posts, known as factories°, along the coast of India. The first of these factories was Surat, which was settled in 1612, and it was soon followed by Madras (1640), Bombay (1661), and Calcutta (1690). There were significant differences between these mercantile outposts and the colonies in the Caribbean and the North American mainland. The number of British settlers in India, most of whom were members of the East India Company, remained extremely small, and they did not establish large plantations like those in the Caribbean colonies and the southern mainland colonies. Consequently they did not introduce slave labor into these countries.

In contrast to the situation in North America and the Caribbean, the British in India had to deal with a large native population. At first they had contact with that population only when they were engaged in trade. In the second half of the eighteenth century, however, the British began to gain direct political control of Indian provinces, and by 1850 they controlled a large portion of the South Asian subcontinent. Not only did the British eventually subject the Indians to their rule, but they also drove out their French and Dutch commercial rivals, who had established their own factories along the coast.

DOCUMENT

Arrival of the British in the Punjab (mid-19th c.)

In addition to their settlements in America and India, the British acquired influence and ultimately political control of the area from Southeast Asia stretching down into the South Pacific. In the late seventeenth century the British began to challenge the Dutch and the Portuguese for control of the trade with Indonesia, and in the second half of the eighteenth century British merchants established a thriving trade with the countries on the Malay peninsula. In the late eighteenth century the British also began to explore the South Pacific, which remained the last part of the inhabited world that Europeans had not yet visited and settled. In 1770 the British naval officer and explorer Captain James Cook (1728–1779) claimed the entire eastern coast of Australia for Great Britain, and in 1788 the British established a penal colony in the southeastern corner of the continent at Botany Bay. Cook also visited New Zealand and many of the islands in the South Pacific, including Fiji, but colonies were not established at those locations until the middle of the nineteenth century.

The British Empire of the late seventeenth and eighteenth centuries possessed little administrative coherence; it was a hodgepodge of colonies, factories, and territories that had different relationships to the royal government in Britain (see Map 17.1). In India the provinces brought un-

---

Map 17.1 European Empires in 1763

This map shows the overseas possessions of Britain, France, the Dutch Republic, Spain, and Portugal. Russian overseas expansion into North America had not yet begun.

European Empires in 1763

- Dutch
- British
- French
- Ottoman Empire
- Portuguese
- Russian
- Spanish

der British control were run by a trading corporation that exercised many functions of government. Some colonies in America, such as Maryland and Pennsylvania, operated under charters granted to members of the aristocracy. Most of the colonies on the North American mainland and in the Caribbean had their own legislatures. None of these colonies, however, sent representatives to the British Parliament. The only bond of unity among all the colonists is that they, like British subjects living in England or Scotland, owed their allegiance to the monarch and were under the monarch's protection. All of these colonists were therefore British subjects.

The Scattered French Empire

French colonization of North America and India paralleled that of Great Britain, but it never achieved the same degree of success. As the British were establishing footholds in the West Indies and the mainland of North America, the French acquired their own islands in the Caribbean and laid claim to large sections of Canada and the Ohio and Mississippi River valleys in the present-day United States. In the West Indies the French began the process of colonization by introducing indentured servants for periods of three years, but in the eighteenth century they began to follow the British and Spanish pattern of importing slaves to provide the labor for the sugar plantations. In North America French settlers did not require a large labor supply, as their main economic undertakings were the fur trade and fishing. Consequently slaves were not introduced to those areas. The European population of French possessions in North America also stayed well below that of the British colonies.

The parallel between French and British overseas expansion extended to India, where in the early eighteenth century the French East India Company established factories at Pondicherry, Chandenagar, and other locations. Rivalry with the British also led the French to make alliances with native governors of Indian provinces, and with this support the French fought the British both on land and at sea at different critical times between 1744 and 1815. The British ultimately prevailed in this struggle, and by the turn of the nineteenth century the French presence in India had been reduced to a few isolated factories.

The waning of French influence in India coincided with a series of territorial losses in the New World. Defeats suffered at the hands of the British during the Seven Years' War (1756–1763) resulted in the transfer of French Canada and the territory east of the Mississippi River to Great Britain. During that conflict France also ceded the vast region of Louisiana between the Mississippi River and the Rocky Mountains to Spain. France regained Louisiana in 1801 but then promptly sold the entire territory to the United States in 1803. The following year the French Caribbean colony of Saint Domingue became independent, although France retained possession of its other West Indian colonies.

The only overseas area where France continued to expand after 1800 was much closer to home, on the Mediterranean shores of North Africa. French influence in this area had begun in the seventeenth century, and it persisted until the twentieth century. France occupied Egypt briefly from 1798 until 1801, and it acquired Algeria in 1830. It was not until the third stage of imperialism in the late nineteenth century that France took possession of large territories in the interior of Africa and in Asia (see Chapter 23).

The Commercial Dutch Empire

The tiny Dutch Republic acquired almost all of its overseas possessions in the first half of the seventeenth century, at about the same time that the British and French were establishing their first colonies in Asia and the New World. The formation of the Dutch empire went hand in hand with the explosive growth of the Dutch economy in the seventeenth century. At that time the Dutch Republic became the center of a global economy, and its overseas colonies in the New World, Asia, and Africa helped the republic maintain its commercial supremacy. Dutch overseas settlements, just like the port cities of the metropolis, were dedicated almost exclusively to serving the interests of trade.

The Dutch were more eager than other European powers to use military and naval power to acquire and fortify trading depots. They also used military force to seize factories that had been established earlier by other countries, especially Portugal. With more than 1,400 vessels that could be used as warships and 250,000 sailors, they had a distinct military advantage over the Portuguese, who could not muster half those numbers. They seized two trading posts from the Portuguese on the West African coast in 1637, and in 1641 they also acquired from Portugal the African islands of São Tomé and Principe. In 1624 the Dutch, operating through their West Indian Company, seized the northern coast of Brazil, and after its return to Portugal in 1654 they acquired two small West Indian islands and a number of small plantation colonies on the Guiana coast of South America, mainly in present-day Surinam. From these small settlements in Africa and the Caribbean the Dutch carried on trade with the Spanish, Portuguese, French, and British colonies. Through these ports the Dutch brought more than 500,000 slaves to Brazil, the Spanish colonies, and the French and British West Indies.

In addition to their African and Caribbean possessions, the Dutch established a presence in three other parts of the world. In the early seventeenth century they settled a colony in the Hudson River valley on the North American mainland. They named the colony New Netherland and its main port, at the mouth of the river, New Amsterdam. In 1664 the Dutch lost the colony to the English, who renamed the colony and the port New York. The second area was in Asia, where the Dutch East India Company established a fort at Batavia (now Jakarta in Indonesia) and factories in India,

The Trial of the Mutineers on the *Bounty*

In December 1787 a British ship named the *Bounty,* under the captainship of William Bligh, left Portsmouth, England, on a momentous journey to Tahiti, an island in the South Pacific that Captain James Cook had first visited in 1769. The goal of the voyage of the *Bounty* was neither exploration nor colonial expansion but to bring home breadfruit trees that Cook had discovered on his second trip to the island in 1773. The trees, so it was hoped, would be introduced to the West Indies as a source of food for the slaves and hence the survival of the plantation economy. The voyage of the *Bounty* was therefore part of the operation of the new global economy that European expansion had made possible. The total size of the crew, all of whom had volunteered for service, was forty-six. The master's first mate, who became the main leader of a mutiny against Bligh, was Fletcher Christian.

The mutiny did not take place until after the ship had remained at Tahiti for a number of months, loaded its cargo of more than a thousand breadfruit plants, and begun its return voyage. The main reason for the mutiny was Captain Bligh's abusive and humiliating language. Unlike many other officers who faced the task of maintaining order on their ships and commanding the obedience of their crews, Bligh did not flog his men. In that regard Bligh's behavior was mild. Instead he went into tantrums and verbally abused them, belittling them and calling them scoundrels. Just before the mutiny Bligh called Fletcher Christian a cowardly rascal and falsely accused him of stealing from him. On the morning of April 28, 1788, Christian arrested Bligh at bayonet point, tied his hands

behind his back, and threatened him with instant death if he should speak a word. Claiming that "Captain Bligh had brought all this on himself," Christian and his associates put Bligh and eighteen other members of the crew into one of the ship's small launch boats and set them adrift, leaving them to reach a nearby island by their own power.

The mutineers sailed on to the island of Tubuai, where after a brief stay they split into two groups. Nine of them, headed by Christian and accompanied by six Tahitian men and twelve women, established a settlement on Pitcairn Island. The remaining sixteen mutineers returned to Tahiti. All but two of these men were apprehended in 1791 by Captain Edwards of the H.M.S. *Pandora,* which had been sent to Tahiti with the objective of arresting them and returning them to England for trial. At the beginning of its return voyage the *Pandora* was shipwrecked, and four of the prisoners drowned. The rest reached England aboard another ship in 1792. They were

promptly charged before a navy court-martial with taking the *Bounty* away from its captain and with desertion, both of which were offenses under the Naval Discipline Act of 1766.

The trial took place aboard a British ship, H.M.S. *Duke,* in Portsmouth harbor in September 1792. The proceeding had all the markings of a state trial, one initiated by the government for offenses against the Crown. Mutiny and desertion represented challenges to the state itself. During the second period of imperial expansion navies became major instruments of state power. Even when ships were used for purposes of exploration rather than naval combat, they served the interests of the state. The captain of the ship represented the power of the sovereign at sea. Because of the difficulty of maintaining order in such circumstances, he was given absolute authority. He could use whatever means necessary, including the infliction of corporal punishment, to preserve order. To disobey or challenge

Sextant
Eighteenth-century ships like the *Bounty* used this instrument to determine nautical position by means of the stars.

***The Mutineers Casting Bligh Adrift in the Launch,* Engraving by Robert Dodd (1790)**
This was the central act in the mutiny led by Fletcher Christian. Captain Bligh is standing in the launch in his night-clothes. Some of the breadfruit trees loaded on the ship at Tahiti can be seen on the top deck.

him was interpreted as an act of rebellion.

The trial was based on the assumption that the mutiny was illegal and seditious. The only question was the extent of individual involvement in the act itself. The degree of involvement was measured by evidence of one's co-operation with Christian or his loyalty to Bligh. The mere fact that some men had remained with Christian on the *Bounty* did not prove that they had supported the mutiny. Four of those men gave little evidence of having voluntarily cooperated with Christian, and those four men were eventually acquitted. The testimony of Captain Bligh, who declared that those four crew members had been reluctant to put him in the launch boat, was decisive in securing their nonguilty verdicts.

The remaining six men were convicted and sentenced to die by hanging. Three of those men were

eventually spared their lives. Peter Heywood and James Morrison were well connected to influential people in the navy and the government and received royal pardons. William Muspratt, one of only three mutineers to hire a lawyer, entered a protest against the procedures of the court. In a court-martial, unlike a criminal trial at the common law, a prisoner could not call witnesses in his own defense. At the time of his conviction Muspratt protested that he had been "debarred calling witnesses whose evidence I have reason to believe would have tended to prove my innocence." The difference between the two systems of criminal justice, he claimed, "is dreadful to the subject and fatal to me." On this ground Muspratt was reprieved.

The three men who were executed died as model prisoners, proclaiming the illegality of their rebellion. Although the govern-

ment had executed only a small minority of the mutineers, by securing their conviction and dramatizing it with a widely publicized hanging, it had upheld its authority and thus reinforced the power of the Crown.

Questions of Justice

1. How would you characterize the different ideals of justice adhered to by the mutineers on the *Bounty* and the British admiralty court that tried them?
2. What does the journey of the *Bounty* tell us about the role of the British navy in the process of imperial expansion? What problems were inherent in using British ships for these purposes?

Taking It Further

Rutter, Owen, ed. *The Court-Martial of the "Bounty" Mutineers.* 1931. Contains a full transcript of the trial.

The Dutch Factory of Batavia in Indonesia, ca. 1665
The Dutch Republic dominated the Asian trade in the seventeenth century. Batavia (now Jakarta) was the most important of their settlements in Southeast Asia. The efforts of the Dutch to transplant their culture is evident in this building's Dutch style of architecture.

China, and Japan. These possessions allowed the Dutch to engage in trade throughout Asia. In the eighteenth century, however, the British began to take control of Dutch trading routes.

The third area was the southern tip of Africa, where in 1652 the Dutch settled a colony at the Cape of Good Hope, mainly to provide support for ships engaged in commerce with the East Indies. In this colony some 1,700 Dutch settlers, most of them farmers known as boers°, developed an agricultural economy on plantations that employed slave labor. The loss of this colony to the British at the end of the eighteenth century reflected a more general decline of Dutch military and imperial strength.

The Vast Spanish Empire

Of all the European overseas empires, the lands under the control of the Spanish monarchy were the most extensive. At the height of its power in 1650, the Spanish Empire covered the western part of North America from California to Mexico and from Mexico down through Central America.

It also included Florida and the Caribbean islands of Cuba, San Domingo, and Puerto Rico. It embraced almost all of South America except Brazil, which was under Portuguese control. In Asia the main Spanish possessions were the Philippine Islands, named for the future King Philip II in 1542 and conquered with little bloodshed after 1564. The Philippines served as the main base from which the Spanish engaged in trade with other Asian countries.

Spanish overseas possessions were never ruled as closely as the royal government in Madrid ruled the smaller kingdoms and principalities on the Iberian peninsula. Spanish overseas possessions were, however, integrated into a much more authoritative imperial system than were those of the British. Until the eighteenth century a hierarchy of councils, staffed by men appointed by the Crown, exercised political control of the various large territories or viceroyalties into which the empire was divided. Like all mercantilist enterprises, the Spanish colonial empire was designed to serve the purposes of trade. Until the eighteenth century a council known as the House of Trade, situated in Seville, exercised a monopoly over all colonial commerce. It funneled trade with the colonies from the southwestern Spanish port of Cadiz and to selected ports on the eastern coasts of Spanish America, from which it was then redirected to other ports. The ships returned to Spain carrying the gold and silver that had been extracted from the mines of Mexico and Peru. The entire journey was made under the protection of Spanish warships.

The Bourbon kings of Spain, who were installed on the throne in 1700, introduced a number of political reforms that were intended to increase the volume of the colonial trade and prevent the smuggling that had always threatened to undermine it. On the one hand, they opened up the colonial trade to more Spanish and American ports and also permitted more trade within the colonies. On the other hand, the Bourbons, especially Charles III (r. 1759–1788), brought the viceroyalties under more direct control of Spanish royal officials and increased the efficiency of the tax collection system. These Bourbon reforms made the empire more manageable and profitable, but they also created tension between the Spanish-born bureaucrats and the creoles°, the people of Spanish descent who had been born in the colonies. These tensions eventually led in the early nineteenth century to a series of wars of independence from Spain that we shall discuss in a later section.

The Declining Portuguese Empire

The Portuguese had been the first European nation to engage in overseas exploration and colonization. During the late fifteenth and sixteenth centuries they had established colonies in Asia, South America, and Africa (see Chapter 12). By the beginning of the eighteenth century, however, the Portuguese Empire had declined in size and wealth in relation to its rivals. The Portuguese continued to hold a few ports in India, most notably the small island of Goa. They also retained a factory at Macao off the southeastern coast of China. In the New World the major Portuguese plantation colony was Brazil, which occupied almost half the land mass of South America and which supplied Europe with sugar, cacao (from which chocolate is made), and other agricultural commodities. Closely linked to Brazil were the Portuguese colonies along and off the West African coast. These possessions were all deeply involved in the transatlantic trade, especially in slaves. The Portuguese also had a series of trading stations and small settlements on the southeastern coast of Africa, including Mozambique.

The contraction of the Portuguese Empire in the seventeenth and eighteenth centuries resulted in the transfer of land to other European countries. A relatively weak European power, Portugal did not fare well in the fierce military conflicts that ensued in South America and Asia over control of the colonial trade. Portugal's main military and economic competition came from the Dutch, who seized many of its Asian, African, and South American colonies, and who acquired many Portuguese trading routes. Most of those losses took place in Asia between 1600 and 1670. The Portuguese Empire suffered further losses when the crown relinquished Bombay and the northern African port of Tangier to the English as part of the dowry for the Portuguese princess Catherine of Braganza when she married King Charles II in 1661.

Brazil remained by far the most important of the Portuguese possessions during the late seventeenth and eighteenth centuries. The colony suffered from an unfavorable balance of trade with Portugal, but it expanded in population and wealth during this period, especially after the discovery of gold and diamonds led to large-scale mining in the interior. The slave trade increased in volume in order to provide additional labor in the mines and on the sugar plantations. In the first quarter of the nineteenth century, as the British slave trade declined and came to an end, Portuguese ships carried 871,600 slaves to Brazil. Between 1826 and 1850 the number increased to an astonishing 1,247,700. As a result of this massive influx of Africans, slaves accounted for approximately 40 percent of the entire Brazilian population by the beginning of the nineteenth century.

Like most other European countries, Portugal tightened the control of its imperial possessions during the second half of the eighteenth century. During the ministry of the dictatorial Marquis of Pombal from 1755 to 1777, efforts were made to increase the control exercised by the Crown over all aspects of colonial life. Pombal also took steps to encourage the growth of the colonial trade, and he legalized intermarriage between whites and indigenous peoples. Like the Bourbon reforms in Spanish America, this legislation created considerable resentment among the creoles against the Portuguese bureaucrats who controlled the govern-

ment. As in Spanish America, these tensions led to demands for Brazil's autonomy in the nineteenth century.

The Russian Empire in the Pacific

The only eastern European state that established an overseas empire during the eighteenth century was Russia. Between the fifteenth and the early eighteenth centuries Russia had gradually acquired a massive overland empire stretching from St. Petersburg in the west across the frigid expanse of Siberia to the Pacific Ocean. The main impulse of Russian expansion had been the search for exotic furs that were in high demand in the colder climes of Russia and northern Europe. During the reign of the empress Catherine the Great (r. 1762–1796), Russia entered a period of further territorial expansion. On its western frontier it took part in the successive partitions of Poland between 1772 and 1795, while to the south it held the Crimean region within the Ottoman Empire between 1783 and 1792.

During the late eighteenth and early nineteenth centuries Russia also extended its empire overseas. Russian traders and explorers undertook numerous expeditions to Hawaii and other islands in the Pacific Ocean, sailing as far south as Mexico. They did not, however, establish colonies in these locations. Further expeditions brought Russia across the northern Pacific, where they encroached upon the hunting grounds of the native Aleuts in Alaska. The Russian-American Company, established in 1789, built a number of trading posts along the Pacific seaboard from Alaska down to Fort Ross in northern California. These claims led to a protracted territorial dispute with Spain, which had established a string of missions and settlements on the California coast as far north as San Francisco. In this way the two great European empires of Russia and Spain, advancing from opposite directions, confronted each other on the western coast of North America. Russian expansion into Alaska and California also led to territorial disputes with the United States, which was engaged in its own process of territorial expansion westward toward the Pacific during the nineteenth century.

Warfare in Europe, North America, and Asia

■ In what ways did the wars waged by European powers during this period involve competition for overseas possessions and trading routes?

Until the middle of the seventeenth century, European states engaged each other in battle almost exclusively within their own continent. The farthest their armies ever traveled was to the Middle East to fight the Turks or to Ireland to conquer the native Celts. The acquisition of overseas empires and the conflicts that erupted between European powers over the control of global trade brought those European conflicts to new and distant military theaters. Wars that began over territory in Europe were readily extended to America in one direction and to Asia in the other. The military forces that fought in these imperial battles consisted not only of metropolitan government troops but also those of the colonists. These colonial forces were often supplemented by the troops drawn from the local population, such as when the French recruited Native Americans to fight with them against the British in North America. This pattern of recruiting soldiers from the indigenous population, which began in the eighteenth century, became the norm during the third and final phase of empire building in the nineteenth and early twentieth centuries.

Wars fought overseas placed a premium on naval strength. Ground troops remained important, both in Europe and overseas, but naval power increasingly proved to be the crucial factor. All of the Western imperial powers either possessed or acquired large navies. Great Britain and the Dutch Republic rose to the status of world powers on the basis of sea power, while the French strengthened their navy considerably during the reign of Louis XIV. The Dutch used their naval power mainly against the Portuguese and the British, while the British directed theirs against the French and the Spanish as well as the Dutch. The overwhelming success that the British realized in these conflicts resulted in the establishment of British maritime supremacy.

Mercantile Warfare

An increasingly important motive for engaging in warfare in the late seventeenth and eighteenth centuries was the protection and expansion of trade. The theory that underlay and inspired these imperial wars was mercantilism. As we discussed in Chapter 15, those who subscribed to this theory, such as Louis XIV's minister Jean-Baptiste Colbert, believed that the wealth of the state depended on its ability to import fewer commodities than it exported and thus to acquire the largest possible share of the world's monetary supply. In order to achieve this goal, mercantilists encouraged domestic industry and placed heavy customs duties or tariffs on imported goods. Mercantilism was therefore a policy of protectionism°, the shielding of domestic industries from foreign competition. Mercantilists also sought to increase the size of the country's commercial fleet, establish colonies in order to promote trade, and import raw materials from the colonies to benefit domestic industry. The imperial wars of the seventeenth and eighteenth centuries, which were fought over the control of colonies and trading routes, thus formed part of a mercantilist policy.

Of course the older, more traditional motives for waging war, especially the desire of rulers for territorial expansion, did not disappear. The acquisitive impulses of France, Prussia, Austria, and Russia remained a recurrent source of international conflict throughout this period. But the mercantile motive, which began to emerge only in the 1650s, soon became a major feature of European warfare, and it explains why military conflict was extended from Europe to the colonies. As this motive for going to war became more important, wars fought primarily for religious or ideological reasons, which had been the norm during the period of the Reformation, virtually disappeared.

The first of the great mercantile wars that involved conflict overseas arose between England and the Dutch Republic in the middle and late seventeenth century (1652–1654, 1664–1667, 1672–1675). As these wars were fought between two Protestant powers, little about these conflicts could be attributed to religious zeal. Instead they were fought mainly for mercantile advantage between the two emerging commercial giants of Europe. The two countries were engaged in heated competition for control of the transatlantic trade, and the Dutch resented the passage of English laws, known as the Navigation Acts, that excluded them from trade with the English colonies. The Dutch claimed the right to trade with all ports in the world as well as to fish in the waters off British shores. Not surprisingly, many of the engagements in these wars took place at sea and in the colonies. The most significant outcome of these Anglo-Dutch wars was the loss of the port city of New Amsterdam to the English. That city, renamed New York, later became the leading port and financial center in the Western Hemisphere.

Shortly after the first Anglo-Dutch War, England also went to war against Spain (1655–1657). Although this conflict pitted a Protestant against a Catholic power, it too reflected the new emphasis on mercantile objectives. The main battles of this war were not fought in the English Channel, as they had been when the Spanish Armada had descended on England in 1588, but in the Caribbean. The war resulted in the British acquisition of one of its most important Caribbean colonies, Jamaica, in 1655. The Anglo-Spanish tensions that surfaced in this conflict continued into the eighteenth century, when Britain tried to smuggle more goods than it was allowed by the Treaty of Utrecht (1713) into the Spanish trading post of Portobelo on the isthmus of Panama. The Spanish retaliated by cutting off the ear of Robert Jenkins, an English captain, and this incident led to the War of Jenkins' Ear in 1739. In 1762, during another war against Spain (as well as France), armed forces from Britain and the North American colonies seized the Cuban port of Havana as part of an effort to monopolize the Caribbean trade. The following year, however, Britain returned the city to Spain in exchange for Florida. This acquisition gave the British control of the entire North American eastern seaboard.

Anglo-French Military Rivalry

Anglo-Spanish conflict paled in comparison with the bitter commercial rivalry between Great Britain and France during the eighteenth century. Anglo-French conflict was one of the few consistent patterns of eighteenth-century European warfare. It lasted so long and had so many different phases that it is known as the second Hundred Years' War, a recurrence of the bitter period of warfare between England and France from the middle of the fourteenth to the middle of the fifteenth century. The great difference between the two periods of warfare was that the first Hundred Years' War involved military conflicts in France, while the second was marked by periodic naval and military engagements not only in Europe but in Asia and North America as well.

The Wars of the Spanish and Austrian Successions, 1701–1748

This eighteenth-century Anglo-French rivalry had its roots in the war of the Spanish Succession (1701–1713). The war began as an effort to prevent France from putting Louis XIV's grandson, Philip, on the Spanish throne (see Chapter 15). The implications of this dynastic conflict for the British and French colonial empires were monumental. By uniting French and Spanish territory the proposed succession would have created a massive French-Spanish empire not only in Europe but in the Western Hemisphere as well. This combination of French and Spanish territory and military power threatened to eclipse the British colonies along the North American coast and deprive British merchants of much of their valuable trade.

The ensuing struggle in North America, known by British colonists as Queen Anne's War, was settled in Britain's favor by the Treaty of Utrecht in 1713. Philip V, the first Spanish king from the Bourbon dynasty (r. 1700–1746), was allowed to remain on the throne, but French and Spanish territories in Europe and America were kept separate. Even more important, the French ceded their Canadian territories of Newfoundland and Nova Scotia to the British. The treaty, which also gave Britain the contract to ship slaves to the Spanish colonies for thirty years, marked the emergence of Britain as Europe's dominant colonial and maritime power.

The next phase of Anglo-French warfare, the War of the Austrian Succession (1740–1748), formed part of a European conflict that engaged the forces of Austria, Prussia, and Spain as well as those of Britain and France. In this conflict European dynastic struggles once again intersected with competition for colonial advantage overseas. The ostensible cause of this war was the impetuous decision by the new king of Prussia, the absolutist

CHRONOLOGY

A Century of Anglo-French Warfare

1701–1713	War of the Spanish Succession (Queen Anne's War in North America): Spain is allied with France
1740–1748	War of the Austrian Succession (Europe): France is allied with Spain and Prussia; Britain is allied with Austria and the Dutch Republic
1744–1748	King George's War (North America)
1754–1763	French and Indian War (North America): French and British are allied with different Indian tribes
1756–1763	Seven Years' War (Europe): France is allied with Austria; Britain is allied with Prussia
1775–1783	American War of Independence: France is allied with United States against Britain in 1778
1781–1783	Warfare in India
1792–1815	French Revolutionary and Napoleonic Wars: Britain is allied at various times with Austria, Prussia, Spain, and the Dutch Republic; warfare at times in the West Indies as well as in India

Frederick II (r. 1740–1786), to seize the large German-speaking province of Silesia from Austria upon the succession of Maria Theresa (r. 1740–1780) as the ruler of the hereditary Habsburg lands (see Map 17.2). Using the large army that his militaristic father Frederick William I had assembled, Frederick struck with devastating effectiveness, and by terms of the treaty that ended the war he acquired most of the province.

Frederick's aggression enticed other European powers to join the conflict. Eager to acquire some of the Habsburg territories in different parts of Europe, France and Spain both declared war on Austria. Britain then entered the war against France, mainly to keep France from acquiring Austria's possessions in the Netherlands. Britain's main concern in the European phase of this war, as it had been in the War of the Spanish Succession, was to maintain the balance of power among European states.

The colonial phase of this war, known in British North America as King George's War, opened in 1744, when the French supported the Spanish in a separate war that Spain had been waging against Britain since 1739 over the Caribbean trade. Clashes between French and British trading companies in India also began in the same year. The main military engagement of this war was the seizure of the French port and fortress of Louisbourg on Cape Breton Island in Canada by 4,000 New England colonial troops and a large British fleet. At the end of the war, however, the British returned Louisbourg to the French in exchange for

Map 17.2 The War of the Austrian Succession, 1740–1748
Austria lost Silesia to Prussia during the War of the Austrian Succession in 1742. Maria Theresa's efforts to regain the province in the Seven Years' War were unsuccessful.

the factory of Madras in India, which the French had taken during the war.

The Seven Years' War, 1756–1763

European and colonial rivalries became even more entangled in the next round of Anglo-French warfare, known as the Seven Years' War (1756–1763) in Europe and the French and Indian War (1754–1763) in North America. In Europe the conflict arose as a result of Maria Theresa's eventually unsuccessful attempt to regain Silesia. In this encounter, however, she joined forces with her former enemies, France and Russia, after Great Britain signed a defensive alliance with Prussia. This "diplomatic revolution" of 1756 shifted all the traditional alliances among European powers, but it did not affect Anglo-French rivalry in the colonies, which continued unabated.

The fighting in this North American theater of the war was particularly brutal and inflicted extensive casualties. In their struggle to gain control of eastern port cities and interior lands, the British and the French secured alliances with different Indian tribes. Among the many victims were some

of France's Indian allies who contracted smallpox when British-American colonists sold them blankets deliberately contaminated with the disease—the first known use of germ warfare in the West. This colonial war also had an Asian theater, in which French and British forces, most of them drawn from the trading companies of their respective countries, vied for mercantile influence and the possession of factories along the coast of the Indian Ocean. This conflict led directly to the British acquisition of the Indian province of Bengal in 1765.

The Treaty of Paris, which ended this round of European and colonial warfare in 1763, had more profound implications in the colonies than in Europe. In Europe, Prussia managed to hold on to Silesia, although its army incurred heavy casualties and its economy suffered from the war. In North America, however, monumental changes occurred. As a result of British naval victories, all of French Canada east of the Mississippi, including the entire province of Quebec, with its predominantly French population and French system of civil law, passed into British control (see Map 17.3). Even more important, the treaty secured British naval and mercantile superiority in the Atlantic, Caribbean, and Indian oceans. By virtue of its victories over France, Britain gained control of the lion's share of world commerce. This commercial superiority had profound implications for the economic development of Britain. Partially because of its ability to acquire raw materials from its colonies and to market its products throughout the world, Britain became the first country to experience the Industrial Revolution, as shall be discussed fully in Chapter 20.

The American and French Revolutionary Wars, 1775–1815

Despite the British victory over the French in 1763, the long conflict between the two countries continued into the early

nineteenth century. During the American War of Independence (1775–1783), which we shall consider later, the North American colonists secured French military aid. During that war a British fleet attacked the French colony of Martinique, while the French dispatched an expedition against the British at Savannah that included hundreds of Africans and mulattos, or people of mixed race, drawn from the population of the West Indies. In India further conflicts between the French and British occurred, mainly between 1781 and 1783. These simultaneous military engagements in various parts of the world turned this phase of Anglo-French conflict into the first truly global war.

Anglo-French rivalry entered yet another phase between 1792 and 1815, during the era of the French Revolution (see Chapter 19). The British were able to

Map 17.3 British Possessions in North America and the Caribbean After the Treaty of Paris, 1763

The British acquisition of French territory marked a decisive moment in the expansion of the British Empire.

maintain their military and naval superiority, although once again it required an alliance with many European powers and the creation of a new balance of power against France. Even during this later phase of this French-British rivalry the British pursued imperial objectives. They expanded their empire in India and consolidated their territory there under the governorship of Richard Wellesley (1760–1842). In 1795, in the midst of the war against France, the British also acquired the Dutch colony at the Cape of Good Hope, giving them a base for their claims to much larger African territories in the nineteenth century.

The Atlantic World

■ How did European empires create an Atlantic economy in which the traffic in slaves was a major feature?

By the beginning of the eighteenth century, the territorial acquisitions of the five European maritime powers had moved the geographical center of the West from the European continent to the Atlantic Ocean itself. The Atlantic, rather than separating large geographical land masses, became a central, unifying geographical entity. The boundaries of this new Western world were the four continents that bordered the Atlantic: Europe, Africa, North America, and South America. The main thoroughfares that linked them were maritime routes across the Atlantic and up and down its coasts. The main points of commercial and cultural contact between the four continents, until the end of the eighteenth century, were the coastal areas and ports that bordered on the ocean. Within this Atlantic world arose new patterns of trade and economic activity, new interactions between ethnic and racial groups, and new political institutions. The Atlantic world also became the arena in which political and religious ideas were transmitted across the ocean and developed within a new environment.

The Atlantic Economy

The exchange of commercial goods and slaves between the western coasts of Europe, the African coasts, and the ports of North and South America created an economic enterprise that became one of the most active in the entire world (see Map 17.4). The ships that had brought the slaves from Africa to the Americas used the profits gained from their transactions to acquire precious metals and agricultural products for the European market. They then returned to western European Atlantic ports, where the goods were sold.

This Atlantic economy was fueled ultimately by the demand of a growing European population for agricultural products that could not be obtained in Europe and were more costly to transport from Asia. Sugar was the most important of these commodities, but tobacco, cotton, rice,

cacao, and coffee also became staples of the transatlantic trade. At the same time the North and South American colonists created a steady demand for manufactured goods, especially cutlery and metal tools, that were produced in Europe.

Two of the commodities that were imported from the colonies, tobacco and coffee, were criticized for the harmful effects they had on the human body. Tobacco, which came from the Americas, was the target of a number of criticisms in the seventeenth century. Even at that early date critics recognized the adverse physical effects of this product, which had been used widely among Native Americans. "Tobacco, that outlandish weed," read one popular rhyme, "It spends the brain and spoils the seed." Critics also believed that it had a hallucinatory effect on those who inhaled its smoke.

Coffee was a stimulant that originally came exclusively from the Middle East but later began to be shipped from Haiti and after 1809 from Brazil. Like tobacco, coffee was controversial because of the effects it had on the human

A Satire Against Coffee and Tobacco
A seventeenth-century satirical depiction of two European women smoking tobacco and drinking coffee. Turkey, represented by the figure to the right, was the main source of coffee in the seventeenth century. An African servant, to the left, pours the coffee. Tobacco came from the Americas.

Map 17.4   The Atlantic Economy in the Mid-Eighteenth Century

Commodities and African slaves were exchanged between the four continents of North America, South America, Europe, and Africa.

body. In the late seventeenth and eighteenth centuries it was believed to be a source of political radicalism, probably because the coffeehouses where it was consumed served as gathering places for political dissidents. Contemporaries also identified coffee's capacity to produce irritability and depression.

The Atlantic economy had its own rhythms, but it was also part of a global economy that had taken shape during the seventeenth century. As Europeans had expanded the volume of their imports from Asia, those markets were fully integrated into this world system. The system was capitalist in the sense that the production and distribution of

Chocolate in the New World and the Old

One product of the encounters that took place between Spaniards and the indigenous people of the New World was the widespread consumption of chocolate among western Europeans in the seventeenth century. Chocolate was produced from the seeds of the cacao tree, which was indigenous to South America. Consumed mainly as a beverage, chocolate had been in widespread use among Aztecs and Mayans for centuries before the Spanish Conquest in the sixteenth century; like another native American plant, tobacco, it was used in religious and political ceremonies as well as for medicinal purposes. Spanish colonists received gifts of chocolate from Indians and soon began to enjoy the pleasurable physiological effects of this commodity, which contains chemical agents that act like amphetamines. Because it had such pleasurable effects, it was used in rituals of worship, friendship and courtship.

By the beginning of the seventeenth century, chocolate made its way from colonial America across the Atlantic to Spain. Shortly thereafter it became available in other western European countries. Its widespread use prepared the way for the introduction of two stimulants that came originally from the Middle East and Asia in the latter half of the seventeenth century: coffee and tea.

Because chocolate was grown in non-Christian lands where Spaniards believed that demons inhabited the landscape, and because it was associated with sexual pleasure, it met with harsh disapproval. Clerics denounced it—together with tobacco—as an inducement to vice and the work of Satan. Gradually, however, chocolate came to be viewed in purely secular terms as a commodity, without any religious significance.

The European demand for chocolate contributed to three major transformations of Western life. The first was the growth of the Atlantic trade and a global economy. Among the products that were shipped from the Americas to Europe in exchange for slaves and manufactured goods, cacao was second only to sugar in volume. In preconquest America cacao had often served as an exchange currency; now it was assigned a specific value in the world marketplace. As the price of chocolate escalated Spain established a monopoly over the trade, thus integrating it into the mercantilist system.

Second, the introduction of chocolate into Europe transformed the drinking patterns of Europeans. There had been nothing like chocolate in the diets of Europeans before its arrival, and when it was introduced, new rituals of consumption developed around its use. Cups with handles were designed specifically for drinking the hot beverage, the same cups later used for coffee and tea. The Aztec custom of scooping the foam from the top of a chocolate drink was adopted in Europe. The European desire to sweeten chocolate, as well as coffee and tea, increased the demand for sugar, which in turn encouraged the growth of slavery on the sugar plantations in the West Indies. Sweetened chocolate eventually began to be served as a candy, and by the nineteenth century chocolate candy became the main form in which the commodity was consumed.

Finally, chocolate became a part of the emerging bourgeois sexual culture of eighteenth-century France and England. Just as in preconquest Spanish America, it began to play a role in rituals of sexual seduction. It is no accident that boxes of chocolate are popular gifts on Valentine's Day and that the most well-known chocolate candy in the United States, Godiva, features the English noblewoman who rode naked through the streets of Coventry in 1140. The sustained exchange of a delectable commodity between the New World and the Old World thus contributed to a transformation of Western culture.

For Discussion

To what extent did the tastes of European consumers determine the nature of the Atlantic economy in the seventeenth and eighteenth centuries?

The Chocolate House (1787)
Men and women drinking chocolate, tea, and coffee at the White Conduit House, Islington, London.

commodities were undertaken by private individuals, in a systematic way, for the purposes of profit. European governments had an interest in this capitalist economy because as mercantilists they wanted their countries to acquire the largest possible share of world trade, but they did not control the actual operations of the marketplace. Their role was mainly to authorize individuals or trading companies to conduct trade in a particular geographical area.

The Atlantic Slave Trade

The slave trade became the very linchpin of the Atlantic economy, and all five Western European imperial powers—Britain, France, the Dutch Republic, Spain, and Portugal—engaged in it. The trade arose to meet the demand of plantation owners in the New World for agricultural labor. In the seventeenth century, after the indigenous Indian population had been ravaged by disease and the indentured whites who had emigrated from Europe in search of a more secure future had gained their freedom, this demand became urgent. Slave labor possessed a number of advantages over free labor. Slaves could be disciplined more easily, they could be forced to work longer hours, and they could be used to build a plantation economy in which the growing, harvesting, and processing of sugar and other agricultural commodities could be directed by one authority. The use of slave labor also allowed the economies of

European countries, especially Great Britain, to develop. Those who had invested in the colonial trade received attractive returns on their investment, while agricultural profits acquired from crops produced by slaves encouraged the growth of domestic manufacturing.

The slave trade formed the crucial link in the triangular pattern of commercial routes that began when European vessels traveled to ports along the western coast of Africa. There they exchanged European goods, including guns, for slaves that African merchants had captured in the interior and had marched to the sea. At these ports the slaves were branded with initials indicating to which nation they belonged. They were then crowded into ships that transported them across the Atlantic to the coast of South America, to the Caribbean, or as far north as Maryland. This was the famous and often deadly Middle Passage, the second leg of the triangular journey, which was completed when the ships returned to their point of origin. Once they had arrived in the Americas, the slaves were sold to the owners of plantations in the tropical areas of the Caribbean and the south Atlantic and in the more moderate climates of the North American mainland.

Mungo Park on Slavery in the Atlantic (late 1700s)

Slavery has been present throughout world history. It was a major feature of classical civilization and it was also present in medieval Europe before 1200. In Greece and Rome it had often been the result of captivity in war, whereas in the Middle Ages it was reserved for individuals

---

DOCUMENT

A Former Slave Protests African Slavery

In 1787 Quobna Ottobah Cugoano (1757–1791), a former slave, published an abolitionist treatise, Thoughts and Sentiments on the Evil and Wicked Traffic of the Slavery and Commerce of the Human Species. *Like the narrative written by Olaudah Equiano quoted at the beginning of this chapter, Cugoano's account describes the horrors of the African slave trade that he himself had experienced. In this passage Cugoano deplores the effect that the slave trade had on his native Africa.*

That base traffic of kid-napping and stealing men was begun by the Portuguese on the coast of Africa, and as they found the benefit of it for their own wicked purposes, they soon went on to commit further depredations. The Spaniards followed their infamous example, and the African slave trade was thought most advantageous for them, to enable themselves to live in ease and affluence by the cruel subjection and slavery of others. The French and English, and some other nations in Europe, as they founded

settlements or colonies in the West Indies or in America, went on in the same manner, and joined hand in hand with the Portuguese and Spaniards to rob and pillage Africa as well as to waste and desolate the inhabitants of the western continent. But the European depredators and pirates have not only robbed and pillaged the people of Africa themselves; but, by their instigation, they have infested the inhabitants with some of the vilest combinations of fraudulent and treacherous villains, even among their own people, and have set up their forts and factories as a reservoir of public and abandoned thieves and as a den of desperadoes, where they may ensnare, entrap and catch men. So that Africa has been robbed of its inhabitants, its freeborn sons and daughters have been stole, and kid-napped and violently taken away and carried into captivity and cruel bondage. And it may be said in respect to that diabolical traffic which is still carried on by the European depredators, that Africa has suffered as much and more than any other quarters of the globe.

Source: Quobna Ottobah Cugoano, *Thoughts and Sentiments on the Evil and Wicked Traffic of the Slavery and Commerce of the Human Species* (London, 1787).

who had been denied certain liberties. As Islam expanded in the ninth century, Arabs began the enslavement of foreign peoples, including black slaves from eastern Africa, and they continued that traffic into the early modern period. In the sixteenth and seventeenth centuries Barbary pirates in the Mediterranean captured approximately 850,000 white Europeans during sea raids and forced them into slavery in Muslim North Africa.

Within this long history of world slavery, the African slave trade conducted by Europeans is unique in three respects. The first distinction is its size. As a demographic phenomenon this involuntary transportation of Africans to the New World is without parallel in world history. It is the largest transoceanic migration recorded in written documents. Between 1519 and 1867 more than 11 million slaves were shipped from Africa to the New World. Deaths at sea reduced the number of slaves who actually arrived in the Americas to about 9.5 million. The peak years of the trade were from 1751 to 1800, when nearly four million slaves left African shores. As the volume of the slave trade increased during the eighteenth century, the percentage of African slaves among all immigrants arriving in the New World rose to more than 75 percent. Nine out of every ten slaves were sent to Brazil or the Caribbean region, including the northern coast of South America. The great majority of these slaves were sold to the owners of sugar and coffee plantations. Only about 4 percent of all slaves were destined for the British colonies on the North American mainland (after 1776 the United States), and almost all of those slaves were sent to the southern colonies.

The second distinctive feature of African slavery in the Americas was its racial character. It differed from the forms of slavery that had existed in ancient Greece and Rome as well as in medieval Europe, in which people of different races and ethnicities had been enslaved. It even differed from Muslim slavery, which involved the enslavement of European Christians as well as black Africans. As the slave trade brought millions of Africans into the Americas, and as indigenous Indian slavery diminished in size, slavery came to be equated with being black, while race was used to justify the inferiority of all African slaves.

The third distinctive feature of the Atlantic slave trade was its commercial character. Its sole function was to provide slave traders with a profit and slave owners with a supply of unfree labor. From the very beginning of their captivity African slaves were considered objects to be sold and their labor exploited. Acting in concert with African chieftains, European slave traders seized people who had performed no acts of aggression in their homelands, transported them overseas, and sold them to the highest bidders. Theories of private property developed in Europe in the seventeenth and eighteenth centuries established the right of slave masters to own their slaves as they would other pieces of property. In this way African slaves were turned into commercial commodities and treated in a manner that

Volume of the Transatlantic Slave Trade from Africa, 1519–1867	
1519–1600	266,100
1601–1650	503,500
1651–1675	239,800
1676–1700	510,000
1701–1725	958,600
1725–1750	1,311,300
1751–1775	1,905,200
1776–1800	1,921,100
1801–1825	1,645,100
1826–1850	1,621,000
1851–1867	180,800
Total	11,062,000

Source: David Eltis, "The Volume and Structure of the Transatlantic Slave Trade: A Reassessment," *William and Mary Quarterly*, 3rd series, 58 (2001), Table II.6.

deprived them of all human dignity. To justify such treatment their owners insisted that they "were beasts and had no more souls than beasts."[3] Slaves have never been treated well in any society, but slavery in the Americas acquired a reputation for being particularly exploitative and barbaric, and this has much to do with its commercial character.

One harrowing incident on the British slave ship *Zong* reveals the way in which financial calculations determined the fate of slaves. The *Zong* set sail in 1781 from the African island of São Tomé with 442 African slaves on board. When the slaves began to fall ill and die from malnutrition and disease, the captain of the ship, Luke Collingwood, feared that the owners of the ship would suffer a financial loss. If, however, the slaves were to be thrown overboard on the pretext that the safety of the crew was in jeopardy, the loss would be absorbed by those who had insured the voyage. Accordingly Collingwood decided to tie 132 slaves together, two by two, and fling them into the sea. When the ship owners went to court to collect the insurance, they argued that slaves were no different from horses and that they had a perfect right to throw the slaves overboard in order to preserve the safety of the ship.

Differences in the treatment and survival of slaves in the various parts of the New World had more to do with economic conditions, climate, and population trends than with the nationality or the religion of the slave masters. The crucial factor was the nature of the labor to which the slaves were subjected. Slaves who worked on plantations, especially those growing sugar, usually died within a few years. They were—simply said—worked to death. In the French colony of Saint Domingue, more than 500,000 of the 800,000 slaves brought to the colony between 1680 and 1780 perished. As long as the slave trade was still open, it was more profitable simply to replace those who died with new slaves than to try to extend the life of those the plantation owners already had. It was for this reason that the slave population did not start to grow internally in most areas until the slave trade ended in the nineteenth century.

Another factor influencing the treatment and survival of slaves was the ratio of the black to the white populations. When that ratio was high, as in all the Caribbean colonies, the codes regulating slave life were particularly harsh and created a reign of terror within the slave community. Yet another factor was climate. The absence of tropical diseases in the more temperate zone of the North American colonies provides the best explanation why in these colonies the numbers of births equaled and eventually exceeded the number of deaths long before they did in the Caribbean and South American colonies.

The slave trade itself became the object of intense competition, as each country tried to establish a monopoly over certain routes. During the seventeenth century the British managed to make inroads into the French slave trade, and eventually they surpassed the Portuguese and the Dutch as well. By 1700 British ships were transporting more than 50 percent of all slaves to the Americas. The dominance that Britain established in the slave trade was closely related to its growing maritime and commercial strength. With an enormous merchant marine and a navy that could support it, the British came to dominate the slave trade in the same way they came to dominate the entire world economy. Both revealed how far mercantile capitalism had triumphed in Britain and its overseas possessions.

For the British merchants who engaged in this trade there was no conflict between their traditional beliefs in individual liberty and their subjugation of African slaves. Theories of racial and national superiority removed Africans as well as other non-Europeans from the category of human beings who lived in a free society and who enjoyed individual rights. As long as those rights were tied to a particular national or racial group, such as freeborn Englishmen, slavery presented no challenge to British political ideas.

Not until the late eighteenth century did the enslavement of black Africans become a source of widespread moral concern. The movement to end the slave trade and slavery itself arose almost simultaneously in all European countries. It was inspired mainly by religious zeal, especially from evangelical Protestants in Great Britain and

***The Slave Ship* by J. M. W. Turner (1840)**
The English painter J. M. W. Turner captured the horror of the incident that took place aboard the slave ship *Zong,* when the crew threw 132 slaves overboard in 1781.

the Jesuits in Spain and Portugal. Societies were formed to campaign for the legislative prohibition of the transportation and sale of slaves. These appeals found support in the calculations by European capitalists, especially in Britain, that slavery was no longer economically advantageous. Goods produced by free labor, especially by machine, made slavery appear less cost-effective than in the past, and the entire system of slavery began to be viewed as a costly encumbrance.

By the first decade of the nineteenth century opposition to slavery began to achieve limited success, and by 1851 it had brought about an end to the entire slave trade. The United States refused to allow any of its ports to accept slave ships after 1808, the same year in which the British parliament legislated an end to the trade within its empire. The Dutch ended their slave trade in 1814, the French in 1815, and the Spanish in 1838. The Portuguese continued to import slaves to Brazil until 1851 and ended the practice only because the British were subjecting Portuguese slave traders to constant harassment. Liberation of the slaves generally came later, except in Haiti (formerly Saint Domingue), where slavery was abolished in 1794. The British dismantled the system within their empire between 1834 and 1838. Slavery persisted until 1848 in the French Caribbean, 1863 in the southern United States, 1886 in Cuba, and 1888 in Brazil.

Carlos Julião, *Extraction of Diamonds*
In addition to their labor on plantations, slaves in Latin America were put to work mining precious metals and jewels. This watercolor depicts African slaves mining diamonds in eighteenth-century Brazil.

Cultural Encounters in the Atlantic World

European countries had always possessed some ethnic diversity, but the emigration of people from many different parts of Europe and Africa to America, followed by their intermarriage, created societies of much greater complexity. Even the composition of the white European communities in the colonies was more varied than in the metropolis. In the British colonies, for example, English, Scots, and Irish were joined by large numbers of Germans, French, and Swiss. In 1776 Thomas Paine argued that all of Europe, rather than just England, was the true parent country of North American colonists. Ethnic divisions were further complicated by those of religion, especially in North America, where Protestants of many different denominations, as well as Roman Catholics, lived in close proximity to each other.

The ethnicity of colonial populations was more varied in Latin American colonies than in North America. The higher proportion of Africans in those colonies, more extensive patterns of intermarriage, and the free status achieved by large numbers of blacks and mulattos created highly stratified societies by the end of the eighteenth century. In these colonies divisions arose not only between the recently arrived Europeans and the creoles, but between the various groups considered by Europeans to be below them. The social structure of Brazil was more complex than that of any other country in the New World. At the top of the social hierarchy were Portuguese bureaucrats and below them was a large and wealthy group of planter creoles. These two elite groups dominated a lower-class social hierarchy of mestizos (people of mixed white and Indian ancestry), indigenous people, mulattos, freed blacks, and slaves.

Encounters between Europeans and Africans in the New World fostered the growth of ideas of white racial superiority that were grounded in the unbalanced power relationship between the dominant white and subordinate black populations. The circumstances under which physical contact between the races took place made the imbalance of this relationship readily apparent. Blacks appeared at the slave-trading stations having already been beaten into submission by their captives and forced to march hundreds of miles. The demeaning medical exams to which the slaves were subjected and their reduction to the status of a commodity for sale could readily deprive them of any sense of pride or self-respect. Their lack of formal education and literacy put them in a position of cultural inferiority, further reducing them to the status of beasts in the eyes of their white masters. In such circumstances references to the reputed blackness of the biblical Cain (Adam and Eve's first son, who murdered his brother Abel) only confirmed or reinforced the sense of superiority that white people took for granted.

The Transmission of Ideas

The Atlantic Ocean became a corridor for the transmission of political and religious ideas. Political ideologies that developed in Europe were spread from the Old World to the New World mainly by the large volume of printed works that were exported during the eighteenth century. The ancient idea that a republic was the best form of government, which had found widespread support in Renaissance Italy and in seventeenth-century England, appealed to many political leaders in colonial North America. Eighteenth-century French and Scottish ideas regarding the rights of man and the responsibility of the government to bring about the improvement of society found fertile ground in many parts of North and South America. At the time of the French Revolution, ideals of liberty and equality spread not only throughout Europe but in the Americas as well. Legal ideas embodied in English common law, French civil law, and Spanish customary law were also transported to the New World and became the legal foundation of the new societies that were formed there.

The traffic in political ideas did not flow in only one direction. Political ideologies that were formed out of British and European ideas of liberty at the time of the American Revolution were sent back to European countries in a new form, where they inspired reform and revolution in Britain, France, and Ireland. These same ideas of liberty exerted a powerful influence in the Caribbean colonies and in South America. In Haiti, where French and American ideas of liberty inspired a revolution in the 1790s, radical ideas of racial equality developed within the new republic and then spread outward to other colonies and the United States.

Religious ideas experienced a similar transmission and transportation. The Calvinist belief in predestination, which had been formulated in Switzerland and modified by Puritans in England during the sixteenth century, was adopted and further modified by colonists in New England during the seventeenth century. Catholic theological ideas that were introduced into Spanish and Portuguese America, including those regarding the role of the Devil in human society, interacted with those of indigenous peoples and African slaves and produced new religious syntheses. In religion as well as politics, these exchanges of ideas enriched the intellectual worlds of Europeans and colonists alike.

Encounters Between Europeans and Asians

■ What cultural encounters took place between European and Asian peoples during this period of empire building, and how did these encounters change Western attitudes toward outsiders?

The period from 1650 to 1815 was decisive in the development of European empires in Asia. These overseas possessions, like the American colonies, formed important components of the empires of European states and were also essential to the operation of the global economy. European dominance of world trade was exercised not only in the Atlantic world but also in the Middle East and Asia. The history of the European presence in these areas, however, is very different from that which occurred in the New World. A first difference was that of simple numbers. Prior to the eighteenth century the European presence in Asia had been limited to the activities of missionaries and merchants in places such as Jakarta, Macao, and Manila. During the eighteenth century the number of European colonists in Asia, even in India, remained relatively small in comparison with the numbers who settled in America, especially in British North America.

A second major difference between European empires in the East and in the West during the period from 1650 to 1850 is that in Asia European powers initially did not try to acquire and govern large land masses and subjugate their populations. Europeans first came to Asia to trade, not to conquer. They did not engage in fixed battles with Asians, take steps to reduce the size of their populations, or force them to migrate, as they did in the New World. Only in a handful of Southeast Asian islands did a pattern of conquest, similar to that which had occurred in the New World, take place. When Europeans used military force in Asia, it was almost always against rival European powers, not the indigenous population. When European countries did eventually use force against Asians, they discovered that victory was much more difficult than it had been in the New World. Indeed, Asian peoples already possessed or were acquiring sufficient military strength to respond to European military might. In China and Japan the possession of this military power prevented Europeans from even contemplating conquest or exploitation until the nineteenth century. Establishment of European hegemony in Asia, therefore, took longer and was achieved more gradually than in the Americas.

Political Control of India

Despite their original intentions, Europeans eventually began to acquire political control over large land masses in Asia and subject Asians to European rule. The first decisive steps in this process took place in India during the second half of the eighteenth century. Until that time the British in India, most of whom were members of the British East India Company, remained confined to the factories that were established along the Indian coast. The main purpose of these factories was to engage in trade not only with Europe but also with other parts of Asia. In conducting this trade the British had to deal with local Indian merchants and to compete with the French, the Portuguese and the Dutch, who had established factories of their own. They also found it advantageous to make alliances with the provincial governors, known as nawabs°, who controlled the interior of the country. It became customary for each European power to have its own candidate for nawab, with the expectation that he would provide favors for his European patrons once he took office.

Military Conflict and Territorial Acquisitions, 1756–1856

In 1756 this pattern of trading and negotiating resulted in armed military conflict in the city of Calcutta in the northeastern province of Bengal. The British had established a factory at Calcutta in 1690, and they continued to carry on an extensive trade there with Indian merchants, many of whom were Hindus. The nawab of Bengal, the Muslim

Warren Hastings

Warren Hastings (1732–1818), who was appointed the first governor-general of India in 1773, represented the ambiguities of early British rule in that country. An officer in the British East India Company, he was sympathetic to Indian culture. He was, however, accused of gross misconduct in the management of Indian affairs. His impeachment by the British Parliament in 1786 for corruption in his administration and cruelty toward some of the native people in Bengal lasted 145 days but resulted in an acquittal in 1787.

Siraj-ud-Daulah, had contempt for all Europeans, especially the British, and he was determined that he would not be beholden to any of them. He was also deeply hostile to the Hindu merchants who were trading with the British. In June 1756 he sent an army of 50,000 Muslims against Calcutta, burning and plundering the city and beginning a siege of the East India Company's Fort William, which was manned by 515 troops in the service of the company. The entire British population of the city, together with more than 2,000 Hindus, had taken refuge in the fort. After a long struggle, which resulted in the death of hundreds of Indians, the fort fell to the nawab's forces, and some of the British officers and magistrates, including the governor of Calcutta, fled by sea.

During this siege the shooting death of a Bengali guard led to an incident that became permanently emblazoned on the emerging imperial consciousness of the British people. Officers in the nawab's army crammed the entire remaining British contingent, a total of 146 men and women, into the fort's lockup or prison, known as the Black Hole of Calcutta. Measuring 18' × 14' 10", it was meant to hold only three or four prisoners overnight. The British prisoners were stifled by the insufferable heat and a lack of water and air. The stench was so bad that many prisoners vomited on the people squeezed next to them. Only twenty-two men and one woman survived until the next morning, when the nawab released them. The remainder either had been trampled to death or had asphyxiated.

The deaths of these British men and women in the Black Hole of Calcutta led the British to seek swift and brutal retribution against the nawab. In 1757, under the direction of the British military officer Robert Clive, a force of 800 British troops and 2,000 native Indian soldiers known as sepoys° retook Calcutta and routed Siraj-ud-Daulah's army of 50,000 men at the battle of Plassey. Siraj-ud-Daulah was executed and replaced by a nawab more amenable to the British. A few years later the British East India Company secured the right to collect taxes and thus exercised political control over the entire province of Bengal. The enormous revenue from these taxes enabled the company to acquire a large army, composed mainly of sepoys. This force grew to 115,000 men by 1782. The British then used these military forces, which were equipped with Western military technology, to gain control of other provinces in India as well as to defeat their French rivals in subsequent engagements during the early nineteenth century.

These further acquisitions of Indian territory led to the eventual establishment of British rule throughout the South Asian subcontinent (see Map 17.5). New territories were brought under British control in the early years of the nineteenth century, and during the tenure of Lord Dalhousie as governor-general of India from 1848 to 1856 the British annexed eight Indian states, including the great Muslim state of Oudh in 1856. This policy of annexation went hand in hand with the introduction of Western technology and literature, the English language, and British criminal procedure.

The Sepoy Mutiny

The British policy of annexation in India, coupled with the attitude of cultural superiority it encouraged, lay at the root of the greatest act of rebellion by Indians against British rule in the nineteenth century. This rebellion, which began in 1857, is often known as the Sepoy Mutiny, because it originated in the ranks of the Indian troops serving in the armed forces of the British East India Company. The main source of resentment was the British annexation

Map 17.5 The Sequence of British Territorial Acquisitions in India, 1765–1856

British political control of large territories on the South Asian subcontinent began more than a century after the establishment of the first factories along the coast.

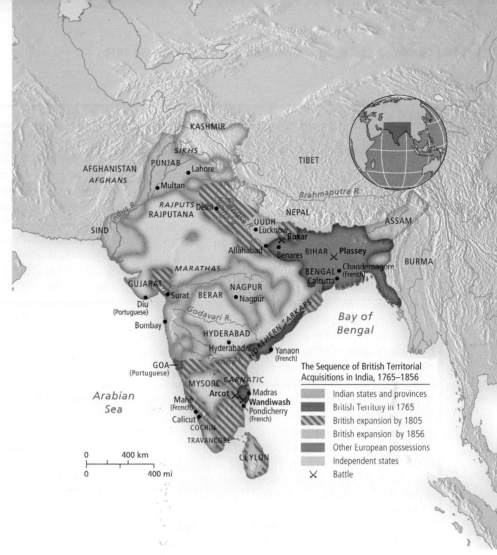

The Sequence of British Territorial Acquisitions in India, 1765–1856

- Indian states and provinces
- British Territory in 1765
- British expansion by 1805
- British expansion by 1856
- Other European possessions
- Independent states
- ✕ Battle

of Oudh, which many sepoys considered their homeland. The incident that actually provoked the rebellion was the issue of rifle cartridges coated with beef fat, which violated Hindu law, and pork fat, which violated Muslim law. Although this insensitivity to native Indian culture was not unprecedented, in this case it struck a particularly raw nerve and led to a mutiny by the Bengali army. The cities of Delhi and Lucknow came under siege, and dreadful atrocities, including the hacking to death of British women and children, occurred. British reprisals were equally savage and eventually succeeded in suppressing the rebellion.

In the wake of the mutiny the British government abolished the British East India Company and assumed direct rule of India. Queen Victoria (r. 1837–1901), the constitutional monarch of the United Kingdom, acquired much greater power over her Indian empire. Although the British government did take steps to confirm the lands and titles of Indian princes and to give them local power, their relationship with their British overlords remained one of strict subordination.

Changing European Attitudes Toward Asian Cultures

This second phase of European imperialism in Asia played a crucial role in the formation of Western identity. The steadily increasing numbers of Europeans who had contact with these lands—merchants, missionaries, writers, and colonial administrators—and to a lesser extent the public who read about these foreign places gained a clearer sense of who they were once they compared themselves to Indians, Chinese, and Polynesians. Until the seventeenth century Europeans thought of "the East" mainly as the Middle East, an area that was largely subsumed within the Ottoman Empire. Europeans expressed a generally negative

view of the culture of this region (see Chapter 15), and over the years that perception had not changed. The political system of the Ottoman Empire was considered despotic and its religion, Islam, the antithesis of Christianity. The Far East, comprising South Asia (India), East Asia (China, Japan), and Southeast Asia (Burma, Siam, Indonesia), generally did not enter into these perceptions of "the Orient." There was little contact with this part of the world, and much of what was known about it was shrouded in mystery. During this period Europeans viewed the Far East mainly as an exotic land, rich in spices, silk, and other luxury commodities.

As Western missionaries and merchants made more frequent contacts with Asian society, Europeans developed more informed impressions of these distant lands and peoples. Some of those impressions were negative, especially when the power of Asian rulers was discussed, but many other characterizations of the East were positive. Interest in and admiration for both Indian and Chinese culture were most widespread during the middle years of the eighteenth century. The systematic study of Asian languages, especially Chinese and Sanskrit, began during this period. A preference for things Asian became characteristic of Enlightenment thinkers such as Voltaire (1694–1778), who regarded Asian cultures as superior to

American people that included racial difference as one of its main components. This ideology prepared Europeans intellectually and emotionally for the conquest of numerous countries in Asia and Africa in the second half of the nineteenth century. This third and final period of European imperial expansion, which began around 1870 and reached its peak around 1900, brought 84 percent of the Earth's surface under Western control.

The Crisis of Empire and the Atlantic Revolutions

■ Why did European powers begin to lose control of some of their colonies, especially those in the Americas, between 1775 and 1825?

During the period from 1780 to 1825, European empires experienced a crisis that marked the end of the second stage of European overseas expansion. As a result of this crisis British, French, and Spanish governments lost large segments of their empires, all in the Americas. New states and nations were carved out of the older sprawling empires. The crisis was to some extent administrative. Having acquired large expanses of territory overseas, European states were faced with the challenging problem of governing them from a distance. They not only had to rule large areas inhabited by non-European peoples (Indians and African slaves), but they also faced the difficulty of maintaining the loyalty of people of European descent who were born in the colonies.

These European colonials or creoles became the main protagonists in the struggles that led to the independence of the North American colonies from Britain in 1776 and the South American colonies from Spain a generation later. In the French colony of Saint Domingue, the location of the only successful revolution in the Caribbean region during this period, a very different set of pressures led to independence. In this colony, which became the republic of Haiti in 1804, the revolution was led not by white creoles but by people of color, including the slaves who worked on the plantations. In Britain's European colony of Ireland, where an unsuccessful revolution against British rule took place in 1798, the urge for independence came both from settlers of British descent and the native Irish population.

The American Revolution, 1775–1783

The first Atlantic revolution was the revolt of the thirteen North American colonies and the establishment of their independence from British rule. During the second half of the eighteenth century, a number of tensions arose between the British government and its transatlantic colonies. All of these overseas colonies had developed traditions of self-government, and all of them had their own representative assemblies. At the same time the colonies were controlled by various governmental bodies responsible to the British Parliament, such as the Board of Trade. The colonies had their own militias, but they also received protection from British troops when conflicts developed with the French or other hostile powers.

The crisis that led to the American Revolution had its roots in the situation that emerged at the end of the French and Indian War. In order to maintain the peace agreed to in 1763, the government stationed British troops on the frontiers of the colonies. It argued that because the troops were protecting the colonists, they should contribute financially to their own defense. To this end the government began imposing a number of new taxes on the colonists. In 1765 the British Parliament passed the Stamp Act, which forced

***The Bostonian's Paying the Excise Man or Tarring and Feathering* (1774)**
This satirical engraving reflects the hatred of colonial Americans at the collection of taxes levied on them without their consent. The Boston Tea Party is depicted in the background. The colonists are forcing the tax collector to drink the tea on which he is trying to collect taxes.

The British Surrender at Yorktown In 1781
This battle ended the American War of Independence, although the peace treaty was not signed
for another two years.

colonists to purchase stamps for almost anything that was printed. This piece of legislation raised the central constitutional issue of whether Parliament had the power to legislate for British subjects in lands that did not elect members of that Parliament. "Taxation without representation is tyranny" became the main rallying cry of the colonists. Opposition to the Stamp Act was so strong that Parliament repealed the act the following year, but at the same time it passed a statute declaring that it had the authority to tax the colonists as it pleased. When the government imposed new taxes on the tea imported from Britain in 1773, a number of colonists, dressed as Indians, threw the tea into the Boston Harbor.

The government responded to this "Boston Tea Party" by passing a series of statutes, known in the colonies as the Intolerable Acts, in 1774. One of these acts specified that the port of Boston be closed until the colonists had repaid the cost of the tea. The Intolerable Acts led to organized resistance to British rule, and in the following year military conflict broke out at Lexington and Concord in Massachusetts. On July 4, 1776, thirteen of the colonies on the North American mainland, stretching from New Hampshire to

Georgia, approved a Declaration of Independence from Great Britain. A long revolutionary war, in which the colonists received assistance from France in 1778, ended with the defeat of British troops at Yorktown in 1781 and the recognition of the republic of the United States of America in the Treaty of Paris in 1783.

The case that the American colonists made for independence from Britain drew upon the political theories of John Locke, who justified resistance against the Stuart monarchy at the time of the Glorious Revolution. Locke, who placed limits on legislative as well as executive power, became the main inspiration of the Declaration of Independence, which was drafted by Thomas Jefferson. The Revolution also found support in the customs and traditions embodied in the English common law, especially the principle that men could not be deprived of their rights without their own consent. Republican ideas, drawn both from ancient Greece and Rome and revived at the time of the Renaissance, gave colonists a model of a community of virtuous men joined in a commitment to the body politic, which they defined in colonial terms. Finally there was the influence of the ideas of the Enlightenment, which empha-

DOCUMENT

Thomas Paine Supports the American Cause

Thomas Paine (1737–1809) was a radical Whig reformer who supported the cause for American independence. In Common Sense *(1776), a pamphlet written to support the American cause in the year of the Declaration of Independence, Paine refutes the arguments of the British that they served the interests of the American colonists. Paine protests not only the commercial exploitation of the colonies but also the way in which Great Britain has involved them in warfare with continental rivals.*

I have heard it asserted by some, that as America has flourished under her former connection with Great Britain, the same connection is necessary towards her future happiness, and will always have the same effect. Nothing can be more fallacious than this kind of argument. We may as well assert that because a child has thrived upon milk, that it is never to have meat, or that the first twenty years of our lives is to become a precedent for the next twenty. But even this is admitting more than is true; for I answer roundly that America would have flourished as much, probably much more, had no European power taken any notice of her. The commerce by which she hath enriched herself are the necessaries of life and will always have a market while eating is the custom of Europe.

But she has protected us, say some. That she hath engrossed us is true, and defended the Continent at our expense as well as her own, is admitted; and she would have defended Turkey from the same motive, *viz.* for the sake of trade and dominion.

Alas! We have been long led away by ancient prejudices and made large sacrifices to superstition. We have boasted the protection of Britain without considering that her motive was *interest,* not *attachment;* and that she did not protect us from *our enemies* on *our account* but from *her enemies* on *her own account,* from those who had no quarrel with us on any *other account,* and who will always be our enemies on the *same account.* Let Britain waive her pretensions to the Continent, or the Continent throw off the dependence, and we should be at peace with France and Spain, were they at war with Britain. The miseries of Hanover last war ought to warn us against connections.

Source: From Thomas Paine, *Common Sense* (Philadelphia: W. T. Bradford, 1776).

sized the natural right of all men to life, liberty, and the pursuit of happiness (see Chapter 18).

Although the American Revolution was inspired by many of the ideas that had originated in the two English revolutions of the seventeenth century, it differed from those earlier revolutions in that it was directed more against the British Parliament than the king. The Declaration of Independence severed the bonds between the colonists and King George III, to whom they formally owed allegiance, but the constitutional powers against which they protested, especially that of taxation, were those of Parliament. It was taxation by the British Parliament, rather than nonparliamentary taxes like those levied in the 1640s, that led to the American Revolution.

The Haitian Revolution, 1789–1804

The second successful revolution in the Atlantic world took place in the French Caribbean colony of Saint Domingue, known later as Haiti, which occupied the western portion of the island of Hispaniola. This revolution resulted in the establishment of the colony's independence, but the revolt was directed not so much against French rule as against the island's white planters. Just like their counterparts in Spanish and British Caribbean colonies, these planters, known in Haiti as colons°, had little desire for national independence. They wished to remain within the protective custody of the French state. Because they formed a distinct minority of the total population, they did not think of themselves as constituting a separate national community. Any resistance to imperial rule, moreover, would have required that they arm their slaves in order to make the movement succeed, and that would have threatened their control of the black population.

The real threat of revolution in all the Caribbean colonies came not from the elite or ruling class but from the subordinate members of the population. In Saint Domingue the revolution began in 1789 with a rebellion of people defined legally as free coloreds, most of whom were mulattos. The development that triggered this revolt, organized under the leadership of Vincent Ogé, was the refusal of the white planters, who were creoles, to give the free coloreds representation in the revolutionary French National Assembly as well as in local assemblies in Saint Domingue.

The free colored rebellion of 1789 led directly to a massive slave revolt in 1791. At that time slaves constituted about 90 percent of the population. Their uprising took place after the French National Assembly voted to abolish slavery in France but not in the French colonies. In this revolt 12,000 African slaves, armed with machetes and reacting to their brutal treatment by their masters, destroyed a thousand plantations and killed hundreds of whites. Their tactics, which included cutting white planters in half, raping their wives and daughters, and decapitating their children, were matched by those of the planters, who retaliated by torturing blacks and hanging them in the streets.

Spanish and British armies, frightened that this slave rebellion would spread to their colonies, occupied Saint Domingue and massacred thousands of slaves, many of them after they surrendered. In 1795, however, the Spanish withdrew from Saint Domingue and ceded their portion of the island of Hispaniola to France. The British were likewise forced to leave the colony in 1798, having lost as many as 40,000 soldiers, most of them from disease. The man who had assumed the leadership of the slave revolt, the freed slave Toussaint L'Ouverture, then proceeded to conquer the entire island in 1801, abolish slavery, and proclaim himself the governor-general of an autonomous province.

In 1801, after Napoleon had assumed control of the French government and the idealism of the French Revolution had evaporated, a French army of 20,000 men occupied Saint Domingue. The purpose was to make the colony the centerpiece of a restored French Empire, including Florida, Louisiana, French Guiana, and the French West Indies. This assertion of French imperial control secured the surrender of L'Ouverture. When it was learned that the French were planning to reintroduce slavery, however, two black generals, Jean-Jacques Dessalines and Henri Christophe, whom the French had enlisted to suppress the revolt, united freed blacks and slaves against the French forces. In 1803 these united forces drove the French out of the colony, and in 1804 they established an independent state of Haiti.

This new state of Haiti was far different from the United States, in that it was governed entirely by people of color and it banned slavery. It proclaimed racial equality by defining all Haitians as black. The plantation system was destroyed and the land was redistributed among free blacks; foreigners were forbidden to hold property. Deciding upon the form of government took time, however, as the new rulers of the country were divided between those who wished to establish a monarchy and those who favored a republic. Those divisions led to a prolonged civil war from 1807 until 1822, when the warring northern and southern provinces were integrated into a single republic.

The Haitian revolution was the most radical and egalitarian of the Atlantic revolutions of the late eighteenth and early nineteenth centuries. Whereas the American Revolution was mainly a political movement that established a new republic, the Haitian revolution was a genuine social and economic revolution as well. Its unqualified declaration of human equality and its abolition of slavery served as an inspiration to abolitionist movements in other countries, including the United States, throughout the nineteenth century. The destruction of the plantation system, however, brought about a revolutionary transformation of the country's economy. As a French possession Saint Domingue was quite possibly the richest colony in the world, producing about two-fifths of the world's sugar and half of its coffee. After the revolution, with its economy severed from that of France, the country could no longer compete successfully in the Atlantic economy.

The Irish Rebellion, 1798–1799

Within the British Empire the country that was most directly inspired by the success of the American Revolution was the kingdom of Ireland. Unlike the residents of the thirteen colonies in North America, the Gaelic people of Ireland had long thought of themselves as a distinct nation. The English, however, had begun a conquest of this Irish nation in the twelfth century, and during the next 500 years they had struggled to rule it effectively. One of their methods was to settle English landlords on Irish lands. They had done this in the Middle Ages by giving large estates to English feudal lords, but those old Anglo-Irish families had gradually begun to think of themselves as Irish, and after the Reformation they had remained Catholic, while most English people had become Protestant.

In the sixteenth century the English government had begun to settle colonies of English Protestants on plantations in various parts of Ireland. The purpose of this policy was to gain tighter control over the country and to promote the loyalty of Irish landowners to the English government. In the early seventeenth century James VI of Scotland (who had also become James I of England in 1603) had settled both Scottish Presbyterians, later known as the Scots Irish, as well as English Anglicans, in the northern Irish province of Ulster. These Protestants of Scottish and English descent had become the core of the ruling establishment throughout Ireland, especially after Catholic rebellions in 1641–1649 and again in 1689–1690 had failed.

In the eighteenth century Irish Protestants began to resent their subservient relationship to the British government. Just like the American colonists, they recognized the way in which the Irish economy was serving British rather than Irish interests, and they resented the control that Britain had over the Irish parliament. A reform association known as the Society of United Irishmen, led by the Protestant Ulsterman Wolfe Tone, succeeded in building common ground between Protestants and Catholics. The United Irishmen demanded the repeal of the laws that denied Catholics the right to hold office and sit in the Irish parliament.

The ideals of the United Irishmen drew on many different sources. A long tradition of Presbyterian republican radicalism found reinforcement in the ideals of the American Revolution. The Irish objected to paying tithes to the established Anglican church, and like the American colonists in the 1760s they resented the taxes they were asked to pay to aid in the British war against the French during the 1790s.

French revolutionary ideas of liberty, equality, and fraternity had a pervasive influence in Ireland as well.

In 1798 the United Irishmen aligned themselves with lower-class Catholic peasants known as Defenders, and these Irish groups staged a rebellion against British rule with the intention of establishing an Irish republic. Like the American colonists, the Irish revolutionaries sought French aid, but it came too little and too late, and the rebellion failed. The revolt, which was marred by atrocities on both sides, resulted in the deaths of 30,000 people.

The British government recognized that its arrangement for ruling Ireland, in which the nationalist republican movement had originated, could no longer work. The British government decided therefore to bring about a complete union between Great Britain and Ireland. By the terms of this arrangement, which took effect in 1801, Ireland's parliament ceased to meet; instead the Irish were to elect a limited number of representatives to sit in the British parliament. Ireland thus became a part of the United Kingdom, just as Scotland had done in 1707. The proximity of Ireland to Britain, which made the prospect of Irish independence much more dangerous, was a major factor in making the British determined to hold on to this "internal colony." The forces of Irish nationalism could not be contained, however, and during the nineteenth century new movements for Irish independence arose.

National Revolutions in Spanish America, 1810–1824

The final set of revolutions against European imperial powers occurred between 1810 and 1824 in a number of Spanish American colonies. These struggles, like the American Revolution, turned colonies into new states and led to the building of new nations. The first of these revolutions began in Mexico in 1810; others soon arose in Argentina, Colombia, Chile, and Peru. In these revolutions creoles played a leading role, just as they had in the American War of Independence. The main sources of creole discontent were the Bourbon reforms, which ironically had been intended to make the Spanish Empire more efficient and thus to preserve it. The reforms had achieved this goal, however, by favoring commercial interests at the expense of the traditional aristocracy, thereby reversing or threatening the position of many creole elites. The creoles also faced increasingly heavy taxation, as the Spanish government sought to make them support the expenses of colonial administration.

During the late eighteenth century Spanish creole discontent had crystallized into demands for greater political autonomy, similar to the objectives of British American colonists. South American creoles began to think of themselves as Spanish Americans and sometimes simply as Americans. Like British American colonists, they also read and were inspired by the works of Enlightenment political philosophers. They protested against the Bourbon reforms. Nevertheless, the Spanish creole struggle against imperial rule did not commence until some thirty years after the North American colonies had won their independence. One reason for this slow development of revolutionary action was that Spanish American creoles still looked to the Spanish government to provide them with military support against the threat of lower-class rebellion. When, for example, a rebellion of this sort against Spanish rule occurred in Peru in 1780, creole planters not only refused an invitation to join the revolt but also supported the Spanish forces that crushed it. Faced with this lower-class threat, which continued to plague them even after independence, creoles were cautious about abandoning the military and police support provided by the metropolis.

The event that eventually precipitated these wars for national independence was the collapse of the Spanish monarchy after Napoleon's French army invaded Spain in 1808 (see Chapter 19). This development left the Spanish Empire, which had always been more centralized than the British Empire, in a weakened position. In an effort to reconstitute the political order in their colonies, creoles sought to establish greater autonomy. Once the monarchy was restored, this demand for autonomy led quickly to armed resistance. This resistance began in Mexico, but it soon spread throughout Spanish America and quickly acquired popular support.

DOCUMENT

The Plan of Iguala (1821)

The man who took the lead in these early revolts against Spanish rule was the fiery Venezuelan aristocrat Símon Bolívar (1783–1830). Educated in the ideas of the Enlightenment, Bolívar led uprisings in his homeland in 1812 and 1814 and eventually defeated the Spanish there in 1819. Unlike most creoles, Bolívar was not afraid to recruit free coloreds and blacks into his armies. His hatred of European

CHRONOLOGY

The Atlantic Revolutions, 1775–1824

1775–1783	United States of America
1789–1804	Haiti
1798–1799	Ireland
1810–1821	Mexico
1810–1819	Colombia
1810–1821	Venezuela
1810–1816	Argentina
1810–1818	Chile
1821–1824	Peru

Símon Bolívar Presenting the Flag of Liberation to Soldiers After the Battle of Carabobo, 1821
Bolívar was the man most directly responsible for liberating South American countries from Spanish rule. He liberated his native Venezuela in 1821 and defeated Spanish forces in Peru in 1824.

colonial governors knew few boundaries. At one point he reportedly commanded his soldiers to shoot and kill any European on sight. He vowed never to rest until all of Spanish America was free. Bolívar carried the struggle for liberation to Peru, which became independent in 1824, and created the state of Bolivia in 1825. Often compared to George Washington, he was more responsible than any one individual for the liberation of Spanish America from Spanish rule. Independent states were established in Argentina in 1816, Chile in 1818, Colombia in 1819, and Mexico in 1821. By then the Spanish, who in the sixteenth century had the largest empire in the world, retained control of only two colonies in the Western Hemisphere: Puerto Rico and Cuba.

Conclusion

The Rise and Reshaping of the West

During the second period of European empire building, the West not only expanded geographically but also acquired a large share of the world's resources. By dominating the world's carrying trade, and by exploiting the agricultural and mineral resources of the Americas, Western states gained control of the world economy. The slave trade, with all its horrors, formed an important part of this economy and served as one of the main sources of Western wealth.

Western economic power laid the foundations for Western political control. In Asia European states assumed political control over territories slowly and reluctantly, as Britain's gradual and piecemeal acquisition of territory in India revealed. In the Americas, European powers acquired territory with relative ease, and European possessions in the New World soon became part of the West. By 1700, as we have seen, the geographical center of the West had become the Atlantic Ocean.

The American territories that were brought under European political control also became, at least to some extent, culturally part of the West. The European colonists who settled in the Americas preserved the languages, the religions, and many of the cultural traditions of the European countries from which they came. When some of the British and Spanish colonies in the Americas rebelled against European regimes in the late eighteenth and early nineteenth centuries, the identity of the colonists who led the resistance remained essentially Western. Even the political ideas that inspired national resistance to European regimes had their origins in Europe.

The assertion of Western political and economic power in the world cultivated a sense of Western superiority. The belief that Europeans, regardless of their nationality, were superior to those from other parts of the world originated in the encounters that took place between Europeans and both African slaves and the indigenous peoples in the

Americas. In the late eighteenth century a conviction also developed, although much more slowly, that the West was culturally superior to the civilizations of Asia. This belief in Western superiority became even more pronounced when the economies of Western nations began to experience more rapid growth than those of Asia. The main source of this new Western economic strength was the Industrial Revolution, which will be the subject of Chapter 20.

Suggestions for Further Reading

For a comprehensive listing of suggested readings, please go to www.ablongman.com/levack2e/chapter17

Bailyn, Bernard. *Ideological Origins of the American Revolution.* 1967. A probing analysis of the different intellectual traditions upon which the American colonists based their arguments for independence.

Blackburn, Robin. *The Making of New World Slavery: From the Baroque to the Modern, 1492–1800.* 1997. Places European slavery in a broad world perspective.

Boxer, C. R. *The Dutch Seaborne Empire, 1600–1800.* 1965. A thorough account covering the entire period of Dutch expansion.

Davis, Ralph. *The Rise of the Atlantic Economies.* 1973. A readable study of economic development on both sides of the Atlantic.

Eltis, David, *The Rise of African Slavery in the Americas.* 2000. An analysis of the different dimensions of the slave trade based on a database of slave ships and passengers.

Goody, Jack. *The East in the West.* 1996. Challenges the idea that Western cultures are more rational than those of Asia.

Greene, Jack P. *Peripheries and Center: Constitutional Development in the Extended Polities of the British Empire and the United States, 1607–1788.* 1986. A study of the composition of the British Empire and its disintegration in North America.

Kamen, Henry. *Empire: How Spain Became a World Power.* 2003. Explains how Spain established the most extensive empire the world had ever known.

Langley, Lester D. *The Americas in the Age of Revolution, 1750–1850.* 1996. A broad comparative study of revolutions in the United States, Haiti, and Latin America.

Liss, Peggy K. *The Atlantic Empires: The Network of Trade and Revolutions, 1713–1826.* 1983. Places the American Revolution in a broader comparative setting and includes material on early Latin American independence movements.

Mungello, D. E. *The Great Encounter of China and the West, 1500–1800.* 1999. Studies China's acceptance and rejection of Western culture as well as the parallel Western reception of China.

Pagden, Anthony. *Lords of All the World: Ideologies of Empire in Spain, Britain and France, ca. 1500–ca. 1800.* 1996. Discusses the theoretical foundations of the Atlantic Empires.

Said, Edward. *Orientalism.* 1979. A study of the way in which Western views of the East have assumed its inferiority.

Notes

1. Olaudah Equiano, *The Interesting Narrative of the Life of Olaudah Equiano, or Gustavus Vassa the African* (1789).

2. Thomas Rymer (ed.), *Foedera* (1704–1735), vol. 18, 72.

3. Quoted in Robin Blackburn, *The Making of New World Slavery* (1997), 325.

4. Samuel Johnson, *Rasselas* (1759), 47.

Eighteenth-Century Society and Culture

18

N 1745 THOMAS BROWN AND ELEVEN OTHER MEN LIVING ON THE ESTATE OF the Earl of Uxbridge, an English nobleman, were jailed for up to one year for shooting deer and rabbits on the earl's land. All twelve defendants were poor. Brown eked out a living as a coal miner in the earl's mines and rented a cottage and five acres of land from him. Like many of his fellow villagers, Brown supplemented his family's diet by shooting game from time to time, usually as he was walking to work through the earl's vast estate. This poaching violated a set of English parliamentary statutes known as the game laws, which restricted the shooting or trapping of wild animals to the members of the landed class.

The earl and other noblemen defended the game laws on the grounds that they were necessary to protect their property. The laws, however, served the even more important purpose of maintaining social distinctions between landowners and the common people. Members of the landed class believed that only they should have the right to hunt game and to serve deer, pheasants, and hares at lavish dinners attended by their social equals. For a poor person like Thomas Brown, who was described in a court document as "a rude disorderly man and a most notorious poacher," to enjoy such delicacies was a challenge to the social order.

This mid-eighteenth-century encounter between the Earl of Uxbridge and his tenants, which took the form of a criminal prosecution, reflected the tensions that simmered beneath the calm surface of eighteenth-century European society. These tensions arose between the members of the aristocracy, a small but wealthy governing elite, and the masses of tenants and laborers who formed the overwhelming majority of the European population. The aristocracy occupied a dominant position in eighteenth-century society. They controlled an enormous portion of the wealth in their countries, much of it in land. They staffed the state bureaucracies, the legislative assemblies, the military officer corps, and the judiciaries of almost all European states. They dominated and set the tone of high cultural life in Europe. Together

First Lecture in the Salon of Madame Geoffrin, 1755 The speaker is lecturing on Voltaire's *The Orphan of China* before a predominantly aristocratic audience of men and women.

with the monarchy and the church, with which they were socially and politically linked, the aristocracy formed what today is often referred to as "the Establishment."

By 1800 the social and political dominance of the aristocracy had begun to wane. Their legitimacy as a privileged elite was increasingly called into question. In a few countries political power began to pass from them to different social groups. The aristocracy did not surrender all their power, but they lost their stranglehold over society. This change began during a period of political stability between 1750 and the outbreak of the French Revolution in 1789.

The decline of the aristocracy was the result of a series of cultural encounters. The first were the tense and occasionally violent interactions between landowners and peasants who resented the repressive features of upper-class rule. The second were criticisms of the aristocracy and the demands for reform that came from the increasingly literate, politically active people from the middle ranks of society, such as merchants, financiers, industrialists, and skilled artisans. The third was the cultural and intellectual movement known as the Enlightenment. Even though many of the Enlightenment's most prominent thinkers came from the ranks of the aristocracy, they advanced a set of political, social, economic, and legal ideas that ultimately inspired the creation of a more egalitarian society.

The aristocracy did not relinquish power willingly or quickly. Although they faced severe criticism and challenges to their dominance, they managed to preserve much of their wealth and maintain at least some of their political influence. To insulate themselves from criticisms from less powerful social groups, they adopted many of the values of the people who occupied the middle ranks of society and subscribed to many of the ideas of the Enlightenment, including those that criticized their own class. Internal encounters between different social groups, just like external encounters between Western and non-Western peoples, rarely result in total domination of one group over the other. Instead both parties change their thinking and behavior as a result of their interaction.

These encounters, especially those that took place at the time of the Enlightenment, resulted in a redefinition of the West. In Chapter 16 we saw how the Scientific Revolution completely changed the face of Western culture. In the eighteenth century the Enlightenment, which was inspired to a great extent by the ideas of the Scientific Revolution, produced a set of political and social ideals that served as the basis for a new Western identity.

This chapter will explore the ways in which these social and cultural encounters changed the political and intellectual culture of the West. In doing this the individual sections of the chapter will address the following questions:

- **What social groups belonged to the aristocracy and how did they exercise their power and influence during the eighteenth century?**

- How did subordinate social groups, most notably the rural peasantry and those who lived in the towns, challenge the aristocracy during the late eighteenth century?
- What were the main features of Enlightenment thought and how did it present a threat to the old order?
- What impact did the Enlightenment have on Western culture and politics?

The Aristocracy

- **What social groups belonged to the aristocracy and how did they exercise their power and influence during the eighteenth century?**

During the eighteenth century a relatively small, wealthy group of men dominated European society and politics. This social and ruling elite is often referred to as the aristocracy°, a term derived from a Greek word meaning the people who were the most fit to rule. In the eighteenth and nineteenth centuries the term *aristocracy* began to be applied not just to those few men who exercised political power but to the wealthiest members of society, especially those who owned land.

Within the aristocracy those who received official recognition of their hereditary status, including their titles of honor and special legal privileges, were known as the nobility°. In the Middle Ages the nobility consisted mainly of warriors who prided themselves on their courage and military skill. Over the course of many centuries these military functions became less important, although many noblemen, especially in central and eastern Europe, continued to serve as military officers in the armies of the state during the eighteenth century.

The aristocracy for the most part lived on their estates in the countryside, but they also spent time in the cities and towns, where many of them maintained townhouses or even large palaces. In cities that were centers of national government, such as Madrid and Berlin, aristocrats were prominent members of the royal court. As royal judges, some members of the aristocracy also took an active part in the administration of the law in the cities, just as they did in the provinces. The aristocracy, therefore, maintained a visible and powerful presence in urban society.

By the eighteenth century most European aristocracies included a relatively small group of titled noblemen (such as dukes and counts) who possessed great wealth and political influence and a much larger group of lesser aristocrats, occasionally referred to as gentry, who sometimes did not even bear hereditary titles. In Spain a vast gulf separated a few hundred titled noblemen, the *titulos*, and thousands of sometimes poverty-stricken *hidalgos*. In Britain a few hun-

DOCUMENT

Merchants Become Members of the Aristocracy in England

Daniel Defoe is most famous for his novels, such as Robinson Crusoe *(1719) and* Moll Flanders *(1722), but he also wrote commentaries on contemporary English politics and society. In* The English Tradesman *(1726), which is excerpted here, Defoe argued that the wealth of England "lies mainly among the trading part of the people." To support his argument he presented evidence that many members of the English aristocracy came from trading backgrounds. England was unusual in the opportunities it offered for this type of upward social mobility, but Defoe nonetheless overstated his case. Even the English aristocracy of the eighteenth century was not open to such frequent entry from below.*

This being the case in England, and our trade being so vastly great, it is no wonder that the tradesmen in England fill the lists of our nobility and gentry; no wonder that the gentlemen of the best families marry tradesmen's daughters, and put their younger sons' apprentices to tradesmen; and how often do these younger sons come to buy the elder sons' estates, and restore the family, when the elder and head of the house, proving rakish and extravagant, has wasted his patrimony, and is obliged to make out the blessing of Israel's family, where the younger son brought the birthright, and the elder was doomed to serve him?

Trade is so far here from being inconsistent with a gentleman, that in short trade in England makes gentlemen, and has peopled this nation with gentlemen; for after a generation or two the tradesmen's children, or at least their grand-children, come to be as good gentlemen, statesmen, parliament-men, privy counselors, judges, bishops and noblemen, as those of the highest birth and the most ancient families; and nothing too high for them. Thus the earl of Haversham was originally a merchant; the late Secretary Craggs was the son of a barber; the present Lord Castlemaine's father was a tradesman, the great grandfather of the present Duke of Bedford the same, and so of several others. . . .

We see the tradesmen of England, as they grow wealthy, coming every day to the herald's office, to search for the coats of arms of their ancestors, in order to paint them upon their coaches, and engrave them upon their furniture, or carve them upon the pediments of their new houses; and how often do we see them trace the registers of their families up to the prime nobility, or the most ancient gentry of the kingdom?

Source: From Daniel Defoe, *The Complete English Tradesman,* Volume I, 1726.

---

dred titled noblemen, known as peers, took precedence over some 50,000 families that belonged to the gentry. In Poland the nobility, known as the *szlachta,* was divided between a tiny, powerful group of magnates and some 700,000 noblemen of much more modest means who constituted more than 10 percent of the entire population.

The aristocracy was not completely closed to outsiders. Commoners could gain entrance to it, especially its lower ranks, on the basis of acquired wealth or government service. It was not unusual for lawyers, wealthy merchants, or accomplished state servants to accumulate wealth during their careers, use that wealth to purchase land, and then receive a recognition of their new status in the form of a title of nobility. Many of the men to whom Peter the Great of Russia gave titles of nobility in the early eighteenth century were commoners. In France, where the old "nobility of the sword" could be distinguished from the "nobility of the robe" that ascended through state service, more than 20 percent of mid-eighteenth-century noblemen could not trace their noble status back further than two generations.

It was also possible for prosperous farmers to enter the aristocracy by purchasing land, hiring manual laborers to perform agricultural work, and then adopting the leisured lifestyle, dress, and manners of aristocrats. These men did not bear titles, but they expected to be regarded as having the same status as other members of the lesser aristocracy. Occasionally women of nonnoble birth gained entry into aristocratic society by marriage. This usually occurred when a nobleman who was greatly in debt arranged to marry his son to the daughter of a wealthy merchant in order to secure the dowry from the father of the bride. The dowry became the price of the daughter's admission to the nobility.

In the sixteenth and seventeenth centuries the size of the aristocracy had grown faster than the general population, as a result of both economic prosperity and the expansion of the state bureaucracy. In eastern Europe monarchs had increased the number of hereditary noblemen in order to gain their services for the state. In the eighteenth century the size of the aristocracy stabilized and in many countries declined, as nobles took steps to restrict the number of newcomers from the lower orders. It was never a very large social group. The number of titled nobles was almost always less than 1 percent of the total population, and even when lesser nobles or gentry are taken into account, their total numbers usually amounted to no more than 4 percent. Only in Poland and Hungary did the percentages climb to more than 10 percent. Because of the small size of this social group, many nobles knew each other, especially those who were members of the same political assembly or who served together at court. The aristocracy was in fact the only real class° in European society before the early nineteenth century, in the sense that they formed a cohesive social group with similar economic and political interests, which they were determined to protect.

The Wealth of the Aristocracy

The aristocracy was without question the wealthiest social group in all European countries, and during the eighteenth century many members of this group became even wealthier. The most prosperous aristocratic families lived in stupendous luxury. They built magnificent homes on their country estates and surrounded them with finely manicured gardens. In the cities, where service at court demanded more of their time, they built spacious palaces, entertained guests on a lavish scale, and purchased everything from expensive clothes to artistic treasures. They consumed the best food and wines they could find at home or abroad. This ostentatious display of wealth was intended to confirm their social importance and status.

Most of the income that supported the lifestyle of the aristocracy came directly or indirectly from land. In all European countries the aristocracy owned at least one-third of all the land, and in some countries, such as England and Denmark, they owned more than four-fifths of it. Even in the Italian states, where many of the nobility had come from families of merchants, they controlled large estates. Land provided the aristocracy with either feudal dues or rents from the peasants who lived and worked on their estates. Because noblemen did not engage in manual labor themselves, it is not surprising that they later came to be seen as unproductive parasites living off the labor of others.

During the first half of the eighteenth century the collective wealth of the European aristocracy reached new heights. In eastern Europe that increase in wealth derived mainly from the dramatic increase in the size of the population. With more serfs under their control, the landed nobility could increase the wealth they gained from their labor and dues. In western European countries, most notably Britain and France, the members of the aristocracy increasingly participated in other forms of economic activity. They operated rural industries such as mining and forestry. They entered the financial world by lending money to the government, thus serving the state in the process. They became involved in urban building projects and in the economic development of overseas colonies. Those who came from old families considered these pursuits to be beneath the status of a nobleman, but by investing at a distance nobles could give the impression that they were not actually engaged in the sordid transactions of the marketplace.

Size of the Aristocracy in European States in the Eighteenth Century

Country	Date	Number of Nobles and Lesser Aristocrats	Percent of the Population
Austria	1800	90,000	1.15%
France	1775	400,000	1.60
Great Britain & Ireland	1783	50,000	3.25
Hungary	1800	400,000	11.25
Poland	1800	700,000	11.66
Russia	1800	600,000	1.66
Spain	1797	402,000	3.80
Sweden	1757	10,000	0.50
Venice	1797	1,090	0.80

Sources: A. Corvisier, *Armies and Society in Europe, 1494–1789* (1976), pp. 113, 115; J. Meyer, *Noblesses et pouvoirs dans l'Europe d'Ancien Régime* (1973); M. Reinard and A. Armenguard, *Histoire Générale de la Population Modiale* (1961); J. Dewald, *The European Nobility* (1996), pp. 22–27.

The members of the eighteenth-century aristocracy are often described as social and economic conservatives who were unable or unwilling to act in an entrepreneurial manner. The financial and commercial projects that many noblemen engaged in suggest that this reputation of the aristocracy is not fully deserved. Even on their landed estates, the aristocracy often behaved in a capitalistic manner during the seventeenth and eighteenth centuries. Many members of the aristocracy, both titled and untitled, adopted capitalist techniques of estate management to make their lands more productive. In England a nobleman, Charles Townshend, became widely known as "Turnip Townshend" when he introduced a crop rotation that included the lowly turnip. This type of agrarian entrepreneurship accounts for the accumulation of many great eighteenth-century aristocratic fortunes.

The Political Power of the Aristocracy

The mid-eighteenth century also marked the apex of political power for the aristocracy in Europe. Having recovered from the economic and political turmoil of the mid-seventeenth century, when they suffered economic losses and experienced a temporary eclipse of their power, noblemen pursued various strategies to increase or preserve their share of local and national political power. In

Marriage into the Nobility

This painting by William Hogarth, in a series titled *Marriage à la Mode*, depicts the negotiation of a marriage contract between an English earl and a wealthy London merchant. The earl, seated to the left and pointing to his family tree, is negotiating with the merchant sitting across the table. The marriage will take place between the earl's vain son, sitting to the far right, and the distracted daughter of the merchant, sitting next to him. The two individuals who are about to be married have no interest in each other. The earl has incurred large debts from building the large mansion depicted in the rear, and he intends to use the dowry to recover financially. By virtue of this trans-action the daughter will enter aristocratic society.

England, where royal power was greatly restricted as a result of the Glorious Revolution, the aristocracy gained political dominance. A small group of noblemen sat in the House of Lords, while the gentry formed the large majority of members of the House of Commons. After 1689 the English king could not rule without the cooperation of these two Houses of Parliament. The monarchy tried to control the proceedings of that assembly by creating parties of royal supporters within both houses. Because those parties were controlled by the king's ministers, who were themselves members of the nobility, the system allowed the aristocracy to dominate.

A similar situation prevailed in Poland and Hungary, where only the nobility were represented in the legislative assemblies of those countries. In Sweden and most German states the nobility formed a separate group that voted by themselves within the representative assemblies of those kingdoms. The country in Europe where members of the aristocracy exercised the least power and influence was the Dutch Republic. The traditional Dutch landed nobility remained a force to be reckoned with in eighteenth-century politics, but wealthy merchants and bankers held the balance of power in the seven Dutch provinces.

In absolute monarchies, where rulers had succeeded in restricting independent aristocratic power, members of the aristocracy exercised political power by controlling the institutions through which royal power was exercised. As we have seen in Chapter 15, absolute monarchs appeased the aristocracy by giving them control over provincial government and by recruiting them to occupy offices in the central bureaucracy of the state. The large bureaucracy of the eighteenth-century French state, for example, was run mainly by noblemen of the robe, a privileged group of approximately 2,000 officials who owed their noble status to their appointment to office rather than to heredity. In Russia during the early eighteenth century, tsars granted the nobility privileges and strengthened their powers over their serfs in order to secure the assistance the tsars needed to administer the Russian state at the local level.

The aristocracy also exercised political power through the judiciary. Members of the aristocracy often served as judges of the law courts of their kingdoms. In England noblemen and gentry served as the judges of almost all the common law courts, hearing cases both at the center of government at Westminster and in the provinces. In France noblemen staffed the nine regional *parlements* that registered royal edicts and acted as a court of appeal in criminal cases. The nobility controlled the central tribunals of the German kingdoms and principalities. At the local level the nobility exercised either a personal jurisdiction over the peasants who lived on their lands or an official jurisdiction as magistrates, such as the justices of the peace in each English county.

Britain provides a vivid example of the way in which the members of the landed class could use their judicial power to keep the lower classes in line: punishing petty crimes with harsh penalties. During the eighteenth century the incidence of crimes against property increased, especially when war created shortages of basic commodities. Those who occupied the middle ranks of society were the most frequent victims of these crimes, but as men of great wealth the aristocracy believed that all crimes against property threatened them as well. The aristocracy responded to this threat by passing legislation making even minor crimes against property, such as petty theft, capital offenses punishable by death. One victim of this harsh policy was John Burton, a lowly paid wagon driver who was hanged in 1744 for stealing two woolen caps.

Not all those convicted of such petty crimes suffered the same punishment as Burton. A few public executions every year were deemed sufficient to deter crime in a country that did not have a police force. Most convicted criminals were pardoned or had their sentences reduced. These displays of judicial mercy also served the purposes of the aristocracy by making people from the lower ranks of society dependent upon them for their lives. Exercising the power of pardon also strengthened their authority and made them appear sympathetic to the poor. In this way the British aristocracy helped to maintain the traditional deference paid to them from the lower ranks of society.

The Cultural World of the Aristocracy

During the eighteenth century the aristocracies in western European countries followed a lifestyle that emphasized their learning, refinement, and appreciation of the fine arts. It had not always been that way. As late as the fifteenth century the aristocracy, which in the Middle Ages had been a warrior class, had a reputation for their indifference or

even hostility to learning, and their conduct was often uncouth if not boorish. In eastern Europe a tradition of aristocratic illiteracy persisted into the eighteenth century. In western and central Europe, however, the pattern began to change in the sixteenth century, when members of the aristocracy started providing for the education of their children either at universities or in private academies. Even more important, aristocratic families began to acquire the manners and social graces that would be acceptable at court. By the eighteenth century the aristocracy, especially its upper ranks, became the backbone of what was then called "polite society."

The aristocracy also developed a sophisticated appreciation of high culture. Their homes housed large private collections of artwork that occasionally rivaled or even surpassed those of contemporary European monarchs. They were the main participants in the cultural life of European cities, especially Paris, London, Rome, Vienna, and Berlin. They formed the audiences of musical recitals, attended plays and operas in large numbers, and frequented the art galleries that were established in all the capitals of Europe. They also became the patrons of musicians, writers, and artists.

The homes of the eighteenth-century aristocracy reflected their preference for classicism°, a style in art, architecture, music, and literature that emphasizes proportion, adherence to traditional forms, and a rejection of emotion and enthusiasm. The classicism of the eighteenth century marked a step away from the more dynamic, imposing baroque style, which had flourished in the seventeenth century. Classicism celebrated the culture of ancient Greece and Rome. The revival of that culture in the eighteenth century in art and architecture is often referred to as neoclassicism°. The residences of the eighteenth-century aristocracy built in the classical style were perfectly proportioned and elegant without being overly decorated. Their Greek columns and formal gardens, lined with statues of classical figures, served as symbols of their cultural heritage. The classical architecture of the eighteenth century reflected the quiet confidence of the aristocracy that they, like their Greek and Roman forebears, occupied a dominant position in society.

Eighteenth-century music, which is likewise referred to as classical, reflected a concern for formal design, proportion, and concise melodic expression. The two greatest composers of the eighteenth century, Franz Joseph Haydn (1732–1809) and Wolfgang Amadeus Mozart (1756–1791), whose music was played before predominantly aristocratic audiences, became the most famous composers in this tradition. Classical music appealed less to the emotions than either the baroque music of the seventeenth century or the romantic music of the nineteenth century. The dominance of classicism in music as well as architecture during the eighteenth century reflected broader cultural currents in

Chiswick House
This house was built by Lord Burlington as a library and reception hall on his estate near London about 1725. Symmetrical, balanced, and restrained, the building embodies many of the features of classicism. Chiswick House was modeled on the architecture of the Italian Andrea Palladio (1518–1580), who in turn drew his inspiration from the buildings of ancient Rome.

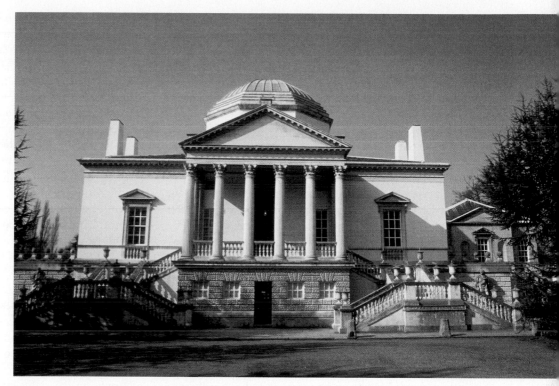

European intellectual life, when science and philosophy placed the highest value on the rationality and order of all material and human life.

Challenges to Aristocratic Dominance

■ How did subordinate social groups, most notably the rural peasantry and those who lived in the towns, challenge the aristocracy during the late eighteenth century?

Starting around the middle of the eighteenth century, the aristocracy endured increasingly acrimonious challenges to their power and criticisms of their values and lifestyles. They gradually lost the respect that they commanded from the lower ranks of society. By the end of the century European aristocracies had been significantly weakened. Their values had been called into question, while their political power and privileges had been eroded. A claim of nobility began to be viewed more as a sign of vanity than as a natural right to rule. The revolution that took place in France in the last decade of the eighteenth century, followed by the reform movements that developed in its wake throughout Europe in the early nineteenth century, brought the age of aristocracy to an end. Members of the aristocracy managed to regain some of what they had lost

in the French Revolution, and they also showed their resourcefulness by accommodating themselves to the new order, but they never recovered the dominant position they had held in the eighteenth century.

Encounters with the Rural Peasantry

One set of challenges to the aristocracy came from the peasants and serfs who lived and worked on landed estates. This was the social group over whom the aristocracy exercised the most direct control. The control was most oppressive in central and eastern Europe, where the rural masses were serfs and therefore had no personal freedom. Landlords not only determined where serfs lived and when they married, but they also collected burdensome financial duties from them. Their plight was relieved only partially by the elimination of some of the burdens of serfdom. In Prussia and Austria these obligations were abolished by royal edict. The monarchs who instituted these reforms may have been responding to the demands of philosophes°, the intellectuals and writers of the age, who condemned the institution of serfdom for its cruelty and inefficiency. (See the section on the Enlightenment later in this chapter.) A more powerful motive, however, was the desire of monarchs to collect taxes from a peasantry that was spending the greater part of its income on financial duties owed to aristocratic landowners. Because the peasants still remained overburdened by financial obligations, emancipation did little to improve their lot.

In western Europe, where serfdom had for the most part given way to tenant ownership and leasehold tenure, the condition of the rural masses was only marginally better. After 1720, famines became less common than they had been in the late seventeenth century, making it possible for peasants to eke out an existence, but other economic pressures, including the elimination of common pasture rights and an increase in taxation, continued to weigh down on them. Over the course of the eighteenth century the number of peasants owning small plots of land declined. Many of those who leased land were forced to sell it as landowners consolidated their holdings. Consequently the number of landless laborers who worked for wages increased. By 1789 almost half the peasants in France had no land at all.

Under these circumstances the relationship between peasants and landowners continued to deteriorate. The realities of the marketplace gradually eroded the paternalistic concern that the nobility had traditionally shown for the welfare of their serfs or tenants. As the relationship between landlord and peasant became predominantly economic, the two parties became more distant. At the same time the gap between the culture of the elite and that of the common people, which as we have seen in Chapter 16 began in the seventeenth century, became more pronounced. The distance between landlord and peasant assumed real geographical form as landlords built their mansions away from the local village. By surrounding their homes with acres of parkland and gardens, they shielded themselves from the sight of the peasants working in the fields. Visual and personal contact between lord and peasant therefore became less frequent. The most direct contact a landlord made with the members of the lower classes was with the servants who worked in their homes.

As economic pressures on the peasants mounted, conflict between them and the aristocracy increased. Peasant resistance to their landlords could take a number of different forms. In some countries, most notably France, peasants could bring their grievances before village assemblies. These democratic institutions often succeeded in upholding peasants' demands, especially when royal officials in the provinces, who wished to collect their own taxes from the peasants, sided with them against the nobility.

Another option was to file a lawsuit against the lord, often with the assistance of the royal government. In Burgundy numerous peasant communities hired lawyers to take their seigneurs° or lords to court in order to prevent the imposition of new financial dues or the confiscation of communal village land. They were often aided in these efforts by the agents of the royal government, who wanted the peasants to be able to pay higher taxes imposed by the king. In these lawsuits, which became very common in the second half of the eighteenth century, peasants challenged not only the imposition of seigneurial dues but the very institution of aristocratic lordship. In 1765 one lawyer representing a peasant community in Champagne argued that the

rights claimed by landowners "derive from the violence of seigneurs" and had always been "odious." The language used in these cases inspired much of the rhetoric employed in the abolition of feudal privilege at the time of the French Revolution (see Chapter 19).

Peasants occasionally took more direct action against their landlords. In eastern France the number of incidents of rural violence against the property of seigneurs who tried to collect new duties increased toward the end of the eighteenth century. In Ireland a group known as the Whiteboys maimed cattle and tore down fences when landowners denied tenants their common grazing rights. Other forms of peasant action included poaching on the lands of landowners who claimed the exclusive right to hunt or trap game on their estates. The hunting activities of the tenants of the Earl of Uxbridge discussed at the beginning of this chapter are just one example of this type of lower-class resistance to aristocratic privilege.

In western Europe these acts of resistance did not develop into widespread peasant rebellion until the outbreak of the French Revolution in 1789. During the late eighteenth century incidents of rural violence were largely confined to individual villages. The reduction in the incidence of famine in the eighteenth century provides one possible explanation for this pattern of isolated, localized resistance. Without recurrent subsistence crises, the plight of the rural masses was not sufficiently desperate to provoke large-scale rebellion. The only expressions of collective unrest over the supply of food in western Europe during the eighteenth century were urban riots. These food riots usually took place in market towns or ports where grain was being exported. The violence was not directed against landlords but merchants or officials who were suspected of hoarding grain or fixing the price of bread.

The economic and social situation in eastern Europe differed from that of France, Britain, and other western European countries. In the east the deteriorating economic condition of the peasantry led to large-scale rebellion. Bohemia, Hungary, and Croatia, all of which lay within the boundaries of the Austrian Habsburg monarchy, witnessed large peasant revolts in the 1780s. The bloodiest of these revolts occurred in the province of Transylvania in 1784, when 30,000 peasant rebels butchered hundreds of noblemen and their families after those landowners had raised the dues owed to them as much as 1,000 percent.

The largest eastern European rural rebellion took place in Russia between 1773 and 1774. Pretending to be the murdered Tsar Peter III (d. 1762), the Cossack Emelian Pugachev (1726–1775) set out to destroy the Russian government of Catherine the Great and the nobility that served it. Pugachev assembled an army of 8,000 men, which staged lightning raids against government centers in the southern Urals. The most serious phase of this uprising took place when these troops marched into the agricultural regions of the country and inspired as many as three million serfs to revolt. Pugachev promised to abolish serfdom, end taxation, and eliminate the lesser aristocracy. The rebellion took a heavy toll, as the serfs and soldiers murdered some 3,000 nobles and officials. The Russian upper class feared that the rebellion would spread and destroy the entire social order, but government troops prevented that from happening by brutally suppressing the rising. Pugachev was transported to Moscow in an iron cage, where he was hanged, quartered, and burned.

Neither Pugachev nor the serfs who joined his rebellion envisioned the creation of a new social order. They still spoke in conservative terms of regaining ancient freedoms that had been lost. But this massive revolt, like others that resembled it, reflected the depth of the tension that prevailed between landlord and peasant, between nobleman and serf, in the apparently stable world of the eighteenth century. That tension serves as one of the most striking and ominous themes of eighteenth-century social history.

The Social Position of the Bourgeoisie

In the cities and towns the most serious challenges to the aristocracy came not from the urban masses, who posed an occasional threat to all urban authorities, but from the bourgeoisie°. This social group was more heterogeneous than the aristocracy. It consisted of untitled people of property who lived in the cities and towns. The word *bourgeoisie* refers to those who were burghers—or those who had voting rights in the towns. Prosperous merchants and financiers formed the upper ranks of the bourgeoisie, while members of the legal and medical professions, second-tier government officials, and emerging industrialists occupied a social niche just below them. The bourgeoisie also included some skilled artisans and shopkeepers, sometimes referred to as the "petty bourgeoisie," who were far more prosperous than the large mass of urban laborers. The size of the bourgeoisie grew as the urban population of Europe expanded during the eighteenth century, even before the advent of industrialization. This social group was far more numerous in the North Atlantic countries of France, the Dutch Republic, and Britain than in the states of central and eastern Europe. In England the bourgeoisie accounted for about 15 percent of the total population in 1800, whereas in Russia they constituted no more than 3 percent.

Because it was possible for some members of the bourgeoisie to achieve upward social mobility and join the ranks of the aristocracy, the social and economic boundaries separating these wealthy townsmen from the lower ranks of the nobility could become blurred. In French towns it was often difficult to distinguish between wealthy financiers and noble bureaucrats. Although the two groups received their income from different sources, they both belonged to a wealthy, propertied elite. The middle and lower ranks of the

Joshua Reynolds, *Mary, Duchess of Richmond* (ca. 1765)
At a time when most European noblewomen were attracting criticism for their luxury and vanity, this prominent English duchess was depicted as being engaged in the simple domestic task of needlepoint. Some members of the aristocracy were able to deflect criticism of their lifestyle by adopting the habits of the bourgeoisie.

bourgeoisie, however, gradually emerged as a social group that acquired its own social, political, and cultural identity distinct from that of the aristocracy.

Bourgeois identity was rooted in the towns, which had their own political institutions and their own social hierarchies. The bourgeoisie also possessed the means of effectively communicating with each other and thus were capable of forming common political goals. Their high rates of literacy made them the core of the new political force of public opinion that emerged in the cities and towns in the eighteenth century. The bourgeoisie made up the main audience of the thousands of newspapers, pamphlets, and books that rolled off the presses during the eighteenth century. A "public sphere" of activity, in which politically conscious townsmen participated, became a peculiar feature of bourgeois society. During the eighteenth and early nineteenth centuries the bourgeoisie became the leaders of movements seeking political change. They organized and became the main participants in the protest movements,

Bathing in the West

One of the personal habits that members of the European aristocracy and bourgeoisie began to adopt in the eighteenth century was frequent bathing. Until that time people in the West had been reluctant to immerse their bodies in water. In this respect there was a clear difference between Western and Eastern practice. Among Asians who practiced the Hindu religion, bathing had deep religious significance and was a daily ritual. The same was true for Muslims, for whom water possessed a sacred purifying role and prepared the bather for prayer or sacrifice. In the West bathing was not invested with similar religious significance. Christianity had emphasized purity of heart, not of the body. Without a religious inspiration, bathing the body rarely occurred in Western nations during the early modern period. Europeans might wash various parts of their body, especially the hands and face, but total immersion was almost unheard of. The few who did bathe usually did so no more than once a year, and tubs and basins were not widely available. Swimming in rivers and lakes was dangerous and often resulted in drowning. Even medical opinion conspired against bathing. According to one seventeenth-century French doctor, "bathing outside the practice of medicine was not only superfluous but very damaging to health."

By the beginning of the nineteenth century, many Europeans had begun to take regular baths. The sale of washbasins and commercially produced soap soared. This change occurred as a result of three distinct factors. The first was the insistence by many eighteenth-century Protestants that Christianity did indeed demand a clean body as well as a clean soul. The eighteenth-century founder of Methodism, the English preacher John Wesley, coined a new proverb when he declared that "cleanliness is indeed next to godliness."

A second reason was that cleanliness became associated with gentility and good manners. Bodily cleanliness became one of the ways in which members of society who considered themselves civilized made themselves attractive to the people with whom they associated. This explains why bathing the body all over was first adopted by the upper classes, who contrasted themselves with the dirty lower classes. It also became more common among women than men. The third reason was a change in medical opinion, which began to view bathing as a means to keep the pores of the skin open and thus promote perspiration. Bathing came to be viewed as a means of curing numerous diseases and as a key to long life.

The acceptance of bathing in the West owed something to Eastern influence. Eighteenth-century Western writers often commented on the daily bathing of Turks and Hindus, and Europeans who lived in the East had the opportunity to witness firsthand a custom that contrasted strikingly with their own. The period of most pronounced influence was the mid-eighteenth century, when many other features of Eastern culture penetrated the West. In the early nineteenth century a Hindu noted that bathing in the West was still very different from that practiced in his own country. Nevertheless, the reluctant European adoption of immersing the body in water had brought about a minor accommodation between Eastern and Western practice.

For Discussion

What does the widespread practice of bathing in Asia and the reluctance of Europeans to adopt this practice tell us about the differences between Eastern and Western cultures in the eighteenth century?

Jean-Jacques Henner, *Chaste Susanna at Her Bath* (1865)
By the nineteenth century, Europeans had adopted the practice of bathing the entire body.

petitioning drives, and ultimately the revolutionary steps taken to challenge and replace established regimes.

The Bourgeois Critique of the Aristocracy

At the core of bourgeois identity lay a set of values that contrasted with those attributed to the aristocracy, especially the noblemen and noblewomen who gathered at court. Not all members of the bourgeoisie shared these values, nor did all members of the nobility embody those attributed to them. Nonetheless, the bourgeois critique of aristocratic society, which flourished mainly among the lower or petty bourgeoisie rather than the great merchants and financiers, contributed to the formation of bourgeois identity and helped to erode respect for the traditional aristocracy.

The bourgeois critique of the aristocracy consisted of three related themes. First was the allegation that the aristocracy lived a life of luxury, hedonism, and idleness that contrasted with the thrifty, sober, hardworking petty bourgeoisie. Unlike the aristocracy, the bourgeoisie did not display their wealth. Second, court nobles were accused of being sexually promiscuous and immoral, while their wives were depicted as vain flirts. There was some foundation to this charge, especially because the predominance of arranged marriages within the nobility had induced many noble husbands and wives to seek sexual partners outside marriage, a practice that was widely tolerated within aristocratic circles. By contrast, the bourgeoisie tended to enter into marriages in which both partners remained faithful to each other. Third, the members of the aristocracy were considered participants in a decadent international culture that often ignored or degraded the more wholesome, patriotic values of the bourgeoisie.

This critique of the aristocracy had profound political implications. It laid the foundation for the demands for equal political rights and the advancement of careers on the basis of talent rather than inherited wealth. These demands came not from the wealthy financiers, merchants, and capitalists who had the opportunity to ascend into the ranks of the nobility but from men of more modest wealth: holders of minor political offices, shopkeepers, and even skilled artisans. These people from the middle ranks of society, especially those who lived in the cities and towns, were most responsible for eventually reducing the influence of the aristocracy in European political and social life.

Criticism of aristocratic values and demands for liberty and equality received support from intellectuals who are usually identified with the movement known as the Enlightenment°. Not all of these thinkers and writers came from the middle ranks of society. Many of them were in fact members of the aristocracy or the beneficiaries of aristocratic patronage. Nevertheless their goal was to bring about the reform of society, and that inevitably led to a critique of aristocratic values and practices.

The Enlightenment

■ **What were the main features of Enlightenment thought and how did it present a threat to the old order?**

The Enlightenment was the defining intellectual and cultural movement of the eighteenth century. This complex movement had roots in the seventeenth century; the Scientific Revolution and the growth of philosophical skepticism were particularly important influences (see Chapter 16). Contemporaries used the word *Enlightenment* to describe their own intellectual outlook and achievements. For Immanuel Kant (1724–1804), the renowned German philosopher and author of *Critique of Pure Reason* (1781), enlightenment was the expression of intellectual maturity, the attainment of understanding solely by using one's reason without being influenced by dogma, superstition, or another person's opinion. For Kant enlightenment was both the process of thinking for oneself and the knowledge of human society and human nature that one achieved as a result. His famous exhortation, "Have the courage to know!" could serve as a slogan for the entire Enlightenment.

The Enlightenment is often referred to as a French movement, and it is true that the most famous of the European writers and thinkers of the Enlightenment, known as philosophes, were French. It was also in France that the Enlightenment first became a campaign to change people's minds and reform institutions. But French philosophes were inspired by seventeenth-century English sources, especially the writings of Isaac Newton (1647–1727) and John Locke (1632–1704), while German, Scottish, Dutch, Swiss, and Italian writers made their own distinctive contributions to Enlightenment thought. The ideas of the Enlightenment also spread to the Americas, where they inspired movements for political reform and national independence. The men and women of the Enlightenment thought of themselves not so much as French, British, or Dutch but as members of an international Republic of Letters, not unlike the international community of scholars that had arisen within the ancient Roman Empire and again at the time of the Renaissance. This cosmopolitan literary republic knew no geographical boundaries, and it was open to ideas from all lands (see Map 18.1). Its literary achievements, however, bore a distinctly Western stamp, and the ideas its members promoted became essential components of Western civilization.

Themes of Enlightenment Thought

Because the Enlightenment spanned the entire continent and lasted for more than a century, it is difficult to establish characteristics that all its participants shared. The Enlightenment was more a frame of mind, an approach to

Map 18.1 The European Enlightenment

The map shows the birthplaces of thinkers and writers of the Enlightenment. The greatest number of them came from France and Britain, but all European countries were represented, and the men and women of the Enlightenment thought of themselves as belonging to an international "Republic of Letters" that knew no political boundaries.

obtaining knowledge, as Kant claimed, than a set of clearly defined beliefs. Enlightenment writers, however, emphasized several intellectual themes that gave the entire movement a certain degree of unity and coherence.

Reason and the Laws of Nature

The first theme emphasized by Enlightenment thinkers was the elevation of human reason to a position of paramount philosophical importance. Enlightenment thinkers placed almost unlimited confidence in the ability of human beings to understand how the world operates. In previous ages philosophers had always found a place for human reason, but they also placed limits on it, especially when it came into conflict with religious faith. Medieval scholastic philosophers had tried to reconcile faith and reason, and that effort continued through the seventeenth century, par-

ticularly in scientific circles. In the eighteenth century, however, greater emphasis was placed on reason alone, which was believed to be superior to religious faith and the final arbiter of all disputes.

Confidence in human reason was closely associated with the belief that the operation of the entire universe was governed by natural laws that human reason could discover. This belief in natural law can be traced back to the ancient Greeks and to its revival and assimilation to Christian theology by the scholastics in the Middle Ages. Natural law acquired a distinctive character at the time of the Scientific Revolution. The search for and discovery of the laws governing such phenomena as gravitation, the circulation of the blood, and dynamics gradually led to the belief that all activity, including the behavior of human beings, was governed by similar laws.

The application of natural law to human society was the most novel and distinctive feature of Enlightenment thought. According to Enlightenment thinkers, scientific laws governed the functioning of society. There were even laws governing the passions and the operation of the human psyche. In his *Treatise of Human Nature* (1739–1740),

the Scottish philosopher David Hume (1711–1776) offered a science of the human mind, which could be applied to politics and other human endeavors. Economics, too, received the same treatment. The Scottish economist Adam Smith (1723–1790), who described the operation of economic life in *The Wealth of Nations* (1776), believed that the economy was subject to inviolable laws, just like those that governed the movement of the heavens. The Enlightenment therefore gave birth to modern social science. Economics, political science, sociology, anthropology, and psychology all trace their origins as intellectual disciplines to this time. They were all based on the premise that reason could discover the laws or principles of human nature.

The search for natural laws governing all human life provides one explanation for the unprecedented interest of eighteenth-century writers in non-European cultures. During the Enlightenment a vast literature subjected the peoples of the world to detailed description, classification, and analysis. The first thorough, scholarly studies of Indian, Chinese, and Arab cultures were published during the middle and late eighteenth century. Egypt, a country that had been a part of the Ottoman Empire and isolated from the West since the sixteenth century, became the subject of a sizable literature, especially after the French occupied the country in 1798. There also was an increase in travel literature describing the societies that Europeans were encountering, some of them for the first time. Descriptions of the indigenous peoples of northwestern Canada, Australia, and Tahiti became readily available in the bookshops of Paris and London.

This cross-cultural scholarship, which was facilitated by the rapid growth of overseas empires after 1660, served the purpose of providing intellectuals with information enabling them to discover laws governing the behavior of all people. Some of the non-European countries that these scholars studied, such as China, had highly developed civilizations, whereas those of Native Americans and the indigenous people of the South Sea islands were far less developed. In both cases, however, educated people in the West began to consider these non-Western societies valid subjects of intellectual inquiry.

Religion and Morality

The spread of scientific knowledge in the eighteenth century gave the thinkers of the Enlightenment a new understanding of God and his relationship to humankind. The Christian God of the Middle Ages and the Reformation period was an all-knowing, personal God who often intervened in the life of human beings. He could be stern and severe or gentle and merciful, but he was always involved in the affairs of humankind, which he governed through Providence. The gradual recognition that the universe was of unfathomable size and that it operated in accordance with natural laws made God appear more remote. Most philosophes believed that God was still the creator of the universe and the author of the natural laws that governed it, but they did not believe that he was still actively involved in its operation. God was the playwright of the universe, but not its director. This belief that God had created the universe, given it laws, and then allowed it to operate in a mechanistic fashion is known as deism°. In deism there was no place for the traditional Christian belief that God became human in order to redeem humankind from original sin.

Enlightenment thinkers, especially those who were deists, believed that human beings could use reason to discover the natural laws God had laid down at the time of creation. This inquiry included the discovery of the principles of morality, which no longer were to be grounded in Scripture. To observe the laws of God now meant not so much keeping his commandments but discovering what was natural and acting accordingly. In a certain sense God

David Hume, Scottish Philosopher
Like John Locke, Hume explored the process by which the human mind reaches an understanding of the material world. Hume was committed to the application of science to the human psyche.

was being remade in a human image and was being identified with the natural instincts of human beings. In this way religion could become equated with the pursuit of human happiness.

If one believed that God established natural laws for all humanity, then doctrinal differences between religions became less important. All religions were valid to the extent that they led to an understanding of natural law. There was no one true religion, a point that the German dramatist and philosopher Gotthold Lessing (1729–1781) made in his play *Nathan the Wise* (1779) in response to the persistent questioning of a fictional Turkish sultan. This denial of the existence of one true religion led naturally to a demand for toleration of all religions, including those of non-Western peoples.

Enlightenment thinkers were highly critical of the superstitious and dogmatic character of contemporary Christianity, especially Roman Catholicism. French philosophes in particular had little use for priests, whom they castigated relentlessly in their letters and pamphlets. They minimized the importance of religious belief in the con-

duct of human life and substituted rational for religious values. They had little respect for the academic discipline of theology. The German-born Parisian writer Baron d'Holbach (1723–1789), one of the few philosophes who could be considered an atheist—denying the existence of God at all—dismissed theology as a "pretended science." He claimed that its principles were "only hazardous suppositions, imagined by ignorance, propagated by enthusiasm or knavery, adopted by timid credulity, preserved by custom which never reasons, and revered solely because not understood."[1]

Epitomizing the new religious outlook of the Enlightenment was the Scottish moral philosopher David Hume, who is most famous for his treatise *An Enquiry Concerning Human Understanding* (1748). In that work he challenged the argument of the great rationalist philosopher René Descartes that God implants a number of clear and distinct ideas in our minds, from which we are able to deduce other truths. Hume's position was that our understanding derives from sense perceptions, not innate ideas. Even more important, he denied that there was any certain knowledge,

CREDULITY, SUPERSTITION, & FANATICISM.

Hogarth pinx. *I. Cook sculp.*

Published by Longman, Hurst, Rees, & Orme, Jan. 1st 1809.

William Hogarth, *Credulity, Superstition, and Fanaticism* (1762)

Hogarth was a moralist who embodied the rationalism and humanitarianism of the Enlightenment. In this engraving he exposes the effects of fanatical religion, witchcraft, and superstition. The sermon has whipped the entire congregation into a highly emotional state. The woman in the foreground is Mary Tofts, who was believed to have given birth to rabbits. The boy next to her, allegedly possessed by the Devil, vomits pins. The Protestant preacher's wig falls off, exposing the shaven head of a Roman Catholic monk. An unemotional Turk observes this scene from outside the window.

thereby calling into question the authority of revealed truth and religious doctrine.

Hume's writing on religion reflected his skepticism. Raised a Presbyterian, he nevertheless rejected the revealed truths of Christianity on the ground that they had no rational foundation. The concept of Providence was completely alien to his philosophical position. An avowed deist, he expressed contempt for organized religion, especially Catholicism in France and Anglicanism in England. Organized religion, according to Hume, "renders men tame and submissive, is acceptable to the magistrate, and seems inoffensive to the people; till at last the priest, having firmly established his authority, becomes the tyrant and disturber of human society."[2]

Progress and Reform

Theories regarding the stages of human development, coupled with the commitment of philosophes to the improvement and ultimate transformation of society, contributed to a belief in the progress of civilization. Until the eighteenth century the very notion of progress was alien to even the most highly educated Europeans. Those who held political power had dedicated themselves to maintaining the social and political order, not its transformation. Programs of reform were almost always associated with the restoration of a superior golden age rather than the realization of something new and different. If movement took place, it was cyclical rather than progressive. Even the original meaning of the word *revolution* was the path of a planet that came full circle in its orbit, not the creation of a new order. Now, however, the possibility of improvement began to dominate philosophical and political discussion. The Enlightenment was largely responsible for making this belief in progress, especially toward the attainment of social justice, a prominent feature of modern Western culture.

Some Enlightenment thinkers, using evidence gained from encounters with non-Western people, argued that all civilizations progressed gradually from relatively simple to more complex economies and societies. David Hume, Adam Smith, and their fellow Scotsman Adam Ferguson (1723–1816) identified four stages of human development. The first was characterized by hunting and gathering, the second by pastoral farming, the third by agriculture, and the last by commerce. The French philosophe the Marquis de Condorcet (1743–1794) focused more on intellectual progress. In *A Sketch for a Historical Picture of the Progress of the Human Mind* (1795), Condorcet identified nine distinct epochs in human history. He predicted that in the tenth and final epoch humankind would achieve a state of perfection in which rational moral judgments would inform efficient government policy.

Another source of the Enlightenment's belief in progress was the conviction that corrupt institutions could be reformed, thereby allowing societies to advance to a higher level and realize their full potential. The system of taxation, bureaucratic institutions, established churches, and the institution of monarchy itself all became the targets of Enlightenment reformers. The judicial institutions of government were particularly susceptible to this type of reforming zeal. Campaigns arose to eliminate the administration of judicial torture as well as capital punishment. All of this was intended to establish a more humane, civilized society.

The intellectual inspiration to this movement for legal reform was the work of the Italian jurist Cesare Beccaria (1738–1794). In his *Essay on Crimes and Punishments* (1764), Beccaria argued that punishment should be used not to exact retribution for crimes but to rehabilitate the criminal and to serve the interests of society. "In order that every punishment may not be an act of violence committed by one or by many against a private member of society," wrote Beccaria, "it should be above all things public, immediate, and necessary, the least possible in the case given, proportioned to the crime, and determined by the laws."[3] He called for the abolition of capital punishment and the imprisonment of convicted felons. The prison, which prior to the eighteenth century had been little more than a jail or holding facility, was now to become a symbol of the improvement of society.

Voltaire and the Spirit of the Enlightenment

The philosophe who captured all the main themes as well as the spirit of the Enlightenment was the writer and philosopher François Marie Arouet (1694–1778), known universally by his pen name, Voltaire. Born into a French bourgeois family, Voltaire became one of the most prominent and prolific writers of the eighteenth century. Although he wrote for a fairly broad, predominantly bourgeois audience, and although he waged war against the injustices of aristocratic society, he was comfortable in the homes of the nobility and at the courts of European monarchs, especially that of Frederick the Great of Prussia. Voltaire's main career was as an author. He wrote plays and novels as well as poems, letters, essays, and history. These writings revealed his commitment to scientific rationality, his contempt for established religion, and his unflagging pursuit of liberty and justice.

DOCUMENT

Voltaire on the Relations Between Church and State (mid-18th c.)

Like many men of the Enlightenment, Voltaire developed a deep interest in science. He acquired much of his scientific knowledge from a learned noblewoman, Madame du Châtelet (1706–1749), a scientist and mathematician who translated the works of Newton into French. Madame du Châtelet became Voltaire's mistress, and the two lived together with her tolerant husband in their country estate in eastern France. The sexual freedom they experienced was characteristic of many Enlightenment figures, who rejected the Christian condemnation of

A Case of Infanticide in the Age of the Enlightenment

A mid-eighteenth-century trial of a young French woman charged with killing her newborn child provides a window into the life of women who occupied the lower rungs of French society, in contrast to those who frequented the court and met in salons. The trial also raises the larger questions, debated in French and European judicial circles during the time of the Enlightenment, of how society should deal with the mothers of illegitimate children and whether the punishments prescribed for infanticide, or the killing of a young child, were proportionate to the crime.

In August 1742 Marie-Jeanne Bartonnet, a 21-year-old unmarried woman from a small French village in Brie, moved to Paris, where she took up residence with Claude le Queux, whom she had known in her youth, and Claude's sister. At that time Bartonnet was seven months pregnant. On October 22 Bartonnet caused a ruckus in the middle of the night when she went to the toilet and began groaning loudly and bleeding profusely. When her neighbors found her, and when she asked for towels for the blood, they suspected that she had had a miscarriage and called for a midwife. By the time the midwife arrived, it was clear that the delivery had already taken place and that the infant had fallen down the toilet to the cesspool five stories below. Suspecting that Bartonnet had killed the baby, the proprietress of the building reported her to the nearest judicial officer. The next day judicial authorities returned to the building and found the dead infant in the cesspool. An autopsy revealed that the child's skull had been dented by either a blunt instrument or a fall. After a med-ical examination of Bartonnet revealed the signs of having just delivered a baby, she was arrested and imprisoned for the crime of infanticide.

Bartonnet came very close to being executed, but the strict procedures of French justice saved her from paying the ultimate price for her apparent crime. In the seventeenth and eighteenth centuries French criminal justice had established clear criteria for determining the guilt or innocence of a person accused of a crime. These procedures involved a systematic interrogation of the accused (only rarely under torture), the deposition of witnesses, the evaluation of physical evidence, and the confrontation of the accused with the witnesses who testified against her. There also was a mandatory review of the case, which involved a further interrogation of the defendant, before the Parlement of Paris, the highest court in northern France.

The interrogations of Bartonnet did not give her judges much evidence on which they could convict her. When asked the name of the village where she had lived in Brie, she told her interrogators, "It's none of your business." She denied that she had even known she was pregnant, refused to name the man with whom she had had intercourse, and claimed that she had mistaken her labor pains for colic or diarrhea. She denied picking her baby off the floor of the toilet after the delivery and throwing it into the cesspool. When presented with the baby's corpse, she claimed she did not recognize it.

After this interrogation, Bartonnet was given the opportunity to challenge the testimony of the witnesses who had seen her the night of the delivery. The most damning testimony came from Madame Pâris, the wife of the proprietor, who had found Bartonnet on the toilet and thus could verify the circumstances of the clandestine delivery. Bartonnet's inability to challenge the testimony of Madame Pâris led directly to her initial conviction. After reviewing the entire dossier of evidence, the king's attorney recommended conviction for concealing her pregnancy, hiding her delivery, and destroying her child. French criminal procedure entrusted the decision of guilt or innocence to the judges themselves, and on November 27 they voted that Bartonnet should be executed by hanging.

Marie-Jeanne Bartonnet's fate, however, was not yet sealed. When her case went on appeal to the Parlement of Paris, Bartonnet repeated her statement that she had gone to the toilet but did not know whether she had given birth. Even though her execution was warranted by terms of an edict of 1557 that defined the crime of infanticide, the judges of this court voted to commute her sentence to a public whipping, banishment from the jurisdiction of the Parlement of Paris, and confiscation of her property. The basis of this decision appears to have been the absence of any proof that she had deliberately killed her baby. Indeed, its injuries could have been caused by its fall down the drain pipe into the cesspool. There was also the persistent refusal of the defendant to make a confession. She may have been lying, but it is equally possible that once she had delivered the baby, which happened very quickly, she convinced herself that it had not happened.

Bartonnet's trial for infanticide stands at the end of a long period of intense prosecution of this crime. Trials of this sort declined as cities and towns built foundling hospitals for abandoned infants and as the moral outrage for illegitimacy was redirected from the pregnant mother to the illegitimate father. The new legal values promoted at the time of the Enlightenment, moreover, made it less likely that any woman or man would be executed for this or any other crime.

Questions of Justice

1. As in many trials, the facts of this case can be used to support different claims of justice. If you had been the prosecutor in this trial, what position would you have taken to prove the crime of infanticide? If you had been defending Marie-Jeanne Bartonnet, what arguments would you have used in her defense?

2. In his *Essay on Crimes and Punishments* (1764), Beccaria recommended that punishments be determined strictly in accordance with the social damage committed by the crime. What would Beccaria have said about the original sentence of death in this case? What would he have said about the modified sentence handed down by the Parlement of Paris?

Taking It Further

Michael Wolfe, ed. *Changing Identities in Early Modern France.* 1997. Gives a full account of Marie-Jeanne Bartonnet's trial for infanticide.

A Woman Accused of Murder in the Eighteenth Century
With the exception of infanticide—the crime for which Marie-Jeanne Bartonnet was tried and convicted—few women were tried for capital crimes in the eighteenth century. One exception was Sarah Malcolm, a 22-year-old Englishwoman, shown here in a portrait by William Hogarth (1733). Malcolm was executed for slitting the throat of a wealthy lady in London.

sexual activity outside marriage and who justified their behavior on the basis of natural law and the pursuit of happiness. From Madame du Châtelet, Voltaire acquired not only an understanding of Newton's scientific laws but also a commitment to women's education and equality. Voltaire lived with her until she died in 1749 while giving birth to a child that was fathered neither by Voltaire nor her husband.

Voltaire's belief in a Newtonian universe—one governed by the universal law of gravitation—laid the foundation for his deism and his attacks on contemporary Christianity. In his *Philosophical Dictionary* (1764), he lashed out at established religion and the clergy, Protestant as well as Catholic. In a letter to another philosophe attacking religious superstition he pleaded, "Whatever you do, crush the infamous thing." In Voltaire's eyes Christianity was not only unreasonable; it was vulgar and barbaric. He condemned the Catholic Church for the slaughter of millions of indigenous people in the Americas on the grounds that they had not been baptized, as well as the executions of hundreds of thousands of Jews and heretics in Europe. All of these people were the victims of "barbarism and fanaticism."[4]

Voltaire's indictment of the Church for these barbarities was matched by his scathing criticism of the French government for a series of injustices, including his own imprisonment for insulting the regent of France. While living in England for three years, Voltaire became an admirer of English legal institutions, which he considered more humane and just than those of his native country. Using England as a model, he appealed for the implementation of various political reforms in France. He deplored those "who reduce men to a state of slavery by force and downright violence." A tireless advocate of individual liberty, he became a regular defender of victims of injustice, including Jean Calas, a Protestant shopkeeper from Toulouse who had been tortured and executed for allegedly murdering his son because he had expressed a desire to convert to Catholicism. The boy had in fact committed suicide.

Voltaire showed a commitment to placing his knowledge in the service of humanitarian causes. In his most famous novel, *Candide* (1759), the character by that name challenges the smug confidence of Dr. Pangloss, the tutor who repeatedly claims that they lived in "the best of all possible worlds." At the end of the novel Candide responds to this refrain by saying that "we must cultivate our garden." Voltaire, instead of being content with the current condition of humankind, was demanding that we work actively to improve society.

Madame du Châtelet

In her *Institutions de physique* (1740) this French noblewoman, the mistress of Voltaire, made an original and impressive attempt to give Newtonian physics a philosophical foundation.

Enlightenment Political Theory

Enlightenment thinkers are known most widely for their political theories, especially those that supported the causes of liberty and reform. The men and women of the Enlightenment did not, however, share a common political ideology, nor did they agree on the most desirable type of political society. They did share a belief that politics was a science that, like the cosmos, had its own natural laws. The title of one of David Hume's treatises, *That Politics May Be Reduced to a Science* (1741), reflects a belief that most Enlightenment political writers endorsed. They also thought of the state in secular rather than religious terms. There was little place in Enlightenment thought for the divine right of kings. Nor was there a place for the Church in the government of the state. On other issues, however, there was little consensus. Three thinkers in particular illustrate the range of Enlightenment political thought: Montesquieu, Rousseau, and Paine.

Baron de Montesquieu: The Separation of Powers

The most influential political writer of the Enlightenment was the French philosophe Charles-Louis de Secondat, Baron de Montesquieu (1689–1755). The son of a nobleman of the robe from Bordeaux, Montesquieu had a legal education and also developed an early interest in science. His political thought owed as much to his study of history and anthropology as to the study of law and science. His first book, *The Persian Letters*, published anonymously in Holland in 1721, was a brilliant satire of Western government and society through the eyes of two Persian aristocrats traveling in Europe. It laid the groundwork for a much more scholarly and substantial contribution to political theory, *Spirit of the Laws* (1748). Often compared to Aristotle because of the range of his thought, Montesquieu interwove commentaries on natural law, religion, morals, virtue, climate, and liberty. Unlike Hobbes, Locke, and the other natural-law philosophers who preceded him, Montesquieu was not concerned with the origin of government or with the establishment of a universal model of politics. Rather, he treated the laws of a country in historical perspective and within the context of that country's religion, morality, climate, geography, and culture. His political writing was scientific mainly in its empirical approach to its subject, and in the comparisons it made between politics on the one hand and Newtonian physics on the other.

Montesquieu argued that there were three forms of government: republics, monarchies, and despotisms, each of which had an activating or inspirational force. In republics that force was civic virtue, in monarchies it was honor, and in despotisms it was fear. In each form of government there was a danger that the polity could degenerate: The virtue of republics could be lost, monarchies could become corrupt, and despotisms could lead to repression. The key to maintaining moderation and preventing this degeneration of civil society was the law of each country. Ideally the law of a country should provide for the separation and balance of political powers. Only in that way could degeneration be avoided and moderation ensured.

Montesquieu used his knowledge of the British political system, which he had studied firsthand while living in England for two years, to propose that the key to good government was the separation of executive, legislative, and judicial power. He was particularly concerned about the independence of the judiciary. Montesquieu was unaware of

CHRONOLOGY

Literary Works of the Enlightenment

1687	Isaac Newton, *Mathematical Principles of Natural Philosophy*
1690	John Locke, *An Essay Concerning Human Understanding*
1721	Baron de Montesquieu, *The Persian Letters*
1738	Voltaire, *Elements of the Philosophy of Newton*
1739	David Hume, *Treatise of Human Nature*
1748	Baron de Montesquieu, *Spirit of the Laws*
1748	David Hume, *An Enquiry Concerning Human Understanding*
1751	First volume of Diderot and d'Alembert's *Encyclopedia*
1755	Jean-Jacques Rousseau, *Discourse on the Origin of Inequality Among Men*
1759	Voltaire, *Candide*
1762	Jean-Jacques Rousseau, *The Social Contract* and *Emile, or on Education*
1763	Voltaire, *Treatise on Toleration*
1764	Cesare Beccaria, *Essay on Crimes and Punishments*
1764	Voltaire, *Philosophical Dictionary*
1776	Adam Smith, *The Wealth of Nations*
1781	Immanuel Kant, *Critique of Pure Reason*
1791	Thomas Paine, *The Rights of Man*
1792	Mary Wollstonecraft, *A Vindication of the Rights of Woman*
1795	Marquis de Condorcet, *Progress of the Human Mind*

how legislative and executive powers actually overlapped in eighteenth-century Britain, but his emphasis on the importance of a separation of powers became the most durable of his ideas. It had profound influence on the drafting of the Constitution of the United States of America in 1787.

Jean-Jacques Rousseau: The General Will

Also influential as a political theorist was the Swiss philosophe Jean-Jacques Rousseau (1712–1778), who as a young man moved from Geneva to Paris and became a member of a prominent intellectual circle. Rousseau does not conform to the model of the typical Enlightenment thinker. His distrust of human reason and his emotionalism separated him from Hume, Voltaire, and another

Differences Among the Philosophes

This satirical print shows Rousseau, to the left, and Voltaire engaged in heated debate. The two men were both major figures in the Enlightenment, but they differed widely in temperament and in their philosophical and political views. Rousseau was very much the rebel; unlike Voltaire, he distrusted reason and articulated highly egalitarian political principles.

of recreating an idealized golden age when they were not yet alienated from themselves and their environment.

Rousseau's political theories were hardly conventional, but they appealed to some segments of the reading public. In his *Discourse on the Origin of Inequality Among Men* (1755) and *The Social Contract* (1762) he challenged the existing political and social order with an uncompromising attack on aristocracy and monarchy. He linked absolute monarchy, which he referred to as despotism, with the court and especially with the vain, pampered, conceited, and overdecorated aristocratic women who wielded political influence with the king and in the salons. As an alternative to this aristocratic, monarchical, and feminized society Rousseau proclaimed the sovereignty of the people. Laws were to be determined by the General Will, by which he meant the consensus of a community of citizens (but not necessarily the vote of the majority).

As a result of his writings Rousseau became associated with radical republican and democratic ideas that flourished at the time of the French Revolution. One indication of that radicalism was the fact that *The Social Contract* was banned not only in absolutist France but in the republics of the Netherlands and Switzerland as well. Rousseau was also criticized for justifying authoritarian rule. His argument that the General Will placed limits on individual civil liberty encouraged autocratic leaders, such as the radical Maximilien Robespierre

great French philosophe, Denis Diderot (1713–1784). That distrust laid the foundations for the romantic reaction against the Enlightenment in the early nineteenth century (see Chapter 21). Instead of celebrating the improvement of society as it evolved into higher forms, Rousseau had a negative view of the achievements of civilization. In his novel *Emile, or on Education* (1762) he wrote, "All our wisdom consists of servile prejudices, all our customs are but enslavement, constraint, or bondage. Social man is born, lives and dies enslaved. At birth he is bound up with swaddling clothes; at his death he is nailed down in a coffin. For the whole of his existence as a human being he is chained up by our institutions."[5] Rousseau idealized the uncorrupted condition of human beings in the state of nature, supporting the theory of the "noble savage." Human beings could not ever return to that original natural state, but Rousseau held out the hope

at the time of the French Revolution, to claim that their dictatorial rule embodied that General Will.

Thomas Paine: The Rights of Man

Of all the Enlightenment political theorists, the English publicist and propagandist Thomas Paine (1737–1809) was arguably the most radical. Paine was influenced by Rousseau, Diderot, and Voltaire, but his radicalism was cultivated mainly by his intense involvement in the political world of revolutionary America, where he became politically active in the 1770s. In *Common Sense* (1776) Paine presented the case for American independence from Britain. This included a passionate statement of human freedom, equality, and rationality. It also involved a vicious attack on hereditary monarchy and an eloquent statement for the sovereignty of the law. At the time of the French Revolution, Paine continued to call for the establishment

DOCUMENT

Rousseau Places Limits on Civil Liberty

In his Social Contract *(1762) Rousseau discussed the effect that the formation of the civil state had on individual liberty. Rousseau is careful to distinguish between the liberty one enjoys in the state of nature and the liberty one acquires by entering civil society. As he explains in this passage, the establishment of the civil state limits one's natural liberty, but contrary to what some scholars have maintained, he does not justify totalitarian rule. Passionately committed to human liberty, Rousseau claims that the democratic and egalitarian society he envisions would serve as an alternative to the despotic systems of government that existed in late-eighteenth-century Europe.*

The passage from the state of nature to the civil state produces a very remarkable change in man, by substituting justice for instinct in his conduct and giving his actions the morality they had formerly lacked. Then only, when the voice of duty takes the place of physical impulses and right of appetite, does man who so far had considered only himself, find that he is forced to act on different principles, and to consult his reason before listening to his inclinations. Although in this state he deprives himself of some advantages which he got from nature, he gains in return others so great, his facilities are so stimulated and developed, his ideas so extended, his feelings so ennobled, and his whole soul so uplifted that, did not the abuses of this new condition often degrade him below that which he left, he would be bound to bless continually the happy moment which took him from it forever and, instead of a stupid and unimaginative animal, made him an intelligent being and a man.

Let us draw up the whole account in terms easily commensurable. What man loses by the social contract is his natural liberty and an unlimited right to everything he tries to get and succeeds in getting; what he gains is civil liberty and the proprietorship of all he possesses. If we are to avoid mistake in weighing one against the other, we must clearly distinguish natural liberty, which is bounded only by the strength of the individual, from civil liberty, which is limited by the general will; and possession, which is merely the effect of force or the right of the first occupier, from property, which can be founded only on a positive title.

Source: Jean-Jacques Rousseau, *The Social Contract* (1762).

of a republic in France and in his native country. In his most widely circulated work, *The Rights of Man* (1791), he linked the institution of monarchy with the aristocracy, which he referred to as "a seraglio of males, who neither collect the honey nor form the hive but exist only for lazy enjoyment."

The title of *The Rights of Man* identified a theme that appeared in much Enlightenment writing. Like Diderot and Rousseau, Paine spoke the language of natural rights. Until the Enlightenment, rights were considered legal privileges acquired by royal charter or by inheritance. One had a right, for example, to a particular piece of land or to elect representatives from one's county or town. Those rights could be surrendered under certain circumstances, such as when a person sold land. The new emphasis on natural law, however, led to the belief that simply by being a human being one acquired natural rights that could never be taken away. The American Declaration of Independence (1776), drafted by Thomas Jefferson, presented an eloquent statement of these God-given inalienable rights, which included "life, liberty and the pursuit of happiness." In defending that independence, Paine claimed that "a government of our own is our natural right." Since the eighteenth century those rights have been extended to include newly defined activities, such as the right to privacy, but the language in which such rights are asserted is a legacy of the Enlightenment.

Women and the Enlightenment

The claim advanced by Enlightenment thinkers that all human beings are equal in a state of nature did not lead to a widespread belief that on the basis of natural law men and women are equal. Quite to the contrary, many philosophes, including Diderot and Rousseau, argued that women are different in nature from men and that they should be confined to an exclusively domestic role as chaste wives and mothers. Rousseau also insisted on the separate education of girls.

This patriarchal argument supported the emerging theory of separate spheres°, which held that men and women should conduct their lives in different social and political environments. The identification of women with the private, domestic sphere laid the foundation for the ideology of female domesticity, which became popular in bourgeois society in the nineteenth century. But it denied them the freedom that aristocratic women in France had acquired during the eighteenth century, especially those who participated in polite society. It also continued to deny them civil rights. Like women in ancient Sparta, whose situation served as the model for a number of Enlightenment thinkers, eighteenth-century women could not vote and could not initiate lawsuits on their own authority. They were not full members of civil society.

DOCUMENT

Montesquieu Satirizes European Women

Montesquieu's first publication, The Persian Letters *(1721), is a clever satire on French society. The book consists of a series of letters written to and from two fictional Persian travelers, Usbek and Rica. Because the characters come from a radically different culture, Montesquieu was able to avoid official censure for presenting his irreverent views. The Persians refer to the king as a great magician who has the power to persuade men to kill one another though they have no quarrel, and to the pope as "an old idol worshipped out of habit." Montesquieu's satire was all the more biting because Europeans harbored deep contempt for the world of the Middle East, which they thought of as a region ruled by oriental despots and inhabited by people with lax standards of sexual morality. In this passage from one of Usbek's early letters to one of his wives in the harem, Montesquieu presents a favorable image of the oriental harem to contrast with the aristocratic women of eighteenth-century France.*

Usbek to Roxana, at the seraglio in Ispahan

How fortunate you are, Roxana, to live in the gentle land of Persia and not in these poisoned regions where neither shame nor virtue are known! You live in my seraglio as in the bower of innocence, inaccessible to the assaults of mankind; you rejoice in the good fortune that makes it impossible for you to fall. No man has sullied you with lascivious glances;

even your father-in-law, during the freedom of the festivals, has never seen your lovely mouth, because you have never failed to cover it with a sacred veil . . . .

If you had been raised in this country, you would not have been so troubled. Women here have lost all restraint. They present themselves barefaced to men, as if inviting conquest; they seek attention, and they accompany men to the mosques. On walks, even to their rooms; the service of eunuchs is unknown. In place of the noble simplicity and charming modesty which is the rule among you, one finds here a barbaric impudence, to which one cannot grow accustomed. . . .

When you enhance the brilliance of your complexion with lovely coloring, when you perfume all your body with the most precious essences, when you dress in your most beautiful garments, when you seek to distinguish yourself from your companions by the charm of your dancing or the delight of your song, when you graciously compete with them in beauty, sweetness and vivacity, then I cannot imagine that you have any other object than that of pleasing me. . . .

But what am I to think of European women? Their art in making up their complexions, the ornaments they display, the care they give to their bodies, their preoccupation with pleasing are so many stains on their virtue and outrages to their husbands.

Source: From Baron de Montesquieu, *The Persian Letters,* translated by George R. Healy (Hackett, 1999), Letter 26. Reprinted by permission of Hackett Publishing Company, Inc. All rights reserved.

Only in the 1790s did writers begin to use the language and ideas of the Enlightenment to advance the argument for the full equality of men and women. The first of these appeals came from Condorcet, who published *On the Admission of Women to the Rights of Citizenship* in 1789. In that pamphlet he proposed that all women who own property be given the right to vote. He later called for universal suffrage for all men and women on the grounds that they all shared a common human nature. A similar appeal came from the French dramatist and revolutionary activist Marie Olympe Aubrey de Gouges (1748–1793). At the very beginning of the French Revolution, de Gouges, the daughter of a butcher, proposed that the revolutionary manifesto adopted by the French National Assembly, *Declaration of the Rights of Man and Citizen* (1789), be extended to include women as well as men.

De Gouges drafted her most famous publication, *The Rights of Woman* (1791), as a proposed appendix to that constitutional document. She took the authors of the *Declaration* to task for their failure to address the problem of women's civil rights and responsibilities with the same

determination and enthusiasm they had manifested in proclaiming the rights of men. Revealing her debt to Rousseau, she proposed in Article VI of her document that "the law must be the expression of the general will. All citizens, men and women, must concur, personally or through their representatives, in its creation. It must be the same for everyone: every citizen, man and woman, being equal in its eyes, must be equally eligible for all high honors, public offices, and positions according to their merits. . . . " Using more of Rousseau's language, she went on to propose a "social contract" between man and woman that recognized, among other things, common ownership of property. None of de Gouges's proposals were implemented by the French government, but she did succeed in drawing attention to the contradictions between the rhetoric and the reality of natural rights.

De Gouges's English contemporary, Mary Wollstonecraft (1759–1797), was the most famous of the Enlightenment's advocates of women's rights. Inspired by the events of the French Revolution and angered by the conservative English response to the events taking place in France,

Wollstonecraft wrote *A Vindication of the Rights of Woman* (1792). This treatise, which embodies a stinging critique of eighteenth-century polite society, has become a founding document of modern feminism. In it Wollstonecraft made an eloquent appeal for extending civil and political rights to women and even proposed that women elect their own representatives to legislatures. Her most original and innovative proposals, however, dealt with education. She claimed that in order for women to take control of their lives and to become the full equals of men within marriage and in the political realm, girls had to acquire greater knowledge and skill and learn how to support themselves. Wollstonecraft insisted that the education of women must be made equal and identical to that of men. In this way she challenged the arguments presented by Rousseau and many other male Enlightenment thinkers that cultural and social differences between men and women should be maintained because they were "natural."

The Enlightenment and Sexuality

One facet of Enlightenment thought that had a profound effect on the position of women in society was the appeal for greater sexual permissiveness. Many philosophes, including Voltaire, Diderot, and Holbach, remained openly critical of the strict standard of sexual morality enforced by Christian churches. The basic argument of the philosophes was that sexual activity should not be restricted, because it was pleasurable and a source of happiness. The arbitrary prohibitions imposed by the Church contradicted human nature. European encounters with pagan natives of the South Pacific, who were reported to have enjoyed great sexual permissiveness, were used to reinforce this argument based on human nature. Diderot appealed to the sexual code of the Tahitians in his attack on Christian sexual morality.

Many philosophes, including Voltaire, practiced what they preached and lived openly with women out of wedlock. Other members of wealthy society adopted an even more libertine lifestyle. The Venetian adventurer and author Giacomo Casanova (1725–1798), who was expelled from a seminary for his immorality, gained fame for his life of gambling, spying, and seducing thousands of women. To one young Spanish woman, who resisted his advances in order to protect her virginity, he said: "You must abandon yourself to my passion without any resistance, and you may rest assured I will respect your innocence." Casanova's name soon became identified with sexual seduction.

The violent excesses to which this type of eighteenth-century sexual permissiveness could lead can be seen in the career of Alphonse Donatien François, the Marquis de Sade (1740–1814). The author of licentious libertine narratives, including his own memoirs and an erotic novel, *Justine* (1793), de Sade described the use of violence in sexual en-

counters and thus gave rise to the word *sadism* to describe the pleasurable administration of pain. He spent twenty-seven years in prison for his various sexual offenses.

It makes sense that noblemen like Casanova and de Sade would have adopted the libertine values of the Enlightenment thinkers. Somewhat more remarkable was the growth of public sexual permissiveness among all social groups, including the rather prim and proper bourgeoisie and the working poor. Erotic literature, such as John Cleland's *Memoirs of a Woman of Pleasure* (1749), and pornographic prints achieved considerable popularity in an increasingly commercialized society, while prostitution became more open and widespread. Voltaire and Diderot might not have approved of this literature or these practices, but their libertine, anti-Christian, materialist outlook helped to prepare the ground for their acceptance.

The Impact of the Enlightenment

■ What impact did the Enlightenment have on Western culture and politics?

The ideas of the Enlightenment spread to every country in Europe as well as to the Americas. They inspired programs of reform and radical political movements. Enlightenment thought, however, did not become the property of the entire population. It appealed mainly to the educated and the relatively prosperous and failed to penetrate the lower levels of society.

The Spread of Enlightened Ideas

The ideas of the Enlightenment spread rapidly among the literate members of society, mainly by means of print. During the eighteenth century, print became the main medium of formal communication. The technology of printing allowed for the publication of materials on a scale unknown a century before. Pamphlets, newspapers, and books poured off presses, not only in the major cities but in provincial towns as well. Literacy rates increased dramatically throughout western Europe. The highly educated still constituted a minority of the population, but the better part of the aristocracy and many of those who occupied the middle ranks of society could read and write. By 1750 more than half the male population of France and England could read basic texts. The foundation of public libraries in all the major cities of western Europe made printed materials more widely available. In many bookshops, rooms were set aside for browsing in the hope that readers would eventually purchase the books they consulted.

One of the most widely circulated publications of the Enlightenment was the *Encyclopedia* compiled by the philosophe Denis Diderot and the mathematician Jean le Rond d'Alembert. This massive seventeen-volume work, which was published between 1751 and 1765, contained thousands of articles on science, religion, politics, and the economy. The entries in the *Encyclopedia* were intended not only to promote knowledge but also to advance the ideas of the Enlightenment. Included, for example, were two entries on natural law, which was described as being "perpetual and unchangeable." The entry on intolerance makes a passionate plea against religious persecution, asserting that "If we may tear out one hair of anyone whose opinions differ from ours, we could also claim the whole head, for there is no limit to injustice." Other articles praised the achievements of science and technology and gave special attention to industrial crafts and trades. Underlying the entire enterprise was the belief that knowledge was useful, that it could contribute to the improvement of human life. In these respects the *Encyclopedia* became the quintessential statement of the worldview of the Enlightenment, and its publication stands as a crowning achievement of the entire movement.

Diderot's *Encyclopedia*, Plate Illustrating Agricultural Techniques

Encyclopedias, pamphlets, newspapers, and novels were not the only means by which the ideas of the Enlightenment spread. A number of informal institutions promoted the exchange of ideas. Literary societies and book clubs, which proliferated in the major cities of western Europe, encouraged the public reading and discussion of the latest publications. Scientific societies sponsored lectures on the latest developments in physics, chemistry, and natural history. One of the most famous of these lectures demonstrated the power of electricity by charging a young boy, suspended from the ground, with static electricity. This "electrified boy," who was not harmed in the process, attracted objects from a stool placed below him. Lectures like this one attracted large crowds.

Equally important in the spread of the scientific and cultural ideas of the Enlightenment were museums, where scientific and cultural artifacts, many of them gathered from around the world, could be viewed by an increasingly curious and educated public. The museums often sponsored exhibits and lectures. Paris became home to a number of these museums in the 1780s, and they could be found in all the major cities of Europe by the end of the eighteenth century. A more informal set of cultural institutions were the coffeehouses that sprang up in cities across Europe. These commercial establishments were open to everyone who could pay the fare, and therefore they proved immensely successful in facilitating the spread of ideas within the bourgeoisie. Newspapers were often read aloud at coffeehouses, and they became the setting for many political debates.

Another set of institutions that promoted the ideas of the Enlightenment were the secret societies of men and women known as freemasons°. Freemasons strove to create a society based on reason and virtue, and they were committed to the principles of liberty and equality. Freemasonry first appeared in England and Scotland in the seventeenth century and then spread to France, the Dutch Republic, Germany, and as far east as Poland and Russia during the eighteenth century. Some of the most famous figures of the Enlightenment, including Voltaire, belonged to masonic lodges. In the 1770s there were more than 10,000 freemasons in Paris alone. The lodges were places where philosophes interacted with merchants, lawyers, and government leaders. The pope condemned the freemasons in 1738, and many civil authorities expressed deep suspicion of the political and religious ideas they fostered.

The most famous informal cultural institutions of the Enlightenment were the salons, the private sitting rooms or parlors of wealthy women where discussions of philosophy, science, literature, and politics took place. Salons became particularly prominent in Paris, where the salons of Madame Geoffrin and Madame du Deffand won international fame. The women who hosted these meetings invited the participants, entertained those who attended, and used their conversational skills to direct and facilitate the discussions that took place in the salons. They also used their influence to secure aristocratic patronage of the young male writers and scientists whom they cultivated. The success of a new book was often determined by its initial reception in the salon. Most of the prominent male figures of the French Enlightenment participated in these meetings, at least during the early years of their careers. (See the illustration at the beginning of this chapter.)

Madame Geoffrin
Her salon was called "one of the wonders of the social world."

The salons became the target of contemporary criticism not only because they allowed women to participate in public life but also because they were bastions of aristocratic society. While most of the salon women came from the aristocracy, many of their fathers had recently risen into the nobility or had merely purchased their noble status. The men who attended the meetings had even fewer ties to the traditional aristocracy. The salons were places where old and new noble blood intermingled, where social refinement was even more important than inherited nobility. What mattered most in the salons was the quickness of one's wit, the quality of one's conversational skills, and the appeal of one's views. Thus the salon succeeded in opening elite society to the talented. In this way the salons helped to dissolve the bonds that held together the Old Regime and contributed to the creation of a society based on merit rather than birth alone.

The Limits of the Enlightenment

The ideas of the Enlightenment spread rapidly across Europe, but their influence was limited. The market for books by philosophes such as Voltaire and Rousseau was quite small. Diderot and d'Alembert's *Encyclopedia* sold a remarkable 25,000 copies by 1789, but that was exceptional, and many sales were to libraries. Paine's *The Rights of Man* also reached a fairly broad audience, mainly because it was written in a simple direct style and its price was deliberately kept low. Most books on social and political theory, however, like scholarly works on science, did not sell very well. Rousseau's *The Social Contract* was a commercial failure.

Books on other topics had much better sales. Inspirational religious literature continued to be published in large quantities, indicating the limits of Enlightenment secularism. Novels, a relatively new genre of fiction that appealed to the bourgeoisie, were almost as successful. We can readily see why Rousseau and Voltaire both used novels to advance their radical social views. In France, books that were banned because of their pornographic content or their satirical attacks on the monarchy, the clergy, or ministers in the government also proved to be best-sellers in the huge underground French book market.

One segment of the popular press that revealed a limited influence of the Enlightenment was the literature on popular science. The reading public did not show much interest in technical scientific books, but they did purchase publications on such technological developments as hot-air balloons, which became a new fad in the 1780s. Descriptions of monsters found in distant lands and other extraordinary natural occurrences also sold thousands of copies. Some of this interest in the preternatural originated in the work of highly educated scholars, but the reports of new discoveries increasingly lent themselves to sensational treatment in the popular press.

Another subject of popular literary interest was mesmerism°. The Viennese physicist and physician Franz Anton Mesmer (1734–1815), who moved to Paris in 1778, claimed that he had discovered a fluid that permeated and surrounded all bodies and was the source of heat, light, electricity, and magnetism. Sickness was caused by the obstruction to the flow of this fluid in the human body. To restore this flow patients were massaged, hypnotized, or "mesmerized" with the intention of producing a convulsion or crisis that restored health. Mesmerism developed into a form of spiritualism in which its patients engaged in séances with spirits, and its practitioners dabbled in the occult. This pseudoscience, which was rejected by the French Academy of Science as a hoax, became the subject of numerous pamphlets and newspaper articles that fascinated the reading public.

Those who read books about mesmerism had only a tenuous connection with the learned world of the Enlightenment. Among those who were illiterate or barely literate, Enlightened ideas made even fewer inroads. The only exposure these people may have had to the ideas we associate with the Enlightenment would be through the actions and attitudes of their social superiors. From the elitist perspective of the philosophes, the intellectual world of the illiterate was characterized by the superstition and ignorance that the philosophes were determined to eliminate.

The growing gap between a learned culture shared by philosophes and members of salons on the one hand and the popular culture of the lower classes on the other can be seen in the perpetuation of beliefs regarding magic and witchcraft among the uneducated. During the late seventeenth and eighteenth centuries, educated people in Europe gradually abandoned their belief in magic and witchcraft. As we have seen in Chapter 16, belief in the operation of a mechanical universe, religious skepticism, and rationalism had gradually eroded many beliefs regarding the operation of a supernatural realm, especially the possibility of demonic intervention in the natural world. Among the lower classes, however, this skeptical outlook found very little fertile ground. Popular belief in a world charged with supernatural and magical forces continued to lead villagers to accuse their neighbors of having harmed them by means of witchcraft. After European courts stopped prosecuting witches in the late seventeenth and early eighteenth centuries, local communities often took justice into their own hands and lynched the suspects themselves. It was left to the government to prosecute those who engaged in this illegal form of local justice.

The gap between the high culture of the Enlightenment and that of the lower classes can also be seen in the condemnations of certain sports and amusements. Popular culture was known for its blood sports, especially cockfighting, and the baiting of bulls, bears, and badgers by tying the animals down and allowing dogs to attack them. These blood sports, which could attract thousands of spectators at a single event, resulted in the serious injury or death of animals. Enlightenment thinkers, especially those from the bourgeoisie, condemned this activity for its cruelty and its barbarism. Just like the torture and execution of criminals, these "barbarous" pastimes had no place in polite society. Popular sports, however, could not be easily eradicated. It was not until the nineteenth century that they began to disappear, often as the result of campaigns conducted by clergymen rather than philosophes. The persistence of blood sports reveals the strength of popular culture and the inability of the Enlightenment to transform it.

Enlightened Absolutism

When we turn to Enlightened political ideas, we confront an even more difficult task of determining the extent of their impact. The main figures of the Enlightenment were intellectuals—men of letters who did not occupy positions of great political importance and who did not devote much thought to the challenging task of putting their theories into practice. The audience for their books did not always include people with the power to implement their proposals. Rulers often treated Enlightenment thinkers with suspicion, if only because they criticized established authority. Nevertheless, Enlightenment thought did make its mark on eighteenth-century politics in two strikingly different ways.

The first was through the reforms enacted by rulers who are often referred to as enlightened despots°. These rulers exercised absolute power and used that power to implement changes that Enlightenment thinkers had proposed. The term *despot* is misleading, as these enlightened rulers were rarely despotic in the sense of exercising power cruelly and arbitrarily. The connection between Enlightenment and royal absolutism is not as unnatural as it might appear. It is true that philosophes tended to be critical of the Old Regime°, the eighteenth-century political order that was dominated by an absolute monarch and a privileged nobility and clergy. But many of them, including Voltaire, had little sympathy with democracy and social equality, and preferred to entrust absolute monarchs with the implementation of the reforms they advocated. Among the philosophes the prospect of a philosopher-king had widespread appeal.

Rulers of central and eastern European countries were particularly open to Enlightenment thought. These monarchs had read widely in the literature of the Enlightenment and introduced Western intellectuals to their courts. The most famous of the enlightened absolutists was King Frederick II of Prussia, known as Frederick the Great (r. 1740–1786). Frederick, a deist who wrote poetry and played the flute, was enamored of all things French. When the French philosophe d'Alembert visited his court, the king hosted a dinner at which he spoke only French, leav-

ing many of the Prussian guests to sip their soup in stunned silence. Frederick corresponded extensively with Voltaire and invited him to take up residence at his French-style royal palace, "Sans Souci," at Potsdam. The relationship between king and philosopher, however, was often stormy, and when Frederick publicly burned a publication in which Voltaire had lampooned a royal favorite, Voltaire left Potsdam in 1752.

The departure of Voltaire did not weaken Frederick's determination to implement a number of policies that reflected the ideals of the Enlightenment. The most noteworthy of these was the introduction of religious toleration throughout his predominantly Lutheran kingdom. Protestants of all denominations and Catholics (but not Jews) received the protection of the law and even benefited from royal patronage. Frederick also introduced a number of legal reforms with the intention of realizing the Enlightenment ideal of making the law both rational and humane. He authorized the codification of Prussian law (which was completed after his death in 1794), abolished judicial torture, and eliminated capital punishment. In order to provide for the training of future servants of the state, he began a system of compulsory education throughout the country. Like most enlightened rulers, Frederick never abandoned his commitment to absolute rule, which he strengthened by winning the support of the nobility. He also remained committed to the militaristic and expansionist policies of his father, Frederick William I. For him there was no contradiction between his style of rule and his commitment to Enlightenment ideals.

In neighboring Austria two Habsburg rulers, Maria Theresa (r. 1740–1780) and her son Joseph II (r. 1780–1790), pursued reformist policies that gave them the reputation of being enlightened monarchs. Most of Maria Theresa's reforms were of an administrative nature. Stunned by the Prussian invasion and occupation of the Habsburg province of Silesia in 1740, Maria Theresa set out to strengthen the Habsburg monarchy by gaining complete control over taxation and by reorganizing the military and civil bureaucracy. She also took steps to make the serfs more productive, mainly by restricting the work they performed on their lords' lands and by abolishing the feudal dues they paid.

These efforts won the applause of philosophes, but the policies of Maria Theresa's that most clearly bore the stamp of the Enlightenment were her legal reforms. Inspired by Beccaria and Montesquieu, she established a commission to reform the entire corpus of Austrian law. A new code of criminal law was promulgated in 1769, and seven years later Maria Theresa issued an edict abolishing judicial torture. Joseph continued this program of legal reform by reorganizing the entire central court system and by eliminating capital punishment. He also revealed the influence of the Enlightenment by granting religious toleration, first to Protestants and eastern Orthodox

Torture

The torture of a defendant as depicted in the published version of the criminal code promulgated by Empress Maria Theresa in 1769. This form of torture, the *strappado,* used a pulley to hang the accused from the ceiling. Weights could be attached to the feet to make the pain more excruciating. The purpose of judicial torture was to extract a confession. Torture was eliminated from the law codes of most continental European countries during the Enlightenment.

Christians in 1781, and then to Jews in 1782. With respect to social issues, he completed his mother's work of abolishing serfdom altogether.

The efforts of Catherine II of Russia (r. 1762–1796) to implement the ideas of the Enlightenment followed a different course from those of Maria Theresa and Joseph. The daughter of a German prince, Catherine received an education grounded in a traditional curriculum of history, geography, and Lutheran theology. In 1745 she was married to a distant cousin, Peter, who was in line to inherit the Russian throne from his aunt, the childless Empress Elizabeth (r. 1741–1762). After arriving in St. Petersburg Catherine

not only acquired a knowledge of Russian language, literature, and religion but also read widely in western European sources, including the works of Enlightenment thinkers. She later corresponded with Voltaire and d'Alembert and employed the famous salon hostess Madame Geoffrin at her court. At Catherine's invitation Diderot visited St. Petersburg for six months.

Early in her reign, Catherine embarked on a program of reform similar to those of other enlightened absolutists. In 1767 she appointed a commission to codify Russian law on the basis of western European principles. Her recommendations to the commission included the abolition of torture and inhumane punishment and the establishment of religious toleration. She was eventually forced to disband the commission, which could not agree on a new code, but she later abolished torture and capital punishment on her own authority. Like Maria Theresa, she instituted a number of administrative and educational reforms, including the introduction of primary schooling in the provinces. Catherine, who became known as Catherine the Great, also tried unsuccessfully to provide for the education of girls as well as boys.

DOCUMENT

Catherine the Great's Constitution (1767)

Catherine gained a reputation for being an enlightened European monarch, but her acceptance of traditional Russian culture and the need to maintain her rule prevented her from fully embracing the ideals of the Enlightenment. She even admitted that it was much easier to subscribe to the ideals of the Enlightenment than actually to implement them. The strength of vested interests within Russian society accounted for the failure of the law commission of 1767. After putting down the Pugachev rebellion in 1774, she began to question the desirability of social reform, and the experience of the French Revolution in the 1790s (see Chapter 19) led her to disavow the ideals of the Enlightenment.

On the issue of serfdom, which most Enlightenment thinkers wished to see abolished, she would not yield. She preserved that social system in order to secure the loyalty of the Russian nobility, and she extended it to Ukraine and parts of Poland after Russia incorporated those regions into the empire. Catherine also catered to the imperialistic ambitions of the Russians, gaining vast territories in eastern Europe, East Asia, and Alaska. Thus she expanded the Russian Empire at the very time when the ideals of the Enlightenment were leading some philosophes to call for the dissolution of large imperial structures.

The Enlightenment and Revolution

The second mark that Enlightenment thought made on eighteenth-century politics was the inspiration it gave to movements for reform and revolution in western Europe and the Americas. The emphasis placed by Enlightenment

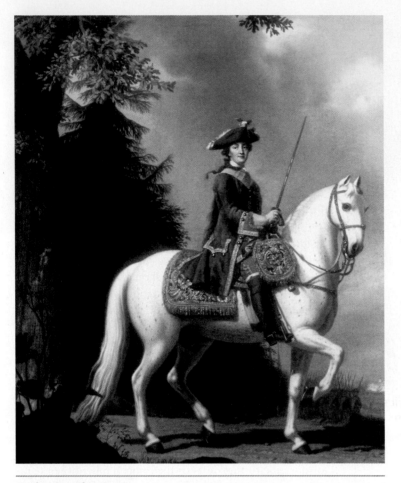

Catherine the Great

Catherine II of Russia on the day she succeeded in taking the throne from her husband, Peter III, at Peterhof in 1762. Catherine, who despised her husband, joined a conspiracy against him right after his accession to the throne. Catherine, like Peter, had a number of lovers, and her two children, including the future emperor Paul, were reputedly conceived by members of the nobility.

reforms were inspired by ideals born of the Enlightenment.

In France the influence of the Enlightenment on the momentous changes that took place during the French Revolution (1789–1799) has been a matter of debate among historians. The complexity of the revolution, which will be discussed in Chapter 19, and the diversity of Enlightenment thought make this a particularly difficult debate to resolve. Many of the revolutionaries of the 1790s were steeped in the ideas of the Enlightenment, but those ideas did not necessarily inspire the revolution itself. The French philosophes of the eighteenth century denounced the evils of the Old Regime and proposed many ideas about how governments should function, but they did not make serious efforts to introduce actual reforms, much less topple the government. Many philosophes, including Voltaire, had personal connections with aristocratic society, and very few shared the democratic and egalitarian ideas that came to the fore at the time of the Revolution. Some lesser journalists and literary hacks were more successful than the most renowned philosophes in fostering contempt for the Old Regime before the Revolution. Their merciless satires of the court and the clergy were more responsible than the grand treatises of the philosophes for stimulating a crisis of confidence in the French government and eroding the traditional respect for authority that made possible the violent overthrow of the Old Regime.

We can nevertheless establish some connections between the ideas and programs of the philosophes and the events that transpired in France during the 1790s. Some of the figures of the Enlightenment contributed to the new critical spirit evident after 1750 or provided some inspiration for the creation of a new political culture once the revolution began. The towering reputation of Voltaire during the French Revolution—and the anger of conservatives who exhumed and burned his bones after it had ended—suggest that his passionate criticisms of the Old Regime and his pleas for human freedom at the very least helped to set the stage for the revolutionary events of the 1790s. The same is true of the radical Rousseau, whose concept of the General Will served as the basis of a revolutionary ideology. Rousseau's democratic and republican ideas were used to justify some of the most important changes that took place during the revolution. Contemporaries glorified or attacked him, depending on their political philosophy, for having actually caused the revolution. One book published in 1791 was titled *On Jean-Jacques Rousseau Considered as One of the First Authors of the Revolution.*

thinkers on individual liberty, natural rights, and political reform put pressure on both monarchs and the traditional nobility either to make concessions or to relinquish power altogether.

In Britain, for example, the movement for parliamentary reform and the expansion of the franchise°, as well as the first appeals for women's rights, were partially inspired by the Enlightenment. The radical democrat Thomas Paine, the feminist Mary Wollstonecraft, and the parliamentary reformer Joseph Priestley all based their demands for political reform on Enlightenment ideas of natural rights and civil liberty. It took considerable time, however, for these reforms to be realized. Only in 1832 did the British Parliament agree to a modest extension of the franchise, and women did not receive the vote until the early twentieth century. Nevertheless the movements to achieve these

Yet another application of enlightened ideas to politics took place in the Americas. The advocates of colonial independence from their mother countries, such as Thomas Jefferson in Virginia and Símon Bolívar in Venezuela and Colombia, were all deeply influenced by the Enlightenment concepts of natural law, natural rights, liberty, and popular sovereignty. The Declaration of Independence, which was written by Jefferson, betrayed its debt to the Enlightenment in its reference to the inalienable rights of all men and to the foundation of those rights in "the law of nature and Nature's God." Of course the American Revolution cannot be explained solely in terms of these Enlightenment ideas. The colonists found inspiration in many different sources, including English common law. But the American colonists did wish to create an entirely new world order, just as did many Enlightenment thinkers. They also adopted some of the most radical political ideas of the Enlightenment, which identified the people as the source of political power.

More generally, the Enlightenment fostered a critique of all efforts to establish overseas empires. The French priest Guillaume Thomas Raynal, mentioned in Chapter 17, wrote a condemnation of colonialism titled *The Philosophical and Political History of the Settlement and Commerce of Europeans in the Two Indies* (1770). Diderot and a number of lesser-known philosophes contributed to the final version of this massive work, which was published at Geneva in 1780. The book, which was the first to treat European imperialism in both hemispheres in the same context, praised the civilizing effects of commerce but condemned colonialism for the effects it had on those who emigrated. Cut off from their homeland, colonists brought with them only the prejudices of the civilizations they left behind and became hopelessly corrupt and degenerate. The English political theorist Richard Price developed a similar critique of all overseas empires, claiming that simply by their size and their diversity they could not promote the happiness of a community and the "fellow-feeling that takes place between persons in private life." According to Price, sprawling overseas empires by their very nature violated the standards of humanity.

Conclusion

The Enlightenment and Western Identity

The Enlightenment was a distinctly Western phenomenon. It arose in the countries of western Europe and then spread to central and eastern Europe (Germany, Austria, Poland, and Russia) and to the Americas. Most traditions that are identified today as "Western values" either had their origin or received their most cogent expression in the Enlightenment. In particular, the commitment to individual liberty, civil rights, toleration, and rational decision making all took shape during this period.

It would be misleading to make a simple equation between the ideas of the Enlightenment and the Western intellectual tradition. First, the ideals of the Enlightenment have never been fully accepted within Western societies. Ever since their original formulation, the ideas of the philosophes and publicists of the Enlightenment have been challenged by conservatives who argued that those ideas would lead to the destruction of religion and the social order. Those conservative criticisms, which are voiced even today, became intense at the time of the French Revolution and during the early years of the nineteenth century, and we shall discuss them in Chapters 19 and 21. Second, claims that the ideas promoted by the Enlightenment are exclusively Western can also be disputed. A celebration of reason and an insistence on religious tolerance, for example, can be found in the cultures of ancient India and China. The claim that the West is more rational than the East is itself a product of long-standing Western prejudice, an assertion that studies of other cultures undertaken by Enlightenment writers only served to strengthen.

Nevertheless, the ideas and traditions of the Enlightenment, despite the challenges they have endured, have become deeply ingrained in Western law and politics. They are less often found embedded in the political and legal traditions of non-Western lands, and when they are, such as in the twentieth-century socialist legal system of China, their presence is more often the result of Western influence than the legacy of native Eastern thought.

The acquisition of the values of the Enlightenment, even though they were never universally adopted, gave Europeans a clear sense of their own identity with respect to the rest of the world. Educated people who prided themselves on being enlightened knew that their scientific, rational worldview was not shared by Asians, Africans, indigenous Americans, or South Pacific islanders. It did not matter whether Enlightenment thinkers had a positive view of those other cultures, like Voltaire or Rousseau, or a negative one, like Montesquieu. What mattered was that they shared a similar mental outlook and a commitment to individual liberty, justice, and the improvement of civilization. For all of them religious faith was less important, both as an arbiter of morality and as a source of authority, than it was in these other cultures. The men and women of the Enlightenment all looked to the law as a reflection of natural law and as the guardian of civil liberty. Their writings helped their European and colonial public audiences think of themselves as even more distinct from non-Western people than they had in the past.

As these enlightened Western cultural values were spreading, the boundaries between East and West remained fluid and contested. The geographical region where this contest took place was what we now call eastern Europe. As we have seen in Chapter 15, the countries that occupied this buffer zone between East and West had long-standing cultural ties with Asia, especially the Middle East, but they also developed an attraction to Western culture beginning in the late seventeenth century. In Russia, this process of westernization began with Peter the Great, who integrated his country into European social, political, and diplomatic life. But it was carried further by Catherine the Great, who invited *philosophes* to her court and introduced Western reforms. This adoption of Western ideas made her appear to be a model Enlightened ruler and her country part of the Western world, but Russia's inclusion became and has remained a matter of debate. The very term "eastern Europe," which was coined during the Enlightenment, reflected the ambiguous relationship between this part of the world and the West. It provides a further illustration of the fact that the West was a cultural realm whose geographical boundaries have frequently changed.

Suggestions for Further Reading

For a comprehensive listing of suggested readings, please go to www.ablongman.com/levack2e/chapter 18

Alexander, John T. *Catherine the Great: Life and Legend.* 1989. A lively biography of the remarkable "enlightened despot."

Beckett, J. V. *The Aristocracy in England, 1660–1914.* 1986. A comprehensive study of this landholding and governing elite. Makes the important distinction between the aristocracy and the nobility.

Darnton, Robert. *The Forbidden Best-Sellers of Pre-Revolutionary France.* 1995. A study of the salacious, blasphemous, and subversive books that sold more copies than those of the philosophes in eighteenth-century France.

Dewald, Jonathan. *The European Nobility, 1500–1800.* 1996. A comprehensive study of this social class that emphasizes its adaptability.

Doyle, William. *The Old European Order, 1660–1800.* 2nd ed. 1999. The best general study of the period.

Houston, R. A. *Literacy in Early Modern Europe: Culture and Education.* 1991. The best survey of the subject for the entire period.

Lugee, Carolyn. *Le Paradis des Femmes: Women, Salons and Social Stratification in 17th-Century France.* 1976. A social study of the women of the salons.

Outram, Dorinda. *The Enlightenment.* 1995. A balanced assessment of the major historiographical debates regarding the Enlightenment.

Root, Hilton. *Peasants and King in Burgundy: Agrarian Foundations of French Absolutism.* 1979. A study of peasant communal institutions and their relationship with the crown as well as the nobility.

Williams, David, ed. *The Enlightenment.* 1999. An excellent collection of political writings with a long introduction.

Notes

1. Baron d'Holbach, *Good Sense* (1753).

2. David Hume, *Essays Moral, Political, and Literary* (1742), Essay X: "Of Superstition and Enthusiasm."

3. Cesare Beccaria, *An Essay on Crimes and Punishments* (1788), Chapter 47.

4. Voltaire, "Religion," in *The Philosophical Dictionary* (1802).

5. Jean-Jacques Rousseau, *Emile, or on Education* (1762).

The Age of the French Revolution, 1789–1815

19

ON JULY 12, 1789, THE FRENCH JOURNALIST CAMILLE DESMOULINS addressed an anxious crowd of Parisian citizens gathered outside the Palais-Royal, where public debate often took place. Playing upon fears that had been mounting during the past two months, Desmoulins claimed that the royal government of Louis XVI was preparing a massacre of Parisians. "To arms, to arms," Desmoulins cried out, as he roused the citizens to their own defense. That night Parisians responded to his call by invading arsenals in the city in anticipation of the violence they thought was about to descend upon them. The next day they continued to seize weapons and declared themselves members of the National Guard, a volunteer militia of propertied citizens.

On the morning of July 14, crowds of Parisians moved into a district of the city where royal troops were stationed in an ancient fortress known as the Bastille. The Parisians feared that the troops in the Bastille would take violent action against them, and they also wanted to capture the ammunition stored inside the building, which served as both an arsenal and a prison. Negotiations with the governor of the Bastille were interrupted when some of the militia, moving into the courtyard of the fortress, demanded the surrender of the troops. Shots were fired from both sides, and the exchange led to a full-scale assault upon the Bastille by the National Guard.

After three hours of fighting and the death of eighty-three people, the governor surrendered. He was then led by his captors, bearing the arms they had seized, to face charges before the officers of the city government. The crowd, however, crying for vengeance against their oppressors, attacked the soldiers and crushed some of them underfoot. The governor was stabbed hundreds of times, hacked to pieces, and decapitated. The chief magistrate of the city suffered the same fate for his reluctance to issue arms to its citizens. The crowd then placed the heads of the two men on pikes and paraded through the city.

Jacques-Louis David, *The Oath of the Tennis Court* The oath taken by the members of the Third Estate not to disband until France had a constitution led to the creation of the National Assembly and the legislation that destroyed royal absolutism and feudalism.

The storming of the Bastille was the first of many violent episodes that occurred during the sequence of events called the French Revolution. That revolution brought about some of the most fundamental changes in European political life since the end of Roman rule. It heralded the destruction of the Old Regime, the eighteenth-century political order that had been dominated by an absolute monarch and a privileged nobility and clergy. It led to the submission of the Catholic Church to state control. A more radical phase of the revolution, beginning in 1792, resulted in the destruction of the French monarchy and the declaration of a republic. It also led to a period of state-sponsored terrorism in 1793 and 1794, during which one group of revolutionaries engaged in a brutal campaign to eliminate their real and imagined enemies.

The excesses of the revolution led to a conservative reaction. Between 1795 and 1799 a moderate republican government, known as the Directory, modified the egalitarianism of the revolution by limiting the right to vote to men of property. Between 1799 and 1814 the reaction continued under the direction of Napoleon Bonaparte, a military officer who dominated the Consulate, a new political structure established in 1799, and then proclaimed himself emperor in 1804. Although Napoleon declared his loyalty to many of the principles of the revolution, his authoritarian rule undermined or reversed many of its achievements. In 1815 Napoleon fell from power and the monarchy was restored, marking the end of the revolutionary period. The ideas of the revolution, however, especially its commitment to democratic republicanism and its concept of the nation, continued to dominate politics in the West for the next hundred years. The French Revolution permanently changed the political culture of the West.

This chapter will address the question of how the encounters between different political and social groups in France at the end of the eighteenth century brought about some of the most important and far-reaching changes in the history of the West. In pursuing this broad objective, the individual chapter sections will address the following questions:

The Storming of the Bastille, July 14, 1789
The Bastille was attacked not because it was a symbol of the Old Regime, but because it contained weapons that the Parisian citizens needed to protect themselves from royalist troops.

- Why did the Old Regime in France collapse in 1789, and what revolutionary changes took place in French government and society during the next two years?
- How did a second, more radical revolution, which began with the establishment of the Republic in 1792, lead to the creation of a regime that used the power of the state to institute the Reign of Terror?
- In what ways did the political events of the revolution change French cultural institutions and create a new political culture?
- How did the authoritarian rule of Napoleon Bonaparte from 1799 to 1814 confirm or betray the achievements of the French Revolution, and what impact did his military conquests have on Europe and the world?

■ What did the French Revolution ultimately achieve and in what ways did it change the course of European and Western history?

The First French Revolution, 1789–1791

■ Why did the Old Regime in France collapse in 1789, and what revolutionary changes took place in French government and society during the next two years?

One of the main characteristics of political revolutions is that they involve a fundamental change in the political *system*, not simply in the personnel of government. On the basis of this criterion the French Revolution consisted of two distinct revolutions. The first revolution, which began in 1789, resulted in a destruction of royal absolutism and the drafting of a constitution. The second and more radical revolution began in 1792 with the abolition of the monarchy and the formation of the French Republic.

Like all revolutions, the first French revolution had deep-seated causes. As we discussed in Chapter 18, a constant barrage of satirical literature directed at the royal family and the court lowered the prestige of the government and thus weakened its authority. The publication of thousands of pamphlets advocating reform, including many written by philosophes of the Enlightenment, fostered a critical attitude toward the French government and led to demands for political and economic change. Conflicts between the nobility and the crown over constitutional issues, a source of tension throughout the age of absolutism, led to charges that the government was acting despotically. Encounters between the landowning nobility and the peasantry, which increased in the last half of the eighteenth century, also contributed to the disaffection with the Old Regime and played a major role in stimulating demands for a restriction of the privileges enjoyed by the nobility. Ongoing food shortages in the cities created a militant citizenry ready to take action against authorities they considered responsible for the high price of bread.

DOCUMENT

De Stael on the Ancien Regime (1789)

The immediate cause of the revolution was a major economic crisis that bankrupted the monarchy and deprived it of its authority. This crisis led to a revolt of the nobles against the crown and brought down the entire system of royal absolutism. Only after this collapse of royal government did various groups that had had long-standing grievances against the regime take the initiative and establish a new political system. These groups never actually planned the revolution; they simply filled a void created by the absence of effective governmental power.

The Beginning of the Revolution

The financial crisis that brought about the collapse of the French government peaked in the late 1780s. The government of Louis XVI (r. 1774–1792) had inherited considerable debts from that of his grandfather, Louis XV (r. 1715–1774) as a result of protracted periods of warfare with Great Britain. The opening of a new phase of this warfare in 1778, when France intervened in the American War of Independence on the side of the United States, pushed the government further into debt and put a strain on the entire French economy. Attempts to solve the crisis by implementing financial reforms made the situation only worse. In 1787 the government had a revenue of 475 million livres and expenses of just under 600 million livres. More than half of the revenue went to pay interest on the accumulated debt. As the crisis deepened, protests from the ranks of the nobility against royal policy became more vocal.

In 1787 the king made efforts to win the support of the nobility by convening an Assembly of Notables, a hand-picked group of 144 nominees, the great majority of whom were noblemen. The purpose of the meeting was to gain approval for a new system of taxation that would include a direct tax on all landowners. These proposals encountered formidable opposition from the members of the assembly, and the meeting was adjourned. Some of the nobles in the assembly had been willing to pay the taxes, but only if the king would convoke the Estates General, a national legislative body that had not met since 1614. Convening the Estates General, they argued, would provide them with guarantees against royal despotism. Louis resisted these pressures because he did not want to give up the right to make law by his own authority.

The king then tried to gain approval of new taxes from the regional parlements, the provincial law courts whose powers included the registration of royal edicts. There too the crown met resistance. The Parlement of Paris, which was the most important of all the parlements, refused to comply with the king's request. The other parlements followed suit, claiming that only the Estates General had the power to approve new taxes. Constitutional tension was heightened when the king demanded the registration of edicts for new loans without the approval of the parlements, a step that even he acknowledged was illegal. He then suspended the parlements, thereby deepening the constitutional crisis.

The deterioration of the government's financial condition finally forced the king to yield to the demands of the nobles and the increasingly hostile popular press. When tax returns dried up as the result of an agricultural crisis in the summer months of 1788, the government could no longer pay its creditors. In a desperate effort to save his regime, Louis announced that he would convene the Estates General. By this time there was little hope for Louis. His absolutist government had completely collapsed.

CHRONOLOGY

The First French Revolution, 1789–1791

1787

February 22	Convening of the Assembly of Notables

1788

August 8	Announcement of the meeting of the Estates General

1789

May 5	The Estates General opens at Versailles
June 17	The Third Estate adopts the title of the National Assembly
June 20	Oath of the Tennis Court
July 11	The king dismisses his finance minister, Jacques Necker
July 14	The storming of the Bastille
Late July	The Great Fear in rural areas
August 4	Abolition of feudalism and privileges
August 26	*Declaration of the Rights of Man and Citizen*
October 5	March to Versailles; Louis XVI and National Assembly move to Paris
November 2	Church property is nationalized

1790

July 12	Civil Constitution of the Clergy
July 14	Feast of the Federation
November 27	Decree requiring oath of loyalty from the clergy

1791

June 20	Royal family flees to Varennes, is apprehended by the National Guard
October 1	Newly elected Legislative Assembly opens

The meeting of the Estates General was set for May 1789, and during the months leading up to its opening, public debates arose over how the delegates should vote. The Estates General consisted of representatives of the three orders or social groups, known as estates, that made up French society: the clergy, the nobility, and the Third Estate. The Third Estate technically contained all the commoners in the kingdom (about 96 percent of the population), ranging from the wealthiest merchant to the poorest peasant. The elected representatives of the Third Estate, whose num-

bers had doubled by a recent order of the king, were propertied nonnoble elements of lay society, including many lawyers and military officers.

Before the meeting a dispute arose among the representatives whether the three groups would vote by estate, in which case the first two estates would dominate the assembly, or by head, in which case the Third Estate would have numerical parity. Each side claimed that it was the best representative of the "nation," a term meaning the entire body of French people. The nobles maintained that the nation was represented by the nobility and clergy from all the provinces, especially the members of the provincial parlements, who had been critical of royal power during the past few decades. The members of the Third Estate advanced the claim that *they* represented the nation. The cleric Emmanuel-Joseph Sieyès (1748–1836), who joined the Third Estate during this dispute, claimed that it "has within itself all that is necessary to constitute a nation. . . . Nothing can go on without it, and everything would go on far better without the others. . . . This privileged class (nobility and clergy) is assuredly foreign to the nation by its do-nothing uselessness."[1]

The question of voting within the Estates General was not resolved when that body met at Versailles on May 5, 1789. After the king indicated that he would side with the clergy and nobility, the Third Estate took the dramatic step of declaring itself a National Assembly and asking members of the other estates to vote with them on the basis of "one man, one vote." Many members of the lower clergy and a few noblemen accepted this invitation. In a conciliatory response to this challenge, the king planned to summon all three estates to a special "royal session" to announce some concessions. In preparation for this meeting, however, he locked the Third Estate out of its meeting hall without explanation. The outraged members of the Third Estate went to a nearby indoor tennis court and took a solemn oath that they would not disband until the country had been given a constitution. One week later, after more clerics and noblemen had joined the ranks of the Third Estate, the king ordered the nobility and the clergy to join the National Assembly.

As this political crisis was reaching a climax, a major social crisis fueled by the high price of bread was causing a breakdown of public order. For many years French agriculture had had difficulty meeting the demands of an expanding population. These problems, aggravated in the 1780s by a succession of poor harvests, climaxed in a widespread harvest failure in 1788. As the price of bread soared, demand for manufactured goods shrank, thus causing widespread unemployment among artisans. An increasing number of bread riots, peasant revolts, and urban strikes contributed to a sense of panic at the very time that the government's financial crisis deepened. In Paris the situation reached a critical point in June 1789.

At this point the king, a man with little political sense, made two ill-advised decisions. The first was to send 17,000 royal troops to Paris to restore order. The arrival of the troops gave the impression that the government was planning an attack on the people of the city. The second decision was the dismissal of the king's popular finance minister, Jacques Necker, who had favored the meeting of the Estates General and demonstrated real concern for the welfare of the populace. His dismissal sent a signal that the king was contemplating a move against the National Assembly. It was in this atmosphere of public paranoia that Parisians formed the National Guard and stormed the Bastille.

The fall of the Bastille unnerved the king. When he asked one of his aides, "Is it a revolt?" the aide replied, "No, sire, it is a revolution." The revolution had just begun. It moved into high gear two weeks later when the National Assembly responded to the outbreak of social unrest in the provinces. The scarcity of grain in the countryside gave rise to false rumors that the nobles were engaged in a plot to destroy crops and starve the people into submission. Peasants armed themselves and prepared to fight off the hired agents of the nobility. Some of these peasants burned the mansions of noblemen, together with the deeds that gave the nobles title to their lands and the right to collect dues from their tenants. A widespread panic, known as the "Great Fear," gripped many parts of the country. Townspeople and peasants amassed in large numbers to defend themselves and save the harvest. In response to this panic, which reached its peak in the last two weeks of July, the National Assembly began to pass legislation that destroyed the Old Regime and created a new political order.

The Creation of a New Political Society

Between August 1789 and September 1790 the National Assembly took three revolutionary steps. The first was the elimination of noble and clerical privilege. In August the assembly abolished the feudal dues that peasants paid their lords, the private legal jurisdictions of noblemen, the collection of tithes by the clergy, and the exclusive rights of noblemen to hunt game on their lands. The privileges of provinces and local towns met the same fate, and ten months later the nobility lost their titles. Instead of a society divided into various corporate groups, each with its own privileges, France would now have only citizens, all of them

equal at law. Social distinctions would be based on merit rather than birth. There were no longer any intermediary powers between the king and the individual subject.

The second step, taken on August 26, was the promulgation of the *Declaration of the Rights of Man and Citizen.* This document reveals the main influence of the Enlightenment on the revolution. It declared that all men, not just Frenchmen, had a natural right to liberty, property, equality before the law, freedom from oppression, and religious toleration. The statement that the "law is the expression of the general will" reflects the influence of Rousseau's *The Social Contract* (1762), while the statement that every citizen has the right to participate in the formation of that law either personally or through a representative embodies the basic principle of democracy. The *Declaration* differed from the English Bill of Rights of 1689 by grounding the rights it proclaimed in natural law rather than in the law of one country. The provisions of the French document therefore serve as statements of broad principle rather than as confirmations of specific rights that the government had allegedly been violating.

The third step in this revolutionary program was a complete reorganization of the Church. In order to solve the problem of the national debt, the National Assembly placed land owned by the Church (about 10 percent of all French territory) at the service of the nation. The Civil Constitution of the Clergy of July 1790 in effect made the Church a department of the state, with the government paying the clergy directly. In order to retain their positions, the clergy were required to take an oath of loyalty to the nation. At the same time the Church was reorganized into eighty-three dioceses, one for each of the departments or administrative units into which the country was also now divided. The bishops of these dioceses were to be elected by laymen. The parishes, which were the basic units of ecclesiastical administration, would become uniform in size, each administering to some 6,000 parishioners.

In 1791 a newly elected Legislative Assembly—replacing the National Assembly—confirmed and extended many of these changes. A constitution, put into effect in October, formalized the end of royal absolutism. The king became a constitutional monarch, retaining only the power to suspend legislation, direct foreign policy, and command the armed forces. The constitution did not, however, give all men the right to vote. Only "active citizens," who paid the equivalent of three days' wages in direct taxes, had the right to vote for electors, who in turn chose representatives to the legislature.

The new constitution formally abolished hereditary legal privileges, thus providing equality of all citizens before the law. Subsequent legislation granted Jews and Protestants full civil rights and toleration. A law eliminating primogeniture (inheritance of the entire estate by the eldest son) gave all heirs equal rights to inherited property.

DOCUMENT

Declaration of the Rights of Man and Citizen (1789)

The passage of the Declaration of the Rights of Man and Citizen *by the National Assembly on August 26, 1789, is one of the earliest and most enduring acts of the French Revolution. A document of great simplicity and power, it was hammered out during many weeks of debate. Its concern with the natural rights of all people and equality before the law reflected the ideas of the Enlightenment.*

1. Men are born free and remain free and equal in rights. Social distinctions may be founded only on the common good.

2. The aim of all political association is the preservation of the natural and imprescriptible rights of man. These rights are liberty, property, security and resistance to oppression.

3. The principle of all authority rests essentially in the nation. No body nor individual may exercise any authority which does not emanate expressly from the nation.

4. Liberty consists in the freedom to do whatever does not harm another; hence the exercise of the natural rights of each man has no limits except those which assure to the other members of society the enjoyment of the same rights. These limits can only be determined by law. . . .

6. Law is the expression of the general will. Every citizen has the right to participate personally or through his representative in its formation. It must be the same for all, whether it protects or punishes. All citizens, being equal in the eyes of the law, are equally eligible to all dignities and to all public positions and occupations, according to their abilities, and without distinction except that of their virtues and talents.

7. No man may be indicted, arrested, or imprisoned except in cases determined by the law and according to the forms prescribed by law. . . .

10. No one should be disturbed for his opinions, even in religion, provided that their manifestation does not trouble public order as established by law.

11. The free communication of thoughts and opinions is one of the most precious of the rights of man. Every citizen may therefore speak, write, and print freely, but shall be responsible for any abuse of this freedom in the cases set by the law. . . .

17. Property being an inviolable and sacred right, no one may be deprived of it except when public necessity, determined by law, obviously requires it, and then on the condition that the owner shall have been previously and equitably compensated.

Source: From P.-J.-B. Buchez and P.-C. Roux, *Histoire parlementaire de la Révolution française.* (Paris: Paulin, 1834).

The establishment of marriage as a civil contract and the right to end a marriage in divorce supported the idea of the husband and wife as freely contracting individuals. The largely symbolic abolition of slavery in France was consistent with the proclamation of equality of all men, but the failure to extend that emancipation to French colonies suggests that there were limits to the concept of liberty proclaimed by the assembly.

This body of legislation amounted to nothing less than a revolution. The Old Regime had been destroyed and a new one had taken its place. Although the form of government remained a monarchy, the powers of that monarchy were drastically curtailed. Unlike the English revolutions of the 1640s and 1688, this revolution did not disguise the extent of the changes that had transpired by using the language of conservatism, claiming that the revolution had recovered lost freedoms. It did not appeal to the French past at all. It promoted a new view of French society as a nation composed of equal citizens possessing natural rights, in place of the older concept of a society consisting of different corporate groups, each with its own privileges. Contemporaries recognized the significance of these changes. The Portuguese ambassador to France, who witnessed the events of 1789 firsthand, reported back to his government, "In all the world's annals there is no mention of a revolution like this."

Responses to the First French Revolution

During the early years of the revolution, events in Paris and Versailles dominated the political scene. The revolution was not confined, however, to the metropolis. In the provinces groups of ordinary townspeople and peasants, frightened that the members of the nobility might be taking counteraction against them, took the law into their own hands and brought about a new revolutionary political and social order. In many places the local rulers who had exercised political power in towns and villages were overthrown and replaced by supporters of the new regime. At the same time there was considerable opposition to the revolutionary government. In many parts of the country the clergy's refusal to take the oath of loyalty to the nation led to violent clashes with the provincial authorities. In the south nobles began to organize resistance to the new regime, while militant Catholics attacked Protestants, who had been granted toleration and who generally supported the revolution.

The revolutionary events of 1789–1791 quickly gained the attention of countries outside France. In England the nonconformist Protestant minister Richard Price urged members of the British Parliament to follow the example of their French neighbors and abolish the laws that restricted

DOCUMENT

Edmund Burke Deplores the Events of the French Revolution

The first French Revolution met with both praise and criticism abroad. The strongest attack came from Edmund Burke, an Irish-born lawyer who sat in the British Parliament. Burke, who is recognized as the father of modern conservatism, attacked the leaders of the revolution for destroying religion and the social order in the interests of an abstract philosophy, subverting the law, and introducing a new tyranny.

. . . France has bought undisguised calamities at a higher price than any nation has purchased the most unequivocal blessings. France has bought poverty by crime. France has not sacrificed her virtue to her interest; but she has abandoned her interest that she might prostitute her virtue. All other nations have begun the fabric of a new government, or the reformation of an old, by establishing originally, or by enforcing with greater exactness, some rites or other of religion. All other people have laid the foundation of civil freedom in severer manners and a system of a more austere and masculine morality. France, when she let loose the reins of regal authority, doubled the license of a ferocious dissoluteness in manners, and of an insolent religion in opinions and practices; and has extended through all ranks of life, as if she were communicating some privilege or laying open some secluded benefit, all the unhappy corruptions that usually were the disease of wealth and power. This is one of the new principles of equality in France.

France, by the perfidy of her leaders, has utterly disgraced the tone of lenient council in the cabinets of princes, and disarmed it of its most potent topics. She has sanctified the dark, suspicious maxims of tyrannous distrust, and taught kings to tremble at . . . the delusive plausibilities of moral politicians. Sovereigns will consider those who advise them to place an unlimited confidence in their people as subverters of their thrones—as traitors who aim at their destruction, by leading their easy good—nature, under specious pretenses, to admit combinations of bold and faithless men into a participation of their power. . . . They have seen the French rebel against a mild and lawful monarch, with more fury, outrage, and insult than ever any people has been known to rise against the most illegal usurper or the most sanguinary tyrant. . . .

They have found their punishment in their success. Laws overturned; tribunals subverted; industry without vigour; commerce expiring; the revenue unpaid, yet the people impoverished; a church pillaged, and a state not relieved; civil and military anarchy made the constitution of the kingdom; everything human and divine sacrificed to the idol of public credit, and national bankruptcy the consequence. . . .

Were all these dreadful things necessary? Were they the inevitable results of the desperate struggle of determined patriots, compelled to wade through blood and tumult to the quiet shore of a tranquil and prosperous liberty? No! Nothing like it. The fresh ruins of France, which shock our feelings wherever we can turn our eyes, are not the devastation of civil war: they are the sad, but instructive monuments of rash and ignorant counsel in a time of profound peace. . . .

Source: Edmund Burke, *Reflections on the Revolution in France* (1790).

---

hunting on aristocratic lands. Prussian reformers took heart that the events of the revolution would portend the destruction of absolutism in their country and in other European lands. A Prussian official who had studied with the philosopher Immanuel Kant called the revolution "the first practical triumph of philosophy . . . the hope and consolation for so many of those ancient ills under which mankind has suffered."

Not all foreign assessments of the revolution were positive. In November 1790 the British politician Edmund Burke published *Reflections on the Revolution in France,* in which he expressed horror at the way in which abstract philosophy had destroyed the traditional social order in France. Pope Pius VI condemned the *Declaration of the Rights of Man and Citizen* and then, outraged at the attack upon the Roman Catholic Church, issued a sweeping condemnation of the Civil Constitution of the Clergy. The absolute monarchs of western Europe, sensing rightly that their regimes were in danger of a contagious revolutionary ideology, not only planned an invasion of France to restore the old order but took action against dissent in their own territories. When Polish legislators wrote a new constitution in 1791, modeled on that of France, Catherine the Great of Russia, who controlled a portion of Poland at the time, claimed that it was the product of French radicalism. She shut down the presses, revived censorship, turned against the philosophes whom she had admired, and banned the works of Voltaire.

The French Republic, 1792–1799

■ How did a second, more radical revolution, which began with the establishment of the Republic in 1792, lead to the creation of a regime that used the power of the state to institute the Reign of Terror?

Beginning in 1792 France experienced a second revolution that was much more radical than the first. During this revolution France was transformed from a constitutional monarchy into a republic. The state claimed far greater power than it possessed under the constitutional monarchy established in 1791, and it used that power to bring about a radical reform of French society.

The Establishment of the Republic, 1792

During the first two years of the revolution it appeared that the building of a new French nation would take place within the framework of a constitutional monarchy. Absolutism had suffered an irreversible defeat, but there was little sentiment among the members of the Legislative Assembly, much less among the general population, in favor of abolishing the institution of monarchy. The only committed republicans—those supporting the establishment of a republic—in the Legislative Assembly belonged to a party known as the Jacobins°, who found support in political clubs in Paris and in other parts of the country. By the late summer of 1792 this group of radicals, drawing upon the support of militant Parisian citizens known as *sans-culottes* (literally, those without breeches, the pants worn by noblemen), succeeded in bringing about the second, more radical revolution.

King Louis himself was in part responsible for this destruction of the monarchy. The success of constitutional monarchy depended on the king's willingness to play the new role assigned to him as a constitutional figurehead. In October 1789 Louis had agreed, under considerable pressure, to move his residence from Versailles to Paris, where the National Assembly had also relocated. The pressure came mainly from women, who formed the large majority of 10,000 demonstrators who marched from Paris to Versailles demanding a reduction in the price of bread. The king yielded to their demands and came to Paris. As he entered the city, accompanied by soldiers, monks, and women carrying guns and pikes, he reluctantly agreed to wear the tricolor cockade (a badge) to symbolize his acceptance of the revolution. Louis, however, could not disguise his opposition to the revolution, especially to the ecclesiastical settlement. This opposition led many people to suspect that he was encouraging the powers of Europe to invade France to restore the Old Regime.

Louis XVI had few personal resources upon which he might draw to win the confidence of his subjects. He was not as intelligent as his grandfather, Louis XV, nor did he have the skills necessary to dispel his subjects' growing distrust of him. Neither Louis nor his Austrian wife, Marie Antoinette, commanded much respect among the people. For many years the royal couple had been the object of relentless, sometimes pornographic satire. He had been lampooned for his rumored sexual inadequacies and she for a series of alleged infidelities with the king's brother and a succession of female partners. Whatever confidence Parisian citizens might have retained in the royal couple evaporated in June 1791, when the king and queen attempted to flee the country. The National Guard apprehended them at Varennes, close to the eastern French border, and forced them to return to Paris, where they were kept under guard at the palace of the Tuileries. Even that development, however, failed to destroy the monarchy,

Sans-Culottes

Male and female dress of the *sans-culottes,* the armed Parisian radicals who supported the Republic. The men did not wear the breeches (*culottes*) that were in style among the members of the French nobility.

which had been preserved in the constitution implemented in October.

The development that actually precipitated the downfall of the monarchy and led to the establishment of a republic was the decision to go to war. Until the summer of 1791 European powers had been involved in various conflicts and had resisted pleas from French émigrés to support a counterrevolutionary offensive against the new French regime. After the flight to Varennes and the capture of the royal family, however, Frederick William II of Prussia (r. 1786–1797) and Emperor Leopold II of Austria (r. 1790–1792), the brother of Marie Antoinette, signed an alliance and called upon the other monarchs of Europe "to restore to the King of France complete liberty and to consolidate the bases of monarchical government." No action would be taken, however, unless all European sovereigns agreed to cooperate.

The actual declaration of war came not from the monarchs of Europe but from the French Legislative Assembly. A small group of republicans, headed by the eloquent orator Jacques-Pierre Brissot (1754–1793), convinced the assembly that an international conspiracy against the revolution would end in an invasion of their country. Brissot and his supporters also believed that if France could be lured into a foreign war, the king and queen would be revealed as traitors and the monarchy would be destroyed. Exploiting xenophobic as well as revolutionary sentiment, and claiming that the strength of a citizen army would win a quick and decisive victory, Brissot and his allies won the support of the entire assembly. They also appealed to the international goals of the revolution, claiming that the French army would inspire revolution against "the tyrants of Europe" everywhere they went.

The Legislative Assembly declared war on Austria in April 1792. Instead of a glorious victory, however, the war resulted in a series of disastrous defeats at the hands of Austrians and their Prussian allies in the Netherlands. This military failure contributed to a mood of paranoia in France, especially in Paris. Fears arose that invading armies, in alliance with nobles, would undermine the revolution. In May members of the assembly learned that the Austrian minister, in cooperation with a group of the king's advisers, was plotting the destruction of the assembly itself. In July the assembly officially proclaimed the nation to be in danger, calling for all citizens to rally against the enemies of liberty at home and abroad. Women petitioned for the right to bear arms. When the Austrians and Prussians threatened to

Tricolor Cockade
Louis XVI wearing the red liberty bonnet with the tricolor cockade on October 20, 1792. Refusing to be intimidated by a crowd of 20,000 people outside the royal palace, he donned the cap and proclaimed his loyalty to the constitution.

torch the entire city of Paris and slaughter its population if anyone laid a hand on the royal family, citizens in Paris immediately demanded that the king be deposed.

On August 10 a radical republican committee overthrew the Paris commune, the city government that had been installed in 1789, and set up a new, revolutionary commune. A force of about 20,000 men, including volunteer troops from various parts of the kingdom, invaded the Tuileries, which was defended by about 900 Swiss guards. When the members of the royal bodyguard fled, they were pursued by members of the Paris crowds, who stripped them of their red uniforms and hacked 600 of them to death with knives, pikes, and hatchets. The attack on the Tuileries forced the king to take refuge in the nearby Legislative Assembly. The assembly promptly suspended the monarchy and turned the royal family over to the commune, which imprisoned them in the Temple, a medieval fortress in the northeastern part of the city. The assembly then ordered its own dissolution and called for the election of a new legislative body that would draft a new constitution.

The fall of the monarchy did nothing to allay the siege mentality of the city, especially after further Prussian victories in early September escalated fears of a Prussian invasion. Individuals suspected of plotting against the regime were imprisoned, and when it was rumored that they would escape and support the Prussian enemy, angry crowds pulled 1,200 prisoners (most of whom were being held for nonpolitical crimes) from their cells and killed them. The feared foreign invasion that had inspired this "September Massacre" never did materialize. On September 20, 1792, a surprisingly well-disciplined and well-trained army of French citizens, inspired by dedication to France and the revolution, repulsed the armies of Austria and Prussia at Valmy. This victory saved the revolution. The German poet Johann Wolfgang von Goethe (1749–1832) claimed that the battle marked the beginning of "a new epoch in the history of the world." Delegates to a new National Convention, elected by universal male suffrage°, had already arrived in

The Attack on the Palace of the Tuileries

On the night of August 10, 1792, Parisian crowds and volunteer soldiers attacked the royal palace in Paris. The puffs of smoke in the building are coming from the Swiss guards, who were entrusted with the defense of the royal family and the palace. The royal family escaped and took refuge in the Legislative Assembly, but 600 of the Swiss guards were killed. Those that retreated were hunted down in the streets of Paris and stripped of their uniforms, and their heads were placed on the ends of pikes.

Paris to write a new constitution. On September 22 the convention declared that the monarchy was formally abolished and that France was a republic. France had now experienced a second revolution, more radical than the first, but dedicated to the same principles of liberty, equality, and fraternity.

The Jacobins and the Revolution

Before the Republic was established, different political factions had begun to vie for power, both in the Legislative Assembly and in the country at large. The first major division to emerge was between the Feuillants, who supported a constitutional monarchy, and the Jacobins, many of whom favored the creation of a democratic republic. By the time the Republic had been declared, the Jacobins had become

the major political party. Soon, however, factional divisions began to develop within Jacobin ranks. The main split occurred between the followers of Brissot, known as Girondins°, and the radicals known as Montagnards°, or "the Mountain." The latter acquired their name because they occupied the benches on the side of the convention hall, where the floor sloped upward. The Girondins occupied the lower side of the hall, while the uncommitted deputies, known as "the Plain," occupied the middle. Both the Mountain and the Girondins claimed to be advancing the goals of the revolution, but they differed widely on which tactics to pursue. The Mountain took the position that as long as the state was endangered by internal and external enemies, the government needed to centralize authority in the capital. The Mountain thought of themselves as the representatives of the common people, especially the *sans-culottes* in Paris. Many of their leaders, including

Georges-Jacques Danton (1759–1794), Jean-Paul Marat (1743–1793), and Maximilien Robespierre (1758–1794), were in fact Parisians. Their mission was to make the revolution even more egalitarian and to establish a republic characterized by civic pride and patriotism, which they referred to as the Republic of Virtue.

The Girondins, known as such because many of their leaders came from the southwestern department of Gironde, took a more conservative position than the Mountain on these issues. Favoring the economic freedom and local control desired by merchants and manufacturers, they were reluctant to support further centralization of state power. They believed that the revolution had advanced far enough and should not become more radical. They were also afraid that the egalitarianism of the revolution, if unchecked, would lead to a leveling of French society and result in social anarchy.

The conflict between the Girondins and the Mountain became apparent in the debate over what to do with the deposed king. Louis had been suspected of conspiring with the enemies of the revolution, and the discovery of his correspondence with the Austrian government led to his trial for treason against the nation. The Girondins had originally expressed reluctance to bring him to trial, preferring to keep him in prison. Once the trial began, they joined the entire National Convention in voting to convict him, but they opposed his execution. This stance led the Mountain to accuse the Girondins of being secret collaborators with the monarchy. By a narrow vote the convention decided to put the king to death, and on January 21, 1793, Louis was executed at the Place de la Révolution.

The instrument of death was the guillotine, an efficient and merciful but nonetheless terrifying decapitation machine first pressed into service in April 1792. It took its name from Dr. Joseph-Ignace Guillotin, who had the original idea for such a device, although he did not invent it. The guillotine was inspired by the conviction that all criminals, not just those of noble blood, should be executed in a swift, painless manner. The new device was to be put to extensive use during the next eighteen months, and many Girondins fell victim to it.

The split between the Mountain and the Girondins became more pronounced as the republican regime encountered increasing opposition from foreign and domestic enemies. Early in 1793 Great Britain and the Dutch Republic allied with Prussia and Austria to form the First Coalition against France, and within a month Spain and the kingdoms of Sardinia and Naples joined them. The armies of these allied powers defeated French forces in the Austrian Netherlands in March of that year, and once again an invasion seemed imminent. At the same time internal rebellions against the revolutionary regime took place in various outlying provinces, especially in the district of the Vendée in western France. These uprisings were led by noblemen and clerics, but they also had popular support, especially from

tenant farmers who resented the increased taxation imposed by the new revolutionary government.

In the minds of Robespierre and his colleagues, the Girondins were linked to these provincial rebels, whom they labeled as federalists° because they opposed the centralization of the French state and thus threatened the unity of the nation. In June twenty-nine Girondins were expelled from the convention for supporting local officials accused of hoarding grain. This purge made it apparent that any political opponent of the Mountain, even those with solid republican credentials, could now be identified as an enemy of the revolution.

CHRONOLOGY

The French Republic and the Terror, 1792–1794

1792

April 20	Declaration of war against Austria
August 10	Attack on the Tuileries; monarchy is suspended
September 2–6	September Massacre of prisoners in Paris
September 20	French victory at the Battle of Valmy
September 21	National Convention meets
September 22	Abolition of the monarchy and establishment of the Republic

1793

January 21	Execution of Louis XVI
February 1	Declaration of war against Great Britain and the Dutch Republic
March 11	Beginning of rebellion in the Vendée
June 2	Purge of Girondins from the Convention
June 24	Ratification of a republican constitution
July 27	Robespierre elected to the Committee of Public Safety
August 23	The Convention decrees the *levée en masse*
October 5	Adoption of the revolutionary calendar
October 16	Execution of Marie Antoinette

1794

July 28	Tenth of *Thermidor;* execution of Robespierre
November 12	Jacobin clubs are closed

The Trial of Louis XVI

After the abolition of the monarchy and the proclamation of the French Republic in September 1792, the National Convention considered the fate of the deposed king. There was a broad consensus that Louis was guilty of treason against the nation and that he should answer for his crimes, but how he should do so was a matter of heated debate. The convention was divided between the Girondins and the Mountain. Of the two, the Girondins were more inclined to follow legal forms, whereas those of the Mountain considered themselves to be acting as a revolutionary tribunal that should adhere to standards of justice not specifically included in the law of the land. The convention thus became a forum where Louis's accusers expressed competing notions of revolutionary justice.

The most divisive and revealing issue was whether there should be a trial at all. The Mountain originally took the position that because the people had already judged the king on August 10, when the monarchy had fallen and the king taken prisoner, there was no need for a second judgment. They should proceed immediately to carrying out the death sentence. Robespierre argued that to have a trial would be counter-revolutionary, for it would allow the revolution itself to be brought before the court to be judged. A centrist majority, however, decided that the king had to be charged with specific offenses in a court of law and found guilty by due process before being sentenced.

A second issue, closely related to the first, was the technical legal question of whether the king could be subject to legal action. Even if the legislative branch of the government was considered the equal of the king in a constitutional monarchy, it did not possess authority over him. A further argu-

ment was that the king could not be tried for actions for which he had already suffered abdication. This claim was challenged on the most basic principle of the revolution—that the nation was higher than the king and his crimes were committed against that nation, which is the people. The king, moreover, was no longer king but was now a citizen and therefore subject to the law in the same way as anyone else.

The third issue was Louis's culpability for the specific charges in the indictment. These crimes included refusing to call the Estates General, sending an army to march against the citizens of Paris, and conducting secret negotiations with France's enemies. The journalist and deputy Jean-Paul Marat added that "he robbed the citizens of their gold as a subsidy for their foes" and "caused his hirelings to hoard, to create famine, to dry up the sources of abundance that the people might die from misery and hunger."

Nonetheless the king, who appeared personally to hear the indictment and then to respond to the charges on December 26, presented a plausible defense. He based it on the laws in force at the various times he was supposed to have committed his crimes. Thus he defended his sending of troops to Paris on the grounds that in June and July 1789 he could order troops wherever he wanted. In the same vein he argued that he had used force solely in response to illegal intimidation. These legalisms, however, only made the members of the convention more contemptuous of the king. His defense failed to persuade a single convention deputy. He was convicted of treason by a vote of 693–0.

This unanimous conviction of the king did not end the factional debates over the king's fate. Knowing that there was extensive

support for the king in various parts of the country, the Girondins asked that the verdict be appealed to the people. Their argument was that the convention, dominated by the Mountain and supported by militants in Paris, had usurped the sovereignty of the people. Pierre-Victurnien Vergniaud, a lawyer from Bordeaux, pleaded that "To take this right from the people would be to take sovereignty from them, to transfer it . . . to the hands of the representatives chosen by the people, to transform their representatives into kings or tyrants." Vergniaud's motion to submit the verdict to the people for ratification lost by a vote of 424–283.

The last vote, the closest of all, determined the king's sentence. Originally it appeared that a majority might vote for noncapital punishment. The Marquis de Condorcet, for example, argued that although the king deserved death on the basis of the law of treason, he could not bring himself to vote for capital punishment on principle. The radical response to this argument came from Robespierre, who appealed to the "principles of nature" in stating that the death penalty could be justified "only in those cases where it is vital to the safety of private citizens or of the public." Robespierre's impassioned oratory carried the day. By a vote of 361–334 the king was sentenced to "death within 24 hours" rather than the alternatives of imprisonment followed by banishment after the war or imprisonment in chains for life. The following day Louis was led to the guillotine.

All public trials, especially those for political crimes, are theatrical events, in that the various parties play specific roles and seek to convey certain messages to their audiences. The men who voted to put Louis XVI on trial

MORT DE LOUIS CAPET 16ᵉ DU NOM, LE 21 JANVIER 1793.

Execution of Louis XVI, January 21, 1793
Although the king was convicted of treason by a unanimous vote, the vote to execute him carried by a slender majority of only twenty-seven votes.

wanted to create an educational spectacle in which the already deposed monarch would be stripped of any respect he might still have commanded among the people. Louis was to be tried like any other traitor, and he was to suffer the same fate, execution by the guillotine. The attempt to strip him of all privilege and status continued after his death. His corpse, with his head placed between his knees, was taken to a cemetery, placed in a wooden box, and buried in the common pit. The revolutionaries were determined to guarantee that even in death the king would have the same position as the humblest of his former subjects.

Questions of Justice

1. How would you describe the standard of justice that the members of the National Convention upheld in voting to execute the king? How did this standard of justice differ from the standard to which King Louis XVI appealed?

2. Evaluate the argument of Robespierre that the death penalty can be justified only in cases of public safety. Compare his argument to that of Enlightenment thinkers such as Cesare Beccaria that capital punishment was an unjust, unnecessary, and uncivilized punishment.

Taking It Further

Jordan, David P. *The King's Trial: The French Revolution vs. Louis XVI.* 1979. The most thorough account of the trial.

Walzer, Michael, ed. *Regicide and Revolution: Speeches at the Trial of Louis XVI.* 1974. A valuable collection of speeches with an extended commentary.

In order to repel the coalition of foreign powers, the convention ordered a *levée en masse,* a conscription of troops from the entire population. This step, taken in August 1793, created an unprecedented military force, a massive citizen army drawn from all segments of the population and committed to the prosecution of the war. In the past the rank and file of European armies, whether mercenaries or regular troops, had been filled with men on the margins of society: the poor, the unemployed, and even criminal outcasts. The conscription of males from all ranks of society might have promoted a sense of national unity among the troops, but it also caused resentment and resistance against this use of state power. It led to increased federalist resistance to the radical Jacobin government.

The Reign of Terror, 1793–1794

In order to deal with its domestic enemies, the republican government claimed powers that far exceeded those exercised by the monarchy in the age of absolutism. The convention passed laws that set up special courts to prosecute enemies of the regime and authorized special procedures that deprived those accused of their legal rights. These laws laid the legal foundation for the Reign of Terror°, a campaign to rid the state of its internal enemies. A Committee of Public Safety, consisting of twelve members entrusted with the executive power of the state, superintended this process. Although technically subordinate to the convention, the Committee of Public Safety became in effect a revolutionary dictatorship.

The man who emerged as the main figure on the Committee of Public Safety was Maximilien Robespierre. A brilliant student as a youth, Robespierre was affronted when the king's carriage splashed him with mud as he was waiting to read an address to the king. A man with little sense of humor, he was passionate in his quest for justice. As a lawyer who defended indigent clients, Robespierre was elected to the Third Estate in 1789 and became a favorite of the *sans-culottes,* who called him "The Incorruptible." That he may have been, but he was also susceptible to the temptation to abuse power for partisan political purposes. Like Rousseau, whose work he admired, he was also willing to sacrifice individual liberty in the name of the collective General Will. His logic was that since the General Will was indivisible, it could not accommodate dissent. Robespierre was primarily responsible for pushing the revolution to new extremes and for establishing the program of state repression that began in the autumn of 1793.

Saint-Just on Democracy, Justice and the Terror (1790s)

The most intense prosecutions of the Terror took place between October 1793 and June 1794, but they continued until August 1794. By that time the revolutionary courts had executed 17,000 people, while 500,000 had suffered imprisonment. Another 20,000 either died in prison or were killed without any form of trial. Among the victims of the Terror were substantial numbers of clergy and nobility, as we might expect, but the overwhelming majority were artisans and peasants. One Parisian stableboy was guillotined for having said "f . . . the Republic," while a baker from Alsace lost his head for predicting that "the Republic will go to hell with all its partisans."[2] Many of the victims came from the outlying regions of the country, especially the northeast, where foreign armies were threatening the Republic, and the west, where a brutal civil war between the French army and Catholics and Royalists was raging. These provincial enemies of the regime were identified by special surveillance committees and then were tried by revolutionary tribunals. The guillotine was by no means the only method of execution. In November and December 1793, about 1,800 rebels captured during the uprising in the Vendée were tied to other prisoners, placed in sinking boats, and drowned in the chilly waters of the Loire River.

The most visible and alarming of the executions took place in the capital. The execution of Marie Antoinette and other royalists might have been justified on the basis of their active subversion of the regime, but trumped-up charges against Girondins exposed a process that would destroy republicans as well. As one Girondin said in a speech to the Convention, the revolution, like the mythical Roman god Saturn, devoured its own children. Some of the most prominent figures of the Enlightenment fell victim to this paranoia. Among them was the Marquis de Condorcet, who believed passionately that all citizens, including women, had equal rights. Having campaigned against capital punishment, he committed suicide in a Parisian prison, just before he was to be executed. Another figure of the Enlightenment, the famous chemist Antoine Lavoisier (1743–1794), who had devoted himself to improving social and economic conditions in France, was executed at the same time. So too was the feminist Olympe de Gouges, who as we discussed in Chapter 18 had petitioned for the equal political rights of women. Many French revolutionaries, including Robespierre, used the political ideas of the Enlightenment to justify their actions, but the Terror struck down some of the most distinguished figures of that movement. In that sense the Terror marked the end of the Enlightenment in France.

The Committee of Public Safety then went after Danton and other so-called "Indulgents," who had decided that the Terror had gone too far. Danton's execution made everyone, especially moderate Jacobins, wonder who would be the next victim of a process that had spun completely out of control. In June 1794 the Terror reached a climax, as 1,300 people were sent to their deaths. In order to stop the process, a group of Jacobins in the convention, headed by Joseph Fouché (1759–1820) and Paul Barras (1755–1829), organized a plot against Robespierre. Calling him a tyrant, they arrested him and more than 100 of his followers and guillotined them in late July 1794. An equally swift retaliation was exacted against the Jacobins in the provinces, when members of the White Terror, so named for the white Bourbon flag they displayed, executed leaders of the local revolutionary tribunals. With these reprisals, which used the very same methods that had been perfected by Robespierre and his followers, the most violent and radical phase of the French revolution came to an end.

The Reign of Terror had ended, but its memory would never be extinguished. Its horrors served as a constant warning against the dangers inherent in revolutionary movements. The guillotine, the agent of a dysfunctional and indiscriminate state terrorism, became just as closely identified with the French Revolution as its famous slogan of "Liberty, Equality, Fraternity." The contrast between those two symbols, each of them emblematic of a different stage of the revolution, helps to explain how both conservatives and liberals in the nineteenth century would be able to appeal to the experience of the revolution to support their contradictory ideologies.

The Directory, 1795–1799

A desire to end the violence of the Terror allowed moderates in the National Convention to regain control of the state apparatus that Robespierre and his allies had used to such devastating effect. The Paris Commune was dismantled and the Committee of Public Safety stripped of most of its powers. In November 1794 the Jacobin clubs throughout the country, which had provided support for the Terror, were closed. The moderates who now controlled the government still hoped to preserve the gains of the revolution, while returning the country to more familiar forms of authority. A new constitution of 1795 bestowed executive power on a five-man Directorate, while an assembly consisting of two houses, the Council of Elders and the Council of Five Hundred, proposed and voted on all legislation. The franchise was limited to property holders, allowing only 2,000,000 men out of an adult male population of 7,000,000 to vote. A system of indirect election, in which a person voted for electors who then selected representatives, guaranteed that only the wealthiest members of the country would sit in the legislative assembly.

The establishment of the Directory formed part of a more general reaction against the culture of the republic. The austere, egalitarian dress of the *sans-culottes* gave way once again to fancy and opulent clothes, at least among the bourgeoisie. Low necklines, officially out of favor during the Reign of Terror, once again came back into fashion among wealthier members of society. The high social life of the capital experienced a revival. Some dances took place on the sites of churches that Jacobins had desecrated. Jacobin theaters were shut down and Jacobin works of art destroyed. France was still a republic, but it was no longer Robespierre's Republic of Virtue.

Some of the more entrepreneurial citizens of Paris welcomed the new regime, but opposition soon arose, mainly from Jacobins and *sans-culottes*. When the government relaxed the strict price controls that had been in effect under the Jacobins, the soaring price of bread and other commodities caused widespread social discontent among the population. This situation was aggravated by the continuation of the interminable war against the foreign powers in the First Coalition. Wherever French troops went, their constant need of food and other goods resulted in serious shortages of these commodities.

By the end of 1798 conditions had grown even worse. Inflation was running out of control. The collection of taxes was intermittent at best. The paper money known as *assignats*, first issued by the government in 1791 and backed by the value of confiscated church lands, had become almost worthless. Late in 1797 the Directory had been forced to cancel more than half the national debt, a

---

CHRONOLOGY

The Directory, 1795–1799

1795

August 22	The National Convention approves a new constitution
October 5	Napoleon suppresses a royalist insurrection in Paris
October 26	End of the Convention; beginning of the Directory

1796

February 19	The issuing of *assignats* is halted
April 12	Beginning of a series of victories by Napoleon in Italy

1798

May 13	Napoleon's expedition departs for Egypt
May	Second Coalition (Britain, Austria, Russia, Naples, and Turkey) is formed against Napoleon
July 21	Napoleon wins the Battle of the Pyramids
August 1	Nelson destroys the French fleet at the Battle of the Nile

1799

November 9–10	Napoleon's coup on the eighteenth of *Brumaire;* Consulate is established

The 25th December 1799. The Three Consuls: Bonaparte, Cambecérès and Lebrun (1856)

This painting by Louis-Charles-Auguste Couder shows the three consuls taking the oath of office before the presidents of the Assembly on December 25, 1799. Napoleon, the First Consul, stands at the center of the three to the left.

step that further alienated wealthy citizens who had lent money to the government. Military setbacks in 1798 and 1799 brought the situation to a critical point. An expedition to Egypt, which was intended to gain for France a foothold in the Middle East, had resulted in a number of victories against the Turks, but the British destroyed the French fleet at the Battle of the Nile in 1798. The next year a series of revolts against French rule in Italy and in the Austrian Netherlands pushed the French armies back to France's earlier boundaries. The formation of a Second Coalition of European powers in 1799, which included Russia, Naples, and Turkey as well as Britain and Austria, represented a formidable challenge to French power and ensured that the war would not end soon. These military events produced a swing to the political left and raised the specter of another Jacobin coup.

In the face of this instability, Emmanuel-Joseph Sieyès, who had been elected as one of the directors two years earlier, decided to overthrow the government. Sieyès provided a link between the early years of the revolution, when he had defended the Third Estate, and the current government of the Directory. Unlike many other prominent political figures, he had managed to avoid prosecution as the revolution had become more radical. When asked what he had done during the Reign of Terror, Sieyès replied, "I survived." The goal of the planned coup was to provide the country with strong government, its greatest need in a period of political, economic, and social instability. The person Sieyès selected as his partner in this enterprise, and the man who immediately assumed leadership of the coup, was Napoleon Bonaparte (1769–1821), a 30-year-old general who in 1795

had put down a royalist rebellion in Paris with a "whiff of grapeshot."

Napoleon had already established impressive credentials as a military leader. In 1796 and 1797 he had won major victories in Italy, leading to the Treaty of Campo Formio with Austria in 1797. Those victories and his short-lived success at the Battle of the Pyramids in Egypt had made him enormously popular in Paris, where he was received as a hero when he assumed command of the armed forces in the city in 1799. His popularity, his demonstrated military leadership, and his control of a large armed force made this "man on horseback" appear to have the best chance to replace the enfeebled civilian regime of the Directory.

On November 9, 1799, Napoleon addressed the two legislative councils. He reported that another Jacobin conspiracy had been uncovered and that in order to deal with such insurrections a new constitution must be written to give the executive branch of the government more authority. Napoleon encountered resistance from some members of the Council of Five Hundred, who demanded that he be declared an outlaw. At this stage the president of the council, Napoleon's brother Lucien, intervened and called in troops to evict the members who opposed him. The following day France had a new government, known as the Consulate.

Executive power in the new government was to be vested in three consuls. It soon became clear, however, that Napoleon would be the dominant member of this triumvirate, and in the new constitution of December 1799, which the electorate ratified by means of a plebiscite, Napoleon was named First Consul. This appointment made him the most powerful man in France and for all practical purposes a military dictator. Republican forms of government were preserved in the new constitution, but they were easily manipulated to produce what the consuls desired. A Senate appointed by the consuls chose men from a list of 6,000 "notables" to form a body known as the Tribunate, which would discuss legislation proposed by the consuls. Another assembly, the Legislative Body, would vote on those measures without debate.

With the establishment of the Consulate the French Republic was a thing of the past. It had been replaced by a military dictatorship in all but name. This transformation of the republic into a military dictatorship had been predicted by both the radical democrat Robespierre and the British conservative Edmund Burke many years before. The dictatorship became more apparent in 1802, when Napoleon was named Consul for Life, and in 1804, when he crowned himself emperor of the French.

Cultural Change in France During the Revolution

■ In what ways did the political events of the revolution change French cultural institutions and create a new political culture?

The French Revolution was primarily a political revolution. It brought about fundamental change in the system of government. It resulted in the destruction of the monarchy and the establishment of a republic. It inspired the drafting of new constitutions, led to the creation of new legislative assemblies, and endowed the state with unprecedented power. The French revolution also brought about profound changes in French culture. It transformed the cultural institutions of the Old Regime and created a new revolutionary culture.

The Transformation of Cultural Institutions

Between 1791 and 1794 most of the cultural institutions of the Old Regime were either destroyed or radically transformed, and new institutions under the control of the state took their place.

Schools

The confiscation of church property in 1790, followed by the abolition of the monastic religious orders, had a devastating effect on the traditional parish schools, colleges, and universities, most of which were run by the clergy. Without sufficient endowments, many of these schools were forced to close. During the Terror, schools suspected of having

aristocratic associations and teaching counterrevolutionary doctrines came under further assault. Thousands of teachers lost their salaries and sought employment elsewhere. In September 1793 the universities were suppressed.

The government gradually realized that the entire educational process was collapsing. Recognizing the necessity of using education to encourage loyalty to the republican regime, the National Convention established a system of universal primary education. Instruction would be free, and the teachers would receive their salaries from the state. Unfortunately, the state did not have enough money to pay for the system, so the schools continued to languish.

The state was only slightly more successful in providing secondary education by converting abandoned colleges, monasteries, and libraries into "central schools," which were intended to provide a standardized form of state education. By 1799, the central schools had 10,000 students, 40,000 fewer than were in the colleges in 1789. The system was improved significantly during the Napoleonic period when the government established thirty-six secondary schools known as *lycées* while also allowing private and religious schools to continue to function.

Academies

The Parisian scientific and artistic academies established by Louis XIV (see Chapter 15) had a monopoly over the promotion and transmission of knowledge in the sciences and the visual arts. The academies were the epitome of privilege. They controlled their own membership, determined the recipients of their prizes, and had a monopoly of their particular branch of knowledge. They were also heavily aristocratic institutions; as many as three-quarters of their members were nobles or clergy.

During the revolution the academies were abolished as part of a general attack on corporate bodies. The work they did was taken over by various government committees. For example, the Commission on Weights and Measures, which had been part of the Academy of Science, became an independent commission. Its task had been to provide uniform weights and measures for the entire kingdom. In 1795 it established the meter, calculated as one ten-millionth of the distance from the North Pole to the equator, as the standard measure of distance. The metric system and the decimal system, which were introduced at the same time, have subsequently been adopted as universal standards in all European countries except Great Britain.

The Royal Academy of Arts, dissolved by a vote of the National Convention in 1793, was replaced by the Popular and Republican Society of the Arts. The inspiration for this new republican society, which was open to artists of all social ranks, was Jacques-Louis David (1748–1825), the greatest painter of his generation. Employed at the court of Louis XVI, David became a vocal main critic of the academy at the time of the revolution. He painted some of the most memorable scenes of the revolution, including the oath taken at the tennis court by the members of the National Assembly in 1789. During the Republic David depicted heroes of the revolution such as Jean-Paul Marat, and after the empire was established he was appointed First Painter to Napoleon. David presided over a revival of classicism in French painting, employing Greek and Roman motifs and exhibiting a rationalism and lack of sentiment in his work.

Libraries

Shortly after the revolution had begun, thousands of books and manuscripts from the libraries of monasteries, royal castles, residences of the nobility, and academies came into the possession of the state. Many of these were funneled into the Royal Library, which grew five times in size between 1789 and 1794 and was appropriately renamed the National Library. The government also intended to inventory and catalog all the books held in libraries throughout the country. This effort to create the General Bibliography of France was never completed, and while the books were being cataloged, the government decided to get rid of those that dealt with "theology, mysticism, feudalism, and royalism" by sending them to foreign countries. This decision did not lead to the export of books to other parts of Europe, but it initiated a frenzy of book sales, mainly to private individuals. Altogether about five million books were lost or sold during these years.

Museums and Monuments

The day after the abolition of the monarchy the National Assembly created a Commission of the Museum, whose function was "to collect paintings, statues and other precious objects from the crown possessions" as well as from the churches and houses of the émigrés. The museum was to be located in the Louvre, a royal palace that also served as an art gallery. When it opened in August 1793 the Louvre included a majority of paintings with religious themes, most of them confiscated from royal and émigré residences. The incompatibility of these religious works of art with the republican rejection of Christianity can be explained only by the assumption that this museum was intended to be entirely historical and to have no relevance to contemporary politics. The Louvre and the Museum of French Monuments represented an attempt to quarantine the religious French past from its secular present, lest it contaminate the revolution itself.

The revolutionaries did not have the same respect for the bodies of their former kings. On August 10, 1793, the first anniversary of the deposition of Louis XVI, the National Convention ordered the destruction of all the tombs of past French kings. One by one the tombs were opened and the corpses, embalmed in lead, were removed. Metals and valuables were melted down for use in the war effort. The corpses were either left to disintegrate in the atmosphere or dragged unceremoniously to the cemetery, where they were

Le XI Aout 1792, les parisiens reprenant une mesure qu'ils avoient eu tort de ne pas mettre à exécution le 20 Juin 1791. Ils abbatirent les Statues de Louis XIV, Place des victoires, et place vendôme.

Destruction of the Statue of Louis XIV in the Place de Victoires, August 11, 1792

The leaders of the Republic attempted to eliminate the memory of the institution of monarchy by destroying statues as well as the tombs of France's kings.

thrown into the common pit. The corpse of Louis XIV landed on top of that of Henry IV. This disrespectful treatment of the remains of France's former kings was intended to erase the memory of monarchy.

The Creation of a New Political Culture

As the state was taking over and adapting the cultural institutions of the Old Regime, revolutionaries engaged in a much bolder and original undertaking: the production of a new, revolutionary political culture. Its sole purpose was to legitimate and glorify the new regime. It symbolized the political values of that regime: liberty, equality, and fraternity in 1789 and republicanism after 1792. This culture was almost entirely political; all forms of cultural expression were subordinated to the realization of a pressing political agenda.

One of the main characteristics of this culture was that it was popular—it was shared by the entire populace, not simply by a small upper-class or literate elite. The fundamental political doctrine of the revolution was popular sovereignty°: the claim that the people were the highest political power in the state. The revolutionaries claimed that this power could never be alienated. The move of the National Assembly from Versailles to Paris actually enabled the people to be present in the gallery during political debate, and deputies were always conscious of their presence. "Learn," claimed one of them in 1789, "that we are deliberating here in front of our masters and we are answerable to them for our opinions." The political culture that emerged—the textual and literary symbols spoken, written, and drawn to reflect this sovereignty of the people—would become the property of the entire population, especially in Paris, where the revolutionary cause found its most passionate popular support. The very words used to identify revolutionary institutions, such as the National Assembly and the National Guard, formed the texture of this new political culture.

The common people who embraced this new culture most enthusiastically were the *sans-culottes*—the radical shopkeepers, artisans, and laborers of Paris. The dress of these people influenced a change in fashion among the wealthier segments of society. A simple jacket replaced the ruffled coat worn by members of the upper classes, their powdered wigs gave way to natural hair, and they too now wore long trousers. They also donned the red liberty cap, to which a tricolor cockade was affixed. The tricolor, which combined the red and blue colors of Paris with the white symbol of the Bourbon monarchy, identified the adherents of the revolution.

Symbols of revolution could be found everywhere. The commercialization of the revolution guaranteed that the tricolor flag, portraits of revolutionary figures, and images of the Bastille would appear on household objects as con-

stant reminders of the public's support for the revolution. By an order of the government in 1792 all men were required to wear the tricolor cockade. Liberty trees, first planted by peasants as protests against local landlords, became a symbol of the revolution. By May 1792 more than 60,000 had been planted throughout the country.

The press, no longer tightly controlled by the government and the printers' guild, became a crucial agent of revolutionary propaganda and a producer of the new culture. Pamphlets, newspapers, brochures, and posters all promoted a distinctive revolutionary language, which became one of the permanent legacies of the revolution. Political leaders used the same rhetoric in their political speeches. *Sans-culottes* sang satirical songs and ballads, many of them to the same tunes well known in the Old Regime. The most popular of the songs of the revolutionary period was the *Marseillaise*, first sung by soldiers preparing for battle against the Austrians but soon adopted by the civilian population and sung at political gatherings. The theaters, which had been privileged corporations in the Old Regime but also carefully regulated, were now free to engage in political satire that strengthened the ties of the people to the revolution.

Much of this new political culture stemmed from the conviction that the doctrine of popular sovereignty should be practiced in everyday life. *Sans-culottes* did this by joining the political clubs organized by different factions within the National Assembly, by addressing others as citizens, and by using the more familiar form of the pronoun *you* (*tu* rather than *vous*) in all conversations. They also participated in the revolution by taking public oaths. On the first anniversary of the fall of the Bastille, as many as 350,000 people, many of them members of the "federations" of National Guards throughout the country, gathered on the royal parade ground outside Paris to take an oath "to the Nation, to the Law, to the King." Direct democracy was not possible in a society of 27 million people, but these cultural practices allowed people to believe that they were participating actively in the political process.

The new revolutionary culture was emphatically secular. In its most extreme form, it was blatantly anti-Christian. In September 1793 the radical Jacobin and former priest Joseph Fouché inaugurated a program of de-Christianization°. Under his leadership, radical Jacobins closed churches and removed religious symbols such as crosses from cemeteries and public venues. In an effort to establish a purely civic religion, they forbade the public practice of religion and renamed churches "temples of reason." In their public pronouncements the architects of de-Christianization avoided reference to the Christian period of French history, which covered the entire national past.

This de-Christianization campaign became the official policy of the Paris Commune, and the National Convention issued a few edicts to enforce it. The program, however, did not win widespread support, and even some Jacobins

Oath Taking

On July 14, 1790, the first anniversary of the fall of the Bastille, as many as 350,000 people gathered on a field outside Paris to take an oath of loyalty to the new French nation. The event was referred to as the Feast of the Federation, because most of the oath takers were members of the regional federations of National Guards. The oath taking, which had many characteristics of a religious gathering, was led by the king himself, and it marked the most optimistic period of the revolution.

claimed that in rejecting Christianity it had undermined a belief in God and the afterlife. In 1794 Robespierre attempted to modify the excesses of de-Christianization by launching the Cult of the Supreme Being. He promoted a series of festivals acknowledging the existence of a deity and the immortality of the soul. This new cult paid lip service to traditional religious beliefs, but it still served secular purposes. In fact, the cult was designed to direct the spiritual yearnings of the French people into patriotic undertakings and promote republican virtue.

The new secular revolutionary culture incorporated many elements of the Christian culture that had prevailed before the revolution began. The new pageants and festivals designed to promote a civic religion were modeled on traditional Catholic processions. Revolutionaries co-opted some of the religious holy days for their own purposes. Churches were converted to temples honoring revolutionary heroes. An effigy of Jean-Paul Marat, who was murdered in 1793, appeared on the altar of a Parisian church, next to a female statue of liberty. Jacques-Louis David's portrait of the murdered Marat depicted the slain victim in the manner of the dead Christ in Michelangelo's *Pietà*. Meetings of revolutionaries often took on the atmosphere of religious revivals, as men and women wept in response to orations. Secular catechisms taught young children the virtues of republicanism in the same way that they had in-

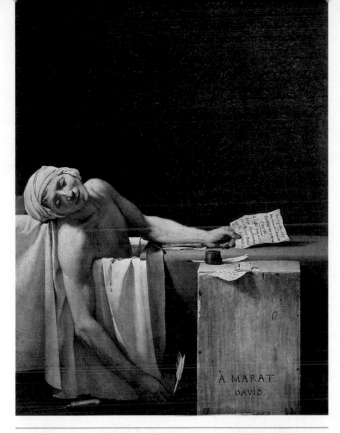

Jacques-Louis David, *The Death of Marat* (1793)
The Jacobin journalist Jean-Paul Marat was stabbed to death in his bathtub by a noblewoman, Charlotte Corday, in July 1793. The painting depicts Marat as having suffered a martyr's death. Marat holds the letter from his murderer that gave her entrance to his residence.

structed them in Christian doctrine during the Old Regime.

In order to destroy all vestiges of the Old Regime, the government also instituted a new calendar in October 1793. The dates on the calendar began with September 22, 1792, the day the Republic was established. That became the first day of the year I, while the weeks now had ten days instead of seven. The new months were given names to evoke the different seasons, such as *Brumaire* for the first month of wintry weather, *Germinal* for the season of planting, and *Thermidor* for the warmest month of the summer. Hostile British contemporaries gave their own humorous renditions of these names, translating them as Freezy, Flowery, Heaty, and so on. The new calendar was intended to make the revolution a part of people's everyday consciousness. It remained in effect until the last day of 1805.

The new revolutionary culture was disseminated widely, but it was always contested. Royalists trampled on the tricolor cockade, refused to adopt the new style of dress, and pulled up the liberty trees. This resistance from counterrevolutionary forces guaranteed that when the revolution was reversed, much of the new political culture would disappear. Napoleon did little to perpetuate it, and the restored monarchy was openly hostile to it. Like the political revolution, however, some elements of revolutionary culture, such

as the tricolor and the rhetoric of the revolutionary press, could never be suppressed. Not only did these cultural innovations inspire revolutionaries for the next hundred years, but they also became part of the mainstream of Western civilization.

Cultural Uniformity

One of the most striking features of the new revolutionary culture was its concern for standardization and simplicity. The division of France into *départements*, all roughly equal in size, population, and wealth, and the further subdivision of each *département* into uniform districts and communes, serves as one manifestation of this compulsion. The establishment of a national school system, at least on paper, serves as another. When the *lycées* were founded by Napoleon, each of the schools was given the exact same curriculum, and the same 3,000 books, chosen by a central committee, were deposited in all *lycée* libraries. The adoption of the metric system and the decimal system and the plan to establish one body of French law for the entire country, eventually brought to fruition by Napoleon, reflected the same impulse. So too did the efforts begun during the Terror to make French the official language in regions of the country that spoke Breton, Occitan, Basque, or other regional dialects.

The main source of this drive toward cultural uniformity was the desire to build a new French nation composed of equal citizens. Linguistic, legal, educational, or administrative diversity only made the realization of that program more difficult. The quest for cultural and political standardization did not, however, originate during the revolution. Many of the projects of the 1790s, especially the desire to establish standard weights and measures, began during the Old Regime. They were often the product of the rationalism of the Enlightenment, which, as we have seen in Chapter 18, sought to make society conform to the operation of universal laws.

The Napoleonic Era, 1799–1815

■ How did the authoritarian rule of Napoleon Bonaparte from 1799 to 1814 confirm or betray the achievements of the French Revolution, and what impact did his military conquests have on Europe and the world?

The coup d'état on November 9, 1799, or the eighteenth of *Brumaire* on the revolutionary calendar, marked a turning point in the political history of France. The Consulate ushered in a period of authoritarian rule. Liberty was restricted in the interest of order; republicanism gave way to dictatorship. The French Revolution had apparently run its course. But the period between 1799 and 1815 was also a time of considerable innovation, especially in the realm of politics and diplomacy. Those innovations were primarily the work of one man, Napoleon Bonaparte, who controlled the French government for the next fifteen years.

Napoleon's Rise to Power

Napoleon Bonaparte was born on the Mediterranean island of Corsica. His father, Charles-Marie de Buonaparte, was an attorney who had supported the Corsican patriot Pascale de Paoli in winning the independence of the island from the Italian state of Genoa. His mother, Letizia, had come from an old noble family from Lombardy in Italy. In 1770 the new French government, which had gained control of the island the previous year, accepted the Buonaparte family as nobility. In 1779 the young Napoleon, whose native language was Corsican, received an appointment to a French military school. He survived both the rigors of the course of study and the taunting of his classmates, who mocked him for his accent and his poverty. Displaying a natural gift for military science, he won a position in the artillery section of the national military academy in Paris.

Until the beginning of the French Revolution, Napoleon seemed destined to pursue a successful but unspectacular career as an officer in the royal army. The events of the revolution made possible his rapid ascent to military prominence and political power. When the revolution broke out, Napoleon returned to Corsica, where he organized the National Guard and petitioned the government to grant full rights of citizenship to his people. As the revolution became more radical he became a Jacobin, and he was commissioned to attack federalist and royalist positions in the south of France. Unlike many of his fellow Jacobins, he managed to survive the Terror and then found favor with the Directory. In 1796 Napoleon was given command of the Army of Italy, at which time he abandoned the Italian spelling of his name for Bonaparte. His decisive victories against the Austrians and his popularity in Paris attracted the attention of Sieyès and others who wished to give the country strong, charismatic leadership.

Napoleon's personality was ideally suited to the acquisition and maintenance of political power. A man of unparalleled ambition, he was driven by an extraordinarily high assessment of his abilities. After one of his military victories he wrote, "I realized I was a superior being and conceived the ambition of performing great things." To the pursuit of his destiny he harnessed a determined and a stubborn will. Temporary setbacks never seemed to thwart his single-minded pursuit of glory. He brought enormous energy to his military and political pursuits. He wrote more than 80,000 letters during his life, many of them transmitting orders to his officers and ministers. Authoritarian by nature, he used intimidation as well as paternal concern to cultivate the loyalty of his subordinates. Like many authoritarian leaders, he had difficulty delegating authority, a trait that was to weaken his regime. Finally, in an age dominated by high-minded causes, he exhibited an instinctive distrust of ideology and the doctrinaire pronouncements of philosophes such as Rousseau. Napoleon's military training led him to take a pragmatic, disciplined approach to politics, in which he always sought the most effective means to the desired end.

Napoleon's acquisition of power was systematic and shrewd. Playing on the need for a strong leader, and using the army he controlled as his main political tool, he maneuvered himself into the position of first consul in 1799. In 1802 he became consul for life, and two years later he crowned himself emperor of the French and his wife Josephine empress. The title of emperor traditionally denoted the height of monarchical power. It identified a ruler who not only ruled more than one kingdom or state but also did not share power with any other political authority. That was certainly the case with Napoleon. During his rule the Legislative Body, the Senate, and the Tribunate, all of which had been instituted during the Consulate, were reduced to performing only ceremonial functions.

It is certainly ironic that Napoleon, while continuing to hunt down and execute royalists, accepted a title of royalty himself and made his position, just like the French kingship, hereditary. In 1804 a group of royalists, including the members of the Bourbon family, were convicted of and executed for trying to assassinate Napoleon. One of them declared ironically, "We have done more than we hoped. We meant to give France a king, and we have given her an emperor." That emperor, moreover, appeared to the royalists and to many others to be a tyrant who would trample on the rights of the French people. Napoleon's coronation also made a negative impression outside France. The great German composer Ludwig van Beethoven, having dedicated his *Third Symphony* (1803) to Napoleon for overthrowing tyranny in France, scratched Napoleon's name from the dedication after Napoleon assumed his new position as emperor.

Napoleon and the Revolution

What was the relationship between Napoleon's rule and the French Revolution? Did Napoleon consolidate the gains of the revolution or destroy them? Did he simply redirect the revolutionary commitment to liberty, equality, and fraternity into new and more disciplined channels of expression after 1799? Or did he reverse the political trends that had prevailed from 1789 to 1799, crushing liberty in all its forms and establishing a ruthless, authoritarian dictatorship? Napoleon always thought of himself as the heir of the

Emperor Napoleon Crowning His Wife, Josephine, Empress of the French in the Cathedral of Notre Dame, 1804

This painting by Jacques-Louis David depicts secular and religious figures gathered around Napoleon not as members of privileged orders but as representatives of the nation. Pope Pius VII remains seated as Napoleon places the crown on Josephine's head. Napoleon had already crowned himself emperor of the French.

revolution rather than its undertaker. Certainly he was able to use the radical vocabulary of the revolution to characterize his domestic programs and his military campaigns. He presented himself as the ally of the common man against entrenched aristocratic privilege. He proclaimed a love for the French people and gave his support to the doctrine of popular sovereignty. He often referred to the rulers of other European countries as tyrants and presented himself as the liberator of their subjects.

This view of Napoleon as a true revolutionary, however, ignores the fact that his commitment to liberty was almost entirely rhetorical. Behind the appeals to the slogans of the revolution lurked an authoritarian will that was far stronger than that of any eighteenth-century absolute monarch. He used the language of liberty and democracy to disguise a thoroughgoing authoritarianism, just as he used the rhetoric of republicanism to legitimize his own dictatorial regime. The practice of holding carefully orchestrated and controlled elections to ratify the changes he made in French government guaranteed that his rule would appear to have

emanated from the will of the people. At the establishment of the Consulate, Napoleon paid lip service to representative forms of government, which he maintained but then proceeded to render totally ineffective. When the empire was established he told his troops that they had the freedom to vote for or against the new form of government but then told them that if they voted against it, they would be shot.

We can make a stronger case for Napoleon's egalitarianism. He spoke of equality of opportunity. He synthesized the egalitarianism of the revolution with the authoritarianism of the Old Regime. He supported the equality of all Frenchmen (but not Frenchwomen) before the law. This egalitarianism laid the foundation for the support he received from the peasants, soldiers, and workers. It might be said that he brought both equality and political stability to France in exchange for political liberty.

There are two other ways in which we might legitimately consider Napoleon the heir of the revolution. The first is that he continued the centralization and growth of state power and the rational organization of the administration

DOCUMENT

The French People Accept Napoleon as Emperor, 1804

The Countess de Rémusat was the wife of one of Napoleon's chamberlains. In this letter she explains why the French people accepted Napoleon as their emperor. Her comments reflect the fear of disorder that permeated French society at the end of the eighteenth century.

I can understand how it was that men worn out by the turmoil of the Revolution, and afraid of that liberty which had long been associated with death, looked for repose under the dominion of an able ruler on whom fortune was seemingly resolved to smile. I can conceive that they regarded his elevation as a decree of destiny and fondly believed that in the irrevocable they should find peace. I may confidently assert that those persons believed quite sincerely that Bonaparte, whether as Consul or Emperor, would exert his authority to oppose the intrigues of faction and would save us from the perils of anarchy.

None dared to utter the word Republic, so deeply had the Terror stained that name, and Directorial Government had perished in the contempt with which its chiefs were regarded. The return of the Bourbons could only be brought about by the aid of a revolution; and the slightest disturbance terrified the French people, in whom enthusiasm of every kind seemed dead. Besides, the men in whom they had trusted had one after the other deceived them; and as, this time, they were yielding to force, they were at least certain that they were not deceiving themselves.

The belief, or rather the error, that only despotism could at that epoch maintain order in France, was very widespread. It became the mainstay of Bonaparte; and it is due to him to say that he also believed it. The factions played into his hands by imprudent attempts which he turned to his own advantage; he had some grounds for his belief that he was necessary; France believed it too; and he even succeeded in persuading foreign sovereigns that he constituted a barrier against Republican influences which, but for him, might spread widely. At the moment when Bonaparte placed the imperial crown upon his head, there was not a king in Europe who did not believe that he wore his own crown more securely because of that event. Had the new emperor granted a liberal constitution, the peace of nations and of kings might, in sober seriousness, have been for ever secured.

Source: *Memoirs of Madame de Rémusat*, translated by C. Hoey and John Lillie (D. Appleton and Co., 1880).

---

that had begun in 1789. Each of the successive regimes between 1789 and 1815, even the Directory, had contributed to this pattern of state building, and Napoleon's contribution was monumental. The second was his continuation and extension of France's military mission to export the revolution to its European neighbors. The two achievements are related to each other, because the war effort necessitated the further growth and centralization of state power.

Napoleon and the French State

Once Napoleon had gained effective control of the French state, he set about the task of strengthening it, making it more efficient, highly organized, and powerful. In addition to turning the government into a de facto dictatorship, he settled the long struggle between Church and state, laid down an entirely new law code that imposed legal uniformity on the entire country, and made the civil bureaucracy more centralized, uniform, and efficient. All of this was done with the intention of making the state an effective instrument of social and political control.

Concordat with the Papacy

Napoleon's first contribution to the development of the French state, achieved during the Consulate, was to bring about a resolution of the bitter struggle between Church and state. A committed secularist, Napoleon was determined to bring the Church under the direct control of the state. This had been the main purpose of the Civil Constitution of the Clergy of 1790. Napoleon also realized, however, that this policy had divided the clergy between those who had taken an oath to the nation and those who had refused. Clerical independence had also become a major rallying cry of royalists against the new regime, thereby threatening the stability of the country.

Napoleon's solution to this problem was to reach an agreement with the Church that would satisfy clerics and royalists yet not deprive the state of its authority over the Church. With the Church safely under state control, Napoleon could also use religion to maintain respect for authority and to encourage loyalty and service to the state. "In religion," he wrote, "I do not see the mystery of the Incarnation but the mystery of the social order." In a new catechism published after Napoleon became emperor, children were taught: "Christians owe to the princes who govern them, and we owe in particular to Napoleon I, our Emperor, love, respect, obedience, fidelity, military service, and the tributes laid for the preservation and defense of the Empire."

The death of Pope Pius VI (r. 1775–1799), the implacable foe of the revolution, gave Napoleon the opportunity to address this problem. The new pope, Pius VII (r. 1800–1823), who was more sympathetic to liberal causes, was eager to come to terms with a French government that had become more moderate under the Consulate. The Concordat, which Napoleon and Pope Pius agreed to in 1801 and which was published the following year, gave something to both sides, although Napoleon gained more than he conceded. The pope agreed that all the clergy who refused to swear their loyalty to the nation would resign their posts, thus ending the bitter divisions of the past twelve years. The pope would appoint new bishops, but only with the prior approval of Napoleon. The state would pay all clerical salaries, and the Church would abandon any claims it still had to the ecclesiastical lands seized by the state at the beginning of the revolution.

These provisions represented formidable concessions to state power, and many French bishops found the terms of the Concordat too unfavorable to the Church. But the pope did manage to secure a statement that Roman Catholicism was the religion of the majority of citizens, and Napoleon agreed to scrap the secular calendar introduced in 1793, thereby restoring Sundays and holy days. Church attendance began to increase, having reached historic lows during the period of the Republic. The Church regained its respect as well as its legitimacy and its freedom to function in French society. More young recruits joined the clergy. Napoleon did not make many concessions to the Church, but they were significant enough to alienate a group of liberal philosophers and writers known as the Ideologues°, who objected to what they saw as the return of "monkish superstition."

With the pope at least somewhat appeased, Napoleon took unilateral steps to regulate the administration of the French Church. In a set of regulations known as the Organic Articles, which were added to the Concordat in 1802, the French church became a department of state, controlled by a minister of religion, just like the treasury or any other bureaucratic ministry. Pronouncements from the pope required prior government approval, and the clergy were obliged to read government decrees from the pulpit. Protestant congregations, which were also given freedom of worship and state protection by the terms of the Concordat, were likewise brought under state control, and their ministers were paid by the state. Jews received the protection of the state, but the government did not pay the salaries of rabbis.

The Civil Code

Napoleon's most enduring achievement in the realm of state building was the promulgation of a new legal code, the Civil Code of 1804, later known as the Napoleonic Code°. A legal code is an authoritative and comprehensive statement of the law of a particular country. The model for modern legal codes in Europe was the *Corpus Juris Civilis* of the Roman Empire, which Justinian decreed at Constantinople

between 529 and 534 C.E. That code had replaced the thousands of constitutions, customs, and judicial decisions that had been in effect during the Roman Republic and Empire. In compiling the new French code Napoleon, who had just proclaimed himself emperor of the French, was imitating Justinian's legal achievement.

The Napoleonic Code also met a long-standing set of demands to reform the confusing and irregular body of French law. Ever since the Middle Ages, France had been governed by a multiplicity of laws. In the southern provinces of the country, those closest to Italy, the law had been influenced by Roman law. The *Corpus Juris Civilis* had been revived in the Middle Ages and had been incorporated into the written law of these southern French provinces and municipalities. In the north the law was based on local or provincial customs that had not originally existed in written form. France needed a common law for all its people. Efforts to produce an authoritative written code began during the revolution, but Napoleon completed the project and published the code.

The Civil Code, which consisted of more than 2,000 articles, reflected the values that were ascendant in Napoleonic French society. The ideals of the revolution were enshrined in the articles guaranteeing the rights of private property, the equality of all people before the law, and freedom of religion. The values it promoted, however, did not include the equality of the sexes. It granted men control of all family property. Women could not buy or sell property without the consent of their husbands. Only adult men could witness legal documents. All male heirs were entitled to inherit equal shares of a family estate, but daughters were excluded from the settlement.

The Civil Code, which dealt only with the rights and relationships of private individuals, was the first and most important of six law codes promulgated by Napoleon. Others dealt with civil procedure (1806), commerce (1807), and criminal law (1811). Renamed the Napoleonic Code in 1806, the Civil Code had an impact on the law of several countries outside France. It became the basis for the codification of the laws of Switzerland, northern Italy, and the Netherlands, and it served as a model for the numerous codes that were compiled in the German territories controlled by France during the Napoleonic period. The Napoleonic Code also influenced the law of French-speaking North America, including the civil law of the state of Louisiana, which bears signs of its influence even today.

Administrative Centralization

Napoleon laid the foundation of modern French civil administration, which acquired the characteristics of rational organization, uniformity, and centralization. All power emanated from Paris, where Napoleon presided over a Council of State. This body consisted of his main ministers, who handled all matters of finance, domestic affairs, and war and oversaw a vast bureaucracy of salaried,

CHRONOLOGY

The Consulate and the Early Years of the Empire, 1799–1806

1799

December 15	Proclamation of the Constitution of the Consulate

1801

July 15	Signing of the Concordat with the Papacy

1802

March 27	Peace of Amiens
April 8	Organic Articles added to the Concordat

1803

May	Renewal of the war with Britain

1804

March 21	The Civil Code is promulgated
December 2	Napoleon is crowned emperor of the French

1805

August	Third Coalition (Britain, Austria, and Russia) is formed against France
October 21	Defeat of the French navy in the Battle of Trafalgar
October 29	The French defeat the Austrian army at Ulm
December 2	The French defeat Russian and Austrian armies at Austerlitz
December 31	End of the revolutionary calendar

1806

October 14	French victories at the battles of Jena and Auerstädt
November 21	Proclamation of the Continental Blockade of British goods
August 6	Formal dissolution of the Holy Roman Empire

The men who served in the government of the French Empire belonged to one of two elaborate, hierarchical institutions: the civil bureaucracy and the army officer corps. The two were closely related, because the main purpose of the administrative bureaucracy was to prepare for and sustain the war effort. Both institutions were organized hierarchically, and those who held positions in them were trained and salaried. Appointment and promotion were based primarily on talent rather than birth.

The idea of "a career open to all talents," as Napoleon described it, ran counter to the tradition of noble privilege. This was one of the achievements of the revolution that Napoleon perpetuated during the empire. All of the twenty-six marshals who served under him in the army were of nonnoble blood. Three of them had been sergeants in the army before 1789 and another three had been privates. The new system did not amount to a pure meritocracy, in which advancement is determined solely by ability and performance, because many appointments were made or influenced by Napoleon himself on the basis of friendship or kinship. Napoleon's brother, Lucien, for example, became minister of the interior. The system did, however, allow people from the ranks of the bourgeoisie to achieve rapid upward social mobility. In order to recognize their new status, Napoleon created a new order of nonhereditary noblemen, known as *notables*. As men ascended through the ranks of the bureaucracy and army they were given the titles of duke, count, baron, and chevalier. Instead of earning status based on their ancestry, these men acquired their titles by virtue of their service to the state. Napoleon created more than 3,500 notables during his rule. In this way he encouraged service to the state while also strengthening loyalty to it.

Napoleon, the Empire, and Europe

Closely related to Napoleon's efforts to build the French state was his creation of a massive European empire. The French Empire was the product of a series of military victories against the armies of Austria, Prussia, Russia, and Spain between 1797 and 1809. By the latter date France controlled, either directly or indirectly, the Dutch Republic, the

trained officials. The central government also exercised direct control over the provinces, which lost the local privileges they had possessed under the Old Regime. In each of the departments an official known as a *prefect*, appointed by the central government, implemented orders emanating from Paris. Paid the handsome annual salary of 20,000 francs, the prefects were responsible for the maintenance of public order. The power of the prefects was far greater than that of the *intendants* of the Old Regime. The prefects enforced conscription, collected taxes, and supervised local public works, such as the construction and improvement of roads.

Austrian Netherlands, Italy, Spain, and large parts of Germany and Poland. The instrument of these victories was the massive citizen army that Napoleon assembled. Building on the *levée en masse* of 1793, which he supplemented with soldiers from the countries he conquered, Napoleon had more than one million men under arms by 1812. More than three times the size of Louis XIV's army in 1700, it was the largest military force raised under the control of one man up to this time in European history.

These troops engaged in a military offensive that was more massive, wide-ranging, and sustained than Alexander the Great's invasion of Egypt, Persia, and northern India between 334 and 326 B.C.E. Napoleon's invasion began with the great victories against Austria and Prussia in 1797. Two years later, shortly after Napoleon had become first consul, he directed his army to further military successes that paved the way to French dominance of Europe. The defeat of Austria in 1800 confirmed earlier territorial gains in Italy as well as French control over the southern Netherlands, now called Belgium. With Austria defeated and Russia involved with the Ottoman Turks, France and Britain concluded peace at Amiens in 1802. This peace gave Napoleon free rein to reorganize the countries that bordered on France's eastern and southeastern boundaries. In Italy he named himself the president of the newly established Cisalpine Republic, and he transformed the cantons of Switzerland into the Helvetic Republic. These acquisitions gave substance to the title of emperor that he assumed in 1804, because now he controlled many different kingdoms. France had not had an emperor since the ninth century, when Charlemagne and his heirs had ruled as Roman emperors, and Napoleon's territories were more extensive than those under Charlemagne's jurisdiction.

These stunning military successes as well as those that were to follow have secured Napoleon's reputation as one of the most brilliant and successful military leaders in modern history. The reasons for that reputation are a matter of some controversy. Napoleon made terrible strategic blunders in many of his campaigns and tactical mistakes in many of his battles. Somehow he seemed to make up for these mistakes by his careful planning, unbounded energy, and decisive moves. He spent hours studying his opponents' position beforehand but made quick decisions once the battle had begun. "Everything," he once said, "is in the execution." The combination of infantry, artillery, and cavalry in the same units or *corps* allowed him to move these forces easily on the battlefield. He struck quickly, usually at the center of enemy lines, using superior numbers to overwhelm his opponent. Attacks on enemy lines of communication often prevented his opponents from calling up reinforcements. Once they began their retreat, he would pursue them rather than stop to celebrate. In his campaigns he benefited from the loyalty of his troops and the ideological zeal that continued to inspire them, even as his wars lost their ideological purpose of exporting the ideals of the revolution.

Napoleon was far less successful at sea than on land. With no real experience in naval warfare, he could not match the dominance of the British navy, which retained its mastery of the seas throughout the entire revolutionary period. Only in the West Indies, where Britain was never able to send sufficient naval forces, did the French navy manage to hold its own. This naval weakness also explains Napoleon's failure to build or regain an overseas empire. His expedition to Egypt in 1798, which was dominated by dreams of colonial conquest in the Middle East and South Asia, was checked by the British destruction of the French fleet at the Battle of the Nile. In the Western Hemisphere financial problems and a false hope of limiting British power induced Napoleon to sell the vast North American territory of Louisiana, which he had regained from Spain in 1800, to the United States in 1803. The following year the French Caribbean colony of St. Domingue became independent as the result of the violent revolution staged by free blacks and slaves, as discussed in Chapter 17. Informed of that loss, Napoleon shouted "Damn sugar, damn coffee, damn colonies!"

The most significant French naval defeat came in 1805, shortly after Britain, Austria, and Russia had formed the Third Coalition against France. As Napoleon was preparing for an invasion of Britain from northern French ports, the British navy, under the command of the diminutive, one-eyed Admiral Horatio Nelson, won one of the most decisive battles in the history of naval warfare. Nelson broke the line of a Franco-Spanish fleet that was preparing to strike off the Cape of Trafalgar near Gibraltar. The British destroyed or captured half the enemy ships, thus breaking the back of French sea power. The battle is commemorated at Trafalgar Square in London, which is overlooked by a towering statue of Nelson, who died of wounds inflicted during the battle. Nelson might have survived if he had not insisted on wearing glimmering medals on his uniform, thereby attracting the notice of French marksmen.

The monumental naval defeat at Trafalgar did not prevent Napoleon from continuing his wars of conquest in central Europe. In October 1805 he defeated an Austrian army at Ulm, and in December of that year he overwhelmed the combined forces of Austria and Russia at Austerlitz. These victories brought him new German and Italian territory, which he ceded to some of the larger German states; the smaller German states became satellites of France and fought with him until the collapse of his empire. A defeat of Prussian forces at Jena and Auerstädt in 1806 and the subsequent occupation of Berlin gave him the opportunity to carve the new German kingdom of Westphalia out of Prussian territory in the Rhineland and to install his brother Jerome as its ruler. In the East he created the duchy of Warsaw out of Polish lands controlled by Prussia. In 1806

The French Encounter the Egyptians, 1798–1801

Napoleon's expedition to Egypt in 1798 marked one of the few times during the revolutionary period that the French came in direct contact with non-Western peoples. The expedition resulted in the military occupation of the country for three years and set the stage for the first extensive encounters between Egyptians and Europeans since the Ottoman conquest of Egypt in the sixteenth century. At that time Egypt had become a semiautonomous province of the Ottoman Empire and had very little contact with the West. Egypt's isolation from the West meant that it had little exposure to the scientific and technological discoveries that had taken place in western Europe during the previous 300 years.

In addition to 38,000 soldiers, Napoleon brought with him 165 scholars who were organized in a Commission of Science and Arts. These men came from virtually every branch of learning: surveyors, cartographers, civil engineers, architects, botanists, physicians, chemists, and mineralogists. The commission also included artists, archaeologists, writers, and musicians. Their purpose was to give Napoleon information on the people and the resources of the country so that he could more easily subject it to French domination. A small group of these scholars set up an Institute of Egypt, whose mission was to propagate the Enlightenment and to undertake research on the history, people, and the economy of the country. This involved the scholarly study of Egyptian antiquities, including the pyramids.

This work of the institute ushered in a long period in which many artifacts of Egyptian antiquity were taken from the country and transported to European museums and palaces. Members of the institute encouraged this cultural plundering, arguing that their addition to the collections of the Louvre would embellish the glory of France. This plundering of native Egyptian antiquities represented a form of cultural imperialism that continued unabated during the nineteenth century.

Cultural imperialism of a different sort can be found in a widely disseminated description of Egypt, *Travels in Upper and Lower Egypt* (1802), by a member of the institute, Dominique Vivant-Denon. This two-volume work contained extensive descriptions of the different "races" of people in Egypt whom the expedition encountered in the thriving port town of Rosetta. Vivant-Denon described the Copts, the most ancient Egyptians, as "swarthy Nubians" with flat foreheads, high cheekbones, and short broad noses. They displayed the moral qualities of "ignorance, drunkenness, cunning, and finesse." The Arabs, who were the most numerous group, and the Turks had more appealing physical and personal characteristics, although they were often reduced to the "degraded state of animals."

Expressions of French cultural superiority permeate other contemporary accounts of Napoleon's expedition. A multivolume work, *The Description of Egypt,* claimed that Napoleon wanted to procure for Egyptians "all the advantages of a perfected civilization." It praised him for bringing modern knowledge to a country that had been "plunged into darkness." These attitudes provided a justification for the subsequent economic exploitation of Egypt, first by the French and later by the British, during the nineteenth century.

For Discussion

In what ways did Vivant-Denon's work reflect the values that were cultivated during the Enlightenment?

Jean Charles Tardieu, *The French Army Halts at Syene, Upper Egypt, on February 2, 1799*
This painting depicts a cultural encounter between French soldiers and Egyptians in the city of Syene (now Aswan) during the Egyptian campaign of 1798–1799. The soldiers are scribbling on the ruins of ancient Egypt, indicating a lack of respect for Egyptian culture.

Map 19.1 The Empire of Napoleon in 1812

By establishing dependent states in Spain, Italy, Germany, and Poland, France controlled far more territory than the areas technically within the French Empire.

he formally dissolved the ancient Holy Roman Empire and replaced it with a loose association of sixteen German states known as the Confederation of the Rhine. By 1807, in the words of one historian, Napoleon had "only allies and victims" on the Continent (see Map 19.1).

Napoleon inserted the last piece in this imperial puzzle by invading and occupying the kingdom of Spain in 1808. This campaign began as an effort to crush Portugal, the ally of Britain, which he was never able to defeat. In May 1808, as French armies marched through Spain en route to Lisbon, the Portuguese capital, a popular insurrection against Spanish rule occurred in Madrid. This spontaneous revolt, which led to the abdication of King Charles IV and the succession of his son Ferdinand VII, was the first of many developments that caused the collapse of the Spanish Empire in America. In Europe it led to the absorption of Spain into the French Empire. Sensing that he could easily add one more territory to his list of conquests, Napoleon forced Ferdinand to abdicate and summoned his own brother, Joseph Bonaparte, who was then ruling the dependent kingdom of Naples, to become king of Spain.

Joseph instituted some reforms in Spain, but the abolition of the Spanish Inquisition and the closing of two-thirds of the Spanish convents triggered a visceral reaction from the Spanish clergy and the general populace. Fighting for Church and king, small bands of local guerillas subjected French forces to intermittent and effective sabotage. An invasion by British forces under the command of Arthur Wellesley, later the Duke of Wellington (1769–1852), in what has become known as the Peninsula War (1808–1813), strengthened Spanish and Portuguese resistance.

The reception of the French in Spain revealed that the export of revolution, which had begun with the French armies of 1792, was a double-edged sword. The overthrow of authoritarian regimes in other European states won the support of progressive, capitalist, and anticlerical forces in those countries, but it also triggered deep resentment against French rule. The ideology of nationalism in Germany and Italy arose more because of a reaction against French rule than because the armies of France had tried to stimulate it. In Italy during the 1790s young educated *patrioti*, imbued with enthusiasm for liberty, equality, and progress, supported the newly proclaimed republics and envisioned the establishment of a single Italian state, at least in the north of Italy. By the middle of the Napoleonic years that vision had changed. Many of the *patrioti* had become disillusioned and joined secret societies to press for further political and social change and to plot insurrections against the new republics.

In Germany many of those who supported the French cause during the early years of the Republic turned away from it during Napoleon's wars of expansion. In 1809 a German student who attempted to assassinate Napoleon shouted "Long live Germany!" at his execution. In 1813 the German writer Johann Gottlieb Fichte (1762–1814) appealed to the German nation to resist Napoleon in order to regain their liberty. For all his political astuteness, Napoleon could not comprehend that his own policies were responsible for the growth of this reactive sentiment, which formed one of the foundations of nineteenth-century nationalism. We shall discuss this topic more fully in Chapter 21.

The Downfall of Napoleon

The turning point in Napoleon's personal fortunes and those of his empire came in 1810. After securing an annulment of his marriage to Josephine in late 1809, he married Marie-Louise, the daughter of the Habsburg emperor. This marriage, which the following year produced a son and heir to the throne, should have made the French Empire more secure, but it had the opposite effect. For the first time during his rule, dissent from both the right and the left became widespread. Despite the most stringent efforts at censorship, royalist and Jacobin literature poured off the presses. The number of military deserters and those evading conscription increased. Relations with the papacy reached a breaking point when Napoleon annexed the Papal States, at which point Pope Pius VII, who had negotiated the Concordat of 1801, excommunicated him.

Dissent at home had the effect of driving the megalomaniacal emperor to seek more glory and further conquests. In this frame of mind Napoleon made the ill-advised decision to invade Russia. The motives for engaging in this overly ambitious military campaign were not completely irrational. Victory over Russia promised to give France control of the Black Sea, and that in turn would ultimately lead to the control of Constantinople and the entire Middle East. More immediately, defeating Russia would be necessary to enforce the French blockade of British goods, which Russia had refused to support.

The problem with a Russian invasion was that it stretched Napoleon's lines of communication too far and his resources too thin, despite the support of the Austrians and Prussians whom he had defeated. Even before the inva-

Francisco Goya, *The Third of May 1808*
This painting of the suppression of the popular revolt in Madrid in 1808 captures the brutality of the French occupation of Spain. A French unit executes Spanish citizens, including a monk in the foreground. Goya was a figure of the Enlightenment and a Spanish patriot.

VIDEO
The Art of Francisco Goya

sion it was becoming increasingly difficult to feed, equip, and train the huge army he had assembled. The Grand Army that crossed from Poland into Russia in 1812 was not the efficient military force that Napoleon had commanded in the early years of the empire. Many of his best soldiers were fighting in the guerilla war in Spain. Casualties and desertions had forced Napoleon to call up new recruits who were not properly trained. Half the army, moreover, had been recruited from the population of conquered countries, making their loyalty to Napoleon uncertain.

The tactics of the Russians contributed to the failure of the invasion. Instead of engaging the Grand Army in combat, the Russian army kept retreating, pulling Napoleon further east toward Moscow. On September 7 the two armies clashed at Borodino, suffering a staggering 77,000 casualties in all. The Russian army then continued its retreat eastward. When Napoleon reached Moscow he found it deserted, and fires deliberately set by Muscovites had destroyed more than two-thirds of the city. Napoleon, facing the onset of a dreaded Russian winter and rapidly diminishing supplies, began the long retreat back to France. Skirmishes with the Russians along the way, which cost him 25,000 lives just crossing the Beresina River, conspired with the cold and hunger to destroy his army. During the entire Russian campaign his army lost a total of 380,000 men to death, imprisonment, or desertion. In the midst of this horror Napoleon, oblivious to the suffering of his troops, reported back to Paris, "The health of the emperor has never been better."

Not to be discouraged, Napoleon soon began preparing for further conquests. Once again his enemies formed a coalition against him, pledging to restore the independence of the countries that had become his satellites or dependents. Napoleon scored a few victories in the late summer of 1813, but in October allied forces inflicted a crushing defeat on him in the Battle of the Nations at Leipzig. Austrian troops administered another blow to the French in northern Italy, and the British finally drove them out of Spain. As a result of these defeats, Napoleon's army was pushed back into France. A massive allied force advanced into Paris and occupied the city. After extensive political maneuvering, including a vote by the Senate to depose Napoleon, the emperor abdicated on April 6, 1814. The allies promptly exiled him to the Mediterranean island of Elba. As he made the journey to the coast, crowds surrounding his coach shouted "Down with the tyrant!" while some villagers hanged him in effigy.

This course of events led to the restoration of the Bourbon monarchy. By the terms of the first Treaty of Paris of May 1814, the allies restored the brother of Louis XVI, the Count of Provence, to the French throne as Louis XVIII (r. 1814–1824). Louis was an implacable foe of the revolution, and much of what he did was intended to undermine its achievements. The white Bourbon flag replaced the revolutionary tricolor. Catholicism was once again recognized as the state religion. Exiled royalists returned to their high-ranking positions in the army. Nonetheless, Louis accepted a Constitutional Charter that incorporated many of the changes made between 1789 and 1791. Representative government, with a relatively limited franchise, replaced the absolutism of the Old Regime. Equality before the law, freedom of religion, and freedom of expression were all reaffirmed. Even more important, the powers of the state that the National Assembly and the Directory had extended and Napoleon had enhanced were maintained. The administrative division of France into departments continued, and the Napoleonic Code remained in force. France had experienced a counterrevolution in 1814, but it did not simply turn the political clock back to 1788. Some of the political achievements of the previous twenty-five years were indeed preserved.

Despite his disgrace and exile, Napoleon still commanded loyalty from his troops and from large segments of the population. While in power he had constructed a legend that drew on strong patriotic sentiment. Supporters throughout France continued to promote his cause in the same way that royalists had maintained that of the Bourbon monarchy since 1792. The Napoleonic legend held great appeal among the lower classes, who were persuaded that Napoleon, the patriot and the savior of the revolution, had made it possible for every Frenchman to achieve wealth and fame. The strength of the Napoleonic legend became apparent in March 1815, when Napoleon escaped from Elba and landed in southern France. Promising to rid the country of the exiled royalists who had returned and to save the revolutionary cause that he claimed had been abandoned, he won over peasants, workers, and soldiers. Regiment after regiment joined him as he marched toward Paris. By the time he arrived, Louis XVIII had gone into exile once again, and Napoleon found himself back in power.

CHRONOLOGY

The Downfall of Napoleon, 1807–1815

1807
November–December	French military intervention in Spain and Portugal begins

1808
| May | Beginning of the Spanish rebellion |
| July 20 | Joseph Bonaparte appointed king of Spain |

1809
| December 15 | Annulment of marriage of Napoleon and Empress Josephine |

1810
| April 2 | Marriage of Napoleon to Marie-Louise |

1812
September 7	Battle of Borodino
September 14	Napoleon enters Moscow
October	Retreat from Moscow begins

1813
| October 16–19 | Battle of the Nations at Leipzig |

1814
April 6	Abdication of Napoleon
May 30	First Treaty of Paris
September	Congress of Vienna assembles

1815
March	Napoleon escapes from Elba
June 18	Battle of Waterloo
November 20	Second Treaty of Paris

But not for long. The allied European powers quickly began to assemble yet another coalition. Fearing that the allies would launch a massive invasion of France, Napoleon decided to strike first. He marched an army of 200,000 men into the Austrian Netherlands, where the allies responded by amassing 700,000 troops. Near the small village of Waterloo, south of Brussels, he met the British forces of the Duke of Wellington, who had turned the tide against him during the Peninsula War. Reinforced by Prussian troops, Wellington inflicted a devastating defeat on the French army, which lost 28,000 men and went into a full-scale retreat. Napoleon, captured in the battle, abdicated once again. He was

DOCUMENT

Napoleon's Exile to St. Helena (1815)

exiled to the remote South Atlantic island of St. Helena, from which escape was impossible. He died there in 1821.

Even before the battle of Waterloo, the major powers of Europe had gathered in Vienna to redraw the boundaries of the European states that had been created, dismembered, or transformed during the preceding twenty-five years (see Map 19.2). Under the leadership of the Austrian foreign minister, Prince Clemens von Metternich (1773–1859), this conference, known as the Congress of Vienna°, worked out a settlement that was intended to preserve the balance of power in Europe and at the same time uphold the principle of dynastic legitimacy. By the terms of a separate Treaty of Paris (the second in two years) the boundaries of France

Map 19.2 Europe After the Congress of Vienna, 1815

The four most important territorial changes that took place in 1815 were the scaling back of the boundaries of France to their status in 1790, the Austrian acquisition of territory in western and northeastern Italy, the establishment of the new kingdom of the Netherlands, and the formation of the new German Confederation.

were scaled back to what they had been in 1790, before it had begun its wars of expansion. To create a buffer state on the northern boundary of France, the Congress annexed the Austrian Netherlands to the Dutch Republic, which now became the kingdom of the Netherlands with William I, a prince of the House of Orange, as its king. Territory along the Rhineland in the state of Westphalia was ceded to Prussia, while Austria gained territory in Italy, both along the French border in the west and in northern Italy to the east. In place of the defunct Holy Roman Empire, the Congress established a new German Confederation, a loose coalition of thirty-nine separate territories with a weak legislative assembly, whose members were appointed and instructed by their governments. The five major powers that had drawn this new map of Europe—Britain, Austria, Prussia, Russia, and France—agreed to meet annually to prevent any one country, especially France but also Russia, from achieving military dominance of the European Continent.

The Legacy of the French Revolution

■ What did the French Revolution ultimately achieve and in what ways did it change the course of European and Western history?

With the conclusion of the Congress of Vienna a tumultuous period of European and Western history finally came to an end. Not only had France experienced a revolution, but every country in Europe and America had felt its effects. Governments were toppled in countries as far apart as Poland and Peru. Added to this turbulence was the experience of incessant warfare. France was at war for more than twenty years during the period of the Republic and the empire, and it had brought almost all European powers into the struggle. With armies constantly in need of provisions and supplies, high taxation, galloping inflation, and food shortages inflicted economic hardship on a large portion of the European population.

The cost of all this instability and warfare in terms of human life was staggering. Within the space of one generation almost two million European soldiers were killed in action, wasted by disease, or starved or frozen to death. In France alone just under 500,000 soldiers died during the revolutionary wars of 1792–1802 and another 916,000 during the wars of the empire. Internal political disturbances took the lives of hundreds of thousands of civilians from all ranks of society, not only in France but throughout Europe. The violence was fed at all levels by unprecedented fears of internal and external subversion. Government officials, col-

laborators, counterrevolutionaries, and imagined enemies of the state were all executed. This spate of violence and death—much of it in the name of liberty—was inflicted almost entirely by the state or its enemies.

What was achieved at this extraordinary price? How did the France of 1815 differ from the France of 1788? What on balance had changed? For many years historians, especially those who believed that economic forces determined the course of history, claimed that as a result of the revolution the bourgeoisie, composed of merchants, manufacturers, and other commoners of substantial wealth, had replaced the nobility as the dominant social and political class in the country. The bourgeoisie, so they argued, had started the revolution in order to acquire political power that was commensurate with their economic power, and they had ultimately prevailed.

This assessment can no longer be sustained. The nobility certainly lost many of their privileges in 1789, and many of them went into exile during the revolutionary period, but the position they had in French society in 1815 did not differ greatly from what it had been under the Old Regime. In both periods there was considerable blurring of the distinctions between nobility and bourgeoisie. Nor did the revolutionary period witness the emergence of a new class of industrial entrepreneurs. The only group who definitely profited from the revolution in the long run were men of property, regardless of their membership in any social category or "class." Men of property emerged triumphant in the Directory, found favor during the Napoleonic period, and became the most important members of political society after the monarchy was restored.

It would be difficult to argue that *women* of any social rank benefited from the revolution. During the early years of the revolution, women participated actively in public life. They were involved in many demonstrations in Paris, including the storming of the Bastille and the march to Versailles to pressure the king to move to Paris. Women as well as men filled the ranks of the *sans-culottes*, and women donned their own female version of nonaristocratic dress. During the early years of the revolution, many women joined patriotic clubs, such as the Club of Knitters or the unisex Fraternal Society of Patriots of Both Sexes. In 1790 the Marquis de Condorcet published *On the Admission of Women to the Rights of Citizenship*, and the following year Olympe de Gouges published *The Rights of Women*, in which she called for the granting of women's equal rights. Both of these advocates of women's rights had been influenced by Enlightenment thought, as we have discussed in Chapter 18.

The goal advanced by Condorcet and de Gouges was not to be realized. The radical Jacobins dealt it a terrible setback when they banned all women's clubs and societies on the grounds that their participation in public life would harm the institution of the family. This action, coupled with the imprisonment and death of both de Gouges and Condorcet during the Terror, signaled an end to the extensive participation of women in political life, which had begun during the eighteenth century, especially in the salons. During the nineteenth century women were generally considered to occupy a separate sphere of activity from that of men. They were expected to exercise influence in the private sphere of the home, but not in the public sphere of politics. As we shall discuss in Chapter 20, the changes wrought by the Industrial Revolution reinforced this segregation of men and women by excluding many married women from the workforce.

It is even more difficult to identify permanent economic changes as a result of the revolution. The elimination of the remnants of feudalism may have made France marginally more capitalist than it had been before the revolution, but agricultural and mercantile capitalism had long been entrenched in French society. Nor did the Continental System, the blockade of British goods from all European ports initiated in 1806, allow French industry to catch up with that of Great Britain. Whatever economic gains were made under the protective shield of the state were offset by the adverse economic effects of twenty-two years of nearly continuous warfare. In the long run the revolutionary period delayed the process of industrialization that had entered its preliminary stages in France during the 1780s and retarded the growth of the French economy for the remainder of the nineteenth century.

The permanent legacy of the French Revolution lies in the realm of politics. First, the period from 1789 to 1815 triggered an enormous growth in the competence and power of the state. This trend had begun before the revolution, but the desire of the revolutionaries to transform every aspect of human life in the service of the revolution, coupled with the necessity of utilizing all the country's resources in the war effort, gave the state more control over the everyday life of its citizens than ever before. Fifteen years of Napoleonic rule only accentuated this trend, and after 1815 many of those powers remained with the government.

An even more significant and permanent achievement of the French Revolution was the promotion of the doctrine of popular sovereignty. The belief that the people constituted the highest political authority in the state became so entrenched during the revolution that it could never be completely suppressed, either in France or in the other countries of Europe. Napoleon recognized its power when he asked the people to approve political changes he had already made by his own authority. He also arranged for such plebiscites to secure approval of the new states he had set up in Europe. After the restoration of the monarchy the doctrine of popular sovereignty was promoted mainly by the press, which continued to employ the new revolutionary rhetoric to keep alive the high ideals and aspirations of the revolution. The doctrine also contributed to the forma-

tion of two nineteenth-century ideologies, liberalism and nationalism, which will be discussed in Chapter 21.

The third permanent political change was the active participation of the citizens in the political life of the nation. This participation had been cultivated during the early years of the revolution, and it had been accompanied by the creation of a new political culture. Much of that culture was suppressed during the Napoleonic period, but the actual habit of participating in politics was not. The franchise was gradually expanded in Europe during the nineteenth century. The press spread political ideas to a large segment of the population. People from all walks of life participated in marches, processions, and demonstrations. All of this followed from the acceptance of the French revolutionary doctrine that the people are sovereign and have a right therefore to participate in the political life of the state.

Conclusion

The French Revolution and Western Civilization

The French Revolution was a central event in the history of the West. It began as an internal French affair, reflecting the social and political tensions of the Old Regime, but it soon became a turning point in European and Western history. Proclamations of the natural rights of humanity gave the ideals of the revolution widespread appeal, and a period of protracted warfare succeeded in disseminating those ideals outside the boundaries of France.

Underlying the export of French revolutionary ideology was the belief that France had become the standard-bearer of Western civilization. French people believed they were *la grande nation,* the country that had reached the highest level of political and social organization. They did not believe they had acquired this exalted status by inheritance. Unlike the English revolutionaries of the seventeenth century, they did not claim that they were the heirs of a medieval constitution. French republicans of the 1790s attributed none of their national preeminence to the monarchy, whose memory they took drastic steps to erase. They considered the secular political culture that emerged during the French Revolution to be an entirely novel development.

The export of French revolutionary political culture during the Republic and the empire brought about widespread changes in the established order. Regimes were toppled, French puppets acquired political power, boundaries of states were completely redrawn, and traditional authorities were challenged. Liberal reforms were enacted, new constitutions were written, and new law codes were promulgated. The Europe of 1815 could not be mistaken for the Europe of 1789.

The ideas of the French Revolution, like those of the Enlightenment that had helped to inspire them, did not go unchallenged. From the very early years of the revolution they encountered determined opposition, both in France and abroad. As the revolution lost its appeal in France, the forces of conservatism and reaction gathered strength. At the end of the Napoleonic period, the Congress of Vienna took steps to restore the legitimate rulers of European states and to prevent revolution from recurring. It appeared that the revolution would be completely reversed, but that was not the case. The ideas born of the revolution would continue to inspire demands for political reform in Europe during the nineteenth century, and those demands, just like those in the 1790s, would meet with fierce resistance.

Suggestions for Further Reading

For a comprehensive listing of suggested readings, please go to www.ablongman.com/levack2e/chapter19

Andress, David. *The French Revolution and the People.* 2004. Focuses on the role played by the common people of France—the peasants, craftsmen and those living on the margins of society—in the revolution.

Blanning, T. C. W. *The French Revolutionary Wars, 1787–1802.* 1996. An authoritative political and military narrative that assesses the impact of the wars on French politics.

Chartier, Roger. *The Cultural Origins of the French Revolution.* 1991. Explores the connections between the culture of the Enlightenment and the cultural transformations of the revolutionary period.

Cobban, Alfred. *The Social Interpretation of the French Revolution.* 1964. Challenges the Marxist interpretation of the causes and effects of the revolution.

Doyle, William. *The Oxford History of the French Revolution.* 1989. An excellent synthesis.

Ellis, Geoffrey. *Napoleon.* 1997. A study of the nature and mechanics of Napoleon's power and an analysis of his imperial policy.

Furet, François. *The French Revolution, 1770–1814.* 1992. A provocative narrative that sees Napoleon as the architect of a second, authoritarian revolution that reversed the gains of the first.

Hardman, John. *Louis XVI: The Silent King.* 2000. A reassessment of the king that mixes sympathy with criticism.

Higonnet, Patrice. *Goodness Beyond Virtue: Jacobins During the French Revolution.* 1998. Explores the contradictions of Jacobin ideology and its descent into the Terror.

Hunt, Lynn. *Politics, Culture and Class in the French Revolution.* 1984. Analyzes the formation of a revolutionary political culture.

Kennedy, Emmet. *The Culture of the French Revolution.* 1989. A comprehensive study of all cultural developments before and during the revolution.

Landes, Joan B. *Women and the Public Sphere in the Age of the French Revolution.* 1988. Explores how the new political culture of the revolution changed the position of women in society.

Lefebvre, Georges. *The Great Fear of 1789: Rural Panic in Revolutionary France.* 1973. Shows the importance of the rural unrest of July 1789 that provided the backdrop of the legislation of August 1789.

Schama, Simon. *Citizens: A Chronicle of the French Revolution.* 1989. Depicts the tragic unraveling of a vision of liberty and happiness into a scenario of hunger, anger, violence, and death.

Notes

1. Emmanuel-Joseph Sieyès, *What Is the Third Estate?* (1789).

2. H. Wallon, *Histoire du tribunal révolutionnaire de Paris* (1880–1882), Vol. 4, 511.

Glossary

Credits

Index

Glossary

absolutism (p. 478) A form of government in the seventeenth and eighteenth centuries in which the ruler possessed complete and unrivalled power.

agrarian capitalism (p. 404) A form of economic organization characteristic of European colonialism in which Europeans organized the production of certain kinds of commercial crops (such as sugar, tobacco, and indigo) on land expropriated from native peoples and with slave labor.

alchemy (p. 518) A form of learned magic that was intended to turn base metals into precious ones.

aldeias (p. 396) Settlements for natives who had converted to Christianity in Brazil. In these settlements the Jesuit fathers protected the natives from enslavement.

Anabaptism (p. 425) Meaning "to rebaptize"; refers to those Protestant radicals of the sixteenth century who rejected infant baptism and adopted adult baptism. Anabaptists treated the Bible as a blueprint for reforming not just the church but all of society, a tendency that led them to reject the authority of the state, to live in self-governing "holy communities," and in some cases to practice a primitive form of communism.

aristocracy (p. 576) A term that originally applied to those who were considered the most fit to rule and later identified the wealthiest members of society, especially those who owned land.

auto-da-fé (p. 451) Meaning literally a "theater of faith," an *auto* was practiced by the Catholic Church in early modern Spain and Portugal as an extended public ritual of penance designed to cause physical pain among the sinful and promote fear of God's judgment among those who witnessed it.

Babylonian Captivity of the Church (p. 329) Between 1305 and 1378 seven consecutive popes voluntarily chose to reside in Avignon, France, in order to escape anarchy in the streets of Rome. During this period the popes became subservient to the kings of France.

balance of power (p. 487) An arrangement in which various countries form alliances to prevent any one state from dominating the others.

baroque (p. 483) A dynamic style in art, architecture, and music intended to elicit an emotional response. It was closely associated with royal absolutism in the seventeenth century.

boers (p. 548) Dutch farmers in the colony established by the Dutch Republic in South Africa.

bourgeoisie (p. 583) A social group, technically consisting of those who were burghers in the towns, that included prosperous merchants and financiers, members of the professions, and some skilled craftsmen known as "petty bourgeoisie."

bubonic plague (p. 310) An epidemic disease spread from rats to humans via flea bites. The infection enters the bloodstream, causing inflamed swellings called buboes (hence, "bubonic" plague) in the glands of the groin or armpit, internal bleeding, and discoloration. Although disputed by some, most experts consider bubonic plague the cause of the Black Death, which killed at least one-third of the population of Europe between 1348 and the early 1350s. Bubonic plague reappeared recurrently in the West between 1348 and 1721.

calling (p. 423) The Calvinist doctrine that God calls the Elect to perform his will on earth. God's calling gave Calvinists a powerful sense of personal direction.

caravels (p. 381) Hybrid three-masted ships developed about 1450 in the Iberian peninsula by combining the rigging of square with triangular lateen sails. These ships could be sailed in a variety of winds, carry large cargoes, be managed by a small crew, and be defended by guns mounted in the castle superstructure.

Carnival (p. 455) The most popular annual festival in much of Europe before modern times. Also known as Mardi Gras, the festival took place for several days or even weeks before the beginning of Lent and included all kinds of fun and games.

Catholic Reformation (p. 430) A series of efforts during the sixteenth century to purify the Church that evolved out of late medieval spirituality and that included the creation of new religious orders, especially the Society of Jesus.

chinoiserie (p. 564) A French word for an eighteenth-century decorative art that combined Chinese and European motifs.

Christian humanists (p. 413) During the fifteenth and sixteenth centuries these experts in Greek, Latin, and Hebrew subjected the Bible to philological study in an attempt to understand the precise meaning of the founding text of Christianity.

civic humanism (p. 356) A branch of humanism introduced by the Florentine chancellor Leonardo Bruni who defended the republican institutions and values of the city. Civic humanism promoted the ethic of responsible citizenship.

class (p. 578) A large and often cohesive social group that was conscious of its shared economic and political interests.

classicism (p. 580) A style in art, architecture, music, and literature that emphasizes proportion, adherence to traditional forms, and a rejection of emotion and enthusiasm.

colons (p. 568) White planters in the French Caribbean colony of Saint Domingue (Haiti).

Columbian exchange (p. 400) The trade of peoples, plants, animals, microbes, and ideas between the Old and New Worlds that began with Columbus.

Columbian question (p. 402) The debate among historians and epidemiologists about whether syphilis or its ancestor disease originated in the Americas and was brought to the Old World after Columbus's voyages.

Conciliar Movement (p. 330) A fifteenth-century movement that advocated ending the Great Schism and reforming church government by calling a general meeting or council of the bishops, who would exercise authority over the rival popes.

Confessions (p. 450) The formal sixteenth-century statements of religious doctrine: the Confession of Augsburg for Lutherans, the Helvetic Confessions for Calvinists, the Thirty-Nine Articles for Anglicans, and the decrees of the Council of Trent for Catholics.

Congress of Vienna (p. 638) A conference of the major powers of Europe in 1814–1815 to establish a new balance of power at the end of the Napoleonic Wars.

conquistadores (p. 388) Spanish adventurers in the Americas who explored and conquered the lands of indigenous peoples, sometimes without legal authority but usually with a legal privilege granted by the king of Spain who required that one-fifth of all things of value be turned over to the crown. The conquistadores extended Spanish sovereignty over new lands.

cosmology (p. 514) A theory concerning the structure and nature of the universe such as those proposed by Aristotle in the fourth century B.C.E. and Copernicus in the sixteenth century.

creoles (p. 548) People of Spanish descent who had been born in Spanish America.

cultural relativism (p. 404) A mode of thought first explored during the sixteenth century to explain why the peoples of the New World did not appear in the Bible. Cultural relativism recognized that many (but not necessarily all) standards of judgment are specific to particular cultures rather than the fixed truths established by natural or divine law.

de-Christianization (p. 625) A program inaugurated in France in 1793 by the radical Jacobin and former priest Joseph Fouché that closed churches, eliminated religious symbols, and attempted to establish a purely civic religion.

deduction (p. 521) The logical process by which ideas and laws are derived from basic truths or principles.

deists (p. 529) Seventeenth- and eighteenth-century thinkers who believed that God created the universe and established immutable laws of nature but did not subsequently intervene in the operation of nature or in human affairs.

demonic magic (p. 531) The invocation of evil spirits with the goal of utilizing their supernatural powers to change the course of nature or to alter human behavior.

dualistic (p. 522) A term used to describe a philosophy, such as that of René Descartes, in which a rigid distinction is made between body and mind or between the material and the immaterial world.

Dutch Revolt (p. 466) The rebellion against Spanish rule of the seven northern provinces of the Netherlands between 1579 and 1648, which resulted in the independence of the Republic of the United Provinces.

Edict of Nantes (p. 463) Promulgated by King Henry IV in 1598, the edict allowed the Huguenots to build a quasi-independent state within the kingdom of France, giving them the right to have their own troops, church organization, and political autonomy within their walled towns, but banning them from the royal court and the city of Paris. King Louis XIV revoked the edict in 1685.

empires (p. 542) Large political formations consisting of different kingdoms or territories outside the boundaries of the states that control them.

encomienda (p. 391) The basic form of economic and social organization in early Spanish America, based on a royal grant awarded to a Spaniard for military or other services that gave the grantee and his successors the right to gather tribute from the Indians in a defined area.

enlightened despots (p. 600) The term assigned to absolute monarchs who initiated a series of legal and political reforms in an effort to realize the goals of the Enlightenment.

Enlightenment (p. 585) An international intellectual movement of the eighteenth century that emphasized the use of reason and the application of the laws of nature to human society.

factories (p. 544) Trading posts established by European powers in foreign lands.

fanatic (p. 460) Originally referring to someone possessed by a demon, a fanatic came during the sixteenth century to mean a person who expressed immoderate enthusiasm in religious matters or who pursued a supposedly divine mission, often to violent ends.

federalists (p. 617) The name assigned by radical Jacobins to provincial rebels who opposed the centralization of the state during the French Revolution.

franchise (p. 602) The right to vote; also called suffrage.

freemasons (p. 598) Members of secret societies of men and women that flourished during the Enlightenment, dedicated to the creation of a society based on reason and virtue and committed to the principles of liberty and equality.

French Wars of Religion (p. 461) A series of political assassinations, massacres, and military engagements between French Catholics and Calvinists from 1560 to 1598.

Girondins (p. 616) The more conservative members of the Jacobin party who favored greater economic freedom and opposed further centralization of state power during the French Revolution.

Great Schism (p. 329) The division of the Catholic Church (1378–1417) between rival Italian and French claimants to the papal throne.

guilds (p. 319) Professional associations devoted to protecting the special interests of a particular trade or craft and to monopolizing production and trade in the goods the guild produced.

haciendas (p. 391) Large landed estates that began to be established in the seventeenth century replaced encomiendas throughout much of Spanish America.

Huguenots (p. 461) The term for French Calvinists, who constituted some 10 percent of the population by 1560.

humanists (p. 365) During the Renaissance humanists were writers and orators who studied Latin and sometimes Greek texts on grammar, rhetoric, poetry, history, and ethics.

Hundred Years' War (p. 321) Refers to a series of engagements (1337–1453) between England and France over England's attempts to assert its claims to territories in France.

Ideologues (p. 631) A group of liberal writers and philosophers in France who objected to Napoleon's religious policy on the grounds that it would inaugurate a return of religious superstition.

induction (p. 521) The mental process by which theories are established only after the systematic accumulation of large amounts of data.

indulgences (p. 329) Certificates that allowed penitents to atone for their sins and reduce their time in purgatory. Usually these were issued for going on a pilgrimage or performing a pious act, but during the Babylonian Captivity of the Church (1305–1378) popes began to sell them, a practice Martin Luther protested in 1517 in an act that brought on the Protestant Reformation.

intendants (p. 481) French royal officials who became the main agents of French provincial administration in the seventeenth century.

Jacobins (p. 614) A French political party supporting a democratic republic that found support in political clubs throughout the country and dominated the National Convention from 1792 until 1794.

Junkers (p. 493) The traditional nobility of Prussia.

justification by faith alone (p. 415) Refers to Martin Luther's insight that humanity is incapable of performing enough religious good works to earn eternal salvation. Salvation is an unmerited gift from God called grace. Those who receive grace are called the Elect.

linear perspective (p. 361) In the arts the use of geometrical principles to depict a three-dimensional space on a flat, two-dimensional surface.

magic (p. 457) Learned opinion described two kinds of magic: natural magic, which involved the manipulation of occult forces believed to exist in nature, and demonic magic, which called upon evil spirits to gain access to power. Widely accepted as a reality until the middle of the seventeenth century.

Magisterial Reformation (p. 421) Refers to Protestant churches that received official government sanction.

mercantilism (p. 484) The theory that the wealth of a state depended on its ability to import fewer commodities than it exported and thus acquire the largest possible share of the world's monetary supply. The theory encouraged state intervention in the economy and the regulation of trade.

mesmerism (p. 599) A pseudoscience developed by Franz Anton Mesmer in the eighteenth century that treated sickness by massaging or hypnotizing the patient to produce a crisis that restored health.

metropolis (p. 542) The parent country of a colony or imperial possession.

Modern Devotion (p. 331) A fifteenth-century religious movement that stressed individual piety, ethical behavior, and intense religious education. The Modern Devotion was promoted by the Brothers of the Common Life, a religious order whose influence was broadly felt through its extensive network of schools.

Montagnards (p. 616) Members of the radical faction within the Jacobin party who advocated the centralization of state power during the French Revolution and instituted the Reign of Terror.

nabobs (p. 564) Members of the British East India Company who made fortunes in India and returned to Britain, flaunting their wealth.

natural magic (p. 525) The use of magical words and drawings to manipulate the occult forces that exist in nature without calling on supernatural beings for assistance.

nawabs (p. 561) Native provincial governors in eighteenth-century India.

neoclassicism (p. 580) The revival of the classical art and architecture of ancient Greece and Rome in the eighteenth century.

Neoplatonism (p 522) A philosophy based on the teachings of Plato and his successors that flourished in Late Antiquity, especially in the teachings of Plotinus. Neoplatonism influenced Christianity in Late Antiquity. During the Renaissance Neoplatonism was linked to the belief that the natural world was charged with occult forces that could be used in the practice of magic.

nobility (p. 570) Members of the aristocracy who received official recognition of their hereditary status, including their titles of honor and legal privileges.

Old Regime (p. 600) The political order of eighteenth-century France, dominated by an absolute monarch and a privileged nobility and clergy.

opera (p. 366) A musical form invented in the final decades of the sixteenth century by a group of humanist-musicians who thought the power of ancient Greek music could be recovered by writing continuous music to accompany a full drama. The drama was performed as a kind of speech-song with the range of pitch and rhythms closely following those of natural speech.

paradigm (p. 525) A conceptual model or intellectual framework within which scientists conduct their research and experimentation.

parlements (p. 481) The highest provincial courts in France, the most important of which was the Parlement of Paris.

personal rule (p. 500) The period from 1629 to 1640 in England when King Charles I ruled without Parliament.

philology (p. 355) A method reintroduced by the humanists during the Italian Renaissance devoted to the comparative study of language, especially to understanding the meaning of a word in a particular historical context.

philosophes (p. 581) The writers and thinkers of the Enlightenment, especially in France.

plantation colony (p. 382) First appearing in the Cape Verde Islands and later in the tropical parts of the Americas, these colonies were established by Europeans who used African slave labor to cultivate cash crops such as sugar, indigo, cotton, coffee, and tobacco.

popular sovereignty (p. 625) The claim that political power came from the people and that the people constituted the highest political power in the state.

portolanos (p. 381) Books of sailing directions that included charts and descriptions of ports. Portolanos appeared in the Mediterranean in the Late Middle Ages.

predestination (p. 423) The doctrine promoted by John Calvin that since God, the all-knowing and all-powerful being, knew everything in advance and caused everything to happen, then the salvation of any individual was predetermined.

prerogative (p. 499) The set of powers exercised by the English monarch alone, rather than in conjunction with Parliament.

Price Revolution (p. 448) After a long period of falling or stable prices that stretched back to the fourteenth century, Europe experienced sustained price increases between about 1540 and 1640, causing widespread social and economic turmoil.

priesthood of all believers (p. 417) Martin Luther's doctrine that all those of pure faith were themselves priests, a doctrine that undermined the authority of the Catholic clergy over the laity.

protectionism (p. 550) The policy of shielding domestic industries from foreign competition through a policy of levying tariffs on imported goods.

Radical Reformation (p. 421) Refers to Protestant movements that failed to gain official government recognition and were at best tolerated, at worst persecuted, during the sixteenth century.

Reign of Terror (p. 620) A purging of alleged enemies of the French state between 1793 and 1794, superintended by the Committee of Public Safety, that resulted in the execution of 17,000 people.

Religious Peace of Augsburg (p. 420) In 1555 this peace between Lutherans and Catholics within the Holy Roman Empire established the principle of *cuius regio, eius religio*, which means "he who rules determines the religion of the land." Protestant princes in the Empire were permitted to retain all church lands seized before 1552 and to enforce Protestant worship, but Catholic princes were also allowed to enforce Catholic worship in their territories.

Renaissance (p. 344) A term meaning "rebirth" used by historians to describe a movement that sought to imitate and understand the culture of antiquity. The Renaissance generally refers to a movement that began in Italy and then spread throughout Europe from about 1350 to 1550.

republicanism (p. 345) A political theory first developed by the ancient Greeks, especially the philosopher Plato, but elaborated by the ancient Romans and rediscovered during the Italian Renaissance. The fundamental principle of republicanism as developed during the Italian Renaissance was that government officials should be elected by the people or a portion of the people.

requerimiento (p. 388) A document read by conquistadores to the natives of the Americas before making war on them. The document briefly explained the principles of Christianity and commanded the natives to accept them immediately along with the authority of the pope and the sovereignty of the king of Spain. If the natives refused, they were warned they would be forced to accept Christian conversion and subjected to Spain anyway.

rhetoric (p. 356) The art of persuasive or emotive speaking and writing, which was especially valued by the Renaissance humanists.

seigneur (p. 582) The lord of a French estate who received payments from the peasants who lived on his land.

separate spheres (p. 595) The theory that men and women should conduct their lives in different social and political environments, confining women to the domestic sphere and excluding them from the public sphere of political involvement.

sepoys (p. 562) Indian troops serving in the armed forces of the British East India Company.

settler colony (p. 382) A colony authorized when a private person obtained a license from a king to seize an island or parcel of land and occupied it with settlers from Europe who exported their own culture to the new lands. Settler colonies first appeared among the islands of the eastern Atlantic and portions of the Americas.

Spanish Armada (p. 465) A fleet of 132 ships, which sailed from Portugal to rendezvous with the Spanish army stationed in the Netherlands and launch an invasion of England in 1588. The English defeated the Armada as it passed through the English Channel.

spiritualists (p. 428) A tendency within Protestantism, especially Lutheranism, to emphasize the power of personal spiritual illumination, called the "inner Word," a living form of the Scriptures written directly on the believer's soul by the hand of God.

states (p. 542) Consolidated territorial areas that have their own political institutions and recognize no higher political authority.

Time of Troubles (p. 474) The period from 1604 to 1613 when Russia fell into chaos, which ended when the national assembly elected Tsar Michael Romanov, whose descendants ruled Russia until they were deposed in 1917.

trading posts (p. 388) Built by European traders along the coasts of Africa and Asia as a base for trade with the interior. Trading posts or factories were islands of European law and sovereignty, but European authority seldom extended very far beyond the fortified post.

troubadours (p. 302) Poets from the late twelfth and thirteenth centuries who wrote love poems, meant to be sung to music, which reflected a new sensibility, called courtly love, about the ennobling possibilities of the love between a man and a woman.

Unitarians (p. 429) A religious reform movement that began in the sixteenth century and rejected the Christian doctrine of the Trinity. Unitarians (also called Arians, Socinians, and Anti-Trinitarians) taught a rationalist interpretation of the Scriptures and argued that Jesus was a divinely inspired man, not God-become-man as did other Christians.

universal law of gravitation (p. 518) A law of nature established by Isaac Newton in 1687 holding that any two bodies attract each other with a force that is directly proportional to the product of their masses and indirectly proportional to the square of the distance between them. The law was presented in mathematical terms.

universal male suffrage (p. 615) The granting of the right to vote to all adult males.

witch-hunt (p. 457) Refers to the dramatic increase in the judicial prosecution of alleged witches in either church or secular courts from the middle of the sixteenth to the middle of the seventeenth centuries.

Credits

Unless otherwise acknowledged, all photographs are the property of Pearson Education, Inc.
Page abbreviations are as follows: (T) Top, (B) Bottom, (L) Left, (R) Right, (C) Center.

Index

Este family, 345 (map), 348; Isabella d', 349

Ethics: of moderation, 455

Ethiopia, 379–380

Ethnic diversity: in Middle Ages, 337

Ethnic groups and ethnicity: Statues of Kilkenny and, 338; in Venice, 347–348; of colonial peoples, 560

Eucharist, 330; Zwingli on, 422. *See also* Communion

Eugenius IV (Pope), 330, 410

Europe. *See* Europe and Europeans

Europe and Europeans: 14th-century demographics and, 308; Black Death in, 309–313; state system in, 366–373; culture of, 376 (illus.); expansion by, 377–406, 383 (map); voyages along African coast, 380–381; Americas and, 384–397; North American colonization by, 396–397; Asia and, 397–399, 561–566; agriculture in, 405; early modern period in, 444–450; religion and, 461 (map); absolutism in, 479; after Treaty of Westphalia, 493 (map); Peter the Great (Russia) and, 497; overseas empires of, 541–542; in 1742, 552 (map); aristocracy in, 578; Enlightenment in, 585–603, 586 (map); after Congress of Vienna (1815), 638 (map)

Evangelicals: Luther's followers as, 417

Exchange Bank (Amsterdam), 508

Excommunication: Calvinism on, 423; of Napoleon, 636

Executions: by guillotine, 617; of Louis XVI (France), 618–619, 619 (illus.)

Expansion: European, 377–406, 383 (map); Ethiopian, 379–380; Russian, 399. *See also* Empire(s)

Experimentation: scientific, 521

Exploration and discovery: by Columbus, 369; Portuguese in Africa, 383–384; European, 386–388; English, 396–397; voyages of, 527

Extraction of Diamonds (Julião), 560 (illus.)

Factories: English, 561, 564

Factors and factories (trading posts): in trading post empires, 398; English, 544; Dutch, 545; French, 545

Faerie Queen, The (Spenser), 468

Fairs: European, 379

Faith. *See* Confessions; Justification by faith; Theology

Falloppio, Gabriele, 358

Families: patriarchal, 351–354, 451, 454; Calvin on, 423; peasant, 445; limiting sizes of, 451; regulation of, 451–455; children in, 454–455; ideal, 454 (illus.)

Famine: in 14th century, 307, 308–309; decline of, 582. *See also* Starvation

Fanatic and fanaticism: use of term, 460; assassination of Henry IV (France) and, 463

Far East: European perceptions of, 563. *See also* East, the; specific countries

Farel, Guillaume, 435

Farms and farming: forests cleared for, 308; movement to cities from, 447; farmers in

aristocracy and, 577. *See also* Agriculture; Peasants

Farnese family: Paul III of, 434

Fathers, 454. *See also* Families

Faust (Goethe), 470

Feast of the Federation (France), 626 (illus.)

Federico II da Montefeltro (Urbino), 348–349, 349 (illus.)

Fedor (Russia), 497

Feminism: of Christine de Pisan, 337; of humanist women, 358. *See also* Women

Ferdinand I (Holy Roman Empire), 470

Ferdinand II (Aragon), 368; Isabella of Castile and, 369, 369 (map), 488; Loyola and, 431

Ferdinand II (Bohemia, Hungary, Holy Roman Empire), 493, 496

Ferdinand VII (Spain), 635

Ferguson, Adam: on human development, 589

Ferrara, 345 (map), 348; Duke of, 360

Feudal dues, 578, 611

Feudalism: armies and, 367

Fichte, Johann Gottlieb, 636

Ficino, Marsilio, 347

Fiefs: in Russia, 473

Fiji: England and, 544

Finances: in France, 323, 367, 484, 609; sale of indulgences and, 416; in Spain, 490; slavery and, 558. *See also* Taxation

Financing: of military, 480–481

First Coalition: against France, 617

First Consul: Napoleon as, 622–623, 622 (illus.)

Fisher, John, 424

Fishing industry, 396, 545

Flagellation, 311 (illus.); in Spanish America, 392, 392 (illus.)

Flanders: worker rebellions in, 320; painting in, 364–365

Flemish language, 465

Flemish painting, 364–365

Florence, 345 (map); Black Death in, 311; banking in, 319; guilds in, 319; Ciompi revolt in, 319–320; Machiavelli in, 343; Italian Renaissance in, 345–347; Medici family in, 346–347; vendettas in, 352; Baptistery in, 360 (illus.), 361, 361 (illus.); sculpture in, 363; cathedral of, 363 (illus.)

Florida, 550; colonization of, 396, 543

Florin (coin), 319

"Flowery war": by Aztecs, 384–385

Fontenelle, Bernard de, 535–536

Food: costs of, 307; insufficiency of, 308–309

Foot soldiers: in Hundred Years' War, 328

Forests: destruction for farming, 308

Fortescue, John, 499

Forts. *See* Trading posts

Fort William, India, 562

Fouché, Joseph, 620, 625

Four Books on the Family (Alberti), 351

Fourth Crusade, 315

Fox, George, 543

France: Hundred Years' War and, 308, 321–328, 323 (illus.), 324 (map); Black Death in, 311; England and, 319, 325, 545, 551; worker rebellions in, 320; jurisdiction of

kings in, 322–323; Aquitaine and, 323; Edward III (England) and, 323; papacy and, 329; Italian Wars and, 366; Church in, 367; state (nation) in, 367–368; Estates General in, 368; dynastic marriage encircling, 369–370, 369 (map); Holy Roman Empire and, 370; Italy invaded by, 370; Verrazano and, 396; popes in, 410; after wars of religion, 445; Huguenots in, 460–461; literature in, 467–468; absolutism in, 481–488; economy in, 484; territorial acquisitions of, 486–487, 486 (map); Spain and, 488 (map); Dutch Republic and, 508; overseas empire of, 543; trading companies of, 543; War of the Austrian Succession and, 551; Anglo-French wars and, 551–554; slave trade and, 559; civil law in, 561; Haitian Revolution and, 568–569; nobility in, 577; aristocracy in, 579; peasants in, 582; bourgeoisie in, 583; philosophes in, 585; criminal justice in, 590; Voltaire and, 592; women in, 595; republic in (1792-1799), 613–623; Consuls in, 622 (illus.); academies in, 623–624; cultural change in, 623–627; political culture in, 625–627; revolutionary calendar in, 627; under Napoleon, 627–639; administration of, 631–632; boundaries of, 638–639, 638 (map); after Congress of Vienna, 639; after Revolution, 639–640. *See also* French Empire; Old Regime (France)

Franche Comté, 486 (map)

Franchise: expansion of, 602. *See also* Voting and voting rights

Francis I (France), 368, 461

Francis II (France), 425, 460, 461

Franciscans, 311, 393, 399; in Mexico, 389, 392

Francis of Alençon (France), 462

Francogallia (Hotman), 463

Frederick I (Prussia), 494, 495

Frederick II (the Great, Prussia), 551, 589, 600

Frederick V (Bohemia Palatinate), 493

Frederick the Wise (Elector of Saxony), 416, 417

Frederick William (Great Elector), 494, 495

Frederick William I (Prussia), 494, 551, 600

Frederick William II (Prussia), 615

Free coloreds: in Haiti, 568

Freedom(s): spiritual and fiscal, 410–411; of religion, 428, 429–430. *See also* Rights

Freedom of a Christian, The (Luther), 417, 418

Freedom of the Sea, The (Grotius), 508

Freemasons, 598

Freethinking: of Spinoza, 529

Free will: Luther on, 416

French Academy of Sciences, 535–536, 536 (illus.)

French and Indian War. *See* Seven Years' War

French Army Halts at Syene, Upper Egypt..., The (Tardieu), 634 (illus.)

French East India Company, 545

French Empire, 545; under Napoleon, 632–636, 635 (map)

French language, 486

French Revolution (1789 and 1792), 553–554, 560, 607–627; aristocracy and, 581;

Navarre, 368; Huguenots in, 461; Bourbon family in, 462; kingdom of, 489

Navies, 550; Chinese, 397–398; trading post empires and, 398–399; in absolutist age, 480; Dutch, 507; mutiny on *Bounty* and, 546–547, 547 (illus.); warfare and, 550; British, 633; French, 633

Navigation: maritime technology and, 381–382

Navigation Acts (England), 550

Nawabs (India), 561–562

Necker, Jacques, 611

Negus (Ethiopian emperor), 380

Nelson, Horatio, 633

Neoclassicism, 580

Neoplatonism, 522, 524, 525; education and, 528; on role of humans in universe, 535

Netherlands, 370; Black Death in, 311; woolen cloth and, 319; painting in, 364–365; iconoclasm in, 436 (illus.); Catholic Reformation and art in, 438; assassination of Prince of Orange in, 443; English support for, 464; provinces in, 465; Dutch Revolt in, 465–466, 466 (map); Spain and, 465–466, 189; Austria and, 187, 195; kingdom of, 639. *See also* Dutch; Dutch Republic (United Provinces of the Netherlands); Holland

Neva River, 498, 499

New Amsterdam, 545, 550

New Astronomy (Kepler), 516

New England: Puritans in, 543

Newfoundland, 551; fishing industry in, 396

New Mexico, 393, 396

New Model Army (England), 501

New Netherland, 545

New Organon (Bacon), 521, 527

New Spain, 389

Newspapers: in Enlightenment, 598

New Testament. *See* Bible (Christian)

Newton, Isaac, 517–518, 518 (illus.), 585; mathematics and, 522; on religion, 531

New World, 388; use of term, 382; cultures in, 401; cosmology and, 403; peoples of, 403; Africans in, 558. *See also* America(s)

New York City, 545, 550

New Zealand: England and, 544

Nicaea, Council of, 429

Nile, Battle of the, 622, 633

Niña (ship), 387

Ninety-Five Theses (Luther), 417

Nobility, 576; lifestyle of, 333–334; women in convents from, 433; in France, 461–462, 481, 482, 484, 609, 611, 632, 639; in Poland-Lithuania, 471–472; in Russia, 473, 499; in absolutist states, 480; in Spain, 490, 576; in England, 577; in Poland, 577; marriage into, 579 (illus.); as French estate, 610. *See also* Aristocracy

Nobility and Excellence of Women, The. . . . (Marinella), 467

"Noble savage": Rousseau on, 594

Nogarola, Isotta, 357–358

Noguerol de Ulloa, Francisco, 394–396

Nomads: Mongols and Turks as, 313–314

North Africa: European trade with, 380; Spanish fortresses in, 464

North America, 543; before Europeans, 384; Spanish missionaries in, 393; colonization of, 396–397; England and, 396–397, 543–544, 550, 553 (map); French colonies in, 545; Spain and, 548; Napoleon and, 633

North Carolina, 543

Northern Europe: settlement of, 444; demographic and economic shift to, 445; cities in, 446; marriage in, 451

Northern Renaissance: art in, 364–365, 365 (illus.); Christian humanists and, 413–415

Northwest Passage: search for, 396

Norway: Black Death in, 311

Notables (France), 632

Nova Scotia, 551; French in, 396

Novels: *Don Quixote* as, 468; in Enlightenment, 598, 599. *See also* Literature

Novgorod, 473

Nunneries. *See* Convents

Nuns: Black Death and, 311; Modern Devotion and, 331; Teresa of Avila as, 432; religious orders and, 433–434

Nuremberg: guilds in, 319

Nutmeg, 398

Oath of the Tennis Court (David), 606 (illus.)

Oaths: in France, 625, 626 (illus.)

Observation: empirical, 521, 523

Occult, 457

Ochino, Bernardino, 434

Ogé, Vincent, 568

Old Regime (France), 599; Enlightenment and, 602; destruction of, 608; end of, 611–612. *See also* French Revolution (1789 and 1792)

Old Testament. *See* Bible (Hebrew)

Oligarchy: Dutch, 507

Olivares, Count-Duke of, 489

"On Cannibals" (Montaigne), 404

On Disciplining Children:. . . ., 454

On Jean-Jacques Rousseau Considered as One of the First Authors of the Revolution, 602

On the Admission of Women to the Rights of Citizenship (Condorcet), 596, 639

On the Fabric of the Human Body (Vesalius), 358

On the Revolution of the Heavenly Spheres (Copernicus), 524

Opera: in Renaissance, 366

Optics, 358–359, 535

Orange, House of, 507, 639

Orders (of knights), 333–334; of the Garter, 333; of the Golden Fleece, 333, 334; of the Passion, 333; of St. Michael, 333; of the Stars, 333

Orders (social groups): in France, 610

Organic Articles of Confederation, 631

Orleans, battle at, 325

Orphanages, 448

Orphan of China (Voltaire), 574 (illus.)

Orthodox Christianity: Ottomans and, 316; in Transylvania, 430; in Lithuania, 472; in Russia, 473

Osman I (Ottoman dynasty), 315

Other World, The (Bergerac), 535

Ottoman Empire, 315–318, 316 (map), 491, 496–497, 542, 543; in East, 478; Hungary and, 495; Russia and, 549; Egypt in, 634

Ottoman Turks, 314, 315–318, 496; conquest of Constantinople, 317; Byzantine fall to, 348; in Mediterranean region, 377–378; Christian Ethiopia and, 379; Philip II (Spain) and, 464; Russia and, 497

Oudh, India, 563

"Outer Word," 429

Overseas empires. *See* Empire(s); Imperialism

Oxford University, 412

Pachacuti Inca Yupanqui (Inca), 385

Pacific Ocean region: navigation across, 381; Magellan and, 388; Russia in, 549

Pacifism: of Baptists, 428

Paine, Thomas, 560, 568, 594–595, 599, 602

Painting: humanists on, 356; optics, perspective, and, 358–359; Roman, 360; linear perspective in, 363–364; portraits in, 363 (illus.); with oil paint, 364–365; in Spain, 490–491; Dutch, 508–509

Pajamas, 564–565

Palace of the Popes (Avignon), 329 (illus.)

Palaces: El Escorial as, 464; at Versailles, 483–484, 483 (illus.)

Palestrina, Giovanni Pierluigi da, 439

Palladio, Andrea, 581 (illus.)

Pamphlets: in Enlightenment, 598

Panama, 390; Spain and, 550

Pandora (ship), 546

Papacy: Babylonian Captivity of the Church, Great Schism and, 329–330; Conciliar Movement and, 330; protests against, 330–331; Council of Trent and, 435; Napoleon and, 630–631. *See also* Pope(s); specific popes

Papal States, 410, 636; after Great Schism, 350; Donation of Constantine and, 413

Paper, 359; print revolution and, 412

Pappenheimer family: witchcraft trial of, 458

Paprika, 402

Paracelsus, 518, 524

Paradigms: collapse of scientific, 525

Paraguay, 393

Pardons: in England, 580

Paris: Black Death in, 311; *Maillotins* revolt in, 320; in Hundred Years' War, 325; blockade of (1649), 482; Parlement of, 482; salons in, 598; French Revolution and, 607, 615; French monarch in, 614; National Assembly in, 625

Paris, Treaty of: of 1763, 552; of 1783, 567; in 1814, 637; of 1816, 638

Paris Commune: of 1792, 615, 625

Parlement of Paris (court), 590, 609; *Fronde* of, 482

Parlements (French courts), 580, 609

Parliament: French Estates General as, 368

Parliament (England), 480, 499; Charles I and, 500–501; in English civil war, 500–504; Charles II and, 504–505;

160°W 140°W 120°W 100°W 80°W 60°W 40°W 20°W

80°N

GREENLAND
(KALAALLIT NUNAAT)
(Den.)

Arctic C

ALASKA
(U.S.)

ICELAND

60°N

UN
KING

C A N A D A

IRELAND

FR

40°N

UNITED STATES

ATLANTIC
OCEAN

AZORES (Port.)

PORTUG

MOR

CANARY IS. (Sp.)

Tropic of Cancer

WESTERN SAHARA
(Mor.)

HAWAII (U.S.)

BAHAMAS

20°N

MEXICO

CUBA

DOMINICAN
REPUBLIC

HAITI

PUERTO RICO (U.S.)

MAURITAN

JAMAICA

ST. KITTS AND NEVIS

BELIZE

ANTIGUA AND BARBUDA

CAPE
VERDE

GUATEMALA

GUADELOUPE (Fr.)

DOMINICA

SENEGAL

HONDURAS

MARTINIQUE (Fr.)

ST. VINCENT AND THE GRENADINES

THE GAMBIA

EL SALVADOR

NICARAGUA

ST. LUCIA

BARBADOS

GUINEA-BISSAU

GRENADA

GUINEA

COSTA RICA

TRINIDAD AND TOBAGO

SIERRA LEONE

PANAMA

VENEZUELA

GUYANA

SURINAME

LIBERIA

FRENCH GUIANA (Fr.)

CÔTE D'IVO

COLOMBIA

GALÁPAGOS IS.
(Ec.)

ECUADOR

BURKINA

0° Equator

PACIFIC OCEAN

B R A Z I L

PERU

WESTERN
SAMOA

AMERICAN
SAMOA (U.S.)

BOLIVIA

TONGA

FRENCH
POLYNESIA (Fr.)

20°S

PARAGUAY

Tropic of Capricorn

CHILE

ATLANT
OCEA

URUGUAY

ARGENTINA

FALKLAND IS. (U.K.)

40°S

**Contemporary
Political Map
of the World**

0   1,500   3,000 Miles

0   1,500   3,000 Kilometers

60°S

Antarctic Circle

80°S

RCTIC OCEAN

SWEDEN
FINLAND
NORWAY
LITH.
ESTONIA
LATVIA
RUS.
ARK
ER.
POLAND
BELARUS
X.
CZ. REP.
SLVK.
UKRAINE
AUS.
HUNG.
MOLDOVA
SLOV.
ROMANIA
CRO.
YUGO.
BULGARIA
GEORGIA
B.-H.
GREECE
ALB.
TURKEY
ARMENIA
TUNISIA
MALTA
CYPRUS
SYRIA
LEB.
AZERBAIJAN
ITALY
MAZ.
ISRAEL
IRAQ
IRAN
RIA
LIBYA
EGYPT
JORDAN
KUWAIT
BAHRAIN
AFGHANISTAN
PAKISTAN
NGER
CHAD
SUDAN
SAUDI ARABIA
QATAR
UNITED ARAB
EMIRATES
OMAN
YEMEN
ERITREA
DJIBOUTI
ERIA
CENTRAL
AFRICAN REP.
ETHIOPIA
AMEROON
SOMALIA
GABON
CONGO
RWANDA
UGANDA
KENYA
DEM. REP. OF
THE CONGO
PE
BURUNDI
TANZANIA
DA
COMOROS
MAYOTTE (Fr.)
SEYCHELLES
ANGOLA
ZAMBIA
MALAWI
NAMIBIA
ZIMBABWE
MADAGASCAR
BOTSWANA
MOZAMBIQUE
RÉUNION
(Fr.)
MAURITIUS
SOUTH
AFRICA
SWAZILAND
LESOTHO

RUSSIA

KAZAKHSTAN
MONGOLIA
UZBEKISTAN
KYRGYZSTAN
TURKMENISTAN
TAJIKISTAN
CHINA
N. KOREA
S. KOREA
JAPAN
NEPAL
BHUTAN
INDIA
BANGLADESH
MYANMAR
(BURMA)
TAIWAN
Hong Kong
Macao (Port.)
LAOS
THAILAND
VIETNAM
CAMBODIA
MALDIVES
SRI
LANKA
BRUNEI
PHILIPPINES
PALAU
MALAYSIA
SINGAPORE
INDONESIA
PAPUA
NEW
GUINEA

PACIFIC
OCEAN

NORTHERN
MARIANA
IS. (U.S.)
GUAM (U.S.)
MARSHALL
IS.
FEDERATED STATES
OF MICRONESIA
NAURU
KIRIBATI
SOLOMON
IS.
TUVALU

INDIAN
OCEAN

AUSTRALIA

VANUATU
FIJI
NEW
CALEDONIA
(Fr.)

NEW
ZEALAND

NTARCTICA